The Illustrated Encyclopedia of Zen Buddhism

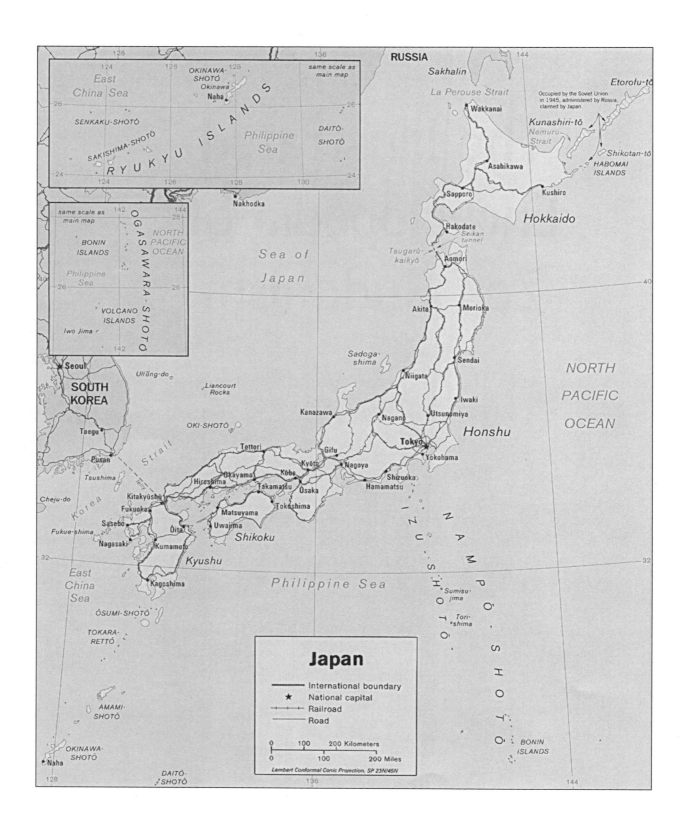

Japan

International boundary
★ National capital
Railroad
Road

0 — 100 — 200 Kilometers
0 — 100 — 200 Miles
Lambert Conformal Conic Projection, SP 23N/45N

The Illustrated Encyclopedia of Zen Buddhism

Helen J. Baroni, Ph.D.

The Rosen Publishing Group, Inc.
New York

To my students at the University of Hawai'i, past, present, and future.

Published in 2002 by The Rosen Publishing Group, Inc.
29 East 21st Street, New York, NY 10010

First Edition

Library of Congress Cataloging-in-Publication Data

Baroni, Helen Josephine.
The illustrated encyclopedia of Zen Buddhism / Helen J. Baroni.
   p. cm.
   Includes bibliographical references and index.
   ISBN 0-8239-2240-5
   1. Zen Buddhism—Dictionaries—English. I. Title.
BQ9259 .B37 2002
294.3'927'03—dc21
                        99-053421
                        CIP

Manufactured in the United States of America

Staff Credits

Editors: Michael Isaac, Christine Slovey
Editorial Assistant: Rob Kirkpatrick
Book Design: Olga M. Vega
Cover Design: MaryJane Wojciechowski
Production Design: Erica Clendening, MaryJane Wojciechowski

Table of Contents

Introduction

In the one hundred years since Zen Buddhism was introduced to the West, many of its traditions have become a part of our culture. When I tell people that I study Zen, they often tell me about their familiarity with Zen arts such as haiku poetry, martial arts, or flower arranging. At the same time, many people also learn about Buddhism by experiencing meditation. Yet despite the growing popularity of Zen arts and practices, the ancient religious beliefs that formed them remain largely unfamiliar to those in the West.

In the Western vocabulary, the word *zen* has taken on a broad array of meanings. The philosophy of Zen is often recast to Westerners as a freedom from social norms and ordinary religious restrictions. It may be suggested, for example, that Zen practitioners do not need to concern themselves with good and bad behavior because they have risen above distinctions such as right and wrong. In East Asia, the impression of Zen could not be more different. Zen Buddhism is regarded as a religion of strict religious practice because there it is concentrated in monasteries where monks and nuns live their lives guided by a special code of conduct. This understanding of Zen is based on its tradition of scholarship and religious discipline.

In Japanese, the term *zen* means "meditation." Zen is an abbreviation of the word *zenna*, which is derived from a Chinese term for meditation, *ch'anna*. The Chinese term is a translation of the Sanskrit word *dhyana*, a term for meditation that is found in Buddhist texts. The introspective and contemplative practice of meditation is a part of many religious traditions and is a fundamental element of all schools of Buddhism. In both the Chinese and Japanese languages, one may use the words *ch'anna* or *zen* to refer to any form of meditation, whether Buddhist, Confucian, or even Christian. Most often the terms refer to the styles of seated meditation (zazen) practiced in Zen Buddhist monasteries. Zazen specifies the way a person should sit and includes techniques to allow one to release control of his or her thoughts. When a new East Asian form of Buddhist monastic practice centered on seated meditation took shape in China during the T'ang Dynasty (618–907) and then spread to Korea and Japan, it became known as the Meditation School of Buddhism (the Ch'an school in Chinese, the Son school in Korean, and the Zen school in Japanese). The term *zen*, therefore, refers not only to the practice of meditation but also refers to the many schools of Buddhism that practice seated meditation.

The History of Zen

Traditional Account

Buddhism first arose in India, based on the teachings of Siddharta Gautama (566–486 B.C.E.), the Buddha. Born as a prince, Siddharta abandoned his regal life and began a lifelong search for religious insight. After a period of intense meditation, he arrived at the core beliefs and practices of Buddhism and established a community of followers and disciples, including pre-Hindu monks and nuns, as well as laypeople. This community was responsible for propagating Siddharta's teachings after his death. In the centuries that followed, several forms of Buddhism took shape in India. The two largest of these schools of Buddhism are known today as Theravada Buddhism and Mahayana Buddhism. As Buddhist missionaries traveled east, they spread the teachings throughout the rest of Asia. The style of Buddhism that became dominant in East Asia is Mahayana, and Zen is one of the many forms of Mahayana Buddhism that developed there.

According to traditional Zen accounts, the teachings of Zen are said to date back to this historical Buddha, who wordlessly transmitted them to Mahakashyapa, one of his most talented disciples. The tradition names a series of twenty-eight Indian patriarchs who passed the teachings on, beginning with the historical Buddha and Mahakashyapa and culminating with the patriarch Bodhidharma. In the fifth century, Bodhidharma traveled to China, where he took on Chinese disciples. From among these, Bodhidharma is said to have selected Hui-k'o to be his official successor. The tradition then traces its lineage through six generations of Chinese patriarchs, concluding with Sixth Patriarch Hui-neng. After the sixth generation, the lineage of patriarchs branches into a large and ever-expanding family tree of teachers and disciples. All forms of Zen Buddhism existing today trace their origins back to the sixth patriarch, Bodhidharma, and the historical Buddha.

Historical Account

Scholars have come to realize that the history of Zen is much more complicated than the story related in these traditional accounts. For example, we now know that Zen actually first developed in China as a distinctly Chinese form of Buddhism. The basic teachings of Zen Buddhism emerged in China during the sixth and seventh centuries as Chinese scholars translated Buddhist texts and began to fuse Buddhist practices with indigenous Chinese beliefs. By the eighth and ninth centuries, Zen had taken on a distinctive identity, with numerous monastic communities developing the teachings we now know as Zen Buddhism. Specifically, the emphasis in Zen is more on meditation and less on the study of texts, philosophical discussion, and other practices such as chanting texts.

From China, Buddhist monks transmitted Zen teachings and practices throughout East Asia to Korea, Japan, and Vietnam. Today it is among the largest schools of Buddhism in Japan and one of the most popular forms of Buddhism in Western countries.

In Japan today, there are three large denominations of Zen Buddhism: the Sôtô, Rinzai, and Obaku sects. There are also several other smaller groups.

- Sôtô Zen is the largest of the three denominations. The Japanese monk Dôgen Kigen (1200–1253) founded the Sôtô sect in the thirteenth century. He traveled to China, where he practiced with a Chinese Zen master from the Sôtô lineage, known as Ts'ao-tung.

- The founding of Rinzai Zen, known in Chinese as the Lin-chi lineage, involved the efforts of several Chinese and Japanese monks over many decades. Traditional accounts usually simplify matters by saying that the Rinzai sect was founded by a single person, the monk Eisai, who was Dôgen's teacher.

- Obaku Zen is the smallest and most recent of the larger denominations. The Chinese monk Yin-yüan Lung-ch'i (1594–1673) founded the Obaku sect in the seventeenth century. Yin-yuan regarded himself as a descendent of the Rinzai lineage, and the two groups' teachings and practices are closely related.

In the last century, numerous Sôtô and Rinzai teachers have traveled to the West and introduced their teachings and practices to Western audiences. One of the most influential Zen movements in the West, Sanbô Kyôdan, originated in Japan as only one of many small modern groups. Harada Sogaku (1871–1961) and Yasutani Hakuun (1885–1973) founded Sanbô Kyôdan in 1954 to encourage the practice of seated meditation among laypeople outside of the monastic setting. Sanbô Kyôdan combines some aspects of both the Sôtô and Rinzai practices. While the movement remains very small in Japan, it has greatly influenced the development of Zen in the West through the efforts of such teachers as Robert Aitken, Philip Kapleau, Bernard Glassman, Maureen Stuart, and Richard Baker, who have written, and are discussed in, books about American Zen and American Buddhism. A large percentage of Zen teachers in the United States were affiliated with Sanbô Kyôdan at one time or studied with its teachers.

Zen Teachings

Zen, along with all other forms of Buddhism, is fundamentally concerned with the problem of human suffering. The Buddha determined that the root of our suffering is our desire for and attachment to things, people, ideas, and experiences. These needs are problematic because in the Buddhist view of the world, nothing remains stable—all things constantly change and will eventually pass away. We cannot possess those things to which we have formed attachments; thus all of our desires will inevitably lead to frustration and suffering.

Aside from the daily frustrations that our attachments cause, Buddhism asserts that human suffering also occurs on a cosmic level. Buddhists believe that after death each being will be reincarnated into a new life, the quality of which depends on the religious merit (karma) earned in the last life. Despite the rewards one may acquire through rebirth, the unending cycle of death and reincarnation on Earth is seen as a burden and another form of suffering. This suffering will end only when a person is able to break from the cycle of reincarnation.

The Buddhist solution to the problem of suffering requires a shift in our perception of the world. By understanding the impermanence of all things and eliminating all desires, we can break our attachments. This means that one sees the world as a buddha, or enlightened person, would. In fact, Zen masters are fond of reminding us that we are all actually buddhas, even though most of us do not yet see ourselves or reality in that way. The ultimate goal is to attain enlightenment, or satori. This is described as a blissful state of awareness in which one has relinquished all attachments and recognizes the underlying unity of all things. As an enlightened being, one exists in a state of nirvana, in which one is liberated from the cycle of death and rebirth.

Zen Practice

Zen masters say that Zen practitioners do not depend on written words to teach or grasp the Zen teachings. This means that reading and interpreting the Buddhist scriptures will not lead to enlightenment. As one Chinese master said, the scriptures are like a road map—while the map can show you where you would like to go and even set out the quickest route, you still must travel the road for yourself. Not depending on written words requires that students learn through practice and experience, with the aid of a qualified teacher. Zen Buddhism places great emphasis on the religious rituals and practices a student must perform to gain proper insight into Zen teachings.

According to Zen, meditation is one of the most effective practices for attaining a proper understanding of reality. Meditation allows a person to experience the self as interconnected with all other things. One realizes that distinctions between one's self and other people are not absolute and that every action one takes affects everyone else. In Zen meditation, the practitioner sits in the lotus position—cross-legged with each foot placed on the opposing thigh. Beginners generally learn to concentrate the mind by focusing on their breathing, noticing the intake and exhalation of the breath. Other meditation techniques may include focusing on a single syllable of sound assigned to them by their teacher.

In Zen meditation, students may also concentrate on a kôan, a cryptic saying or story from Zen literature that is intended to focus one's mind and challenge ordinary ways of thinking. Kôan often take the form of puzzles that defy logical solution, such as "What is the sound of one hand clapping?" Students meditate with their assigned kôan in mind; they are said to "work on the kôan." When they have questions about the kôan or feel that they have mastered it, they approach their teacher in a private interview. In these face-to-face encounters, Zen teachers evaluate the students' understanding.

The Zen Monastery

The Zen monasteries I have visited in Japan are all places that engage the senses. The smell of incense pervades many halls, since incense is regularly offered to the images of the Buddha and bodhisattvas. Outside, one often encounters the scent of burning leaves as the novices clean the grounds in the afternoon. Colorful silk banners stream down pillars within graceful wooden structures with smooth polished floors and ornately carved rafters. One may glimpse the flashing eyes of a painted dragon on the ceiling. Some of the most treasured examples of Asian painting, sculpture, and calligraphy may be viewed within temple walls, rather than in secular museums. During the morning and evening services, a monk beats a hollow drum carved in the shape of a fish in time with the novices chanting verses from Buddhist scripture; hand chimes punctuate breaks during the service.

Many rules govern the appropriate conduct of life within the monastery community. Life in the monastery may be described as a series of ritual acts, from bathing oneself in the morning to laying out one's bedding in the evening. New monks and nuns must learn to behave properly, to chant the Buddhist scriptures, to offer incense, and to bow. There is a proper manner of walking into the meditation hall, a proper way to eat one's food, and even a proper way to take a bath and use the toilet. There are also set manners for drinking tea, meeting with one's teacher, and requesting entry into the monastery.

The typical daily routine at a Zen monastery is highly structured. The monks or nuns rise early and follow a regular schedule of eating, meditating, working outside, studying, and chanting scriptures. Much of the day is spent in silence. Ritual takes several forms in the monastery. Monks and nuns participate in morning and evening services. They recite particular prayers and scriptures, make offerings, and bow down before images of the Buddha and other religious figures.

Ritualizing all aspects of life serves several purposes. First of all, it allows the many people practicing within the monastery to live together harmoniously because it is always clear what one should be doing and how one should behave. Second, the constant attention to detail transforms all the activities of the day, even mundane ones such as eating and bathing, into a kind of meditation.

Throughout the United States, Canada, and Europe, Zen is practiced predominantly by laypeople in Zen centers, but in East Asia the situation is quite different. In Japan, for example, Zen meditation is most often practiced by monks and nuns. Buddhist temples do not generally offer weekly services for laypeople, as is common at Christian churches, Jewish synagogues, and Muslim mosques. Laypeople may be members of a local Zen congregation, but they rarely practice meditation in a temple or at home. In Japan, Zen monasteries provide for the religious needs of laymembers. Most laypeople rely primarily on the Zen clergy to perform religious rituals such as funerals and memorial services for deceased family members. They may also visit their local temple on special holidays, such as the Buddha's birthday or the Festival of the Dead.

Encyclopedia Entries

The majority of the Zen vocabulary in this book is rendered in both English and Japanese. However, some Buddhist terms also appear in Sanskrit, Pali, or Chinese, reflecting Buddhism's influence across Asian cultures. Many terms, therefore, are listed in several languages. These alternative entries include cross-references to the basic English and Japanese listings.

It should be noted that translations are not entirely standardized in the field of Buddhist studies or Japanese religions. In each case, I have tried to select the most common and accurate translations. I selected transliterations that reflect English pronunciation, avoiding extensive use of diacritical markings. In certain cases, more than one transliteration is included.

• The Contents by Subject lists related entries in the following categories: Art, Architecture, and Iconography; Biographical Entries; Buddhas and Bodhisattvas; Concepts; Geography; Monastic Life; Mythology and Cosmology; Rituals; Sects, Schools, and Groups; and Texts.

• Parenthetical citations are used to refer to selections from primary Buddhist texts. Citations preceded by (T.) denote the Taisho edition of the *Daizôkyô*, a Japanese version of the Buddhist scriptures used by most scholars for referencing texts. The first number is the volume, and the second number is the document number (each document has a unique number).

• Abbreviated bibliographic citations appear at the end of some entries. The full citations are grouped together in the bibliography.

• Cross-referenced terms within entries are in boldface type.

• Transliterated Chinese, Japanese, and Sanskrit terms are identified by (C.), (J.), and (Sk.), respectively.

• Words with distinctive pronunciations are identified by diacritical marks—symbols above the letters to indicate their proper pronunciations. They are pronounced as follows:

â	*father*
ö	*saw*
ô	*old*
û	*put*
üe	*oo-eh* (merged into one syllable)

Contents by Subject

Art, Architecture, and Iconography

Biographical Entries

Buddhas and Bodhisattvas

Concepts

Geography

Monastic Life

Mythology and Cosmology

Rituals

Sects, Schools, and Groups

Texts

Abbot

The chief administrative officer within a monastery or large temple. The most common Japanese terms for the post are **jûji** and chôrô. The English term "abbot" is appropriately applied to head **monks** or **nuns** at training monasteries and large temples, where the monastic community practices **Zen meditation**. In the case of small local temples where there is only one monk in residence, the term "head monk" would be more appropriate.

The abbot's duties include management of the monastery as a whole, handling both the administrative work and the spiritual direction of the community. He or she oversees the work done by the other administrative officers (**seihan** and **tôhan**). Since the abbot's primary responsibility is to ensure the smooth operation of the monastery, he or she may pass on a large portion of the spiritual guidance of the resident **novices** and monks to another Zen master. In addition, the abbot represents the monastery in all dealings with the outside world, including relations with the government and with other monasteries or religious bodies.

The abbot serves as the primary teacher of the **Dharma** at the monastery. On several occasions each month, the abbot lectures on the Dharma to the entire monastic community. For these "great assemblies" (**daisan**), the abbot mounts the podium in the Dharma hall (**hattô**), takes his or her place in the Dharma chair (**hôza**), and speaks to the community. At the end of the lecture, the abbot typically invites members of the community to engage in a question-and-answer session (**mondô**). At the great assemblies, the abbot is said to teach in the place of the **buddhas** and Zen **patriarchs**.

An abbot is the primary teacher and manager of a Buddhist monastery.

Abbots of major monasteries are usually selected from among a group of qualified Zen masters. The selection process and exact qualifications differ throughout the world, but in general, the qualified candidate has practiced for at least ten years and has held other high-ranking administrative positions. In the **Gozan temples** of medieval Japan (1185–1600), for example, candidates were required to have served as the chief seat (**shuso**) of a monastery and to have passed a qualifying exam (**hinpotsu**). In Japan, the abbot of a major Zen monastery was traditionally appointed by either the emperor or the military government (**bakufu**). In Korean temples today, the abbot is elected by the assembly of monks at the monastery.

The abbot formally assumes his post with an installation service (**shinsan-shiki**). In some cases, an abbot serves for a specified term of office. Since the responsibilities of the post are quite heavy, many Zen monasteries prefer to rotate qualified candidates to reduce the strain on any one individual. This is the norm in Korean temples today. In other cases, the length of time an abbot serves is left to his or her own discretion. The abbot at **Mampuku-ji**, the main monastery for the **Obaku sect** in Japan, usually assumes the post permanently, stepping down only if he or she can no longer fulfill his or her duties.

Buswell, Robert E., Jr. *The Zen Monastic Experience: Buddhist Practice in Contemporary Korea*. Princeton, NJ: Princeton University Press, 1992.

Collcutt, Martin. *Five Mountains: The Rinzai Zen Monastic Institution in Medieval Japan*. Cambridge, MA: Harvard University Press, 1981.

Abhidharma

The abbreviated name for the Abhidharma Pitika, one of the three sections of the **Buddhist scriptures**. "The Basket of Scholasticism" (another name for the Abhidharma) is the third and latest section of the **Tripitaka**, representing commentaries on the **Buddha's** teachings written by later Buddhist scholars. The Abhidharma texts were written over a period of several centuries, between 350 B.C.E. and 450 C.E. The Abhidharma texts deal with teachings from the earlier **sermons** of the Buddha, written in a scholastic and systematic manner. This means that the texts do not provide the teaching aids employed in the discourses (or **sutras**), such as images, parables, and stories, which help to make the concepts more understandable.

The Pali Abhidharma, one version of the Abhidharma that represents the teachings of **Theravada Buddhism**, is comprised of seven texts related to Buddhist psychology and philosophy. They include: 1) Dhamma-sangani (Enumeration of **Dharmas**), which analyzes things into categories of mental and physical factors; 2) Vibhanga (Divisions), a discussion of the skandhas (**five skandhas**); 3) Dhatu-katha (Discussion of Elements), which classifies elements of reality; 4) Puggala-pannatti (Designation of Persons), which classifies various types of individuals; 5) Katha-vatthu (Subjects of Discussion), a discussion of various controversies in early Buddhist philosophical teachings; 6) Yamaka (The Pairs), which deals with issues in a dual fashion—positive and negative; and 7) Patthana (Activations) dealing with causal relations.

Other schools of **Buddhism** also composed their own Abhidharma literature in Sanskrit, but most have been lost. Some have been preserved in Chinese translations and are included as a separate section of the **Chinese Tripitaka**. The Abhidharma of the Sarvastivada tradition, for example, survives in Chinese. It contains seven works: "Jnana-prasthana" ("Method of Knowledge"); "Sangitiparayaya", a summary of the Buddha's teachings; "Dhatukaya" ("Book of Elements"); "Vijnanakaya" ("Synopsis of Consciousness"); "Prakaranapada", a collection of verses; "Dharmaskandha" ("Book of Things"); and "Prajnapti Sastra" ("Treatise on Communication").

Abhidharma literature is known in Japanese as the Taihôzô or the Ronzô, or transliterated as Abidatsumazô.

Acts of the Buddha

The *Buddhacharita* of Ashvaghosha, the earliest formal biography of Shakyamuni **Buddha** (**Siddharta Gautama**). See *Buddhacharita*.

Afflictions

Any working of the mind, such as a **delusion** or an evil passion, or an action resulting from such thoughts, that interferes with the attainment of **enlightenment**. Affliction is a translation for the terms *klesha* in Sanskrit and *bonnô* in Japanese. The Buddhist tradition identifies the afflictions as the root cause of human **suffering**. The six fundamental afflictions are greed, anger, ignorance, arrogance, doubt, and false views. Greed and anger are two opposite forms of craving; greed is an **attachment** to something pleasurable, while anger is an aversion to something unpleasant. Ignorance is lack of understanding of Buddhist teachings and the way things are. The first three fundamental afflictions—greed, anger and ignorance—are called the **three poisons**. Arrogance refers to a self-centered view of the world based on a false sense of self. Doubt means to be uncertain about the validity of Buddhist teachings. The tradition identifies five specific false views, including belief in a false self and rejection of the workings of cause and effect.

Agama Sutras

Discourses of the historical **Buddha** preserved in Buddhist scripture. In the tradition of **Mahayana Buddhism**, the term *Agama Sutras* is used to distinguish the ancient sutras of **Theravada Buddhism** from the later Mahayana sutras. The word *Agama* literally means "tradition" in Sanskrit. Other Indian religious traditions, including Hinduism and Jainism, also refer to their teachings and sacred texts as Agama. In Buddhist tradition, the Agama Sutras (J. Agongyô) are the four collections of discourses attributed to the Buddha, which were originally composed in Sanskrit. These sutras are now preserved in Chinese translation as the first segment of the **Chinese Tripitaka**. The four collections include the Long Agama Sutras, the Middle Length Agama Sutras, the Item-More Agama Sutras and the Miscellaneous Agama Sutras. The four Agama collections correspond to four of the five Nikayas, the collections of discourses preserved in the *Pali Canon* (**Tripitaka**).

Age of the Degenerate Dharma
See **Latter Age of the Dharma**.

Agyo

Words spoken about the **Dharma** (Buddhist teachings) by a **Zen** master when teaching his or her students. The term also refers to a student's expression in understanding the teachings in response to a question by the master. The term originally referred to the immediate and spontaneous exchanges between master and disciple during lectures or question-and-answer sessions (**mondô**). In the broadest sense, the term may be used as a generic reference of various responses to a **kôan** that students of Zen are called upon to make, such as capping verses (**jakugo**) or **turning words** (**ittengo**). These responses were originally intended to be spontaneous expressions of a Zen practitioner's understanding of a kôan; masters would determine the disciples' progress based on their responses. Later, agyo became stylized responses, memorized by the students for the various kôan they studied.

Ahimsa

(J. fugai) Non-injury of living beings. The concept of ahimsa prohibits killing, injuring, or wishing to harm **sentient beings** (those capable of thought or feeling). Ahimsa is the primary virtue in several Indian religious traditions, including **Buddhism**, Jainism, and Hinduism. The importance of ahimsa in Buddhist morality is seen in the **precepts** taken by lay people and the monastic community against killing. It is, in fact, the first precept of the five taken by lay practitioners and the first of ten taken by **novices**.

Buddhism interprets the practice of ahimsa as the active expression of **compassion** for other sentient beings. According to the Buddhist understanding of ahimsa, intent is the crucial element; accidentally injuring or causing death would not be seen as a violation of the precept against killing.

In Jainism, any taking of life or injury, even unintentional or accidental, is thought to incur karmic repercussions.

Lay Buddhists and the monastic community approach the practice of ahimsa somewhat differently. While lay Buddhists refrain from causing intentional injury to other sentient beings,

monks and **nuns** seek to reduce inadvertent injury. Lay Buddhists often choose a vegetarian diet so as not to participate in the killing of animal life, but they nevertheless farm the land. Buddhist monks and nuns traditionally refrained from farming because it inevitably caused injury to small creatures living in the soil. See also **lay believer**.

Aikuô

Japanese for King **Ashoka**. See **Ashoka**.

Ajari

A senior **monk** who teaches students; often abbreviated to jari. The term is a Japanese rendering of the Chinese transliteration for the Sanskrit "âcârya," one who knows and teaches the rules. In ancient **Buddhism, novices** had two masters, one who taught them the **Dharma**, and one who taught them the rules of conduct (**vinaya**). The term does not retain this connotation in the Japanese context: it is used in many sects to indicate seniority or high rank among monks who instruct disciples. It is most often associated with masters from the esoteric schools, Tendai and Shingon Buddhism.

In Sôtô **Zen**, the term is used as a title of respect for any senior monk. It is not limited to teachers, but applies to any monk who has practiced Zen for more than five years. **Dôgen Kigen** (1200–1253) composed a text, the *Tai Taikogoge Jarihô*, in which he delineates the proper behavior of junior monks in the presence of their seniors, the ajari who had passed at least five summer retreats. See also **Shingon sect**, **Sôtô sect**, and **Tendai sect**.

Shohei, Ichimura. *Zen Master Eihei Dôgen's Monastic Regulations*. Washington, DC: North American Institute of Zen and Buddhist Studies, 1993.

Ako

"Lowering the flame," the ritual action of starting the cremation fire at a funeral service. Today, the ako is a symbolic gesture performed by the Buddhist **monk** leading the funeral service. The officiant symbolically lights the cremation fire with a torch. Ako is performed as one of the nine ritual actions (**kubutsuji**) comprising the funeral services for an **abbot** or another prominent member of the monastic community. It is also one of three ritual actions characterizing Buddhist funerals for ordinary monks and **lay believers**. Also known as hinko. See also **sanbutsuji**.

Akudô

Japanese for **evil paths**. The term refers to the lower three of the six realms of existence, those of **hell** (**jigoku**), **hungry ghosts** (**gaki**), and animals (chikushô). See **evil paths**.

Alaya Consciousness

(J. Arayashiki) The storehouse consciousness, the eighth and deepest level of consciousness in the Yogachara (Hossô) schema of human psychology. The term can also be used in reference to the schema as a whole. The **Yogachara school's** psychology analyzes human perception of the world at eight levels: sight consciousness, sound consciousness, smell consciousness, taste consciousness, tactile consciousness, mind consciousness, ego consciousness, and the storehouse consciousness. The first five levels correspond to five senses. Mind consciousness corresponds to the Western idea of consciousness; at this level, the information gathered from the previous five levels is coordinated. Ego consciousness is the level at which personal **attachments** are formed, either positive or negative. For example, the ego consciousness determines if an object of sight is pleasant to behold, and begins to crave possession of the object; on the

Amida buddha, the Buddha of "Infinite Light," is closely associated with the Pure Land Sutras. This statue was built in Kamakura, Japan in 1252 and stands more than eleven meters high.

other hand, it may find an object repulsive and seek to avoid contact with it. The eighth level of consciousness stores all previous experiences and impressions as seeds, which are the basis for evaluating all present and future experience.

Ordinary human beings create their subjective perception of the world through the workings of the alaya consciousness. Although human consciousness may not create the external objects, the process does create the image that an individual perceives. For this reason, different individuals will not necessarily experience the same external object in the same manner. For example, an individual learns to associate a certain aroma with burning **incense**; the experience is stored as a seed in the storehouse consciousness. In some cultures, incense may be associated with funeral services; a person raised in such a culture, may associate the smell of incense with the sorrow of personal loss. The scent of incense burning may then elicit feelings of melancholy, thus he or she may find the aroma unpleasant, even repulsive. Another person, without a comparable previous experience, may find the aroma of incense pleasant or soothing. See also **Fa-hsien school** and **Hossô school**.

Ama No Hakkikai

The eight **parajika** offenses of a Buddhist **nun**. Parajika offenses, the most serious in the **monastic code**, are punished with expulsion from the monastic order.

Amida Buddha

The **Buddha** of "Infinite Light." The Japanese rendering of the Sanskrit "Amitabha" and the Chinese "Amita", the name is also translated as Muryôkô. Amida buddha is one of the most popular celestial buddhas in **Mahayana Buddhism**. Amida buddha resides in the **Western Pure Land** (Sk. Sukhâvtî), a wondrous world and an ideal location for Buddhist practitioners to attain **enlightenment**. Veneration for Amida dates back to the first century C.E. in India, although Amida attained more popularity in East Asia. Buddhists throughout East Asia, regardless of their schools, consider Amida a primary object of veneration. Amida is credited with infinite **compassion** for suffering **sentient beings**, even the worst offenders of Buddhist ethical norms. For many Buddhists, faith in Amida and his saving powers are the crucial elements in the practice of Buddhism.

Amida's story begins when he was a king, long before he became a buddha. Having heard the **Dharma** preached by the buddha Lokeshvara, the king desired to attain enlightenment (**bodhichitta**). He left behind his secular life and became a **monk**, taking the name Dharmakara. Dharmakara practiced the **bodhisattva** way for ten million years under the guidance of Lokeshvara. He visited innumerable **Buddha Lands** (similar to **heavens**) and took note of the good qualities of each. Finally, he decided to concentrate all of his accumulated **merit** to produce a Buddha Land which possessed all of the positive qualities he had observed in the others. He then took **bodhisattva vows** promising that he would not attain **buddhahood** unless his Buddha Land had the desired qualities and was accessible to all sentient beings. Since Dharmakara became the buddha Amida, his vows guarantee that his Western Pure Land exists.

Amida's Western Pure Land is described in great detail in Buddhist literature. The birds sing the Dharma; even the sounds of running streams proclaim the Dharma. Everything about the land is conducive to enlightenment. There are no evil destinies in the **Pure Land**, no **hungry ghosts** or **hell** dwellers. Any person born into the Pure Land is assured that they will not regress in the path toward enlightenment.

The primary scriptural accounts of Amida and his Western Pure Land are found in three so-called **Pure Land Sutras**: the larger Pure Land Sutra, the Smaller Pure Land Sutra (also known as the Amida Sutra), and the Sutra of the Buddha of Infinite Light (also called the Contemplation Sutra). The Larger Pure Land Sutra recounts the story of the bodhisattva Dharmakara, and spells out the forty-eight vows that he took, explaining the means for attaining **rebirth** in his Pure Land. These vows have come to be called the Original Vow of Amida. The Smaller Pure Land Sutra explains the simplest form of practice to assure rebirth in the Pure Land—the recitation of the name of Amida. In the Sutra of the Buddha of Infinite Light, Sakyamuni Buddha appears to a human queen imprisoned by her wicked son; the text teaches her several methods of **meditation** on Amida buddha and the Pure Land.

There are various opinions of what is necessary to assure rebirth in his Pure Land. The scriptural accounts suggest that a combination of faith in Amida and the practice of good works lead to rebirth. Interpretations of the scriptures by East Asian Pure Land believers, especially by the Japanese schools, reject the notion that good works are necessary. They stress faith in Amida buddha and the power of his Original Vow to save ordinary sentient beings. See also **dual practice** and **koshin mida**.

Cowell, E. B. et al., eds. *Buddhist Mahayana Texts*. New York: Dover Publications, 1969.

Matsunaga, Daigan, and Alicia Matsunaga. *Foundation of Japanese Buddhism*. 2 vols. Los Angeles, CA: Buddhist Books International, 1976.

Ueda, Yoshifumi and Dennis Hirota. *Shinran: An Introduction to His Thought*. Tokyo: Hongwanji International Center, 1989.

Amida's Vows

Vows taken by the **Amida buddha** while he was still a **bodhisattva** named Dharmakara. This is also known as the Original Vow. Dharmakara took forty-eight great **bodhisattva vows** in an effort to save **sentient beings** and create a **Pure Land**, ideal for practicing **Buddhism**. The vows are elaborated in the Larger **Pure Land Sutra**. The vows are interpreted somewhat differently by various sects of Pure Land Buddhism; in particular, the requirements for attaining **rebirth** into the Pure Land stated in the vows have been an object of controversy. See also **Amida buddha**.

Amitayus

The **buddha** of "Infinite Life." Another Sanskrit name for **Amida buddha**, translated as Muryôju in Japanese. See **Amida buddha**.

Ananda

(J. Anan) One of the ten distinguished disciples of Shakyamuni **Buddha** (**Siddharta Gautama**). Ananda was a younger cousin of the Buddha and became his favorite disciple in the later part of the Buddha's life. Ananda served as the Buddha's personal attendant for the last twenty years of his life and was present at the Buddha's death. Ananda is renowned for his exceptional memory; he is said to have memorized every sermon that he heard the Buddha deliver. For this reason, he is known as the Foremost in Hearing the **Dharma**. Ananda is also known as a strong advocate for female disciples: He helped convince the Buddha to establish the female order of **nuns**.

Ananda was the only one of the great disciples who did not attain **arhat** before the Buddha passed away. (Arhatship is usually confirmed by another enlightened master.) He still had not done so when **Mahakashyapa** convened the First Council, and therefore was not initially allowed to attend. Ananda meditated through the night and by morning was admitted to the council. According to tradition, he contributed to the assembly by reciting several **sermons** of the Buddha. This collection of sermons became the Sutra Pitaka, one of the three portions of the **Tripitaka**.

The **Zen** tradition reveres Ananda as the second of the twenty-eight Indian **patriarchs**. Ananda is said to have inherited the Dharma from Mahakashapa. The story of his enlightenment is recorded as a **kôan** in Case 22, of the *Mumonkân*: "Ananda asked Mahakashyapa, 'Did the **World-Honored One** transmit anything to you other than the golden monastic robe?' Mahakashyapa shouted in reply, 'Ananda!' Ananda responded. Mahakashyapa said, 'Knock down the flagpole in front of the gate!'" See also **arhat**.

Ishigami, Zenno. *Disciples of the Buddha*. Trans. Richard L. Gage and Paul McCarthy. Tokyo: Kosei Publishing Co., 1989.

Anatman

(J. Muga) The teaching of No-Self, the most basic and distinctive teaching of **Theravada Buddhism**. According to tradition, the historical **Buddha** discovered the truth of Anatman during **meditation** and taught it to others, beginning with his first sermon. The teaching denies the existence of **atman**, or soul, which is eternal, abiding, and unchanging. **Attachment** to the concept of such a false self is the fundamental cause of human **suffering**. Realization that no such self exists is the basis for the attainment of **nirvana**, or release.

According to the Buddhist understanding of Anatman, the true self can be understood as the ever-changing configuration of five elements, known as the **five skandhas**. Rather than possessing an eternal and unchanging soul, the individual is actually an on-going process of transformation. The classical text explaining the concept of Anatman is the *Questions of King Milinda*. In the text, Nagasena, the Buddhist **monk**, uses the image of a chariot made from a configuration of interdependent parts to express this concept.

Anatman is a basic concept in **Mahayana Buddhism**, although in an altered form. The Mahayana tradition extends the analysis of an individual's No-Self applying it to all things (**Dharmas**). This led to the Mahayana teaching of shunyata, or **emptiness**.

Conze, Edward. *Buddhist Scriptures: A Bibliography.* Ed. Lewis Lancaster. New York: Garland, 1982.

Andae

The five-strip inner garment worn by Buddhist **monks** and **nuns**. Andae is the Japanese transliteration of the Sanskrit term *antarvasa*. See **gojôe**.

Andô

Attendants hall—the living quarters for **novices** at **Zen** monasteries of the Sung dynasty (960–1279). Used as an alternative term for the **anjadô**. See **anjadô**.

Ango

The **rainy-season retreat**. A three-month period during the summer when **monks** and **nuns** stay at a temple or monastery for an intensive practice session. Traditionally the summer retreat was observed from the middle of the fourth lunar month through the middle of the seventh lunar month (roughly April through July). The term literally means "peaceful dwelling" and is the Japanese rendering of the Sanskrit "vârsika." The custom dates back to the time of the historical **Buddha**, before the establishment of permanent monastic dwellings. During the Buddha's lifetime, he and his disciples traveled throughout the year, teaching and lecturing in the villages they visited along the way. They settled down temporarily during the annual rainy season when travel was inconvenient and sometimes unsafe. Eventually, the Buddhist **monastic code** (**vinaya**) forbade travel during the rainy season, a period of ninety days.

Today, the **Zen** community in Japan observes the summer retreat as one of two annual retreats. Major monasteries hold the summer retreat from April 16 through July 15 and a winter retreat from November through January. During the retreat, monks and nuns strictly observe the Zen monastic rules (**shingi**), concentrating their efforts on **meditation**. In many cases, up to fourteen hours of each day are dedicated to seated meditation. Travel outside the temple is strictly limited for the duration of the retreat; even word of a parent's death will not be passed along until the end of the retreat.

The rainy-season retreat is commonly called "ge-ango" (summer retreat), or "u-ango" (rainy retreat) in Japanese. **Dôgen Kigen** (1200–1253) discusses the Sôtô customs for the ango in the seventy-ninth chapter of the *Shôbôgenzô*, called "Ango." See also **Sôtô sect**.

Buswell, Robert E., Jr. *The Zen Monastic Experience: Buddhist Practice in Contemporary Korea.* Princeton, NJ: Princeton University Press, 1992.

Angya

Literally meaning "to go on foot;" the **Zen** practice of **pilgrimage**. Pilgrimage is a traditional aspect of the Zen lifestyle. Historically, angya referred to the common practice of Zen **monks** and **nuns** travelling from master to master, or monastery to monastery. Pilgrimage served a number of purposes. Initially, a monk or nun traveled in search of a comparable master with whom to begin the practice of Zen. Student and teacher alike needed to evaluate the other. Masters often tested a potential disciple's resolve before admitting him or her to the assembly. In earlier centuries, pilgrimage was not limited to beginners; advanced practitioners also traveled. Masters often encouraged disciples who had attained some level of maturity to experience the Zen styles of other teachers as a means to further their practice. Monks and nuns sometimes spent years travelling, becoming familiar with the styles of various Zen masters of the day. In this case, pilgrimage played an essential role in preparing a Zen practitioner to become a master who would guide the practice of others.

Angya, the Zen practice of pilgrimage, requires a traditional dress that includes robes and a straw hat.

In modern Japan, however, angya usually applies to the initial journey made by a new trainee (**unsui**) seeking admission to a main monastery for formal training. The experience has now been ritualized and follows a set pattern. The trainee, already ordained, will approach the monastery dressed as a pilgrim monk and formally ask for admission. The traditional dress for a pilgrim includes a bamboo hat (kasa), straw sandals, and cotton leggings. The pilgrim carries all necessary items, including a full set of monastic robes (**kesa**), **begging bowls**, a razor to shave the head, and a straw raincoat (mino). Inevitably, the monastery refuses the initial request for entry with a set explanation. The monastery officer usually explains that the monastery has no space to accommodate a new trainee or is too poor to support one. The trainee must then wait patiently outside the entrance gate (**niwa zume**) until he is finally admitted on a probationary basis (**tanga zume**) after a number of days.

Anja

An attendant or lay **novice**. Historically, anja were lay people who lived on temple grounds before being ordained. In China, it was quite common for lay novices to live and work on temple grounds for extended periods of time without ever seeking **ordination**. In Japan, that practice was less common; in most cases, Japanese anja were young men or boys who had not yet completed their training for ordination. At a **Zen** temple, novices serve a variety of functions and perform most of the **manual labor** for the monastic community—tending fields, assisting with preparation and serving of meals, cleaning temple buildings (**shichidô garan**) and grounds. Traditionally anja had their own quarters within the temple grounds (**anjadô**), separate from those of the ordained **monks**. Today, younger monks in training at **Zen** monasteries (also called anja) serve the same functions.

The same Chinese characters which spell the word *anja* are also pronounced *gyôja* when used in an unrelated context. See also **lay believer**.

Anjadô

Assistants' hall. A separate residence on temple grounds for **anja**, the unordained **novices** who traditionally served in a variety of roles in Chinese **Zen** monasteries. In temples, the anjadô were often quite large and elaborate, since it was common practice for large numbers of lay novices to reside and work at the monastery for many years without seeking **ordination**. In addition to sleeping quarters, the complex included a **meditation hall**, reading room, latrine, and wash stand. Only vestiges of the anjadô survived in the Japanese Zen context, since Japanese monasteries did not perpetuate the practice of having lay novices in residence for extended periods of time. See also **lay believer**.

Anroku

Brief biographical account of any **Zen** master's **pilgrimages** and **enlightenment** experience. Anroku is the Japanese rendering of the Chinese term *hsing-lu*. Also pronounced gyôroku or kôroku.

Anuruddha

One of the ten distinguished disciples of Shakyamuni **Buddha** (**Siddharta Gautama**), Anuruddha is renowned for his divine insight. Anuruddha (J. Anaritsu) came from the Shakya family and was a cousin of Shakyamuni. Like Shakyamuni, he had been raised in great luxury and found the monastic life difficult. Although he persevered in his practice, on one occasion he fell asleep while the Buddha was preaching. Ashamed of his weakness, Anuruddha took a vow of sleeplessness. As a result of his intense practice and lack of sleep, Anuruddha eventually lost his eyesight. The loss of his physical vision led to his attainment of spiritual insight. According to some traditions, Anuruddha recited the **Abhidharma** Pitaka, one of the three sections of the **Tripitaka**, at the First Council.

Ishigami, Zenno. *Disciples of the Buddha*. Trans. Richard L. Gage and Paul McCarthy. Tokyo: Kosei Publishing Co., 1989.

Anuttara Samyak Sambodhi

Supreme perfect **enlightenment**. This is the Sanskrit term for the perfect, unsurpassed enlightenment experienced by the buddhas. The term is often left untranslated in Buddhist texts. The Japanese transliteration is "anokutara sammyaku sambodai."

Arada Kalama

One of two Indian **meditation** masters with whom **Siddharta Gautama** studied before he attained **enlightenment**. Kalama taught a form of yogic meditation leading to a state of deep concentration beyond sensory perception. According to traditional accounts, Siddharta mastered Kalama's teachings easily, and Kalama was prepared to accept him as his equal and co-teacher. Feeling that the meditative states that he had attained were not yet the enlightenment he sought, Siddharta left Kalama.

Arayashiki

Japanese transliteration for the Sanskrit term *Alaya vijnana*. See **alaya consciousness**.

Archery

Known in Japanese as **kyûdô**, archery is one of the traditional East Asian martial arts most closely associated with the **Zen** sect of **Buddhism**. See **kyûdô**.

Arhat

"Holy one worthy of veneration"; one who has attained release (**nirvana**) from the cycle of **suffering** by following the **Eightfold Path** of **Buddhism**. According to the tradition of **Theravada Buddhism**, the arhat is the ideal practitioner of Buddhism—one who has attained the same level of

慶友尊者

Statue of an arhat housed in the Daiyûhôden at Mampukuji in Uji, Japan.

enlightenment as the historical **Buddha**, **Siddharta Gautama**. Theravada Buddhism recognizes four stages along the path to enlightenment; the arhat has attained the highest stage. Like the Buddha, the arhat has nothing left to learn and is worthy of veneration by others. At death, the arhat achieves ultimate release (**parinirvana**) from **samsara**, the ongoing cycle of birth, death, and **rebirth**. The term is also one of the ten epithets of respect used for the Buddha.

The tradition of **Mahayana Buddhism** generally regards the arhat as inferior to the **bodhisattva**, the Mahayana ideal of a Buddhist practitioner. According to Mahayana, arhats selfishly aspire to their own enlightenment, without compassionate concern for others. In contrast to this, bodhisattvas are presented as compassionate beings who simultaneously seek enlightenment for themselves and all other **sentient beings**.

During the T'ang dynasty (618–907), Chinese artists depicted the arhat as grotesque figures, often with exaggerated features. Chinese Buddhists came to favor a group of sixteen disciples of the historical Buddha who attained enlightenment as a subject of their art. The Sixteen Arhats became a common theme in East Asia Buddhist painting, sculpture, and other styles of sacred imagery. In some cases, the group depicted was the Five Hundred Arhats mentioned in the **Lotus Sutra**. Although the arhats were not originally intended as positive images within the iconography of Mahayana art, in popular understanding they were regarded as guardian figures who protect the Buddha and the **Dharma** from evil forces.

Like the early tradition, the **Zen** school tends to regard the arhat as a figure worthy of respect and admiration. Indeed, Zen masters extol the arhat as an ideal worthy of emulation. Like the arhat, the Zen practitioner must rely upon the self alone, struggling toward the attainment of enlightenment without reliance on any external assistance. Portrayals of the Sixteen Arhats are depicted in Zen art. Many Zen temples even have a separate hall in which their images are enshrined.

The Chinese and Japanese terms *Lohan* and *Rakan* became a title of respect used in reference to enlightened Zen masters.

Kent, Richard K. "Depictions of the Guardians of the Law: Lohan Painting in China." In *Latter Days of the Law: Images of Chinese Buddhism, 850–1850.* Ed. Marsha Weidner. Honolulu, HI: University of Hawaii Press, 1994.

de Visser, Marinus Willem. *The Arhats in China and Japan.* Berlin: Oesterheld and Co., 1923.

Ascetic Practices

Ascetic practices are forms of self-denial undertaken for religious purposes. The most common forms of religious asceticism include fasting, celibacy, and sleep deprivation. Extreme forms of asceticism include self-mutilation (especially castration), and fasting to the point of starvation. While Buddhist monastic life can be characterized as a modified form of ascetic practice, the tradition rejects extreme forms. This rejection can be traced to the teachings of the historical **Buddha**. After six years of harsh ascetic practice, which brought him to the brink of death, **Siddharta Gautama** concluded that the extreme path of self-denial was not helpful in attaining **enlightenment**. He devised a path balancing extreme asceticism and hedonism (the quest for complete self-gratification). The Buddha called his path the middle way, the traditional name for what is now known as **Buddhism**.

The **Zen** tradition maintains many of the modified forms of ascetic practice observed by other forms of Buddhism, especially within the monastic setting. Like other Buddhist **monks** and **nuns**, Zen monastics traditionally remain celibate, consume food only before the noon hour, limit their diet to exclude liquor, intoxicants, some spices and meats, and maintain a strict schedule of early rising and relatively short periods of sleep. These practices are intended to promote concentration during **meditation** and to reduce **attachment** to worldly values. At the same time, they are designed to maintain the physical health of the body, which the Buddha felt contributed positively to the meditative life.

Nevertheless, there are a number of notable examples in the Zen literature of practitioners who displayed extraordinary levels of ascetic practice in their single-minded quest for enlightenment. **Bodhidharma**, the First **Patriarch**, is said to have spent nine years facing a wall in meditation; he was so intent on attaining his goal that he lost the use of his arms and legs. **Hui-k'o** (487–593), the Second Patriarch, is said to have cut off his own arm in order to demonstrate to Bodhidharma his absolute dedication to pursuing the **Dharma**. Other Zen monks, such as the Japanese monk **Bankei Yôtaku**, followed the Buddha's example and practiced forms of extreme asceticism until it threatened their lives. Like the Buddha, Bankei found that the answer was not achieved through self-punishment.

Ashita

(J. Ashida) An Indian holy man and seer who visited the newborn **Siddharta Gautama**. Ashita examined the child and found marks of greatness. He told **Suddhodana**, the child's father, that his son would become either a great religious leader (**buddha**) or a great king (Cakravarti).

Ashoka

(J. Aikuô) The Indian king who ruled the Maurya empire in the third century B.C.E. Ashoka inherited the throne circa 269 B.C.E. from his father, Bindusara, and extended the empire to encompass most of the Indian subcontinent. According to Buddhist legend, Ashoka defeated the Kalingas in a bloody war. After witnessing the **suffering** he inflicted on the Kalingas, he chose to forsake violence and devote himself to the peaceful study and teachings of the **Dharma**. He became a devout Buddhist and spent the rest of his life promoting **Buddhism** throughout India. Ashoka had several stone pillars engraved with edicts declaring the Dharma. Additionally, he is believed to have erected 84,000 **stupas** and temples throughout India, many of them marking religiously significant sites from the **Buddha's** life. Ashoka promoted religious tolerance, denounced both hunting for sport and the sacrifice of animals, and commanded his administrators to protect the welfare of the people. He supported the Buddhist **sangha** and public welfare projects such as sponsoring hospitals, building rest houses along major roads, and digging wells.

Ashoka is also credited with convening the Third Buddhist Council, held in the Mauryan capital of Pataliputra. Ashoka sent out emissaries to spread the teachings of Buddhism to other lands, including Egypt, Syria, and Sri Lanka. He is sometimes regarded as the second founder of Buddhism, one who embodies the qualities of the ideal lay devotee, and serves as the model for the perfect Buddhist ruler. See also **lay believer**.

Strong, John S. *The Legend of King Ashoka: A Study and Translation of the* Asokavadana. Princeton, NJ: Princeton University Press, 1983.

Ashura

Fierce, pugnacious supernatural beings, or demi-gods; often translated as "titan." According to the Hindu tradition, ashura are evil spirits who continually engage in warfare with the gods, especially **Indra**. In this context, they are regarded as demons or anti-gods. The Buddhist tradition has reinterpreted the concept, transforming ashura into protective spirits who guard the Buddhist **Dharma**. While they remain fond of fighting, they are no longer seen as evil.

In **Buddhism**, existence as an ashura is considered one of the six realms (rokudô) into which an individual may be reincarnated. The level of the ashura in the hierarchy of beings is generally regarded as a higher realm than that of human because they are supernatural in power and activity. In other contexts, the ashura are interpreted as one of the **evil paths** (akudô) in which one suffers punishment for past misdeeds.

Ashvaghosha

Indian **monk** who lived during the late first and early second centuries C.E. Ashvaghosha was a poet, Buddhist philosopher, and proponent of Mahayana teachings. He is best known as the author of the *Buddhacharita* (*Acts of the Buddha*), one of the first biographies of Shakyamuni **Buddha** (**Siddharta Gautama**). He is known to have composed a number of treatises on Mahayana thought; several more are attributed to him.

The **Zen** school reveres Ashvaghosha as one of the twenty-eight Indian **patriarchs** of Zen. In the *Ching-te Ch'üan-teng Lu*, for example, he is included as the twelfth Indian patriarch.

Atman

(J. ga) The Hindu concept of a soul or true self within a human being. According to Hindu philosophy, the atman is the eternal and non-physical aspect of a person, identified with the cosmic soul, or Brahman. In the classical philosophical tradition, release (moksha) is attained by contemplating the nature of the atman and realizing its identification with Brahman.

Buddhism denies the existence of the atman, rejecting the concept that any eternal, abiding, and unchanging aspect exists (**Anatman**). According to tradition, the **Buddha** sought an atman, as the Hindu tradition suggests, but discovered that it did not actually exist. In Buddhism, the atman is a false sense of self to which human beings become attached. This **attachment** leads inevitably to **suffering**. Release from suffering is attained with the realization that there is no atman.

Attachment

Buddhism regards attachment—the desire for things or pleasure, or obsession with ideas and concepts—as one of the basic **afflictions** (bonnô) that cause human **suffering** and hinder progress toward **enlightenment**. The tradition recognizes various kinds of attachments, from very coarse to very subtle. The crudest forms of attachment are to sensual pleasures, including cravings for sex, food, and wealth. The basic Buddhist **precepts**, including the **five precepts** of **lay believers** and the **ten precepts** of **novices**, are designed to reduce these coarser attachments. People also form more subtle attachments, however, to intangible things like ideas. One of the most persistent attachments, for example, is the human tendency to cling to a false concept of the self (**atman**). To overcome this sort of attachment, one must learn meditative techniques, which help to expose the emptiness of the concept. Advanced practitioners of Buddhism sometimes become attached to the Buddhist teachings themselves. In this case, the very **Dharma** can become a hindrance to enlightenment, since it is a means to an end and not enlightenment itself. The traditional image describing attachment to the teachings compares them to a raft, carrying the believer from this shore of **samsara** to the other shore of **nirvana**. Upon reaching the far shore, however, the raft becomes useless and can be abandoned. Clinging to the teachings is the same as insisting on carrying the raft on one's back.

Avalokiteshvara

The **bodhisattva** of infinite **compassion** and mercy; one of the most important bodhisattvas, or beings seeking enlightenment, in the pantheon of **Mahayana Buddhism**. Avalokiteshvara is revered throughout the Mahayana world by Buddhists of all schools. The exact meaning of the Sanskrit name is somewhat obscure and is debated by scholars. It may mean "one who looks upon the **suffering** of the world," or "one who hears the cries of those suffering in the world." The bodhisattva appears in several Mahayana **sutras**, including the **Heart Sutra** and the **Lotus Sutra**, in which one chapter is devoted to Avalokiteshvara's special powers to rescue those in need.

In China, Avalokiteshvara is known as **Kuan-yin**, "one who observes the sounds." In Japan, the bodhisattva is called **Kannon**, the Japanese pronunciation of the Chinese characters. Changes occurred in the presentation and description of Avalokiteshvara as devotion to the bodhisattva spread throughout East Asia. Although Avalokiteshvara was portrayed as masculine in Indian images and texts, female images emerged in China and Japan.

Avalokiteshvara Sutra

A brief Buddhist text dedicated to a description of the power of the **bodhisattva** named **Avalokiteshvara** (Ch. **Kuan-yin**; J. **Kannon**). Although the text has circulated as a single work, it appears in the original Sanskrit version of the **Lotus Sutra** (Saddharma-pundarika-sutra) as Chapter 24. In the Chinese translation of the Lotus Sutra prepared by **Kumarajiva**, the most popular version used in East Asia, the Avalokiteshvara Sutra is Chapter 25. It is known as the **Kuan-yin Ching** in Chinese and the **Kannonkyô** in Japanese. The text is commonly chanted at **Zen** temples throughout East Asia, especially at ceremonies where lay practitioners are present. There have been many English translations based on the Chinese, including those by Hurvitz and Watson.

The text begins with a bodhisattva asking Shakyamuni **Buddha** (**Siddharta Gautama**), why Avalokiteshvara, literally called "One Who Perceives the Sounds of the World," is so named. Shakyamuni responds by recounting all calamities from which Avalokiteshvara will save a believer who calls out to him for help. The bodhisattva then asks in what form Avalokiteshvara appears to

perform these acts of **compassion**. The Buddha explains that Avalokiteshvara assumes any form that is appropriate to the situation of the person in need, listing thirty-three different manifestation. See also **lay believer**.

Hurvitz, Leon, trans. *Scripture of the Lotus Blossom of the Fine Dharma.* New York: Columbia University Press, 1982.
Watson, Burton, trans. *The Lotus Sutra.* New York: Columbia University Press, 1993.

Avatamsaka Sutra

The "Flower Garland Sutra;" a Mahayana sutra originally composed in Sanskrit but now preserved in the Chinese translation known as the Hua-yen Sutra. It became the central text of the Chinese **Hua-yen school** (J. **Kegon school**) and had widespread influence and popularity in various other schools of East Asian **Buddhism**. There are three Chinese translations of the text: Buddhabhadra in 418–421 (T. 9, no. 278), Shiksananda in 695–699 (T. 10, no. 279), and **Prajna** in 759–762 (T. 10, no. 293). According to tradition, the Avatamsaka Sutra represents the **Buddha's** first sermon, given almost immediately after he attained **enlightenment**. His audience found the concepts so difficult to grasp that the Buddha decided to alter his teaching strategy and begin with the simpler Theravada concepts.

The sutra contains a number of chapters that once circulated as independent texts, including a chapter describing the **ten stages of a bodhisattva**. Another major segment of the text, known in Sanskrit as the "Gandavyuha," describes the travels of a pilgrim, Sudhana, who seeks guidance from numerous teachers in his quest to learn the way of the bodhisattva. The Gandavyuha has been translated into English by Thomas Cleary under the title *Entry into the Realm of Reality*.

The Avatamsaka Sutra presents the teachings of the **Mâdhyamaka** and **Yogachara schools** of **Mahayana**

Buddhism, as well as important new concepts. Its prominent teachings include the notion that all **sentient beings** possess **Buddha Nature**, that Absolute Truth and **Relative Truth** are not mutually exclusive or mutually denying, and that all phenomena are interdependent and interpenetrating.

The **Zen** tradition makes extensive use of teachings and images drawn from the Avatamsaka Sutra. From the beginning, Zen teachings were heavily influenced by Hua-yen thought—so much so, that the modern Zen scholar, **D. T. Suzuki** (1689–1966), maintained that Zen emerged from the philosophical basis of Hua-yen thought.

Avici Hell

The lowest and harshest region of **hell**, where the **suffering** is interminable. Avici is the worst of the **eight hot hells** (hachinetsu jigoku) reserved for those who have committed one of the five deadly acts (**gogyakuzai**) or slandered the **Dharma**. The inhabitants of Avici hell constantly cry out in pain. In Japanese, the Avici hell is called Muken jigoku, the Hell of Incessant Suffering.

Awakening of Faith

Known in Chinese as the Ta-ch'eng Ch'i-hsin lun, and in Japanese as the Daijô Kishinron, a comprehensive summary of Mahayana teachings traditionally attributed to **Ashvaghosha**, an Indian **Zen** patriarch. Modern scholars have concluded that Ashvaghosha probably did not compose the original Sanskrit texts, as none survive. Scholars believe it was composed originally in Chinese. There are two Chinese versions believed to be translations completed by Paramartha (T. 32, no. 1666) around 550 C.E. and by Shiksananada (T. 32, no. 1667) around 700 C.E. Despite its brevity, the treatise is among the most influential texts in all of East Asian **Buddhism**. Approximately 170 commentaries were written to explicate its tersely argued contents. The most important of the traditional commentaries was written by Fa-tsang (643–712), **patriarch** of the **Hua-yen school**. Other schools, including Shingon, Zen, and **Pure Land**, hold the text in high regard. See also **Shingon sect**.

Hakeda, Yoshito S., trans. *The Awakening of Faith*. New York: Columbia University Press, 1967.

A-yu-wang-shan

(J. Aikuô-zan) Mount A-yu-wang, an important religious site for Zen, located in present-day Chekiang, China. A-yu-wang is the Chinese name for the Indian Buddhist monarch, **Ashoka**. According to tradition, the Buddhist **monk** Hui-tah discovered an old **stupa** on the mountain in 281 C.E. Believing it to be one of the 84,000 stupas erected by Ashoka centuries earlier, Hui-tah named the mountain for King Ashoka. Centuries later, the mountain became the site of the **Zen** monastery **Kuan-li-ssu**; A-yu-wang-shan became known as one of the Five Mountains (Ch. wu-shan; J. **Gozan temples**), the most prestigious Zen monasteries in China.

B

Baitô

Plum tea, a sweet beverage made by steeping plums and sugar. At some **Zen** temples in Japan, it is served daily to the resident **monks** or **nuns** after the morning service.

Baiyû Jikushin

(1633–1707) A Japanese Sôtô **monk** of the Tokugawa period (1600–1867), who participated in reform movements within the **Sôtô sect**. Baiyû was born in Osaka, Japan and became a Buddhist monk at age eleven. He became the **Dharma heir** of Ryûban Shôun of **Kôshô-ji** and joined with **Manzan Dôhaku**, the reformer, to petition the Japanese government for permission to restore the original system of Dharma succession within the Sôtô sect. They were successful in their efforts, and **isshi inshô** became the norm once again.

Bakufu

A military government in Japan under the leadership of a **shôgun**. The term literally means "tent government," referring to the field headquarters of a military leader during wartime. Later, the term referred to a permanent military government headquarters. Gradually it became the common term for the military government itself. There have been several bakufu in Japanese history, established under successive **lineages** of shôgun. Bakufu existed during the Kamakura (1185–1333), Ashikaga (1392–1568), and Tokugawa (1600–1867) periods. The bakufu is also called shogunate in English.

During each period, the bakufu maintained close relations with the **Zen** school, acting as supporters for various Zen masters and monasteries. It is commonly noted that during the Kamakura period, the bakufu sponsored the newly imported Zen school because Zen was better suited to military culture than older, more established forms of **Buddhism**. The Ashikaga ordered the construction of an extensive network of Zen temples throughout the country, which served as state temples (kokubunji). See also **samurai**.

Ball of Doubt

(J. gidan) A **Zen** expression for the tension that builds up in a Zen practitioner, especially when teaching or working on a **kôan**. According to **Hakuin Ekaku** (1685–1768) the formation of this ball of doubt is one of the essential elements of Zen practice. When the ball of doubt finally shatters, the practitioner has an experience of **satori**, or **enlightenment**. Zen texts sometimes use the phrase "to smash the ball of doubt" as an expression for attaining enlightenment.

Yampolsky, Philip B., trans. *The Zen Master Hakuin: Selected Writings.* New York: Columbia University Press, 1971.
Miura, Isshû, and Ruth Fuller Sasaki. *Zen Dust: The History of the Kôan and Kôan Study in Rinzai (Lin-chi) Zen.* New York: Harcourt, Brace & World, 1967.

Banka

Evening services; one of three periods of ritual **chanting**, along with morning and midday services, held daily in a **Zen** monastery. The evening service is held before dusk in the main hall (**Butsuden**). It includes the chanting of various **sutras** and other prayers. It is known more fully as banka fugin.

Bankei Yôtaku

(1622–1693) Japanese Rinzai **monk** from the early Tokugawa period (1600–1867), officially recognized as a member of the lineage of **Myôshin-ji**. Bankei was born to a **samurai** family of Confucian scholars. He rebelled against the Confucian education that his family expected of him, turning instead to the **Zen** sect of **Buddhism** to answer his religious doubts. He practiced under several important masters of the day, including **Umpo Zenjô** (1572–1653) and the Chinese monk **Tao-che Ch'ao-yüan** (d. 1660). Nevertheless, he regarded himself as self-taught, refusing to accept official sanction (J. **inka**) from Tao-che. He became Umpo's **Dharma heir** fulfilling Umpo's dying wish. Although Bankei established several temples and accepted disciples, he did not officially transmit the Dharma to any successor and establish a lineage. Nevertheless, Bankei had a deep influence on the Zen Buddhism of his day, primarily through his public **sermons**, which were later published.

Later in life, Bankei became a popular preacher, opening his Dharma talks to the general public and attracting large crowds. Thus, he promoted his unique style of Zen to Buddhist monks and **nuns** from other sects and to all social classes. In his sermons, Bankei explained the Unborn Buddha Mind as innate within every individual. Human beings have no need to struggle to become buddhas; they need only trust in the **unborn**. Instead of recommending seated **meditation** (**zazen**) or contemplation based on a **kôan** as is the norm in Rinzai practice, Bankei encouraged his audience to simply abide in the Unborn Buddha Mind. See also **Rinzai sect**.

Haskell, Peter. *Bankei Zen: Translations from the Record of Bankei*. New York: Grove Press, 1984.

Waddell, Norman. *The Unborn: The Life and Teaching of Zen Master Bankei, 1622–1693*. New York: North Point Press, 2000.

Baranashi

A kingdom in central India at the time of the historical **Buddha**. The capital city, also called Baranashi, was the site of the Deer Park, where the Buddha gave his first sermon to the five mendicants. The Deer Park is near the present-day city of **Benares**.

Barbarian

(J. koshu) In Chinese texts, the term may apply to any foreigner. In **Zen** materials, the expression refers almost exclusively to **Bodhidharma**, the traditional founder of Zen in China. He is often called the Barbarian with a Red Beard (J. Shaku Koshu), since it was commonly believed that all foreigners had red hair.

Bashô

See **Matsuo Bashô**.

Basô Dôitsu

Japanese transliteration of **Ma-tsu Tao-i** (709–788), one of the most influential Chinese Zen masters of the T'ang dynasty (618–907). See **Ma-tsu Tao-i**.

Bassui Tokushô

(1327–1387) Japanese Rinzai **monk** of the third generation of the **Hottô-Ha**, who lived during the Kamakura period (1185–1333). Bassui was born in Sagami, in present-day Kanagawa Prefecture. He was plagued by religious doubts in his early years, and did not take the **tonsure** until he was twenty-eight years old. Later, he regarded doubt as the crucial factor in the struggle for **enlightenment**. After becoming a monk, he set out on a **pilgrimage** seeking a master. He met **Kohô Kakumyô** and almost immediately became his **Dharma heir**, although he only remained with the master for two months. Bassui then continued on his pilgrimage until 1380, when patrons constructed a monastery for him in Enzan, present-day Yamanashi Prefecture. He named the temple Kôgoku-ji and established a community of disciples. He is regarded as the founder of the Kôgoku-ji branch of Rinzai Zen. He received the posthumous title Ekô Daien **Zenji**, which means **Zen** Master Great Perfection of the Light of Wisdom. See also **Rinzai sect**.

Begging Alms

The practice of making begging rounds, during which Buddhist **monks** and **nuns** accept donations of food, clothing, and other necessities from lay supporters. Begging alms, or mendicancy, dates back to the lifetime of the historical **Buddha** in ancient India, but the Buddha was not the first or only religious leader to encourage the practice as a regular part of monastic life. At the time, many religious groups embraced mendicancy as a form of ascetic practice. For Buddhist monks and nuns, mendicancy was traditionally a regulated part of the monastic life. It is required by the **vinaya**, the Theravadan **monastic code** which governs life within Buddhist monasteries. The vinaya explicitly forbids monks and nuns to earn a living through means other than begging. It defines begging as the "right livelihood" for monks and nuns. Although the Buddhist monastic community continues to rely on lay support, begging rounds remain an active part of monastic life in only a few parts of the Buddhist world.

According to the vinaya, monks and nuns should beg for alms each morning, silently visiting the houses of lay people. The rules require them to keep their eyes cast downward and to make no special requests. They are not allowed to refuse any offering, regardless of the food's quality. Even meat is to be accepted, provided the animal was not slaughtered specifically for the monk or nun. After making the begging rounds, they return to the monastery before the noon hour to eat whatever was offered to them. The vinaya regulates the types of **offerings** lay people may make. For example, monks and nuns traditionally could not accept cash donations, since they were forbidden to handle money. However, modern cash economies have forced the monastic community to develop various means to accept monetary donations in order to purchase goods and services.

Within the Buddhist monastic context, begging for alms serves a number of related purposes. It is one of the **ascetic practices** that the vinaya imposes on monks and nuns to reduce their **attachment** to wealth and material things. **Buddhism** regards attachment to material possessions as one of the basic obstacles to **enlightenment**. In addition, begging is often a humbling experience that can help to reduce one's attachment to the false self (**atman**). Also of great importance is the opportunity which mendicancy provides for lay people to build **merit**. Begging allows for a mutually beneficial relationship to develop between the ordained and lay portions of the Buddhist **sangha**. While lay people provide for the physical necessities of monks and nuns, the monastic community provides lay people with spiritual benefits.

In East Asian Buddhism, begging for alms has never been common practice except in the case of the **Zen** school. The reasons for this are not completely clear, but they probably include differences in culture and climate. First, the practice of monks and nuns living from the labor of lay supporters conflicts with the dominant Confucian principle of productive labor by all members of society. In addition, unlike India, the weather in many parts of East Asia makes mendicancy a severe hardship. Throughout the region, Buddhist monasteries and temples relied on two basic sources of income: land ownership and financial assistance from government sponsorship and wealthy lay patrons.

In the Zen sects of East Asia today, begging for alms is not practiced universally as a regular part of the monastic life. When it does occur, monks and nuns do not follow the ancient pattern of daily rounds to receive prepared food for the day's sustenance. Japanese Zen monks and nuns go out on begging rounds several days each month. They typically beg in small groups, walking through the streets single file, calling out the word *Hô*, meaning **Dharma**. **Lay believers** offer them donations, usually money or uncooked rice. The exchange is marked by mutual respect and gratitude, with both parties bowing to each other. The practice is known as jihatsu in Japanese.

Wijayaratna, Mohan. *Buddhist Monastic Life: According to the Texts of the Theravada Tradition.* Trans. Claude Grangier and Steven Collins. New York: Cambridge University Press, 1990.

Begging Bowl

The bowl that Buddhist **monks** and **nuns** traditionally used to collect donations of food from lay people. The begging bowl is one of the few basic possessions allowed to monks and nuns. Traditionally they used the same bowl for begging and for eating the food. According to the early **monastic code (vinaya)**, the bowl should be made of iron or clay; materials such as gold, silver, bronze, glass, and wood were forbidden. Each morning, monks and nuns went out to beg food (jihatsu) from lay people living in the vicinity. Monks and nuns were required to accept whatever type of food lay people put into their bowls; they were strictly forbidden to request special foods. They returned to the monastery before the noon hour to consume the food they had collected.

In **Zen** monasteries, monks and nuns generally own a set of nested bowls which they receive at **ordination** as a part of their personal possessions. They use this set of bowls for all meals eaten at the monastery. The largest of the set, also called jihatsu or ôryôki, is comparable to the historical begging bowl used in India. Although technically forbidden by the vinaya, most bowls used by Zen monks and nuns today are made from red or black lacquered wood. See also **begging alms** and **lay believer**.

Wijayaratna, Mohan. *Buddhist Monastic Life: According to the Texts of the Theravada Tradition.* Trans. Claude Grangier and Steven Collins. New York: Cambridge University Press, 1990.

Benares

Present-day city in India, which is the site of the Deer Park, where the **Buddha** gave his first sermon after attaining **enlightenment**. During the time of the Buddha, the city was known as **Baranashi**, the capital city of the kingdom bearing the same name.

Bendôwa

"Discourse on the Practice of the Way," the first chapter of **Dôgen Kigen's** *Shôbôgenzô*. Dôgen composed his first major composition in 1231, while living in Fukukusa. Dôgen employs a question and answer format to structure the text, answering the doubts and queries of a fictitious beginner. He includes an autobiographical account of his own search for **enlightenment**. He also explains his style of **zazen**, distinguishing it from other forms of meditation, and invites serious practice by lay people, **monks**, and **nuns** alike. Dôgen argues that zazen is not just another style of **meditation**, but enlightenment itself. He presents zazen as the original way of the **Buddha** and all the **patriarchs**. See also **lay believer**.

The Bendôwa has been translated into English by Abe and Waddell, in *Eastern Buddhist*, Vol. 4, No. 1 (1971), pp. 124–157.

Benzaiten

A river goddess from Hindu and Buddhist mythology, known as Sarashvati in Sanskrit. Benzaiten (often shortened to Benten) is associated with eloquence, learning, and music. She is depicted playing a lute (biwa), or carrying the sword of wisdom and a wish-granting jewel (**mani**). In **Mahayana Buddhism**, she is regarded as the female counterpart of Manjusri, the **bodhisattva** of wisdom. In Japan, she is worshipped as one of the **seven lucky gods** (shichifukujin), and regarded as a patron deity of the performing arts.

The begging bowl, one of the few basic possessions allowed to Buddhist monks,
is traditionally used to collect donations of food.

Betsugo

An alternative answer that a master provides for a **kôan**, one which differs from the answer given in the original exchange. Literally, the word means "to offer a different response." When **Zen** masters compiled collections of historical kôan cases, they often appended different types of answers of their own devising. (The other basic type of answer is the **daigo**.) The betsugo was one such type, given when the master disagreed with the original answer. The practice of adding on alternative answers is said to have originated in Yunmen's school during the Sung dynasty (960–1279) in China.

Miura, Isshû, and Ruth Fuller Sasaki. *Zen Dust: The History of the Kôan and Kôan Study in Rinzai (Lin-chi) Zen.* New York: Harcourt, Brace & World, 1967.

Bhikkhu

A wandering **monk** or mendicant; one who has renounced home life and lives as a wandering holy man, begging for alms. Bhikkhu is the Pali term, related to the Sanskrit "bhiksu" (J. Biku). In **Buddhism**, the term refers to a male member of the **sangha**, the community of Buddhist believers who have accepted the approximately 250 **precepts** of the **monastic code** and received full **ordination**.

In most schools of **Mahayana Buddhism**, bhikkhu applies to any male who has received full ordination, usually based on the **vinaya**—the same monastic code used in the tradition of **Theravada Buddhism**. In the **Zen** school, this is true of Zen monks in China and Korea, as well as for Obaku Zen monks in Japan, all of whom are fully ordained when they receive the 250 precepts. Sôtô and Rinzai monks in Japan are not ordained using the Theravada precepts. Nevertheless, the term is used in reference to them. See also **Obaku sect**, **Rinzai sect**, and **Sôtô sect**.

Wijayaratna, Mohan. *Buddhist Monastic Life: According to the Texts of the Theravada Tradition.* Trans. Claude Grangier and Steven Collins. New York: Cambridge University Press, 1990.

Bhikkhuni

(J. bikuni) A wandering **nun** or mendicant; one who has renounced home life and lives as a wandering holy woman, begging for alms. Bhikkhuni is the Pali term, related to the Sanskrit "bhiksuni." In **Buddhism**, it applies to a female member of the **sangha**, the community of Buddhist believers who have received full **ordination**. Following the Theravada **monastic code** (**vinaya**), full ordination for women involves accepting some 500 **precepts**. According to traditional accounts, the first Buddhist nun was the **Buddha's** foster mother and maternal aunt, Maha **Prajapati**. When she asked the Buddha to accept her as an ordained member of the sangha, he refused. He finally conceded to admitting women to the ordained orders of the sangha after one of his principal disciples, **Ananda**, intervened on his foster mother's behalf. The Buddha accepted the admission of nuns, provided that they undertake a set of precepts in addition to those taken by **monks**. These precepts require that nuns remain subservient to monks.

In many parts of the Buddhist world, the order of nuns died out sometime after the tenth century C.E. In some areas, women continued to wear robes and live the life of ordained members of the sangha without having access to ordination. The vinaya requires that a minimum community of at least ten fully ordained, senior nuns be present to perform ordinations. In areas lacking that number, the formal ordination became an impossibility. For this reason, surviving communities of bhikkuni in East Asia today are sometimes called upon to reintroduce women's monastic orders in Southeast Asian Buddhist communities.

Barnes, Nancy J., "Women in Buddhism." In *Today's Woman in World Religions.* Ed. Arvind Sharma. Albany, NY: State University of New York Press, 1994.

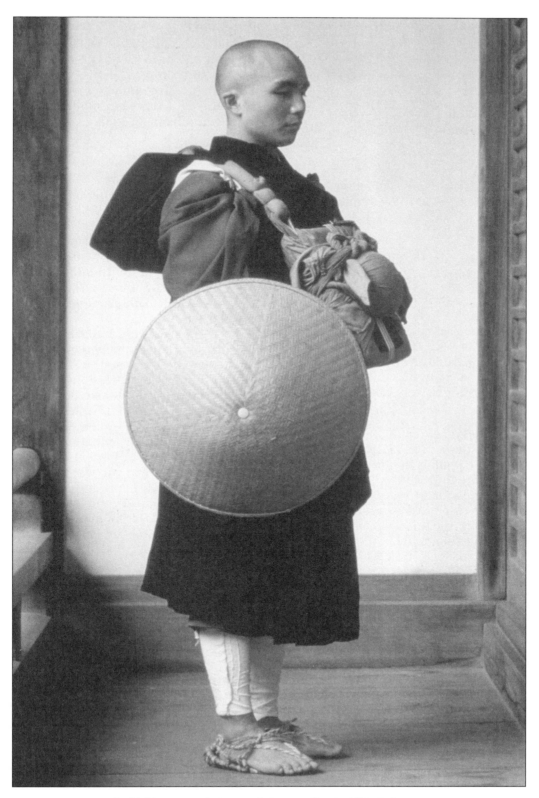

The bhikku, or wandering monk, is a traveling Buddhist holy man.

Paul, Diane Y. *Women in Buddhism: Images of the Feminine in Mahayana Tradition.* Berkeley, CA: University of California Press, 1985.

Bien-li Wen
See **Pien-wen**.

Biku
A Buddhist **monk**; the Japanese transliteration for *bhikkhu*. See **bhikkhu**.

Bikuni
A Buddhist **nun**; the Japanese transliteration for *bhikkhuni*. See **bhikkhuni**.

Binzuru
The Japanese name for **Pindola**, the first of the Sixteen **Arhats** venerated in East Asian **Buddhism**. Binzuru has been popular in Japan for centuries because of his healing powers. See **Pindola**.

Biography
The life stories of the historical **Buddha** and other famous Buddhists are a standard genre in Buddhist literature. Such stories are used to instruct Buddhists in the basic beliefs of the tradition and the principles of Buddhist morality. In addition to biographies of the historical Buddha such as the *Buddhacharita*, there are also stories of the Buddha's previous lifetimes, known as **Jataka tales**. Biographies of enlightened masters play an especially important role in **Zen** literature. Traditionally, the early history of the Zen school is taught through collections of biographies of prominent masters. This form of Zen literature is sometimes known as "transmission of the lamp literature," since it relates the passing of the **Dharma** through generations of Zen leaders. It is a common practice in the Zen world for a disciple to record the life story of his or her teacher after the teacher's death.

Birushana
Japanese transliteration of Vairochana **Buddha**, the primary object of veneration in the **Shingon sect** of Japanese **Buddhism**. Also known as **Dainichi Nyorai**, the Great Sun Buddha. See **Mahavairochana Buddha**.

Bishamon
(Sk. Vaishravana) One of the **four guardian kings** (J.shitennô) of the four directions, Bishamon is associated with the north. He is also called Tamonten in Japanese, meaning "the King who hears much," because he enjoys listening to the **Buddha** preach the **Dharma**. The four guardian kings live on **Mount Sumeru** and protect people living in the four quarters; in particular, they guard places where **Buddhism** is taught. Images of the four guardians kings, dressed in full armor and having fierce expressions, appear in almost every Buddhist temple in East Asia. Bishamon is traditionally pictured as having green skin. He wears jeweled armor and often carries a three-tined fork in his left hand; in other images, he carries a small **pagoda** in his left hand and a halbert (a combination spear and battle-axe) in his right hand. In Japan he is venerated apart from the other three guardian kings as one of the **seven lucky gods** (shichifukujin) and is regarded as the patron of doctors, travelers, and missionaries.

Black Mountains
(J. kokusan) An expression used in **Zen** for **attachment** to discriminating thinking, which hinders practice. A master might say, for example, that a student is caught in the black mountains, if the student seems determined to resolve a **kôan** with reason. The phrase is an allusion to a legendary region of the world inhabited by demons. According to Indian mythology, there are black mountains to the north of the continent. The area within the mountains is

Bishamon, one of the four guardian kings, is traditionally depicted with green skin and jeweled armor.

completely black and infested with evil demons. In many cases, masters use a longer version of the phrase, "living in a demon's cave in the black mountain."

Blue Cliff Record

(*J. Hekiganroku*) *Pi-yen Lu*, a classic **Zen** text comprised of one hundred traditional **kôan**, or teachings, with verse and commentary, compiled by the Rinzai master **Yüan-wu K'o-ch'in** (1063–1135). See *Hekiganroku*.

Bodai

Enlightenment, wisdom. The Japanese translation for the Sanskrit term *bodhi*. See **bodhi**.

Bodaidaruma

The Japanese pronunciation of **Bodhidharma**, the Indian Buddhist **monk** traditionally regarded as the founder of Zen in China. The name is more often abbreviated in Japanese to Daruma. See **Bodhidharma**.

Bodaiju

Bodhi tree, in Japanese. See **bodhi tree**.

Bodaishin

The mind of **enlightenment**, sometimes translated as **bodhi**-mind. Japanese for **bodhichitta**. See **bodhichitta**.

Bodhi

(J. bodai) Commonly translated as **enlightenment** or wisdom, this Sanskrit term refers to the ultimate goal of Buddhist practice. The historical **Buddha** attained bodhi while meditating under the **bodhi tree**. In the Theravada tradition, practitioners strive to emulate that experience by following the **Eightfold Path**. **Theravada Buddhism** describes bodhi as the point at which one has cut off all **afflictions** and illusory misconceptions realizing the **four noble truths**. The Mahayana tradition describes the **Bodhisattva** Path as the way to attain bodhi. While the various schools of **Mahayana Buddhism** describe the content of bodhi wisdom in various ways, one of the most common is to identify it as the realization of **emptiness**, which leads to a recognition of the unity of **samsara** and **nirvana**.

Bodhichitta

(J. bodaishin) The thought of **enlightenment** or the aspiration to attain **buddhahood**, sometimes translated as **bodhi**-mind. In **Mahayana Buddhism**, acquiring bodhichitta is a crucial first step on the **Bodhisattva** Path. It involves a twofold resolve: the desire to attain enlightenment oneself and the desire to assist all other **sentient beings** in escaping the **suffering** of **samsara** (the cycle of birth, death, and **rebirth**). Arousing bodhichitta is a meritorious act—one which builds good **karma** and destroys previously accumulated bad karma.

Dôgen Kigen (1200–1253) wrote extensively on the concept of bodhichitta and its relationship to Zen practice, dedicated one essay in the *Shôbôgenzô*, "Hotsu mujô shin," to the subject. He identifies the mind that gives rise to bodhichitta with the enlightenment mind: "Within this kind of life just as it is the act of sitting like a **buddha** and making an effort like a buddha, which is called 'arouses the thought of enlightenment.' The conditions for arousing the thought of enlightenment do not come from anywhere else. It is the enlightened mind which arouses the thought of enlightenment." (Cook, p. 116)

Cook, Francis Harold. *How to Raise an Ox: Zen Practice as Taught in Zen Master Dôgen's* Shobogenzo. Los Angeles, CA: Center Publications, 1978.

Robinson, Richard H. and William L. Johnson. *The Buddhist Religion: A Historical Introduction*. Belmont, CA: Wadsworth Publishing. Co., 1996.

Williams, Paul. *Mahâyâna Buddhism: The Doctrinal Foundations*. New York: Routledge, 1989.

Bodhi Day

The East Asian festival commemorating the day on which the historical **Buddha**, **Siddharta Gautama**, attained **enlightenment**. Traditionally observed on the eighth day of the twelfth lunar month, it is now commonly observed on December 8. In East Asia, Buddhists celebrate the birth (hanamatsuri), death, and enlightenment of the Buddha on separate days. In the Theravadan tradition of South and Southeast Asia, the three events are commemorated on a single day, called Visakha, observed on the full moon in May.

Bodhidharma

(d. 532; J. Bodaidaruma) An Indian Buddhist **monk** traditionally regarded as the founder of the **Zen** sect of **Buddhism** in China. He is considered the Twenty-eigth Indian **Patriarch** in a direct **lineage** from Shakyamuni

Buddha (**Siddharta Gautama**) and is also counted as the first of the six Chinese Zen Patriarchs. Scholars can confirm few details about his **biography**, many doubting that the historical Bodhidharma had any connection with the Zen school. Nevertheless, he is a central figure in the traditional Zen accounts of the school.

According to Zen biographies, Bodhidharma was born to a Brahminclass family in southern India; some alternative accounts say that he was the third son of a king. He studied Buddhism under Prajnatara, the Twenty-seventh Patriarch of Zen, from whom he received **Dharma transmission**. In 520, he made his way east to China where he attended an interview with Emperor Wu (502–550), founder of the Liang dynasty. The emperor asked Bodhidharma what **merit** he had accrued from his many donations to the Buddhist order, including the construction of numerous temples. Bodhidharma replied that there was no merit in these external activities; the only useful practice was **meditation**. The emperor did not understand Bodhidharma's teachings and banished him. Bodhidharma then took up residence at **Shao-lin-ssu**, where he sat continuously in meditation facing a wall for nine years until his legs withered away. He eventually accepted the Chinese monk Hui-k'o as his disciple and recognized him as the Second Patriarch of Zen in China. Bodhidharma miraculously survived many attempts to poison him in China. When he had completed his mission, he allowed the sixth attempt on his life to succeed and passed away while sitting in meditation. He was granted the posthumous title Yüan-shüeh Ta-shih, or Great Master of Perfect Enlightenment (J. Engaku Daishi), by Emperor Tai-tsung.

Bodhidharma's Six Gates

A collection of six **Zen** essays in Chinese, traditionally attributed to **Bodhidharma**. See *Shôshitsu Rokumon*.

Bodhisattva

(J. bosatsu) The term literally means "a being (striving for) **enlightenment**." In the tradition of **Theravada Buddhism**, it is used exclusively in reference to **Siddharta Gautama**, the historical **Buddha**, before he attained enlightenment. In the later Mahayana tradition, it came to mean anyone striving for enlightenment who works tirelessly for the sake of other **sentient beings**.

The bodhisattva became the Mahayana ideal for the Buddhist practitioner. A bodhisattva's goal is twofold: to become a Buddha and to lead all sentient beings to **buddhahood**. According to tradition, the bodhisattva may be capable of attaining **nirvana**, but will refuse to leave the realm of **samsara**— the cycle of birth, death, and **rebirth**— in order to help others. Mahayana proposes this view of the bodhisattva in sharp contrast to its rendering of the Theravada ideal of the **arhat**. **Mahayana Buddhism** generally portrays Theravadan arhats as selfish beings, single-mindedly seeking their own enlightenment without a trace of concern for other sentient beings. Although the Mahayana version of the arhat is unfair, it serves to highlight the guiding principle for the bodhisattva's practice of Buddhism—**compassion** for the **suffering** of other sentient beings.

According to Mahayana teaching, the Bodhisattva Path is accessible to all, including **lay believers**. Again, this is said to differ sharply from the way of the arhat which is accessible only to **monks** and **nuns** who devote their lives to the monastic life. Bodhisattvas build **merit** through their compassionate activities, which they share with others. The bodhisattva does not selfishly retain the benefits of good **karma** but transfers the benefits to all other beings. Thus, beginners on the Bodhisattva Path can rely on more advanced practitioners for assistance.

The path of the bodhisattva begins when an individual hears the **Dharma** from a good spiritual friend (**Zenchishiki**). After pondering the

This bronze Bodhisattva head and torso is from the Kamakura period, 1185–1336.

Dharma, the new bodhisattva gives rise to the thought of enlightenment (**bodhichitta**). This thought is twofold: the desire to attain enlightenment for oneself and the desire to help others. Bodhisattvas then take the **bodhisattva vows** expressing their intention. Bodhisattva practice is described in terms of the **six perfections**, which include the virtues of generosity, morality, patience, vigor, **meditation**, and wisdom. The bodhisattva continues to practice the virtues until attaining the stage of perfection, when the virtues become spontaneous. The tradition has also described the path of the bodhisattva in terms of stages of development. The standard list includes ten stages, which are said to take three great eons to complete. Names for the stages differ somewhat in various sources, but a typical listing of the ten stages would be: joyous, immaculate, luminous, radiant, hard-to-conquer, face-to-face, fargoing, immovable, sagely, and the cloud of the Dharma.

The concept that bodhisattvas can transfer merit to others provides a promise of relief and assistance for ordinary people who feel they lack capabilities of their own. Ordinary individuals can rely on the merit accumulated by buddhas and advanced bodhisattvas. Mahayana developed a pantheon of cosmic bodhisattvas, including figures like **Kannon** and **Jizô**, with stores of merit sufficient to assist any living being who called upon them for help. Thus, there is a distinction to be made when using the term *bodhisattva* as it applies to ordinary Mahayana Buddhists and to the great cosmic figures.

Strong, John S. *The Experience of Buddhism: Sources and Interpretations*. Belmont, CA: Wadsworth Publishing Co., 1995.

Bodhisattva Precepts

(J. bosatsukai) A set of **precepts** or rules derived from the Bonmôkyô (**Brahma Net Sutra**), a Mahayana sutra. They are used exclusively within the tradition of **Mahayana Buddhism** as the guiding principles for a **bodhisattva**. The sutra details "**ten heavy**" **precepts** (jûjûkinkai) and "forty-eight light" precepts (**shijûhachikyôkai**). All Mahayana Buddhists are required to follow the ten heavy precepts, which include prohibitions against killing, stealing, sexual misconduct, lying, using intoxicants, finding fault in others, boasting about oneself, envy, anger and ill will, and slandering the **three treasures**. The so-called light precepts involve a longer list of less serious offenses.

Most Mahayana **monks** and **nuns** in East Asia continue to be ordained according to the full set of Theravada monastic precepts found in the **vinaya**. While the Theravada precepts were designed to regulate the details of monastic life in practical terms, the bodhisattva precepts establish the mindset of Mahayana practice. The focus of the bodhisattva precepts is **compassion**, which is the guiding principle of the bodhisattva path. The concern in fulfilling these precepts rests in one's striving to help other **sentient beings**. Both lay people and monks receive the bodhisattva precepts at **ordination** ceremonies and other special events. Receiving the bodhisattva precepts reaffirms one's commitment to **Buddhism**; people can participate in bodhisattva ordination ceremonies on more than one occasion.

Some changes in the use of the bodhisattva precepts occur in Japanese Buddhism. First, **Saichô** (767–822), the founder of the **Tendai sect** of Japanese Buddhism, introduced a new ordination practice for his sect—the final ordination of Tendai monks was based on the bodhisattva precepts from the Bonmôkyô. Monks in the Tendai sect take the bodhisattva precepts at ordination, but not using vinaya precepts, and so they are without recourse to the Theravada vinaya code. **Dôgen Kigen** (1200–1253) likewise rejected the use of the Theravada precepts for his **Sôtô sect**. However, Sôtô Zen has its own set of bodhisattva precepts used at ordinations including a set of sixteen articles (**jûrokujôkai**): the three refuges (**sankikai**), the three pure precepts (sanshujôkai), and the ten heavy precepts from the Bonmôkyô. See also **lay believer**.

Bodiford, William M. *Sôtô Zen in Medieval Japan*. Honolulu, HI: University of Hawaii Press, 1993.

Stevens, John. *The Marathon Monks of Mount Hiei*. Boston, MA: Shambhala, 1988.

Groner, Paul. *Saichô: The Establishment of the Japanese Tendai School*. Honolulu, HI: University of Hawaii Press, 2000.

Bodhisattva Vows

In the Mahayana tradition, each practitioner embarks upon the **Buddhist path** by taking certain **vows** which guide his or her practice. The most important of these is the vow to attain **enlightenment**. The desire or thought of attaining enlightenment (**bodhichitta**) is a logical first step in becoming a Buddhist. The **bodhisattva** does not think selfishly, however, so the vow expresses a dual intention: not only to strive for oneself, but at the same time, to aid all other **sentient beings** toward enlightenment. The two parts of the vow are held together inseparably by the guiding principle of **compassion**.

All practitioners of **Mahayana Buddhism**, recite the bodhisattva vows. They do this first as a symbol of their initial commitment to **Buddhism**, but continue to recite the vows many times throughout their lives. In **Zen** monasteries, **monks** and **nuns** recite a version of the bodhisattva vows every day as a part of the regular daily rituals. For lay people, reciting the vows is often done on special occasions; this is understood as an opportunity to reaffirm their commitment to Buddhism.

The following is a translation of the standard set of bodhisattva vows used in Zen monasteries:

1. Sentient beings are beyond number; I vow to save them all.
2. The passions (**afflictions**) are inexhaustible; I vow to extinguish them all.
3. The Buddhist **Dharmas** (teachings) are infinite; I vow to master them all.
4. The Buddhist Way is unsurpassed; I vow to attain it.

In addition to the vows recited by ordinary Mahayana Buddhists, certain celestial buddhas and bodhisattvas are known for the extraordinary vows they have taken for the sake of other sentient beings. For example, while **Amida buddha** was still a bodhisattva named Dharmakara, he took a series of forty-eight vows, among which was the establishment of a **Pure Land** (Jôdo) in the West. Since he stipulated that he would only attain enlightenment if his vows were fulfilled, his vows are understood by many Mahayana Buddhists, especially those in the **Pure Land schools**, as a guarantee that his Pure Land exists. See also **lay believer**.

Bodhi Tree

(*Ficus religiosa*; J. bodaiju) The fig tree in Bodhgaya under which **Siddharta Gautama** sat and meditated until he had attained **enlightenment**. Literally "the tree of enlightenment," the tree is commonly called the bo-tree or pipal tree. Early in Buddhist history, the bodhi tree became a popular **pilgrimage** site and the object of devotion by **lay believers**. Believers offered flowers, then bowed and walked clockwise around the tree. Cuttings from the bodhi tree were distributed widely by early Buddhist missionaries. A descendant of the original tree, planted by the daughter of King **Ashoka**, still stands in Anuradhapura in Sri Lanka. Shashanka, a seventh-century Indian king devoted to the god Shiva, destroyed the original tree in Bodhgaya during a violent persecution of **Buddhism**. The tree that stands in Bodhgaya today descends from a cutting brought back from the tree in Sri Lanka.

The Bodhi tree is the type of tree under which Siddharta Gautama,
who became known as the Buddha, is believed to have gained enlightenment.

Basham, A. L. *The Wonder That Was India: A Survey of the History and Culture of the Indian Sub-Continent Before the Coming of the Muslims.* New York: Taplinger Publishing Co., 1968.

Bôkatsu

Literally, a stick and a shout. An expression used to describe a particular style of **Zen** characterized by the use of sticks and shouts. This style of Zen practice dates back to the classical period of Zen, during the T'ang dynasty in China (618–907). At that time, Zen masters introduced such devices as hitting disciples with a stick (kyoshaku) or staff (**shippei**), or answering them with a loud shout (**katsu**). The purpose of these actions was to shock disciples out of the ordinary, analytical style of thinking and push them toward an **enlightenment** experience (**satori**). In particular, **Te-shan Hsuan-chien** (782–685) and **Huang-po Hsi-Yün** (d. 850) were famous for their use of the stick, and **Lin-chi I-hsüan** (d. 867) perfected the use of the shout.

Bokuseki is the calligraphy art of Zen masters.

Bokuseki

"Ink trace," a piece of **calligraphy** or an ink drawing executed by a **Zen** master. Bokuseki are said to be expressions of the artist's understanding of the **Dharma**. They are often mounted on brocade and hung as art.

Bonbai

To chant verses or hymns. The term usually refers to the highly melodic **chanting** of sacred texts accompanied by music, which **monks** perform in front of an image of the **Buddha** as a part of a ritual service. Bonbai is generally performed in a stylized fashion, with the voice rising and falling. The chanting is alternatively known as **shômyô**. In the **Zen** school, there are a number of bonbai chanting styles, including Obaku bonbai. Obaku bonbai, or Obaku shômyô, is unique in Japanese Zen because the monks chant the verses in an approximation of the Fukien dialect of Chinese, the language used by the Obaku founders in the 17th century. See also **Obaku sect**.

Bongyô

Morally pure actions. Literally, the word means the acts of the god Brahma, one of the Hindu deities. Bongyô is the Japanese term that comes from the Sanskrit *brahma-caryâ*, which was first used in India in reference to the religious practices of the Brahmin, or priestly class. It later came to mean religiously motivated action in keeping with religious **precepts**, especially chastity or sexual purity. In **Buddhism**, bongyô refers specifically to those actions which are conducive to attaining **enlightenment**. Most especially, in **Mahayana Buddhism**, it is used to convey the actions taken by a **bodhisattva** out of **compassion** to save other **sentient beings**.

Bonmôkyô

The **Brahma Net Sutra**, the Japanese title for the Brahmajala Sutra. The sutra presents ten major and forty-eight minor **precepts**, commonly known as the **bodhisattva precepts**, that govern the life and practice of a bodhisattva. See **Brahma Net Sutra**.

Bonnô

Afflictions or **delusions**. A Japanese translation of the Sanskrit term *klesha*. The term is commonly translated as passions, although the English word is not broad enough in its general usage to encompass the various types of delusions denoted by the original. Bonnô refers to any passion, **attachment**, working of the mind, or subsequent action that hinders the attainment of **enlightenment**. The afflictions cause **suffering** and traditionally are thought of as impurities. These impurities are eliminated by the practice of **Buddhism**. **Nirvana** can be understood as the extinction of all klesha.

The Buddhist tradition identifies six states of mind as the fundamental afflictions (konpon bonnô). These include greed, anger, ignorance, arrogance, doubt, and false views. The first three are known collectively as the **three poisons**. A large number of minor afflictions, such as laziness, shamelessness, and deceit, arise in conjunction with the basic forms.

Bonpu

An ordinary or foolish person. The expression is used to contrast an unenlightened individual with an enlightened one. The Japanese characters may also be pronounced "bonbu." According to **Zen** teaching, the difference between an ordinary or foolish person and an enlightened **buddha** is a shift in perception, since all **sentient beings** possess the **Buddha Nature** and are originally enlightened. In the **Platform Sutra**, the Sixth **Patriarch Hui-neng** (638–713) said, "If you cling to your previous thoughts and are deluded, then you are ordinary. But if the next thought is enlightened, then you are a buddha."

Bosatsu

Japanese for **bodhisattva**. See **bodhisattva**.

Bosatsukai

Japanese for the **bodhisattva precepts**. See **bodhisattva precepts**.

Boxwood Zen

(J. Kôyôboku no Zen) The boxwood tree is said to grow an inch a year, but to shrink an inch in leap years. The expression "boxwood Zen" is used in reference to students' progressing erratically in their practice of **Zen**. A master will use the expression to reproach a disciple who is overly attached to the notion of **enlightenment**.

Bôzu

The head **monk** or resident monk of a Japanese Buddhist temple. The term may apply to the resident monk at a small temple, most of which have only one monk in residence. In a larger temple, with several monks in residence, the term technically applies only to the head monk or **abbot**. In common usage today, however, people use the term for any Buddhist monk or priest, regardless of status. The term is often rendered in English as *bonze*.

Brahma Net Sutra

The Brahmajâla Sutra (J. Bonmôkyô), a Mahayana sutra that sets out the moral code for the **bodhisattva**, consisting of ten major and forty-eight minor **precepts**. **Kumarajiva** translated the text into Chinese (T. 24, no. 1484) in 406 C.E. The precepts described by the text are intended for all Buddhist practitioners, lay people and monastics alike. Unlike the **vinaya**, which presents a **monastic code** designed to govern all aspects of life in a monastic setting, the Brahma Net Sutra emphasizes the quality of **compassion** that governs the actions of a bodhisattva. Throughout East Asia, lay people, **monks**, and **nuns** participate in precept ceremonies in which they receive the **bodhisattva precepts** based on the Brahma Net Sutra. In Japan, following the example set by the Tendai school, several schools of **Buddhism** ordain monks and nuns using the bodhisattva precepts in place of the vinaya code. See also **lay believer** and **Tendai sect**.

Branch Temple

A Buddhist temple that has institutional ties to a larger **main temple** or main monastery. The pattern of affiliation between main and branch temples (J. honji matsuji) emerged in Japan during the medieval period (1185–1600) and was later systematized in the early modern (1600–1867) and modern (1868–present) periods. During the Tokugawa period (1600–1867), the government required all Buddhist temples throughout the country to be organized in a hierarchy, limiting the number of main monasteries. The practice continues today; most Buddhist temples in Japan are branches under the administrative leadership of a main monastery.

Buddha

(J. butsu or butsuda) A title that means "**enlightened one**." In its broadest sense, the title can refer to any fully enlightened being. It most often refers specifically to **Siddharta Gautama**, also called Shakyamuni Buddha, the founder of **Buddhism**. Although it was recognized early on that many of Shakyamuni's disciples also attained **enlightenment**, he was still considered the only one worthy of the title because he had fashioned the path that the others merely followed.

Shakyamuni is believed to be the only buddha of the present epoch, but the idea that other historical buddhas existed before him emerged early in Buddhist history. The most common listing of historical buddhas of past ages includes seven, with Shakyamuni listed last. In many cases, a future buddha (**Maitreya**), who will appear in the next age, is also mentioned. Other historical buddhas played the same role in previous ages as Shakyamuni does during the present age: teaching the **Dharma**. It is believed that only one buddha exists in the world in any given age and that his teachings live on far beyond the time of his death. Gradually, however, the Dharma is forgotten. When it has completely disappeared, the next buddha appears to reintroduce the Dharma into the world. One tradition says at least 12,000 years span the time between the appearances of buddhas.

Mahayana Buddhism expanded the general concept of the buddha beyond the notion of historical buddhas, encompassing many eternal and cosmic buddhas. First, ideas about Shakyamuni Buddha underwent change. Traditionally, the Buddha had not been worshipped as a deity but was regarded as an enlightened human being who could serve as a guide and inspiration for other human beings. Over time, however, veneration of the Buddha as a human being became more and more like worship of a god. Early schools of Mahayana began teaching that the historical Buddha was not just an ordinary person but the human manifestation of an eternal Buddha; the eternal Buddha did not pass into extinction when Shakyamuni died but remained eternally active in the world.

Next, concepts of celestial buddhas (buddhas living in the **Pure Lands**) operating in other worlds developed. Just as the earlier tradition suggested that historical buddhas emerged in this world to teach in different ages, Mahayana taught that other buddhas existed to serve the beings in the innumerable other worlds in the cosmos. Like Shakyamuni, these celestial buddhas were manifestations of the eternal Buddha. More important, many of them were powerful enough to offer assistance to **sentient beings** in this world.

Buddha, or "enlightened one," most often refers to Siddharta Gautama, the founder of Buddhism. The Great Buddha shown above is located at the Todai-ji Temple in Nara, Japan.

Belief in powerful celestial buddhas led to the worship and veneration of a number of noted buddhas, including **Amida buddha** and Vairocana.

The Mahayana tradition developed the idea of the **three bodies of the Buddha** to clarify the various types of buddhas. First, the Dharma, or Truth Body, is the eternal Buddha from which all other buddhas are created. The Dharma Body is closely identified with the Mahayana concept of **emptiness** (shunyata). Second, the Bliss Body of the Buddha is associated with the celestial buddhas who dwell in **Buddha Lands**. Amida is an example of this type of buddha. Third, the transformation body (**nirmanakaya**) represents the historical appearances of the Buddha in this world. Siddharta Gautama was one instance of the transformation body.

Reynolds, Frank E., and Charles Hallisey. "The Buddha." In *Buddhism and Asian History*. Ed. Joseph M. Kitagawa and Mark D. Cummings. New York: Macmillan, 1987.

Robinson, Richard H. and William L. Johnson. *The Buddhist Religion: A Historical Introduction*. Belmont, CA: Wadsworth Publishing Co., 1996.

Buddhacharita

(J. *Busshogyôsan*) *The Acts of the Buddha*, the earliest formal **biography** of Shakyamuni **Buddha** (**Siddharta Gautama**). The Buddhist poet **Ashvaghosha** composed the text in Sanskrit verse around 100 C.E. Although

Ashvaghosha was a supporter of Mahayana teachings, he stresses the basic teachings of the historical Buddha, such as the **four noble truths** and the **Eightfold Path**. A complete Sanskrit version of the *Buddhacharita* does not survive today; however, it is preserved in full in Tibetan and Chinese translations.

Buddha Day

In East Asian **Buddhism**, the day commemorating the birth of Shakyamuni **Buddha** (**Siddharta Gautama**). East Asian Buddhists traditionally observe Buddha Day on the eighth day of the fourth lunar month. Some communities now celebrate it on April 4th, according to the Western calendar. Buddhists in South Asia and Southeast Asia celebrate Buddha Day somewhat differently, combining the Buddha's birth, **enlightenment**, and death in a one-day celebration; they believe that Shakyamuni Buddha miraculously experienced these events on the same day of the year. Their observance of Buddha Day is now usually held in May, shortly before the beginning of the **rainy-season retreats**. East Asian Buddhists, on the other hand, observe the three events as three separate holidays, with the Buddha's enlightenment celebrated on December 8 and Death on February 15. See also **Hana Matsuri** and **kanbutsu**.

Buddha Dharma

The teachings of the **Buddha**. Sometimes referred to as the Law of the Buddha. See **Buppô**.

Buddha Hall

One of the seven primary buildings of a **Zen** temple or monastery, known as a **Butsuden** in Japanese. It is called the Buddha hall because it contains a shrine housing the primary **Buddha** image (**honzon**) of the temple. See **Butsuden**.

Buddhahood

An expression used within **Mahayana Buddhism** that means the attainment of perfect **enlightenment**—a characteristic of all buddhas. Unlike **Theravada Buddhism**, Mahayana Buddhism does not reserve the title *buddha* for Shakyamuni Buddha (**Siddharta Gautama**) alone. Mahayana teaches that all believers as **bodhisattvas** are striving to become buddhas.

Mahayana Buddhism uses the concept of buddhahood to indicate the highest goal of Buddhist practice. In Mahayana scriptures such as the **Lotus Sutra**, buddhahood is portrayed as the supreme goal, one that surpasses **Hinayana Buddhism's** goal of **nirvana**. According to the Mahayana view, the struggle to attain nirvana and become an **arhat** is an inherently selfish endeavor in contrast to the path of the **bodhisattva** who seeks buddhahood for the self and for all other **sentient beings**.

Buddha Land

A world in which a **buddha** is living and teaching the **Dharma**. The tradition believes that hearing the Dharma directly from a buddha greatly enhances one's ability to progress toward **enlightenment**. Although the present world currently has no buddha preaching the Dharma, it will someday become the Buddha Land of the **bodhisattva** named **Maitreya**, traditionally believed to be the next buddha of our world.

In addition to our world, **Mahayana Buddhism** asserts that there are tens of thousands of other worlds, many of which have buddhas. These cosmic **Buddha Lands** share many characteristics with the **heavens** in which gods reside, since they are places of ease and comfort. The primary distinction between a Buddha Land and a heaven is that, unlike heaven dwellers, individuals born in Buddha Lands can practice **Buddhism** and make progress toward enlightenment. Many Buddhist believers hope to be reborn into a Buddha Land in order to enjoy the benefits of practicing Buddhism directly under a buddha's guidance. The tradition commonly refers to these cosmic Buddha Lands as **Pure Lands** (J. Jôdo). The most famous Buddha Land is the **Western Pure Land** of **Amida buddha**. Buddhas reigning in the Pure Lands usually took **vows** as bodhisattvas to create a Pure Land specifically for the sake of their devotees.

Buddha Nature

An expression of the Mahayana Buddhist teaching that all **sentient beings** innately possess the potential to attain perfect **enlightenment** and become buddhas. (Some schools of **Mahayana Buddhism** extend the concept to include non-sentient objects.) Buddha Nature (J. Busshô) is sometimes referred to as intrinsic enlightenment or **original enlightenment**: the basic quality within the individual that makes the practice of Buddhism possible. Buddha Nature can be understood as a seed, which if cultivated by Buddhist practice, will eventually bear the fruit of acquired enlightenment.

The Mahayana teaching that all sentient beings possess the Buddha Nature found early expression in the **Nirvana Sutra**, which rejected the notion that some sentient beings, known as **icchantika**, lack the potential to become enlightened. The concept of Buddha Nature became one of the most basic teachings within the **Zen** school. Zen masters and texts commonly refer to seeing one's innate Buddha Nature, or **kenshô**, to describe the experience of enlightenment. Buddha Nature, in the Zen context, is seen not so much as a seed that holds potential, but an existing reality. Seeing one's nature or enlightenment is not so much becoming a buddha, but the realization that one already is a buddha.

It should be noted that Buddha Nature is not the same as an eternal, abiding, and unchanging self, like the Hindu understanding of the soul or **atman**. The Zen master **Dôgen Kigen** (1200–1253) warned against the dangers of misinterpreting Buddha Nature as an essential core that underlies all things. To avoid this trap, Dôgen stressed that Buddha Nature be identified with **impermanence**, the characteristic of **emptiness** that typifies all phenomena.

Buddha Patriarch

A term applied to any **buddha** or **patriarch** of **Zen** who transmits the **Dharma**. It applies especially to the **lineage** extending from Shakyamuni **Buddha** (**Siddharta Gautama**) to **Bodhidharma**, the traditional founder of Zen in China, and on to **Hui-neng** (638–713), the Chinese Sixth Patriarch. See **busso**.

Buddhism

General name for the religious traditions (J. Bukkyô) that developed from the teachings of **Siddharta Gautama**, the original **Buddha**, or **Enlightened One**. Siddharta (circa 566–486) lived in the northeast region of the Indian subcontinent, teaching in the area along the Ganges River and establishing a community of followers (**sangha**) comprised of both ascetics and lay people. After the Buddha's death, his teachings were drawn together in the early scriptures known as the **Tripitaka**. Buddhist teachings eventually spread from India throughout Asia.

Today, there are many schools and forms of Buddhism throughout the world, and therefore no single, unified tradition. The Buddhist world is most commonly divided into three schools: **Theravada Buddhism**, **Mahayana Buddhism**, and Vajrayana Buddhism (**esoteric Buddhism**). Two of these divisions flourish in distinct geographical areas of the world: Theravada Buddhism predominates in South and Southeast Asia, while Mahayana predominates in East Asia. While Theravada preserves the teachings of the historical Buddha and the early Buddhist community, Mahayana arose several centuries later and upholds some modifications and innovations on the earlier tradition. Mahayana Buddhism can be further subdivided into several distinctive schools of thought and styles of practice, including **Zen, Pure Land,** Hua-yen, and Tendai. In addition, some scholars regard the Vajrayana tradition as a distinct and separate division; others classify it as a form of Mahayana Buddhism. Vajrayana represents the tantric or esoteric portion of the Buddhist tradition, and flourishes today in Tibet and in certain schools of Japanese Buddhism. See also **Hua-yen school, lay believer,** and **Tendai sect**

Buddhist Name

Buddhist practitioners traditionally accept a new Buddhist name when they are ordained as a **monk** or a **nun**. The new name replaces the person's secular name, serving as a symbol that the individual has departed from the life of a lay person. In Japan, Buddhist names are conferred posthumously on lay people as a part of the Buddhist funeral and **memorial services**. See **kaimyô**.

Buddhist Path

(J. **butsudô**) The way set out by the **Buddha** leading to **enlightenment**. The term may refer to the teachings and the practice of **Buddhism** which lead to enlightenment, or to enlightenment itself. According to the tradition of **Theravada Buddhism**, the path set out by the Buddha is summarized by the **four noble truths** and the **Eightfold Path. Mahayana Buddhism** describes the path in terms of the career of a **bodhisattva**, who seeks enlightenment for him- or herself and for all other **sentient beings**.

Buddhist Scriptures

The Buddhist scriptures include a wide variety of related collections of texts preserved in several languages, including Sanskrit, Pali, Tibetan, and Chinese. Buddhist scripture collections are distinguished by the portion of the religious tradition they discuss or the cultural area in which they are recognized. The most basic division in the Buddhist scriptures is that between the ancient, or Theravada scriptures, and the later scriptures of **Mahayana Buddhism**. The canon of **Theravada Buddhism**, commonly known as the **Tripitaka**, represents the oldest collection of Buddhist scriptures, portions of which date back to the second century B.C.E. The Tripitaka is divided into three segments, representing three distinct types of writing. The first portion is the **vinaya**, which provides the **monastic code** governing the lives of Buddhist **monks** and **nuns**. The second portion, known as the **sutras**, preserves the **sermons** attributed to the historical **Buddha**. Third, the **Abhidharma** portion includes commentaries on the Buddha's teachings written by later Buddhist scholars. The Tripitaka is preserved in both Sanskrit and Pali, with related Tibetan and Chinese translations. Since it was originally recorded in Pali, it is sometimes known as the *Pali Canon.*

The Mahayana scriptures include the original Tripitaka as well as a large number of later texts composed by Mahayana thinkers. The Mahayana texts include sutras, commentaries, and philosophical treatises composed over many centuries beginning around the year 100 B.C.E. The early Mahayana texts were composed in Sanskrit and later translated into Tibetan and Chinese. As **Buddhism** spread throughout the cultures of North and East Asia, additional texts composed in Tibetan, Chinese, and other local languages were added to the collection. For this reason, there is variation among the Tibetan, Chinese, Japanese, and Korean versions of the Mahayana scriptures. See also **Chinese Tripitaka** and **Daizôkyô**.

Buppô

The Japanese translation of Buddha Dharma. The term is translated into English as the Buddha's Law or the Buddhist Teachings. Buppô is Shakyamuni's (**Siddharta Gautama**) understanding of reality or truth, which he realized for himself when he became enlightened. The term also signifies the teachings of Shakyamuni through which he conveyed to others the path to **enlightenment**; in this sense, the Buddha's **Dharma** is preserved in the **Buddhist scriptures**, which present the teachings of the historical **Buddha** and his disciples. According to the **Zen** understanding, Buppô cannot be expressed in ordinary human language, but must be realized for oneself through a first-hand experience. Zen maintains that the Buddha Dharma is transmitted from mind to mind, master to disciple.

Burning House

A reference to a parable found in the third chapter of the **Lotus Sutra**, explaining the use of **expedient means** (Sk. upaya, J. hôben) in Buddhist teachings. In the sutra, the **Buddha** tells his disciples about a father's efforts to get his children safely out of their burning house. At first, the children are so engrossed in playing with their toys that they ignore their father's pleas. Having failed with a direct approach, the father devises another plan of action. The father resorts to an expedient means to save their lives, promising them more wondrous toys if they will only go outside to collect them. The children race outside to receive the promised carriages, each drawn by a goat, a deer, or an ox. The Buddha then explains that ordinary people, like children, cannot always hear and understand the teachings of the Buddha, which are designed to save them from the **suffering** of **samsara** (the cycle of birth, death, and **rebirth**). Therefore, the Buddha sometimes resorts to expedient means, such as teaching devices that take into account what people can understand and that shock them out of everyday existence. When using expedient means, the Buddhist tradition does not intend to mislead believers with partial truths. Like the father in the parable, the purpose is to help them: in this case to assist them in their progress along the **Buddhist path**.

Hurvitz, Leon, trans. *Scripture of the Lotus Blossom of the Fine Dharma.* New York: Columbia University Press, 1982.

Watson, Burton, trans. *The Lotus Sutra.* New York: Columbia University Press, 1993.

Bushi

Japanese warrior; **samurai**. See **samurai**.

Busshi

A disciple of the **Buddha**; a Buddhist. The Japanese term literally means "child of the Buddha." In some Mahayana contexts, it refers specifically to **bodhisattvas**. It is said that all **sentient beings** are busshi, since they all possess the **Buddha Nature**.

Busshin'in

Seal of the Buddha Mind. A symbol indicating that authentic transmission of the **Dharma** has taken place: The seal, sometimes represented by an object such as a certificate, is conferred by a master upon a disciple. See **inka**.

Busshô

Buddha Nature, in Japanese. The Mahayana teaching that all **sentient beings** innately possess the potential to become a buddha. See **Buddha Nature**.

Busshogyôsan

Japanese title for the *Buddhacharita*. See *Buddhacharita*.

Busso

The **Buddha** and the **patriarchs**, the founding masters who transmitted the **Dharma** from generation to generation. The term may refer specifically to the **lineage** within the **Zen** sect that begins with Shakyamuni (**Siddharta Gautama**), the historical Buddha, and includes twenty-eight Indian patriarchs and six Chinese patriarchs. It may also refer more generally to any and all masters who perpetuate a Zen lineage, especially those designated as founders of specific lines. In some contexts, the term *busso* is more accurately translated as Buddha-Patriarch, since there is no real distinction between buddhas, patriarchs, and other enlightened masters, all of whom transmit the same Dharma.

Butsu

Japanese for **Buddha**. The same character may also be transliterated **hotoke**. See **Buddha**.

Butsuda

Full Japanese transliteration of **Buddha**. More commonly abbreviated to Butsu. See **Buddha**.

Butsudan

A Buddhist altar. A platform or altar on which a Buddhist image, usually depicting a **buddha** or **bodhisattva**, is enshrined. **Incense**, flowers, and other **offerings** may be made before the image. The term is most commonly applied to family altars kept in Japanese homes, on which the memorial tablets (**ihai**) of deceased family members are enshrined. In many cases, lay people are encouraged to include a Buddist image on their family butsudans. The family butsudan is typically a cabinet made from lacquered wood; sizes vary from large pieces of furniture to small items which fit into the limited space of modern apartments.

Family members may pay their respects daily to both ancestors and the buddhas; it is traditional to offer rice, water, incense, or flowers. Many families announce to the butsudan important events, including graduations, marriages, and the birth of a child. In this way, the family symbolically includes deceased relatives in the life of the surviving family. **Memorial services** for the deceased are generally held in front of the butsudan, with the ihai as the central focus. The altar also receives special attention during the **Obon** season. See also **lay believer**.

Smith, Robert. *Ancestor Worship in Contemporary Japan.* Stanford, CA: Stanford University Press, 1974.

Butsuden

The Buddha hall, where the **Zen** temple or monastery's primary image of the **Buddha** is enshrined, along with other images of the buddhas and **bodhisattvas**. The Butsuden is one of the seven monastic halls (**shichidô garan**) that form the core of a Zen monastery. The Buddha hall corresponds to golden hall (kondô) found in the temples of other Buddhist schools. Traditionally, it is located at the center of the monastery grounds. The style of the Zen Buddha hall was developed in China, probably during the Sung dynasty (960–1279), and transmitted to Japan where it is still preserved.

The main image (**honzon**) in most Zen temples is Shakyamuni Buddha (**Siddharta Gautama**), the historical Buddha. The main image is usually flanked by two other statues, forming a triad. The other figures are either buddhas from the past and future, or two attendants from the historical Buddha's lifetime. The images are placed on a pedestal representing **Mount Sumeru**, the sacred mountain at the center of the Buddhist cosmos. The main image is set off by a large tapestry in gold or purple brocade. Three lacquered wooden tablets, with inscriptions dedicating the temple to its patrons and to the emperor, are place in front of the honzon. Daily **chanting** services are held in the Buddha hall.

Collcutt, Martin. *Five Mountains: The Rinzai Zen Monastic Institution in Medieval Japan.* Cambridge, MA: Harvard University Press, 1981.

Butsudô

The Way of the **Buddha**; the Japanese term for **Buddhism**, or the teachings of

In the Butsuden, or Buddha hall, the main image of the historical Buddha is surrounded either by images of Buddhas of the past and future, or two attendants from the historical Buddha's lifetime.

Buddhism. The expression may refer to the path leading to **enlightenment** as taught by the Buddha; it may also refer to enlightenment itself. According to the tradition of **Theravada Buddhism**, the way set out by the Buddha is summarized by the **four noble truths** and the **Eightfold Path**. The tradition of **Mahayana Buddhism** describes the way in terms of the career of a **bodhisattva**, who seeks enlightenment for him- or herself and for all other **sentient beings**. In some contexts, the term *Butsudô* is used as an alternative term for **Buppô**, or the Buddha Dharma.

Buttsû-ji

A rural Rinzai temple in Aki, Hiroshima Prefecture. It was founded by **Guchû Shûkyû** (1323–1409) in 1399. It serves as the main monastery for the **Buttsû-ji Ha**, the Buttsû-ji branch of Rinzai. See also **Rinzai sect**.

Buttsû-ji Ha

The **Buttsû-ji** branch of Rinzai, one of the fourteen contemporary branches of the Japanese **Rinzai sect**. The main monastery for the branch is Buttsû-ji, located in Aki, Hiroshima Prefecture. **Guchû Shûkyû** (1323–1409) is regarded as the founder. The branch has fifty-one temples throughout Japan and claims approximately 98,500 followers.

Byakushi Butsu

Pratyeka buddha, the Japanese rendering of a Chinese transliteration of the original Sanskrit term. See **pratyeka buddha**.

Byakutsui

"White mallet;" the religious implement used to call an assembly of **monks** or **nuns** to order while making a special announcement. The term may also refer to the high-ranking monk or nun who wields the mallet and officiates at important ritual occasions.

Byôdô

The Japanese expression meaning "**equality**." The term refers to the **non-duality** and non-differentiation of all things as seen from the perspective of **enlightenment**. The teaching of equality is based upon the realization that all phenomena are essentially the same. See **equality**.

Strong, John S. *The Legend of King Ashoka: A Study and Translation of the* Asokavadana. Princeton, NJ: Princeton University Press, 1983.

Cakravartin

(J. Tenrinô) "The Wheel-Turning King," the ideal universal monarch according to Indian mythology. The myth of the Cakravartin existed in India before the formation of **Buddhism**. The Cakravartin reigns by turning a wheel, which was presented to him by the gods at his enthronement. As he turns the wheel, all lesser kings accept his authority. He is said to possess the **thirty-two marks of a buddha**—the marks of greatness characterizing all buddhas. In Buddhist tradition, if a Cakravartin were to leave his home life to become a holy man, he would become a buddha.

According to the Cakravartin myth, there are four types of universal monarchs, distinguished by the type of wheel each turns: gold, silver, copper, or iron. The king with a golden wheel rules all four of the continents (understood by the ancient Indians to be the entire world). The king with a silver wheel rules only three continents, the king with a copper wheel rules two, and the one with an iron wheel rules one continent. Only one type of king rules at any one given time.

According to the Buddhist interpretation of the Cakravartin myth, the monarch rules by virtue of **turning the Wheel of the Dharma**—his rule is benevolent because it is based on Buddhist teachings and **precepts**. If **Siddharta Gautama**, the historical Buddha, had chosen to remain in the secular life, he would have become a Cakravartin. The historical figure King **Ashoka**, a Buddhist monarch, is sometimes interpreted as a Cakravartin.

Calligraphy

The art of writing is among the most highly developed artistic forms in East Asia, valued in both the secular and the religious realms. Calligraphy is associated with the **Zen** sect of **Buddhism**, although it predates the development of Buddhism in China and Japan. Calligraphy executed by Zen masters is said to reveal their understanding of the **Dharma**. It is common practice for Zen **monks** and **nuns** to learn the art of calligraphy as a part of their **monastic training**. Calligraphy is known in Japanese as either shodô (the Way of Writing), or shojutsu (the Art of Writing).

Capping Verse

A verse offered by a **Zen** practitioner to his master as a response to a **kôan**. The verse expresses the practitioner's understanding of the kôan, and hence of the **Dharma**. See **jakugo**.

Causality

In **Buddhism** every action has consequences, and everything that happens is caused by something. Cause and effect functions like an impersonal moral law, without dependence on the workings of a personal god. Actions can be likened to seeds, which an individual sows. The seeds eventually mature and produce a related fruit: Good actions produce good effects and bad actions produce bad effects. Punishment for evil actions and reward for good actions are the natural consequence of the action itself. See also **codependent origination**, **inga**, and **karma**.

Cave of the Dharma

(J. kokkutsu no sôge) A place where **Buddhism** is practiced, especially a **meditation hall** at a **Zen** monastery. **Hakuin**

Chanoyû, or Zen tea ceremony, is associated with many art forms, including ceramics. The tea ceremony bowls shown here are from the Middle Edo period of eighteenth-century Japan.

Ekaku (1685–1768), the Zen Master of the Tokugawa period (1600–1867), used the expression "talons and teeth of the Cave of the Dharma" to describe the powers acquired through Zen meditation, which could then be used to aid others.

Chadô

The Way of Tea, a Japanese art form closely associated with the **Zen** sect of **Buddhism**. See **chanoyû**.

Ch'an-kuan Ts'e-chin

(J. *Zenkan Sakushin*) *To Encourage Zealous Study of the Zen Barriers*, a compilation put together by the Chinese Buddhist **monk** Yun-chi **Chu-hung** (1535–1615; J. Renchi Shukô), during the Ming dynasty (1368–1644). Chu-hung collected **sermons** and talks from **Zen** monks, stories about **enlightenment** experiences, and quotations from various **sutras**. He intended the work to encourage the practice of Zen **meditation**, especially the use of **kôan**; the "barriers" referred to in the title are kôan. Chu-hung not only promoted the practice of Zen **Buddhism** in the text, but also encouraged the combined practice of Zen medi-

tation and **Pure Land** devotion. The text was first published in China in 1600. It prompted the Japanese Rinzai master **Hakuin Ekaku** (1685–1768) to become a Zen monk. The text was published in Japan in 1762 by **Tôrei Enji** (1721–1792), Hakuin's disciple, who added an epilogue. See also **Rinzai sect**.

Ch'an-men Kuei-shih

(J. Zenmon Kishiki) "Zen **monastic code**," an early **Zen** monastic code written during the Sung dynasty (960–1279) in China, circa 1004. The text is very brief and appears as an addendum to the **biography** of **Pai-chang Huai-hai** (720–814) in the *Transmission of the Lamp* (Ch. **Ching-te Ch'üan-teng-Lu**). The text explains the reasons for the production of the first distinctively Zen monastic code, traditionally attributed to Pai-chang, and briefly describes life in an early Zen monastery.

Chanoyû

The tea ceremony, a Japanese art form associated with the **Zen** sect of **Buddhism** since it originally developed from the practice of serving tea within Zen monasteries. The term literally means "boiling water for tea." The tea ceremony involves a small gathering of guests for whom the host carefully prepares and serves green tea (J. matcha). The entire process is closely choreographed and performed with simple grace. In many cases, the tea ceremony is carried out in a specially designed tea room or hut (J. sukiya), with specially selected utensils. Chanoyû is associated with many art forms, including ceramics, tea gardens, painting, **calligraphy**, and flower arranging.

Tea was introduced to Japan by **Eisai**, the Rinzai Zen **monk**, after his travels to China during the twelfth century. In China, Zen monks used tea as a part of their monastic practice because of its medicinal value and its effects as a stimulant, aiding them to stay awake during **meditation** sessions. In Japan, the practice of serving tea spread quickly throughout the populace. By the fourteenth century, tea gatherings were held among the social elite. This practice eventually gave rise to a culture of tea, with tea masters and distinct schools of practice. See also **Rinzai sect**.

Varley, Paul, and Kumakura Isao. *Tea in Japan: Essays on the History of Chanoyu*. Honolulu, HI: University of Hawaii Press, 1989.

Ch'an-shih

"Zen master" or "**meditation** master," a Chinese title of respect used to address accomplished **monks** and **nuns** who practice **Zen**. The Japanese pronunciation of the same characters is "**Zenji**." Originally, the term distinguished masters who instructed others in meditation from **Dharma** masters, or Fa-shih. Historically, Ch'an-shih was also a formal honorific title bestowed on outstanding Zen monks by the imperial courts in China and Japan.

Chanting

The ritual recitation of the **sutras** or other Buddhist texts, names for the **Buddha**, and other religious statements. Chanting forms a regular part of Buddhist practice in all schools of **Buddhism** throughout the world. **Monks**, **nuns** and lay people may participate in chanting as a part of their daily devotions or for special intentions. In **Zen** monasteries, for example, monks and nuns regularly chant sutras as a part of morning and evening services and recite prayers before or after each daily meal. Learning to chant the daily services, funeral and memorial rituals, and other ritual services forms a major portion of the **monastic training** received by **novices** at Zen monasteries. **Lay believers** often learn to chant specific sutras, such as the **Heart Sutra**, the **Avalokiteshvara Sutra**, or Zen prayers, such as the **Zazen wasan** written by **Hakuin Ekaku** (1685--1768).

Buddhist religious chanting takes many forms. In some cases, lay people and monastics may use the chanting of religious formulae, such as **mantras** or **dharani**, as a part of their meditative practice. The rhythmic repetition of sounds has long been known to induce meditative states similar to those achieved through other forms of **meditation**. In other cases, chanting a religious formula is regarded as beneficial because it builds **merit** for the practitioner. Devotees of **Pure Land** Buddhism, for example, may chant the name of the **Amida buddha** (J. **nembutsu**; Ch. nien-fo), in order to achieve **rebirth** in the Pure Land. Buddhist clerics may chant dharani in order to bring rain, prevent the spread of disease, or ward off other natural calamities.

Ch'an-tsung Wu-mên-kuan

The Gateless Barrier of the Zen School, the full Chinese title for the *Wu-mên-kuan*. See *Mumonkan*.

Ch'an-yuan Ch'ing-kuei

(J. *Zen'on Shingi* or *Zen'en Shingi*) "The Zen **monastic code** of the Yüan dynasty," a code composed in ten sections by **Zen** Chinese **monk** Chang-lu Tsung-i in 1103. The *Ch'an-yuan Ch'ing-kuei* is the oldest Zen code in existence. The code is quite lengthy and discusses almost every aspect of life and practice in a Zen monastery. It was used as the basis for subsequent versions of the Zen monastic code produced in China. The text was transmitted to Japan in about 1200 and became very influential there. **Dôgen Kigen** (1200–1253) used it as the basis for his *Eihei Shingi*.

Ch'an-yuan Chu-ch'uan-chi Tu-hsu

(J. *Zengen Shosenshû Tojo*) **Zen** text composed by **Tsung-mi** (780–840) as a preface to a much larger work, which is no longer in existence. In the preface, Tsung-mi distinguishes five types of **meditation** and characterizes three schools of early Chinese Zen. The five types of meditation include non-Buddhist meditation, ordinary meditation, Hinayana meditation, Mahayana meditation, and the ultimate form of meditation associated with the Zen school. The three schools of Chinese Zen he describes are the **Northern school** of **Shen-hsiu** (606?–706), the **Southern school** represented by **Ma-tsu Tao-i** (709–788) and his disciples, and the **Ho-tse school** to which Tsung-mi claimed to belong.

Chao-chou Ts'ung-shen

(778–897; J. Jôshû Jûshin) A T'ang dynasty **Zen** master from the **lineage** of Nan-chüan known for his paradoxical statements and strange actions. Chao-chou was one of the outstanding masters of his day and became the subject of numerous **kôan** from the classical collections, including five in the *Mumonkan* and twelve in the *Hekiganroku*. The most famous is the **Mu kôan**, the first case in the *Mumonkan*, commonly used as the first device for beginning students of Zen.

Chao-chou entered the monastery at an early age and became Nan-chüan's disciple at age eighteen. It is said that he attained his first **enlightenment** experience that year. He remained with Nan-chüan for many years, continually deepening his understanding. After his master's death, when he was in his fifties, Chao-chou set out on a **pilgrimage** to visit other Zen masters. At the age of eighty, he was invited to take up residence at the **Kuan-yin** temple in the city of Chao-chou (from which he took his Buddhist name). There he accepted disciples and taught until he died at the age of 120. He did not use harsh teaching devices, such as the stick or the shout (**bôkatsu**), typical of his day to challenge his disciples; instead he employed quiet, simple words which were, nonetheless, powerful.

Chao-lun

(J. *Jôron*) "The Treatises by **Seng-chao**," a commentary on **Mâdhyamaka** teaching written by Seng-chao (374–414). Seng-chao was a disciple of **Kumarajiva**, the Central Asian translator and scholar-**monk**. He was the first native Chinese to discuss the middle way of Madhyamika thought, and he effectively expressed these sophisticated concepts of Buddhist philosophy in a Chinese manner. The *Chao-lun* comprises four essays, "Things are Without Change," "The Emptiness of the Unreal," "Prajna is Without Knowledge," and "The Namelessness of **Nirvana**." The essays were probably composed between 404 and 414, although it is unknown when the compilation was first completed. The *Chao-lun* served as one of the foundational texts of the **San-lun school** of Chinese **Buddhism**. It was also highly valued by the Hua-yen and **Zen** schools. The entire text appears as one section of the *Transmission of the Lamp* (Ch. **Ching-te Ch'üan-teng Lu**; J. *Keitoku Dentô Roku*). A complete English translation was prepared by Walter Liebenthal in his *Book of Chao*. See also **Hua-yen school**.

Cheng-fa Yen-tsang

"Treasury of the True **Dharma Eye**," a collection of traditional **kôan** compiled by **Ta-hui Tsung-kao** (1089–1163), a Chinese Rinzai master of the Sung dynasty (960–1279) between 1141 and 1150. The title is pronounced *Shôbôgenzô* in Japanese, but the work is unrelated to the more famous *Shôbôgenzô* written by **Dôgen Kigen** (1200–1253). See also **Rinzai sect**.

Chen-jen

(J. shinnin) A Chinese term usually translated as True Person. Chen-jen is a Taoist term used by the philosopher Chuang-tzu to indicate an ideal Taoist adept who understands the **Tao**. The expression was later adopted by Chinese Buddhists to translate the Sanskrit word "arhat," the ideal Buddhist practitioner who has realized **nirvana**. See **true person of no rank**.

Chia-t'ai P'u-teng Lu

"The Chia-t'ai Comprehensive Record of the Lamp" (J. *Katai Futô Roku*), a supplement to earlier historical chronicles of the **Zen** school. It was compiled by Lei-an Cheng-shou (1146–1208) in 1204. The text includes biographies and writings of Zen masters and prominent Buddhist masters from other schools of **Buddhism**, as well as biographies of emperors and government officials who favored Zen. Its primary focus is on the Northern Sung and Southern Sung dynasties. The text is the fifth and final of the five Zen chronicles known collectively as the Five Records of the Lamp (J. *Gotôroku*).

Chiden

Prefect of the Buddha hall, one of the six offices (chôsu) related to the **meditation** and training aspects of life in a **Zen** monastery. The chiden is a senior **monk** responsible for cleaning and preparing the various halls; in particular, he sees that the Buddha hall (**Butsuden**) is ready for all ritual functions.

Chie

Wisdom; Japanese term used as a translation for the Sanskrit term *prajna*. See **prajna**.

Chief Cook

One of the highest and most important officers in a **Zen** monastery, the chief cook is one of six administrative offices which oversee the practical administration of the monastery. See **tenzo**.

Chien-chen

(687–763; J. Ganjin) Chinese Buddhist **monk** who founded the **ritsu** (**vinaya**) school of **Buddhism** in Japan. Japanese monks studying in China during the early eighth century invited the famous vinaya master Chien-chen to visit Japan, since Japan still lacked formal **ordination** procedures. Chien-chen made five unsuccessful attempts to reach Japan over a period of eleven years but finally succeeded in 754; by then he was blind. He took up residence at Tôdai-ji in Nara, where he supervised the construction of the first ordination platform (J. **kaidan**) in the country. At the first formal ordination ceremony, Chien-chen bestowed the **precepts** on more than 400 lay people, including Emperor Shômu, and some 80 monks. See also **lay believer**.

Chien-chung Ching-kuo Hsu-teng Lu

(J. *Kenchû Seikoku Zokutô Roku*) *The Chien-chung Ching-kuo Supplementary Record of the Lamp*, a thirty-section chronicle of early **Zen** history, presented in the biographies, **sermons**, and anecdotes of prominent Zen masters. It was compiled by Fo-kuo Wei-po in 1101 and published in 1103. Fo-kuo was a scholar-**monk** of the **Yun-men school** of Zen. He intended the work to be a continuation of the ***Ching-te Ch'üan-teng Lu***, therefore concentrating the majority of the chapters on Zen masters from the **five houses** (J. goke) of Zen active during the Northern Sung dynasty (960–1279). The text is the third of the five Zen chronicles known collectively as the Five Records of the Lamp (J. ***Gotôroku***).

Chi-fei Ju-i

(1616–1671; J. Sokuhi Nyoichi) An Obaku **monk** from Fukien province who emigrated from Ming China and arrived in Japan in 1657. Chi-fei was one of the leading disciples and **Dharma heirs** of **Yin-yüan Lung-ch'i** (1594–1673), the founder of Obaku Zen in Japan. Chi-fei is known for his poetry and masterful **calligraphy**. Along with Obaku masters Yin-yüan and Mu-an, Chi-fei is known as one of the "Three Brushes of Obaku" (san-hitsu), monks who were regarded as great artists for their calligraphy. See also **Obaku sect**.

Ch'ih-hsiu Pai-chang Ch'ing-kuei

(J. ***Chokushû Hyakujô Shingi***) "The Imperial Compilation of the Pai-chang Monastic Code," a Yüan dynasty (1260–1368) collection of monastic codes prepared for **Zen** monasteries in 1336. Although the title contains the name Pai-chang and it is often abbreviated as the "Pai-chang Code," Pai-chang himself did not compose any part of the text. The text was transmitted to Japan in about 1350 and served as the basis for governing life at Gozan monasteries.

Chih-i

(538–597; J. Chigi) Chinese Buddhist master who founded the **T'ien-t'ai school** of Chinese **Buddhism**; he resided on Mount T'ien-t'ai, for which the school is named. Chih-i is recognized within the T'ien-t'ai tradition as the fourth **patriarch** of the school because he based his work on the teachings of earlier masters. In particular, he systematized the teachings of Hui-wen and Hui-ssu (515–577). Chih-i based his work on the **Lotus Sutra**, which he regarded as the final, perfect teaching of the historical **Buddha**. He developed a system classifying all of the known Buddhist **sutras** into five periods of the Buddha's life and eight styles of teaching. Texts derived from the ancient Buddhist tradition, the Theravada school, and many of the early Mahayana schools of thought had been introduced simultaneously in China without any clear sense of their relative position in the historical development of Buddhism. Chih-i's classification system helped clarify the confusing array of Buddhist teachings encountered by Chinese Buddhists of his time. Chih-i also spelled out the T'ien-t'ai concept of the **Threefold Truth**, based on **Nagarjuna's** understanding of two levels of truth. In addition, he developed chih-kuan, the T'ien-t'ai method of **meditation**.

Chih-wei

(646–722; J. Chii) **Zen** Chinese **monk** of the T'ang period (618–907), regarded as the Fifth **Patriarch** of the **Oxhead school** of early Zen. Along with his master, Fa-ch'ih, Chih-wei practiced under the Fifth Patriarch of Zen, **Hung-jen** (601–674), for a time and received his **Dharma transmission**. He and his master then returned to Niu-t'ou where they led a brief revival of the Oxhead school.

Chih-yen

(600–677; J. Chigan) **Zen** Chinese **monk** of the T'ang period (618–907), regarded as the Second **Patriarch** of the **Oxhead school** of early Zen. He was the **Dharma heir** of founder Fa-yung (594–657).

Chii

(646–722) Japanese transliteration of **Chih-wei**, Fifth **Patriarch** of the **Oxhead school**. See **Chih-wei**.

Chiji

Stewards; the six senior **monks** at a **Zen** monastery who assist the **abbot** in managing the administrative aspects of the community, particularly economic matters. As a group they are also known as the Eastern rank (**tôhan**), since their duties keep them in the eastern portion of the temple grounds most of the time. The stewards include the offices of prior (**tsûsu**), supervisor (**kansu**), assistant supervisor (**fûsu**), chief cook (**tenzo**), labor steward (**shissui**), and supervisor of trainees (**ino**). The Japanese later added a seventh office, that of bursar (**tsûbun**). Their counterparts in the Western ranks (**seihan**) are known as the prefects (**chôshu**), and assist the abbot in the spiritual aspects of the community. See **tôhan**.

Chinese Tripitaka

(J. *Daizôkyô*) The collection of Buddhist texts, written in Chinese, which is regarded as the canon or official scriptures of the Buddhist tradition throughout East Asia. The Chinese Tripitaka incorporates several types of texts: translations from the early tradition of **Theravada Buddhism**, which formed the original Sanskrit Tripitaka; translations of Mahayana **sutras** originally composed in Sanskrit; apocryphal texts composed in Chinese but presented as translations; and texts composed by and attributed to Chinese authors.

Before the development of printing technology—when Buddhist texts still had to be copied by hand—the Chinese devised catalogs listing existing Buddhist texts. The catalogs were expanded over time to include newer translations and texts originally composed in Chinese. Beginning with the T'ang dynasty (618–907), Chinese imperial courts sometimes issued orders that a collection of all texts mentioned in a given catalog be compiled. These collections of hand-written texts were referred to as Ta-tsang-ching (J. Daizôkyô), or Great Storehouse Scriptures, and later became the basis for printed editions of the Chinese Tripitaka.

There have been a number of complete printed editions of the Chinese Tripitaka produced in China, Korea, and Japan. The first complete wood-block edition, known as the Szechuan edition, was begun during the reign of the first Sung emperor. It was completed in 983. The standard edition currently used by most scholars is the *Taishô Shinshû Daizôkyô*, a modern Japanese edition, which adds several volumes of texts composed by Japanese authors to the Chinese Tripitaka.

Chên, Kenneth Kuan Shêng. *Buddhism in China: A Historical Survey.* Princeton, NJ: Princeton University Press, 1964.

Ching-kuei

"Pure regulations," the Chinese form of **monastic codes** used in the practice of **Zen**, which set out the proper conduct for life and practice within the Zen monastic community. See **shingi**.

Chingo Kokka No Sambukyô

"Three **sutras** for the protection of the country," three **Buddhist scriptures** revered in Japan as beneficial for the welfare of the ruler, the nation, and the people. The three sutras are the **Konkômyôkyô** (Golden Light Sutra), the Hokkekyô (**Lotus Sutra**) and the Ninnôkyô (Benevolent Kings Sutra). Japanese emperors ordered these sutras distributed to temples throughout the country, where they were recited and copied for the sake of the nation.

Ching-shan

(J. Kinzan) Mount Ching, a mountain in modern-day Che-chiang province, China, which was traditionally an important religious site for **Zen**. The mountain was the site of the Zen monastery **Wan-shou-ssu**, home to such famous Zen masters as **Ta-hui Tsung-kao** (1089–1163). Ching-shan became known as one of the Five Mountains (Ch. wu-shan; J. **Gozan temples**), the most prestigious Zen monasteries in China.

Ching-shan Tao-ch'in

(714–792; J. Kinzan Dôkin) Chinese **Zen monk** of the T'ang dynasty (618–907), the final master of the **Oxhead school**. He was the **Dharma heir** of Hsüan-su.

Ching-te Ch'üan-teng Lu

(J. *Keitoku Dentô Roku*) *The Ching-te Era Record of the Transmission of the Lamp*, a thirty-section collection of biographies of Indian and Chinese **Zen** masters. It was compiled by Tao-yuan and edited by Yang I (968–1024) in 1004, during the Ching-te era of the Sung dynasty (960–1279). The collection contains the biographies of Zen **patriarchs**, **monks**, **nuns**, and important lay disciples, arranged chronologically. The title is commonly abbreviated to *Ch'üan-teng Lu* (J. *Dentô Roku*). The text begins with the **seven buddhas of the past**, the last of whom is Shakyamuni **Buddha** (**Siddharta Gautama**), and continues to the time of Tao-yuan at the end of the tenth century. The chronology presents a traditional Zen history of the authentic transmission of the **Dharma** through the generations. Tao-yuan based his version of the Zen **lineage** on the *Pao-lin Chuan*, an earlier compilation. The *Transmission of the Lamp* is the first and earliest of the five texts known collectively as the Five Records of the Lamp (J. *Gotôroku*).

The Transmission of the Lamp includes a total of 1,701 biographies—960 biographical sketches and a listing of another 740 names. In addition to biographical details such as place of birth and family name, it also includes poetry attributed to the various masters, stories of encounters between masters and disciples, and stories about **enlightenment** experiences drawn from **recorded sayings** and other sources. Later Zen masters used the text as a resource for training students. Many of the **kôan** traditionally used within the Zen school were drawn from its pages.

Scholars no longer regard the lineage presented in the *Transmission of the Lamp* as historically accurate, but the text remains a basic resource for early Zen history. Only portions of the text have been translated into English. See also **lay believer**.

Sohaku, Ogata, trans. *The Transmission of the Lamp: Early Masters*. Wolfeboro, NH: Longwood Academic, 1989.

Ching-te-ssu

(J. Keitoku-ji) An important Chinese **Zen** monastery on T'ai-po-shan (Mount T'ai-po), located in modern-day Chekiang. The monastery's full name was T'ien-t'ung Ching-te-ch'an-ssu; it became known as one of the Five Mountains (Ch. wu-shan; J. **Gozan temples**), the most prestigious Zen monasteries in China.

Ching-tzu-ssu

(Jinzu-ji) An important Chinese Sôtô **Zen** monastery on **Nan-shan** (Mount Nan) in Che-chiang. The monastery's full name was Ching-tzu Pao-en-kuang-hsiao-ssu; it became known as one of the Five Mountains (Ch. wu-shan; J. **Gozan temples**), the most prestigious Zen monasteries in China. See also **Sôtô sect**.

Chinsô

The portrait of a **Zen** master, a traditional form of Zen art, alternatively pronounced Chinzô. Chinsô include realistic portraits of prominent Zen **abbots** painted during the subject's life or shortly after death, as well as traditional depictions of famous Zen **patriarchs**

Chinsô, a traditional form of Zen art, includes realistic portraits of Buddhist abbots and Zen masters. This is a painting of Bodhidharma, the legendary founder of Zen Buddhism.

from the past, especially **Bodhidharma**. Formal portraits typically present the master in formal ceremonial dress, seated in a chair. It has long been held that Zen masters bestowed chinsô onto their disciples as a symbol of **Dharma transmission**. Scholars also believe that chinsô were used in many different ritual contexts, especially to represent the deceased during **memorial services**.

Chishiki

A good friend. Literally, the term means knowledge or wisdom. It is often used as a polite form of address for worthy or prominent **monks** who practice **Zen**. Sometimes used synonymously with **Zenchishiki**.

Chiyoku

The bathkeeper at a **Zen** monastery. One of six offices of the monastery of the Western rank (**seihan**), held by a

senior **monk**. In a traditional monastery, the bathkeeper is responsible for preparing the bath and supervising conduct within the bathhouse. (Some members of the community were children.) Bathing days, the only time hot water is available in large quantities, are scheduled every two weeks. The bathkeeper heats the water over a fire, traditionally using leaves and other refuse from cleaning the grounds as fuel.

Chizô

Chief librarian at a **Zen** monastery, one of the six senior officers from the Western rank (**seihan**) of the monastery. Also known as the sutra prefect, or **zôsu**, the librarian is responsible for the proper care of the monastery's collection of books and scrolls, including the preservation of texts and the acquisition of new materials. The chizô is usually a **monk** educated in Buddhist literature, especially Zen. In a contemporary Zen monastery, the position is often held by a highly trained scholar-monk.

Chôka

Morning services, one of three periods of ritual **chanting** held daily in a **Zen** monastery. The morning service is held before sunrise in the main hall (**Butsuden**). It includes the chanting of various **sutras** and other prayers. It is known more fully as Chôka fugin.

Chôka

(2) "Long verse," a genre of Japanese poetry; one of two standard forms of **waka**, or poetry. Chôka may be any length and are composed of alternating lines of five and seven syllables, concluding with a couplet of 7-7.

Chokushû Hyakujô Shingi

Japanese title for the *Ch'ih-hsiu Pai-chang Ch'ing-kuei*. See *Ch'ih-hsiu Pai-chang Ch'ing-kuei*.

Chôrô

An alternative Japanese term for **jûji**, the **abbot** or chief **monk** at a monastery or temple. See **jûji**.

Chôshu

The prefects of a **Zen** monastery. The prefects include a group of six senior **monks** who assist the **abbot** in the spiritual aspects of the monastic community. Prefects participate in training members of the community in **meditation**, monastic discipline, ritual procedures, and the study of religious texts. The prefects include the offices of chief seat (**shuso**), scribe (**shoki**), sutra prefect (**zôsu**), guest prefect (**shika**), bathkeeper (**chiyoku**), and prefect of the Buddha hall (**chiden**). They are also referred to as the Western rank (**seihan**), because their duties keep them in the western precincts of the monastery. Their counterparts on the administrative side are called the stewards (**tôhan**). See **seihan**.

Ch'uan Fa-pao Chi

(J. *Den Hôbôki*) "The Annals of the Transmission of the **Dharma** Treasure," a compilation of the biographies of seven Chinese **Zen** masters. These include **Bodhidharma**, **Hui-k'o** (487–593), **Seng-ts'an** (d. 606), **Tao-hsin** (580–651), **Hung-jen** (601–674), Fa-ju, and **Shen-hsiu** (606?–706), who are considered the Chinese **patriarchs** of the **Northern school** of Zen. The text was written by a lay practitioner, Tu Fei. See also **lay believer**.

McRae, John R. *The Northern School and the Formation of Early Ch'an Buddhism*. Honolulu, HI: University of Hawaii Press, 1986. (McRae includes a complete English translation of the text as an appendix.)

Ch'uan-hsin Fa-yao

(J. *Inshû Obaku-zan Dansai Zenji Denshin Hôyô*) "The Principles of the Transmission of Mind," a collection in one section of **Huang-po Hsi-yün's** (d. 850) **recorded sayings** which was compiled by P'ei-hsiu in 857. The text's full title is *Yun-chou Huang-po-shan Tuan-chi Ch'an-shih Ch'uan-hsin Fa-yao*. It appears as a part of the *Ssu-chia Yu-lu*, the *Record of the Four Houses*. See also **Huang-po-shan** and **Zenji**.

Ch'uan-teng Lu

(J. *Keitoku Dentô Roku*) A common abbreviation for the *Ching-te Ch'üan-teng Lu*, the *Transmission of the Lamp*. See *Ching-te Ch'üan-teng Lu*.

Chü-chih

(J. Gutei) A T'ang dynasty **Zen monk** from **Ma-tsu Tao-i's** (709–788) **lineage**, who lived during the ninth century. Chü-chih was known for his "One-finger Zen." When asked by disciples for instruction, Chü-chih would reply by silently raising a single finger. Little else is known about Chü-chih, except that he made use of unusual and shocking behavior to push disciples toward **enlightenment**. According to a classical kôan preserved in the *Mumonkan* and *Hekiganroku*, when a young attendant once imitated the master's teaching technique without yet grasping its importance, Chü-chih cut off the young man's finger. In the shock and pain of the experience, the attendant attained enlightenment.

Chûganha

Japanese name for the **Mâdhyamaka** school. See **Mâdhyamaka**.

Chûhô Myôhon

The Japanese pronunciation for **Chung-feng Ming-pen** (1263–1323), a Yüan dynasty Rinzai **monk**. See **Chung-feng Ming-pen**.

Chu-hung

Yün-ch'i Chu-hung (1535–1615; J. Unsei Shukô), also known as Lien-ch'i Chu-hung (J. Renchi Shukô), was a leading Chinese Buddhist **monk** of the Ming dynasty (1368–1644). Chu-hung did not become a monk until he was thirty-two years old. Before that time, he lived as a **householder**, marrying twice. He is called Yün-ch'i after the temple of that name, which he founded in Hang-chou. He resided for most of his monastic life at Yün-ch'i-ssu. Within the monastery, he studied **Zen**, Hua-yen, and T'ien-t'ai thought, but he took the **tonsure** at a Zen monastery and is therefore generally regarded as a Zen monk. Since he regularly chanted the **nembutsu** (Ch. nien-fo) and wrote many texts recommending that practice, he is sometimes also regarded as a **Pure Land** master. He left behind numerous important treatises and was the founder of a popular lay Buddhist movement based on the concept of meritorious and demeritorious behavior.

Like other Buddhist masters of his time, Chu-hung combined various religious teachings, arguing that **Buddhism**, Taoism, and Confucianism were all compatible. He also advocated a combined practice of Zen **meditation** and Pure Land devotion, a trend in Chinese Buddhism at the time. Chu-hung not only advocated the simple recitation of the nembutsu, but recommended that practitioners contemplate the nembutsu in a **kôan**-like fashion, concentrating on the **Amida buddha** within the self and the Pure Land of the Mind. Chu-hung is also known for his response to the teachings of Jesuit missionaries in China. He composed the essay "T'ien-shuo ssu-p'ien," in which he gave a Buddhist refutation of Christian beliefs. See also **dual practice**, **Hua-yen school**, **T'ien-t'ai school**, and **lay believer**.

Chûin

The interim period between death and the next **rebirth**, usually believed to last 49 days. During this period of time, the karmic energy or residue from the previous life is believed to exist in a suspended state before taking on its next form. In more popular terms, the karmic residue is thought of as the spirit or soul of the deceased, which escapes from the body at death but retains some semblance of the individual's personality. At the end of the interim period, the karmic residue or spirit takes on another form, being reborn into one of the six realms of existence. Rebirth is based upon the accumulated **karma** and **merit** from the previous existence, so that goodness is rewarded and evil actions punished.

In East Asian cultures, the chûin is observed as the initial period of mourning after the death of a loved one. Since the exact outcome of the next rebirth is not yet determined, it is commonly believed that the chûin period provides a final opportunity to improve the person's prospects. Specifically, meritorious actions undertaken by the living during this time can benefit the deceased. In Japanese **Buddhism**, for example, the mourning period is marked by a series of **memorial services** conducted every seven days. Traditionally, the merit accumulated from these services is believed to be transferred to the deceased in the hope of insuring a better rebirth.

Chung-feng Ho-shang Kuang-Lu

(J. *Tenmoku Chûhû Osho Kôroku*) *The Comprehensive Record of Master Chung-feng*, a text of thirty sections, including the **recorded sayings** (goroku) and writings of **Chung-feng Ming-pen**, a Yüan dynasty (1260–1368) Chinese Rinzai master. The work was compiled by Po-t'ing Tz'u-chi and other disciples. The full title for the text is *T'ien-mu Chung-feng Ho-shang Kuang-lu*, which is sometimes abbreviated to *Chung-feng Kuang-Lu*. In 1334, the completed work was presented to the last Yüan emperor, Shun-ti (r. 1333–1368), who ordered it included in the **Chinese Tripitaka**. See also **Rinzai sect**.

Chung-feng Ming-pen

(1263–1323; J. Chûhô Myôhon) A Yüan dynasty (1260–1368) **monk** who practiced **Zen** and worked to restore a vigorous form of Rinzai practice in China. He was called "the old **buddha** south of the sea" by his contemporaries because he once fled the monastery by boat when he was appointed to serve as **abbot**: He preferred a solitary life of **meditation** to the busy life of a senior monk at an established monastery, and he was respected for his act because it indicated a dedication to practice rather than a lust for power. For most of his career he lived without a permanent residence, taking up temporary lodging in various huts on Mount T'ien-mu. Although he refused an invitation from Emperor Jen-tsung to become a court monk, he received from the emperor an honorific robe and the title Fo-tz'u Yüan-chao Kuang-hui Ch'an-shih.

Chung-feng exerted considerable influence on Japanese Rinzai of the Kamakura period (1185–1333), despite the fact that he never left China. Several Japanese monks traveled to China to study with him. His Japanese **Dharma heirs** then established his **lineage** in Japan, where it was known as the Genjû line of Rinzai Zen. Chung-feng's style was distinctive in Japan because he allowed some blending of **Pure Land** practice into his Zen style. See also **Rinzai sect**.

Codependent Origination

(J. engi) The Buddhist teaching that all mental and physical things come into being a result of causes and conditions—none are self-existent. A thing passes out of existence when its causes and conditions cease to exist. This means that all things lack an essential self-nature, such as an eternal soul, and are thus impermanent. All things are characterized by perpetual change.

Traditionally a Twelve Link Chain of Causation illustrated how human **suffering** arises from a series of interrelated conditions. A standard rendering of the Twelve-Link Chain begins with ignorance. Ignorance leads to dispositions, consciousness, name and form, six senses (the five senses plus the mind), sensory stimulation, feeling, desire, **attachment** to things and persons, becoming, birth, and finally aging, dying, and sorrow.

In **Theravada Buddhism**, the teaching of codependent origination is closely related to the **four noble truths**, especially the second and third truths, which explain the cause and relief of suffering. When the chain is explained as above, it describes the causes of suffering. When the chain is reversed, it illustrates how eliminating spiritual ignorance will alleviate suffering.

In **Mahayana Buddhism**, the teaching of codependent origination is closely related to the teaching of **emptiness**. The concept of emptiness recognizes that all things are mutually interdependent.

Harvey, Peter. *An Introduction to Buddhism: Teachings, History and Practices*. Cambridge: Cambridge University Press, 1990.

Cold Ashes and Dead Trees

Zen masters sometimes use expressions such as cold ashes and dead trees as metaphors for the Zen practice of seated **meditation** (zazen), in which one transcends the hindrances of ordinary passions and desires.

Compassion

Primary virtue of Buddhist practitioners, especially **bodhisattvas**. Compassion (J. **jihi**) is the motivation to help other **sentient beings** to alleviate their **suffering** and lead them toward **enlightenment**. Within the Buddhist tradition, compassion is always paired with wisdom. Compassion is said to arise from wisdom because it is based on one's awareness of the interdependence and interconnectedness of all things. Conversely, wisdom is demonstrated in compassion. Compassion requires taking action that will alleviate suffering and lead other sentient beings toward enlightenment. It can be demonstrated in many ways, especially through teaching and transferring **merit** to others.

According to the tradition of **Mahayana Buddhism**, there are three degrees of compassion. First, there is the "small compassion" in which ordinary individuals, **pratyeka buddhas**, and **shravakas** display upon observing the suffering of other sentient beings. Second, **arhats** and bodhisattvas in the early stages of the **Buddhist path** produce the "middle compassion," which is based on their awareness of the teaching of No-Self (Sk. **Anatman**). Finally, advanced "bodhisattvas and buddhas give rise to great compassion" as a result of their thorough grasp of **emptiness**.

Consciousness Only

The Mahayana teaching that all phenomena that one experiences as external realities are manifestations of one's consciousness or mind (J. yuishiki).

This teaching, which became a great influence on **Zen** thought and practice, constituted the basic doctrine for the **Yogachara school** of **Mahayana Buddhism** which arose in India, as well as the later Ti-lun (J. Jiron), She-lun (J. Shôron), and Fa-hsiang (J. Hossô) schools in China and Japan. The teaching was developed and set out in the **Avatamsaka Sutra**, **Lankavatara Sutra**, and treatises attributed to the Indian scholar monks Maitreyanatha, Asanga, and Vasubandu.

According to the Yogachara school's psychology of the human mind, each individual has eight levels of consciousness. The first five are related to the five senses and the sixth to the ordinary mind, which processes the sensory perceptions. The seventh level of consciousness is the ego, the source of desire and other emotional responses. At the deepest level, there is the unconscious mind, known in Yogachara thought as the storehouse consciousness (**alaya consciousness**), in which all previous experiences and impressions are stored as seeds. These seeds become the basis for evaluating all present and future experience and are projected outward, creating the false impression of an external reality outside the mind. The "Consciousness Only" teaching is not intended to function simply as a philosophical position that denies the existence of any external reality. Rather, its understanding of human perception and the workings of the mind are intended to serve as a meditative device to promote the experience of **enlightenment**. See also **eight conciousnesses**, **Fa-hsien school**, and **Hossô school**.

Daibontennô Monbutsu Ketsugikyô

"The Sutra of King Mahabrahman's Questions to the Buddha and Resolution of Doubts," a sutra in one or two sections purported to be the words of Shakyamuni Buddha (**Siddharta Gautama**), at the time of the first transmission of the Zen Dharma. According to tradition the Buddha raised a flower instead of preaching, and **Mahakashyapa** responded with a smile. The title is commonly abbreviated to "Monbutsu Ketsugikyô." The text's authenticity is now doubted; based on its contents, it was probably composed in China. The Chinese title is "Ta-fan-t'ien-wang Wen-fo Chuen-i-ching." The two existing versions are different in length and content; the one-section text was probably composed later than the two-section version.

Daibutchô-ju

The **Shuramgama dharani**, a spell derived from the seventh section of the **Shuramgama Sutra**, was used to exorcise evil spirits and ward off calamities. The full title of the spell in Japanese is Daibutchô Mangyô Shuryôgon Darani; it is sometimes abbreviated as the Ryôgon-ju. The Shuramgama Dharani is one of the most commonly used **dharani** in the **Zen** school. It often appears as a part of Zen rituals, including **memorial services** and funerals. See **Shuramgama dharani**.

Daie

"Great robe," the formal outer garment which **monks** and **nuns** wear over their other monastic robes. The daie is the largest of the three monastic robes, or **kesa**. It was originally donned whenever a monk or nun needed to leave the monastic community to beg or teach. Daie are constructed of strips of cloth, numbering from nine to twenty-five, which are sewn together. It is alternatively known as the sôgyari (**kujôe**) in Japanese.

Daie Sôkô

The Japanese pronunciation for **Ta-hui Tsung-Kao** (1089–1163), a Chinese Rinzai **monk**. See **Ta-hui Tsung-Kao**.

Daifunshi

Great resolve or determination. According to **Zen** teachings, Great Resolve is one of the three essential traits necessary for Zen practice, along with Great Doubt (**Daigi**) and Great Trust (**Daishinkon**). The Zen practitioner must produce deep and abiding resolve to persevere in the practice of Zen, to overcome the doubts that arise, and to attain **enlightenment**. The term is discussed in *Zen Essentials* (*Kao-feng Ho-shang Ch'an-yao*; J. *Kôhô Ôshô Zen'yô*), a text composed by the Yüan dynasty (1260–1368) Rinzai master Kao-feng Yüan-miao (1238–1295). See also **Rinzai sect**.

Daigi

Great doubt or great questioning. According to **Zen** teachings, Great Doubt is one of three necessary traits for the practice of Zen. Great Resolve (**Daifunshi**), Great Trust (**Daishinkon**), and Great Doubt motivate the practitioner. The term is discussed in *Zen Essentials* (*Kao-feng Ho-shang Ch'an-yao*; J. *Kôhô Ôshô Zen'yô*), a text composed by the Yüan dynasty (1260–1368) Rinzai master Kao-feng Yüan-miao (1238–1295). Like others before him, the Rinzai master, **Hakuin Ekaku** (1685–1768), believed that every practitioner must produce great doubt, sometimes called "the **ball of doubt**," as the first step toward attaining

enlightenment. He and other masters formulated **kôan** and other Zen devices to elicit great doubt in their disciples. See also **Rinzai sect**.

Daigo

An alternative saying or answer that a commentator appends to a **kôan** to complete the case. The term literally means "words offered in place of another" and refers specifically to cases in which the commentator provides an answer of his own devising when the disciple in the original exchange (**mondô**) was unable to reply. The term is used for one of two basic kinds of answers that masters would traditionally provide for kôan in compilations of historical cases. The other major style of appended answer is the **betsugo**, a saying with a different opinion.

The term *daigo* originally referred to the spontaneous comments that masters made during actual question-and-answer sessions with their disciples. If the students failed to respond to a question, the master would make a comment in their stead. In the *Hekiganroku*, Case 86, for example, Yunmen answered his own question in place of his students. When he asked, "Each person possesses their own light, but if one tries to search for it, all is darkness. What is this light?" he received no response. He then gave two answers, "The monastery halls and gate;" and "Even something one enjoys is not better than nothing."

Daigu Sôchiku

(1584–1669) A Japanese Rinzai **monk** from the **Myôshin-ji lineage**. Daigu was born in Mino to a **samurai**-class family. He is one of the **Zen** reformers who tried to revitalize Rinzai Zen during the early Tokugawa period (1600–1867). After achieving considerable success within the Rinzai institutional hierarchy, Daigu set out to attain **enlightenment** through the practice of **meditation**. Believing that there were no qualified

masters in Japan to confirm his experience, Daigu regarded himself as a "self-confirmed" master. He is best known for his efforts in restoring ruined temples. See also **Rinzai sect**.

Daihannya Haramitsukyô

Mahaprajna Paramita, "The Great Perfection of Wisdom Sutra," the massive Chinese translation (T. 4–7, no. 220) in 600 sections of the entire collection of the **Perfection of Wisdom** literature. Hsuan-tsang (600–664), the Chinese Buddhist **monk**, completed the original translation between 661 and 663 C.E. The **sutra**, which includes such texts as the **Heart Sutra** and the **Diamond Sutra**, is extremely important to many East Asian schools of **Buddhism**, including **Zen**. At many Zen monasteries, monks and **nuns** read the entire sutra at ceremonies for the New Year. They also read it to acquire **merit** for special intentions, using the **tendoku** method, a form of speed-reading.

Daihatsu Nehangyô Shuge

Japanese title for the Parinirvana Sutra, a **sutra** which explains itself to be the final sermon given by the **Buddha** before his death. See **Nirvana Sutra**.

Daiji

The "Great Matter," a common **Zen** expression. It is often used to indicate the **Ultimate Truth** of **Buddhism**, which is realized when one attains **enlightenment**. Also, it may refer specifically to the experience of enlightenment (J. **satori**), when one sees one's own **Buddha Nature**, or to the practice of **meditation** that leads to enlightenment. A Zen master may tell his disciples to attend to the Great Matter, in which case any or all the above meanings may apply. The term is actually the common abbreviation for the Japanese expression **ichidaiji innen**, "the most important cause." The most important cause for the Buddha to appear in the world was to lead others to enlightenment.

Founded in 1282, the monastery Daiji-ji was the headquarters of the Higo branch of Sôtô.

Daiji-ji

An important Sôtô **Zen** monastery, located in Kumamoto Prefecture on the island of Kyûshû, Japan. The temple was founded in 1282 by Kangan Giin (1217–1300), a leading disciple of **Dôgen Kigen** (1200–1253). It was constructed with financial assistance from Kawajiri Yasuaki, a **samurai** warrior from Kyûshû. Daiji-ji became the headquarters of the Higo branch of Sôtô. See also **Sôtô sect**.

Daijô

"Great vehicle," the Japanese translation of Mahayana, one of the two major divisions within **Buddhism**. **Mahayana Buddhism** proliferates throughout East Asia and includes many distinctive schools and styles of practice, including **Zen**. See **Mahayana Buddhism**.

Daijô-ji

An important Sôtô **Zen** monastery, located in Kanazawa, Ishikawa Prefecture, Japan. The temple was founded in 1263 by Togashi Iehisa (d. 1329), as his family temple (J. ujidera). It was originally a Shingon temple, and its first **abbot** was the Shingon **monk** Chôkai. Tettsû Gikai (1219–1309), a direct disciple of **Dôgen Kigen** (1200–1253), converted the temple to a Zen monastery in 1293. See also **Shingon sect** and **Sôtô sect**.

Daijô Kishinron

The Awakening of Faith in Mahayana, a Mahayana treatise traditionally attributed to **Ashvaghosha**. There are two Chinese versions of the text preserved in the **Chinese Tripitaka**. The first translation is believed to have been completed by Paramartha (T. 32, no. 1666) around 550 C.E.; the second translation was done by Shiksananada (T. 32, no. 1667) around 700 C.E. See *Awakening of Faith*.

Daikaku Ha

An alternative name for the **Kenchô-ji** branch of Japanese Rinzai, headquartered at Kenchô-ji in Kamakura. *Daikaku Zenji* was the honorific title conferred posthumously on Chinese master **Lan-ch'i Tao-lung** (1213–1278; J. Rankei Dôryû), who founded the **lineage**. See also **Rinzai sect**.

Daikyû Shônen

The Japanese pronunciation for **Ta-hsiu Cheng-nien** (1215–1289), a Chinese Rinzai **monk**. See **Ta-hsiu Cheng-nien**.

Dainichi Nônin

A twelfth-century Japanese **monk** who founded the *Daruma sect*, the earliest school of **Zen** in Japan. Little can be confirmed about Nônin's life and teachings. Originally, he was a Tendai monk who practiced Zen **meditation** on his own before Zen was established in Japan as an independent school. Nônin apparently attained some degree of proficiency and proclaimed himself a self-enlightened teacher. In that capacity, he established the temple of Sambô-ji in Osaka. There he accepted disciples and trained them according to his own system of thought. Nônin did not adhere to the typical style of either the Rinzai or the Sôtô schools of Zen, but followed meditation practices compatible with the Tendai tradition he had studied at Mount Hiei. Although he eventually received recognition as a Rinzai **lineage** master, he did not make use of **kôan** in training his disciples. Based on criticism of his teachings from other Zen masters, it appears that Nônin believed that keeping the monastic **precepts** was not a necessary part of Zen practice.

Nônin eventually sought confirmation of his **enlightenment** experience from a qualified master in order to establish his credibility as a Zen teacher. He dispatched two disciples to China in 1189, with gifts and a letter addressed to the Chinese Rinzai master Cho-an Te-kuang (1121–1203). In response, Te-kuang sent to Nônin a certificate of enlightenment, a **Dharma robe**, and other gifts. This form of indirect **Dharma transmission** was not universally accepted in Japan, and Nônin became the target of severe criticism from other Japanese Zen leaders. The Daruma sect did not survive long after Nônin's death (circa 1195). Several of Nônin's disciples later joined **Dôgen Kigen's** Sôtô Zen community. See also **Rinzai sect**, **Sôtô sect**, and **Tendai sect**.

Dainichi Nyorai

Japanese for the Great Sun **Buddha**, a translation of the Sanskrit name Mahavairochana Tathagata. Dainichi Nyorai, also known as Birushana (**Mahavairochana Buddha**), is the primary object of veneration in the **Shingon sect** of Japanese **Buddhism**. Early in its history, Japanese Buddhism came to associate Dainichi Nyorai with Amaterasu, the Sun Goddess and the central deity within the Shinto tradition. For this reason, large images of Dainichi, such as the magnificent example at Tôdai-ji in Nara, were enshrined at national temples (kokubunji) in Japan.

Daiô Kokushi

The posthumous honorific title by which **Nampô Jômyô** (1235–1309), a Japanese Rinzai **monk** of the Kamakura period (1185–1333), is commonly known. The full title is actually Enzû Daiô Kokushi. See **Nampô Jômyô**.

Daisan

"Great assemblies;" the formal **Dharma** lectures and subsequent discussion sessions held in the Dharma hall (**hattô**), of a **Zen** monastery with the entire monastic community in attendance. At the great assembly, the **abbot** "ascends the hall" (**jôdô**), meaning that he mounts the central dais in the Dharma hall and speaks to the community from his Dharma chair (**hôza**). At this time, the abbot represents the buddhas and Zen **patriarchs** who taught the Dharma before him. Most Dharma halls have no Buddhist images, since the abbot serves the same role at a great assembly.

The abbot typically gives a formal lecture, known in Japanese as a **teishô**. The sermon is usually a commentary on a few passages from one of the Zen classics, such as the *Lin-chi Lu* (*Sayings of Lin-chi*). After the formal portion of the lecture, the abbot invites questions from the assembly; the audience then has an opportunity to engage in **mondô** with the master. In rare cases, a member of the assembly will challenge the abbot to debate. According to the **monastic codes**, great assemblies should be scheduled every five days. In most modern monasteries, however, they are held during the summer and winter retreats.

Daisetsu Sonô

(1313–1377) Japanese Rinzai **monk** of the Kamakura period (1185–1333) who traveled to China to study Zen. Sonô was a member of the Fujiwara family and was born and raised in Kamakura, Japan. When he was fourteen he took the **tonsure** as a Tendai monk on Mount Hiei. At seventeen he joined the **Zen** assembly at **Tôfuku-ji** in Kyoto, where he studied with several leading Zen masters before leaving for China in 1344. He went to Sheng-shou-ssu and became the disciple of Ch'ien-yen Yüan-ch'ang, a **Dharma heir** of **Chung-feng Ming-pen** (1263–1323) of the Yang-ch'i (J. Yôgi) **lineage**. He received **inka** in 1346, and was given a **Dharma robe** belonging to Chung-feng as a symbol of Dharma transmission. He traveled in China for ten years returning home to Japan in 1358, where he founded several temples and served as **abbot**. It is said that as many as 3,000 disciples joined his assembly at Ryôgon-ji in Ibaraki. Sonô also served as the **abbot** of two prestigious Zen temples, **Kenchô-ji** and **Engaku-ji**. Because of his experience in China and impressive lineage, he was in demand from the Ashikaga government. Although he could not refuse a direct summons from the shogun, it is said that on one occasion he served as abbot of Kenchô-ji for only ten days before resigning. Sonô was the last of the Japanese monks who studied in China, and his transmission represented the final influx of Chinese teachings for several hundred years. His posthumous title is Kôen Myôkan **Zenji**. See also **Rinzai sect**, **Tendai sect**, and **Yang-ch'i school**.

Daishi

A great master. An honorific title which refers primarily to Shakyamuni (**Siddharta Gautama**), the historical **Buddha**. By extension it is often used as a title of respect for a **bodhisattva** or a Buddhist **patriarch**, the founder of a school of **Buddhism**. It may also be used more generally for any extraordinarily talented Buddhist teacher.

In China and Japan, it became the custom for emperors to confer the title "great master" on outstanding Buddhist **monks**, usually as a posthumous honor. The first Buddhist monk to be so honored in Japan was **Saichô** (767–822), the founder of the **Tendai sect**, in 856. In some instances, Japanese make use of the expression as an abbreviation for Kôbô Daishi, the honorific title conferred on the monk **Kûkai** (774–835), founder of the **Shingon sect** in Japan.

Daishinkon

Great trust or great belief. According to **Zen** teachings, Great Trust is one of the three essential traits necessary for Zen practice, along with Great Doubt (**Daigi**), and Great Resolve (**Daifunshi**). The Zen practitioner must have a deep faith in Buddhist teachings and in the historical **Buddha**. In addition, the individual must place a great deal of trust in his or her own teacher. The term is discussed in *Zen Essentials* (*Kao-feng Ho-shang Ch'an-yao*; J. *Kôhô Ôshô Zen'yô*), a text composed by the Yüan dynasty (1260–1368) Rinzai master Kao-feng Yüan-miao (1238–1295). See also **Rinzai sect**.

Daitoku-ji, the main monastery for the Daitoku-ji branch of the Japanese Rinzai sect.

Daitô Kokushi

The posthumous honorific title by which **Shûhô Myôchô** (1282–1337), a Japanese Rinzai **monk** of the Kamakura period (1185–1333), is commonly known. See **Shûhô Myôchô**.

Daitoku-ji

A major **Zen** monastery in Kyoto, Japan, which serves as the main monastery for the Daitoku-ji branch of the Japanese **Rinzai sect**. The temple's formal name is Ryûhô-zan Daitoku-ji, "Dragon's Treasure Mountain, Great Virtue Temple." It was founded by the Zen master **Shûhô Myôchô** (1282–1337)

with the patronage of the retired **Emperor Hanazono** and the reigning **Emperor Go-Daigo**. Shûhô first built a small hermitage for himself in the area of Kyoto, known as Mushashino, in 1315. In 1324, Go-Daigo granted him land to build a large monastery. A group of patrons raised the necessary funds, and the temple was consecrated in 1327. Daitoku-ji was designated as one of the highest-ranking temples in the **Gozan system** for a period of time, but voluntarily withdrew from the system in 1431.

The temple was destroyed by fire and war during the fifteenth century, and was rebuilt later in that century.

Many of the present buildings date to that period. Daitoku-ji has strong associations with the tea ceremony (**chanoyû**) and other artistic forms; famous tea masters including **Sen no Rikyû** took up residence at the temple. The temple houses magnificent works of religious art, donated by wealthy patrons during the Ashikaga (1392–1568) and Tokugawa (1600–1867) periods. Although the temple suffered some damage during the persecution of **Buddhism** in the Meiji period (1868–1912), it remains a vital monastic community for Rinzai practice.

Daitoku-ji Ha

The **Daitoku-ji** branch of Rinzai, one of the fourteen contemporary branches of the Japanese **Rinzai sect**. The main monastery for the branch is Daitoku-ji, located in Kyoto. **Shûhô Myôchô** (1282–1337) is regarded as the founder. The branch has 198 temples throughout Japan and claims approximately 15,000 adherents.

Daizôkyô

The most commonly used Japanese name for the entirety of the **Buddhist scriptures**. The word is derived from the Chinese expression "Ta-ts'ang-ching," which literally means "the Great Storehouse of **Sutras**," and is synonymous with **issaikyô**; it is used somewhat loosely, and may refer to the ancient Sanskrit or Pali Tripitaka, the more extensive **Chinese Tripitaka**, or Japanese editions which include additional materials. There are many complete editions of the Buddhist scriptures, including the most recent Japanese edition, the *Taishô Daizôkyô*.

Danka Seido

The Parishioner System, a policy of social control devised by the Japanese military government during the Tokugawa period (1600–1867). Under a series of regulations introduced in the early seventeenth century, all Japanese families were required to register as members of a local Buddhist temple. In this way, **Buddhism** became an unofficial state religion; Buddhist **monks** served as quasi-civil servants. Monks issued certificates (terauke), verifying that the temple's parishioners were not members of any illegal organization, particularly Christianity or the Fuju Fuse sect of **Nichiren** Buddhism. In some respects, the system benefitted Buddhism, since it guaranteed Buddhist temples large memberships, which in turn provided a stable economic base. On the other hand, enforced membership did not encourage personal commitment on the part of individual Japanese. The regulations were abolished in the Meiji period (1868–1912).

Dankyô

"The **Platform Sutra**," the abbreviated Japanese title for the Rokuso Dankyô, the Platform Sutra of the Sixth Patriarch **Hui-neng**. See **Platform Sutra**.

Danna

A donation, or a donor who makes an offering to the **Buddha**, a **monk**, a **nun**, or a temple. In some cases, the term is used for a person who sponsors a religious ritual or service. The Japanese word comes from the Sanskrit *dâna*. The **offerings** may be material gifts, such as food, clothing, and shelter for the monastic community, or spiritual gifts, such as instruction in the **Dharma** provided by monks and nuns. The term also has come to be used in various Buddhist cultures as a respectful form of address for lay Buddhists.

Danna, understood as generosity, is the first of the **six perfections** practiced by a **bodhisattva**. Bodhisattvas offer material and spiritual gifts, even their lives, to other **sentient beings**. In this way, bodhisattvas accrue **merit**, which they likewise confer on others rather than retaining the spiritual benefits for themselves. Many jataka stories (tales recounting the previous lives of the historical Buddha) offer examples of this form of **compassion**. See also **lay believer**.

Darani
Japanese transliteration of the Sanskrit term *dharani*. See **dharani**.

Daruma
Japanese term for **Bodhidharma**, the First **Patriarch** of **Zen**. The Zen school traditionally regards Bodhidharma as the founder of Zen in China. The term *daruma* may also refer to small dolls or tumblers called **Dharma dolls** made to resemble Bodhidharma. See **Bodhidharma** and **Dharma doll**.

Daruma Sect
The earliest independent sect of **Zen** established in Japan during the late twelfth century by **Dainichi Nônin**, the Buddhist **monk**. The sect takes its name from **Bodhidharma**, traditionally regarded as the founder of Zen in China. Dainichi practiced Zen **meditation** on his own, becoming a self-enlightened master. He established Sambô-ji temple in the Settsu region as the headquarters for his movement. He eventually sent two disciples to China to request formal recognition for his **enlightenment** experience from Cho-an Te-kuang (1121–1203), and became an indirect **Dharma heir** within a recognized Chinese Rinzai **lineage**. The Daruma school did not survive long after the death of its founder; many of his leading disciples joined **Dôgen Kigen's** Sôtô Zen community.

Until recently, the teachings of the Daruma school were known only through the writings of its critics, including Myôan **Eisai** (1141–1215) and Dôgen, Japanese founders of the Rinzai and **Sôtô sects** respectively. From these texts, it seems that the Daruma school rejected the need to follow any external practice or **monastic code**. However, scholars have recently identified three texts that were authored by members of

the Daruma school indicating its teachings had more in common with the Zen of T'ang dynasty China (618–907) than with the Sung dynasty style characterized in Japanese Rinzai and Sôtô. Dainichi practiced a form of meditation similar to that found in the Tendai school, rather than a style typical of the Rinzai lineage to which he formally belonged. He did not, for example, make use of **kôan**. See also **Rinzai sect** and **Tendai sect**.

Daruma-shû
Literally, "the school or **lineage** of **Bodhidharma**," the Indian **monk** who is said to have brought **Zen** from India to China in the sixth century. The name may be used to designate the Zen school in general, or the teachings of Zen **Buddhism**. In other contexts, it refers to a short-lived sect of Zen founded in Japan by the monk **Dainichi Nônin** in the late twelfth century. See also **Daruma sect**.

Dead Ashes
(J. shikai) A **Zen** expression used metaphorically to describe the mind purified of all the harmful passions and **attachments** of ordinary thought. The term applies especially to practitioners of **Theravada Buddhism** who attain the meditative level of extinction (J. **metsujinjô**), a desirable state.

Dead Sitting
(J. shiza) A derogatory expression used by **Zen** teachers to describe incorrect or ineffective forms of seated **meditation**. **Hakuin Ekaku** (1685–1768), for example, criticized silent illumination Zen, or **mokushô Zen**, as a form of dead sitting.

Defilements
Mental activities such as **attachment** that obstruct the path to **enlightenment**. Also referred to as "outflows" or "binding influences" (J. **ro**). For ordinary

people, defilements arise constantly as a result of the workings of the senses and the mind. Buddhist practice, especially within the tradition of **Theravada Buddhism**, can be thought of as a process of extinguishing defilements. Once all defilements are extinguished, one has attained the level of an **arhat** and the state of **nirvana**.

Defrocking

To be formally expelled from a monastic community. When a **monk** or **nun** commits certain offenses, the religious community may take action to expel the individual. The community will often request that items such as monastic robes, certificates of **ordination**, or **lineage charts** be returned to the monastery, symbolizing that it has revoked membership privileges. In the ancient Buddhist tradition, there were four offenses that called for permanent expulsion from the **sangha**. These actions were engaging in sexual intercourse, stealing, killing a human being, and making false claims about one's spiritual attainments. These offenses correspond to **precepts** accepted by **novices** at their initial ordination; an explanation concerning the punishment for breaking them was a regular part of the ordination process. In the **Zen** school, various sects and monasteries have devised **monastic codes** (**shingi**) to govern the behavior of Zen monks and nuns. In some cases, other offenses have been deemed serious enough to warrant defrocking.

Delusion

Attachment to false views of reality. Delusions are very much like ignorance and are a cause of **suffering** for **sentient beings**. The most basic delusion is the attachment to a false sense of self—the belief that one possesses some eternal and unchanging soul or identity (**atman**).

Dembôin

"Seal of **Dharma Transmission**," an alternative expression for **inka** shômei. The dembôin is an official certification from a **Zen** master that a disciple has attained the same **enlightenment** as the master and is qualified to function as a Zen master. See **inka**.

Dengyô Daishi

The posthumous title for **Saichô** (767–822), the Japanese **monk** and founder of the **Tendai sect** in Japan. In 866, Saichô became the first Japanese monk to receive the title "**daishi**" (Great Teacher), an honor bestowed on him by Emperor Seiwa. See **Saichô**.

Denkôroku

"The Record of the Transmission of the Light," a two-section text written by **Keizan Jôkin** (1425–1500), the Second **Patriarch** of Sôtô in Japan. Keizan patterned the text on the *Keitoku Dentô Roku* (Ch. ***Ching-te Ch'üan-teng Lu***), the eleventh-century collection of early **Zen** biographies. The *Denkôroku*, first published in 1857, recounts the **lineage** of Zen patriarchs of the Sôtô school, beginning with Shakyamuni **Buddha** (**Siddharta Gautama**). The text concludes with the biographies of **Dôgen Kigen** (1200–1253) and Koun Ejô (1198–1309), the 51st and 52nd generation patriarchs. A recent English translation was published by Nearman. See also **Sôtô sect**.

Nearman, Rev. Hubert, O.B.C. *The Denkôroku or The Record of the Transmission of the Light by Keizan Zenji*. Mount Shasta, CA: Shasta Abbey, 1993.

Denshin Hôyô

The Japanese title for the ***Ch'uan-hsin Fa-yao***, or "The Principles of the Transmission of Mind." See ***Ch'uan-hsin Fa-yao***.

Denshô

A medium-sized temple bell that hangs from the eaves of the Buddha hall (**Butsuden**). The Denshô is used to call the **monks** to services in the hall. It is similar in design to the **ogane**, or large monastic bell, although significantly smaller in size. It is rung by striking the side of the bell with a hand mallet or a small swinging mallet (**shumoku**).

Dentôroku

The common Japanese abbreviation for the *Keitoku Dentô Roku* (Ch. ***Ching-te ch'üan-teng Lu***). See ***Ching-te Ch'üan-teng Lu***.

Deshi

A disciple or follower of the **Buddha**; a student who receives instruction from a Buddhist teacher. In some cases, the Japanese term *deshi* is used as a translation for the Sanskrit term *sravaka*, meaning those disciples of the historical Buddha who heard him preach in person. The term has common usage in secular contexts in Japan, indicating a student of some sort. While the term may be used for any student in school, it connotes a close bond between student and teacher; for this reason, it applies most aptly to a teacher's proteges. Students of the fine arts and martial arts who train under a master are also known as deshi.

Devadatta

(J. Daibadatta) A cousin of Shakyamuni (**Siddharta Gautama**), who initially became one of his disciples, but later turned against him. Devadatta hoped to be the leader of the Buddhist **sangha**, or community, but the **Buddha** rejected his request for that position. Devadatta became so resentful that he attempted to kill the Buddha and take the leadership of the sangha by force. According to legend, he attacked the Buddha three times. First, Devadatta sent assassins, but they became so impressed with the Buddha that they refused to complete their assignment. Next, he tried to crush the Buddha with a boulder, but the boulder stopped before it could harm the Buddha. Finally, he attacked the Buddha with an enraged elephant, but the Buddha pacified the beast with his great love and was once again unharmed. Although unsuccessful in his attempts to destroy the Buddha, Devadatta's hostility resulted in the first schism within the Buddhist order.

Devas

The deities. The Sanskrit word *deva* literally means "a shining being." In its plural form, the term originally applied to all Hindu deities. **Buddhism** adopted the basic Indian cosmology, but reinterpreted the existence of the devas. In Buddhism, devas are heaven dwellers and represent one of the six realms of existence in **samsara** (rokudô)—the ongoing cycle of birth and death. Like other **sentient beings**, devas are subject to the workings of **karma**; they have been born into a heavenly realm because of good **merit** accumulated in previous lifetimes. When the store of merit is exhausted, however, they fade and die like other sentient beings, usually falling into one of the lower realms. Devas have the advantage of living in pleasurable circumstances, but unlike human beings, they are unable to make progress toward release from samsara. It is said that, untouched by the **suffering** that characterizes human life, devas have no incentive to progress on the path to **enlightenment**. See also **six paths**.

Devil's Cave

A dark place in which one cannot see anything at all. **Zen** texts use the expression as a metaphor for an **attachment** to false views of reality, especially nihilism. See **Kikutsuri**.

Dharani

Sacred formulas found in the **Buddhist scriptures**. Dharani are chanted in a manner similar to **chanting** mantras. Dharani and **mantras** differ only in length; dharani generally refers to longer formulas. Like mantras, dharani often make little sense literally, but the syllables are believed to contain inherent power. Chinese and Japanese versions of dharani are often transliterations of the Sanskrit sounds, sometimes made without any attempt at literal accuracy. Like mantras, dharani may be chanted repeatedly as a way to focus concentration in certain styles of **meditation**. They may also be used as magic spells to ward off various calamities such as disease, dangerous animals, and drought. Although dharani are associated most commonly with tantric and **esoteric Buddhism**, schools also make some use of dharani in daily ritual and for extraordinary circumstances.

Dharma

(J. hô) A Sanskrit term used in all of the major religious and philosophical systems originating in India, including Hinduism, Jainism, and **Buddhism**. The various traditions apply the term somewhat differently. There is no single English term that adequately translates the full range of meanings and implications of the original Sanskrit; the word is variously translated as Truth, Law, Duty, Teaching, Religion, and Norm. The term may appear in secular contexts and refer to secular laws or a secular sense of justice. In Buddhist contexts, it may be used synonymously with the word *Buddhism*.

Buddhist texts use the term *Dharma* to refer to several different but related concepts. The most common usage references the teachings of Buddhism or the teachings of the **Buddha**, including the **sermons** that the Buddha gave during his lifetime as well as the scriptures recorded later, which are said to reflect the original sermons. When used in this sense, the expression *Buddha-Dharma* is often employed. The term *Dharma* may also refer to the morality associated with the **Buddhist path**.

Traditional Buddhist teachings maintained that morality is necessary for the practice of Buddhism and the eventual attainment of **enlightenment**. Buddhist practitioners are required to live according to the Dharma, abiding by the Buddha's prohibitions against killing, stealing, lying, and other offenses. For **monks** and **nuns** this may be interpreted to mean living according to the entire **vinaya**, or **monastic code**. Within the tradition of **Mahayana Buddhism**, living according to the Dharma would involve abiding by the **bodhisattva precepts**. Finally, the term *Dharma* in its deepest sense refers to reality itself and the awareness of things as they are, characterizing the enlightenment of the Buddha and other perfectly enlightened beings. In this final sense, the Dharma may be understood as the ultimate goal of the Buddhist path.

In contrast to the above usages, which are generally denoted in English with the upper-case "Dharma," the Sanskrit word may also refer to elements of the world: things, mental constructions, and events. In this case, the term means "thing." When referring to all things that exist in the phenomenal world, Buddhist texts will speak of all dharmas. Used in this manner, "dharma" is typically left in the lower case to distinguish it from other uses. See also **lay believer**.

Dharma Combat

An expression used to describe certain intense exchanges between **Zen** masters and disciples, using verbal and nonverbal forms of communication. A typical exchange is initiated when the master issues a challenge to members of the assembly, individually or as a group, to express their understanding of the **Dharma**. Although Dharma combat takes on the general appearance of a debate, usually including a question-and-answer period, accounts of these exchanges rarely make much logical sense to the reader. In most cases, the exchange between the combatants amounts to little more than a few disjointed remarks, or shouts and slaps. The goal of the exchange, however, is not to provide an

Designed without arms or legs, Dharma dolls represent the founder of Zen, Bodhidharma, who according to legend lost use of his appendages in meditation.

analytical expression of the Zen teachings. Rather, the master uses the emotionally charged moment of confrontation as an opportunity to push students toward an immediate realization.

Examples of Dharma combat abound in the classical Zen literature, especially in the genre of the **recorded sayings** (goroku) of the masters. Perhaps the most illustrative cases are seen in the *Lin-chi Lu*, the *Sayings of Lin-chi*. In the first discourse recounted in the text, **Lin-chi I-hsüan** (d. 867) explicitly employs the language of battle in his challenge to the assembly: "'Now is there any adept warrior who forthwith can array his battle-line and unfurl his banners here before me? Let him try proving himself before the assembly!' A **monk** asked, 'What about the cardinal principle of the Buddha-Dharma?' The master gave a shout. The monk bowed low. 'As an opponent in argument this young reverend is rather good,' said the master."

Sasaki, Ruth Fuller. *The Record of Lin-chi*. Kyoto, Japan: The Institute for Zen Studies, 1975.

Dharmadhatu

(J. hokkai; "The Realm of the **Dharma**"). The Sanskrit term is used in the Buddhist tradition to mean a variety of things. Dharmadhatu refers to the realm or sphere of ultimate reality. It may be used also to indicate the entire universe and everything in existence. The two senses of the word are related philosophically. From one perspective, the realm of **Ultimate Truth** is clearly distinct from the realm of ordinary existence. Within the realm of ordinary existence, the various things (dharmas) that exist are differentiated from one another, while the realm of ultimate reality transcends all distinctions. Viewed from another perspective, however, the realm of ultimate reality is identical to the realm of ordinary existence. Indeed, ultimate reality is made manifest in everything that exists.

Dharma Doll

A papier-mâché doll or tumbler representing **Bodhidharma**, the first **patriarch** of **Zen**. A popular item in Japanese culture today, the Dharma doll is known simply in Japanese as Daruma and draws loosely upon the Zen legend of Bodhidharma. The dolls are either round or pear-shaped, without any suggestion of arms or legs. This shape symbolizes Bodhidharma's perseverance in **meditation**. According to popular versions of the legend, Bodhidharma sat facing a wall meditating for nine years without pause. During that time, it is said, he lost the use of his arms and his legs, so determined was he to sit until he attained his goal of **enlightenment**. Since the dolls can tumble without falling over, they represent the proverb, "If you fall down seven times, get up eight times (Nana korobi yaoki)." Most often, the proverb is painted on the doll as a reminder to persevere. The body of the doll is usually painted bright red. In most cases, the face does not have eyes. The person who purchases the doll paints in the first eye when starting out on a major endeavor or making a vow to achieve a specific goal. The second eye is painted in only when the goal has been attained. People often buy darumas at the New Year in a custom comparable to the Western practice of making New Year's resolutions.

Dharma Eye

The insight or wisdom to see the true nature of reality; the eye of **enlightenment** that understands the Buddhist teachings. In the ancient Buddhist tradition, those individuals who had gained direct insight into the **Buddha's** teachings were said to possess the Dharma eye (J. hôgen) and to have achieved the stage of stream-winner (one of the **four fruits**). In T'ien-t'ai thought, the Dharma eye is regarded as one of the **five eyes** associated with five kinds of beings. **Bodhisattvas** are said to possess Dharma eyes, which represent the wisdom to see the differentiation among all things that exist. This wisdom enables bodhisattvas to see the **suffering** of all **sentient beings** and to create **expedient means** to alleviate the suffering.

Zen masters may use the term *Dharma eye* in a manner comparable to those mentioned above, or they may use it more broadly to refer to enlightenment. For example, Zen texts use expressions such as "opening the Dharma eye" in reference to enlightenment experiences. In particular, the Zen tradition uses the related expression True Dharma Eye, or the Treasury of the True Dharma Eye (J. **Shôbôgenzô**), as an expression for the fundamental Buddhist understanding that is transmitted from generation to generation within the Zen school. See also **T'ien-t'ai school**.

Dharma Gate

(J. hômon) The Buddhist teachings are compared to a gate that provides entrance to a deeper understanding of life and to **enlightenment**. The expression *Dharma gate* sometimes refers to the Buddhist teachings as a whole; it may also be used in reference to a particular school or sect of **Buddhism** or to a specific type of practice. For example, one Buddhist text may call the **Zen** and the **Pure Land schools** of Buddhism "Dharma gates," while another may refer to the associated practices of **zazen** and **nembutsu** as the respective Dharma gates. **Hui-neng** (638–713), the Sixth Patriarch of the Zen school, commonly used the expression *Dharma gate* when discussing his own teachings and the teachings of Zen.

Dharma Hall

The main assembly and lecture hall at a **Zen** monastery; known as **hattô** in Japanese. The Dharma hall is one of the seven buildings (**shichidô garan**) that form the core of any Zen monastery. See **hattô**.

Dharma Heir

(J. hassu) A **Zen** practitioner who succeeds his or her teacher as a recognized master of Zen and has been deemed competent to take on and train disciples. In most cases, recognition as a Dharma heir implies official recognition of one's

enlightenment experience through a certificate of **inka** or inshô. Such recognition qualifies the student to continue the teacher's **lineage** and transmit the Dharma to a future generation of students. Males and females may be designated as Dharma heirs. The names of Dharma heirs are recorded in the official **lineage chart** of the sect or temple.

In theory, only those students who have attained the same level of understanding of the Dharma as the master may qualify as Dharma heirs. In actual practice, however, the designation of Dharma heir may serve as an institutional device to establish legitimately ordained individuals who serve local temples within a given Zen sect. Since the modern period in Japan (1868–present), when marriage for Buddhist priests has become the norm, for example, young Sôtô priests are usually designated as Dharma heirs early in their careers, thus qualifying them to succeed their fathers as head of the local home temple.

A master might have more than one Dharma heir, but tradition maintains that from the Buddha down through the sixth **patriarch**, only one heir may be designated as patriarch. See also **Sôtô sect** and **lay believer**.

Dharmakaya

"**Dharma** body," a term used in the tradition of **Mahayana Buddhism** to denote the ultimate nature of the **Buddha** and of reality. It may be rendered in English as Truth-Body or Law-Body. The term refers to the perfectly realized wisdom of all buddhas. In this sense all buddhas are one. It may refer also to the ultimate reality of existence, or things as they really are. In this latter sense, the Dharmakaya (J. hosshin) is synonymous with **emptiness**. Within the Mahayana doctrine of the **three bodies of the Buddha**, the Dharmakaya is the highest aspect of the Buddha—the absolute or eternal Buddha.

Dharma King

(J. **Hôô**) A name for the **Buddha**, from the Sanskrit "Dharma Raja." The expression recognizes that the Buddha fully mastered the **Dharma** and was the preeminent teacher of the Dharma. It contrasts the authority of the Buddha as a religious leader with the secular authority of king. In some contexts, the term may refer to a secular king who guards the Buddhist Dharma through his secular authority.

Dharma Robe

Within the **Zen** tradition, monastic robes (J. hôe) are sometimes used as outward symbols that **Dharma transmission** has taken place between a master and disciple. According to traditional accounts, the conveying of Dharma robes began with **Bodhidharma**. After he had confirmed **Hui-k'o** (487–593) as his **Dharma heir**, Bodhidharma bestowed his robe and bowl to him as a sign of Dharma transmission. With this gift, he officially confirmed that Hui-k'o was his legitimate heir and the Second Chinese **Patriarch** of Zen. In turn, Hui-k'o transmitted the robe to his heir, **Seng-ts'an** (d. 606), and so on through the first six generations of Chinese patriarchs. In the **Platform Sutra**, the Fifth Patriarch bestowed the **robe of transmission** for the final time to **Hui-neng** (638–713), thus designating him as the Sixth Patriarch. There are contradictory passages in the Platform Sutra concerning the original robe of transmission. In the biographical portion of the text, **Hung-jen** (601–674) indicates that the robe will be a symbol throughout the generations (Yampolsky, p. 133). In a later passage describing the preparations for his own death, Hui-neng explains that there is no longer any need to transmit the robe (Yampolsky, p. 176).

Yampolsky, Philip B. *The Platform Sutra of the Sixth Patriarch*. New York: Columbia University Press, 1967.

Dharma Seal

The formal certification within the **Zen** school that **Dharma transmission** has occurred between master and disciple. The English expression may serve as a translation for a variety of Chinese and Japanese terms, most commonly **inka**,

The Diamond-Realm Mandala bears over 1,400 buddhas, bodhisattvas, and other deities.

inka shômei, or denbôin. Receiving the Dharma seal of a Zen master implies that the disciple has attained a mature understanding of the Dharma and is qualified to serve as a Zen master to others. See **inka**.

Dharma Seat

The **abbot's** formal lecture chair, or **hôza**, located on the raised platform in the **hattô**, or Dharma hall of the monastery. See **hôza**.

Dharma Transmission

Transmission of the **Dharma** from master to disciple. Although the language suggests that something is passed from one person to another, the Dharma is not a thing that can be physically or literally passed on from one generation to the next. Dharma transmission is actually the acknowledgment by a master that a disciple has attained an experience of **enlightenment** equal to his or her own. Related traditional expressions such as "mind to mind transmission" and "transmission without reliance on words" attempt to make this clear.

According to the **Zen** tradition, the first example of Dharma transmission occurred on **Vulture Peak** between Shakyamuni **Buddha** (**Siddharta Gautama**), and **Mahakashyapa**. On that occasion, when the Buddha was asked to preach the Dharma to an assembly of disciples, he silently held up a flower. No one in the audience understood his meaning, and none could reply. Only Mahakashyapa grasped the Buddha's meaning and responded with a smile. The Buddha then said, "I have the True **Dharma Eye**, the wondrous mind of **nirvana**. I entrust it to Mahakashyapa." This story is the subject of several **kôan**, including Case 6 of the *Mumonkan* and Case 253 of the *Sanbyakusoku*.

Traditional renderings of Zen history are often referred to as "transmissions of the lamp." These maintain that the Dharma was transmitted from Shakyamuni through twenty-eight generations of Indian **patriarchs**, the last of whom was **Bodhidharma**, who carried the teaching to China. The Dharma was then transmitted through five generations of Chinese Zen patriarchs to the Sixth Patriarch, **Hui-neng** (638–713). Since then, the Dharma has been transmitted by masters throughout the generations of the Zen **lineage**; all surviving Zen lineages trace themselves back to Dharma transmission from the Sixth Patriarch.

The most common expression indicating that an authentic transmission has occurred is for a master to confer **inka**, or a "seal of approval," onto a disciple. There are also a variety of outward symbols used within the Zen tradition to certify a transmission of the Dharma. In some cases, official certificates of transmission are prepared; in other cases, a **Dharma robe**, a portrait of the master, a copy of a text, or a religious implement belonging to the master may serve the same purpose. Only those masters who receive a seal of transmission are eligible to take on disciples, passing on the Dharma to the next generation. In addition the expression is employed as an institutional recognition of office. The Sôtô school in Japan today uses the ritual form of Dharma transmission to indicate valid **ordinations** within the sect. Almost every Sôtô **monk** receives Dharma transmission when he is ordained in order to qualify as the head priest of a local temple. See also **Sôtô sect**.

Dharma Wheel
See **Wheel of the Dharma**.

Dhyana

The Sanskrit word for **meditation** from which the Chinese term *ch'an* and the related Japanese term *Zen* are derived. See **meditation**.

Diamond-Realm Mandala

One of two primary **mandala** used in **esoteric Buddhism**, especially the **Shingon sect**. The Diamond-Realm Mandala represents the power of the diamond (or **vajra**) of wisdom to overcome all ignorance. The textual base for the Diamond-Realm Mandala (J. kongôchô mandara) is the Vajrashekhara Sutra (J. Kongôchôkyô). The mandala graphic consists of nine rectangular assemblies arranged in three rows of three. More than 1,400 buddhas, **bodhisattvas**, and other deities appear on the Diamond-Realm Mandala. **Mahavairochana Buddha** appears more than 400 times in various manifestations throughout the graphic, and appears directly as the central image in two assemblies. In the central rectangle, Mahavairochana is surrounded by four other buddhas, representing the Five Wisdoms of esoteric thought. In the upper central rectangle, Mahavairochana appears as the lone figure in the assembly. The mandala is interpreted in two basic ways: clockwise or counterclockwise. When reading clockwise (begining at the center and spiral outward), the mandala represents the movement of Mahavairochana's **enlightenment** into all aspects of the cosmos. Moving counterclockwise (begining at the outside and spiraling inward), the mandala represents the progress of a sentient being toward the attainment of enlightenment. Another primary mandala used in esoteric Buddhism is the **Womb-Realm Mandala**.

Yamasaki, Taiko. *Shingon: Japanese Esoteric Buddhism*. Trans. Richard and Cynthia Peterson. Ed. Yasuyoshi Morimoto and David Kidd. Boston, MA: Shambhala, 1988.

Ishida, Hisatoyo. *Esoteric Buddhist Painting*. Trans. E. Dale Saunders. New York: Harper & Row, 1987.

Diamond Sutra

The Vajra Sutra, a one-section sutra from **Mahayana Buddhism** composed around the fourth century C.E. The Diamond Sutra is one of the later **Perfection of Wisdom Sutras** (Sk. Prajna-paramita). Its full Sanskrit name is Vajra-cchedika-prajna-paramita-sutra (J. Kongô Hannya Haramitsu Kyô); it is known in English as the Diamond-Cutter Sutra. The text explains the Mahayana teachings of **emptiness** (shunyata) and wisdom (**prajna**). It is one of the most important sutras for the **Zen** school, perhaps because it employs negation, a teaching device much in keeping with Zen. It is said that **Hui-neng** (638–713), the Sixth Patriarch, first attained **enlightenment** when he heard a man reciting verses from the Diamond Sutra.

Dô

"Way" or "path," the Japanese rendering of the Chinese word **Tao**. Sometimes pronounced "Tô," as in Shintô, "the Way of the **kami**." See **Tao**.

Dôban

A hanging banner used as ornamentation for a temple building or at a **memorial service**. The central support is a vertical pole with an ornate top piece, decorated with a dragon pattern and jewels. In traditional dôban, long strips of cloth hang down from the top piece of the pole. Today, strips of gold-colored metal or wooden strips are used instead of cloth. A pictorial description is provided by the *Obaku Shingi*.

Dôgen Kigen

(1200–1253) **Zen monk** who founded the **Sôtô sect** in Japan. Dôgen was the son of a noble family and received a classical education. He was orphaned as a young child, losing his father at age two and his mother at about age seven. He entered monastic life at thirteen, becoming a Tendai monk on Mount Hiei. A few years later, he left Mount Hiei to study Zen with Myôan **Eisai** (1141–1215), founder of the **Rinzai sect**, at **Kennin-ji**. It is not known if the two ever met, since Eisai died at about that time. Dôgen became **Ryônen Myôzen's** (1184–1225) disciple and remained at Kennin-ji from 1217 to 1223. In 1223, he and Myôzen traveled together to China. While in China, Dôgen became the disciple and **Dharma heir** of the Sôtô master **Ju-ching** (1163–1228). He returned to Japan in 1227 and spent several years in the Kyoto area, establishing his first monastery in 1233, called **Kôshô-ji**. In 1244 he and his community of monks moved to Echizen where he established **Eihei-ji**, the main monastery for the Sôtô sect. He died while traveling to Kyoto in 1253. His major literary works include the *Shôbôgenzô* and the *Eihei Shingi*. See also **Tendai sect**.

Dojidô

Hall of the Guardian Deity. A small temple building traditionally positioned to one side of the Buddha hall (**butsudô**) of a **Zen** monastery. A Buddhist protective deity is enshrined inside the dojidô. *Doji*, or *Dojijin*, is the Japanese term for guardian deities, including both Buddhist deities and certain Shintô **kami**. In most cases, the image in a Zen dojidô would be a Buddhist deity such as Daigon Shuri Bosatsu, Bonten, or Gohô Myôô. Traditionally, services were held at the hall twice a month, on the second and sixteenth days. **Offerings** were also made to the guardian deity on other occasions. For example, a new **abbot** offered **incense** before the image of the Dojijin as a part of the installation service. More recently in Zen monasteries in Japan, the dojidô has been replaced by an altar within the Buddha hall, called the Dojidan. It serves the same purpose as the separate hall.

Dôjô

"A place of the way." The term *dôjô* has wide and varied usage. It may mean the place under the **bodhi tree** in Bodhgaya, India, where the **Buddha**, Shakyamuni (**Siddharta Gautama**), attained **enlightenment**; any place where **Buddhism** is practiced; a Buddhist temple or monastery as a whole; or a single hall at a Buddhist temple. In popular usage it may also refer to schools or buildings unrelated to Buddhism where martial arts are taught and practiced.

In the **Zen** school, dôjô usually refers to the training or the **meditation hall** at a monastery where **monks** receive instruction in meditation. In the Rinzai and Obaku sects, it is called the zendô, or meditation hall; in the **Sôtô sect**, it refers to the **sôdô**, or monks' hall. The term *dôjô* may also be used as an abbreviation for **semmon dôjô**, meaning a training monastery for the **Rinzai sect**.

Dokkaku

"Self-enlightened one." A Japanese translation for the Sanskrit term **pratyeka buddha**. **Hsüan-tsang** (ca. 600–664), the Chinese scholar-**monk**, derived the Chinese word *tu-chüeh*, on which the Japanese is based. See **pratyeka buddha**.

Miura, Isshû, and Ruth Fuller Sasaki. *The Zen Kôan*. New York: Harcourt, Brace & World, 1967.

Dokusan

The private interview between a **Zen** master and a disciple; the commonly used abbreviation for nyûshitsu dokusan. The term literally means "going alone" to visit the master. During the course of the morning and evening **meditation** session at a Zen monastery, students have the opportunity to enter the master's quarters and consult with him privately in matters related to their practice. The master may use the meeting as an opportunity to evaluate a disciple's progress in meditation, especially when the disciple is working on a **kôan**. Dokusan is typically practiced in Rinzai and Obaku Zen, since it is associated with the guidance related to kôan contemplation. It is in the context of dokusan that a master assigns a kôan, tests a student's understanding, and offers encouragement to persevere. When a student experiences a breakthrough, the master may test and perhaps affirm the experience during dokusan.

Monasteries observe traditional patterns of etiquette for dokusan. During the period when the master is receiving students for dokusan, disciples wait outside the master's room for their turn to enter. Before going into the master's quarters, the student rings a bell, announcing his or her presence. Once inside, the student bows to pay respect to the master. When the master determines that the interview is over, he signals dismissal with a hand bell. The student bows and departs, making way for the next person. See also **Rinzai sect** and **Obaku sect**.

Kapleau, Philip. "The Private Encounter with the Master." In *Zen, Tradition and Transition*. Ed. Kenneth Kraft. New York: Grove Press, 1988.

Dôkyô Etan

(1642–1721) Japanese Rinzai **monk** from the **Myôshin-ji lineage**, best known as the master of **Hakuin Ekaku** (1768–1768), the great **Rinzai sect** reformer. Etan was the son of a **samurai** and his concubine. He was raised in the household of Lord Matsudaira Tadatomo, where he was first introduced to **Zen**. On a trip to Edo in 1660, Etan became the disciple of **Shidô Bu'nan** (1603–1676), having already attained an experience of **enlightenment**. He received the master's certificate (J. **inka**) after only one year of practice. He then returned to his native Iiyama in Shinano, where he lived a simple life in a small hermitage called Shôju-an. From the hermitage Etan received his nickname, Shôju Rôji, "the old man of the Shôju hermitage." None of Etan's writings were published, although some of his teachings are scattered within Hakuin's work.

Dônai

The areas within a **Zen** monastery in which the **monks** or **nuns** live and practice, especially the zendô or **meditation hall**. The term literally means "inside the hall." The dônai is distinguished from the administrative areas of the monastery, known as **jôjû**.

Donkatsukan

"Stupid blind oaf," an expression used by the Japanese Rinzai master **Hakuin Ekaku** (1685–1768). There are a number of related terms used in a similar manner throughout **Zen** literature such as

Donkonnin ("Dimwit") and Danrusei ("Damn fool!"). Zen masters often addressed disciples with such derogatory terms in order to push them beyond whatever hindrances they had encountered. For example, if a student persisted in analyzing a **kôan** in purely intellectual terms, the master might rebuke him for being a fool. Alternatively, masters sometimes used the term in a positive manner to indicate a splendid disciple. See also **Rinzai sect**.

Dora

A musical instrument used in Buddhist ritual services. The dora is a gong, typically made of bronze. It is shaped like a round dish and attached with a cord to a wooden frame. It is sounded by striking it in the center with a mallet. The dora is used during **memorial services** and **tanbutsu** services.

Dôsha Chôgen

The Japanese pronunciation for **Tao-che Ch'ao-yüan** (d. 1660), a Chinese Rinzai **monk**. See **Tao-che Ch'ao-yüan**.

Dôshin

The Japanese pronunciation for **Tao-hsin** (580–651), the Fourth Chinese **Patriarch** of Zen. See **Tao-hsin**.

Dôshô

One of the early Buddhist **monks** in Japan, Dôshô (628–670) founded the **Hossô school** of Nara **Buddhism**. Dôshô is said to have been the first Japanese **monk** to study **Zen**. While visiting China in 653, he studied Yogachara philosophy with the Chinese scholar monk **Hsüan-tsang** (ca. 600–664), who also introduced him to Zen thought. He then studied **meditation** with Hui-man, a disciple of **Hui-k'o** (487–593), the second Chinese **Patriarch**. When he returned to Japan, Dôshô built the first Zen **meditation hall** at Gangô-ji in Nara. See also **Yogachara school**.

Dôshu

The **monk** in charge of the sick room or infirmary (**enjudô**) at a **Zen** monastery. The term is sometimes used synonymously with the offices of dôsu or **ino**. See **ino**.

Dôsu

The supervisor of trainees at a **Zen** monastery. One of the six stewards (chiji), who assist the **abbot** in overseeing the administration of the monastery, Dôsu is another term for **ino**. See **ino**.

Dropping Off Body and Mind

An expression used in Sôtô Zen for the experience of **enlightenment**, which transcends the mundane experience of self. See **shinjin datsuraku**.

Dual Practice

The combined practice of **Zen meditation** and **Pure Land** devotions. Dual practice was first introduced to the Zen school by disciples of **Hung-jen** (601–674), the Fifth Patriarch, although it did not survive for long. Dual practice later became extremely popular in Chinese **Buddhism** beginning in the late Sung (960–1279) and early Yüan (1260–1368) dynasties; by the time of the Ming dynasty (1368–1644), it was the norm throughout the Chinese Buddhist world, including the Zen school. Chinese Zen **monks** regularly incorporated **chanting** the name of **Amida buddha** (J. **nembutsu**; Ch. nien-fo) into their daily ritual services. In some cases, chanting the Buddha's name was used as a meditative device to facilitate concentration, not unlike the use of **mantra** or **dharani**. In other cases, chanting the name was intended as a means to build **merit** in order to attain **rebirth** in Amida's **Western Pure Land**.

While dual practice was introduced to Japan during the Kamakura period (1185–1333) by the Japanese and Chinese disciples of **Chung-feng Ming-pen** and others, it did not become the norm in Japan. Although Japanese Zen masters sometimes advocated forms of dual practice, especially among **lay believers**, most remained hostile to the mingling of Pure Land elements with Zen practice. The Rinzai reformer **Hakuin Ekaku** (1685–1768), for example, regarded dual practice as a serious threat to the ongoing survival of Zen. The **Obaku sect** in Japan is the primary example of practitioners using dual practice methods. Established by Chinese Zen monks of the late Ming dynasty (1368–1644), Obaku follows the Ming Chinese style of Zen practice. Obaku monks chant nembutsu at ritual services, and Obaku masters have sometimes made use of the so-called **Nembutsu kôan**. See also **Rinzai sect**.

Duhkha

Sanskrit term for **suffering**, one of the basic teachings of **Buddhism**. See **suffering**.

Dust

(J. jin) An expression used within the Buddhist tradition for objects of human perception, including sights, sounds, tastes, textures, aromas, and mental images. The term has negative connotations suggesting contamination, since such sensory perceptions may stimulate desires leading to **attachment**, which ultimately result in **suffering**. Buddhist texts may refer to entry into the **Buddhist path**, especially becoming a **monk** or **nun**, as "shaking off the dust of the world." See also **five dusts** and **six dusts**.

E

Eastern Rank

The administrative officers at a **Zen** monastery. See **tôhan**.

East Mountain School

The teachings and practice of the Chinese **Zen** masters **Tao-hsin** (580–651) and **Hung-jen** (601–674), acknowledged as the Fourth Patriarch and Fifth Patriarch. The school derives its name from East Mountain, the popular Zen name for Mount Feng-mu in present-day Hupeh, where Hung-jen established his monastery. It is known in Chinese as Tung-shan-tsung (J. Tôzan-shû). In certain contexts, the phrase *East Mountain school* may apply to the Zen **lineage** of the Chinese master **Shen-hsiu** (606?–706), which is otherwise known as the **Northern school**.

Easy Path

Pure Land Buddhism. An expression usually used to contrast the path of faith followed in **Pure Land schools** of **Buddhism** with the so-called holy or **steep path** of personal striving, characterized especially by **Zen**. Pure Land Buddhism is regarded as the easy path, because ordinary individuals, even those with limited capabilities, can rely upon the assistance of **Amida buddha**. **Nagarjuna** is said to have originated the distinction between the easy and steep paths in a chapter on easy practice in the *Shih-chu-p'i-p'o-sha-lun* (J. *Jûjûbibasharon*). Zen masters generally reject the easy path as incompatible with Zen, although they may recognize that it has limited benefits for those individuals unable to undertake the more difficult practice of Zen. In the essay "Gakudô Yôjin-shû" ("Points to Watch in Buddhist Training"), **Dôgen Kigen** (1200–1253) observed, "What is the easily practiced and easily understood teaching of which present-day man is so fond? It is neither a secular teaching nor a Buddhist one. It is even inferior to the practice of demons and evil spirits, as well as that of non-Buddhist religions and the **two vehicles**. It may be said to be the great **delusion** of ordinary men and women." (Yûhô Yôkoi, p. 53)

Yôkoi, Yûhô, and Daizen Victoria. *Zen Master Dôgen: An Introduction with Selected Writings*. New York: Weatherhill, 1976.

Ehatsu

"Robes and bowl," an abbreviation for the Japanese term *san'e ippatsu* (**three robes, one bowl**). See **three robes, one bowl**.

Eichô

See **Shakuen Eichô**.

Eigen-ji

A rural Rinzai temple located in Shiga Prefecture, near Kyoto. The temple's formal name is Ryûseki-san Eigen-ji, "Dragon Stone mountain, Eternal Origin temple." It was founded in 1361 for the **Zen** master **Jakushitsu Genkô** (1290–1367) by his patron Sasaki Ujiyori (1326–1370). The temple serves as the main monastery and headquarters for the Eigen-ji branch of Japanese Rinzai (**Eigen-ji Ha**). See also **Rinzai sect**.

Eigen-ji Ha

The **Eigen-ji** branch of Rinzai, one of the fourteen contemporary branches of the Japanese **Rinzai sect**. The main monastery for the branch is Eigen-ji, located in Shiga Prefecture. **Jakushitsu Genkô** (1290–1367) is regarded as the founder. The branch has 121 temples throughout Japan and claims approximately 13,600 adherents.

Eight Cold Hells

(J. hachikan **jigoku**) According to Buddhist mythology, **hell** is divided into a number of different regions, characterized by the type of punishment inflicted. The regions in which the inhabitants suffer from severe cold are known as the eight cold hells. They include Arbuda, the Hell of Swelling; Nirarbuda, the Hell of Tumors; Atata, Hahava, and Huhuva, each named for the cries of their inhabitants; Utpala, the Hell of the Blue Lotus; Padma, the Hell of the Red Lotus; and Mahapadma, the Hell of the Large Red Lotus. In the latter three hells, the freezing conditions cause the skin to develop sores resembling blue or red lotus blossoms.

Eight Consciousnesses

(J. hasshiki) The eight levels of human consciousness with which the Buddhist school of Yogachara explains the workings of human psychology. They are sight consciousness, sound consciousness, smell consciousness, taste consciousness, tactile (touch) consciousness, mind consciousness, ego consciousness, and the storehouse consciousness (**alaya consciousness**). The first five levels are interpreted as the functioning of the five senses. The mind consciousness is generally regarded as ordinary consciousness; at this level, the data gathered through the five senses are coordinated, so that objects of sight, sound, etc., are processed and identified. The seventh or ego consciousness is the level at which personal **attachments**, such as likes and dislikes, are formed. The eighth consciousness is the fundamental level of consciousness, similar to the notion of the subconscious mind developed by modern Western psychology. The storehouse consciousness is that level at which all previous experiences and impressions are stored as seeds. These seeds form the basis for evaluating all present and future experience. See also **Consciousness Only** and **Yogachara school**.

Eightfold Path

(J. hasshôdô) The path of **Buddhism** as taught by the historical **Buddha**. According to the tradition, Shakyamuni (**Siddharta Gautama**), devised a path to **enlightenment** for himself, then taught it to his disciples as the Eightfold Path. The Eightfold Path is the basis of the fourth of the **four noble truths**, which identifies it as the path to enlightenment. The path includes right views, right intention, right speech, right action, right livelihood, right effort, right mindfulness, and right concentration.

Right views, or an understanding of things as they really are, generally begins with learning the basic Buddhist teachings. Right intention involves a dual effort to keep one's thoughts free from destructive emotions and to promote positive states of mind. One avoids such emotions as desire, ill will, anger, jealousy, and hatred, while encouraging thoughts of loving kindness, goodwill, and concern for others. Right speech means abstaining from four kinds of destructive speech: lying, slander, abuse, and idle talk. Right action refers to abstaining from wrongdoing, especially killing, stealing, and sexual misconduct. Right livelihood involves avoiding certain occupations that inevitably cause harm to other **sentient beings**, such as military service, butchering, or fishing. Right effort means to avoid unwholesome actions that create bad **karma** and to encourage good actions that create good karma. Right mindfulness is really a form of **meditation** in which one becomes progressively mindful of the body, of the rising and passing away of feelings, of the activity of the mind, and of mental objects. Right concentration refers to an intense form of mental concentration called "one-pointedness."

The path can be seen as a unified whole, each step to be practiced simultaneously with the others. Also, it can be understood as a progressive movement: One first learns about Buddhist teachings and then begins to practice

Buddhist morality to gain control over one's actions. Finally, the path culminates with the practice of meditation, through which one gains control of the mind. At this stage the path circles back on itself, since through meditation one attains wisdom and comes to fully realize the teachings accepted on faith at the beginning.

It is traditional to teach about the Eightfold Path in terms of the **threefold training**, arranging the steps under the categories of wisdom (**prajna**), morality (**sila**), and concentration (**samadhi**). The practice of wisdom focuses on right views and intention; the practice of morality includes right speech, action, and livelihood; and the practice of concentration covers right effort, mindfulness, and concentration.

The Eightfold Path remains crucial in **Theravada Buddhism** as the basic format of practice. While **Mahayana Buddhism** accepts the Eightfold Path as an important part of the early teachings of the Buddha, it is not a focus of Mahayana teaching. Mahayana texts sometimes make reference to the threefold training, or more rarely the Eightfold Path, but it is the **Bodhisattva** Path which structures Mahayana practice.

Eight Hot Hells

According to Buddhist mythology, **hell** is divided into a number of different regions, characterized by the type of punishment inflicted. The regions in which the inhabitants suffer from heat are known as the eight hot hells (J. hachinetsu **jigoku**). They include the Hell of Repeated Misery, where inhabitants are repeatedly put to death with iron bars or knives, and then revived to be executed again; the Hell of Black Ropes, where sinners are bound with hot iron cords and cut to pieces with hot iron hatchets; the Hell of Mass Suffering, where sinners are crushed between two iron mountains; the Hell of Wailing and the Hell of Great Wailing, where sinners cry out in pain as they are

boiled in a cauldron or roasted in an iron room; and the Hell of Searing Heat, the Hell of Great Searing Heat, and the Hell of Incessant Suffering in which the suffering from the intense heat becomes progressively worse.

Eight Precepts

(J. hakkai or hassaikai) The eight precepts undertaken by lay people on certain days of the month, known as **uposatha** days. On these occasions, lay people abide by the same precepts as ordained **novices**. The eight precepts forbid killing living beings; stealing; sexual conduct; lying; consuming intoxicants; eating after noon; adorning the body with perfume, flowers, or jewelry; participating in public entertainment including dancing, plays, and singing; and sleeping in a luxurious bed. The list is very similar to the **ten precepts** of the novice, with the exception that lay people do not abstain from handling money. Although the first five precepts of the novice correspond to the **five precepts** of lay people, they are not interpreted in exactly the same way on uposatha days. On ordinary days, the prohibition against sexual misconduct for lay people implies abstaining from premarital and extramarital relations. On uposatha days, lay people abstain from all sexual conduct, abiding by the precept in the same manner as **monks** and **nuns**. See also **lay believer**.

Eighty Minor Marks of a Buddha

(J. hachijûshûko) Eighty physical marks of perfection that are said to distinguish the body of a **buddha**. The minor marks are so designated to distinguish them from the thirty-two major marks, but there is some overlap between the major and minor lists.

For a full listing of the Eighty Minor Marks in English, see Robert A.F. Thurman's *The Holy Teaching of Vimalakirti: A Mahayana Scripture* (Pennsylvania State University Press, 1976).

The Eihei-ji monastery serves as a headquarters for the Sôtô sect of Zen Buddhists. It was founded in 1243.

Eihei-ji

A major Sôtô **Zen** monastery in Fukui Prefecture in eastern Japan, which serves as one of the two headquarters for the **Sôtô sect** of Japanese Zen. The temple was founded by **Dôgen Kigen** (1200–1253) in 1243, with patronage from Hatano Yoshishige. It is a matter of some debate exactly what motivated Dôgen to leave the Kyoto area and resettle his monastic community in the remote region of Echizen province, but it is likely that he was responding to pressure from the **Tendai sect** and other established schools of **Buddhism**. Dôgen himself commented that he was following his master's instruction that he practice deep in the mountains and avoid cities. He initially named the temple Daibutsu-ji, "Temple of the Great **Buddha**" but later renamed it Eihei-ji for the Chinese Yung-p'ing era

(58–75 C.E.) when Buddhism is said to have been first introduced in China. The monastery is constructed according to Chinese models familiar to Dôgen from his years of practice in China. At Eihei-ji, Dôgen focused his attention on training his disciples in the monastic practice of Zen. He composed the *Eihei Shingi* to govern life at a monastery.

Eihei Shingi

"Monastic Code for Eihei Monastery," a text in two sections composed by **Dôgen Kigen** (1200–1253), the founder of Japanese Sôtô **Zen**. The text is made up of six essays that originally circulated independently; they were first published together in a single volume by Kôshô Chidô in 1667. The six essays are **Tenzo Kyôkun** ("Instructions for the Cook"), a description of the responsibilities of the head kitchen **monk** written in 1237; "Bendôhô" ("Method of Practicing the Way"), a description of daily conduct in the monastery, written in 1246; "Fushuku Hanbô" ("Manners in Eating"), a description of proper manners for serving and eating food in the monks' hall (**sôdô**), written in 1246; "Shuryô Shingi" ("Code for the Reading Room"), a description of appropriate behavior and interaction with fellow monks, written in 1249; "Taitaiko Gogejarihô" ("Rules for Meeting Senior Monks"), a description of respectful behavior that junior monks should show toward senior monks, written in 1244; and "Chiji Shingi" ("Code for Six Stewards"), a description of the responsibilities of six senior administrative officers in the monastery, written in 1246. See also **Sôtô sect**. There are two recent translations of the entire *Eihei Shingi*: Leighton, Taigen Daniel, and Shohaku Okamura's *Dôgen's Pure Standards for the Zen Community* (State University of New York Press, 1996) and Ichimura Shohei's *Zen Master Eihei Dôgen's Monastic Regulations* (North American Institute of Zen and Buddhist Studies, 1993).

Eisai

The Japanese **Zen** master Myôan Eisai (1141–1215), traditionally credited with founding the **Rinzai sect** in Japan. His name may be alternatively pronounced *Yôsai*. Eisai began his career as a Tendai **monk** and trained in the teachings and practices of **esoteric Buddhism** for many years on Mount Hiei. He journeyed to China twice; on the first trip, a brief visit in 1168, he brought back texts from China in which the Zen school and Zen **meditation** were often mentioned. Eisai later decided to return to China to study Zen, and if possible, continue on to India. In 1187 he returned to China and found that a journey to India would not be possible. He studied under Hsüan Huai-chang on Mount T'ien-t'ai. After receiving **Dharma transmission** within the Rinzai **lineage**, he returned

to Japan in 1191. He founded Shôfuku-ji, the first Zen temple in the country, located in Hakata, Kyûshû. When he returned to the Kyoto area, Eisai encountered considerable resistance from the established schools of **Buddhism**, especially the **Tendai sect** and **Shingon sect**. He wrote the *Kôzen Gokokuron* to defend himself and Zen practice, responding to the accusation that Zen represented a new school of Buddhism. He gained the patronage of the **shôgun** in Kamakura, and founded **Jufuku-ji** there in 1200. In 1202, he was invited by the shôgun to serve as the founding **abbot** of **Kennin-ji** in Kyoto.

The Buddhist practice characteristic of Eisai's communities was not exclusively Zen. He continued to incorporate esoteric teachings and rituals which appealed to his patrons. Eisai is remembered also as the person who introduced tea to Japan. He brought back seeds from China, and initiated the custom of growing tea on temple grounds. He even wrote an essay extolling the virtues of drinking tea. Eisai received the posthumous title Senkô **Kokushi**.

Eka Daishi

Japanese transliteration of **Hui-k'o** Ta-shih (487–593), the Second Chinese **Patriarch** of Zen. See **Hui-k'o**.

Emma

Lord of the realm of the dead; the Japanese rendering of *Yama* in Sanskrit. In Buddhist mythology, Emma reigns over the various hells and judges the dead. He determines what misdeeds each individual has performed while alive and assigns punishment accordingly. Yama originally appeared in ancient Indian mythology and as the king of the dead in Hindu mythology. Yama was the first human being to die. He discovered the way to the underworld, where he assumed power. He became a deity and is regarded as the guardian of the south, the region of deceased souls. Yama is depicted as a terrifying green figure, with red robes.

He rides a buffalo and carries a club and noose to capture souls when they die.

In China, Yama merged with indigenous religious beliefs and emerged as a high-ranking underworld bureaucrat. Taoist mythology depicted **hell** as governed by a lord named T'ai-shan-fu-chün, who was served by ten kings. Eventually, the figure of Yama became associated with T'ai-shan-fu-chün. In Japan, Yama underwent further transformation. He was often identified as a form of the **bodhisattva** named **Jizô**, who helps **sentient beings** who are **suffering** in hell. Based on that interpretation of Yama, Emma became an object of devotion in Japan. In Japanese Buddhist iconography, Emma appears on **mandala** used in **esoteric Buddhism**; on the **Womb-Realm Mandala**, he appears in the southern region. There were also mandala devoted specifically to King Emma in which he is the central figure. Japanese Buddhists made Emma the primary object of worship at esoteric rituals intended to ensure health and long life.

Emmei Jikku Kannonkyô

"Kannon Sutra for Long Life in Ten Statements," an abridged version of the popular Kannon Sutra. The text is also known as the Jikku **Kannonkyô**. It is extremely brief and easily memorized, easily lending itself to constant repetition. In the *Hebiichigo*, **Zen** master **Hakuin Ekaku** (1685–1768) recommended that ordinary Buddhists recite this text as they went about their daily work.

Emmei Jikku Kannonkyô Reigenki

"The Wondrous Powers of the Kannon Sutra for Long Life in Ten Statements," a text composed by **Hakuin Ekaku** (1685–1768) in 1759. The text recounts miracles associated with believing in and reciting the **Emmei Jikku Kannonkyô** and explains that one will experience the power of the sutra after reciting it several hundred times.

Yampolsky, Philip B., trans. *The Zen Master Hakuin: Selected Writings*. New York: Columbia University Press, 1971.

Emperor Go-Daigo

(1287–1339) The ninety-sixth Japanese emperor, a patron and student of the **Zen** school of **Buddhism**. Go-Daigo reigned from 1319 to 1338; during that time he extensively interacted with several important Zen masters of the day, including **Shûhô Myôchô** (1282–1337), and **Musô Soseki** (1275–1351). His attempt to regain political power from the military government in Kamakura led to a brief period of direct imperial rule, known as the Kemmu Restoration (1334–1336). Ultimately, Go-Daigo's efforts failed when Ashikaga Takauji (1305–1358) seized power in 1336. Takauji set in place a new puppet emperor in Kyoto, while Go-Daigo fled to Yoshino. This created a split in the ruling family of Japan, the so-called Southern and Northern Courts, which lasted until 1392. After Go-Daigo's death, Musô Soseki convinced the Ashikaga **shôgun** to dedicate a new Zen temple to Go-Daigo's memory. It became the famous **Tenryû-ji** in western Kyoto.

Emperor Hanazono

(1297–1348) The ninety-fifth Japanese emperor and a patron and student of the **Zen** school of **Buddhism**. Hanazono reigned from 1308 to 1318, then resigned and became a cloistered emperor, or an emperor who has taken Buddhist vows. In 1335, he took the **tonsure** and became a **monk**. Hanazono preferred a strict approach to the practice of Zen. Although he was an accomplished poet, he did not approve of the literary excesses of the Gozan monasteries. Hanazono practiced Zen under the guidance of **Shûhô Myôchô** (1282–1337), for whom he built **Daitoku-ji**, one of the most important Zen monasteries in Japan. When Shûhô died, Hanazono turned to Shûhô's

Dharma heir, Kanzan Egen (1277–1369), the founder of the **Myôshin-ji** line, for instruction in Zen. Hanazono converted one of his imperial villas into a monastic retreat for his own **meditation** and practice; he invited Kanzan to serve as the founding **abbot**. This served as the beginning of the extensive Myôshin-ji monastery.

Empress Wu

(r. 685–704) The Chinese empress Wu Chao, who reigned during the T'ang dynasty (618–907). Wu Chao was a strong proponent of **Buddhism**. Her mother was a devout Buddhist, and the empress was raised as a believer. Under her leadership, Buddhism enjoyed a rise in fortunes and was favored over Taoism; she commissioned many Buddhist works of art, including sculptures at the Lung-men caves. Empress Wu planned to establish a new dynasty to replace the T'ang; since the Confucian tradition disapproved of women holding political power, she turned to Buddhist sources to legitimize her claims. Based on interpretations of certain **Buddhist scriptures**, it was argued that Wu Chao was an incarnation of **Maitreya**, the future **Buddha** and therefore qualified to reign. The empress was forced to resign in 1705 by opponents in the T'ang dynasty, which was then restored.

Emptiness

(J. kû) The fundamental concept of **Mahayana Buddhism** regarding ultimate reality, which asserts that all phenomena are empty of self-nature. Emptiness is an English translation of the Sanskrit term *shunyata*, also rendered as "void" or "nothingness" by some authors. Shunyata is the denial that things in the phenomenal world, including **sentient beings**, inanimate objects, and ideas, have an independent, unchanging, and eternal essence. Emptiness is not a nihilistic denial of reality or existence in absolute terms, but the recognition that all phenomena are relative and dependent on causation. To assert that all things are empty means that they are interdependent, arise out of causal factors, and are continually susceptible to change.

The Mahayana concept of emptiness may be seen as an extension of the early Buddhist concept of No-Self (Sk. **Anatman**), which denies the existence of an eternal, abiding, and unchanging self or soul. The teaching of emptiness was first developed by the Shunyavadins. It is discussed throughout the Perfection of Wisdom literature, also known as the Prajna Paramita **Sutras**. The second-century Buddhist philosopher **Nagarjuna** brought the concept to its full flower in his systemization of Mâdhyamika (**Mâdhyamaka**) thought. Nagarjuna clarified the possible misunderstanding of emptiness as a substance that underlies reality. He asserted that the concept of emptiness is itself empty. Rather than understanding emptiness as a thing, it is perhaps more accurate to conceive of it as a descriptive characterization of things as they really are.

Engaku

The Japanese term for *pratyeka buddhas*, or self-enlightened beings. The characters literally mean "one who realizes causation." The name is derived from the understanding that pratyeka buddhas attain **enlightenment** independently, recognizing on their own the workings of the twelve-link chain of causation. Related Japanese terms are *dokkaku* ("self-enlightened") and *byakushi butsu*, based on the Chinese transliteration of the original Sanskrit. See **pratyeka buddha**.

Engaku-ji

A major Rinzai **Zen** temple in Kamakura, Japan, which serves as the main headquarters for the Engaku-ji branch of Rinzai Zen. Its formal name is Ryûroku-zan Engaku-ji. The temple was founded in 1282 by the Chinese master **Wu-hsüeh Tsu-yüan** (1226–1286;

J. Mugaku Sogen), and constructed under the patronage of the regent **Hôjô Tokimune** (1251–1284). The regent intended the monastery to serve as a memorial to the Japanese warriors who fell during the Mongol invasions of 1281. It was one of the earliest monasteries built according to the Zen style developed during the Sung dynasty (960–1279) in China. At its peak in the fourteenth century, the monastery housed almost 2,000 **monks** and included twenty subtemples (**tatchû**). It was ranked among the **Gozan temples** (Five Mountains) of Kamakura. See also **Rinzai sect**.

Engaku-ji Ha

The **Engaku-ji** branch of Rinzai, one of the fourteen contemporary branches of the Japanese **Rinzai sect**. The main monastery for the branch is Engaku-ji, located in Kamakura. **Wu-hsüeh Tsu-yüan** (1226–1286; J. Mugaku Sogen) is regarded as the founder. The branch has 210 temples throughout Japan and claims approximately 178,000 adherents.

Engi

"Arising from causation," the Japanese technical term for **codependent origination**. The concept explains that all phenomena result from causation, that none are self-existent in an absolute sense. Mental and physical things come into being as a result of causes and conditions. A thing inevitably passes out of existence when its causes and conditions cease to exist. This means that all phenomena lack an essential self-nature, such as an eternal soul, and are thus impermanent. See **codependent origination**.

Engi

(2) Legends and historical accounts associated with a Japanese Buddhist monastery or temple, a Shintô shrine, or a religious image.

Engo Kokugon

Japanese transliteration of **Yüan-wu K'o-ch'in** (1063–1135), a leading Chinese Zen master from the Sung dynasty (960–1279), best known as the compiler of the *Hekiganroku*. See **Yüan-wu K'o-ch'in**.

Enju

The **monks** or **nuns** responsible for tending the monastery's vegetable garden. According to the **vinaya**, the **monastic code** used in Theravada **Buddhism**, monks and nuns are not allowed to till the soil and grow their own food. Tradition requires them to beg for their sustenance from **lay believers**. In East Asia, where begging was not always permitted, the **Zen** school adopted the practice of raising food on temple grounds. All members of the community are expected to take turns tending the garden. Like other forms of **manual labor** (samu), this activity is a form of active **meditation**.

Enjudô

The sick hall or infirmary in a **Zen** monastery. The term literally means the "Hall for the Prolongation of Life." **Monks** and **nuns** who are too ill to maintain the daily routine of monastic life are cared for in the infirmary. The infirmary may also be called the **nirvana hall** (nehandô), or the impermanence hall (mujôdô). When someone in the community falls seriously ill, other members may hold prayer services for the sake of the person's recovery.

Enlightened One

A translation of the title **Buddha**, usually applied specifically to **Siddharta Gautama**, the historical Buddha; one of the ten epithets used for the Buddha. The epithet may also be applied to any individual who has attained **enlightenment**.

Enlightenment

General term used to express the ultimate goal in all schools of **Buddhism**. Enlightenment describes the state of awakened awareness achieved by Shakyamuni (**Siddharta Gautama**), the historical **Buddha**. By following the **Buddhist path**, whether the **Eightfold Path** of **Theravada Buddhism** or the **Bodhisattva** Path of **Mahayana Buddhism**, practitioners seek to attain the same state of awareness. The English word "enlightenment" may be used to translate such technical terminology as the Sanskrit words *nirvana* and *bodhi*, or the Japanese word *satori*.

Enni Ben'en

(1202–1280) Japanese Rinzai **monk** who helped establish Rinzai **Zen** in Japan. Enni began his career in the Tendai tradition, where he learned the synchretic mixture of Zen and esoteric practice taught by **Eisai** (1141–1215). Enni was born in Suruga (present-day Shizuoka). He received his early education at Buddhist temples and took the **tonsure** at Mii-dera, a major Tendai temple, at age 18. At Chôrakuji, he studied the Zen and esoteric mixture introduced by Eisai under the instruction of **Shakuen Eichô** (d.1247). In 1235, Enni went to China, where he remained for seven years, studying at Mount Ching. During that time, he became the **Dharma heir** of the Chinese Zen master Wu-shuh Shin-fan (1177–1249) from the Yang-ch'i (J. Yôgi) **lineage** of Rinzai. When Enni returned to Japan in 1241, he promoted Zen practice, while still incorporating aspects of esoteric ritual that appealed to wealthy patrons. He established a strong lineage, accepting many disciples and recognizing several as Dharma heirs. Under the patronage of Fijiwara Michiie (1192–1252), Enni founded **Tôfuku-ji**, one of the most prominent Zen monasteries in Kyoto. He also served as **abbot** at **Jufuku-ji** and **Kennin-ji**. Among his major writings are the *Jisshûyôdôki* and the *Shôichi Goroku*. See also **Rinzai sect**, **Tendai sect**, and **Yang-ch'i school**.

Dumoulin, Heinrich. *Zen Buddhism: A History*. 2 vols. Trans. James W. Heisig and Paul Knitter. New York: Macmillan Publishing Company, 1994.

Ennin

(793–864) Japanese Tendai **monk** who studied under **Saichô** (767–822), the Tendai founder, on Mount Hiei. Later, Ennin became head **abbot** of the **Tendai sect**. He is better known by his posthumous title, Jikaku **Daishi**. Ennin studied T'ien-t'ai thought in China between 838 and 847. Ennin was living in the city of Chang-an when Emperor Wu-tsung ordered the persecution of **Buddhism**. He kept a diary of his experiences while in China. Later published as *Nittô Guhô Junrei Gyôki*, it provides crucial information about Buddhism in T'ang China before the persecutions of 845, as well as first-hand accounts of the persecutions. See also **T'ien-t'ai school**.

Reischauer, Edwin O., trans. *Diary: The Record of a Pilgrimage to China in Search of the Law*. New York: Ronald Press Co., 1955.
———. *Enniu's Travels in T'ang China*. New York: Ronald Press Company, 1955.

Enô

The Japanese pronunciation for **Hui-neng** (638–713), the Sixth Chinese **Patriarch** of Zen. See **Hui-neng**.

Enryaku-ji

The main monastery and headquarters for the Tendai school of Japanese **Buddhism**, both founded by **Saichô** (767–822) in 788. The temple is located on Mount Hiei, to the east of Kyoto. Saichô originally named the temple Hiei-ji for its mountain location, but the name was later changed to Enryaku-ji by imperial decree. For many centuries, Enryaku-ji was the major center for Buddhist studies in Japan. As many as 3,000 temples comprised the monastery complex at one time. All of the founders

Ensô means "circle," and the image symbolizes enlightenment, emptiness, and perfection.

of the Buddhist schools during the Kamakura period (1185–1333) originally studied at Enryaku-ji, including **Dôgen Kigen** (1200–1253) who founded the **Sôtô sect**, and **Eisai** who founded the **Rinzai sect**. The monastery of Enryaku-ji was also a dominant force in the political and economic life in the Kyoto region for centuries. The temple maintained an army of Warrior Monks (J. **sôhei**) to defend its interests. The monastery was completely destroyed by Oda Nobunaga in 1571, in order to control the significant power accumulated by the Tendai school. The temple complex was restored during the Tokugawa period (1600–1867). See also **Tendai sect**.

Enshû

"Round teachings" or "Round school" of **Buddhism**. In East Asian thought, roundness implies perfection. Therefore, to designate a teaching or school as "round" is to claim that it represents Buddhist perfection. The expression most often applies to Tendai teachings, although it may refer to **Zen** itself. See also **Tendai sect**.

Ensô

Circle, especially an ink drawing of an empty circle. Ensô (also known as ichi ensô) are common figures in **Zen** teaching and art. Zen masters use the image of the circle to represent **enlightenment**, the concept of **emptiness**, or perfection. Ensô are usually executed with a single brush stroke, and are said to reveal the mind (or enlightenment) of the artist.

Equality

(J. byôdô) The **non-duality** and non-differentiation of all things as seen from the perspective of **enlightenment**. The teaching of equality arises out of the realization that all phenomena are essentially the same—that is, all things are characterized by **emptiness**. When the concept is applied to **sentient beings**, or more specifically to human beings, the Buddhist concept of equality goes beyond the ordinary social distinctions of class, gender, and race. This equality is often affirmed within **Mahayana Buddhism** by noting that all sentient beings possess the same **Buddha Nature**. Realizing the sameness or equality of all things has important ethical implications for enlightened behavior. The understanding that "self" and "other" are ultimately the same, breaks down the barriers between the two, encouraging the compassionate behavior characteristic of a **buddha** or **bodhisattva**. The realization of equality is regarded as one of the **four wisdoms**.

Esoteric Buddhism

The common term for East Asian forms of tantric Buddhism, known in Japanese as Mikkyô. This form of **Buddhism** became known as secret or esoteric because the teachings and practices are not open to all. Practitioners are required to undergo initiation under a qualified teacher before they qualify for instruction. Esoteric rituals make use of special devices such as **mantra** (sacred sounds), **mudra** (sacred gestures), and **mandala** (cosmic diagrams).

Tantric Buddhism first arose in India in the sixth century, spreading to Tibet and China in the seventh and eighth centuries. Esoteric Buddhism flourished in China for approximately one hundred years but did not survive the great persecution of 842. During the early ninth century, Japanese **monks** studying in China were introduced to the esoteric teachings and brought them to Japan. The **Shingon sect** and **Tendai sect** of Japanese Buddhism, founded in the ninth century, are esoteric teachings that have survived to the present day.

Evil Paths

(J. akudô) The lower three of the six realms of existence (rokudô) in which **sentient beings** experience great **suffering**. In ascending order, the evil paths are **hell**, the realm of **hungry ghosts**, and the realm of animals. Hell dwellers and hungry ghosts endure a variety of punishments for committing the worst sorts of offenses in a previous life. Animals are regarded as evil because they are subjected to heavy burdens, the dangers of the wild, and cruelty from human beings. In some cases, a fourth realm is added to the list of evil rebirths—that of the **ashura**. Ashura are a class of demigods, who are fierce and pugnatious by nature and fight with other deities. Although the tradition most often regards the realm of the ashura as above that of human beings, their continual participation in violence has sometimes been interpreted as a perpetual form of suffering worse than that of human life.

Buddhism teaches that the three or four evil realms are the worst possible outcomes for **rebirth**. Birth in any of these realms results from accumulating bad **karma** in a previous lifetime. Individuals born into them must endure the suffering entailed as a punishment for their actions, but the punishment is not eternal. Once the accumulated bad karma is exhausted, birth into a better realm becomes possible once again. In practical terms, the Buddhist tradition makes use of the notion of evil rebirths to encourage believers to keep the **precepts** and live a moral life. It should be noted, however, that the Buddhist tradition recognizes that suffering characterizes all six realms of **samsara**, even the pleasurable realms. See also **six paths**.

Expedient Means

Teaching devices employed by a **buddha** or another Buddhist teacher in order to convey aspects of the **Dharma** to individuals. Expedient means (J. hôben) is a teaching style that is tailored to suit the specific learning and spiritual capacities of the audience. The English term is a translation of the Sanskrit *upaya-kaushalya*, which may be translated as "skillful means" or "skill in means." Expedient means is an important concept within **Mahayana Buddhism**, developing the compassionate skill to effectively use expedient means to lead other **sentient beings** to **enlightenment** is part of the **Bodhisattva** Path. It is included as one of the stages of the bodhisattva—as a bodhisattva develops wisdom and insight into the Dharma, he or she becomes able to evaluate the capacities of others and to teach accordingly.

There are two basic ways to interpret the use of expedient means, both of which are regarded as valid within the tradition. It is believed that the historical Buddha simplified his message to suit his audience, especially at the beginning of his teaching career. He did not teach the **Ultimate Truth** of the Dharma at the beginning because his audience was not yet prepared to hear it. He began teaching them provisional versions of the Dharma. He later exposed the provisional nature of these early teachings as his disciples became more advanced and capable of understanding the Dharma on a deeper level. The classical source in the **Buddhist scriptures** describing the Buddha's use of expedient means in this sense is the **Lotus Sutra**. This understanding of expedient means enabled Mahayana Buddhists, especially in East Asia, to explain the changes in Buddhist teaching that occurred between the early scriptures of **Theravada Buddhism** and the later Mahayana **sutras**.

Expedient means may also refer to any teaching device that a Buddhist master employs to assist others in understanding the Dharma; typical devices include parables, stories, and works of art. Within the **Zen** tradition, the skillful use of **kôan** is a prime example of expedient means. Other Zen devices include shouts, slaps, paradoxical comments, unconventional behavior, and even poetry.

Pye, Michael. *Skillful Means: A Concept in Mahayana Buddhism*. London: Duckworth, 1978.

Face-to-Face Transmission

(J. menju shikô) Direct transmission of the **Dharma** from a **Zen** master to a disciple through one-on-one encounters between the two. The expression is based upon the assumption that Zen **enlightenment** cannot be verified through indirect means, such as by letter.

Fa-ch'ih

(635–702; J. Hôji) **Zen** Chinese **monk** of the T'ang dynasty (618–907), the fourth generation **patriarch** of the short-lived **Oxhead school**. Fa-ch'ih practiced for a time under **Hung-jen** (601–674), the Fifth Patriarch of the orthodox **lineage** and received his **Dharma transmission** before returning to Niu-t'ou-shan ("Ox Head Mountain"). Later in life, Fa-ch'ih became a **Pure Land** practitioner, and regularly chanted the **nembutsu**. This is one of the earliest examples of **dual practice** in the Zen school.

Fa-hai

(J. Kôhô) The **Zen monk** named in the Tun-huang edition of the **Platform Sutra** as its compiler. The text identifies Fa-hai as a direct disciple of **Hui-neng** (638–713), the Sixth Patriarch. Also, the text credits Fa-hai as the head monk of the temple, who recorded the master's **sermons** for later editing and publication. Scholars cannot validate that the text represents the actual sermons of Hui-neng, and there is no corroborating evidence that Hui-neng had a disciple named Fa-hai. Hence, Fa-hai's identity has fallen into doubt. Yanagida Seizan, a Zen scholar, theorized that Fa-hai was a member of the **Oxhead school** of Zen and a disciple of Hsüan-su (668–752), who recorded a text which later served as a partial basis for what is now known as the Platform Sutra.

Fa-hsien School

The Chinese name for the **Yogachara school** of **Buddhism**. It was among the thirteen schools of Chinese Buddhism which developed during the T'ang dynasty (618–907). The name Fa-hsien literally means "characteristics of the dharmas," indicating the philosophical interest of the school's practitioners to understand the essential nature of all phenomena (dharmas). The primary teachings of the school include the storehouse consciousness (**alaya consciousness**) and the Three Natures of reality. The school is also known as the Wei-shih, or "**Consciousness Only**" school, because it teaches that the phenomenal world that we experience is actually a product of our conscious minds. Based on the writings of the scholar monks Asanga and Vasubandhu, it is believed that the Yogachara school developed in India during the fourth through the seventh centuries. In the seventh century, the Chinese **monk** Hsuan-tsang (600–664), traveled to India and studied Yogachara thought with Shilabhadra. He then transmitted the teachings and texts to China. The Fa-hsien school was systematized by K'uei-chi (638–682).

Fa-jung

(594–657; J. Hôyû) **Zen** Chinese **monk** of the early T'ang dynasty (618–907) regarded as the founder of the **Oxhead school** (Ch. Niu-t'ou; J. Gozu) of early Zen. The school is also known as Niu-t'ou, literally "Ox Head," for the mountain in present-day Kiangsu, where Fa-jung resided. Traditional biographies indicate that he was a **Dharma heir** of the Fourth Patriarch, **Tao-hsin** (580–651), although historians regard this as doubtful. His Oxhead **lineage** represents the earliest branches of the Zen school in China, as well as the **Southern school** and **Northern school**.

Fa-yen School

(J. Hôgen-shû) A **lineage** of Chinese **Zen** active during the T'ang dynasty (618–907) and known as one of the so-called **five houses** of Zen. The lineage was founded by the Zen master **Fa-yen Wen-i** (885–958), and only survived for a few generations. Fa-yen developed his own distinctive style of Zen, which did not include the harsh methods employed by some of his contemporaries. Instead of striking or shouting (**katsu!**) at his disciples, he usually answered their questions using a form of repetition, simply repeating their original question. The Fa-yen school studied the texts and commentaries of the **Hua-yen school** (J. **Kegon school**). Although the lineage did not survive for long, it left a lasting influence on the later Zen tradition through its writings. Among the most important texts produced within the school was the *Transmission of the Lamp* (Ch. **Ching-te Ch'üan-teng Lu**, J. *Keitoku Dentôroku*), the chronicle of early Zen history, which provided much of the material later used as **kôan**. The teachings of the Fa-yen school were absorbed into the **Lin-chi school** during the early Sung dynasty (960–1279).

Fa-yen Wen-i

(J. Hôgen Bun'eki) A T'ang dynasty Chinese master who founded the Fa-yen **lineage**, one of the **five houses** of Chinese **Zen**; also known as the **Fa-yen school**. Fa-yen gathered disciples at Ch'in-liang-ssu, his monastery in Nanching. He is known for his interest in Hua-yen thought: He studied Hua-yen texts and had his students do the same. See also **Hua-yen school**.

Feng-hsueh Yen-chao

(896–973; J. Fuketsu Enshô) A Chinese Rinzai **monk** of the late T'ang (618–907) and early Five Dynasties (907–960) period. Feng-hsueh studied T'ien-t'ai **Buddhism** after he took the **tonsure**. He later turned to **Zen** when he became the disciple of **Nan-yüan Hui-yung** (d. 930). Feng-hsueh played a crucial role in the preservation of the teachings and style of the Rinzai school. As the sole **Dharma heir** of Nan-yüan Hui-yung, Feng-hsueh was the only fourth-generation master in **Lin-chi I-hsüan's** (d. 867) Dharma **lineage**. Feng-hsueh named several heirs during his teaching career, allowing the school to continue and eventually thrive. His most important Dharma heir was Shou-shan Sheng-nien. See also **Rinzai sect** and **T'ien-t'ai school**.

Feng-mu-shan

(J. Tô-zan) Mount Feng-mu, a mountain in present-day Hupeh, where **Hung-jen** (601–674), the Fifth **Patriarch** of **Zen** established his monastery. The mountain is popularly known as **Tung-shan**, or East Mountain. See **Tung-shan**.

Feng-yang Wu-te Ch'an-shih Yü-lu

The Recorded Sayings of Zen Master Wu-te of Feng-yang (J. *Funyô Mutoku Zenji Goroku*). The three-section text is also known as the *Feng-yang Lu* and contains **sermons**, talks, poetry and miscellaneous writings of the **Zen** Rinzai master Feng-yang Shan-chao. It was compiled by Shih-shuang Ch'u-yuan (986–1039), his **Dharma heir**, who completed the work in 1101. The text played a significant role in the development of **kôan** literature. The first section includes **Fen-yang Shan-chao's** commentary on the **five ranks** (goi) of **Tung-shan**. The second section is made up of three collections of one hundred kôan each. The first of these collections consists of old kôan to which Feng-yang added a verse. The second set is kôan of the master's own devising, including answers. The third set is old kôan to which he added his own answers in place of those previously provided. These collections later served as models for similar collections. See also **Rinzai sect**.

Fen-yang Shan-chao

Chinese Rinzai **Zen** master (947–1024; J. Funyô Zenshô) of the T'ang dynasty (618–907). Fen-yang was the **Dharma heir** of Shou-shan Sheng-nien (926–993). According to tradition, he visited seventy-one masters before practicing with Shou-shan. After receiving his master's recognition, he taught for the rest of his life at T'ai-tzu-yüan. His most important disciple was Shih-shuang Ch'u-yüan (986–1039). Fen-yang introduced the use of the **five ranks** into Rinzai teachings; his teachings are recorded in the *Fen-yang Wu-te Ch'an-shih Yü-lu*. The work includes the earliest **kôan** collection, a series of three sets of one hundred kôan. Two hundred were old cases that Fen-yang compiled and commented upon, adding his own answers; the other one hundred were created by the master himself. Fen-yang received the posthumous title of Wu-te Ch'an-shih (J. Mutoku **Zenji**). See also **Rinzai sect**.

Festival of the Dead

A mid-summer Buddhist festival celebrated throughout East Asia to benefit the deceased. The festival, known in English as the Feast of Lanterns or the Feast of All Souls, is popularly called **Obon** or Urabon-e in Japan, P'u-tu in China, and Manghon-il in Korea. All versions of the festival are said to be based upon the ancient **ullambana** ceremony, but each one also represents a combination of regional Buddhist traditions with local religious beliefs. See **Obon**.

Field of Merit

(J. fukuden) A term used for a **buddha**, **bodhisattva**, **monk**, or **nun**, in reference to the benefits **lay believers** reap from them. This expression exemplifies the mutually beneficial relationship of Buddhist clergy and lay followers. Monks and nuns instruct lay people in the Buddhist teachings and also provide them with opportunities to "repay" their teachers. Metaphorically, the clergy are the fields in which lay believers plant the seeds of **merit** by providing for the material needs of the monastic community and consequently reaping the spiritual benefits of their donations. The term *field of merit* is sometimes applied to the **three treasures**, to which believers offer reverence.

Fifth Patriarch

The Chinese **Zen** master **Hung-jen** (601–674; J. Gunin) of the Sui dynasty. Hung-jen inherited the **Dharma** from **Tao-hsin** (580–651), the Fourth Patriarch. He later acknowledged **Hui-neng** (638–713) as his rightful successor. See **Hung-jen**.

Filial Piety

(J. kô) Respect for one's parents. Filial piety became a major theme of **Buddhism** in East Asia in response to influence from existing religious traditions, especially Confucianism. When Buddhism first entered China, for example, monastic life was criticized by Confucians as a teaching that promoted unfilial behavior. In the Confucian view, leaving home to become a **monk** or **nun** was unfilial, since it meant that basic acts of filial piety such as providing financial support for aging parents, marrying, and having children to carry on the family line would not occur. Even shaving the head was regarded as an unfilial practice, since it was seen as a form of self-inflicted mutilation of the body given by one's parents. In response to these attacks, East Asian Buddhism developed teachings reinterpreting filial behavior in terms of Buddhist practice, often arguing that the **compassion** of the **bodhisattva** constituted the highest form of filial piety. The Buddhist **ullambana** festival became extremely popular in East Asian cultures because of its connections with filial piety and ancestor veneration. Chinese Buddhist apocryphal works such as the Sutra of the Filial Child (Ch. Hsiao Tzu Ching, J. Kôshikyô) were composed, creating a

The Festival of the Dead, also known as the Feast of Lanterns or
the Feast of All Souls, is a Buddhist festival that celebrates the deceased.

body of Buddhist literature dedicated to the theme of filial piety. While not a dominant theme in **Zen** writings, biographies of Chinese and Japanese Zen monks and nuns generally emphasize the filial nature of their subjects.

Strong, John S. *The Experience of Buddhism: Sources and Interpretations.* Belmont, CA: Wadsworth Publishing Co., 1995.

Tzu, Mou. "The Disposition of Error." In *Sources of Chinese Tradition.* Compiled by Wm. Theodore De Bary and Irene Bloom. New York: Columbia University Press, 1999.

First Barrier

The first of three sets of **kôan** used in some **Zen** monasteries in medieval Japan (1185–1600). See **shokan**.

Five Deadly Sins

(J. **gogyakuzai**) Five of the most wicked actions, which result in **rebirth** for many eons in the lowest level of **hell**— **Avici hell**—where the **suffering** is incessant. The sins include killing one's father, killing one's mother, killing an **arhat**, harming the body of a **buddha**, and causing schism within the **sangha**. See **gogyakuzai**.

Five Dusts

A Buddhist expression for the five objects of perception (gojin), which correspond to the five senses. These include: form (color and shape), sound, odor, taste, and texture. They are referred to as the five dusts or **defilements** because sensory perceptions are often distracting; **attachment** to sensory perceptions is said to contaminate the originally pure mind. See also **six dusts**.

Five Eyes

(J. gogen) Five kinds of eyes that are associated with five kinds of beings: the physical eyes of ordinary **sentient beings**; the heavenly eyes of deities; the Wisdom Eyes of those in the **two vehicles** (shravakas and **pratyeka buddhas**); the **Dharma eyes** of **Bodhisattvas**; and the eyes of the **Buddha**. Within **Mahayana Buddhism**, the five eyes describe various levels of spiritual development and are associated with the **T'ien-t'ai school's** doctrine of **Threefold Truth**.

Ordinary physical eyes perceive only color and form within a limited range, while the heavenly eyes of deities can see far and near without any obstruction. In contrast, the latter three types represent different levels of insight or wisdom. Wisdom Eyes represent the attainment of insight related to such teachings as **emptiness** and **codependent origination**. Those who have attained this level of insight have grasped the nature of ultimate reality. Dharma eyes represent the wisdom to see the differentiation among all things that exist in the provisional sphere. **Bodhisattvas** are said to possess this Dharma eye, which enables them to see the **suffering** of all sentient beings and to devise **expedient means** to alleviate the suffering. Buddhas possess all of the first four types of eyes. They are capable of maintaining the middle way, balancing an awareness of ultimate reality while recognizing the relative reality of the phenomenal world.

Five False Views

See **five wrong views**.

Five Houses

(Ch. wu-chia, J. goke) The five lineages of the **Southern school** of **Zen** that existed during the T'ang dynasty (618–907). Each "house" had a distinctive style of Zen practice, which was developed by its founding **patriarchs**. The T'ang Zen master **Fa-yen Wen-i** first used the expression "house" to describe the Zen of his time. The five houses were the **Yun-men school** (J. Ummon-shû), the **Kuei-yang school** (J. Igyô-shû), the **Ts'ao-tung school** (J. Sôtô-shû), the **Lin-chi school** (J. Rinzai-shû) and the **Fa-yen school** (J. Hôgen-shû). The expression was later expanded during the Sung dynasty (960–1279) to the **five houses and seven schools**, which included two additional branches of the Lin-chi school—the Yang-ch'i (J. Yôgi-shû) and the Huang-lung (J. Oryô-shû). See also **Huang-lung school** and **Yang-ch'i school**.

Five Houses and Seven Schools

An expression used to describe the distinctive styles of **Zen** practiced during the T'ang (618–907) and Sung (960–1279) dynasties in China. During the T'ang dynasty, there were five separate lineages (Ch. wu-chia, J. goke) within the **Southern school** of Zen. These **five houses** were the **Yun-men school** (J. Ummon-shû), the **Kuei-yang school** (J. Igyô-shû), the **Tsao-tung school** (J. Sôtô-shû), the **Lin-chi school** (J. Rinzai-shû) and the **Fa-yen school** (J. Hôgen-shû). By the end of the Sung dynasty, only the Lin-chi and Tsao-tung lineages survived. The Lin-chi **lineage** had further developed into two strong subdivisions, the Yang-ch'i line (J. Yôgi-shû) and the Huang-lung line (J. Oryô-shû). When these were added to the five houses, the name was changed to the **seven schools**. See also **Huang-lung school** and **Yang-ch'i school**.

Five Mountains

The highest ranking among the most prestigious **Zen** monasteries in China and Japan. Five Mountains is a literal translation of the Chinese term *Wu-shan*, pronounced "Gozan" or "Gosan" in Japanese. See **Gozan temples** and **Gozan system**.

Five Precepts

(J. gokai) The set of **precepts** traditionally taken by lay Buddhists which govern moral conduct in everyday life. The precepts prohibit the killing of living beings, stealing another's belongings, engaging in sexual misconduct, lying, and ingesting intoxicants. These are also the first five of the **ten precepts** undertaken by ordained **novices**. Although worded in the same way, the precepts are understood differently for lay people than for **monks** and **nuns**. In particular, the third precept against sexual misconduct is interpreted to prohibit premarital and extramarital sexual contact for lay people, but all sexual conduct for monks and nuns. Although they are worded in the negative form, the five precepts are understood to include positive action as well. For example, the first precept not only advocates not killing or injuring living beings, but also the active protection and care of living beings. See also **lay believer**.

Wijayaratna, Mohan. *Buddhist Monastic Life: According to the Texts of the Theravada Tradition*. Trans. Claude Grangier and Steven Collins. New York: Cambridge University Press, 1990.

Five Ranks

(J. goi) The five ranks or stages of practice described by **Zen** master **Tung-shan Liang-chieh** (807–869). The five ranks express the relationship between ultimate reality and phenomenal existence. The Zen tradition has used a variety of means to express this teaching, including verse and symbolic or metaphorical representation. The standard version of the five ranks is derived from Tung-shan's original poem in five stanzas. The first line of each stanza serves as a title for one rank. The five verses may be translated as follows: the real within the apparent (J. shô-chû-hen), the apparent within the real (J. hen-chû-shô), the coming from within the real (J. shô-chû-rai), the arrival within the apparent (J. hen-chû-shi), and mutual interpenetration of real and apparent (J. ken-chû-tô).

Tung-shan Liang-chieh initially developed the teaching of the five ranks, which he loosely based on the Hua-yen doctrine of the four realms of ultimate reality and phenomena. Tung-shan eventually passed the teaching of the five ranks on to his leading disciple, **Ts'ao-shan Pen-chi** (840–901), who then systematized the concepts. They later became a standard characteristic of the teachings of the Ts'ao-tung (J. Sôtô) **lineage** in China. The Chinese Rinzai master **Fen-yang Shen-chao** introduced the five ranks to members of his school in the eleventh century; they have since been used as a **kôan** within the Rinzai tradition. Numerous commentaries based on the five ranks were composed by masters of both major schools of Zen. In Japan, the **Rinzai sect** has used the five ranks kôan as the final level of kôan training since the time of **Hakuin Ekaku** (1685–1768). See also **Hua-yen school** and **Ts'ao-tung school**.

Chung-Yuan, Chang. *Original Teachings of Ch'an Buddhism: Selected from the Transmission of the Lamp*. New York: Vintage Books, 1971.

Five Skandhas

(J. goun) The five aggregates; the component parts that make up all existent things (**dharmas**), including the human self. While seeking enlightenment, the **Buddha** analyzed himself in search of an intrinsic, permanent self (**atman**). He found only an ever-changing configuration of component parts, or skandhas. The five skandhas are form, feelings, conceptions, dispositions, and consciousness. Form refers to the physical properties of an individual. In this context, feelings include the raw sensory perceptions of external things, while conceptions are the mental images drawn from the sensory data. Dispositions are the likes and dislikes formed in relation to conceptions and encompass the emotions. Consciousness means the mental workings commonly referred to as conscious thought.

The five skandhas are characterized by **impermanence** and **suffering**. Although there is no permanent self or soul that exists outside or beyond the ongoing physical and mental processes referred to as the five skandhas, human beings create the notion of such a self. The fundamental **attachment** to a false sense of self is the basic cause of suffering. The true self is nothing other than a convenient label for the process of changing configurations.

Five Types of Zen

(J. goshuzen) The five styles of **meditation** developed by Kuei-feng **Tsung-mi** (780–840). In this context, the term *zen* means meditation in general, not the style of seated mediation (**zazen**), characteristic of the **Zen** school of **Buddhism**. In the treatise entitled *Ch'an-yüan Chu-ch'üan-chi Tu-hsü* (*General Preface to the Collected Writings on the Sources of Zen*), Tsung-mi identified differences in meditation based on the practitioner. The categories are non-Buddhist or unorthodox meditation, meditation by an ordinary person, Hinayana meditation, Mahayana meditation, and meditation of the Supreme Vehicle—Zen meditation itself.

Broughton, Jeffrey. *Kuei-feng Tsung-mi: The Convergence of Ch'an and the Teachings*. New York: Columbia University Press, 1975.

Five Wrong Views

(J. goken) The five types of mistaken views that are contrary to the Buddhist teachings. First is the belief that a permanent and abiding self exists—that is, denying that the self is a temporary and constantly changing configuration of the **five skandhas**. Second is belief in the extremes of naive positivism or in Fihilism—the belief that the self and other things exist eternally in an ultimate sense, or that they have no real existence at all. Third is rejection of the law of cause and effect—the denial of the workings of **karma**. Fourth is **attachment** to a false view as the truth. The fifth mistaken view is adherence to a false set of **precepts** as a means to attain **enlightenment**. The five wrong views are included among the basic set of six **afflictions** (bonnô), which hinder an individual's quest for enlightenment.

Flower Garland Sutra

The **Avatamsaka Sutra**, a sutra of **Mahayana Buddhism** that serves as the scriptural basis for the **Hua-yen school** (J. **Kegon school**) of Chinese **Buddhism**. See **Avatamsaka Sutra**.

Formless Precepts

(J. musô kai) An understanding of the Buddhist **precepts**, which sees them not as an external moral code, but rather as the naturally pure behavior that arises from the enlightened mind. The concept appears first in the Platform Sutra of the Sixth Patriarch.

Formless Repentance

(J. musô zange) An interpretation of the practice of repentance, which is introduced in the Platform Sutra of the Sixth Patriarch. Buddhist **monks** and **nuns** regularly perform some form of repentance as a part of their monastic practice. In **Theravada Buddhism**, monks and nuns traditionally had two opportunities each month to reflect upon their behavior and ritually repent for any wrong actions they performed. **Mahayana Buddhism** retained the practice of repentance, and various repentance rituals developed in Chinese schools of Buddhism. The **Zen** understanding of formless repentance contrasts with the more typical understanding of repentance, since it is based upon an understanding that evil deeds, like all other phenomena, have no ultimate reality.

Forty-Eight Light Precepts

(J. shijûhachi kyôkai) A set of **precepts**, which make up the secondary portion of the **bodhisattva precepts**. The forty-eight light and **ten heavy precepts** together are the full bodhisattva precepts as presented in the Bonmôkyô (**Brahma Net Sutra**). For a full listing, see John Stevens' *The Marathon Monks of Mount Hiei* (Shambhala, 1988).

Founder's Hall

(J. kaisandô) The temple building at a **Zen** monastery, which features an image of the founding **abbot** (**kaisan**) and a memorial tablet (**ihai**) inscribed with his name. **Memorial services** for the founding abbot are held in the hall on the anniversary of his death. The founder's hall is sometimes called the patriarch hall (**soshidô**) or the reflection hall (Eishitsu).

Four Aspects

The four aspects of phenomenal existence. The four aspects are called **shisô** in Japanese. See **shisô**.

Four Assemblies

(Sk. **sangha**; J. shishu) The four parts of the Buddhist community, including **monks**, **nuns**, laymen, and laywomen. The four assemblies date back to the lifetime of the historical **Buddha**, who accepted disciples from all four categories. The four assemblies take refuge (**kie**) in the **three treasures**—the Buddha, the **Dharma**, and the sangha—to establish their connection with **Buddhism**. Each assembly recognizes formal rites of entry. Monks and nuns participate in **ordination** ceremonies to become members of their respective monastic assemblies. They are ordained as **novices**, accepting the **ten precepts**, and then as fully ordained **bhikkhu**

or **bhikkhuni** under the full **monastic code**. Lay people also have a ritual of entry into the Buddhist community, based on their acceptance of the **five precepts**.

The bond between the monastic community and the lay community is a reciprocal relationship. Monks and nuns provide for the spiritual needs of the lay community, teaching the **Dharma** and offering opportunities to lay people to build **merit**. In return, lay people provide for the material needs of the monastic community, supplying donations used for food, clothing, and shelter. See also **lay believer**.

Four Discernments

(J. shiryôken) The four viewpoints used by the Chinese master **Lin-chi I-hsüan** (d. 867), founder of Rinzai **Buddhism**, as a teaching device. In the *Sayings of Lin-chi*, Lin-chi said, "Sometimes I take away the person and do not take away the surroundings; sometimes I take away the surroundings and do not take away the person; sometimes I take away both the person and the surroundings; sometimes I take away neither the person nor the surroundings." This passage is usually summarized as: the negation of subject and the affirmation of object (J. datsunin fudakkyô), the negation of object and the affirmation of subject (J. dakkyô fudatsunin), the negation of both subject and object (J. ninkyô ryôgudatsu), and the affirmation of both subject and object (J. ninkyô gufudatsu). These became known as ssu-liao-chien in Chinese and shiryôken in Japanese. The later Rinzai tradition used the four discernments as a **kôan**.

The four discernments represent a gradually deepening grasp of reality. They are based on the four propositions of Buddhist logic: being, nonbeing, neither being nor nonbeing, and both being and nonbeing. They also correspond to the **four realms of reality** taught by the **Hua-yen school** of Buddhism. The first realm is the realization that without an object, there is no subject. The second is the realization that all objects are the product of one's consciousness. The third realm transcends the distinction between subject and object. The fourth is the realization that neither subject nor object have any ultimate reality, that they are ultimately identical. See also **Rinzai sect**.

Four Encounters

According to tradition, when **Siddharta Gautama**, the historical **Buddha**, was still living a secular life at home with a wife and child, he had four encounters that motivated him to abandon his home life and seek **enlightenment**. Siddharta was sheltered in his youth by his father, protected from any exposure to the ugliness and **suffering** of human life. On a series of outings to see and experience the world, the young Siddharta encountered first an old man, second a diseased individual, and third a corpse. From the first three encounters, the future Buddha learned about the inevitability of old age, illness, and death, which afflict all human beings. He pondered the fleeting nature of sensual pleasures and meditated on the reality of suffering. Finally, he encountered a religious mendicant who was in search of enlightenment. This final encounter convinced Siddharta to leave his secular life and set out in search of a remedy for human suffering.

Four Fruits

The four stages of spiritual attainment recognized in the ancient Buddhist tradition and in **Theravada Buddhism**. They are stream winners, once returners, never returners, and **arhats**. Stream winners have destroyed wrong views. Once returners have destroyed the gross, harmful passions and will only be reborn once more before attaining **nirvana**. Never returners are already in their final life, having destroyed both gross and subtle passions. Arhats are those who have already attained nirvana.

Four Grave Offenses

(J. shijû or shijûzai) The gravest offenses against the traditional Buddhist **monastic code** (**vinaya**) that a **monk** or **nun** can commit. The offenses are: engaging in sexual intercourse, stealing another person's belongings, killing a human being, and lying about one's spiritual accomplishments. Punishment for these offenses is the most severe possible within the monastic community—expulsion from the **sangha**, although it is understood that the deed itself has already cut the person off from the sangha. The four offenses are therefore called *parajika*, a Sanskrit term meaning offenses entailing defeat.

Four Great Elements

(J. shidai or shidaishu) Earth, water, fire, and wind; the four fundamental elements from which all things are comprised. The nature of earth is hardness, so its function is to support things. Water has the quality of moistness and can contain things. The nature of fire is heat, so it can bring things to perfection. Wind has the quality of motion, so it causes things to mature. The human body was traditionally understood to be composed of the four elements, with sickness and death resulting from an improper balance of the four. **Buddhism** adopted this system of classification from Indian thought.

Four Great Vows

(J. **Shigu seigan**) The **vows** undertaken by a **bodhisattva**. The four great vows taken by **Zen** practitioners are "**Sentient beings** are innumerable, I vow to save them all"; "The **afflictions** are inexhaustible, I vow to extinguish them all"; "The Gates of the **Dharma** are countless, I vow to master them all"; and "The Buddhist Way is unsurpassed, I vow to attain it." Zen **monks** and **nuns** recite these vows daily as a part of morning and evening services.

The vows have a long history in **Buddhism**. Originally, they were associated with the **four noble truths**.

The four guardian kings ward off evil wherever the Buddhist Dharma is taught.
Their images appear in almost every East Asian Buddhist temple.

The practitioner vowed to lead all people unfamiliar with Buddhism to an understanding of the four noble truths, so they could attain **enlightenment**. The vows changed over time and have taken on somewhat different forms in different schools of Buddhism. The version used within the Zen school is based upon a passage from the Tun-huang edition of the **Platform Sutra**.

Four Guardian Kings

(J. shitennô) Figures originally taken from Hindu mythology and adopted into Buddhist mythology. The four guardian kings live near **Mount Sumeru** and are dedicated to serving **Indra**. They ward off evil and protect people living in the four quarters; in particular, they guard places where the Buddhist **Dharma** is taught. Jikoku (Dhrtarastra) guards the east, Zôjô (Virudhaka) the south, Kômoku (Virupaksha) the west, and Tamon (Vaishravana) the north. Images of the four guardians kings, dressed in full armor and depicted with fierce expressions, appear in almost every Buddhist temple in East Asia. In many cases, their images are located in the four corners of the main hall of a temple (the Buddha hall at a **Zen** temple), or arranged around the central image of the **Buddha**, symbolizing their role as guardians of the Dharma.

Four Kinds of Birth

(J. shishô) **Buddhism** traditionally recognized four modes of birth: from a womb, from an egg, from moisture, and from metamorphosis. In the premodern period, it was believed that fish, worms, and some insects were born spontaneously from moisture. Certain other types of **sentient beings** were thought to metamorphose through the workings of **karma**. These included the beings that dwell in **heaven** and **hell**, some **hungry ghosts**, and the **ashuras**.

Four Noble Truths

(J. shishôtai) The most basic teachings of **Buddhism**, which the **Buddha** is said to have proclaimed in his very first sermon. They are: the truths of **suffering** (dukkha), the cause of suffering, the cessation of suffering, and the path leading to the cessation of suffering. The Sanskrit word commonly translated as "noble" is actually the term *aryan*, originally an ethnic identification given to people of high caste in Indian society. In Buddhist usage, however, the expression is not related to race or social limitation; it means "holy" or "worthy of respect," qualities which Buddhism regards as independent of social class.

The truth of suffering teaches that human life is characterized by suffering. The Buddha said that birth is suffering, old age is suffering, disease is suffering, and death is suffering. Contact with unpleasantness is suffering, as is separation from the pleasant. This means that every aspect of human experience involves suffering, even the elements that one normally thinks of as pleasurable, since separation is inevitable. The second truth identifies desire or craving as the root cause of suffering. The truth of cessation pro-

vides hope for release from suffering; it teaches that when desire ceases, then suffering will also cease. Finally, the fourth truth explains that the **Eightfold Path** of Buddhism is the means to understanding the nature of human existence, and thus, cutting off the causes of suffering.

The four noble truths are often described using a metaphor drawn from medicine. The Buddha is seen as a great physician treating the disease of suffering that plagues human existence. The first truth is the symptom of the disease; the second truth, identifying the cause, is the diagnosis; third is the prognosis that a cure is possible; and finally, the prescription leading to the cure.

It is important to understand that an intellectual grasp of the four noble truths is not considered sufficient; following the **Buddhist path** requires great effort on the part of the individual, leading to a realization of the truths for oneself. This realization requires the practice of **meditation** and is associated with Buddhist monastic practice rather than lay Buddhism. Although **Mahayana Buddhism** accepts the four noble truths as the basic teachings of the Buddha, they are not generally a primary topic for Mahayana teaching, nor are they typically the focus of Mahayana meditative practices. While lay followers of **Theravada Buddhism** are familiar with the four noble truths, most Mahayana Buddhists are not. See also **lay believer**.

Four Obligations

(J. shion) The East Asian concept that every individual receives four kinds of blessings in this life, and therefore, owes a debt of gratitude for these blessings. This notion is referred to as the four debts of gratitude, emphasizing that the obligation is to express gratitude for received blessings. The concept of blessings and obligations is not exclusive to **Buddhism**, but is also taught by the other major East Asian religious and philosophical systems, such as Confucianism and Shintô. There are many Buddhist versions of the four obligations, each incorporating minor variations. Perhaps the most common version includes gratitude toward one's parents, one's country and its leaders, all other living beings, and the **three treasures** (the **Buddha**, the **Dharma**, and the **sangha**). Another version of the four obligations may include mother, father, the buddhas, and one's Buddhist teachers. In **Zen** monasteries, **monks** and **nuns** fulfill the obligation to express gratitude by remembering four types of benefactors at their daily meals: their country and its leaders, their parents, their teachers and friends, and the lay patrons who support their monastery. See also **lay believer**.

Four Offerings

(J. Shiji no Kuyô) The four kinds of **offerings** that are appropriate for a **buddha**, a **monk**, or a **nun**. There are various listings of the four kinds of offerings. In the "Kuyô Shobutsu" chapter of the *Shôbôgenzô*, **Dôgen Kigen** (1200–1253) lists the offerings as food and drink, clothing, bedding, and medicine. This traditional list coincides with the four daily necessities of monks and nuns enumerated elsewhere. Other traditional lists include such items as shelter, scattered flowers, and burning **incense**.

Four Periods of Meditation

(J. **shiji zazen**) **Monks** and **nuns** in a **Zen** monastery participate in four daily sessions of seated **meditation**. This tradition dates back to the Sung dynasty (960–1279) in China. The times and duration differ from monastery to monastery, but the sessions are generally held before dawn, later in the morning (after breakfast), in the afternoon, and in the late evening.

Four Realms of Reality

(J. shishu hokkai) Hua-yen concept using four levels of existence, or **Dharma** realms, to describe reality.

The first is the realm of phenomena, which can be thought of as the mundane level of reality. At this level, one experiences things as existing in a temporary sense and as having clear distinctions one from another. The second is the realm of reality. At this level, one realizes that all things are the same, since all are characterized by **emptiness**. Third is the realm of interpenetration of phenomena and reality. At this level, one understands that the two previous views of reality are not absolutely opposed. In any individual phenomenon, one may perceive the ultimate reality of emptiness. The fourth and final realm is that of interpenetration of phenomena and phenomena, which describes the complete interconnectedness and interdependence of all things. At this level, one understands that any action taken in relationship with any single phenomenon affects all other phenomena. That is, what affects any one thing affects the whole. This realm is commonly described using the image of **Indra's Jewel Net**.

The teaching of the four realms of reality deeply influenced **Zen** thought. It is expressed in such concepts as the **five ranks** of **Tung-shan Liang-chieh** (807–869) and the **four discernments** of **Lin-chi I-hsüan** (d. 867). Mastery of the concept of the four realms, in the form of the five ranks (J. **Goi Kôan**), serves as the final stage of kôan practice in the Japanese Rinzai school today. See also **Rinzai sect** and **Hua-yen school**.

Four Shouts

(J. shikatsu) The four kinds of shouts that the Chinese master **Lin-chi I-hsüan** (d. 867), founder of Rinzai **Buddhism**, claimed to use with his disciples, based on the individual's needs. In the *Rinzai-roku* (*Sayings of Lin-chi*), Lin-chi compared the shouts to a jeweled sword of a **vajra** king, capable of cutting through any **delusion**; a crouching lion waiting to pounce; a grass-tipped pole used as a decoy for fishing; and finally a shout that does not function as a shout. This formula was sometimes used as a **kôan** in the later Rinzai tradition. See also **Rinzai sect**.

Fourth Patriarch

The title usually refers to **Tao-hsin** (580–651), the Fourth Chinese **Patriarch** of **Zen**. According to tradition, Toa-hsin directly inherited the **Dharma** from the Third Patriarch, **Seng-ts'an** (d. 606). See **Tao-hsin**.

Four Wisdoms

(J. shichi) Within the tradition of **Theravada Buddhism**, the four wisdoms refer to the realization of the **four noble truths** that are said to characterize an **arhat**. Within the **Yogachara school** of **Mahayana Buddhism**, an alternative concept of the four wisdoms of the **Buddha** developed. **Bodhisattvas** strive to attain the four wisdoms in order to save **sentient beings**. The four wisdoms are: the Great Perfect Mirror Wisdom (the ability to see all things as they really are); the Universal Nature Wisdom (the ability to see that all things are equal and undifferentiated, leading to the **compassion** of a bodhisattva); the Marvelous Observing Wisdom (the ability to evaluate the needs of all sentient beings, which allows a buddha to preach the **Dharma** in a way appropriate to each individual); and the Perfecting of Action Wisdom (the ability of a buddha to take on any physical form necessary to instruct sentient beings).

Fucha Ryôri

Vegetarian cuisine typical of the Japanese **Obaku sect** of the **Zen** school of **Buddhism**. The founding **monks** of the Obaku sect emigrated to Japan from southern China in the mid- to late seventeenth century. They preserved the monastic cooking styles of their home culture, including the more elaborate cooking used for **vegetarian feasts**. Fucha ryôri remains a distinctive feature at the main monastery of **Mampuku-ji** in the city of Uji; it is prepared for visi-

tors. Sometimes monks were allowed to enjoy this cuisine if wealthy patrons paid for it as a means to build merit.

Fudô Myôô

The "Immovable Shining King"; one of the fierce guardian deities (**myôô**) who destroy demons, protecting **Buddhism** and human beings from evil. The myôô are regarded as manifestations of Dainichi Nyorai, the **Mahavairochana Buddha**; they are capable of teaching the most stubborn **sentient beings** by means of sacred sounds (**mantra** or shingon). Like the other myôô, Fudô is depicted as a fierce deity, with blazing eyes, surrounded by the fire of anger and wisdom. His skin is blue-black in color; he stands upon a rock, armed and ready for battle. Fudô holds a rope in his left hand to ensnare the wicked, with a sword in his right hand to slay them.

Fudô is the most popular of the myôô class of deities in Japanese Buddhism. His image appears in numerous paintings and **mandala**; statues of this fierce guardian often protect temple halls. In the esoteric traditions, Fudô is associated with the fire ritual, or **goma**, and is sometimes used as the central deity for that ritual. **Suzuki Shôsan** (1579–1655), the **Zen** master of the Tokugawa period (1600–1867), favored Fudô not only as an image to focus one's attention when meditating, but as an ideal for the Zen practitioner to emulate. Shôsan recommended that beginners concentrate on the power and energy of the Fudô image.

King, Winston L. *Death Was His Kôan: The Samurai-Zen of Suzuki Shosan*. Berkeley, CA: Asian Humanities Press, 1986.

Tyler, Royall, trans. *Selected Writings of Suzuki Shosan*. Ithaca, NY: Chinese-Japanese Program, Cornell University, 1977.

Yamasaki, Taiko. *Shingon: Japanese Esoteric Buddhism*. Trans. Richard and Cynthia Peterson. Ed. Yasuyoshi Morimoto and David Kidd. Boston, MA: Shambhala, 1988.

The Fudô Myôô, or "Immovable Shining King," is one of the
fierce guardian deities who protects human beings from evil.

This anonymous painting of Fugen depicts him seated on an elephant, surrounded by acolytes and devotees.

Fugen

The Japanese name for the **bodhisattva** known as Samantabhadra in Sanskrit. Fugen is considered the personification of the mercy, **meditation**, and practice of all the **buddhas**. Fugen is usually depicted riding a white elephant with six tusks. He often appears as one of the attendants of either Shakyamuni (**Siddharta Gautama**) or **Maha-vairochana Buddhas**, standing at the Buddha's right side in a triad of figures (Shaka triad). He is often paired with Manjusri (**Monju**), the left-hand attendant, who represents wisdom and **enlightenment**. In the Hua-yen Sutra (**Avatamsaka Sutra**), Fugen takes ten great **bodhisattva vows**, representing the perfect practice of a bodhisattva. See also **Hua-yen school**.

Fujaku

The Japanese pronunciation for **P'u-chi** (651–739), a Chinese Zen **monk**. See **P'u-chi**.

Fukan Zazengi

"General recommendations for seated **meditation**," a brief essay (T. 82, no. 2580) composed by **Dôgen Kigen** (1200–1253), the founder of Japanese Sôtô **Zen**. The text describes the proper method for seated meditation as well as Dôgen's understanding of meditation as **enlightenment**. The text is traditionally dated to 1227, immediately after Dôgen's return from China, but scholars now question that date. Dôgen probably wrote the first version of the text in 1233 and revised it sometime later in his life. It is the latter version that is best known today. The text sometimes circulates as a single work, but under the title *Zazengi*, it is also included as one chapter in the *Shôbôgenzô*, Dôgen's most important work. See also **Sôtô sect**.

Bielefeldt, Carl. *Dôgen's Manuals of Zen Meditation*. Berkeley, CA: University of California Press, 1988.

Fuke Sect

A sect of **Zen**, traditionally said to have originated during the T'ang dynasty (618–907) in China, which spread in early modern Japan (1600–1867); also called the Komu sect. The Fuke sect is known for its use of the **shakuhachi**—a long bamboo flute with five holes—as a means of attaining **enlightenment**. Most of its members were lay people rather than **monks** and **nuns**. They were commonly called **komusô**, or "monks of nothingness." The komusô lived a wandering life, traveling around the Japanese countryside. They played the shakuhachi, chanted the **nembutsu**, and collected alms.

Traditional accounts maintain that the Zen master **P'u-hua** (J. Fuke) founded the sect and that his lay disciple, Chang Po, spread his teachings. There is no historical evidence, however, that the Fuke sect ever existed in China. It is believed that the Japanese Rinzai Zen master **Kakushin** (1207–1298) learned about the Fuke teachings from Chang Ts'an while he was in China, and later transmitted them to Japan during the Kamakura period (1185–1333). The sect took on definite shape and became popular during the Tokugawa period (1600–1867), when many rônin, or masterless **samurai**, became practitioners. They wore a distinctive costume, including a bamboo hat that covered the face. Because the Fuke hat effectively disguised the face, thieves and other outlaws sometimes adopted the dress of a Fuke **monk** to avoid detection. For this reason, the sect was outlawed by the Meiji government in 1871, and it has not been revived since. See also **lay believer** and **Rinzai sect**.

Fuketsu Enshô

Japanese transliteration for **Feng-hsueh Yen-chao**, a Chinese Rinzai master. See **Feng-hsueh Yen-chao**.

Fuke Zenji

The Japanese name for **Zen** Master **P'u-hua**, a Chinese **monk** from the T'ang dynasty (618–907) who is remembered as the founder of the **Fuke sect** of Zen **Buddhism**. See **P'u-hua**.

Fukuden

Field of merit, in Japanese. The character, pronounced "den," literally means a rice paddy or another cultivated piece of land. See **field of merit**.

Funeral Zen

A popular expression used to describe the extent to which the **Zen** school of **Buddhism** is practiced in Japan today, especially by lay practitioners. Although most Japanese may be considered members of one Buddhist sect or another, most have contact with Buddhism only at funeral or **memorial services**. This is equally true for lay members of the three major Zen sects: Sôtô, Rinzai, and Obaku. Very few Japanese Zen Buddhists receive instruction in the teachings of Zen or in the practice of seated **meditation**. Indeed, only a small minority of Buddhist temples and monasteries in Japan offer to lay people the option of joining in sessions of seated meditation. Few Zen clergy regularly practice meditation after their initial **monastic training** which qualifies them for **ordination**. Most serve as local parish priests, offering services such as funeral and memorial rites for their members.

Historically, the close association of Zen and funeral practices can be explained by studying the rapid spread of Zen during the medieval (1185–1600) and early modern (1600–1867) periods. During the medieval period, Sôtô Zen leaders sought to popularize the sect among the warrior and commoner classes in Japan by offering funeral and memorial services to lay members. Later, in the Tokugawa period (1600–1867), government policies spread the use of Buddhist funerals throughout the entire populace. First, the government required that every Japanese be registered as a member of a Buddhist temple. Second, the government required that, when a death occurred, a Buddhist **monk** examine the body before filing a report and issuing a death certificate. Even today, the vast majority of Japanese make use of Buddhist services to honor the deceased. See also **lay believer**, **Obaku sect**, **Rinzai sect**, and **Sôtô sect**.

Bodiford, William M. *Sôtô Zen in Medieval Japan*. Honolulu, HI: University of Hawaii Press, 1993.

Reader, Ian. "Zazenless Zen: The Position of Zazen in Institutional Zen Buddhism." *Japanese Religion*. Vol. 14, No. 3 (1986), pp. 7–27.

Funyô Roku

The Japanese abbreviated title for the *Feng-yang Wu-te Ch'an-shi Yü-lu*, "The **Recorded Sayings** of Zen Master Wu-te of Feng-yang." See *Feng-yang Wu-te Ch'an-shi Yü-lu*.

Funyô Zenshô

Japanese name for **Fen-yang Shan-chao** (947–1024), a Chinese Rinzai master of the T'ang period (618–907). He is also known in Japanese by his **posthumous name**, Mutoku **Zenji**. See **Fen-yang Shan-chao**.

Funzôe

(Sk. kashaya) A **kesa** or robe made by patching together discarded rags. Funzôe is the Japanese translation for the Sanskrit "pamsu-kula kesa," which means "a robe [made from] rags off a **dust** heap." The Japanese expression is actually somewhat stronger, literally meaning "excrement wiping cloth." In the "Shôbôgenzô Kesa Kudoku," an essay about the religious significance of monastic robes, **Dôgen Kigen** (1200–1253) explains that buddhas have always preferred to use rag robes rather than robes made from finer materials. In fact, the earliest Buddhist **monks** and **nuns** did originally wear funzôe. The historical **Buddha** and his disciples initially constructed their robes from discarded rags that they collected from the streets or from cremation areas. They washed the rags and pieced them together to fashion monastic robes. For health reasons, the Buddha later allowed monks and nuns to accept donations of new clothes from lay people. See also **lay believer**.

Furuna

Japanese rendering of **Purna**. See **Purna**.

Furyû Monji

"Without reliance on words or letters," a Japanese expression used to characterize **Zen**. The Zen tradition maintains that the **Dharma** cannot be adequately expressed through human language. Therefore, transmission of the Dharma from a Zen master to a disciple is said to occur from mind to mind, without any dependence upon the written scriptures of **Buddhism**. The phrase is actually one line of a Chinese verse traditionally attributed to **Bodhidharma**.

Fusatsu

Japanese rendering of the Sanskrit term **uposatha**, or poshadha, the traditional meeting of the Buddhist **sangha**, or community, held twice a month for the purpose of reflection and repentance. The fusatsushiki, or uposatha ceremony, is still observed as a part of **Zen** monastic practice. On the fifteenth day and last day of each month, Zen **monks** and **nuns** renew their commitment to the four **bodhisattva** vows (J. shiguseizan) and repent from any offenses against the **monastic code**. See **uposatha**.

Fusetsu

Zen sermon; a general lecture given by a Zen master to the entire assembly in a Zen monastery. The fusetsu is less formal than the **daisan**.

Fushin

Manual labor, a regular part of the **Zen** monastic life. The Chinese characters are pronounced "fushô" in Japanese. The word literally means "general admonition," since manual labor was required of the entire monastic community. See **manual labor**.

Fushô Fumetsu

"Unborn and undying," or "not arising and not passing into extinction," the Japanese rendering of a common **Mahayana Buddhism** expression for absolute reality. The classical scriptural source for the expression is a passage from the Chinese translation of the **Heart Sutra** which says, "O **Shariputra**, all things are characterized by **emptiness**. They are not born and they do not pass into extinction. . ."

Fûsu

The Assistant Supervisor of a **Zen** monastery. One of the six offices held by senior **monks**, whose role is to oversee the practical administration of the monastery. The fûsu works closely with the Prior (**tsûsu**) and the Supervisor (**kansu**) in handling the economic management of the temple. Along with the other two financial officers, the fûsu has his living quarters within the kitchen-office (**ku'in**). From there it is possible to observe and control the daily consumption of resources and assess the immediate needs of the monastic community. The fûsu's particular responsibility lies in keeping accounts of the day-to-day expenditures of temple resources, both monetary and of other supplies. See also **temple positions**.

G

Ga

Japanese translation of the Sanskrit term *atman*. See **atman**.

Gaki

Japanese for **hungry ghost**, one of the six realms of existence through which individuals travel until they attain release (**nirvana**). Birth into the realm of hungry ghosts was one of the evil outcomes, seen as a form of punishment for wicked deeds performed in a previous lifetime. Japanese and Chinese Buddhists focused on one of several species of hungry ghosts described in earlier texts, a creature with a large belly and a needle-thin neck. Although these gaki have voracious appetites, they cannot fill their bellies due to the narrowness of their throats. Originally, each different species of hungry ghost was associated with specific behavior patterns for which they suffered an appropriate form of retribution. In East Asian accounts, a gaki was an individual who lacked charity and intentionally hindered others from practicing the virtue of giving.

In **Zen** monasteries, a number of rituals are performed to ease the **suffering** of hungry ghosts. On an annual basis, monastic communities make special **offerings** to hungry ghosts at the time of the **ullambana** ceremony in the summer, a festival known in Japan as **Obon**. On a daily basis, Zen **monks** and **nuns** set aside a few grains of rice (**saba**) from every meal as an offering (suisan or **shussan**) to aid the gaki; they also recite a brief verse. In some monasteries, monks and nuns pour off the water left over from rinsing the eating bowls as an additional offering. It is said that the

Gakuji are inscribed tablets that indicate the names of Buddhist monasteries.

tiny particles of food present in the water are the easiest for the hungry ghosts to swallow.

Gakuji

Inscribed tablets used in **Zen** monasteries to indicate the names of monastery buildings and offices; tablets also announce upcoming or ongoing functions, such as **sermons**.

Ganjin

Chien-chen (687–763), the Chinese Buddhist **monk** who founded the **ritsu** (**vinaya**) school of **Buddhism** in Japan. See **Chien-chen**.

Garanbô

Dharma lineages based upon the temple of residence rather than one's actual teacher. Although **Dharma**

transmission in the **Zen** school is theoretically based upon a face-to-face encounter between a master and a disciple, other forms of Dharma transmission may occur. The practice of garanbô was an institutional form of Dharma transmission common within the Sôtô school in Japan beginning in the medieval period (1185–1600). It was later rejected during the reform movements of the Tokugawa period (1600–1867). Although less widespread than in the Sôtô school, the practice was sometimes followed in Rinzai temples during the medieval period.

According to the garanbô process, a **monk** would assume the Dharma **lineage** of the former **abbots** of the temple at which he served as abbot or head monk. If a new head monk was from outside the temple in question, he would change his lineage (**in'in ekishi**). His name would be added to the Dharma lineage of the temple, and he would receive a **lineage chart** of its line. This occurred regardless of his actual connections with the previous abbots. The Dharma lineage of the temple would thus remain constant, while the lineage of an individual monk could change several times in a career. See also **Rinzai sect** and **Sôtô sect**.

Bodiford, William M. "Dharma Transmission in Sôtô Zen." In *Monumenta Nipponica*. Vol. 46, No. 4 (Winter 1991).

Gasan Jitô

(1727–1797) Japanese Rinzai **monk** who trained under **Hakuin Ekaku** (1685–1768) and is generally counted among his **Dharma heirs**. Gasan was born in northeastern Japan in Oshû. He originally practiced **Zen** under the Rinzai master Gessen Zen'e (1702–1781); he came to Hakuin much later in his career. It is unclear whether Gasan actually received **inka** from Hakuin before the master died. Nevertheless, Gasan's disciples constitute the most important **lineage** of Hakuin Zen. Along with his disciples,

Inzan Ien (1751–1814) and **Takujû Kosen** (1760–1833), Gasan continued the reforms of the Rinzai system of **kôan** study that were initiated by Hakuin. Gasan is said to have taught some 500 disciples at Rinshô-in in Edo and did much to promote Hakuin Zen. See also **Rinzai sect**.

Gasô

"Painter-**monk**;" **Zen** monks and **nuns** traditionally use the visual arts, including a variety of painting and **calligraphy** styles, to express their understanding of the **Dharma**.

Gasshô

A gesture of reverence, performed with the hands held palm-to-palm at chest level. In India, the ancient gesture was thought to symbolize sincerity. In Buddhist cultures, it is commonly used as a respectful form of greeting, especially between members of the monastic community. It is also commonly employed as a means to pay homage to an image of a **buddha**. In the **Zen** context, the gesture is understood as a **mudra** which expresses nonduality; specifically, it is interpreted as a symbol of the unity between perception and reality, or "**One mind**."

Saunders, E. Dale. *Mudra: A Study of the Symbolic Gestures in Japanese Buddhist Sculpture*. Princeton, NJ: Princeton University Press, 1985.

Gateless Gate

Wu-men Kuan, known in Japanese as the *Mumonkan*, a classic **Zen** text containing forty-eight traditional **kôan** with commentary, compiled by the Rinzai master **Wu-men Hui-k'ai** (1183–1260). See *Mumonkan*.

Gâthâ

(J. ge) A style of verse or song used to teach concepts from a religious tradition or to praise a religious figure. Gâthâs are used in several Indian religious traditions, including **Buddhism**. Buddhist **sutras** often contain sections of gatha interspersed with prose, while some canonical texts are comprised solely of verse.

Ge

Japanese term for *gâthâ*. See **gâthâ**.

Gedatsu

"Release" or "liberation," a Japanese word commonly used to indicate **enlightenment**, the goal of Buddhist practice. It is sometimes used as the technical term for **nirvana**—the release from ignorance and **suffering**. In other contexts, gedatsu means **meditation**, since enlightenment is achieved through meditation.

Genjô Kôan

"Manifesting Absolute Reality before One's Eyes," an essay composed in 1233 by **Dôgen Kigen** (1200–1253), the founder of Japanese Sôtô **Zen**. The text sometimes circulates as a single work, but is also included as one chapter in the *Shôbôgenzô*, Dôgen's most important work. The term *Genjô kôan* expresses the **Mahayana Buddhism** teaching that ordinary phenomena experienced in everyday life are themselves expressions of absolute reality. Dôgen uses the expression to suggest that Zen practice and Zen **enlightenment** are a part of ordinary life. See also **Sôtô sect**.

Genkan

Literally meaning a dark or mysterious gateway, the term is used metaphorically in **Buddhism** to denote entry by a believer onto the **Buddhist path**, or more specifically, entry into the realm of **enlightenment**. In more concrete terms, it refers simply to the entry gate of a **Zen** temple.

Traditionally, Zen monasteries in China customarily inscribed the word *genkan* on their entryways, suggesting that all who entered the gate were embarking on the Buddhist path to enlightenment. Eventually, the word came to be used almost exclusively for the visitor's entrance to the guest hall of a Zen monastery, and thus associated with the specific architectural style of those entryways. The related customs were brought to Japan along with the transmission of Zen teachings during the Kamakura period (1185–1333). Eventually, the practice of building entry gates in the same style became popular at other Buddhist temples. The style then became widespread throughout the secular world. Almost all Japanese homes today have an entryway referred to as a genkan. In most cases, the genkan is a small area separating the interior living quarters from the outside door. On entering the genkan, one removes one's shoes before stepping up into the raised level of the living quarters.

Genshin

(942–1017) Japanese Tendai **monk** known for his teaching of **Pure Land** devotion. Genshin established a theoretical basis for devotion to **Amida buddha** and the hope for **rebirth** in his **Western Pure Land**. He popularized Pure Land belief and the practice of **chanting** the **nembutsu** through his paintings and writings, especially the *Essentials of Salvation* (J. *Ojôyôshû*). Genshin is revered by the **True Pure Land sect** (Jôdo Shinshû) as the Sixth Pure Land **Patriarch**. See also **Tendai sect**.

Genze Riyaku

"Worldly benefits" that may be gained in this life through the practice of **Buddhism**. These benefits include long life, physical health, monetary wealth, safety in childbirth, and protection from various calamities. Although Buddhist scholars often maintain that worldly benefits are not an important part of the Buddhist faith, promises of them abound in the

Buddhist scriptures and other classical texts. The appeal of worldly benefits has often been used by Buddhist teachers as an **expedient means** to attract lay people to the tradition. See also **lay believer**.

Gesshû Shûko

Japanese Sôtô master (1616–1696) of the Tokugawa period (1600–1867) who inspired reform movements within the **Sôtô sect**. Gesshû was initially a Shingon **monk**, but soon began to study with Zen masters. He became the **Dharma heir** of Hakuhô Genteki, the **abbot** at **Daijô-ji**. He also studied with two Chinese **Zen** masters, **Tao-che Ch'ao-yüan** (d. 1660) and **Yin-yüan Lung-ch'i** (1594–1673), the founder of Obaku Zen. In 1680, he became abbot at Daijô-ji. His primary disciple and Dharma heir, **Manzan Dôhaku** (1636–1715), carried out the monastic reforms that Gesshû hoped to accomplish. See also **Obaku sect** and **Shingon sect**.

Geta

Wooden footwear traditionally worn in Japan. Geta are made from a platform of wood resting on two supporting cross bars which raise the foot off the ground. Geta are held on the foot with cloth straps much like thongs. Although the word *geta* did not come into common usage until the Tokugawa period (1600–1867), the style of footwear dates back to ancient times in Japan.

Gidan

The **ball of doubt**. An expression used by **Zen** masters for the tension that builds up in an individual when he or she practice Zen intensely, especially when working on a **kôan**. The buildup of tension is a necessary precursor to the initial experience of **enlightenment** (kenshô). Enlightenment is said to occur when the ball of doubt shatters. See **ball of doubt**.

Ginkaku-ji

The **Silver Pavilion**, the popular name for Jishô-ji, a Rinzai **Zen** temple in eastern Kyoto. See **Silver Pavilion**.

Ginzan Teppeki

"**Silver mountain, iron wall**," a **Zen** expression for **enlightenment**. See **Silver mountain, iron wall**.

Gô

The Japanese word for **karma**; actions and the resulting consequences of actions. See **karma**.

Goddess of Mercy

Avalokiteshvara, the **bodhisattva** of infinite **compassion** and mercy. Jesuit missionaries to China in the sixteenth century coined the name for female images of **Kuan-yin**. The missionaries noted a striking resemblance between female figures of the bodhisattva, especially the white-robed Kuan-yin, and Catholic images of the Virgin Mary. See **Kuan-yin**.

Goga

"False self," the belief in and **attachment** to a false concept of the self or ego. The Japanese term *goga* refers to the common belief that each individual possesses an eternal and unchanging self or soul. According to Buddhist teachings, there is nothing eternal, unchanging, or abiding within the human self. The historical **Buddha** taught that human beings suffer primarily because they become attached to the false self. The term also refers to selfish attitudes and states of mind. See also **Anatman**.

Gogen

"**Five eyes**," the five kinds of perception associated with ordinary **sentient beings**, deities, **shravakas** and **pratyeka buddhas**, **bodhisattvas**, and buddhas. See **five eyes**.

Gogo

Practice after **enlightenment (satori)**. Training within the Rinzai school of **Zen** can be divided into two parts, the practice leading to enlightenment, known in Japanese as **kenshô**, and subsequent practice after the initial experience, or gogo. During the Tokugawa period (1600–1867), masters in the Rinzai school developed a regular system of Zen practice based on the use of **kôan** as the central focus of seated **meditation**. The reformer **Hakuin Ekaku** (1685–1768) is credited with developing the system of kôan practice still in use in the Rinzai school today. According to this system, the initial goal of the practitioner is to contemplate on the first kôan until attaining an initial experience of enlightenment. Attaining the initial experience of kenshô is not the end of practice under the master's guidance, nor is it sufficient to qualify a practitioner as a Zen master. After enlightenment, the practitioner continues to practice seated meditation, proceeding through a series of other kôan designed to mature the level of practice and prepare the individual to become a teacher. See also **Rinzai sect**.

Gogyakuzai

The five deadly actions of killing one's father, killing one's mother, killing an arhat, harming the body of a **buddha**, and causing dissention within the **sangha**. Committing one of these five acts results in **rebirth** for many eons in the lowest level of **hell**, **Avici hell**, where the **suffering** from intense heat is incessant.

Goi

The Japanese term for the "**five ranks**" developed by **Zen** master **Tung-shan Liang-chieh** (807–869). The standard Japanese version of the five ranks is also known as "henshô goi," the five ranks of the Real and the Apparent. Based on Tung-shan's original poem, this abbreviated version is comprised of five verses of three characters each: shô-chû-hen, the real within the apparent; hen-chû-shô, the apparent within the real; shô-chû-rai, the coming from within the real; hen-chû-shi, the arrival within the apparent; and ken-chû-tô, mutual interpenetration of real and apparent. See **five ranks**.

Goi Kôan

A **kôan** based on the "**five ranks**" developed by the Chinese master **Tung-shan Liang-chieh** (807–869). The five ranks is a formulaic expression of the degrees, or stages, of **Zen** realization. Tung-shan's original statement of the five ranks is a poem in five stanzas. The Japanese Rinzai school uses the Goi kôan as the final stage of formal kôan practice. In the eighteenth century, **Hakuin Ekaku** (1685–1768) and his disciples devised a process of kôan practice to be undertaken after an initial **enlightenment** experience. They based the system on five stages or categories of kôan, designed to lead the practitioner to deeper levels of understanding. In this system, a consideration of the Goi kôan serves as the fifth and final barrier through which potential Zen masters must pass before qualifying to take on disciples of their own. See also **Rinzai sect**.

Miura, Isshû, and Ruth Fuller Sasaki. *The Zen Kôan.* New York: Harcourt, Brace & World, 1967.

Gojin

The "**five dusts**" or **defilements**. A Japanese Buddhist expression for the five objects of perception related to the five senses (J. gokon). See **five dusts**.

Gojôe

"Five-strip robe," one of three basic types of **kesa** or monastic robes worn by Buddhist **monks** and **nuns**. The five-strip robe was originally called the antarvasa in Sanskrit. It is known in Japanese as the naie, literally "inner robe," or andae. The gojôe was originally designed to be worn as an inner garment or undergarment. In the **Zen** school it is sometimes known as the samue, or work garment, because monks often strip down to the inner robe when engaging in physical labor. In Japan, the gojôe is usually worn symbolically on a strap placed around the neck as a reminder of the **Buddha's** patched robe. The strap and five-strip kesa worn together in this manner are known as a **rakusu**. Today, lay practitioners sometimes receive this garment when they take the **precepts**. See also **lay believer**.

Goka

The "rear stands." A wash house located behind the monks' hall (**sôdô**) of a traditional **Zen** monastery. The **monks** used the goka for ordinary daily purposes, such as washing their faces and brushing their teeth. Travelers would also use this facility to wash the dirt from their feet before entering the hall. In most traditional monasteries, hot water for bathing was only provided in the separate bath house (**yokushitsu**) once every two weeks. For daily purposes, the monks used cold water at the goka.

Gokai

Japanese for the **five precepts** undertaken by lay Buddhists. They are fusesshô, not to kill living beings; fuchûtô, not to steal; fujain, to abstain from sexual misconduct; fumôgo, not to lie; and fuonju, not to drink liquor. See **five precepts**.

Goke

"Five houses" (Ch. wu-chia), a Japanese expression used to describe the five distinctive styles of **Zen** based on the five different lineages which developed during the T'ang dynasty (618–907) in China. See **five houses**.

Gokei Sôton

(1416–1500) Japanese Rinzai **monk** of the Ashikaga period (1392–1568). He was a seventh-generation descendant of the **Myôshin-ji** line started by **Kanzan Egen** (1277–1369). He became the **Dharma heir** of **Sekkô Sôshin** (1408–1486) and was one of his four principle disciples. Gokei served as **abbot** at **Daitoku-ji**, Myôshin-ji, and other major Rinzai monasteries. He founded Zuiryû-ji in Mino, present-day Gifu Prefecture. See also **Rinzai sect**.

Goken

The **five wrong views**. The Japanese term literally means the five views. They are the mistaken belief that the self is permanent and abiding (shinken); the mistaken belief that the self exists eternally after death or that it is annihilated (henken); mistaken rejection of the workings of cause and effect (jaken); mistaken attachment to a false view (kenjuken); and adherence to a false set of **precepts** as a means to attain **enlightenment** (kaigonjuken). See **five wrong views**.

Goke Sanshô Yôro Mon

"A Detailed Study of the Fundamental Principles of the Five Houses," a **Zen** text in five sections composed by **Tôrei Enji** (1721–1792). Using anecdotes, portions of **sermons**, and other quotations from classical Zen literature, each section presents the distinctive teachings of one of the Five Schools of Chinese Zen. Two essays by Tôrei, the "**Rôhatsu** jishû" (Instructions for Rôhatsu) and the "Kankin bô" (Sutra **chanting** announcement board) are attached as appendices. The work was completed in 1788 and first published in 1827.

Goke Shichishû

"**Five houses and seven schools**," a Japanese expression used to describe the distinctive styles of **Zen** practice that developed during the T'ang (618–907) and Sung (960–1279) dynasties. See **five houses and seven schools**.

Golden Pavilion

The popular name for Rokuon-ji, a Rinzai **Zen** temple in northwestern Kyoto in the Kitayama area. The temple takes the name Golden Pavilion, a literal translation of the Japanese *Kinkaku-ji*, from the three-story gold-leaf pavilion, which is the centerpiece of the monastery garden. The Golden Pavilion sits beside a small pond, in which it is spectacularly reflected. The temple was originally the site of the retirement villa of the third Ashikaga **shôgun**, Yoshimitsu (1358–1408), which was built in 1397. It was converted into a Zen temple after Yoshimitsu's death. **Musô Soseki** (1275–1351) is regarded as the temple's founding **abbot**, although it was constructed long after his death. With the exception of the Golden Pavilion itself, most of the temple buildings (**shichidô garan**) were destroyed in the Onin War (1466–1477) and later restored. The Golden Pavilion was burned to the ground in 1950 by a resident cleric. It was rebuilt to precisely match plans of the original. Along with its sister structure, the **Silver Pavilion**, the Golden Pavilion is regarded as a fine example of Gozan architecture of the Ashikaga period (1392–1568). See also **Rinzai sect**.

Goma

Fire ritual performed by the esoteric schools of Buddhism, including Tendai and Shingon. The ritual comes from Indian practices in which Brahmin priests offered sacrifices to the gods by burning food **offerings** in a specifically designed section of an altar. In the Buddhist ritual, the fire is said to symbolize the wisdom of **enlightenment**, which burns away any **defilements** that hinder enlightenment. Goma may be offered to gain **merit** and diminish bad **karma**, to pray for a special intention such as recovery from illness, or to pray for the protection of family or nation. See also **Shingon sect** and **Tendai sect**.

Gomi Zen

"Five taste zen," or the "five tastes of zen." An expression used for any form of zen regarded as impure or inconsistent with the zen of the **patriarchs**. In this sense, gomi zen is contrasted with single taste zen (**ichimi zen**), or pure zen. In a more technical sense, the expression refers to five basic varieties of meditative practice identified by **Tsung-mi** (780–840), a Chinese **monk**, who studied both Hua-yen and Ch'an **Buddhism**. According to Tsung-mi's classification, one can distinguish the meditative styles of non-Buddhists (gedô zen), ordinary people (**bonpu** zen), **Hinayana** Buddhists (shôjô zen), Mahayana Buddhists (daijô zen), and followers of the supreme teachings (saijôjô zen). The **Zen** tradition recognizes its own meditative style as the fifth and highest form. See also **five types of zen** and **Hua-yen school**.

Gomizunoo

The 108th Japanese emperor (1596–1680) and a patron and devotee of Zen **Buddhism**. Gomizunoo, the third son of Emperor Go-Yôzei, reigned from 1611 to 1629, the period when Tokugawa rule was firmly established. He was obliged to marry Tokugawa Kazuko, the daughter of the second Tokugawa shogun, Hidetada. Gomizunoo's displeasure led him to resign.

Gomizunoo studied **Zen** under a series of masters. He eventually took the **tonsure** in 1651 under Ryôkei, a Rinzai **monk**, who later became an Obaku master. Gomizunoo assumed the **Dharma** name Enjô Dôkaku; he later became Ryôkei's **Dharma heir** and his name is still listed on Obaku **lineage charts**. See also **Obaku sect** and **Rinzai sect**.

Gonsen Kôan

One type of **Zen kôan** based upon difficult phrases and expressions from the classical texts. The term *gonsen* literally means "the investigation of words."

Gorin Sobota is a five-piece statue that
marks holy and historic sites.

The Zen practitioner contemplates an
expression originally uttered by one of
the great historical Zen masters, seeking insight beyond the literal or technical meaning of the words. The phrases
can be thought of as gates leading to
deeper understanding of the Zen
teachings. Examples of Gonsen kôan
include Cases 24 and 27 from the
Mumonkan, and Cases 13 and 36 from
the **Hekiganroku**.

Since the time of the eighteenth-
century reformer **Hakuin Ekaku**
(1685–1768), the Rinzai school of
Japanese Zen has employed a system
of kôan practice that sets out a regular
pattern for approaching kôan after the
initial **enlightenment** experience
(**kenshô**). The system is designed to
lead practitioners to deeper levels of
understanding by moving through various types of kôan. Within the confines
of this system, Gonsen kôan are the

third of five types. They follow the
Hosshin **kôan** and **Kikan kôan**, and
precede the **Nantô kôan** and **Goi kôan**.
See also **Rinzai sect**.

Miura, Isshû, and Ruth Fuller Sasaki.
The Zen Kôan. New York: Harcourt,
Brace & World, 1967.
Shimano, Eido T. "Zen Kôans." In
Zen, Tradition and Transition.
Edited by Kenneth Kraft. New York:
Grove Press, 1988.

Gorin Sotoba

"Five wheel stupa." A stone or cast
metal **stupa** made in five sections.
Stupas are dome-shaped structures
used to enshrine relics or mark historically important places. Each section of
the Gorin sotoba forms a different
shape, which symbolizes one of the five
great elements: earth, water, fire, wind,
and space (or **emptiness**). Originally

the stupas were intended to house Buddhist **relics**, but in later practice they were used as gravestones. Gorin sotoba were first introduced in Japan during the Heian period (794–1185) and are commonly associated with the esoteric schools of **Buddhism**, the **Tendai sect**, and the **Shingon sect**.

Each section of the Gorin sotoba is inscribed with an associated Sanskrit character as well as the Chinese character for the related element. The bottom section is a cube, representing the earth, inscribed with the Sanskrit letter "A." Next is a sphere, representing water, inscribed with the Sanskrit letter "VA." The third section is a triangular stone, representing fire, inscribed with the Sanskrit letter "RA." The fourth is a half-sphere, representing the wind, inscribed with the Sanskrit letter "HA." The top section is in the shape of a **mani** jewel, representing space or emptiness, inscribed with the Sanskrit letter "KHA."

In the esoteric schools of Buddhism, the five sections of the stupa are also said to represent the Five Buddhas; the cube is associated with Ashuku (Akshobhya), the sphere with **Amida buddha** (Amitabha), the triangle with Hôdô (Ratnasambhava), the half-sphere with Fukûjôju (Amoghasiddhi), and the mani jewel with **Dainichi Nônin** (**Mahavairochana Buddha**).

Goriyaku

Worldly benefits arising from the practice of **Buddhism**. The term is an abbreviation for **genze riyaku**. See **genze riyaku**.

Goroku

The Japanese term for **recorded sayings**, one of the most important and distinctive genres of Zen literature. See **recorded sayings**.

Gosan Jôdô

To go to the lecture hall for the fifth-day sermon. According to **monastic** codes used in the practive of **Zen**, the **abbot** is expected to give public lectures to the entire community every five days, on the 5th, 10th, 15th, 20th, and 25th of each lunar month. Since Zen monasteries hold services for the health of the emperor on the 1st and 15th of the month, fifth-day **sermons** are given only four times each lunar month.

Goshuzen

"**Five types of zen**," the classification of five styles of **meditation** developed by Kuei-feng **Tsung-mi** (780–840). See **five types of zen**.

Goso Hoen

Japanese pronunciation for **Wu-tsu Fa-yen** (d. 1104), Chinese Rinzai master of the Sung (960–1279) dynasty. See **Wu-tsu Fa-yen**.

Gotai Tôchi

The most formal bow performed within the Buddhist community. The word literally means "to cast the five parts of the body (gotai) upon the ground." The five parts of the body are the elbows, the knees, and the forehead. Gotai tôchi is performed as follows: beginning in a standing position, hands held palm-to-palm at chest level (**gasshô**), one makes a slight bow. Then, slowly bending the knees, one lowers the knees to the floor. Bending forward from the waist, one lowers the upper torso until one's forehead rests on the ground, resting the arms on the floor, with the palms facing up. One then raises the palms upward, maintaining the position for a moment. Reversing the process, one returns to the standing position, hands held in gasshô, and concludes with another slight bow.

This bow is used at morning and evening services before the image of the Buddha; other occasions include services where an abbot presides.

Gotôroku

"The Five Records of the Lamp," five chronicles recounting the history of **Zen** and the authentic **lineage** of the school. Composed in China during the Sung dynasty (960–1279), all five texts explain the transmission of the **Dharma** using biographical sketches of important masters. The five texts include ***Ching-te Ch'üan-teng Lu*** (*Ching-te Record of the Transmission of the Lamp*), ***T'ien-sheng Kuang-teng Lu*** (*T'ien-sheng Record of the Widely Extending Lamp*), ***Chien-chung Ching-kuo Hsu-teng Lu*** (*Chien-chung Ching-kuo Supplementary Record of the Lamp*), ***Tsung-men Lien-teng Hui-yao*** (*Collection of Essential Material of the Zen Sect's Successive Records of the Lamp*) and ***Chia-t'ai p'u-teng Lu*** (*Chia-t'ai Comprehensive Record of the Lamp*).

Gottan Funei

Japanese pronunciation of **Wu-an P'u-ning** (1197–1276), a Chinese Rinzai Zen **monk**, who also taught in Japan. See **Wu-an P'u-ning**.

Goun

The five aggregates, the component parts that comprise all things. Japanese for the **five skandhas**. See **five skandhas**.

Goya Zazen

Pre-dawn session of **zazen**, one of the **four periods of meditation** (J. **shiji zazen**) observed daily in **Zen** monasteries. Although the exact hours differ by monastery, Goya zazen is held before breakfast, usually between 3 and 5 A.M. See also **shiji zazen**.

Gozan Jissatsu

"Five mountains and seven temples," the common Japanese designation for the Gozan ranking system for **Zen** monasteries in China and Japan. See **Gozan system**.

Gozan Literature

A general term for the artistic and scholarly writings produced by **Zen monks** in the Gozan (Five Mountain) monasteries in Kyoto and Kamakura during the medieval period (1185–1600). This class of literature is known in Japanese as Gozan bungaku. Beginning in the Kamakura period (1185–1333), Gozan monasteries functioned as cultural and artistic centers in Japan, helping to foster several forms of Chinese art, literature, and philosophy. Gozan literature includes poetry, literary prose, encyclopedias, dictionaries, and other scholarly reference works. With the exception of some poetry composed in Japanese, Gozan literature is written in classical Chinese. In addition to Chinese Buddhist texts, Zen monks of the Japanese **Gozan temples** studied Chinese literature and philosophical systems, especially Confucianism and Sung Confucianism. They often composed literary pieces that imitated Chinese styles. Leading figures in Gozan literature include **Musô Soseki** (1275–1351), **Ikkyû Sôjun** (1394–1481), and Zekkai Chûshin.

Gozan System

The Five Mountain System, an official system of ranking **Zen** monasteries, which originated in China and was later adopted by the Japanese. The system is known in Japanese as Gozan jissatsu, "The Five Mountains and Ten Distinguished Temples." The name is derived from the actual numbers of Zen temples within the two hierarchical levels that characterized the original Chinese system. In China, the Five Mountains referred to the five monasteries (**Gozan temples**) officially recognized by the government as the highest-ranking Zen monasteries. The Ten Temples were ten somewhat lower-ranking monasteries. All fifteen monasteries within the Chinese Gozan system received government patronage. Few details are known of the Chinese system, which started during the late Sung dynasty (960–1279). It seems likely that it was less structured than the later Japanese development bearing the same name.

In Japan, the Gozan system was introduced toward the end of the Kamakura period (1185–1333), and fully developed during the Ashikaga period (1392–1568). The Japanese government treated all temples within the Gozan system, said to number approximately 300, as a single administrative unit. All of the temples and monasteries in the Gozan system shared things in common. For example, they were governed by similar **monastic codes** and all were designed to have a similar physical layout and administrative organization. As the Japanese Gozan system took on definite shape, there were three tiers of temples included in the system: the highest ranking Gozan monasteries, the middle ranking Jissatsu monasteries, and the lowest ranking **shozan** temples.

In the fully developed Japanese Gozan system, eleven monasteries were counted among the Gozan, or "Five Mountain" tier of the system. These included five major monasteries in Kamakura and five in Kyoto, all organized under the administrative leadership of the eleventh monastery. The relative ranking of the eleven temples at the Gozan level shifted over time, as did the actual list of Gozan monasteries. The Jissatsu, or "Ten Temples" tier included somewhat less prestigious monasteries in Kyoto and Kamakura as well as important monasteries from the provinces; the number was not strictly limited to ten. The lowest ranking of shozan temples, literally meaning "various temples," was a looser category of provincial temples; the category had no formal numerical limit.

Over time, the Zen monasteries within the Gozan system became closely identified with cultural pursuits, especially in the areas of literature, tea ceremony (**chanoyû**), Zen gardens, and the fine arts. Indeed, it is not uncommon to speak of a distinctive Gozan culture or **Gozan literature**. Throughout the fourteenth and fifteenth centuries, Gozan temples flourished as artistic and cultural centers for the nobility and **samurai** classes. By this period, they functioned less as religious institutions devoted to Zen practice than as literary and artistic centers.

The Gozan system did not encompass all Japanese Zen monasteries and temples. The vast majority of the temples within the Gozan system were affiliated with a Rinzai **lineage**. Although a few Sôtô monasteries were officially designated as Gozan monasteries for periods of time, the majority were never ranked within the system. Non-Gozan monasteries are commonly designated as **rinka**, or Ringe temples. See also **Rinzai sect** and **Sôtô sect**.

Collcutt, Martin. *Five Mountains: The Rinzai Zen Monastic Institution in Medieval Japan.* Cambridge, MA: Harvard University Press, 1981.

Gozan Temples

"Five Mountains," the highest-ranking **Zen** temples according to the Chinese and Japanese hierarchical system. In the original Chinese system, there were exactly five Zen monasteries at the highest rank. They were **Wan-shou-ssu, Kuan-li-ssu, Ching-te-ssu, Ling-yin-ssu**, and **Ching-tzu-ssu**. These five became known collectively as Wu-shan in Chinese. When the Japanese adopted the system during the late Kamakura (1185–1333) and early Ashikaga (1392–1568) periods, the actual number of Gozan temples varied. There were generally eleven Gozan monasteries, which included the five most influential monasteries located in Kamakura and five in Kyoto, all organized under the eleventh head monastery. The Kamakura Gozan monasteries included **Kenchô-ji, Engaku-ji, Jufuku-ji, Jôchi-ji**, and **Jômyô-ji**. The Kyoto Gozan monasteries included **Tenryû-ji, Shôkoku-ji, Kennin-ji, Tôfuku-ji**, and **Manju-ji**. **Nanzen-ji**, also located in Kyoto, served for many generations as

Tôfuku-ji, one of the Gozan temples in Kyoto.

the head monastery in the system. All of these monasteries were affiliated with the **Rinzai sect**. Lower ranking Rinzai temples that were part of the system were known as **jissatsu temples**. In some cases, the term *Gozan temple* may apply to any temple or monastery that was officially a part of the **Gozan system**, regardless of ranking.

Gozu School

The **Oxhead school**, an important **lineage** of early Chinese **Zen** founded by **Fa-jung** (594–657), a **Dharma heir** of the Fourth Patriarch **Tao-hsin** (580–651). Gozu is the Japanese transliteration of the Chinese name *Niu-t'ou*. See **Oxhead school**.

Gradual Enlightenment

(J. zengo) The concept that **enlightenment** may be attained gradually as a process of stages mastered over an extended period of time. Many schools of **Buddhism** teach a form of gradual enlightenment, although the concept is generally rejected by **Zen** teachers. In Zen texts, gradual enlightenment is regarded as an unorthodox concept; it is contrasted with the orthodox understanding of **sudden enlightenment**. Gradual enlightenment is most often associated with the **Northern school** of early Chinese Zen.

Gradual Teaching

(J. Zengyô) Teachings based on a belief in **gradual enlightenment**, in which enlightenment is seen as a progression through several stages, or levels, of attainment. Within **Zen** context, gradual teaching is generally associated with the **Northern school** of early Chinese Zen, which is contrasted with the **sudden enlightenment** teaching (tongyô) of the orthodox **Southern school**.

Great Assemblies

The formal lectures and discussion sessions held by the **abbot** in the Dharma hall (**hattô**) of a **Zen** monastery on specific occasions. The great assemblies are so called because the entire monastic community attends. See **daisan**.

Great Doubt

One of the three bases for the practice of **Zen**, along with Great Trust (**Daishinkon**) and Great Resolve (**Daifunshi**). According to Zen teachings, a practitioner must break through the Great Doubt to attain **enlightenment**. See **Daigi**.

Great Matter

A common Zen expression used to indicate the **Ultimate Truth** of **Buddhism**. It is used in various ways throughout Zen literature—it may mean the experience of **enlightenment** in one context, and the practice leading to that enlightenment in another. The English expression is a translation of the Japanese term *Daiji* (Ch. Ta-shih). See **Daiji**.

Great Renunciation

A term used in reference to an episode from the life of **Siddharta Gautama**, the historical **Buddha**. According to traditional accounts of his life, Siddharta experienced **four encounters** when he left his home and family to seek **enlightenment**. He saw an old man, a diseased person, and a corpse, which led to his contemplation of the problem of human **suffering**. Finally, his meeting with a religious mendicant motivated him to begin his own search for a solution to suffering. The episode is known as the great renunciation because Siddharta gave up a luxurious life filled with sensual pleasures. Legends maintain that he was raised in a palace, the beloved and pampered son of a ruling king, and was married to a lovely wife who had recently given birth to a son. The story highlights the contrasting values of duty to family and the religious quest for enlightenment; it is intended to stress the permeation of suffering even within the most pleasurable of human situations.

Great Resolve

One of the three essential motivating elements of **Zen** practice, along with Great Doubt (**Daigi**) and Great Trust (**Daishinkon**). The practitioner must have a deep determination to persevere in Zen practice. See **Daifunshi**.

Great Trust

One of the three essential bases of **Zen** practice, along with Great Doubt (**Daigi**) and Great Resolve (**Daifunshi**). The Zen practitioner must place great trust in the Buddhist teachings, the path of Zen, and his or her own teacher. See **Daishinkon**.

Great Vehicle

(J. daijô) **Mahayana Buddhism**. The Sanskrit term *mahayana* literally means "great vehicle." The phrase was coined within the tradition to distinguish newer developments in the first century C.E. from older teachings. See **Mahayana Buddhism**.

Guchû Shûkyû

(1323–1409) Japanese Rinzai **monk**. Guchû studied **Zen** in China and received **Dharma transmission** from Chi-hsiu Chi-liao. When he returned to Japan, he served as founding **abbot** at **Buttsû-ji**, an important independent Rinzai temple in Aki. He received the posthumous title Daitsû **Zenji**. His writings include the *Sôyo Shû* and the *Daitsû Zenji Goroku*. He is regarded as the founder of **Buttsû-ji Ha**, the Buttsû-ji branch of the **Rinzai sect**.

Gudô Tôshoku

(1579–1661) Japanese Rinzai **Zen monk** from the early Tokugawa period (1600–1867). Gudô was a leading figure within the lineage of the **Myôshin-ji**, where he led a reform movement to revitalize the practice of Rinzai. He served three times as **abbot** at Myôshin-ji and trained numerous disciples. Among his leading disciples was **Shidô**

Bu'nan (1603–1676), from whose line came the great Rinzai reformer **Hakuin Ekaku** (1685–1768). Gudô received the posthumous title Daien Hôkan **Kokushi**. He left behind no written works. See also **Rinzai sect**.

Gunin
(601–674) Japanese transliteration of **Hung-jen**, the Fifth Patriarch of Chinese **Zen**. See **Hung-jen**.

Gutei
The Japanese pronunciation for **Chü-chih**, a T'ang dynasty (618–907) master known for his "**One-finger Zen**." See **Chü-chih**.

Gyôdô
A ritual circumambulation around, or in front of the main image of the **Buddha** within the main hall of a **Zen** monastery. The members of the procession chant a sutra. The practice is derived from the ancient custom of walking in a circle around an image to show respect or pay homage. Typically, Zen **monks** and **nuns** no longer walk around the image, but form a procession walking in front of the image.

Gyôja
A Buddhist practitioner, especially Buddhist **monks** in the ancient tradition. The Japanese and related Chinese term was used to translate the Sanskrit term *âcârin*. In Japan, the term especially applies to ascetic practitioners like the **Yamabushi**, who build **merit** and spiritual power by combining strenuous physical training with meditative practices. Although written with the same characters as **anja**, an attendant **novice** at a **Zen** temple, the usage is completely different. See also **ascetic practices**.

Gyô-jû-za-ga
Going, staying, sitting, lying down. A very common **Zen** expression used to indicate all human action or the behavior of everyday life. Zen masters often use the expression to suggest that the practice of Zen is not limited to the hours spent in seated **meditation**, but that all aspects of life, even mundane activities, comprise the Buddhist way.

Gyônyû
"The entrance through practice," Japanese term for one of the **two entrances** (**ninyû**) to Buddhist **enlightenment**. Practice is said to include four basic types: hôongyô (endurance of hardships), zuiengyô (adapting to circumstances), mushogugyô (seeking nothing), and shôbôgyô (practicing in conformity with the **Dharma**). Gyônyû is the opposite of **rinyû**, or the entrance through reason.

Gyôyû
See **Taikô Gyôyû**.

Hachikan Jigoku

Also pronounced "Hakkan jigoku," the Japanese term for the **eight cold hells**, where inhabitants suffer various punishments related to severe cold. The Japanese names for the eight hells are 1) A'buda, 2) Nira'buda, 3) Aseta, 4) Kakaba, 5) Kokoba, 6) Upara, 7) Hadoma or Guren, and 8) Makahadoma or Daiguren. See **eight cold hells**.

Hachiman

The Japanese Shintô **kami** (deity) associated with archery (**kyûdô**) and war, who is revered as a **bodhisattva**, or **enlightened one**, in Japan. Hachiman is the deification of a historical figure, the Emperor Ojin (270–310 C.E.). During the Nara period (710–794), shrines to Hachiman were constructed beside national Buddhist temples (kokubunji), symbolizing Hachiman's role as a special guardian of **Buddhism** in Japan. Hachiman was one of the first Shintô kami to be identified by Buddhism as a bodhisattva; he was also sometimes regarded as a manifestation of the Amida buddha. See also **honji suijaku**.

Hachinetsu Jigoku

The **eight hot hells**, where inhabitants suffer various punishments, including searing heat. The eight hells are 1) Repeated Misery (Tôkatsu), 2) Black Ropes (Kokujô), 3) Mass **Suffering** (shugô), 4) Wailing (Kyôkan), 5) Great Wailing (Daikyôkan), 6) Searing Heat (Shônetsu), 7) Great Searing Heat (Daishônetsu), and 8) Incessant Suffering (Muken).

In Japan, **Genshin** (942–1017) described in detail the sufferings of the various hells in his *Ojôyôshû*, (*The Essentials of Salvation*). The hells are also popular subjects for religious paintings, often used to teach ordinary people the consequences of their actions (**karma**). See **eight hot hells**.

Haiku

Genre of Japanese poetry indirectly associated with **Zen**, alternatively known as **hokku**. Haiku are composed of seventeen syllables arranged in three lines of five, seven, and five syllables. The most famous of the Japanese Haiku poets was **Matsuo Bashô** (1644–1694), a lay practitioner of Zen whose poetry is said to reflect Zen influences. See also **lay believer**.

Hajahadai

Japanese transliteration of **Prajapati**, the Buddha's stepmother. See **Prajapati**.

Hajun

Papiyas, an evil heavenly king, also known in Japanese as Mahajun (the Demon Papiyas) and Maô (the Demon King). Hajun is the Japanese pronunciation of the Chinese transliteration of the original Sanskrit name. See **Papiyas**.

Hakkai

"**Eight precepts**," a Japanese abbreviation for Hassaikai. See **eight precepts**.

Hakuin Ekaku

(1685–1768) The great Japanese **Zen** reformer of the Tokugawa period (1600–1867) who revitalized the practice of Rinzai, one of the three major sects of Zen, in Japan. Hakuin's influence on early modern and modern Rinzai is so strong that many refer to it as Hakuin Zen. Hakuin was born in the village of Hara at the foot of Mount Fuji. His secular name was Sugiyama Iwajirô. Hakuin entered monastic life at age fifteen, when he took the **tonsure** at the local Zen temple, Shôin-ji. He spent many years on **pilgrimage**, beginning in 1705, seeking his way through his many doubts. According to his own account, he determined his fate one day in Gifu Prefecture where he was staying with his friend Baô, a Rinzai monk, at Zuiun-ji. The **abbot** there had a large library comprising Taoist, Confucian, and Buddhist texts. On a day when the books were laid out in the sun, Hakuin picked one up without checking the title. He decided that this random choice would determine his future. His selection was a collection of biographies of Chinese Zen masters, and he decided to pursue the Zen path toward **enlightenment**.

Hakuin achieved his first enlightenment experience in 1708 at Eigan-ji in Niigata. Shôtetsu, the abbot there, refused to acknowledge the experience, as did the other masters he sought out. Eventually, he made his way to Nagano where he became the disciple of **Dôkyô Etan** (1642–1721) at Shôju-an, but he remained only eight months before he was called home by the illness of a former teacher. Throughout his life, Hakuin regarded Dôkyô as his master. It is unclear whether or not he received Dôkyô's formal sanction, but tradition regards Hakuin as Dôkyô's **Dharma heir**, fully qualified to take on Dôkyô's teaching after that master's death. In 1710, he once again took up residence at Shôin-ji in Hara. At that time, Hakuin was practicing a regime so austere that he drove himself to a nervous breakdown, which is often referred to as the "**Zen sickness**" (J. Zenbyô). He sought the help of the Taoist hermit Hakuyûshi and cured himself.

Hakuin continued to travel, practicing in various places with different masters. He later wrote that throughout this period of his life he had many enlightenment experiences, which grew more profound. He spent a short time at **Myôshin-ji** in 1718, where he was appointed abbot. He then returned to Hara and settled down permanently at Shôin-ji. Hakuin had no need to remain at a major monastery since disciples came to him in great numbers. He taught for many years, often lecturing on the important **kôan collections** and **recorded sayings** of earlier Zen masters. He also wrote extensively: a few of his writings have been translated into English by Yampolsky and Waddell.

Hakuin trained his disciples using stern methods. He is credited with formulating the systematic use of kôan still in use within the **Rinzai sect** today, although his immediate disciples no doubt completed the task. Hakuin required students to continue the practice of **zazen** throughout their career, believing that not only should they contemplate kôan in order to attain an initial experience of enlightenment (J. **kenshô**), but use zazen as a lifelong means of deepening that experience. He developed a number of his own kôan, including the famous Sound of One Hand (J. Sekishû), which he used with beginners.

Hakuin did extensive work among the common people, writing several popular hymns, miracle stories, and other religious texts in the vernacular language. He is known as an artist, especially his ink painting, **calligraphy**, and sculpture. His leading disciples include **Tôrei Enji** (1721–1792) and **Gasan Jitô** (1727–1797). He received the title Shinki Dokumyô **Zenji** after his death. His many written works include *Itsumadegusa*, **Orategama**, and *Yasen Kanna*.

Waddell, Norman. *The Essential Teachings of Zen Master Hakuin: A Translation of the* Sokko-roku Kaien-fusetsu. Boston, MA: Shambhala, 1994.

Yampolsky, Philip B., trans. *The Zen Master Hakuin: Selected Writings.* New York: Columbia University Press, 1971.

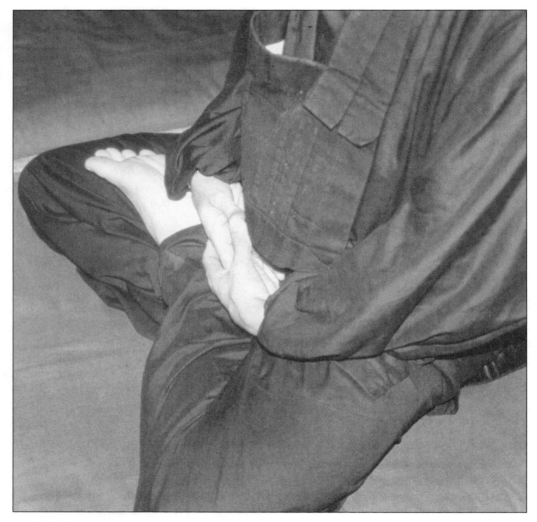

The half-lotus position is a classic meditation posture where the one foot rests upon the other thigh.

Half-Lotus Position

(J. hanka fuza) An alternative posture used for seated **meditation** (**zazen**). When seated in the half-lotus position, the left foot usually rests on the right thigh with both knees resting on the cushion (**zaniku**). Many people find the half-lotus position easier to maintain than the full lotus position over long periods of meditation. It is also possible to alternate the position and rest the right foot on the left thigh. Classical **Zen** texts on seated meditation, including the *Tso-ch'an I* by Ch'ang-lu Tsung-tse and **Dôgen Kigen's** (1200–1253) *Fukan Zazengi* mention this posture.

Han

Sounding boards used to signal various events throughout the monastery, including meal times and the end of **meditation** sessions. The term most commonly refers to rectangular wooden boards that hang outside certain temple buildings (**shichidô garan**), including the **abbot's** hall and the monks' hall (**sôdô**), among others. It may also be used more generically to signify the entire class of sounding instruments, including both the wooden boards and the bronze gongs called **umpan**.

Wooden han are all shaped identically, although they may be distinguished by specific names based on

The han is a rectangular wooden board used to signal various events
in a monastery, such as meal times or meditation sessions.

their location. They are sounded simultaneously at specified times to alert the entire monastic community of an upcoming transition or event. To strike the han, one grasps it by an attached handle and uses a wooden mallet. Typically, the boards have verses inscribed on them, although these may differ by sect and monastery. According to the *Obaku Shingi*, the han outside the **meditation hall** at Obaku temples should read, "Say to the whole assembly that life and death are the great matter. **Impermanence** is swift upon us. Let each one awaken to this. Be reverent, and refrain from self-indulgence." See also **Obaku sect**.

Hana Matsuri

"Flower Festival," the popular Japanese name for **Buddha Day**, the day commemorating the birth of Shakyamuni **Buddha** (**Siddharta Gautama**). The holiday is known more formally in Japanese as Gôtane. Throughout East Asia, the eighth day of the fourth lunar month was traditionally observed as Buddha Day. Today, the Japanese celebrate Hana Matsuri according to the modern calendar on April 8. Typically, images of the infant Siddharta Gautama are placed within a small shrine draped with flowers. Believers then take turns ladling sweetened tea, known as amacha, or perfumed water over the image. This recalls the episode in the birth accounts of the Buddha when the gods and other heavenly beings bathed the newborn with pure water. See also **kanbutsu**.

Hanazonokai

A Japanese lay association of Rinzai **Buddhism**, founded by the **Myôshin-ji** branch of the **Rinzai sect** in 1947. The purpose of the organization is to spread

Zen Buddhism among the general populace. Branches of the association exist in Korea, Mexico, the United States, and other countries. The organization is named for **Emperor Hanazono** (1297–1348), under whose patronage the Myôshin-ji was originally constructed. See also **lay believer**.

Handaikan

The **monk** or **nun** responsible for serving the rice to the rest of the monastic community at mealtime. This responsibility rotates among the monks or nuns in residence. In the **Rinzai sect**, the term sometimes refers to the monks' hall (**sôdô**).

Hanka Fuza

Term that means "sitting in the **half-lotus position**" in Japanese. Also called Bosatsu-za, the **bodhisattva** position. See **half-lotus position**.

Hannya

Wisdom. Hannya is the Japanese transliteration of the Sanskrit term *prajna*. See **prajna**.

Hannya Shingyô

Heart Sutra, an abbreviated Japanese title for the **Prajna**-paramita-hrdaya-sutra (T. 8, no. 251). The full title in Japanese is Maka Hannya Haramitta Shingyô. See **Heart Sutra**.

Hannya Zanmai

The **samadhi**, or state of consciousness of perfect wisdom, in which one realizes the reality of **emptiness** through wisdom. Hannya zanmai is the Japanese transliteration of the original Sanskrit term *prajna samadhi*. The realization of emptiness is regarded within the Buddhist tradition as the moment of **enlightenment**.

Han–shan

(J. Kanzan) Chinese poet and Buddhist practitioner of the T'ang dynasty (618–907) about whom little is known. Scholars tentatively date his life at the late eighth to early ninth century. He lived in Han-shan cave on Mount T'ien-t'ai, from which he drew his name. He is known as an eccentric whose behavior was quite erratic. Tradition maintains, however, that he had a deep understanding of **Buddhism** and that his unusual behavior was intended to express the principles of **Zen**. He is said to have disappeared mysteriously; later generations identified him as an incarnation of the **bodhisattva** Manjusri. Portraits of him were popular among Zen students in China and Japan. He is usually pictured with a writing scroll, and he is often paired with his friend and fellow hermit, Shih-te (J. Jittoku), who holds a broom because he worked in the temple kitchen. His poetry, comprised of approximately three hundred verses, is collected in the *Han-shan Shih* (J. Kanzanshi). The Japanese Rinzai master **Hakuin Ekaku** (1685–1768) wrote a commentary on Han-shan's three hundred poems. See also **Rinzai sect**.

Han-shan Shih

"Poems of Han-shan" (J. Kanzanshi), the collected poems of the Chinese poet and **Zen** practitioner Han-shan. This collection of approximately three hundred verses has long been popular among Zen students, and several commentaries have been written on it. The Japanese Rinzai master **Hakuin Ekaku** (1685–1768), for example, wrote a commentary on the collection, known as the *Kanzanshi Sendai Kimon*. See also **Rinzai sect**.

Han-shan Te-ch'ing

Chinese Rinzai master (1546–1623) of the late Ming period (1368–1644). **Han-shan** was one of a small group of masters who brought about a revival of **Buddhism** in the late Ming period. He advocated a combined practice of Zen **meditation** and **Pure Land** devotion to **Amida buddha**. Although he was a Zen

monk, he continually chanted the name of Amida (Ch. nien-fo; J. **nembutsu**) and claimed that he once had a vision of Amida in a dream. See also **dual practice** and **Rinzai sect**.

Hsu, Sung-peng. *A Buddhist Leader in Ming China: The Life and Thought of Han-shan Te-ch'ing, 1546–1623.* University Park, PA: Pennsylvania State University Press, 1979.

Hanshô

A temple bell shaped like the **ogane**, the largest of the monastery bells, but small enough to hang under the eaves of a temple building. The hanshô is sounded by striking its side with a wooden hand mallet. See also **denshô**.

Hara

The colloquial Japanese term for the lower abdomen, known more formally as **tanden**. Various systems of Asian **meditation** identify the hara as the central core of the individual or as one of the body's energy centers. One method of **Zen** concentration focuses the attention on the hara, especially its movement as one inhales and exhales.

Haraizai

Offenses that consist of defeat, which are the most serious offenses against the **monastic code** a Buddhist **monk** or **nun** can commit. The word *haraizai* is the Japanese transliteration of the Sanskrit term *parajika*. See **parajika**.

Hashin Kyûji

Needle and **moxa**. This term refers to the mundane activities of sewing robes and burning moxa, a flammable substance obtained from the leaves of the mugwort plant. In traditional Zen monasteries, **monks** and **nuns** sewed their own robes. In addition, they patched and repaired damaged robes to extend their wear. The

monastic code limits the number of robes an individual can own at one time and recommends that old robes be completely worn out before a monk or nun acquires a new one. Monks burned moxa on their skin as a medicinal treatment for sore legs and other minor ailments. These activities were typically undertaken on bath day at Zen monasteries, when the regular **meditation** schedule was not observed. Although these activities may seem separate from the Zen practice of meditation, they nevertheless typify the mindfulness of the Zen life.

Hassaikai

The "eight precepts of abstinence" observed by lay people on specific days of the month. The eight precepts are 1) not to kill living beings; 2) not to steal; 3) to abstain from sexual misconduct; 4) not to lie; 5) not to take intoxicants; 6) not to eat after noon; 7) not to adorn the body with perfume, flowers, jewelry, etc., and not to participate in public entertainment, including dancing, plays, singing, etc.; and 8) not to use a luxurious bed. See **eight precepts**.

Hasshiki

Japanese term for the **eight consciousnesses** that make up the human process of perception according to the **Yogachara school** (Hossô) of **Mahayana Buddhism**. The eight consciousnesses are 1) sight consciousness (genshiki), 2) sound consciousness (nishiki), 3) smell consciousness (bishiki), 4) taste consciousness (zesshiki), 5) tactile consciousness (shinshiki), 6) mind consciousness (ishiki), 7) ego consciousness (manashiki) and 8) the storehouse or **alaya consciousness** (arayashiki). See **eight consciousnesses**.

Hasshôdô

"Holy **Eightfold Path**," the Japanese term for the Eightfold Path of **Buddhism**. See **Eightfold Path**.

Hassu

Japanese term for **Dharma heir**. A student who qualifies to succeed his or her master in teaching disciples and transmitting the Dharma. See **Dharma heir**.

Hatsu

Japanese term for **begging bowl**; also pronounced "hachi." The largest of a set of nested eating bowls that **Zen monks** and **nuns** receive at **ordination**. This bowl corresponds to the ancient begging bowl used by Buddhist mendicants to collect donations of food from **lay believers**. There are a number of related Japanese terms, including hou, jihatsu (**begging alms**), and ôryôki.

Hatsui

An alternative pronunciation for "**hoi**," the place where one eats one's meals in a **Zen** monastery. See **hoi**.

Hatsunehan

Japanese transliteration of "**parinirvana**." See **parinirvana**.

Hattô

The **Dharma** hall; the main assembly and lecture hall at a **Zen** monastery. The hattô is one of the seven buildings (**shichidô garan**) that form the heart of any Zen monastery. It is generally located behind the **Butsuden**, or Buddha hall, and replaces the kôdô, or lecture hall, found in monasteries of other Buddhist schools. It is used for lectures, as well as for discussions, question and answer sessions (**mondô**), and ritual services. Unlike other lecture halls, the Zen Dharma hall does not usually have an image of a buddha or **bodhisattva** enshrined within it; instead, the **abbot** is said to represent the buddhas and **patriarchs** when he takes his place on the central dais to instruct the community on the Dharma.

The building is designed to hold the entire monastic community, which gathers there for morning assemblies (**jôdô**) and great assemblies (**daisan**). For this reason, most Dharma halls are large, without much internal furnishing that would take up space. The main focus of the hall is the central dais, from which the abbot addresses the community. The dais is approached by three sets of stairs. The abbot's formal Dharma chair (**hôza**) holds a prominent place on the dais. Many of the Dharma halls in Japanese Zen monasteries have a high circular ceiling adorned with a dramatic painting of a dragon.

Heart Sutra

(J. Hannya Shingyô) Prajna Paramita Hrdaya Sutra, an extremely brief sutra, only a single page in length, which presents the heart or essence of the Mahayana tradition. The original Sanskrit text was probably composed during the fourth century C.E. There are two versions in the Sanskrit, a shorter version with only the main body of the text and a longer version that includes an additional introduction and conclusion. In East Asia, the shorter version is more commonly used. There are several Chinese translations of the sutra; the most popular are those by **Kumarajiva** (T. 8, no. 250), completed in 402, and by Hsuan-tsang (T. 8, no. 251), completed in 648.

The Heart Sutra is among the most important of the **Buddhist scriptures** in China, Korea, and Japan. Buddhist **monks** and **nuns** of many sects, including the **Zen** schools, recite the sutra daily. In addition, many lay Buddhists commit the sutra to memory and recite it as a prayer. See also **lay believer**. An English translation from the Sanskrit can be found in Conze's *Buddhist Scriptures: A Bibliography* and Suzuki's *Manual of Zen Buddhism*.

Conze, Edward. *Buddhist Scriptures: A Bibliography*. Ed. Lewis Lancaster. New York: Garland, 1982.
Suzuki, Daisetz Teitaro. *Manual of Zen Buddhism*. New York: Grove Press, 1960.

Heaven

One of the six realms of existence into which **sentient beings** may be reborn. According to the Buddhist understanding of existence, unenlightened sentient beings are trapped in a continual pattern of birth, death and **rebirth**. Actions in the present life determine the nature of future rebirths. Those who build up sufficient good **karma** may be reborn in one of the various heavens (J. ten). Like other possible rebirths, however, existence as a heaven-dweller is not eternal. Eventually, good karma is exhausted and even deities pass away, to be reborn in another realm. It should be noted that, in religious terms, heaven is not a completely desirable rebirth. While heaven dwellers do not suffer as intensely as sentient beings in the lower realms of existence, they are not able to make spiritual progress toward release from the cycle of rebirth. In that regard, birth as a human being is the most desirable outcome.

In addition to the realm of the gods recognized by all parts of the Buddhist tradition, some schools of **Mahayana Buddhism** believe in the existence of **Buddha Lands**, or **Pure Lands**, which are somewhat reminiscent of heavens. Buddha Lands are envisioned as other worlds, beautiful to all the senses, where sentient beings may readily hear the **Dharma** from a buddha and practice Buddhism.

Hebiichigo

A letter in two segments, written by **Hakuin Ekaku** (1685–1768), a Rinzai **monk**, in 1754. The letter, composed as a sermon on the **Dharma**, was addressed to Ikeda Munemasa, daimyô, or military leader, of Iyo province. In the letter, Hakuin discusses the behavior and virtue of a beneficent ruler and explains the karmic repercussions of tyrannical rule. An English translation can be found in Philip Yampolsky's *The Zen Master Hakuin*. See also **Rinzai sect**.

Yampolsky, Philip B, trans. *The Zen Master Hakuin: Selected Writings*. New York: Columbia University Press, 1967.

Hekiganroku

The Japanese title for the *Pi-yen Lu* (T. 48, no.), a classic Chinese **Zen kôan** collection in ten segments. The full title in Japanese is *Bukka Engo Zenji Hekiganroku, "The Blue Cliff Record of Zen Master Yuan-wu."* **Yüan-wu K'o-ch'in** (1063–1135; J. Engo Kokugon), the Sung dynasty Rinzai **monk** completed the work in 1125; it was first published in 1128. The *Hekiganroku* grew out of a series of **sermons** on an earlier collection of one hundred kôan put together by **Hsüeh-tou Ch'ung-hsien** (J. Setchô Jûken) in the eleventh century. Hsueh-tou originally selected his kôan from the *Ching-te Ch'üan-teng Lu* (J. *Keitoku Dentôroku*) and the **recorded sayings** of **Yun-men Wen-yen** (864–949). To each kôan, Hsueh-tou appended a verse of his own as a commentary. Yüan-wu added an introduction as well as notes and commentaries on each kôan and related verse.

The original edition of the *Hekiganroku* was destroyed by **Ta-hui Tsung-kao** (1089–1163), a disciple of Yuan-wu. Ta-hui, a prominent Rinzai master in his own right, collected all the printed copies of the text that he could find and burned them. He also destroyed the original woodblocks. It is uncertain why Ta-hui took this action, but some scholars believe that he was concerned that Zen practitioners would become too reliant on a written text. The text as we know it was pieced together later by a lay practitioner named Chang Ming-yuan in 1300. See also **lay believer** and **Rinzai sect**.

Hekiganshû

Alternative title for the *Hekiganroku*. See *Hekiganroku*.

Hekigo

Kôan series studied "after the *Hekiganroku*," a classic Chinese **Zen**

kôan collection. During the medieval period (1185–1600), **Zen monks** of the Japanese Rinzai school worked through a series of three hundred kôan. The system included three sets of one hundred kôan each: the **Hekizen**, the *Hekiganroku*, and the Hekigo. The manner in which the kôan were used is unknown, since the medieval system was replaced by the current practice developed in the eighteenth century by the reformer **Hakuin Ekaku** (1685–1768). See also **Rinzai sect**.

Hekikan

"Wall contemplation;" to meditate facing a blank wall. The practice is said to derive from **Bodhidharma**, the traditional founder of **Zen** in China. According to legend, Bodhidharma spent nine years in seated **meditation** (**zazen**) facing a cliff wall outside his small hermitage on Mount Sung. The Zen school preserves that practice for: when a young person first requests entrance to a Zen monastery, he or she must spend up to three days in isolation, doing zazen facing a blank wall.

The term first appears in the *Treatise on the Two Entrances and Four Practices* (Ch. *Erh-ju Ssu-hsing Lun*), traditionally attributed to Bodhidharma. The text reads in part: "If one discards the false and takes refuge in the True, one resides frozen in 'wall contemplation' (pi kuan), [in which] self and other, ordinary person and sage, are one and the same. . ." (McRae, p. 103) Some modern scholars maintain that the expression means not to face a wall while meditating, but to meditate like a wall.

McRae, John R. *The Northern School and the Formation of Early Ch'an Buddhism*. Honolulu, HI: University of Hawaii Press, 1986.

Hekizen

Kôan studied "before the *Hekiganroku*." During the medieval period (1185–1600), **Zen monks** of the Japanese Rinzai school worked through a series of three hundred kôan. The system included three sets of one hundred kôan each: the Hekizen, the *Hekiganroku*, and the **Hekigo**. The Hekizen was the initial set of approximately one hundred kôan to be mastered before moving on to the *Hekiganroku* itself. See also **Rinzai sect**.

Hell

One of the six realms of existence into which **sentient beings** are born. According to the Buddhist understanding of existence, unenlightened sentient beings are trapped in a continual pattern of birth, death, and **rebirth**. Actions in the present life determine the nature of future rebirths. Those who commit serious acts of evil create bad **karma**, which results in birth in one of the various hells (J. **jigoku**). Like other possible rebirths, existence as a hell-dweller is not eternal, and those **suffering** in hell will eventually exhaust their bad karma and attain higher births.

The Buddhist tradition graphically describes the punishments suffered in various hells, especially the **eight cold hells** and the **eight hot hells**. The purpose of these descriptions is to warn people about the karmic consequences of their actions. **Zen** masters sometimes describe the various hells as the present condition of wicked individuals rather than the punishment waiting in a future existence. Those individuals who kill for sport or participate in other evil activities are said to be hell dwellers.

Henshô Goi

"The **five ranks** of the real and the apparent," a standard Japanese re-statement of the five ranks of **Tung-shan Liang-chieh** (807–869), the popular **Zen** name for Mount Feng-mu in present day Hupeh. See **five ranks**.

Henzan

To travel on a **pilgrimage** of visiting **Zen** masters. The term *henzan* may be used synonymously with *angya*. **Dôgen Kigen** (1200–1253) included an essay entitled "Henzan" in his *Shôbôgenzô* (Chapter 62). See **pilgrimage**.

Hiei-zan

Mount Hiei, a mountain situated to the northeast of Kyoto, Japan. Hiei-zan is the site of **Enryaku-ji**, the headquarters for the Tendai school of Japanese **Buddhism**. The Japanese Buddhist monk **Saichô** (767–822) founded the temple there in 782. Because of its auspicious location to the east of Kyoto, Mount Hiei and the temples on its slopes were traditionally regarded as the guardians of the capital city. As many as 3,000 temples at one time stood on the mountain, but all of them were burned to the ground by the military leader Oda Nobunaga in 1571. See also **Enryaku-ji**.

Higan

Literally meaning "the other shore," the Japanese term *higan* derives from a Chinese rendering of the Sanskrit word *pâramitâ*, meaning to cross over from this shore of **suffering** to the other shore of **nirvana**, the realm where suffering ceases. The word *higan* can therefore be used to express the attainment of **enlightenment**.

In Japan, the term *higan* is often used to denote the spring and autumn equinoxes, since rituals known as **higan-e** are held at those times. Alternatively, higan may also be used as an abbreviated reference to the higan-e rituals themselves.

Higan-e

Buddhist rituals held in Japan at the spring and autumn equinoxes, which are observed on March 18–24 and September 20–26 according to the modern calendar. Services are offered at Buddhist temples of all denominations to aid **sentient beings**, especially the spirits of the dead, to pass from this shore of **suffering** to the other shore (**higan**) of **enlightenment**. On a more popular level, Japanese families observe the festival period by visiting family graves, cleaning them, and making **offerings** of flowers, water, and festival foods in honor of deceased family members.

Hijiri

Literally, a holy person or a sage. The Japanese term has a variety of uses in the context of **Buddhism**. Since about the mid-Heian period (794–1185), it has been a term for wandering Buddhist ascetics who spread Buddhism among the common people, as well as for mountain ascetics who practiced austerities in the mountains. In some cases these ascetics were formally ordained **monks**, in other cases they were self-ordained. In the early period most hijiri operated independently, outside the confines of the existing Buddhist monastic system. Buddhism at this time was largely associated with the elite classes and thus under close government scrutiny: the government tried to limit the activities of hijiri in order to control the spread of Buddhism among the common people. Later, in the Kamakura period (1185–1333), various schools of Buddhism incorporated hijiri into their ranks as a part of their program to spread their teachings on a more popular level. In this capacity, groups of hijiri from Mount Kôya helped to popularize Shingon Buddhism, especially popular devotion to its founder **Kûkai** (774–835).

Kûya (903–972), sometimes pronounced Kôya, is a prime example of the early hijiri. Kûya was a Tendai **monk** who traveled throughout the Japanese countryside, mostly working among the common people to promote **Pure Land** practice and belief. He is said to have constantly chanted the **nembutsu**, calling on the name of **Amida buddha**. For this reason, he is called an Amida hijiri. See also **Shingon sect** and **Tendai sect**.

Hô, a wooden gong in the shape of a fish, is sounded to announce meal times in a Zen monastery.

Hori, Ichiro. *Folk Religion in Japan: Continuity and Change.* Ed. Joseph M. Kitagawa and Alan L. Miller. Chicago, IL: University of Chicago Press, 1968.

Hinayana Buddhism

A derogatory name used by the **Mahayana** Buddhist tradition to describe the early Buddhist teachings as well as the surviving Theravada school of **Buddhism**. The term literally means "small vehicle" or "lesser vehicle," and is contrasted with the great vehicle of Mahayana.

Hinko

"Raising the torch," the ritual action of starting the cremation fire at a funeral service. Today, the hinko is a symbolic gesture performed during the service. The Buddhist **monk** leading the funeral service symbolically lights the cremation fire with a torch. In practice, the term sometimes refers to the final words addressed to the deceased by the officiant at the funeral. Hinko is performed as one of the nine ritual actions, (**kubutsuji**) comprising the funeral services for an **abbot** or other prominent member of the monastic community. It is also one of the three ritual actions that characterize Buddhist funerals for ordinary monks and **lay believers**. See **ako**.

Hinpotsu

"Taking hold of the **whisk**," a formal sermon given by a master from the high seat. The name derives from the first action taken by the master after assuming his place on the high seat, which is to take hold of the **hossu** or whisk, a symbol of the master's authority to teach the **Dharma**. According to **Zen monastic codes**, the **abbot** or another senior officer serving the monastery was obliged to give a hinpotsu sermon four times each year, on the opening and closing days of the summer and winter retreats. In the Zen corpus, collections of hinpotsu **sermons** represent a genre in Zen literature.

In the **Gozan system** of Zen temples in medieval Japan (1185–1600), hinpotsu came to refer to a qualifying exam undertaken by **monks** who wished to advance to the highest level of seniority. Senior monks were required to pass the hinpotsu exam before they qualified to serve as abbot at a major temple or monastery. The exam was held on a yearly basis, when senior monks would take the high seat in place of the abbot and engage in an exchange of Zen questions and answers (**mondô**) with younger monks. If an individual's performance was deemed acceptable by the abbot, the monk would receive a hinpotsu certificate.

Hô

A wooden gong in the shape of a long fish with a pearl in its mouth used in **Zen** monasteries. In some cases, the hô may have the shape of a dragon head on a fish body. In modern Zen monasteries, the hô hangs outside the dining hall or monks' hall (**sôdô**). It is sounded by striking it with a wooden stick and is used to announce meal times in a Zen monastery. In former periods, the hô was known as the **mokugyo** (literally, "wooden fish"). For this reason, it is sometimes still called mokugyo today, although that term generally refers to a distinct instrument used during Buddhist ritual services.

Hô

(2) Japanese translation for the Sanskrit word *Dharma*. It may refer to 1) the teachings of the **Buddha** or the **Buddhist scriptures**; 2) Buddhist morality, or the **Buddhist path**; 3) Reality or Truth, the realization of things as they really are; and 4) elements of phenomenal existence, things, mental constructions, and events. See **Dharma**.

Hôben

(**Expedient means**) Any teaching device employed by a **buddha** or another Buddhist teacher in order to convey aspects of the **Dharma** to individuals. *Hôben* is the Japanese translation of the Sanskrit term *upaya* (expedient means) or *upaya-kaushalya*. See **expedient means**.

Hôgen Bun'eki

Japanese rendering of **Fa-yen Wen-i**, a Chinese **Zen monk** who founded the **Fa-yen school**. See **Fa-yen Wen-i**.

Hôgen School

The Japanese name for the **Fa-yen school**, a **lineage** of Chinese **Zen** active during the T'ang dynasty (618–907). See **Fa-yen school**.

Hôgo

Teachings on **Zen** Buddhism presented by a master to disciples either orally (as a sermon) or in writing. Hôgo represent an important genre of Zen instructional literature, which encompasses a wide range of materials, including formal **sermons** in classical Chinese and less formal instructions conveyed in colloquial language. The term is the Japanese rendering of the Chinese word *fa-yu*, which literally means "**Dharma** words." In Japan, it is typical to contrast the more formal hôgo composed in classical Chinese with the more popular **kana hôgo**, informal sermons written in Japanese.

Hoi

The designated place within a **Zen** monastery where a **monk** or **nun** sits to eat daily meals. The term literally means "the place for the **begging bowls**." In Japanese Sôtô monasteries, monks and nuns eat, sleep, and sit in **meditation** at the same spot in the monks' hall (**sôdô**). In Rinzai and Obaku monasteries, there is generally a separate dining hall. In either case, assigned places are determined by length of practice and rank. Also pronounced "hatsui." See also **Obaku sect**, **Rinzai sect**, and **Sôtô sect**.

Hôji

Literally meaning "**Dharma** matter," the term was originally used for any Buddhist ritual observance. It now refers specifically to **memorial services** offered for deceased family members. In Japan, memorial services are conducted at specified intervals from the date of death, continuing for a number of years. During the primary period of mourning (**chûin**), which lasts forty-nine days, services are offered every seventh day. After that, services mark the hundredth day, the first, third, seventh, thirteenth, seventeenth, twenty-third, twenty-seventh, and thirty-third anniversaries of death. In some cases, fiftieth and hundredth anniversaries are likewise marked. In the case of extremely influential people, including founders, memorial services may be observed perpetually every fifty or one-hundred years.

Hôji

(2) Japanese transliteration of **Fa-ch'ih** (635–702), Fourth Patriarch of the **Oxhead school** of early **Zen**. See **Fa-ch'ih**.

Hôjin

"Bliss body," the Japanese translation of the Sanskrit term *sambhogakaya*. Within the **Mahayana** Buddhist doctrine of the **three bodies of the Buddha** (J. sanshin), the sambhogakaya is understood as manifestations of the eternal Buddha (J. hosshin; Sk. **Dharmakaya**) in other celestial worlds. See **sambhogakaya**.

Hoji Zazen

Afternoon session of **zazen**, one of the four periods of meditation (J. **shiji zazen**), observed daily in **Zen** monasteries. Although the exact hours differ by monastery, **sôshin zazen** is held after lunch, sometime between three o'clock and five o'clock.

Hôjô

The **abbot's** quarters at a Buddhist temple or monastery. The **Zen** school uses the expression more regularly than other Buddhist schools. In the Zen sect, the term may also be used as a polite title for the abbot or chief **monk**. The term *hôjô* literally means "ten-foot square," a reference to the bedroom of **Vimalakirti** as described in the **Vimalakirti Sutra**. Vimalakirti, the main character of the sutra, was a wealthy lay Buddhist of deep wisdom who attained **enlightenment** while still a lay person. According to the sutra, he successfully debated with the **bodhisattva** Manjusri and taught a gathering of 32,000 disciples in his small ten-foot square room.

Although the name suggests the cramped quarters of a simple **meditation** hut, Zen hôjô are typically large complexes. The abbot of a Zen monastery traditionally uses his quarters not only for sleep, private meditation, and study, but also as a place of instruction for the entire community. According to Zen **monastic codes**, evening instruction, known as "small assemblies," take place within the abbot's quarters. In the **Rinzai sect**, personal interviews between master and disciples likewise occur in the hôjô. Since the hôjô needed to accommodate the entire monastic community on some occasions, they are often large structures, divided into private inner quarters and outer public areas. See also **lay believer**.

Collcutt, Martin. *Five Mountains: The Rinzai Zen Monastic Institution in Medieval Japan*. Cambridge, MA: Harvard University Press, 1981.

Hôjô

(2) "Releasing living things," or the Buddhist practice of buying captive

animals, such as birds, fish, and turtles, for the sole purpose of releasing them. The term is also used as an abbreviated expression for Hôjôe, the Buddhist ceremony celebrating the release of captive animals. The ritual was typically held on the fifteenth day of the eighth lunar month, and became popular in both China and Japan as a means to promote **compassion** for living beings and to build **merit**.

In China, T'ien-t'ai monasteries commonly held Hôjôe rituals, since the founder of the school, **Chih-i** (538–597), favored the practice. Chih-i designated a specially constructed pond on Mount T'ien-t'ai for the purpose of releasing fish. In Japan, the practice initially gained the support of the imperial family and the aristocracy, who considered it both a merit builder and a pleasant pastime. Special ponds, known in Japanese as hôjô iki, were constructed at some Buddhist temples and Shintô shrines for the ceremonies. The **Zen** master **Yin-yüan Lung-ch'i** (1594–1673), founder of the Obaku Zen sect, favored the ceremony and included a pond for the release of captive fish on the grounds of **Mampuku-ji**, the main Obaku monastery. See also **Obaku sect** and **T'ien-t'ai school**.

Hôjô Regents

The Hôjô family was a **samurai** clan that governed Japan as regents (J. shikken) to the **shôgun** during the Kamakura period (1185–1333). They were patrons of **Zen Buddhism**, beginning with Tokiyori (1227–1263), the fifth regent. The Hôjô helped to establish Zen as an independent school in Japan. They invited prominent Chinese Zen masters to visit and settle in Japan, built many large monasteries in Kamakura and Kyoto, and began the **Gozan** (Five Mountain) **system** of officially sponsored Zen temples throughout the country.

Hôjô Sadatoki

(1271–1311) The seventh **Hôjô regent**; he showed an interest in **Zen** both as a form of personal religious practice and as a cultural resource. He practiced Zen **meditation** under the guidance of the Chinese master **I-shan I-ning** (1247–1317) and invited the Chinese Sôtô master **Tung-ming Hui-jih** (1272–1340) to come to Japan to serve as **abbot** at several of the major monasteries in Kamakura. Sadatoki became involved in issues of monastic discipline, issuing a list of regulations for Zen monasteries in 1294. He also oversaw the first introduction of the **Gozan system** (Five Mountain) of officially sponsored Zen temples. He took the **tonsure**—shaving the head at **ordination** as an indication of the break from ordinary secular life and dedication to monastic practice—in 1301 and continued to govern from retirement until his death in 1311. See also **Sôtô sect**.

Hôjô Tokiyori

The fifth of the **Hôjô regents** who governed during the Kamakura period (1185–1333). Tokiyori (1227–1263) not only patronized **Zen** masters and temples, he undertook the serious practice of seated **meditation** (J. zazen) and of exchanges with a Zen master (J. **mondô**). He assumed the office of regent in 1246, the same year that the prominent Chinese Zen master **Lan-ch'i Tao-lung** (1213–1278) immigrated to Japan. The two men met in 1249, and Tokiyori immediately became the **monk's** patron. He first established Lan-ch'i as the head monk at Jôraku-ji, which he converted to a Zen temple for the master. Tokiyori then began the construction of **Kenchô-ji**, the first full-scale Zen monastery in Kamakura modeled on the Sung Chinese style. Tokiyori invited Lan-ch'i to serve as the founding **abbot**. Tokiyori also practiced Zen under the instruction of the Chinese master **Wu-an P'u-ning** (1197–1276), who granted the regent formal **inka** (official certification that a student has attained the same insight into the Dharma as the master) and a **Dharma robe** as a symbol of the transmission.

The hokkai jôin mudra is a meditative position of the hands and body.

Hôjô Tokimune

(1251–1284) The sixth **Hôjô regent**, and son of Tokiyori. Tokimune became a patron of **Zen** only late in his life; in his early years he was a supporter of the **Ritsu** sect. Like his father, he not only acted as patron, he also practiced Zen **meditation**. Tokimune was in power during the period of the Mongol invasions, and he built the Zen monastery **Engaku-ji** as a memorial for the Japanese warriors who died in battle against the invaders. He died suddenly at the age of thirty-four. On the day of his death, he had taken the **tonsure** and become a Zen **monk**.

Hokekyô

The most commonly used abbreviated Japanese title for the Myôhô rengekyô, the **Lotus Sutra**. See **Lotus Sutra**.

Hôki

A **vessel of the Dharma**. Sometimes pronounced hokki. An expression used to describe an individual with a deep capacity to master the Buddhist Dharma. In the **Zen** school, it refers to a Zen practitioner who is capable of attaining **enlightenment** and is worthy of transmitting the Dharma. A master will often use the term in reference to a prospective disciple who shows great promise. For example, when **Hui-k'o** (487–593), the Second Patriarch, cut off his arm and gave it to **Bodhidharma** to show his determination to practice Zen, Bodhidharma concluded that he was a worthy vessel of the Dharma.

Hokkai

Dharma realm, the Japanese translation of the Sanskrit term *dharmadhatu*. See **dharmadhatu**.

Hokkai Jôin

The "cosmic **mudra**," the body and hand position generally assumed during periods of **Zen meditation**. One forms the hokkai jôin by first crossing the legs either in the **lotus** or **half-lotus position**, with the left foot resting on the right thigh. The right hand rests on the left foot, palm facing up. The left hand rests on the right hand, with the tips of the thumbs lightly touching.

Hokkekyô

An alternative pronunciation for Hokekyô, the common abbreviated Japanese title for the Myôhô rengekyô, the **Lotus Sutra**. See **Lotus Sutra**.

Hokku

Sometimes pronounced "hôku," a term meaning "**Dharma** drum," a drum used during Buddhist services. The hokku found in Sôtô and Rinzai temples is one of two large drums (taiko) found in the Dharma hall (**hattô**). The hokku sits in the northeast corner of the hall, while the **saku**—the "tea drum" used to call monks to tea—sits in the northwest corner. They rest horizontally on wooden platforms and both ends may be played using two wooden sticks. The hokku is sounded at large assemblies of the monastic community, including such occasions as the **abbot** taking the high seat to give a formal sermon (**jôdô**), the small evening assembly (**shôsan**), and informal sermons (**fusetsu**).

The hokku found in Obaku temples is somewhat different in style and usage. Instead of resting horizontally, it sits vertically in a wooden frame, with only one surface for playing. It is used regularly at both morning and evening services. See also **Obaku sect**, **Rinzai sect**, and **Sôtô sect**.

Hokku

(2) See **Haiku**.

Hô Koji

Japanese rendering of "**Layman P'ang**." See **Layman P'ang**.

Hôkô-ji

A major Rinzai **Zen** monastery located in Tôtômi, Shizuoka Prefecture. Its formal name is Shin'ô-zan Hôkô-ji. The monastery was founded by **Mumon Gensen** (1323–1390) in 1384. It was originally an independent monastery (J. **rinka**), not associated with the **Gozan system**, and it now serves as the main headquarters for the Hôkô-ji branch of Rinzai Zen. See also **Rinzai sect**.

Hôkô-ji Ha

The **Hôkô-ji** branch of Rinzai, one of the fourteen contemporary branches of the Japanese **Rinzai sect**. The branch's main monastery, founded by **Mumon Gensen** (1323–1390), for the branch in Hôkô-ji, is located in Tôtômi, Shizuoka Prefecture. The Hôkô-ji Ha has 170 temples throughout Japan and claims approximately 590,000 adherents.

Hômon

"**Dharma** gate," usually a reference to the Buddhist teachings. See **Dharma gate**.

Hômyô

The "**Dharma** name" given to an individual upon taking the **tonsure** and becoming a **monk** or **nun**. The term also often denotes the posthumous Buddhist name granted to a lay person during Buddhist **memorial services** (**hôji**). The term *hômyô* is used less commonly than the related term *kaimyô*. See **kaimyô**.

The Hondô, formally known as Butsuden, is the main hall of a Buddhist temple where morning and evening services are held.

Hondô

The main hall at a Buddhist temple or monastery in which the main image (J. **honzon**) of a **buddha** or **bodhisattva** is enshrined. Morning and evening services are generally held in the Hondô. At **Zen** temples, the Hondô is formally known as the **Butsuden**, or Buddha hall. At other Buddhist temples, it is often known as the kondô, or golden hall. See **Butsuden**.

Hônen

(1133–1212) Japanese **Pure Land monk** of the late Heian (794–1185) and early Kamakura (1185–1333) periods, who founded the Jôdo sect of Pure Land **Buddhism** in Japan. Hônen began his career as a Tendai monk, and it was during his years as a Tendai monk on Mount Hiei that he first became familiar with the practices and teaching of Pure Land devotion. He became a believer in **Amida buddha** and chanted the **nembutsu** constantly. In 1175, after more than twenty years of train-ing and study on Mount Hiei, Hônen left the mountain and moved to the city of Kyoto where he began to publicly teach the exclusive practice of nembutsu (J. **senju** nembutsu). His disciples included people from every social class, Buddhist monks and **nuns**, commoners, and warriors. Conflict with established schools of Buddhism lead to his exile in 1207. He died in 1212 at the age of eighty. See also **Pure Land sect** and **Tendai sect**.

Hongaku

"**Original enlightenment,**" the Japanese term for the innate **Buddha Nature** possessed by all **sentient beings**. See **original enlightenment**.

Honji Suijaku

"Manifestation of the original state," a unique Japanese religious teaching that seeks to harmonize **Buddhism** with the indigenous Shintô belief in **kami** (indigenous Japanese deities or spirits).

According to the Honji suijaku theory, various buddhas and **bodhisattvas** take on specific forms in Japan as the native Japanese kami. The buddhas and bodhisattvas are identified as the honji, or original state, while the Shintô kami represent the suijaku, or localized manifestation. For example, **Amida buddha** is said to become manifest as the kami Kumano Gongen, and the Sun Goddess Amaterasu is a manifestation of the Sun Buddha Dainichi (**Mahavairochana Buddha**). The Honji suijaku theory developed gradually during the Heian (794–1185) and Kamakura (1185–1333) periods and allowed Buddhism to spread among the common people who remained devoted to the local kami. Lists of kami and their associated Buddhist figures date back to at least the twelfth century, but there is no real consistency between existing lists. Although some associations became fairly standard, the Honji suijaku theory was applied mainly at the local level.

Honrai No Menmoku

"**Original Face**," in Japanese. One of the most common **Zen** expressions, meaning **original enlightenment**. See **Original Face**.

Honshin

"**Original Mind**," a Japanese **Zen** expression meaning one's true nature or **Buddha Nature**. The term is contrasted with the deluded mind of ordinary beings. Zen teaches that everyone possesses the Original Mind of **enlightenment**, which is clouded by delusions. Through **meditation**, it is possible to realize the Original Mind, another expression for **satori**.

Honshô

"Original nature," a common Japanese **Zen** expression for **buddhahood** or **original enlightenment**. It is based on the affirmation that all **sentient beings** inherently possess the **Buddha Nature** and are originally buddhas. Enlightenment is the realization of one's original nature.

Honshô

(2) "Original lives," Japanese translation for **jataka tales** of the historical Buddha's previous lives. See **jataka tales**.

Honshôkai

"**Precepts** of the original nature," a **Mahayana** expression indicating that observance of the **bodhisattva precepts** is a natural expression of one's inherent **Buddha Nature**. Since one's true nature is Buddha Nature, the Buddhist precepts are not an external moral code.

Honzan

The main monastery for a school of **Buddhism**. In Japanese Buddhism, every independent sect of Buddhism has one or more honzan, which serve as headquarters for the sect or its branches. In many cases, the honzan also serves as the primary training monastery for Buddhist priests who will serve in local parish temples. Other temples within the sect are generally related to the main monastery as **branch temples**. The term *honzan* may also be used for the **main temple** within a large monastic complex to distinguish it from other subtemples (**tatchû**) on the grounds.

Although the practice of ranking temples is quite old, the hierarchical system of ranking temples as main and branch temples was not formalized until the Tokugawa period (1600–1867). At that time, every Buddhist temple and monastery was required to fit somewhere within a formal sectarian structure. Honzan were designated as the highest level, and as such, represented the sect as a whole to the government. Under the honzan were various levels of primary temples (honji) and branch temples (**matsuji**) that answered directly or indirectly to the honzan. Today, there are eighteen honzan within the **Zen** school. The **Sôtô sect** has two, Rinzai has fifteen (one for each of its main branches), and Obaku has one. See also **Obaku sect** and **Rinzai sect**.

Honzon

The main image at a Buddhist temple or monastery. The term literally means the "main honored one." In most cases, the image is a statue of a **buddha** or **bodhisattva**, but different schools of **Buddhism** favor different images. For example, **Pure Land** temples always have an image of **Amida buddha** enshrined as their honzon. In **Zen** temples, the honzon is most often an image of Shakyamuni (**Siddharta Gautama**), the historical Buddha. Often the central image is flanked by two other statues to form a triad. When Shakyamuni stands in the center, he is flanked by two prominent attendants from his lifetime or by buddhas from the past and future. Other popular images include the bodhisattva **Kannon**, Yakushi Buddha, or the bodhisattva **Jizô**.

Hôô

"The King of the **Dharma**," an epithet used for the **Buddha**. Hôô is the Japanese translation for the Sanskrit *Dharma Raja*. In Japanese history, the Empress Shôtoku (764–770 C.E.) bestowed the title of Hôô on a Buddhist **monk** named Dôkyô (d. 770) in 766 C.E. Dôkyô had designs on ascending the imperial throne himself, and the title conferred upon him the empress's full authority to determine government policy. See also **Dharma King**.

Hôrin

Japanese for **Wheel of the Dharma**. See **Wheel of the Dharma**.

Hôrinden

The Japanese title for the *Pao-lin Chuan*. See *Pao-lin Chuan*.

Hosshi

Dharma master, a Buddhist **monk** or **nun** well-versed in the Buddhist teachings who is competent to instruct others. The Japanese term may also be pronounced "hôshi." In some cases, it is used to distinguish scholar-monks from **meditation** masters (**zenji**) and **vinaya** masters (ritsuji).

Hosshin

"**Dharma** body," the Japanese translation of the Sanskrit term *Dharmakaya*. Within the Mahayana Buddhist doctrine of the **three bodies of the Buddha** (J. sanshin), the Dharmakaya is the highest aspect of the Buddha, and is understood as the absolute or eternal Buddha. In Japanese the other bodies of the Buddha are the hôjin (Sk. **sambhogakaya**), and the ojin (Sk. **nirmanakaya**). See **Dharmakaya**.

Hosshin Kôan

A category of **kôan** comprising those based on sayings from the classical **Zen** texts related to the concept of hosshin, or **Dharmakaya**. The word *hosshin* is the Japanese translation of the Sanskrit term *Dharmakaya*, literally meaning "body of the **Dharma**." Hosshin kôan generally include a comment or verse made by one of the great historical Zen masters when asked about the Dharmakaya. As a category of kôan, they encourage a deep understanding of the **Buddha Nature** that pervades all of reality.

Hosshin kôan represent the first of five stages of Rinzai kôan practice, which follow the initial **enlightenment** experience (**kenshô**). The process of working through five categories of kôan, established by the eighteenth century reformer **Hakuin Ekaku** (1685–1768) and his successors, remains standard practice in the Rinzai school in Japan today. The practitioner undertakes the contemplation of hosshin kôan to expand the initial experience of seeing into one's own nature. See also **Rinzai sect**.

Miura, Isshû, and Ruth Fuller Sasaki. *The Zen Kôan*. New York: Harcourt, Brace & World, 1967.

Shimano, Eido T. "Zen Kôans." In *Zen, Tradition and Transition*. Ed. Kenneth Kraft. New York: Grove Press, 1988.

Hossô School

The Japanese name for the Yogachara or **Fa-hsien school** of **Buddhism**, also known as the Yuishiki or **"Consciousness**

Only" school. The Hossô school was one of the six schools of Nara Buddhism, established in Japan during the Nara period (710–794). The term *Hossô* literally means "characteristics of the dharmas," which reflects the school's philosophical interest in understanding the essential nature of all phenomena (dharmas). The primary teachings of the school include the storehouse consciousness (**alaya consciousness**) and the three natures of reality. The school is also known as the Yuishiki or "Consciousness Only" school, because it teaches that the physical world that we experience through the five senses is actually a product of our conscious minds. The **Yogachara school** developed in India during the fourth through the seventh centuries C.E., based on the writings of Asanga and Vasubandhu, two Indian Buddhist scholar monks. It spread to China in the seventh century, and was first introduced in Japan by **Dôshô** (628–700), the **monk** who studied under the Fa-hsien master Hsuan-tsang (600–664) in China.

Hossu

A fly **whisk**, usually made from horse hair attached to a short staff. Originally, Buddhist **monks** in India carried the whisk to clear the ground in front of them as they walked to avoid inadvertently killing any small insects in their path. In the **Zen** school, the hossu is carried by a Zen master as a sign of teaching authority. The master may use the whisk as a means of nonverbal communication during encounters with disciples, raising the whisk, throwing it to the ground, or even striking students with it. Because the whisk is regarded as a symbol of a master's authority to teach and transmit the **Dharma**, a master may pass a whisk on to a disciple as a physical symbol of **Dharma transmission**.

Hotei

Japanese for **Pu-tai** (d. 916), an eccentric Chinese **monk** from the T'ang dynasty (618–907). In Japan, Hotei is revered as one of the **seven lucky gods** (J. shichifukujin). In that regard, he is considered the patron deity for fortune tellers and liquor merchants. See **Pu-tai**.

Hotoke

Japanese term for the **Buddha** or a buddha. The word can refer generally to any enlightened being or more specifically, to the historical Buddha, and is said to be derived from an ancient Chinese transliteration for the Sanskrit word *buddha*, *futoke*, or *futo*.

The term is also commonly used in Japan in reference to the dead. Although not in keeping with orthodox Buddhist teachings of transmigration, **rebirth** and **nirvana**, in Japanese folk understanding, the spirits of the dead are said to become buddhas after death.

Ho-tse School

An early **lineage** of Chinese **Zen** and one of three lineages founded by disciples of the Sixth Patriarch **Hui-neng** (638–713). The lineage was founded by **Ho-tse Shen-hui** (670–762), the **Dharma heir** of Hui-neng, during the T'ang dynasty (618–907). Although Shen-hui had a lasting impact on Zen history, providing the traditional understanding of the orthodox lineage and the distinction between the **Southern** and **Northern schools**, his lineage was not a dominant force in early Zen. The Ho-tse school (J. Kataku-shû) survived for only five or six generations. The only significant figure to emerge from the school after Shen–hui was Kuei-feng Tsung-mi.

Ho-tse Shen-hui

(670–762; J. Kataku Jinne) Chinese **monk** of the T'ang dynasty (618–907), remembered as the founder of the **Ho-tse school** of early **Zen**. The name Ho-tse derives from the mountain where he had his monastery. Shen-hui was a **Dharma heir** of the Sixth Patriarch **Hui-neng** (638–713).

Nothing is known of Shen-hui's early life. In 699 he became a disciple of **Shen-hsiu** (606?–706), founder of the so-called **Northern school** of Zen. In 701, he joined Hui-neng's Zen community on the advice of his former master. He received Hui-neng's **inka**—or "seal of approval"—in 713, shortly before the master died. Shen-hui played an important role in Zen history, creating the traditional distinction between the Northern and **Southern schools** of early Zen. Shen-hui publicly denounced Zen master Shen-hsiu and his Northern school, accusing them of usurping the patriarchy and promoting a heretical form of **gradual enlightenment**. Shen-hui argued that his own master Hui-neng was the only disciple of the Fifth Patriarch **Hung-jen** (601–674) to receive a valid transmission of the Dharma. Therefore, Hui-neng alone deserved the title Sixth Patriarch. Shen-hui argued that Hui-neng's Southern school preserved the orthodox understanding of **sudden enlightenment** taught by the Fifth Patriarch Hung-jen. Shen-hui's attacks on the Northern school came to a head at the Great Dharma Assembly (J. Daihôe), which he held at Ta-yun-ssu monastery in Honan in 732. Shen-hui's understanding of Zen eventually became the dominant version, and the Southern school became the orthodox school. All currently active lineages of Zen trace their roots through Hui-neng. Scholars now believe that the distinction between the two schools was largely of Shen-hui's own creation.

Hottô Ha

A **lineage** of Japanese Rinzai and one of the twenty-four lineages of Japanese **Zen** active during the Kamakura (1185–1333) and early Ashikaga (1392–1568) periods. The Hottô Ha is a Japanese branch of the Yang-ch'i lineage founded by Shinchi **Kakushin** (1207–1298). Its name comes from Kakushin's honorific title Hottô **Zenji**. After Kakushin traveled to Sung China, where he became the **Dharma heir**

of the Chinese Rinzai master **Wu-men Hui-k'ai** (1183–1260), he returned to Japan and established his own lineage at Saihô-ji, later called Kôkoku-ji. The lineage retained Kakushin's interest in **esoteric** teachings and rituals. It also emphasized the study of Wu-men's *Mumonkan*, which Kakushin introduced to Japan. The Hottô lineage was closely associated with the Southern Imperial Court and therefore received patronage from the Ashikaga **bakufu**. See also **Rinzai sect** and **Yang-ch'i school**.

Hou Hei

"Lord Black," one of two clever robbers from China whose names appear occasionally in **Zen** literature. His partner in crime, **Hou Po** (Lady White), is a female robber. Hou Hei is known as Kô Koku in Japanese.

Hou Po

"Lady White," the clever female robber from China, associated with a male robber named **Hou Hei**. They appear together in **Zen** literature. Hou Po is known as Kô Haku in Japanese.

Householder

A term commonly used to designate Buddhist **lay believers** who have not been ordained as **monks** or **nuns**. The term indicates that the primary concern of lay practitioners remains family life, thus distinguishing them from monks and nuns who leave the home life behind when they enter the monastery.

Hôyû

Japanese transliteration of **Fa-jung** (594–657), the Chinese **monk** who founded the **Oxhead school** of early **Zen**. See **Fa-jung**.

Hôza

The **Dharma** seat, usually the **abbot's** formal lecture chair located on the raised platform in the **hattô**, or Dharma hall of the monastery. The abbot addresses the assembly from this seat for formal lectures and informal discussions about the Dharma. When seated in the chair expounding the Dharma, the abbot is said to represent the **Buddha** and the **patriarchs**, thus the chair is generally the focus of the Dharma hall, which typically houses no other buddha images.

Hsiang-yen Chih-hsien

(d. 898; J. Kyôgen Chikan) Chinese **Zen** master of the T'ang dynasty (618-907) from the **Kuei-yang school** (J. Igyô-shû). He was a **Dharma heir** of **Kuei-shan Ling-yu** (771–853), although he was originally a disciple of **Pai-chang Huai-hai** (720–814). The story of Hsiang-yen's attainment of **enlightenment** is very famous within the Zen tradition. It recounts that although Hsiang-yen was an accomplished scholar of the **Buddhist scriptures**, he did not make progress in his **meditation**. One day, when Kuei-shan asked him about his "**Original Face** before his birth" (J. honrai no memmoku), Hsiang-yen could not respond. His extensive knowledge of scripture did him no good; as he observed, pictures of food cannot satisfy the hungry. He burned his books and concentrated his efforts on the problem, finally, as he was working in the yard, he heard the sound of a tile strike the ground and was suddenly enlightened.

Hsing-hua Ts'ung-chiang

(830–888; J. Kyôgen Chikan) A Chinese Rinzai **monk** of the T'ang dynasty (618–907). Hsing-hua was an important **Dharma heir** of **Lin-chi I-hsüan** (d. 867), the founder of the Rinzai school. He joined Lin-chi's assembly in 861. After he attained **enlightenment**, he set off on a **pilgrimage**. He later returned to care for the master during the last months of his life. Hsing-hua played a crucial role in preserving the teachings and **Zen** style of Lin-chi. His most important Dharma heir was **Nan-yüan Hui-yüng**. See also **Rinzai sect**.

Hsin-hsin-ming

"Hymn of the Sincere Mind," a verse of 146 lines traditionally attributed to **Seng-ts'an** (d. 606), the third Chinese **patriarch**. The verse is an early example of **Zen** poetry and includes many famous lines quoted in subsequent Zen literature. It is known in Japanese as Shinjinmei. **D. T. Suzuki** (1689–1966) published an English translation of the verse in both *Essays in Zen Buddhism* (First Series; Ryder, 1970) and *Manual of Zen Buddhism* (Grove, 1960).

Hsi-shan

"West Mountain," the **Zen** monastery established by **Tao-hsin** (580–651), the fourth Zen **patriarch**. Hsi-shan is a mountain in Lo-ch'ang in modern day Guandong. It is also known as Mount Shuang-feng (J. Sôhô-zan)

Hsüan-tsang

(ca. 600–664; J. Genjô) Chinese Buddhist scholar **monk** who traveled to India on a **pilgrimage** in search of Buddhist texts and translated many texts into Chinese upon his return. Hsüan-tsang left China secretly in 629, having been denied official permission to make the trip to India. He traveled throughout Central Asia and India, studying Sanskrit and Buddhist philosophy. He returned to China in 645, carrying 657 Buddhist texts. He spent the rest of his life translating them from Sanskrit into Chinese, but he completed only seventy-three items. A large portion of the texts that he translated were from the **Yogachara school**. He is credited with founding the Chinese Yogachara school, known as the Fa-hsiang school. Hsüan-tsang is said to have introduced **Zen** to the early Japanese Buddhist monk **Dôshô** (628–670), the first Japanese monk to study Zen in China. He wrote an account of his travels in the *T'a-t'ang Hsi-yü chi* (*Record of the Western Regions*). His journey was also made famous by the popular novel *Monkey* (Ch. *Hsi–yüki*).

Wu, Ch'eng-en. *Monkey*. Trans. Arthur Waley. New York: Grove Press, 1994.

Hsüeh-feng I-ts'un

(822–908; J. Seppô Gison) Chinese **monk** who was one of the most famous and influential **Zen** masters of the late T'ang period (618–907). Hsüeh-feng was the **Dharma heir** of **Te-shan Hsuan-chien** (782–865). He appears in many classical **kôan**, including number thirteen in the *Mumonkan* and numbers five, twenty-two, forty-nine, fifty-one and sixty-six of the *Hekiganroku*. His leading disciples include **Yun-men Wen-yen** (864–949) and Hsüan-sha Shih-pei (835–908), founders of the Yun-men and Fa-yen houses of Zen respectively, and Ch'ang-ch'ing Hui-leng (854–932). See also **Fa-yen school**.

Hsüeh-mo Lun

"Treatise on Blood Lineage," a **Zen** treatise written in Chinese (T. 48, no. 2009). It is known more commonly by its title in Japanese, the *Ketsumyaku Ron*. Although the text is traditionally attributed to **Bodhidharma** (d. 532), the first **patriarch**, it is a later work, probably composed in the early T'ang dynasty (618–907). The sermon stresses the Zen teaching of seeing into one's own nature and thus attaining **enlightenment** without reliance on external practices or written words. The author may have been from **Ma-tsu Tao-i's** lineage or perhaps from the **Oxhead school**. The *Hsüeh-mo Lun* appears in *Bodhidharma's Six Gates* (Ch. *Shao-shih*, J. **Shôshitsu Rokumon Shû**), a collection of six essays attributed to Bodhidharma. An English translation of the essay by Red Pine appears in *The Zen Teaching of Bodhidharma* (North Point Press, 1989).

Hsüeh-tou Ch'ung-hsien

(980–1052; J. Setchô Jûken) Chinese **Zen** master of the early Sung dynasty (960–1279) who was a member of the **Yun-men school** and also one of its last prominent masters. The **Dharma heir** of Chih-men Kuang-tsu (d. 1031), he took his name from Mount Hsüeh-tou, in present day Chekiang, where he taught and wrote for thirty years. Hsüeh-tou was a famous writer and poet of his time, and among his writings is a compilation of the most important classical **kôan**, the *Hsüeh-tou Po-tse Sung-ku*, which included one hundred cases favored in the Yun-men **lineage**. The work later became the basis for the *Hekiganroku*. The collection includes eighteen kôan originally created by **Yun-men Wen-yen** (864–949), the founder of the lineage, which helped to preserve the master's influence on later generations of Zen students. Hsüeh-tou also composed a poem for each of the one hundred cases, which served as his commentary.

Hsü-t'ang Chih-yü

(1185–1269; Kidô Chigu) A Chinese Rinzai **monk** of the Sung dynasty (960–1279). Chih-yü was born in a village in what is now Chekiang Province. He took the **tonsure** at age sixteen at a local temple and then set out on **pilgrimage**. He practiced under the Rinzai master Yü-an P'u-yen (1156–1226) at **Ching-shan** in Hangchow, and eventually became his **Dharma heir**. He was in good favor with the imperial court and held the position of **abbot** at many of the leading monasteries of his time. After he retired to Hsüeh-tou-shan, the Japanese monk **Nampô Jômyô** (1235–1309) became his disciple and later carried his Dharma **lineage** back to Japan. See also **Rinzai sect**.

Hsü-t'ang Lu Tai-pieh

A portion of the *Hsü-t'ang Ho-shang Yu-lu*, the Recorded Sayings of Master Hsü-t'ang, which circulates as an independent work, and contains a collection of one-hundred old kôan with answers. Fifty-three of the kôan have answers in the tai-yu (J. **daigo**) style, in which the master responds for the disciple, and the remaining forty-seven have answers of the pieh-yu (J. **betsugo**) style, in which the master offers an alternative answer to the original. The *Hsü-t'ang Lu Tai-pieh* (J. *Kidô Roku Daibetsu*) is used as an advanced text within the Takujû line of modern Japanese Rinzai. See also **Rinzai sect** and **Takujû school**.

Huang-lung Hui-nan

(1002–1069; J. Oryô or Oryû Enan) Chinese Rinzai master of the Sung dynasty (960–1279) who founded the **Huang-lung school**, one of the two major Rinzai lineages of his time. Hui-nan was the **Dharma heir** of Shih-shuang Ch'u-yuan (986–1039), and he received the posthumous title *Pu-chai Chan-shih*. His **lineage** lasted for about 200 years, and was transmitted to Japan by **Eisai** (1141–1215), the Japanese Rinzai **monk**. See also **Rinzai sect**.

Huang-lung School

A **lineage** of Chinese Rinzai **Zen** active during the Sung dynasty (960–1279) and known as one of the so-called **seven schools** of Zen. The lineage was founded by the Zen master **Huang-lung Hui-nan** (1002–1069; J. Oryô Enan). The school remained active for about 200 years in China before it faded. In the late twelfth century, **Eisai** (1141–1215), the Japanese Zen **monk**, transmitted the lineage to Japan, where it became known as the **Oryô school**. See also **Rinzai sect**.

Huang-mei Hung-jen

(601–674; J. Obai Gunin) An alternative name for the Ffth Chinese **Patriarch** of **Zen**, better known simply as **Hung-jen**. The name Huang-mei derives from the mountain were he lived and taught. See **Hung-jen**.

Huang-mei Shan

"Yellow Plum Mountain" (J. Obai-zan), the mountain in present day Hupeh, China, where the Fifth Patriarch **Hung-jen** (601–674) had his monastery. The mountain is also known by alternative names. It is called Wu-tsu-shan, or Fifth Patriarch Mountain (J. Goso-zan) in honor of Hung-jen. Some texts refer to it as **Tung-shan** (807–869), or East Mountain (J. Tôzan).

Huang-po Hsi-yün

(d. 850; J. Obaku Kiun) Chinese **Zen** master of the T'ang dynasty (618–907), one of the most famous and influential masters of the classical period. Huang-po took his **vows** at Chien-fu-ssu on **Huang-po-shan** in Fukien, then moved north and practiced for a time under Nan-ch'üan P'u-yüan (748–835). Later he became the disciple of **Pai-chang Huai-hai** (720–814), who recognized him as his **Dharma heir**. A lay disciple built a temple for him in the mountains of western Kiangsi. Huang-po named the mountain and the temple Huang-po-shan and Huang-po-ssu after the mountain where he took the **tonsure**, and he later became known by the same name. His most prominent disciple was **Lin-chi I-hsüan** (d. 867), founder of the **Lin-chi** (J. Rinzai) **school**. Huang–po's writings are recorded in the *Huang–po Tuan-chi Ch'an-shih Wan-ling Lu*, which was translated into English by John Blofeld. See also **lay believer** and **Rinzai sect**.

Blofeld, John. *The Zen Teaching of Huang Po on the Transmission of Mind*. Boston, MA: Shambhala, 1994.

Huang-po-shan

"Mount Huang-po." There are two mountains in China that bear the name Huang-po. One is in Fukien province near the modern city of Foochow in southeastern China, and the other in central China in the western part of Kiangsi. The mountain in Fukien has

Hui-k'o is depicted offering his arm to Bodhidharma. He is said to have cut off his arm to demonstrate his sincerity in seeking the dharma.

been the site of a **Zen** temple since the late eighth century. In 789, a Zen **monk** named Cheng-kan, a disciple of the Sixth Patriarch **Hui-neng** (638–713), constructed a **meditation** hut there, which was later expanded to a full Zen monastery called Chien-fu-ssu. The Chinese master later known as **Huang-po Hsi-yün** (d.850; J. Obaku Kiun) took his monastic **vows** at Chien-fu-ssu and later named the other Mount Huang-po after his childhood home. Chien-fu-ssu fell into disrepair during the Sung dynasty (960–1279) and was only a ruin by the late Ming dynasty (1368–1644) when a new Zen monastery, Wan-fu-ssu, was built on the same site. Huang-po-shan Wan-fu-ssu (J. Obaku-san

Mampuku-ji) was the home monastery of **Yin-yüan Lung-ch'i** (1594–1673) who emigrated to Japan in the mid-seventeenth century and founded the **Obaku sect**.

Huang-po Hsi-yün, after receiving **inka** from **Pai-chang Huai-hai** (720–814), established a monastery of his own on a mountain in western Kiangsi. Hsi-yün named both the monastery and the mountain in central China after Mount Huang-po in the south. His own popular name derives from this latter mountain, since it was there that he trained his own disciples, including **Lin-chi I-hsüan** (d. 867), the founder of Rinzai Zen. See also **lay believer** and **Rinzai sect**.

Hua-yen School

"Flower Garden" school, one of the thirteen schools of Chinese **Buddhism** that developed during the T'ang dynasty (618–907). The name derives from the title of the primary scripture of the school, the Hua-yen Sutra (Sk. **Avatamsaka Sutra**; J. Kegonkyô). Although the sutra was written in India, the school has no Indian counterpart. Its primary teachings include the **four realms of reality** and the ten stages of the **bodhisattva**. The school recognizes the Chinese **monk** Fa-shun (557–640) as its founder, although it was the Third **Patriarch** Fa-tsang (643–712) who systematized its teachings.

Hua-yen Sutra

(J. Kegonkyô) The "Flower Garland" Sutra, the Chinese translation of the **Avatamsaka Sutra**. There are three Chinese translations of the text: the first produced by Buddhabhadra from 418–421 in sixty parts (T. 9, no. 278), the second by Shiksananda from 695–699 in eighty parts (T. 10, no. 279), and the third by Prajna from 759–762 in forty parts (T. 10, no. 293). The Hua-yen Sutra was used widely by various schools of East Asian **Buddhism**, including **Zen**. The Buddhabhadra translation served as the scriptural basis for the **Hua-yen school** of Chinese Buddhism, known as the **Kegon school** in Japan. See **Avatamsaka Sutra**.

Hui-k'o

(487–593; J. Eka) Chinese Buddhist **monk** who became known as the Second Chinese **Patriarch** of **Zen**. According to Zen tradition, Hui-k'o inherited the **Dharma** from **Bodhidharma**. The story of the transmission is among the most famous in Zen literature. According to traditional biographies, Hui-k'o was born in Wu-lao (present day Honan). He studied Confucian, Taoist, and Buddhist writings on his own before deciding to become a Buddhist monk. He received the **tonsure** on Lung-men Hsiang-shan and then studied various Buddhist teachings extensively. He practiced **meditation** at Lung-men for eight years before seeking out a master at the age of forty.

Shen-kuang, as Hui-k'o was then called, traveled south and found Bodhidharma living at **Shao-lin-ssu**. In vain he beseeched the master to admit him as a disciple. On a cold winter night, as Hui-k'o stood outside the monastery in a raging blizzard. The master asked him what he wanted. In response, Hui-k'o drew out a sharp knife, cut off his left arm, and handed it to Bodhidharma. This dramatic gesture proved the intensity of his intention to seek the Dharma. Bodhidharma accepted him as his disciple and recognized him as his **Dharma heir**. He also granted him the new name Hui-k'o.

Hui-k'o spent five or six years with Bodhidharma. Before the two parted, Hui-k'o received from the master a robe and bowl as signs of **Dharma transmission**. Hui-k'o then traveled for some years. In 551, he met a lay practitioner of meditation, whom he recognized as his Dharma heir. Hui-k'o bestowed monastic **vows** on him and gave him the name **Seng-ts'an**, thus making him the Third Patriarch. See also **lay believer**.

Hui-neng

(J. Enô) Chinese **Zen** master (638–713) of the T'ang dynasty (618–907), traditionally known as the Sixth Chinese **Patriarch** of Zen. Little is known for certain about Hui-neng except that he was at one time a disciple of the Fifth Patriarch **Hung-jen** (601–674). There are, however, traditional accounts of his life, such as the one found in the **Platform Sutra**. Scholars regard these stories as historically problematic, but they represent the Zen tradition's view of its own history. According to the biography in the Platform Sutra, Hui-neng grew up in poverty, supporting his widowed mother by gathering and selling firewood. He did not receive any formal education and remained illiterate. He decided to enter monastic life after hearing someone recite the **Diamond Sutra**. He made his way to Mount Huang-mei and entered Hung-jen's assembly as a lay person, laboring in the mill, grinding flour. He came to the attention of the Zen master when he composed a poem in response to a verse written by **Shen-hsiu** (606?–706), the senior disciple. Hung-jen recognized Hui-neng's verse as an indication of **enlightenment**. He secretly designated him as the Sixth Patriarch and sent him south to protect the **Dharma**. Hui-neng's **lineage**, which became the orthodox school of Zen, is known as the **Southern school**. Tradition maintains that the latter portions of the Platform Sutra preserve lectures given by Hui-neng later in his teaching career. According to the teachings presented in the sutra, Hui-neng taught the identity of wisdom (**prajna**) and **meditation**, and advocated the concept of **original enlightenment**. His teaching represents the orthodox Zen teaching of **sudden enlightenment**. See also **lay believer**.

Hung-chih Cheng-chüeh

(1091–1157; J. Wanshi Shôgaku) Chinese Sôtô **Zen** master of the Sung dynasty (960–1279). Cheng-chüeh descended from the Yün-chü (J. Ungo) **lineage**. He was born in Hsi-chou in modern day Shansi and became a **monk** at age eleven. He received **inka** from the Sôtô master Tan-hsia Tzu-ch'un. He taught for most of his life at **Ching-te-ssu** on T'ien-lung-shan in Chekiang. He restored the monastery and gathered a large assembly of disciples, said to have numbered up to 1,200 students, and he is sometimes known as T'ien-lung Cheng-chüeh because of his role as restorer.

Cheng-chüeh is remembered primarily for the famous controversy that arose between him and his Rinzai friend and contemporary, **Ta-hui Tsung-kao** (1089–1163), concerning the use of **kôan**. Ta-hui favored the contemplation of kôan during seated **meditation** as the best approach for achieving **enlightenment**. Hung-chih preferred meditation without the use of kôan, striving instead for a mental state of complete tranquillity. His style of meditation became known as "silent illumination Zen" (**mokushô Zen**), which still characterizes practice within the Sôtô school. He received the posthumous title *Hung-chih Ch'an-shih* from the Sung emperor Kao-tsung. Although he did not regard the use of kôan as highly as Ta-hui, his writings include two separate collections of one hundred kôan each, which he compiled. The more famous of the two is the *Sung-ku Po-tse*. His writings were collected in the *Hung-chih Ch'an-shih Kuang-lu*. See also **Rinzai sect** and **Sôtô sect**.

Hung-chou School

An important **lineage** of early **Zen** founded by the T'ang dynasty (618–907) master **Ma-tsu Tao-i**. The name was coined by **Tsung-mi** (780–840) after the region where Ma-tsu had his monastery. The Hung-chou school (J. Kôjû-shû or Kôshû-shû) is one of the main branches of the so-called **Southern school** of Zen, which descended from the Sixth Patriarch **Hui-neng** (638–713). Many of the prominent Zen masters of the T'ang dynasty arose from this lineage, including **Pai-chang Huai-hai** (720–814), Nan-chüan, **Huang-po Hsi-Yün** (d. 850), **Lin-chi I-hsüan** (d. 867), and **Yang-shan Hui-chi** (807–883).

Hung-jen

The Chinese Buddhist master (601–674; J. Gunin) who became known as the Fifth Patriarch of **Zen** in China. He is also known as Huang-mei Hung-jen and Wu-tsu Hung-jen. According to tradition, Hung-jen received the **Dharma** from the Fourth Patriarch **Tao-hsin** (580–651) and later recognized **Hui-neng** (638–713) as the authentic Sixth Patriarch, founder of the **Southern school**. He also formally recognized **Shen-hsiu** (606?–706), who founded the **Northern school**, as a **Dharma heir**.

In this Zen monastery at the Spring Equinox, rice is offered at an altar to hungry ghosts, sentient beings who have been condemned to wander the earth looking for food.

After Tao-hsin's death, Hung-jen established a monastery at Huang-mei-shan in modern day Hupeh, where he trained his own disciples.

According to the account of transmission given in the **Platform Sutra**, Hung-jen asked his disciples at Huang-mei-shan to compose verses so that he could select a Dharma heir who would become the next patriarch. Only Shen-hsiu, the highest ranking disciple, submitted a verse. The master publicly praised the verse and had the others recite it; he privately informed Shen-hsiu that the verse indicated that he had not attained perfect **enlightenment**. Hui-neng, then only a lay disciple working in the threshing room, heard the verse and composed a reply. Based on this verse, Hung-jen secretly acknowledged **Dharma transmission** and bestowed on Hui-neng the robe and bowl of transmission. See also **lay believer**.

Hungry Ghost

(J. **gaki**) A type of **sentient being**, known as *preta* in Sanskrit. After death, **Buddhism** teaches that an individual may be reborn into one of six possible realms of existence (rokudô) ranging from **hell** dwellers and hungry ghosts to **heaven** dwellers. The realm of the hungry ghosts is regarded as an evil outcome because hungry ghosts suffer in a variety of ways. They are said to live either in an area just outside of hell or in a region of hell itself, but unlike other hell dwellers, they leave hell and wander through other regions in search of food, often looking for garbage and human waste on the outskirts of human cities. As their name suggests, they are unable to satisfy their craving for food, and thus are doomed to perpetual hunger. They are said to be invisible during daylight hours but visible at night.

The Buddhist tradition describes several different kinds of hungry ghosts in terms of specific behavior patterns in the previous life, which lead to appropriate punishments. For example, a person who steals food is said to become a hungry ghost that can only eat corpses, while a person who deals harshly with others out of anger will have a mouth of fire that destroys food before it can be consumed. A person who prevents others from practicing the virtue of giving (**danna**), becomes a hungry ghost with a big belly and a neck as thin as a needle. This last species became the basic image for hungry ghosts in East Asian Buddhism. See also **six paths**.

Strong, John S. *The Experience of Buddhism: Sources and Interpretations.* Belmont, CA: Wadsworth Publishing Co., 1995.

Hyakujô Ekai
The Japanese pronunciation for **Pai-chang Huai-hai** (720–814), a Chinese **Zen monk**. See **Pai-chang Huai-hai**.

Hyakujô Shingi
Japanese title for the *Pai-chang Ch'ing-kuei*, a **monastic code** used in the practice of **Zen**, attributed to **Pai-chang Huai-hai** (720–814). See *Pai-chang Ch'ing-kuei*.

Hyôshigi
Wooden clappers used in a **Zen** monastery to signal specific times and events, such as the start of meals.

I

Icchantika

(J. issendai, or sendai) A **sentient being** without the capacity to attain **enlightenment**. This term is also used to describe a **bodhisattva** who willingly chooses not to enter **nirvana** in order to continue living in the world of **samsara** and assist other sentient beings. Some schools of **Theravada** and **Mahayana Buddhism** maintained the theory that certain individuals have so damaged their store of **merit** that they have no root of goodness left; thus these individuals have no hope of ever attaining enlightenment. Other schools of Mahayana denied this teaching. They argued that icchantika do not exist or that even if they do exist, icchantika have the **Buddha Nature**. After Buddhism was transmitted to East Asia, controversy over these teachings continued to be important in several East Asian schools of Buddhism.

The **Buddhist scriptures** can be used to support both arguments, as can be seen by comparing two versions of the **Nirvana Sutra**. One version states that icchantika lack the seed of enlightenment; the other teaches that all sentient beings, including the icchantika, possess the Buddha Nature and are thus capable of attaining enlightenment. In China, the former version of the text was transmitted earlier, setting off the controversy. The **monk** Tao-sheng (360–434 C.E.) rejected the notion that icchantika lacked the Buddha Nature. His position was later vindicated when the latter version of the sutra was translated. Most schools of East Asian Buddhism, including **Zen**, follow Tao-sheng's lead and teach that the Buddha Nature is universal.

Another sutra favored by the Zen school, the **Lankavatara Sutra**, teaches an alternative and more positive understanding of the concept of icchantika. The Lankavatara Sutra applies the term to bodhisattvas who deliberately choose to stay in samsara and serve other sentient beings. Like the earlier concept of icchantika, a bodhisattva who chooses to remain in samsara until all sentient beings have been saved will never attain enlightenment. In this case, however, the cause is **compassion** for others, so the icchantika-bodhisattva is a valiant figure.

Strong, John S. *The Experience of Buddhism: Sources and Interpretations.* Belmont, CA: Wadsworth Publishing Co., 1995.

Ichidaiji Innen

"The most important cause," usually referring to the primary reason the **Buddha** had to appear in the world. The **Lotus Sutra** says that the Buddha's primary purpose was to preach the **Dharma** and thereby save **sentient beings**.

Ichien

An alternative name for **Mujû Dôkyô** (1226–1313), a Japanese Rinzai **monk** who authored the *Shasekishû*. See **Mujû Dôkyô**.

Ichi Ensô

"One circle," an alternative name for *ensô*, the image of a painted circle commonly found in **Zen** art. See **ensô**.

Ichiji Kan

"One-word barrier," a **Zen** teaching device made famous by the master Yunmen. The device entails a master using one sharp word in response to a question asked by a disciple. The single-word answer is sometimes accompanied by a shout or slap. The purpose of this device is to cut off the disciple's rambling flow of rational thought and to prompt an immediate experience or realization. Translators often have difficulty rendering a satisfactory translation with a single word, since the original Chinese character usually encompasses several possible meanings. One of Master Yunmen's famous one-word barriers is the Chinese word *fu*, meaning "everywhere," "universal," or "vast and great." "Someone asked Master Yunmen, 'What is the eye of the genuine teaching?' The Master said, 'It's everywhere [fu]'" (App, p. 91).

App, Urs., trans. and ed. *Master Yunmen: From the Record of the Chan Master "Gate of the Clouds."* New York: Kodansha International, 1994.

Ichijô

"**One vehicle**," the path of **Mahayana Buddhism**. See **one vehicle**.

Ichimi Zen

"One-taste **zen**," an expression used to mean a pure form of zen, the zen transmitted by the buddhas and patriarchs. It is contrasted with "five-taste zen" (**gomi zen**), or impure forms of meditative practice.

Ichinen Fushô

"Nonarising of a single thought," the realm in which no delusions arise. The expression describes the enlightened mind of a **buddha** or the experience of **enlightenment**. In his collection of talks and instructions, the *Shôbôgenzô*, **Dôgen Kigen** (1200–1253) identifies the mental state of ichinen fushô with **zazen**, or meditation itself.

Igan Butsuji

Moving the coffin of a deceased **abbot** or other prominent Buddhist **monk** or **nun** to the lecture hall. Igan is one of the nine ritual acts (**kubutsuji**) performed when a prominent Buddhist monk or nun dies. The coffins of ordinary monks

and nuns are left in the infirmary until cremation. See also **kubutsuji**.

Igyô School

The Japanese name for the **Kuei-yang school**, a **lineage** of Chinese **Zen** active during the T'ang dynasty (618–907). See **Kuei-yang school**.

Ihai

A memorial tablet prepared for the deceased soon after death, according to Japanese Buddhist custom. Inscribed on the tablet is a special Buddhist name, known in Japanese as the **kaimyô**, which is used for the deceased at all **memorial services**. Kaimyô are normally conferred on **monks** or **nuns** at their **ordination**; lay Buddhists usually receive the kaimyô posthumously from members of their family temple shortly after death. Initially, temporary memorial tablets are used, often made of plain wood with the kaimyô written in black ink. Later, permanent tablets, typically black lacquered wood embossed with the name in gold, are prepared.

Memorial tablets are used as physical representations of the deceased at the funeral service and at all subsequent memorial services (**hôji**) performed for the individual. In many cases, two permanent memorial tablets are prepared for each person, one to be kept by the family and the other to be kept at the family temple. **Incense**, prayers, and readings from sacred texts are offered before the ihai in much the same manner that **offerings** are made to other Buddhist images. Temples mark the anniversaries of death (**nenki**) for deceased members by offering services in front of the appropriate ihai on the specified day.

After an initial period of mourning (**chûin**), lasting forty-nine days from the time of death, the family enshrines its copy of the ihai on an altar (**butsudan**), along with the memorial tablets of other deceased family members. Many Japanese families make daily offerings

Ihai are memorial tablets used as physical representations of the deceased at a funeral service.

of food and water before the ihai, and keep flowers on the altar to honor the dead. It is not unusual for important events, such as graduations, new jobs, and marriages to be formally announced to the ihai, particularly if the deceased was the head of the household. According to tradition, the family will keep the ihai until the final memorial service, usually the service marking either the thirty-third or the fiftieth anniversary of death. After that time, the family disposes of the ihai, often returning it to the temple for burning. See also **lay believer**.

Smith, Robert. *Ancestor Worship in Contemporary Japan.* Stanford, CA: Stanford University Press, 1974.

Ikebana

Flower arranging, the popular name for **kadô**, the way of flowers. See **kadô**.

Ikko Hanko

"One person" or "half a person." The expression appears in the *Hekiganroku*, the *Dentôroku* (Ch. *Ching-te Ch'üan-teng Lu*), and other classical **Zen** texts. It refers to a general scarcity of talented people, indicating that it is rare to find a worthy disciple. A master might say that he hopes to find one disciple or even half a disciple to whom he can transmit the **Dharma**.

Ikkyû Sôjun

(1394–1481) Japanese Rinzai **monk** from the Ashikaga period (1392–1568). Ikkyû belonged to the **Daitoku-ji** branch of Rinzai and was a dominant figure in that **lineage**. He is famous for his **calligraphy**, painting, and writing, especially poetry. He was an eccentric and remains a controversial figure. Ikkyû was born in poverty in Saga, in western Kyoto, although he came from a noble family. His mother, a court lady for Emperor Go-Komatsu (1392–1412), was dismissed from court during her pregnancy. When Ikkyû reached the age of five, she entrusted him to a local temple where he received a solid education in the Chinese classics and Buddhist texts. At age thirty he went to **Kennin-ji**, where he studied poetry with the poet monk Botetsu for four years. Disturbed by the worldly atmosphere at Kennin-ji, he moved to a small temple called Saikin-ji where he lived with the hermit monk Ken'ô. Although Ikkyû attained **enlightenment** during this period, Ken'ô was not qualified to certify his experience. After Ken'ô's death, Ikkyû became the disciple of Kasô Sôdon (1352–1428). Although Kasô was officially **abbot** of Daitoku-ji, he resided in a small hermitage on Lake Biwa. Ikkyû practiced with him for nine years, becoming his **Dharma heir** in 1420. It is said that when Ikkyû received his certificate of enlightenment, he threw it onto the fire and destroyed it.

After his master's death, Ikkyû became a wandering monk and spent thirty years travelling throughout the Kyoto and Osaka region, mostly dealing with lay people rather than the **Zen** monastic community. He did not believe that he was bound by any external **monastic code**, and was known to drink sake, eat meat and fish, and enjoy the company of women. Ikkyû was quite critical of monastic life.

Ikkyû settled down at the age of sixty, when he undertook the restoration of **Myôshin-ji**, a major Rinzai monastery in Kyoto. Disciples built him a hermitage within the grounds, which he called Shûon-an. For the first time in his career, he guided a community of students. He later restored Daitoku-ji, which had been badly damaged by fire. In 1474, he was appointed abbot at Daitoku-ji, but continued to reside at Shûon-an. He died there at age eighty-seven. See also **Rinzai sect** and **lay believer**.

Covell, Jon Carter, and Shobin Yamada. *Unraveling Zen's Red Thread: Ikkyu's Controversial Way.* Elizabeth, NJ: Hollym International Corporation, 1980.

Impermanence

According to the Buddhist understanding of reality, impermanence (J. **mujô**) characterizes all of existence. All things are impermanent and subject to perpetual change until they eventually pass out of existence. Things arise, change, and then pass away. Nothing is eternal; indeed, nothing remains constant or unchanging for even a moment. Acceptance of impermanence is part of the process of recognizing the nature of reality. Buddhist **meditation** allows one to observe the impermanence of the mind, following the ongoing flow of thoughts, emotions, and feelings. Impermanence is one of the **three marks** of existence, along with **suffering** (Sk. duhkha) and No-Self (Sk. **Anatman**).

Incense

Buddhists burn incense before images of the **Buddha** and other Buddhist figures as a sign of reverence. One will almost always find incense burning at the various temples of Buddhist schools. The pleasant aroma is said to be a reminder of the Buddha himself who was traditionally described as fragrant. Incense is among the appropriate **offerings** made to a buddha or to Buddhist **monks** and **nuns**. Incense is also regularly offered as a part of funeral and **memorial services** for deceased relatives.

Indaramô

Japanese for **Indra's jewel net**, also called Taimô, an abbreviation for Taishakumô. See **Indra's jewel net**.

Indra

(J. Indara) The god of war in ancient Indian mythology, whose exploits are celebrated in the Rig Veda and other Vedic texts. Indra was the primary deity of the Aryan people who migrated to the Indian subcontinent. He is an atmospheric god who lives in the region between heaven and earth and is described as a powerful warrior, the driver of a chariot whose weapon is the thunderbolt. In his most dramatic exploit, he destroyed the snake demon Vrtra, who was withholding rain and sunlight from the earth. The warrior class (kshastriya) regard him as their special patron. Since Indra enjoys heavy drinking, he is closely associated with the god Soma, the deified form of an intoxicating liquor used in Vedic ritual.

In **Buddhism**, Indra is regarded as a guardian deity for Buddhist teachings and believers. He appears frequently in Buddhist texts, including the ***Buddhacharita***, the story of the historical **Buddha's** life. In that text, Indra appears to the recently enlightened Buddha as he sits in **meditation** under the **bodhi tree**. Along with other Hindu deities, Indra begs the Buddha to venture out to teach the **Dharma** for the sake of all **sentient beings**. Indra is said to reside in a palace in Trayastrimsha **Heaven** above **Mount Sumeru**, where he receives reports from the **four guardian kings** (shittennô) regarding the moral condition of people in the world.

Indra's Jewel Net

(J. Indaramô) According to Buddhist lore, the god **Indra** lives above **Mount Sumeru** in a magnificent palace. Draped over the palace is a wondrous net made with jewels, which hang from each node of intersection on the net. The jewels are perfectly reflective, such that every jewel perfectly reflects every other jewel; thus, any jewel can be taken as the central point, which encompasses the entirety of the net. The image of Indra's Jewel Net is used in **Mahayana** Buddhist texts to teach the concept of **interrelatedness** and the interpenetration of all things. Because of their reflective quality, an alteration made to any single jewel affects them all. For example, painting a dot on one jewel will produce reflected dots on all the others. In the same way, all things in the world are interrelated with one another and interdependent. Most importantly, causing harm to one

sentient being injures all other **sentient beings**. The Hua-yen Sutra (Sk. **Avatamsaka Sutra**) provides the classical description of the image.

Inga

Cause and effect; the law of **causality**. The Japanese word literally means "a cause and its fruits." According to the Buddhist conception of reality, every action inevitably produces consequences. Actions can be likened to seeds which an individual sows. The seeds eventually mature and produce related fruits. Good actions produce good effects and bad actions produce bad effects. Retribution for evil actions and reward for good actions are not meted out by a deity, but are the natural consequence of the action itself. Thus, the workings of cause and effect function like an impersonal moral law. See also **karma** and **Law of Causation**.

Inga Monogatari

Causation stories, or tales of cause and effect; a genre of Buddhist literature used for popular instruction in the workings of **karma**. In particular the stories are told to demonstrate the negative effects of evil or harmful behavior. Inga monogatari also include miraculous tales of salvation brought about by an individual's pious behavior or deep faith in a **buddha**, **bodhisattva**, or **sutra**. *Inga Monogatari* is the title of a text composed by **Suzuki Shôsan** (1579–1655), a Tokugawa period **Zen monk**, which was published in 1661.

Ingen Ryûki

Japanese pronunciation for **Yin-yüan Lung-ch'i** (1594–1673), the Chinese Rinzai master who founded the **Obaku sect** of Japanese **Zen**. See **Yin-yüan Lung-ch'i**.

In'in Ekishi

The practice of changing **Dharma lineage** according to the temple at which a **monk** serves as **abbot**. According to the in'in ekishi process, when a monk moves from his home temple to become abbot at a different temple, he changes lineage. He gives up his initial lineage inherited from his immediate master and adopts the lineage of the former abbots of the new temple. The change takes place even if the monk never practiced under any of the temple's previous abbot. In this manner, a monk could change lineages several times during the course of a career, based solely on the temples he serves. The practice of in'in ekishi is not generally regarded as compatible with the **Zen** ideal of inheriting the **Dharma** (shihô) directly from one's master (**isshi inshô**). According to normal Zen practice, a disciple becomes a part of the Dharma lineage of his master when he receives formal acknowledgment of **enlightenment** (inshô or **inka**). At that time, he is said to inherit the Dharma and become a **Dharma heir**. Lineage of this type, depicted in much the same way as blood lineage on a family tree, does not change based on the temple of residence. Nevertheless, in'in ekishi has been the norm in some periods of Zen history. Before Manzan initiated a reform movement in seventeenth century Japan, for example, in'in ekishi was the common practice for Sôtô Zen. See also **Sôtô sect**.

Bodiford, William M. "Dharma Transmission in Sôtô Zen." *Monumenta Nipponica* Vol. 46 No. 4 (Winter 1991).

Inka

The most commonly used expression in the **Zen** school for a seal of **Dharma transmission**, which confirms the validity of an individual's **enlightenment** experience and indicates that transmission of the Dharma has occurred from master to disciple. Inka is actually an abbreviation of inka shômei, which literally means "seal of approval with clear proof." One typically speaks of a master conferring inka on a disciple, or a student receiving inka. Inka functions as an official

certification or seal of approval from a Zen master that a disciple has attained the same insight into the Dharma as the master and is qualified to serve as a Zen master to others. In some cases, inka is symbolically represented by a written document; in others, it is represented by conferring a personal religious item from the master such as a robe or **whisk**. A disciple who receives inka is formally included in the Dharma **lineage** of the master, which is always traced back through the generations to **Bodhidharma** and Shakyamuni **Buddha** (**Siddharta Gautama**). Inka formally indicates that the disciple has attained a sufficient level of maturity in the Dharma to qualify as a master in his or her own right. Once receiving inka, a Zen teacher may accept students and acknowledge them in turn. For this reason, not all students who attain enlightenment experiences receive inka. Long years of training after an initial enlightenment experience are often required to qualify for inka.

Inkin

A small hand-held bell used at **Zen** monasteries. The bell is bowl-shaped, resting on a small cushion and attached to a wooden handle. It is sounded by striking the side of the bowl with an attached metal stick. Inkin are used in the **meditation hall** to signal the beginning and end of periods of seated **mediation**.

Ino

The supervisor of trainees at a **Zen** monastery in charge of the **meditation** or monks' hall (**sôdô**), sometimes translated as registrar or rector. The same term, usually transliterated *ina*, is used by other Buddhist sects for a high ranking officer who manages the affairs of a temple. In a Zen monastery, the ino is one of the six senior offices of the Eastern rank (**tôhan**), who assist the **abbot** in the administrative aspects of the community. The ino plays a crucial role in managing the daily activities within the monastic community because he oversees activities in the monks' hall. New arrivals register with him, and he determines the relative ranking of seniority among the resident monks. The ino sees to it that the monks keep to the daily mediation and ritual schedule, and leads the monks in some ceremonies. See also **temple positions**.

Inshô

A common abbreviation for the expression "*inka shômei.*" Inshô refers to the formal recognition of a disciple's **enlightenment** experience by a **Zen** master. In some cases, inshô is represented by a written certificate indicating that an authentic transmission of the **Dharma** has taken place. In other cases, a Zen master may bestow another physical object, usually a personal religious implement, such as a robe, a **whisk** (J. **hossu**), a portrait of the master, or a scripture. See **inka**.

Interrelatedness

The Buddhist understanding of reality, which posits that all things and all individuals are mutually dependent on one another. Interrelatedness implies that any action taken toward one individual will impact all others. The concept of interrelatedness is based upon the notion of **emptiness**, that all things exist as a result of causes and nothing is absolutely self-existent. A basic component of interrelatedness is **compassion**, since injuring any other **sentient being** causes injury to all, including the self. See also **emptiness** and **Indra's jewel net**.

Inzan Ien

(1751–1814) Japanese Rinzai **monk** of the Tokugawa period (1600–1867) who is regarded as the founder of the **Inzan school** of Japanese **Zen**. Inzan was the **Dharma heir** of **Gasan Jitô** (1727–1797), a leading disciple of the reformer **Hakuin Ekaku** (1685–1768). Along with his Dharma brother, **Takujû Kosen**

(1760–1833), Inzan is credited with completing the process of systematizing **kôan** practice within the **Rinzai sect**. Inzan was born in Echizen province, where at age nine he entered a Buddhist temple in Gifu. At sixteen, he turned to Zen and practiced with Bankoku, a Rinzai master, who promoted the teachings of the Rinzai master **Bankei Yôtaku** (1622–1693). After three years, he became the disciple of Rinzai master Gessen Zen'e (1702–1781), with whom he remained for seven years. He later spent many years in Mino, before hearing about Gasan. He practiced with Gasan for two years and became his Dharma heir. After receiving **inka**, he spent several years on **pilgrimage**. In 1806, he settled down and established a community at Zuiryô-ji in Gifu, where he taught for most of his final years. He was appointed **abbot** at **Myôshin-ji** in 1808, and served briefly. See also **Rinzai sect**.

Inzan School

One of two major forms of modern Japanese Rinzai **Zen** founded by **Inzan Ien** (1751–1814), a second-generation descendant of **Hakuin Ekaku** (1685–1768). All active lineages of Rinzai Zen in Japan descend from either the Inzan or the **Takujû schools**. The teaching methods and Zen style of the two schools are nearly identical. Together they encompass what is often known as Hakuin Zen. See also **Rinzai sect**.

Ippen

(1239–1289) Japanese Buddhist **monk** of the Kamakura period (1185–1333) who founded the **Ji sect** of **Pure Land Buddhism**. He was originally a Tendai monk and studied for many years on Mount Hiei. He was then known as Zuien. He later left Mount Hiei and became a disciple of Shôtatsu Shônin, a Pure Land teacher. He took the name Ippen in 1276 while visiting the Shinto shrine on Mount Kumano. He traveled throughout the countryside of Japan, spreading Pure Land belief by handing out **nembutsu** amulets (J. fusan). He was popularly known as Yugyô Shônin, "the wandering holy man," because of his itinerant life. See also **Tendai sect**.

Isan Reiyû

Japanese rendering of **Kuei-shan Ling-yu** (771–853). See **Kuei-shan Ling-yu**.

I-shan I-ning

(1247–1317; J. Issan Ichinei) Chinese Rinzai **monk** of the Yüan dynasty (1260-1368) who emigrated to Japan. I-shan was sent to Japan as an emissary by the new Yüan government in 1299. The Japanese suspected him of being a spy and confined him under house arrest at Shuzen-ji in Izu. When Japanese officials realized that they were mistaken, I-shan was welcomed in Kamakura by the regent **Hôjô Sadatoki** (1271–1311). He eventually served as **abbot** at both **Kenchô-ji** and **Engaku-ji**. He attracted disciples in such numbers that he limited entry into his assembly with an entrance exam designed to test the literary skill of the applicants. **Musô Sôseki** (1275–1351) was among his students in Kamakura. I-shan emphasized the literary, artistic, and cultural aspects of **Zen** far more than religious practice. He greatly influenced the rise of Gozan culture in Japan. He also served as abbot at **Nanzen-ji** in Kyoto and influenced the Zen culture of the traditional capital. See also **Gozan literature** and **Rinzai sect**.

Ishin Denshin

Transmission from mind to mind. An expression used to describe the authentic transmission of the **Dharma** in the **Zen** school from master to disciple, generation after generation. The concept of ishin denshin forms one of the basic assumptions of Zen practice: that **enlightenment** passes from one individual to another not through the process of teaching with words, but by an accord of minds. A student attains an intuitive understanding of the Dharma and the master recognizes that intuition, and although no specific teachings have passed from one to the other, they share a realization of the Dharma. The opening line of the *Hsüeh-mo lun* (J. Ketsumyaku **ron**), attributed to **Bodhidharma**, provides a classical statement of the concept: "The Three Worlds arise from and return to **One Mind**. From buddhas of the past to succeeding buddhas, [the Dharma] is transmitted from mind to mind, without reliance on words or letters" (T. vol. 48, p. 373).

Issaikyô

A general Japanese term for the entirety of the **Buddhist scriptures**. The word literally means "all the **sutras**" and is used synonymously with **Daizôkyô**. Since the term is generic, it may refer to the ancient Sanskrit or Pali **Tripitaka**, the more extensive **Chinese Tripitaka**, or Japanese editions, which include additional materials.

Issan Ichinei

Japanese transliteration of **I-shan I-ning** (1247–1317), a Chinese Rinzai **monk** of the Yüan dynasty (1260–1368). See **I-shan I-ning**.

Issendai

Japanese for **icchantika**, a **sentient being** who lacks the capacity to attain **enlightenment**. Also used for **bodhisattvas** who remain indefinitely in the realm of **samsara** in order to lead other sentient beings to enlightenment. See **icchantika**.

Isshi Injô

An alternative pronunciation for **isshi inshô**, to receive the Dharma seal (**inka**) from only one **Zen** master. See **isshi inshô**.

Isshi Inshô

To receive **Dharma transmission** and **inka** from only one **Zen** master. Also pronounced "isshi injô." Isshi inshô

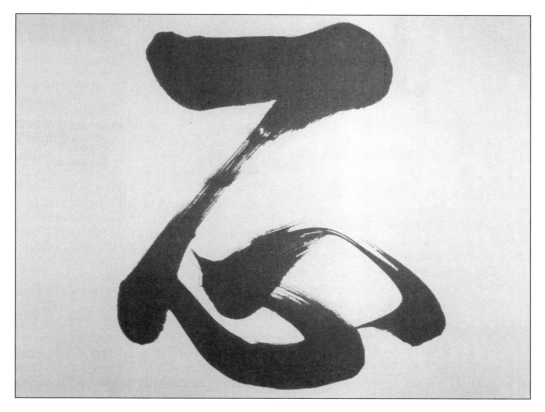

This Zen calligraphy depicts "Isshin," the Japanese term for "one mind," or enlightenment.

became one of the reform themes for Japanese Sôtô during the Tokugawa period (1600–1867). In earlier generations, it was common practice in the Sôtô school for **monks** to change Dharma **lineages** whenever they assumed a new position as **abbot** or head monk (**in'in ekishi**). Rather than maintaining identification with a single master and lineage, they assumed the Dharma seal of their immediate predecessor at each new post. The seventeenth-century Sôtô reformer Manzan opposed this practice and championed a return to the principle of isshi inshô. See also **Sôtô sect**.

Isshin
"**One mind**," Japanese term for the mind of **enlightenment** that perceives ultimate reality and transcends the dualism of ordinary thought and perception.

Isshitô Zen
See **One-finger Zen**.

Isshu
A hand position used during periods of walking **meditation** (**kinhin**). The left hand forms a fist around the thumb, and the right hand covers the left. The hands are held in front of the body with forearms straight.

Ittengo
"One **turning word**," a word or expression usually spoken by a **Zen** master that turns or shifts one's point of view and thereby leads the listener to suddenly attain **enlightenment**.

J

Jakugo

A verse that a **Zen** practitioner offers to his or her master in response to a **kôan**. The verse expresses the practitioner's understanding of the kôan, and hence of the **Dharma**. The practice of using capping verses in this manner developed gradually from a unique genre of Zen commentary found in the Zen kôan literature. In the classical period of Zen in China, the masters who compiled collections of kôan attached verses to each of the historical cases they included in their compendia, thereby expressing in poetic language their own understanding of the meaning of the kôan. Each kôan in the *Mumonkan*, for example, is accompanied by a verse composed by the **monk** who compiled the text.

Later, masters devised the practice of testing their students' progress by asking them for capping verses, which similarly expressed their understanding of a kôan. In eighteenth century Japan, **Hakuin Ekaku** (1685–1768) established a regularized system of kôan study, which applied the same principle, a system that is still used in the **Rinzai sect** today. When a disciple has made sufficient progress in contemplating a particular kôan, the master will ask for a capping phrase. The student then provides a verse, but not an original poem, composed on the spot. Rather, the student draws upon the classical Zen body of religious and secular literature to find an appropriate verse or phrase. The most common resource for this purpose is the *Zenrin Kushû*.

Miura, Isshû, and Ruth Fuller Sasaki. *The Zen Kôan*. New York: Harcourt, Brace & World, 1967.

———. *Zen Dust: The History of the Kôan and Kôan Study in Rinzai (Lin-chi) Zen*. New York: Harcourt, Brace & World, 1967.

Jakumetsu

Tranquility and extinction. Jakumetsu is the Japanese pronunciation of a Chinese compound sometimes used to translate the Sanskrit word *nirvana* in the scriptures. It is used as a synonym for nirvana and **enlightenment**. It can be understood to mean the state of tranquillity in which all of the **afflictions** (bonnô) have been extinguished.

Jakushitsu Genkô

(1290–1367) Japanese Rinzai **monk** of the Kamakura period (1185–1333), regarded as the founder of the **Eigen-ji** branch of the **Rinzai sect**. Jakushitsu was born in Mimasaka. His parents sent him to **Tôfuku-ji** in Kyoto when he was twelve years old so that he could receive a classical education. Two years later, the young man became determined to undertake a serious religious life. He left Tôfuku-ji and joined Yakuô Tokken (1245–1320) in Kamakura. When Tokken became **abbot** at **Kennin-ji**, Jakushitsu accompanied him. He attained **enlightenment** in 1306 and soon began a wandering life. He practiced with many of the Chinese émigré monks, including **Tung-ming Hui-jih** (1272–1340) and **I-shan I-neng** (1247–1317). Under the latter's influence, he became a refined poet.

Jakushitsu traveled to China in 1320 in order to become the disciple of **Chung-feng Ming-pen** (1263–1323). He practiced with the master at T'ien-mu-shan for one year, and then traveled throughout China for several years, visiting various masters. He returned to Japan in 1326, where he spent the next twenty-five years as a wandering monk. In 1361, Sasaki Ujiyori became his patron and built for him the monastery Eigen-ji in Omi province (modern day Shiga prefecture). Jakushitsu gathered a community of disciples at the temple and remained active as abbot for five years. In 1366, he retired in favor of his leading disciple, Miten Eishaku (d. 1406).

Jari

A common abbreviation for **ajari**. In Sôtô **Zen**, it is a title of respect used for a senior **monk** who has practiced Zen for more than five summer retreats. See **ajari**.

Jataka Tales

(J. Jataka or **Honshô**) Stories concerning the previous lives of Siddharta Gautama, the historical **Buddha**. Jataka tales represent a traditional form of Buddhist literature, which has long been used for popular instruction. In particular, the stories are used to illustrate various Buddhist virtues, especially the **six perfections** and the benefits of building good **karma**. They are also a common subject for Buddhist art. One collection of 547 jataka tales forms a part of the **Theravada** Buddhist canon; many other collections, canonical and otherwise, exist throughout the Buddhist world.

Ji

The Japanese term for temple, which commonly refers to Buddhist temples and monasteries. Ji generally appears as a part of any Buddhist temple's name. See **tera**.

Jigoku

The Japanese term for **hell**, one of the six realms of existence (rokudô) into which **sentient beings** are reborn. According to Buddhist teachings, actions in the present life determine one's next **rebirth**. Hell is the lowest and most painful of the six possibilities. If one commits evil acts and accumulates bad **karma**, one may be reborn in one of several hells. The tradition describes **eight hot hells** (hachinetsu jigoku), **eight cold hells** (hachikan jigoku), and various others. Each one entails a form

of **suffering** appropriate for various kinds of evil action performed in a previous existence. See also **six paths**.

Jihatsu

To beg for alms; one of the basic practices of Buddhist monastic life. Jihatsu is more commonly referred to as **takuhatsu** or **kotsu jiki**. The term may also refer to the **begging bowls** that **monks** own and use. See **begging alms**.

Jihi

Japanese Buddhist term for "**compassion**." The mental attitude of compassion toward all **sentient beings** is regarded as an ideal within the **Mahayana** tradition, and is manifested especially by **bodhisattvas** who vow to save all sentient beings from **suffering** and assist them toward **enlightenment**. The Japanese word is a compound of two Chinese characters: "ji" means "to give pleasure" and is related to the Sanskrit word *maitri*; "hi" means "to relieve suffering" and is related to the Sanskrit word *karuna*.

Jiin Hattô

Temple regulations enacted by the Tokugawa military government (**bakufu**) during the Tokugawa period (1600–1867) to control Buddhist temples in Japan. In the era immediately preceding the Tokugawa period, some Buddhist sects and individual temples maintained significant financial influence, and in some cases, impressive military power. The military leaders who unified Japan, leading to the establishment of the Tokugawa regime, opposed these Buddhist centers of power and brought them under secular control. The Tokugawa government intended the jiin hattô to maintain that control by limiting Buddhist groups' access to secular power. Most of the regulations were issued between 1615 and 1640. Although some were issued to regulate specific temples or individual sects of **Buddhism**, many were general in nature and applied to the entire network of sects and temples. Temple regulations forbade the construction of new temples and limited the restoration of dilapidated temples without government permission. They required that every temple claim a sectarian affiliation and be listed within the given sect's hierarchical structure of **main temples** and **branch temples**. In some cases, entire groups were banned, such as the Fujufuse sect of **Nichiren** Buddhism. Other regulations, directed at the clergy, were intended to encourage **monks** and **nuns** to engage in religious and intellectual pursuits. These specifically proscribed certain behaviors for monks and nuns, including inter-sectarian disputes, public debates, and some infractions against the **monastic code**.

Jikai

"Observance of the **precepts**." Keeping the Buddhist precepts is a value throughout the Buddhist world, although Buddhists understand the precepts somewhat differently depending on time, place, sect, and the status of the believer. Within the monastic world, **monks** and **nuns** are generally expected to live according to the code laid out in the **vinaya** texts, especially the **ten precepts** of **novices**. Lay people typically strive to follow the first five of these precepts. This holds true not only for **Theravada** Buddhists but for many Mahayana Buddhists as well. In some schools of **Mahayana Buddhism**, lay people, monks, and nuns strive to uphold the **bodhisattva precepts**, which may replace or supplement the precepts of the vinaya. However the precepts may be interpreted, observing them is generally regarded as one of the basic elements of Buddhist practice for all members of the community. Indeed, many Buddhist teachers regard ethical behavior as the starting point on the **Buddhist path**, the basis on which all other forms of practice are built. In Mahayana descriptions of the Buddhist path of a **bodhisattva**, for example,

observance of the precepts is the second of the **six perfections**. See also **Jikai Zen** and **lay believer**.

Jikai Zen

"Observe-the-precepts Zen," a term which can be applied to any style of **Zen** practice that emphasizes keeping the Buddhist **precepts**, especially the detailed **monastic code** for **monks** and **nuns**. In a Zen monastic context, keeping the precepts often implies living according to special monastic codes (J. **shingi**), developed specifically for Zen temples. In particular, the term applies to movements within the Zen world to reform and revitalize Zen practice by a renewed dedication to keeping the monastic codes.

Although the phrase *Jikai Zen* can be used in a positive manner, in most cases it suggests a negative criticism of overemphasis on the external observance of precepts. Zen monastic practice generally assumes a strict observance of the monastic code, which defines nearly every aspect of life in the monastery. Nevertheless, Zen teachings often take a critical stance against formalistic behavior based on the observance of an external moral code. In the **Platform Sutra** of the Sixth Patriarch, for example, **Hui-neng** (638–713) introduces the concept of preserving "**formless precepts**." This teaching stresses that the origin of the precepts lies within the enlightened mind, not in any external code. If the Zen practitioner becomes overly concerned with fulfilling the letter of the law rather than the motivating spirit within, the monastic code becomes a hindrance to practice rather than an enabling device.

Jikidô

In a **Zen** monastery, the **monk** assigns to watch over the robes and bowls in the **meditation hall**. Any lost items are the jikidô's responsibility. This duty traditionally rotates on a daily basis and is shared by all monks in turn.

Jikijitsu

The manager of the monks' hall, or **sôdô**. Originally, the term applied to the **monk** assigned to care for the robes and bowls of the monastic community. The monks rotated the duty on a daily basis. Today, in the **Rinzai sect**, the jikijitsu serves as the manager for the daily activities within the monks' hall. The manager of the monks' hall keeps track of the timing for **meditation** sessions, mealtimes, and other aspects of the daily schedule. He alerts the other monks through the use of a hand bell and sounding boards (**han**). The position of jikijitsu no longer rotates on a daily basis among the monks, but is an appointed position lasting for an entire retreat period. See also **jikidô**.

Jikishi Ninshin

"Direct pointing to the mind," a Japanese **Zen** expression used to characterize Zen practice and teachings, especially **meditation**. The Zen tradition maintains that one's mind is identical with the mind of the **Buddha**, if one only realizes it. By focusing one's attention inward on the mind, **enlightenment** becomes possible. All Zen teaching devices and practices are intended to serve as aids in attaining enlightenment, or "fingers pointing directly at the mind."

Jikishi Ninshin Kenshô Jôbutsu

"Direct pointing to the mind, seeing one's nature and becoming a **buddha**." The expression is part of a verse traditionally attributed to **Bodhidharma**, which provides the classical characterization of **Zen** practice. According to Zen teachings, all ordinary individuals already possess the buddha mind and are in fact originally buddhas. By focusing one's attention inward through the practice of **meditation**, one may be able to realize this reality and attain **enlightenment**. The process may be understood less as an ordinary person becoming a buddha than as a shift of perspective which allows a person to see his or her true nature.

Jikishi Tanden

Direct transmission of the **Dharma** from a **Zen** master to a disciple. This Japanese expression is used synonymously with **ishin denshin**, "transmission from mind to mind." See **ishin denshin**.

Jikkai

The **ten realms** of living beings, which include, in ascending order, 1) **hell** dwellers (**jigoku**), 2) **hungry ghosts** (**gaki**), 3) animals (chikushô), 4) human beings (ningen), 5) **ashura** (ashura), 6) **heaven** dwellers (tenjô), 7) **shravakas** (shômon), 8) **pratyeka buddhas** (engaku), 9) **bodhisattvas** (bosatsu), and 10) **buddhas** (Butsu). See **ten realms**.

Jikkai

(2) The **ten precepts** accepted by male and female **novices** at their **ordination**. Also pronounced "jukkai." The ten precepts represent the heart of the traditional Buddhist **monastic code**. They include 1) not to kill living beings; 2) not to steal; 3) to abstain from sexual misconduct; 4) not to lie; 5) not to take intoxicants; 6) not to eat after noon; 7) not to adorn the body with perfume, flowers, jewelry, etc.; 8) not to participate in public entertainment, including dancing, plays, singing, etc.; 9) not to use a luxurious bed; and 10) not to handle money. These **precepts** are sometimes known in Japanese as the shamikai, or novice precepts.

The term *jikkai* sometimes refers alternatively to the **ten heavy precepts** (Jûjû kinkai), the most important elements in the **bodhisattva precepts**. The ten heavy precepts are prohibitions against 1) killing, 2) stealing, 3) sexual misconduct, 4) lying, 5) using intoxicants, 6) finding fault in others, 7) boasting about oneself, 8) envy, 9) anger and ill will, and 10) slandering the **three treasures**. The Japanese

Sôtô and Rinzai communities use the ten heavy precepts developed within the **Mahayana** tradition in place of the above novice precepts, which derive from the **Theravada** tradition. See **ten heavy precepts** and **ten precepts**.

Jin

"**Dust**," a Japanese Buddhist expression for the objects of human perception, including sights, sounds, tastes, textures, aromas, and mental images. The term has negative connotations suggesting contamination or defilement, since tradition maintains that sensory perceptions may stimulate desires. Desires lead to **attachment** and ultimately result in **suffering**. See **dust**.

Jinjû

"Steward of purity," the sanitation steward at a **Zen** monastery, responsible for keeping the latrines clean. In a Zen monastery, cleaning the toilets was not traditionally relegated to lay attendants or junior **monks**. Senior monks were expected to hold the position. See also **lay believer**.

Jinne

The Japanese pronunciation for **Ho-tse Shen-hui** (670–762), an early Chinese **Zen monk**. See **Ho-tse Shen-hui**.

Jinshi Eison

(1195–1272) Japanese Buddhist **monk** of the Kamakura period (1185–1333). Eison was born in Echigo, present day Fukuoka Prefecture. He became a Buddhist monk at age seven, studying the Tendai tradition. He was first introduced to **Zen** by **Shakuen Eichô** (d.1247) at Chôraku-ji, a Tendai temple where a combined form of **esoteric** and Zen **Buddhism** were practiced. In 1235, he journeyed to China where he studied an exclusive form of Rinzai Zen. He returned to Japan in 1238. In 1240, he became founding **abbot** at Manjuji in Echizen. See also **Tendai sect**.

Jinshû

The Japanese pronunciation for **Shen-hsiu** (606?–706), an early Chinese **Zen monk**. See **Shen-hsiu**.

Jiri

Phenomena and noumena, or relative and absolute. The Japanese term, based on the Chinese term *shih-li*, is used in technical philosophical discussions on the nature of reality. The character *ji* typically refers to things experienced in the phenomenal world, while *ri* refers to an underlying principle or reality. In a Buddhist context, *ri* is most often associated with the concept of **emptiness**.

Jiriki

"**Self Power**", the Japanese term for seeking **enlightenment** through one's own **merit** and religious practice. See **Self Power**.

Ji Sect

"Time sect," a sect of Japanese **Pure Land Buddhism** founded by the **monk Ippen** (1239–1289) during the Kamakura period (1185–1333). The name is said to signify that members chant the **nembutsu** at all times of the day and night. In the early generations of its history, all members of the Ji sect followed Ippen's example and were expected to practice yugyô, or constant travel to spread the teachings, and fusan, the distribution of nembutsu tablets. Later, the sect allowed for **lay believers** who did not leave the home to devote their lives to religious practice.

Jisha

Attendants to the **abbot**; younger **monks** who serve the abbot as personal assistants. In medieval monasteries, the jisha were selected from among the more talented or promising young monks. The position was coveted because it provided important training in the workings of monastic life. Serving as a jisha prepared a young monk to later assume high-ranking monastic offices.

The abbot typically had five attendants, who served in a variety of roles. They assisted in serving tea, cared for the abbot's **incense** box, served as acolytes at ritual functions, received the abbot's guests, handled the abbot's personal correspondence, kept the abbot's personal financial accounts, and provided medical attention and herbal treatments. The jisha were often assisted in their duties by **anja**, lay attendants who did most of the strenuous physical labor. See also **lay believer**.

Jishô

"Self Nature" or "Original Nature," a Japanese **Zen** expression used to indicate the **Buddha Nature**, which is inherent in all **sentient beings**. Realization of one's original nature, freed from the veil of **delusion**, is **enlightenment**. In Zen contexts, jishô is used synonymously with the terms *Honshô* (Original Nature), *Busshô* (Buddha Nature), and *Nyoraizô* (**Tathagata Garbha**). In most Buddhist contexts, however, the term *jishô* is used quite differently. In **Mahayana** texts it was first used as the Japanese translation of the Sanskrit concept of svabhava, a permanent, unchanging self. According to the Buddhist teaching of **emptiness**, all things are devoid of self-nature in this sense of the word.

Jishô Butsu

"One's self nature is itself **Buddha**." This is a Japanese **Zen** expression for **original enlightenment**, the affirmation that ordinary individuals possess the **Buddha Nature**. If one is freed from all delusions, one will see one's true nature and attain enlightenment.

Jishô Kai

"**Precepts** of the self nature," a **Mahayana** expression in Japanese indicating that observance of the **bodhisattva precepts** is a natural expression of one's inherent **Buddha Nature**. Since one's true nature is Buddha Nature, the Buddhist precepts are not an external moral code. Used as a synonym for **Honshôkai**.

Jishô Shôjô

Self nature, originally pure and free from **delusion**. The Japanese term may be used as a synonym for Nyoraizô (**Tathagata Garbha**) and **Shinshin** (**True Mind**).

Jissatsu Temples

"Ten Distinguished Temples," a designation for a lower ranking within the **Gozan system** of Chinese and Japanese **Zen** monasteries. In the original Chinese system, the Ten Temples referred to a group of ten Zen monasteries, which ranked below the prestigious Five Mountains. Along with the Five Mountains, the Ten Temples received some government patronage. In Japan, the number of Jissatsu temples was not strictly limited to ten. As the second tier in the Gozan system, the Jissatsu designation was at one time limited to ten monasteries in Kyoto and ten monasteries in Kamakura, which were regarded as less prestigious than the Gozan monasteries. The category gradually extended to include a number of temples in Kyoto and Kamakura as well as numerous important provincial monasteries throughout the country. See also **Gozan system**.

Jizô

"Earth womb," the Japanese name for the cosmic **bodhisattva** known as Kshitigarbha in Sanskrit. In China, he is known as Ti-tsang. The name may derive from the popular belief that the historical **Buddha** invoked Kshitigarbha's name to bear witness that he had overcome **Mara's** temptation. In images of that episode, the Buddha is depicted pointing to the earth. Although Kshitigarbha was never a popular figure in Indian and Central Asian **Buddhism**, he became

Jizô is an especially popular bodhisattva in Japan; his image often appears
at temples and roadside shrines.

progressively more popular in East Asia. Devotion to Jizô is strongest in Japan, where his image is commonly found at roadside shrines in the countryside, at city street corners, and at many temples.

As a part of his **bodhisattva vows**, Jizô swore to remain in the realm of **samsara** throughout the difficult period between the death of Shakyamuni Buddha (**Siddharta Gautama**) Buddha, and the birth of the future buddha **Maitreya**. He is said to travel freely among the **six paths** (rokudô) into which **sentient beings** are born, offering assistance to anyone in need. In particular, Jizô willingly journeys down to the realm of **hell**, where he relieves the **suffering** of hell dwellers and **hungry ghosts**. Jizô is understood to be a guide for individuals making the transition from one birth to the next, especially for children. Because of this, Jizô has strong associations with children: women pray to him when they wish to get pregnant or are hoping for an easy childbirth, and bereaved parents request Jizô's help in guiding a deceased child through the afterlife. In modern day Japan, Jizô is a prominent cult image for women who have had abortions.

In Japanese Buddhist iconography, Jizô is depicted as a young **monk** with shaven head and monastic robes. In many cases, he is surrounded by small children, regarded as his special charges. He carries a staff (shakujô) with six rings in his right hand and a **mani** jewel in his left. The six rings represent the six paths of samsaric existence. Grouping six Jizô images together (**roku jizô**) is another popular device for illustrating the same concept.

de Visser, Marinus Willem. "The Bodhisattva Ti-Tsang in China and Japan." *Ostasiatische Zeitschift* 2 (1913).

La Fleur, William R. *The Karma of Words: Buddhism and the Literary Arts in Medieval Japan.* Berkeley, CA: University of California Press, 1983.

————. *Liquid Life: Abortion and Buddhism in Japan.* Princeton, NJ: Princeton University Press, 1992.

Jôchi-ji

An important Rinzai monastery in Kamakura, Japan. Jôchi-ji was founded by the Chinese master **Ta-hsiu Chengnien** (1259–1289) in 1283. It was later designated as one of the Gozan monasteries in Japan. See also **Gozan system** and **Rinzai sect**.

Jôdô

"To go up to the hall," which usually refers to a **Zen abbot** entering the lecture hall and going up to the lecture platform to give a formal sermon to the assembly. Alternatively, it may refer to **monks** and **nuns** entering the **meditation hall** or monks' hall (**sôdô**) for a meal. In some cases the term may also refer to the upper (or eastern) portion of the monks' hall.

Jôdo

(2) **Pure Land**, the Japanese term for the Mahayana Buddhist concept of a celestial world or paradise created by a **buddha**. In most cases, jôdo refers specifically to the **Western Pure Land** of **Amida buddha**. See **Pure Land**.

Jôdô-e

The East Asian Buddhist festival celebrating the **Buddha's enlightenment** under the **bodhi tree**. The holiday is more commonly known as Rôhatsu-e or simply **Rôhatsu**. It was traditionally observed on the eighth day of the twelfth lunar month, but is now celebrated on December 8th in Japan. See **Rôhatsu**.

Jôdo no Sanbukyô

The three **Pure Land Sutras**, which form the scriptural basis for the Pure Land teachings. In Japanese, the three titles are Daimuryôjukyô (Larger Pure Land Sutra), Amidakyô (Amida Sutra, also known as the Smaller Pure Land Sutra), and Kammuryôjukyô (Meditation Sutra).

Jôdo Shinshû

True Pure Land sect of Japanese **Buddhism**, founded by the **monk Shinran** (1173–1262) during the Kamakura period (1185–1333). See **True Pure Land sect**.

Jôdo-Shû

The **Pure Land sect** of Japanese **Buddhism**, founded by the **monk Hônen** (1133–1212) during the Kamakura period (1185–1333). See **Pure Land sect**.

Jôjû

The term literally means permanence, something that remains without change. In a **Zen** monastery, it refers to the public property of the community, those things available for common use as opposed to the private belongings of the **monks** or **nuns**. In this sense, it refers to buildings, grounds, utensils, and food supplies. By extension, the term may also be used as a reference to the administrative office of the monastery. The temple administration bears responsibility for the business of running the monastery, including food preparation, the upkeep of the public property, seeing to visitors, etc.

Jômyô-ji

An important Rinzai monastery in Kamakura, Japan. Jômyô-ji was originally founded as a Shingon temple in 1188, by the shogun Ashikaga Yoshikane (1147–1196). It was later converted to a **Zen** temple by his son Yoshiuji (1189–1254). **Taikô Gyôyû** (1163–1241), a **Dharma heir** of **Eisai** (1141–1215), is officially listed as the founding **abbot**. The monastery was later designated as one of the Gozan monasteries in Japan. See also **Gozan system**, **Rinzai sect**, and **Shingon sect**.

Jôshû Jûshin

The Japanese name for **Chao-chou Ts'ung-shen** (778–897), one of the outstanding **Zen** masters of the T'ang dynasty (618–907). See **Chao-chou Ts'ung-shen**.

Jôza

"High seat," a term for the highest ranking monastic officer in a **Zen** temple after the **abbot**. The term refers to the Jôza's position beside the abbot on the **meditation** platform. It is more commonly referred to as the **shuso**. See **shuso**.

Jûaku

The **ten evil acts**. They are: 1) killing a living being (sesshô); 2) stealing (chûtô); 3) sexual misconduct (jain); 4) lying (môgo); 5) slander (akku), 6) using language that causes dissention among others (ryôzetsu), 7) idle talk (kigo), 8) greed (ton'yoku), 9) giving way to anger (shinni), and 10) holding wrong views (jaken). The jûaku are the opposites of jûzen, the **ten good acts**. See **ten evil acts**.

Ju-ching

(1163–1228; J. Nyojô) Chinese Sôtô master of the Sung dynasty (960–1279) best known as the **Dharma** master of **Dôgen Kigen** (1200–1253), the founder of Japanese Sôtô. He is also known as T'ien-t'ung Ju-ching (J. Tendô Nyojô) after Mount T'ien-t'ung where he was the **abbot** at **Ching-te-ssu**. He was the **Dharma heir** of Tsu-an Chih-chien. Ju-ching stressed the importance of seated **meditation** and the strict observance of proper monastic behavior. See also **Sôtô sect**.

Jûdai Deshi

The ten great disciples of Shakyamuni **Buddha** (**Siddharta Gautama**). Among the immediate disciples of the Buddha, the tradition has singled out ten as outstanding in some respect. Their names, in Japanese, are: 1) Anan (Sk. **Ananda**), known for hearing and recalling the **sermons** of the Buddha; 2) Anaritsu (Sk. **Anuruddha**), known for his divine insight; 3) Kasennen (Sk. **Katyayana**), known for analyzing the teachings; 4) Makakashô (Sk. **Mahakashyapa**), known for his dedication to ascetic practice; 5) Mokuren (Sk. **Maudgalyâyana**), known for his psychic powers; 6) Furuna (Sk. **Purna**), known for his eloquence and skill in debate; 7) Ragora (Sk. **Rahula**), known for his dedication to training young **novices**; 8) Sharihotsu (Sk. **Shariputra**), known for his deep wisdom; 9) Shubodai (Sk. **Subhuti**), known for his deep understanding of the teaching of **emptiness**; and 10) Ubari (Sk. **Upali**), known for his strict observance of the **precepts**.

The **Zen** school reveres Makakashô and Anan as the first and second of the twenty-eight Indian **Patriarchs** of Zen.

Juen

"To enter the temple," an expression for the formal installation of a new **abbot** at a **Zen** temple or monastery. It is alternatively pronounced "nyûin." The ceremony was generally witnessed by honored guests, usually high-ranking **monks** from other monasteries as well as government officials. The most senior visitor officiated as **byakutsui**, calling the assembly to order at each stage of the ceremony. According to ritual protocol, the new abbot would enter through the main gate, offer **incense**, and say a few words to the gathered assembly. He would then proceed to the Buddha hall where he would offer incense and prayers, followed by a short sermon. The abbot would visit various other halls within the monastery, and then formally register at the monks' hall (**sôdô**). Since all newly arrived monks and **nuns** register in a similar manner at the monks' hall, the term *juen* sometimes is used for the entry of a new resident, especially a **novice**, to a Zen monastery. Only after registering did the new abbot take possession of the abbot's quarters. See **shinsanshiki**.

Jufuku-ji

An important Rinzai monastery in Kamakura, Japan, and the first **Zen** monastery in that city. Jufuku-ji was founded by **Eisai** (1141–1215) in 1200. Hôjô Masako (1157–1225), the widow of the founding **shôgun** of the Kamakura period (1185–1333), Minamoto Yoritomo, had the monastery built in the memory of her deceased husband. It was later designated as one of the Gozan monasteries in Japan. See also **Gozan system** and **Rinzai sect**.

Jûgô

The ten epithets or honorific titles of the **Buddha**. In Japanese they are: 1) Nyorai, (**Tathagata** or Thus Come One), 2) Ogu (**arhat**, or a holy one worthy of veneration), 3) Shôhenchi (Fully **enlightened one**), 4) Myôgyôsoku (Possessor of Wisdom and Practice), 5) Zenzei (Well Gone One), 6) Sekenge (Knower of the World), 7) Mujôshi (Unsurpassed), 8) Jôgojôbu (Trainer of Human Beings), 9) Tenninshi (Teacher of gods and human beings), and 10) Butsu seson (the Buddha, the **World-Honored One**).

Jûgyûzu

"Ten **oxherding pictures**," a series of ten drawings of an ox and an oxherder, which describe the process of **Zen** practice and **enlightenment**. The oxherder represents the Zen practitioner seeking enlightenment while the ox represents the true self. The original pictures are attributed to the twelfth-century Chinese Zen **monk** K'uo-an Shih-yuan (J. **Kakuan Shion**; d. 1234). The ten pictures are known in Japanese as: 1) jingyû (seeking the ox); 2) kenshaku (finding its footprints); 3) kengyû (seeing the ox); 4) tokugyû (catching the ox); 5) bokugyû (herding the ox); 6) kigyû kike (riding the ox home); 7) bôgyû zonnin (forgetting the ox, but not the self); 8) ningyû kubô (forgetting both ox and self); 9) henpon gengen (returning to the source); and 10) nitten suishu (entering the marketplace to bestow blessings on others).

Jûji

"One who dwells in the world and maintains the **Dharma**," the Japanese term for an **abbot** or chief **monk** at a monastery or temple. It is said that the abbot teaches the Dharma in place of the **Buddha** and the **patriarchs** of **Zen** and thus makes their **compassion** manifest.

At a training monastery or large temple, the abbot serves as the chief administrative officer for the entire community. At a smaller temple, the jûji may be the only monk in residence. In such cases, it is more appropriate to call him the chief monk. The abbot is responsible for the smooth functioning of both the administrative side of the monastery and the **meditation** and training side, the so-called eastern (**tôhan**) and western (**seihan**) ranks. For this reason, he oversees the work done by the other high-ranking officers of the monastery. In addition, the abbot is the primary teacher of the Dharma for the monastic community. He holds the "great assemblies" (**daisan**) several times each month to instruct the community on the Dharma.

Jûji

(2) **Ten stages of a bodhisattva**. Also pronounced "jucchi." In Japanese, the ten stages are: 1) kangiji (the stage of joy in benefiting oneself and others), 2) rikuji (the stage of freedom from all defilement), 3) hakkôji (the stage of emitting the light of wisdom), 4) enneji (the stage of radiating wisdom), 5) nanshôji (the stage at which one is difficult to conquer), 6) genzenji (the stage at which reality is manifested before one's eyes), 7) ongyôji (the stage of going far), 8) fudôji (the stage of being immovable), 9) zenneji (the stage of attaining expedient wisdom), and 10) hôunji (the stage when one can spread the **Dharma** like a cloud). See **ten stages of a bodhisattva**.

Jûjûkinkai

The **ten heavy precepts**. The primary precepts of the **bodhisattva** path, derived from the Bonmôkyô (**Brahma Net Sutra**). The ten include prohibitions against: 1) killing, 2) stealing, 3) sexual misconduct, 4) lying, 5) using intoxicants, 6) finding fault in others, 7) boasting about oneself, 8) envy, 9) anger and ill will, and 10) slandering the **three treasures**. A secondary set of **forty-eight light precepts** (**shijûhachikyôkai**) fill out the full **bodhisattva precepts** which guide the practice of **Mahayana** Buddhists. See **ten heavy precepts**.

Jukai

"To receive the **precepts**." In most cases, this expression indicates **ordination** as a Buddhist **monk** or **nun**, since monks and nuns accept the **monastic code** at their ordination ceremony. In **Theravada Buddhism** and many parts of the **Mahayana** tradition, **novices** first receive the **ten precepts** of a novice before accepting the full compliment of 250 precepts for monks and 500 precepts for nuns. In Japan, many Buddhist sects, including **Zen**, use an alternative set of precepts known as the **bodhisattva precepts**.

A related Japanese term with the same pronunciation but written with different Chinese characters means "to bestow the precepts." This refers to a Buddhist monk or nun granting some form of the Buddhist precepts on **lay believers**, novices, or monks and nuns.

Jukaie

Ceremony for receiving the **precepts**. In most cases, this refers to a Buddhist **ordination** ceremony for **monks** or **nuns** in which they accept the monastic precepts as a part of joining the monastic community. In some contexts, the term may refer to ceremonies designed for all Buddhist practitioners, lay people and monastics, at which they receive the **bodhisattva precepts** and renew their commitment to **Buddhism**. See also **lay believer**.

Buddhist monks or nuns are ordained during the Jukai ceremony.

Jûrokujôkai

The sixteen article **precepts** that form the basis for Sôtô **ordinations**. The sixteen precepts, sometimes called the **bodhisattva precepts**, include the three refuges (**sankikai**), the three pure precepts (sanshujôkai), and the **ten heavy precepts** (jûjûkinkai). These sixteen precepts are understood to encompass the entire moral code of **Mahayana Buddhism**. **Dôgen Kigen** (1200–1253) spelled out the sixteen precepts and the manner of ordination in a chapter in the *Shôbôgenzô* entitled "**Jukai**" (Receiving the Precepts). See also **Sôtô sect**.

Yôkoi, Yûhô, and Daizen Victoria. *Zen Master Dôgen: An Introduction with Selected Writings*. New York: Weatherhill, 1976.

Jûzen

The **ten good acts**. They are: 1) not killing living beings (fusesshô); 2) not stealing (fuchûtô); 3) abstaining from sexual misconduct (fujain); 4) not lying (fumôgo); 5) not committing slander (fuakku), 6) not using language that causes dissention among others (furyôzetsu), 7) not engaging in idle talk (fukigo), 8) not acting out of greed (futon'yoku), 9) not giving way to anger (fushinni), and 10) not holding wrong views (fujaken). They are the opposites of jûaku, the **ten evil acts**. See **ten good acts**.

K

Kada

Japanese transliteration of the Sanskrit term *gâthâ*, a form of religious verse. See **gâthâ**.

Kadô

"The way of flowers," a traditional Japanese art form, closely associated with the tea ceremony (**chanoyû**). Kadô is popularly known as ikebana, or flower arranging. Although flower arranging predates the introduction of **Zen Buddhism** to Japan, it is now indirectly associated with the Zen tradition.

Kaichin

The **Zen** expression for laying out one's bed and retiring for the night. At the sound of the kaichin bell, resident **monks** or **nuns** take down their bedding, which is stored in the monks' hall, or (**sôdô**). Traditionally, Zen monks and nuns use only one futon, or mattress pad, and no pillow. Since they are allowed no other blankets, they roll themselves into the single futon on cold nights.

Kaidan

Ordination platform; a platform on which one receives the Buddhist **precepts** as a part of the ordination ceremony. The tradition of designating special sites for ordination ceremonies is said to date to the time of the historical **Buddha**. In the ancient tradition, the community would mark out a special area known as a sima for ordination rituals. In East Asia, it became customary to construct platforms with three steps for this purpose. The first ordination platform was constructed in China at Lo-yang in the middle of the third century. The first kaidan in Japan was constructed at Tôdai-ji in Nara under the direction of the Chinese **Vinaya** master **Chien-chen** (688–763; J. Ganjin). Initially, all Buddhist **monks** and **nuns** in Japan received their full ordination at a few officially sanctioned ordination platforms under the supervision of masters from the **Ritsu** school. The Japanese monk **Saichô** (767–822), founder of the **Tendai sect** of **Buddhism**, later altered this pattern. He received permission to construct a **Mahayana** kaidan on Mount Hiei specifically for Tendai ordinations. Unlike ordinations held at the Ritsu kaidan, Tendai monks were ordained using a set of Mahayana precepts known as the **bodhisattva precepts**. After that time, it became common practice for each sect of Japanese Buddhism to maintain its own ordination platforms.

Matsunaga, Daigan, and Alicia Matsunaga. *Foundation of Japanese Buddhism.* 2 vols. Los Angeles, CA: Buddhist Books International, 1976.

Kaidan Seki

A stone tablet posted outside the gates of both the **Zen** and **Ritsu** monasteries, which announces that meat, fish, and alcohol are forbidden within temple grounds. Although the sign only specifies a few items forbidden by the **monastic code**, it is intended to indicate that the monastic community maintains all of the **precepts** received by its members at **ordination**.

Kaigen

"Opening the eyes." The root meaning of the term is the experience of **enlightenment**, when one sees through the delusions of ordinary thinking and opens the **Buddha** eye to see things as they really are. The term also denotes the consecration ritual used for enshrining a new Buddhist image, usually that of a buddha or **bodhisattva**. At the consecration ceremony, the eyes of the image are symbolically opened in some manner. In some cases, the image may be fully draped or the face covered until an appropriate point in the ritual when the image is uncovered. In the **Zen** sect, the eyes may be opened by the officiant drawing a circle (J. ensu) in black ink.

According to traditional accounts within the Obaku Zen sect, a kaigen ceremony was held at **Mampuku-ji** in 1663 to enshrine a set of sixteen life-size statues of **arhats**. The masters **Mu-an Hsing-t'ao** (1611–1684; J. Mokuan Shôtô) and **Chi-fei Ju-i** (1616–1671; J. Sokuhi Nyoitsu) officiated, each consecrating eight of the images. Mu-an is said to have proceeded down the row, politely offering **incense**, bowing, and reciting the appropriate **Dharma** words before each statue. Chi-fei neither bowed nor offered incense. He walked up to each arhat in turn, struck the image squarely between the eyes and said, "This **monk's** eyes are already open." See also **Obaku sect**.

Kaihan

An announcement of the time of day. At Japanese Rinzai monasteries, the time of day is announced three times daily, at daybreak, dusk, and bedtime. This is done by sounding a **han** hanging outside the monks' hall (**sôdô**). See also **Rinzai sect**.

Kaiki

"To open a foundation"; a term for the founding patron of a Buddhist temple or monastery or the founding of a temple by a patron. In most cases, founding patrons were lay Buddhists who donated money to construct a new temple in order to build **merit**. **Buddhism** teaches that **lay believers** accrue merit from such good deeds, especially donations made to a monastic community. Lay believers built temples, thus providing shelter to **monks** and **nuns**, for a variety of spiritual and practical benefits. They could hope to ensure a better **rebirth** in the next life for themselves or for deceased family members. In some cases, patrons built temples in order to promote physical health, to ensure themselves and their family a longer life, or to maintain peace within the country. Emperors, military rulers, and wealthy government officials often provided patronage for the Buddhist monastic order by founding temples.

Kaimyô

A special Buddhist name conferred on an individual at the time of **ordination** as a **monk** or **nun**. The term literally means "precept name," since monks and nuns receive the name when they accept the **precepts** at their ordination. Generally speaking, the name is chosen by the ordinand's teacher, known as the precept master. The name may indicate the **lineage** of the new monk or nun and may suggest an aspect of the person's character. In the **Zen** sect, a master may confer a new kaimyô on a previously ordained individual when first accepting the individual as a disciple.

In Japanese Buddhist practice, the term is also used for the special Buddhist name that most lay people receive after death. For this reason, kaimyô is often referred to as the **posthumous name**. The kaimyô is usually conferred on the deceased at the first seventh day service (**shonan**), held seven days after death. At that service, the presiding monk confers the precepts on the deceased, symbolically ordaining the person as a monk or nun. The name indicates the gender of the individual and may indicate social standing in the community.

Whether referring to a name received posthumously or at ordination, the related term *hômyô*, or "**Dharma** name," may also be used. Hômyô is used more commonly in the **Obaku sect** than in Sôtô or Rinzai. See also **lay believer**, **Rinzai sect**, and **Sôtô sect**.

Kaisan

"To open a mountain," a term for the founding **abbot** of a temple or monastery. All **Zen** temples have a mountain name, regardless of where they actually are built. The practice of mountain names harkens back to the tradition of Zen masters building **meditation** huts in the mountains, removed from the distractions of towns and cities. Disciples wishing instruction would seek out a noted master even in a remote area, and in this way, masters built up a meditative community based on their reputation; construction of a temple complex followed later. The early founding abbots were therefore said to open the mountain. The term now applies to any founding abbot. The term is also used in reference to the founder of a Buddhist sect or a Zen **lineage**.

In many cases, the kaisan may not have initiated construction of the new temple. A founding patron (**kaiki**) may appoint or invite a particular **monk** or **nun** to serve as the first abbot after the building project is complete. It is not uncommon for a monk or nun to name their own Zen master as the founding abbot, sometimes posthumously, as a sign of appreciation and respect.

The fortieth case of the *Mumonkan* recounts how master **Pai-chang Huai-hai** (720–814) selected the kaisan of a new monastery. The master challenged his disciples to respond (**agyo**) to his question, with the understanding that the winner would become the founder. "[Pai-chang] took a water jug and put it on the ground. He asked, 'You must not call this a water jug. So, what will you call it?' The chief seat (**shuso**) answered, 'You can't say it's a wooden post.' Then Pai-chang asked **Kuei-shan Ling-yu** (771–853). Kuei-shan knocked the water jug over and left. Pai-chang laughed and said, 'The chief seat loses to Kuei-shan!' Thereupon, Pai-chang made Kuei-shan the founding abbot."

Kaisandô

Japanese for founder's hall, a monastery building dedicated to the temple's founding **abbot**. See **founder's hall**.

Kaisan Shidô Bu'nan Anju Zenji Anroku

"The **Biography** of the Founder, the Hermitage-dwelling **Zen** Master **Shidô Bu'nan**," composed by **Tôrei Enji** (1721–1792). The brief text provides a basic biographical sketch of Shidô Bu'nan (1603–1676), a Rinzai master from the

lineage of **Kanzan Egen** who was the teacher of **Dôkyô Etan** (1642–1721), the master of **Hakuin Ekaku** (1685–1768). See also **Rinzai sect**.

Kaiyoku

"To open the bath." At traditional **Zen** monasteries, the bath house was prepared and a hot bath provided for the resident **monks** or **nuns** only on specially designated days. According to the *Chokushû Shingi*, the bath was prepared every five days during the winter retreat and daily during the summer retreat. At Sôtô monasteries, bath days were generally observed on days with the numerals 4 or 9, the **shikunichi**. According to Zen **monastic codes**, the bath house is one of three areas within temple grounds where silence is observed. See also **Sôtô sect**.

Kaji Ichige

"To give a forceful shout," an expression used in reference to the moment of attaining **satori** (**enlightenment**). **Zen** masters often use a loud shout, called "**katsu!**" in Japanese, as a teaching device. Shouting serves to shock a student caught up in ordinary thinking into an experience of enlightenment. At the moment of breakthrough, the student may also give a great shout.

Kako Shichibutsu

Japanese for the **seven buddhas of the past**, whose biographies appear at the beginning of the *Transmission of the Lamp* (Ch. *Ching-te Chüan-teng Lu*; J. *Keitoku Dentôroku*) and other traditional accounts of the history of **Zen Buddhism** through the ages. The names of the seven in Japanese are Bibashi Butsu (Sk. **Vipashyin buddha**), Shiki Butsu (Sk. **Shikhin buddha**), Bishabu Butsu (Sk. **Vishvabhu buddha**), Kuruson Butsu (Sk. **Krakucchanda buddha**), Kunagonmuni Butsu (Sk. **Kanakamuni buddha**), Kashô Butsu (Sk. **Kashyapa buddha**), and Shakamuni Butsu (Sk. Shakyamuni Buddha or **Siddharta Gautama**). See **seven buddhas of the past**.

Moss garden of Saihô-ji (later renamed Kôkoku-ji), founded by Kakushin in Wakayama, Japan.

Kakua

(b. 1142) Japanese Buddhist **monk** who traveled to Sung China and became a Rinzai master there. Kakua was originally a Tendai monk who studied on Mount Hiei before he became interested in **Zen**. He went to China in 1171 and practiced under the Rinzai master Hui-yüan (1103–1176), better known as Fo-hai Ch'an-shih, of the Yang-ch'i **lineage**. He received the master's Dharma seal (**inka**) in 1175 and returned to Japan to propagate Zen. Kakua was among the first to attempt to spread Zen teachings in Japan, but he was largely unsuccessful. It is said that when Emperor Takakura (r. 1161–1181) invited him to court to speak about Zen, Kakua responded by playing a single note on his flute. The emperor and his entourage were not convinced, and Kakua eventually retired to a small hermitage on Mount Hiei, where he practiced Zen until his death. See also **Rinzai sect**, **Tendai sect**, and **Yang-ch'i school**.

Kakuan Shion

(d. ca. 1234) A Japanese **monk** from the **Daruma sect**, an early Japanese school of **Zen**. Kakuan Shion was a disciple of the sect's founder, **Dainichi Nônin;** he continued to train disciples at Sambô-ji after Nônin's death. He moved the sect's headquarters and set up a monastery at Tônomine, in the Nara area, to avoid harassment from Tendai monks from Mount Hiei. After Kakuan's death his disciple Ekan (d. 1251) led the group until they joined **Dôgen Kigen's** (1200–1253) community at **Eihei-ji**. Kakuan's former disciples, Ejô (1198–1280) and Ekan, became leading disciples of Dôgen.

Kakushin

(1207–1298) Shinchi Kakushin or Muhon Kakushin was a Japanese Buddhist **monk** of the Kamakura period (1185–1333), regarded as the founder of the **Fuke sect**. Kakushin was born in what is now Nagano Prefecture; at age fourteen, he entered Buddhist orders in the Shingon tradition of **esoteric Buddhism**. Later he went to study at Mount Kôya. He studied **Zen** in Japan under such masters as **Taikô Gyôyû** (1163–1241), **Shakuen Eichô** (d. 1247), and **Dôgen Kigen** (1200–1253), before traveling to China in 1249. In China, he received **Dharma transmission** from **Wu-men Hui-k'ai** (1183–1260), compiler of the *Mumonkan*. Kakushin introduced that important **kôan** collection to Japan when he returned in 1254. After coming home, he founded Saihô-ji (later renamed Kôkoku-ji) in Wakayama, where he remained for the rest of his life. He resisted all attempts by retired, Buddhist-minded emperors to draw him into the Zen community in Kyoto or Kamakura, preferring a life of solitude. His **lineage** was known as the **Hottô-ha**. See also **Shingon sect**.

Kalpa

(J. kô) A world age or a world cycle; a traditional measure of time used in various Indian religions. It indicates an incalculably long period, lasting several thousand eons. In some parts of the Hindu tradition, for example, a kalpa is understood to be a single day for the god Brahma, lasting 4,320 million earth years. The Buddhist tradition metaphorically defines the duration of a kalpa as the time required to empty a ten-mile-square city filled with poppy seeds, if one removes one seed every three years. Alternatively, a kalpa is the time required for a heavenly woman to wear away a ten-cubic-mile rock by rubbing it with her robe once every three years.

Kami

A Shintô spirit or deity. Shintô, the indigenous religious tradition in Japan, recognizes the existence of a wide variety of spiritual beings which are known as kami, including supernatural deities described in mythological terms like stories of the gods from other cultures. The concept of kami is not limited, however, to beings understood as gods in the usual Western sense of the word. Some kami represent forces in nature, such as the sun, the moon, wind and storms, etc. The most important deity of this kind is Amaterasu, the Sun Goddess. Amaterasu is revered as the highest kami in the heavens and is regarded as an ancestor of the imperial family. Other kami are legendary heroes or prominent historical figures who became kami after death. Even living human beings may be regarded as kami under certain extraordinary circumstances. In addition, there are many places identified as kami, including mountains, waterfalls, extraordinary rock formations, and the like. The concept of kami encompasses the understanding that nature is a sacred force. According to the classical definition written by Motoori Norinaga, the leading Shinto scholar of the eighteenth and nineteenth centuries, a kami may be anything extraordinary, mysterious, or awe-inspiring.

Kana Hôgo

Dharma lectures composed in Japanese rather than classical Chinese. Kana hôgo represents a genre of Japanese Buddhist literature designed to make its teachings accessible to a broader audience. Traditionally, Buddhist **monks** wrote about **Buddhism** in classical Chinese, the literary language used by the elite educated classes for all scholarly writing. Kana refers to two Japanese phonetic syllabaries (hiragana and katakana) of approximately fifty characters each, which allow the spoken language to be rendered in written form. Hôgo literally means "words on the Dharma" and refers to a lesson or sermon about the Buddhist teachings.

Kanakamuni Buddha

(J. Kunagonmuni) One of the **seven Buddhas of the past** whose biographies appear at the beginning of the *Transmission of the Lamp* (Ch. **Ching-te Chüan-teng Lu**; J. *Keitoku Dentôroku*) and other traditional accounts of the history of **Zen Buddhism** through the ages. Kanakamuni is the fifth on the list and is identified as the second **buddha** of the present eon.

Kanben

Brief conversations between a **Zen** master and a disciple in which the master tests the disciple's understanding of the **Dharma**. The *Sayings of Lin-chi* includes a selection of kanben, for example. Kanben is the Japanese rendering of the Chinese term *k'an-pien*.

Kanbutsu

"Bathing the **Buddha**;" the ritual of sprinkling perfumed water or sweetened tea over an image of the Buddha. The rituals is also known as Yokubutsu. Throughout the Buddhist world, believers bathe images of the infant **Siddharta Gautama** as part of the observance of his birthday. In East Asia, Buddhists traditionally commemorate the Buddha's birthday on the eighth day of the fourth lunar month. The practice of kanbutsu recalls the description of the Buddha's birth in traditional biographies, which depict gods and other heavenly beings celebrating the birth of the child by bathing him in perfumed water and showering him with flower blossoms.

The practice of bathing images of the Buddha to celebrate his birth originated in India. It became a popular custom in China by the seventh and eighth centuries, when it was transmitted to Japan. Prince **Shôtoku Taishi** (574–622) held the first kanbutsu ritual in Japan to celebrate the Buddha's birthday in 606. See also **Hana Matsuri**.

Kamens, Edward, trans. *The Three Jewels: A Study and Translation of Minamoto Tamenori's* Sanboe. Ann Arbor, MI: Center for Japanese Studies, University of Michigan, 1988.

Kanchô

The head **abbot** responsible for the administration of an entire sect of Japanese **Buddhism**. The position was created by the Japanese government during the modern period (1868–present), as a part of the Meiji government's program of regulations to facilitate its control of Buddhism. Beginning in 1872, government regulations required a reorganization and simplification of the Buddhist monastic world into seven sects, **Tendai**, **Shingon**, **Jôdo**, **Zen**, Shin, **Nichiren**, and **Ji**. At the head of each sect was the kanchô, responsible for the administration of all sub-sects and answerable to the government for the entire sect. Under this initial restructuring, the Rinzai, Sôtô, and Obaku sects were unified under a single head abbot. The government later eased its regulations, allowing sub-sects to gain independence. Under the revised regulations, Rinzai, Sôtô, and Obaku were each independent sects, each with its own head abbot. Since 1946, under the Religious Juridical Persons Law, the position of kanchô has been replaced by a board of at least three officials for any sect that chooses to register under the law for tax purposes. Head abbots of the main monastery for a sect are now known as the kanshu. The term is sometimes translated as bishop, or archbishop. See also **Obaku sect**, **Rinzai sect**, and **Sôtô sect**.

Hori, Ichiro, et. al, eds. *Japanese Religions: A Survey by the Agency for Cultural Affairs*. Tokyo: Kodansha Internatiuonal, 1972.

Kanjizai

"One who observes freely," an alternative Japanese name for the **bodhisattva Kannon** (Sk. **Avalokiteshvara**). See **Kannon**.

Kanki Issoku

"To exhale in a single breath;" a term for exhaling and inhaling to regulate one's breathing at the beginning of seated **meditation**. In the *Fukan Zazengi*, **Dôgen Kigen** (1200–1253) uses this expression to explain the initial process of regulating one's breathing. After adjusting one's body in the correct posture, one opens the mouth slightly and quietly and fully exhales, expelling the air from deep in the abdomen in a single, long breath. One then closes the mouth and breathes in through the nose.

Kanna Zen

"The Zen of seeing into a kôan," the practice of **Zen** using kôan as a **meditation** device. The term, pronounced *K'an-hua Ch'an* in Chinese, was originally coined by the disciples of **Hung-chih Cheng-chüeh** (1091–1157) as a derogatory expression for the Zen style of their rival **Ta-hui Tsung-kao** (1089–1163). Ta-hui was a strong advocate for the use of kôan, regarding kôan as an essential device for attaining enlightenment. Eventually, the term *kanna Zen* lost its negative connotations and is generally used to denote the Rinzai style of Zen practice, which relies upon the use of kôan. The opposite style of practice is known as **mokushô Zen**, or silent illumination Zen. See also **Rinzai sect**.

Kannon

"One who observes the sounds," the Japanese name for **Avalokiteshvara**, the **bodhisattva** of infinite **compassion** and mercy. Kannon is among the most popular Buddhist deities in Japan. She is revered in all sects of Japanese **Buddhism**, including the **Zen** sects. The name is understood to mean that Kannon closely observes the world and can hear all the cries of **suffering** coming from **sentient beings** everywhere. Kannon will respond to save anyone who cries out for help using her name. Kannon can assume any corporeal shape and can enter any region, including **hell**, to rescue a believer. It is also believed that Kannon will appear at death to safely escort a believer to Amida's **Pure Land**. One of the most popular depictions of Kannon in Japan is the Thousand-armed Kannon (J. Senju Kannon), which has an eye in each of its many hands to better watch over the world. Although images of Avalokiteshvara from India are always masculine in form, there are many feminine images for Kannon in East Asia. In Japan, Hidden Christians (J. Kakure Kirishitan), who were forbidden by law to openly practice their Catholic faith for many years, used images of Kannon to represent the Virgin Mary. She became known as Maria Kannon. Also known in Japanese as Kanzeon ("one who observes the sounds of the world") and Kanjizai ("the one who observes freely"). See also **Kuan-yin**.

Kannonkyô

Kannon Sutra, the popular Japanese title for the "Kanzeon Bosatsu Fumon-bon" ("The Universal Gateway of the **Bodhisattva** Perceiver of the World's Sounds"), the twenty-fifth chapter of the **Lotus Sutra**. It is alternatively abbreviated as the "Fumon-bon." The most common version of the sutra used in East Asia is the translation by **Kumarajiva**. The text has circulated independently and is sometimes regarded as a separate sutra. It is often recited at **Zen** rituals involving lay practitioners. See also **Avalokiteshvara Sutra** and **Kuan-yin Ching**.

Kanshi

Poetry composed in Chinese, especially that written by Japanese authors. In Japan, kanshi is contrasted with **Waka**, poetry composed in Japanese.

Kanshiketsu

"A dried outhouse stick." See **shiketsu**.

Kanshô

A small hanging bell used in **Zen** monasteries to announce the opportunity for private instruction with the master (**dokusan**). The bell is sounded

Kannon is among the most popular of the Buddhist dieties.

by striking it with a wooden mallet. The kanshô sits outside the master's quarters, and an assistant sounds the bell at the beginning of the instruction period. Students seeking instruction gather to await their turn. One by one, after the master signals for the next person to enter, students ring the bell twice to announce their entrance.

Kansu

The supervisor, one of the six stewards at a **Zen** monastery who assist the **abbot** in the administrative responsibilities in managing the monastery. Along with the assistant supervisor (**fûsu**) and the prior (**tsûsu**), the kansu is one of three financial officers responsible for the economic management of temple resources. The supervisor and his assistant keep the daily accounts and draw up the annual budget. The economic officers replaced the single office of kan'in (or kannin), previously the sole financial administrator for Zen monasteries. See also **temple positions**.

Kanzan

Japanese rendering of the name **Han-shan**, a Chinese **Zen** poet of the T'ang dynasty (618–907). See **Han-shan**.

Kanzan Egen

(1277–1369) Japanese Rinzai **monk** of the Kamakura period (1185–1333) who founded the important monastery **Myôshin-ji**. He was born in Nakano, in present day Nagano Prefecture, and entered Buddhist orders at a young age to study with his uncle, Gekkoku Sôchû, a **Dharma heir** of **Nampô Jômyô** (1235–1309). At age twenty, his uncle took him to **Kenchô-ji** in Kamakura, where he briefly became a disciple of Nampô Jômyô. When the master died, Kanzan returned to his home and practiced on his own for twenty years. At age fifty, he traveled to Kyoto to study with **Shûhô Myôchô** (1282–1337), the **abbot** at **Daitoku-ji**, and in two years' time he became Shûhô's Dharma heir. In 1337,

following Shûhô's recommendation, the retired **Emperor Hanazono** (1297–1348) invited Kanzan to become founding abbot at a new temple which would become Myôshin-ji. Kanzan continued to live a frugal and austere life at Myôshin-ji, accepting only a few disciples, and training them severely. He acknowledged only one Dharma heir, Juô Sôhitsu (1296–1380). Nevertheless, his **lineage** survived and became one of the most important in Japanese Rinzai. Kanzan left behind no **recorded sayings** or other writings. He received posthumous titles from six emperors, but is best known as Musô **Daishi**, the title conferred on him in 1909 by the Emperor Meiji (1868–1912). See also **Rinzai sect**.

Kanzanshi

Japanese title for the *Han-shan Shih* (*Poems of Han-shan*). See *Han-shan Shih*.

Kanzeon

(Sk. Avalokiteshvara) "One who observes the sounds of the world," an alternative Japanese name for the **bodhisattva Kannon** See **Kannon**.

Kanzeon Bosatsu Fumon-bon

"The Universal Gateway of the **Bodhisattva** Perceiver of the World's Sounds," the twenty-fifth chapter of the **Lotus Sutra**. More popularly known in Japanese as the "Kannonkyô." See **Avalokiteshvara Sutra**.

Kapilavastu

City in present-day Nepal in the foothills of the Himalayas, which was the home of **Siddharta Gautama**. Kapilavastu was the capital city of the kingdom of the **Shakya clan** into which the future **Buddha** was born. Siddharta was born outside the confines of the city, in a garden called Lumbini, and was raised in Kapilavastu.

Kare sansui gardens are dry landscapes that include raked sand, stone, and moss.

Kare Sansui

"Dry mountains and water;" dry landscape gardens constructed of stone, sand, and moss, which represent a traditional form of Japanese art closely associated with **Zen Buddhism**. In most cases, raked sand or pebbles are used to represent flowing water, larger stones represent islands and mountains, and moss suggests forests. Dry landscape gardens are a common feature in Japanese Zen monasteries. The most famous examples include the gardens at **Ryôan-ji**, Daisen-in, and Saihô-ji, all in Kyoto.

Karma

(J. gô) Actions and the personal consequences that accrue from one's actions. The basic concept of karma is shared by the Hindu, Jain, and Buddhist religious traditions, with some variations in interpretation. In the Buddhist teaching of karma, moral actions of the body, speech, and mind that are taken intentionally are said to inevitably bear some fruit for the individual. If an action is good, its resulting effects will be positive and pleasant. If an action is evil, then the consequences will be negative and painful. Karma thus works as an impersonal law of cause and effect, in which good and bad actions produce their own rewards or punishments. No deity metes out punishment or reward, nor does a deity determine the nature of good and evil. In this context, good and bad can be understood in terms of the basic Buddhist **precepts** against killing, stealing, sexual misconduct, and so on.

In the Buddhist understanding of karma, intention is a crucial aspect of the cause and effect process. Indeed, even an intention that does not result in the action itself will, nevertheless, have some karmic consequences for the individual. While the intention to murder may not produce the same evil karma as the act of murder, it does entail some consequences. On the other hand, although unintentional actions may cause some inadvertent effects, they do not produce karmic consequences.

It is possible that the karmic consequences of one's actions may not come to fruition in a single lifetime. Although **Buddhism** denies the existence of a permanent spirit or soul, it nevertheless teaches that karma carries over from one birth to another. The karmic residue accumulated in one lifetime helps to determine the next **rebirth**. An individual who has accumulated good karma, often referred to as **merit**, will be reborn in one of the better realms of existence. A person who has behaved immorally will fall into one of the three **evil paths** and be reborn as a **hell** dweller, a **hungry ghost**, or an animal. It should be noted that whether the sum of one's actions is good or bad, karmic consequences perpetuate the cycle of **samsara**. In this sense, even the production of good karma is not ideal. Breaking the cycle is only possible when one lives without acting out of greed, anger, and ignorance.

Robinson, Richard H. and William L. Johnson. *The Buddhist Religion: A Historical Introduction*. Belmont, CA: Wadsworth Publishing Co., 1996.

King, Winston L. *In the Hope of Nibbana: The Ethics of Theravada Buddhism*. LaSalle, IL: Open Court, 1964.

Kashaku

"To hang up one's staff," to formally enter a **Zen** monastery for practice. Traditionally, Buddhist **monks** and **nuns** carried a staff (shakujô) with them when they traveled on **pilgrimage**. When they entered a monastery to spend a few nights or to stay for a seasonal retreat, they would hang up their staff on a hook above their assigned place in the monks' hall (**sôdô**). The expression is now used primarily for **novices** entering a Zen monastery for training. In certain contexts, however, it may refer to a Zen monk or nun taking up the position as **abbot** or resident priest at a temple.

Kashaya

Buddhist monastic robe. See **kesa**.

Kashin

Hanging a portrait of a deceased **abbot** or other prominent Buddhist **monk** or **nun** in the lecture hall during the funeral services. In addition to the portrait, banners are hung around the coffin and the personal possessions of the deceased, such as the master's **whisk**, **meditation** mat, and razor, are laid out within the hall. Kashin is one of the nine ritual acts (**kubutsuji**) performed when a prominent Buddhist monk or nun dies. The term is also pronounced *Keshin*. See also **kubutsuji**.

Kashô

Japanese transliteration for *Kashyapa*, the common abbreviation for Makakashô, or **Mahakashyapa**. See **Mahakashyapa**.

Kashyapa Buddha

One of the **seven buddhas of the past** whose biographies appear at the beginning of the *Transmission of the Lamp* (Ch. **Ching-te Chüan-teng Lu**; J. *Keitoku Dentôroku*) and other traditional accounts of the history of **Zen Buddhism** through the ages. Kashyapa (**Mahakashyapa**) is sixth on the list and is identified as the third **Buddha** of the present eon.

Kasshiki

A **postulant**; the Japanese term for an individual who lives and trains in a monastery without taking any monastic **vows**. In the Chinese milieu, kasshiki could live in the monastery indefinitely, without ever taking vows. In Japan, most kasshiki came to the temple with the intention of eventually seeking **ordination**, so the English rendering postulant is more appropriate for the Japanese context. In medieval Japan (1185–1600), it was not uncommon for young boys, between the ages of five and seven, to be sent to a monastery to begin their religious training. Ordination was not generally allowed before age fifteen or older, so the boys spent several years as postulants. These youngsters did not shave their heads or wear monastic robes, so they were a distinctive presence within the confines of a monastery. Today, children are not normally accepted into monasteries in the same manner. There are, however, usually determined periods of practice in the monastery before an individual qualifies for initial ordination as a **novice**, so that adults may reside in a temple as postulants.

The term literally means "to announce meals." In Chinese temples, it was originally used in reference to the lay attendants (**anja**) responsible for announcing mealtime and serving the food in the monks' hall (**sôdô**). According to **Dôgen Kigen's** (1200–1253) description in the *Fushuku Hanbô* (*Rules Governing the Morning and Noon Meals*), the kasshiki's announcement included a careful listing of the items on the day's menu. See also **lay believer**.

Kata

The term literally means "to hang up one's bag and staff" and indicates taking up residence at a **Zen** monastery for practice and instruction. When a **monk** or **nun** first requests formal admittance to a Zen monastery and receives permission to enter, a process that may take several days, the newcomer is assigned an appropriate place in the residence hall. Each assigned space includes a hook, upon which the new arrival hangs up both bag and staff. The term is also pronounced *Katô*.

Katai Futô Roku

Japanese title for the *Chia-t'ai Comprehensive Record of the Lamp* (Ch. **Chia-t'ai p'u-teng lu**). See **Chia-t'ai p'u-teng lu**.

Kataku Jinne

The Japanese pronunciation for **Ho-tse Shen-hui** (670–762), a Chinese **Zen monk**. See **Ho-tse Shen-hui**.

Kataku-shû

The Japanese name for the **Ho-tse school** of early Chinese **Zen**, founded by **Ho-tse Shen-hui** (670–762) during the T'ang dynasty (618–907). See **Ho-tse school**.

Katsu!

A shout characteristically used by **Zen** masters, especially in the Rinzai school, to suggest a state beyond distinctions and discursive thought. Katsu is the Japanese pronunciation for the Chinese character read "*Ko!*" The shout was first used as a teaching device by the Chinese T'ang dynasty master **Ma-tsu Tao-i**, but is most often associated with **Lin-chi I-hsuan**, founder of the Rinzai school. Zen masters use a loud shout as a means to shock disciples into cutting off discursive and analytical thought. In some cases, the shout is said to have pushed students into the enlightenment experience.

In a passage found in the *Sayings of Lin-chi* (*Rinzai-roku*), Lin-chi distinguished four types of Katsu in a formula that came to be known as shikatsu, the **four shouts**.

The Master said to a **monk**, "At times my shout is like the precious sword of the Diamond King. At times my shout is like a golden-haired lion crouching on the ground. At times my shout is like the search pole and the shadow glass. At times my shout doesn't work like a shout at all" (Watson, p. 98).

In the first instance, the shout is compared to the sword of wisdom, capable of cutting through any **delusion**. The search pole and the shadow glass refer to lures used by fishermen to draw fish to one spot. See also **Rinzai sect**.

Watson, Burton, trans. *The Zen Teachings of Master Lin-chi: A Translation of the* Lin-chi lu. Boston, MA: Shambhala, 1993.

Kattô

"Creeping vines" or "complications," a Japanese **Zen** expression generally used as a derogatory reference for an overly complex teaching. In the Zen school, it refers to an **attachment** to words, participation in pointless dialogue, or verbal explanations.

Kattôshû

Abbreviated title for the *Shûmon Kattôshû*. See *Shûmon Kattôshû*.

Kattô Zen

A derogatory expression for any **Zen** style which is overly concerned with words and literary pursuits rather than seeking a direct understanding of the **Dharma**. It is used synonymously with **moji Zen**. See **moji Zen**.

Katyayana

(J. Kasennen) One of the ten outstanding disciples of the **Buddha**, renowned for his ability to analyze the Buddhist teachings and to convey them to others. Katyayana was a Brahmin from Avanti, a region in western India far from the Buddha's territory. He is said to have trained under the guidance of **Ashita**, the seer who predicted **Siddharta Gautama's** greatness at his birth. Katyayana served as a court priest for the king in Avanti. When the king sent him on a mission to visit Shakyamuni, he became a disciple and soon attained arhatship (**nirvana**). The Buddha then sent Katyayana back to Avanti to spread the **Dharma** there. See also **arhat**.

Ishigami, Zenno. *Disciples of the Buddha*. Trans. Richard L. Gage and Paul McCarthy. Tokyo: Kosei Publishing Co., 1989.

Kechimyaku

"Blood vessel," a term for **lineage charts**, especially those within the **Zen** school, which illustrate the succession of the teachings through generations of masters and disciples. **Dharma transmission** is likened to a blood lineage linking the present generation with all previous generations of masters going back to the **Buddha**. The charts typically delineate all generations of Zen **patriarchs** and masters from the Buddha or **Bodhidharma**, through the particular sectarian lineage of a Zen master down to a newly recognized disciple. These documents were traditionally presented to disciples either at the time of **ordination** or when they were officially designated as **Dharma heirs**. During the medieval period in Japan (1185–1600), it became a common practice in the **Sôtô** school to distribute kechimyaku to lay practitioners who participated in precept ceremonies. See also **lay believer** and **Sôtô sect**.

Kegonkyô

The "Flower Garland Sutra," the Japanese title for the Hua-yen Sutra, the Chinese translation of the **Avatamsaka Sutra**. See **Avatamsaka Sutra**.

Kegon School

"Flower garland school," the Japanese name for the **Hua-yen school** of Chinese **Buddhism**. The Kegon school was one of the six schools of Nara Buddhism, established in Japan during the Nara period (710–794). The name derives from the title of the primary scripture of the school, the Hua-yen Sutra (Sk. **Avatamsaka Sutra**; J. Kegonkyô). The primary teachings of the school include the **four realms of reality** and the **ten stages of the bodhisattva**. The founder of the school was the Chinese **monk** Fa-shun (557–640), although it was the Third **Patriarch** Fa-tsang (643–712) who systematized its teachings. The school was transmitted to Japan by the Korean monk Shen-hsiang (d. 742).

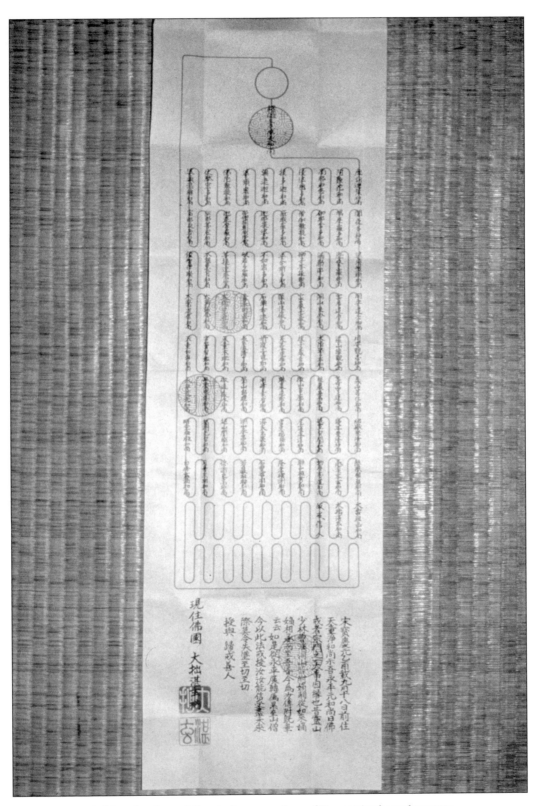

Kechimyaku charts delineate the generations of Zen patriarchs and masters.

The keisaku is a long wooden staff used during meditation to strike those who are becoming drowsy or otherwise preoccupied.

Keisaku

The warning staff or admonition staff used during periods of seated **meditation (zazen)** to ward off drowsiness, to discipline a mind that is wandering, or to encourage the efforts of a meditator striving for **enlightenment**. Keisaku is the Japanese reading of the Mandarin term, pronounced "ching-ts'e," which is preferred by the Rinzai school. In the Sôtô school, the same term, is more often pronounced Kyôsaku. Keisaku typically are made from wood, with a rounded handle at one end for gripping and a flat portion at the other end which strikes the body. They come in various lengths, from two to five feet. The flat end is usually about two to three inches wide. Heavier weight keisaku are used in colder weather when heavier clothing provides extra padding, while lighter keisaku are used in warm weather.

The **jikidô**, the person in charge of the **meditation hall**, wields the keisaku during sessions of seated meditation. Use of the stick is not intended as a form of punishment, although its use may appear quite harsh or painful.

Indeed, it is regarded as a crucial aid for those who sit in meditation, especially in the hands of a skillful jikidô. Not only does the keisaku assist meditators to stay awake and focused, it relieves some of the muscular tension and discomfort that may build up during longer sessions. Individuals may request a blow from the keisaku when they feel sleepy or distracted by lifting their hands in **gasshô**, the Buddhist gesture of reverence. In other instances, the jikidô may recognize the signs of sleepiness and offer the blow. Generally, the jikidô gives a warning tap on the shoulder to prepare the individual to receive the blow. The meditator leans forward and the keisaku falls across the shoulder and back muscles. Afterward, the meditator thanks the jikidô by bowing, and the jikidô responds with a bow. See also **Rinzai sect** and **Sôtô sect**.

Keisen Sôryû

(1425–1500) Japanese Rinzai **monk** of the Ashikaga period (1392–1568). He was a seventh-generation descendant of **Kanzan Egen's** (1277–1369) **Myôshin-ji** line. He became the

Dharma heir of **Sekkô Sôshin** (1408–1486) and was one of his four principal disciples. He served as **abbot** at Myôshin-ji, **Ryôan-ji**, and other major Rinzai monasteries. See also **Rinzai sect**.

Keisu

A large, bronze percussion instrument used during sutra **chanting** and other rituals in the Buddha hall (**Butsuden**). In the **Zen** sect, the keisu is made from cast bronze and is shaped very much like a **begging bowl**. It rests on a pillow, supported by a wooden stand. The keisu is sounded by striking the rim with a padded stick. It is used throughout ritual ceremonies to punctuate the chanting. It is also called a **kin**. Smaller versions are called **shôkei**.

Keitoku Dentôroku

The Japanese title of the *Ching-te Ch'üan-teng Lu*, a compilation of **Zen** biographies recounting the history of the Zen school from the **seven buddhas of the past** through the Chinese masters of the Sung dynasty (960–1279). See *Ching-te Ch'üan-teng Lu*.

Keizan Jôkin

(1268–1325) Japanese Sôtô **monk** of the Kamakura period (1185–1333), who founded **Sôji-ji**, one of the main monasteries for the **Sôtô sect**. Keizan played a crucial role in the early development and spread of Sôtô. He is sometimes regarded as the second founder of the sect. Keizan was born in what is now Fukui Prefecture and became a monk at age twelve, when he entered **Eihei-ji**. He first practiced under Koun Ejô (1198–1280) and later became the disciple and **Dharma heir** of Tettsû Gikai (1219–1309). He became **abbot** at **Daijô-ji** after his master Gikai retired in 1303. He remained there for ten years, before passing on the leadership to a disciple and setting out to found other temples. In 1322, he inherited a Shingon temple that he renamed Sôji-ji.

The **Emperor Go-daigo** (1287–1339) later elevated Sôji-ji to the same rank as Eihei-ji, and it remains the second main monastery for the sect. Keizan popularized Sôtô among the common people and rural **samurai** class by incorporating some esoteric rituals into Sôtô practice and introducing funeral and **memorial services** for lay members. Keizan's written works include the *Denkôroku*, *Zazen Yôjinki*, and the *Keizan Shingi*. He received the posthumous title *Jôsai daishi* from the Meiji emperor. See also **lay believer** and **Shingon sect**.

Keizan Shingi

A Sôtô **monastic code** of two sections composed by **Keizan Jôkin** (1268–1325), the Second Patriarch of the **Zen** sect in Japan. Keizan wrote the code in 1325 to govern life at **Yôkô-ji**, a monastery he founded in Noto. The text is also known as the *Keizan Oshô Shingi* or the *Tôkoku Shingi*. It was first published in 1680 by the Sôtô scholar-monk Manzan. See also **Sôtô sect**.

Kekka Fuza

To assume the full **lotus position**, the body posture most commonly used during Buddhist **meditation**. One sits cross-legged, placing the right foot on the left thigh and the left foot on the right thigh. In most schools of **Buddhism**, one places the hands palm up, the right hand resting on the left foot and the left hand on the right foot. In the case of **Zen** meditation, the right hand rests palm up on the left foot, and the left hand is placed above the right hand with the tips of the thumbs touching.

Kekkaiji

Restricted area, the Japanese term for monastery grounds that were restricted to practitioners only. In Japan, the term applied especially to Buddhist monastery complexes such as those on Mount Hiei and Mount Kôya, where

Kendô practice in a class held at Hanazono College, a Buddhist college in Kyoto, Japan.

women were not allowed to enter. These were also known as nyonin kekkai, areas restricted from women.

Kenchô-ji

A major Rinzai **Zen** monastery located in Kamakura, Japan. Its formal name is Kofuku-zan Kenchô-ji. It was named in honor of the Kenchô era (1249–1256). The temple was founded under the patronage of the regent **Hôjô Tokiyori** (1227–1263), who planned to construct the first full-fledged Rinzai monastery in Japan. He invited the Chinese master **Lan-ch'i Tao-lung** (1213–1278; J. Rankei Dôryû) to serve as the founding **abbot**. The temple was consecrated in 1253. Kenchô-ji was the first major Zen monastery constructed in Kamakura, and unlike Rinzai monasteries already standing in Kyoto, it did not include any structures for **esoteric** Buddhist rituals. It was modeled after the **Ching-shan** monastery built during the Sung dynasty (960–1279) in China and included a monks' hall (J. **sôdô**), the first in the country. It ranked first among the **Gozan** (Five Mountain) **temples** in Kamakura. It serves today as the main headquarters for the Kenchô-ji branch of Rinzai Zen. See also **Rinzai sect**.

Kenchô-ji Ha

The **Kenchô-ji** branch of Rinzai, one of the fourteen contemporary branches of the Japanese **Rinzai sect**. The main monastery for the branch in Kenchô-ji, located in Kamakura. **Lan-ch'i Tao-lung** (1213–1278; J. Rankei Dôryû) is regarded as the founder. The branch has 407 temples throughout Japan and claims approximately 89,000 adherents.

Kenchû Seikoku Zokutô Roku

Japanese title for the *Chien-chung Ching-kuo Supplementary Record of the Lamp* (C. *Chien-chung Ching-kuo Hsu-teng Lu*). See *Chien-chung Ching-kuo Hsu-teng Lu*.

Kendô

"The way of the sword," a Japanese martial art popularly associated with **Zen Buddhism**. It is also known as Kenjutsu, "the art of the sword." The connection between swordsmanship and Zen first emerged in the medieval period (1185–1600), when some sword masters took up the practice of Zen. The steadfastness, concentration, and composure in the face of death of an accomplished Zen practitioner is often compared to the mindset needed by a warrior in battle. Kendô became widely popular during the Tokugawa period (1600–1867), when the arts of war were learned as sport. The Zen master **Takuan Sôhô** (1573–1645) wrote about the relationship between Zen and kendô among other martial arts. In the modern period (1868–present), kendô is practiced using wooden swords and protective clothing.

Kennin-ji

A major Rinzai monastery, located in Kyoto, Japan. It was founded by Myôan **Eisai** (1141–1215) in 1202 and named for the era. It was built under the patronage of Minamoto Yoriie (1182–1204), the second Kamakura **shôgun**, and was modeled after the Po-chang-shan monastery in China. It was not originally an independent Rinzai monastery but a **branch temple** of **Enryaku-ji**, the headquarters for the **Tendai sect**. Some of the temple structures were intended to house **esoteric** rituals of both the Shingon and Tendai schools, rather than strictly Rinzai services. Under the guidance of the Chinese master **Lan-ch'i Tao-lung** (1323–1390; J. Rankei Dôryû) it became a strictly Rinzai monastery. It later ranked among the **Gozan** (Five Mountain) **temples** in Kyoto. The monastery was completely destroyed during the Onin War in the late fifteenth century, and was later rebuilt. The temple serves today as the main headquarters for the Kennin-ji branch of the **Rinzai sect**. See also **Shingon sect**.

Kennin-ji Ha

The **Kennin-ji** branch of Rinzai, one of the fourteen contemporary branches of the Japanese **Rinzai sect**. The main monastery for the branch is Kennin-ji, located in Kyoto. Myôan **Eisai** (1141–1215) is regarded as the founder. The branch has seventy-two temples throughout Japan and claims approximately 25,000 adherents.

Kenshô

"Seeing one's nature," that is, realizing one's own original **Buddha Nature**. Kenshô is a Japanese term commonly used for an **enlightenment** experience; in many cases it is used synonymously with **satori**. In the Rinzai school, it most often refers more specifically to one's initial enlightenment experience attained through **kôan** practice. See also **Rinzai sect**.

Kenshô Jôbutsu

"Seeing one's nature and attaining **buddhahood**." The phrase first appeared in a commentary on the **Nirvana Sutra**, the *Ta-po Nieh-p'an-ching Chi-chieh* (J. *Daihatsu Nehangyô Shuge*; T 37:377–611). It is best known as one line in a poem, attributed to **Bodhidharma**, which describes **Zen Buddhism**. According to Zen teachings, all ordinary individuals already possess the **Buddha** mind, or **Buddha Nature**, and are originally buddhas. By focusing one's attention inward through the practice of **meditation**, one may be able to realize this reality and attain **enlightenment**. The process may be understood less as an ordinary person becoming a buddha than as a shift of perspective, which allows a person to see his or her true nature.

Kesa

Buddhist monastic robes worn by **monks** and **nuns**. The Japanese term derives from the Sanskrit word *kashaya*. There are three primary types of kesa used in the **Zen** school, those made with five, seven, or nine strips of cloth. The five-strip robe (Sk. antarvasa; J. **gojôe**) was originally designed to be worn as an inner garment or undergarment. It is sometimes known as the work garment, because monks often stripped down to the inner robe when engaging in physical labor. The seven-strip robe (Sk. uttarasanga; J. **shichijôe**) is an outer garment intended to be worn as the basic monastic robe within the monastic community. The nine-strip robe (Sk. samghati; J. **kujôe**) was originally designed as a formal outer garment to be worn when outside the monastery.

In China and Japan, kesa are worn in a more symbolic fashion, with the long monastic robe, called the **Koromo**, serving as the basic monastic robe. Buddhist monks generally wear a kesa draped over the koromo. In many cases, the gojôe is worn on a strap placed around the neck as a symbolic reminder of the **Buddha's** patched robe and his **enlightenment**. The strap and five-strip kesa worn together in this manner are known as a **rakusu**. Alternatively, a shichijôe is worn over the shoulder as a tunic or sash.

Kesa Bukuro

The bag or box designed to carry monastic robes, alternatively known as the kesa gôri or kesa bunko. Traditionally, **monks** used a large cloth bag to carry their robes and other possessions. In East Asia, boxes made of bamboo or lacquered wood are also commonly used. **Zen** monks always carry the kesa bukuro with them when they go out on **pilgrimage**. See also **kesa**.

Kesa Kudoku

"**Merit** of the monastic robe." There are three types of monastic robes traditionally worn by **monks**, which are called **kesa** in Japanese. It is said that each type of kesa brings a specific benefit with its use. The five-strip kesa frees one from greed. The seven-strip kesa destroys anger, while the nine-strip kesa alleviates ignorance. **Dôgen Kigen** (1200–1253) wrote an essay entitled "Kesa kudoku," which is included as a chapter in the *Shôbôgenzô*. In it, he explains that all the buddhas and **patriarchs** of **Zen** have worn the monastic robe which symbolizes the **Dharma**. Monks and **nuns** receive their robes at **ordination**, clothing which marks them as members of the monastic community and links them back to the buddhas and patriarchs.

Ketsumyaku Ron

Japanese title of the Chinese text the *Hsüeh-mo Lun*, attributed to **Bodhidharma**. Also pronounced "**kechimyaku ron**." See *Hsüeh-mo Lun*.

Kidô Chigu

Japanese rendering of the name **Hsü-t'ang Chih-yü** (1185–1269), a Chinese Rinzai **monk** of the Sung dynasty (960–1279), known in Japan as the **Dharma** master of **Nampô Jômyô** (1235–1309), better known as Daiô Kokushi. See **Hsü-t'ang Chih-yü**.

Kidô Roku Daibetsu

The Japanese title for the *Hsü-t'ang Lu Tai-pieh*, a collection of 100 old kôan with answers composed by **Hsü-t'ang Chih-yu**. The *Kidô Roku Daibetsu* is still used today as an advanced text within the Takujû line of modern Japanese Rinzai. See *Hsü-t'ang Lu Tai-pieh*.

Kie

To take refuge. The practice of taking refuge dates back to ancient India. In Indian culture, to take refuge in a person or concept indicates that one has made a deep personal commitment. Taking refuge usually involved publicly reciting an oath or some other statement of commitment. In a religious context, refuge does not imply a place to hide but rather a source of strength. Buddhists of all denominations speak of taking refuge in the **Buddha** as an expression of their commitment to the Buddhist tradition. They regularly recite a brief ritual prayer stating their reliance on the Buddha, the **Dharma**, and the **sangha**. Buddhists repeat the formula, "I take refuge in the Buddha, I take refuge in the Dharma, I take refuge in the sangha" three times. This is known as taking refuge in the **three treasures**.

Yampolsky, Philip B. *The Platform Sutra of the Sixth Patriarch*. New York: Columbia University Press, 1967.

Kie Sambô

To take refuge (**kie**) in the **three treasures**. Buddhists express their commitment to **Buddhism** by verbally confirming their trust in the **Buddha**, the **Dharma**, and the **sangha**. The brief ritual formula, "I go to the Buddha for refuge, I go to the Dharma for refuge, I go to the sangha for refuge" is recited three times. The triple repetition indicates that this prayer is not a form of ordinary speech and allows the speaker to dwell on the meaning of each phrase at least once. **Dôgen Kigen** (1200–1253) wrote an essay entitled "Kie sambô", which is included as a chapter in the *Shôbôgenzô*.

Kigan

The procession accompanying the coffin of a prominent Buddhist **monk** or **nun** as it is carried from the lecture hall to the cremation grounds. During the procession, attendants carry the coffin on their shoulders, while other members of the monastic community follow behind, carrying banners, gongs, **incense** burners, and other items needed at the cremation site. Kigan is one of nine ritual actions (**kubutsuji**) performed during the funeral services for **abbots** and other high-ranking members of the monastic community. See also **kubutsuji**.

Kikai

The center of breathing, located approximately 1½ inches below the navel. During periods of contemplation and introspection, attention is focused on an area below the navel, between the kikai and the **tanden**.

Kikan

A teaching device used by a **Zen** master to help a disciple overcome a hindrance to **enlightenment**. The term is derived from the Japanese words *konki*, which means "capacity," and *kanmon*, which means "barrier gates." The master sets up barrier gates in accordance with the individual capacities of his disciples.

Kikan

(2) "Tortoise mirror," a term for the admonitions addressed to a **Zen** community at the beginning of a long period of **meditation**. The term originally implied a magical mirror or device that could foretell the future but later came to mean an example or model to be emulated. It is in this context that kikan is used in Zen. In Chinese Zen temples, it was customary for masters to begin long periods of intensive practice by telling exemplary stories of earlier Zen masters who struggled to attain **enlightenment**. They hoped to encourage the assembled community to strive with comparable devotion. In Japan, the custom later changed, and masters offered personal words of encouragement and guidance to their community. In some cases, the admonitions of a master were preserved, passed down within the monastery, and read aloud by successive generations of masters. Kikan usually spell out guiding principles for the resident **monks** or **nuns** and offer encouragement in their practice. In Japan, they are traditionally read aloud at the beginning of the summer and winter retreats and the night before **Rôhatsu sesshin**, the period of intensive meditation that commemorates the enlightenment of the historical **Buddha**.

Miura, Isshû, and Ruth Fuller Sasaki. *Zen Dust: The History of the Kôan and Kôan Study in Rinzai (Lin-chi) Zen*. New York: Harcourt, Brace & World, 1967.

Kikan Kôan

One of five categories of **kôan** distinguished by the Rinzai school. Kikan kôan deal with differentiation and distinction. The eighteenth-century Japanese Rinzai reformer **Hakuin Ekaku** (1685–1768) and his successors developed a system for kôan practice still in use today. Students who have already experienced an initial breakthrough (**kenshô**) are guided through a series of kôan intended to deepen their understanding. Kikan kôan are the second category in the series. They follow the **hosshin kôan**, which stress the realization of the essential oneness of the self and all reality. In order to prevent students from getting trapped at a superficial level of understanding, Kikan kôan encourage the contemplation of multiplicity and differentiation, while still acknowledging the underlying unity. It is said that holding together the sense of oneness and multiplicity allows the freedom to deal spontaneously with phenomena in the here and now. See also **Rinzai sect**.

Miura, Isshû, and Ruth Fuller Sasaki. *The Zen Kôan*. New York: Harcourt, Brace & World, 1967.

Shimano, Eido T. "Zen Kôans." In *Zen, Tradition and Transition*. Ed. Kenneth Kraft. New York: Grove Press, 1988.

Kikutsuri

"Devil's cave," a place of total darkness where one can see nothing. The term appears in **Zen** writings in reference to living in a state of **delusion**, attached to a false conception of reality. Zen masters apply the term *kikutsuri no kakkei*, living in a devil's cave, to those students who become obsessed with nihilism, a false understanding of the concept of **emptiness**. Kikutsuri is also used in the game of gô for the stalemate of being trapped in seki.

Kimô

Tortoise hair, a **Zen** expression for something that does not exist. See **tortoise hair**.

Kimô Tokaku

Tortoise hair and rabbits' horns, a **Zen** expression for something that does not exist. See **tortoise hair**.

Kin

A percussion instrument used during Buddhist ritual services. In Japanese, it is alternatively called **keisu**. The kin is made from cast bronze and is shaped like a bowl or cauldron. It rests on a cushion; larger instruments sit on wooden stands. It is sounded by striking the side or rim with a padded mallet called a bai. The instrument is used during sutra **chanting**.

King Ashoka

(J. Aikuô) An Indian ruler who governed the powerful Maryan empire from 269 to 232 B.C.E. The Buddhist tradition reveres King **Ashoka** as an ideal lay practitioner and an example for Buddhist rulers. See **Ashoka**.

Kinhin

A form of walking **meditation**, used as a break between periods of **zazen** (seated meditation). Generally speaking, a ten minute period of kinhin follows a fifty minute period of zazen. The word literally means the "warp of a woven cloth," and refers to the pattern of walking characteristic of kinhin. The individual walks straight forward, makes a pivot turn, and walks straight back. In the slow-paced kinhin preferred by the Sôtô tradition, the meditator walks a half step with each complete breath (exhalation and inhalation). The hands are held in front of the chest, the right hand in a fist, left hand loosely covering the right, and forearms parallel to the floor. Faster-paced kinhin is performed with the hands loosely held at one's sides, moving almost at a run. See also **Sôtô sect**.

Kinkaku-ji

The **Golden Pavilion**, the popular name for Rokuon-ji, a Rinzai temple in northwestern Kyoto, Japan. See **Golden Pavilion**.

Kitchen-office

One of the seven primary buildings forming the core of a **Zen** temple or monastery, known as the ku'in in Japanese. The Kitchen-office housed both the kitchen areas and related staff as well as all of the administrative offices for the monastery. See **ku'in**.

Kitô

Prayers recited to buddhas, **bodhisattvas**, or Shintô **kami** (deities) for a special intention. Typical intentions traditionally included requests for fair weather or for rain, relief from various natural disasters, recovery from illness, or a person's birthday. In some cases, lay people make special requests to temples and monasteries to have kitô performed in exchange for a donation. In the **Zen** sect, the purpose of the prayer service is posted on an announcement board (kitôhai). Zen communities most often perform a **tendoku** service, reading the Daihannyakyô (Great Wisdom Sutra). See also **lay believer**.

Kô

A world age or a world cycle; the Japanese term for *kalpa*. See **kalpa**.

Kôan

(Ch. kung-an) "Public case," Term for a teaching device used within the **Zen** school, especially associated with the

Koden is the offering of incense before an image of Buddha in honor of Zen patriarchs and founders.

Rinzai style of practice. Practitioners use kôan as the focus of **meditation** in order to transcend dualistic thinking and promote **enlightenment** experiences. Generally kôan take the shape of a short episode from Zen literature, depicting an encounter between a master and disciple or a traditional account of an important event in Zen history. Although commonly thought of as puzzles, kôan are not intended to elicit rational responses. Rather, they represent challenges to discursive and rational thought.

The term derives from the Chinese governmental tradition of publishing juridical cases that set precedent in law. Chinese Zen masters of the Sung dynasty (960–1279) developed kôan practice by drawing upon famous cases of the earlier T'ang dynasty masters. According to traditional accounts of the development of the kôan, Zen masters in the early periods spontaneously invented teaching devices to aid their disciples, drawing upon some aspect of the immediate situation. Eventually, stories about these encounters were recorded in Zen biographies and **recorded sayings**. By the ninth or tenth century, Zen masters started to use these stories, presenting them to their own students as a means to promote enlightenment and to test their students' understanding of Zen. By the eleventh century, collections of traditional stories of masters and disciples were being compiled, along with poetic and prose commentaries; **kôan collections** became a distinct genre of Zen literature. The most famous of these collections are the *Mumonkan* and the *Hekiganroku*.

In Chinese Zen, kôan practice came to full flower under the inspiration of **Ta-hui Tsung-kao** (1089–1163), who championed its active use as a meditative device and rejected the literary study of kôan. Kôan have often been studied in a literary fashion in the Zen school, especially as a means to learn the classical style of poetry. The modern practice of kôan employed by the Japanese Rinzai school was systematized by **Hakuin Ekaku** (1685–1768) and his disciples. This system includes five types or progressive levels of kôan: **hosshin**, kikan, gonsen, **nantô**, and go-i kôan. See also **Rinzai sect**.

Kôan Collections

One of the most important genres of **Zen** literature. Most kôan collections draw sayings and incidents from the classical tradition. Many are famous stories about the interaction between Zen masters and their disciples. Kôan collections were originally compiled by Zen masters of the Sung dynasty (960–1279) in China as aids in training disciples. Collections often include the compiler's prose and poetic commentary on each case. The most important collections include the *Wu-men Kuan* (J. **Mumonkan**) and the *Pi-yen Lu* (J. **Hekiganroku**).

Kôan-gazing Zen

Style of seated **meditation** characteristic of the Rinzai school of **Zen**, which uses **kôan** as the focus of meditation. See **kanna Zen**.

Kôbô Daishi

The posthumous honorific title, which means "Great Teacher Who Spreads Widely the Dharma," by which **Kûkai** (774–835), the founder of the **Shingon sect** in Japan, is popularly known. The emperor bestowed the title on him in 921. Kôbô daishi has long been the object of popular veneration for the Japanese, regardless of sectarian affiliation. Throughout Japan, there are numerous **pilgrimage** routes dedicated to Kôbô daishi, who functions for believers very much like a saint in Roman Catholicism. There are many miracle stories associated with Kôbô daishi, especially those regarding his saving powers for believers on pilgrimage. See **Kûkai**.

Kôden

To offer **incense**. Throughout the Buddhist world, incense is commonly burned in front of an image of a **buddha** or **bodhisattva** as a symbol of reverence. The term *kôden* is also used in East Asia for the practice of offering incense for the sake of one's deceased relatives and ancestors. Such **offerings** are often made as a part of **memorial services** (**hôji**) marking anniversaries of death. In the **Zen** sect, the term primarily denotes offerings of incense made to the **patriarchs** and founders, since they are regarded as ancestors.

In the context of modern Japanese **Buddhism**, the term *kôden* has come to mean the monetary offerings made to the bereaved family by those who attend a funeral. The money is used to defray the cost of the funeral and the subsequent memorial services.

Kôgaku-ji

An important rural Japanese Rinzai **Zen** temple, located in Enzan, Yamanashi Prefecture. Its formal name is Enzan Kôgaku-ji. It was founded by Bassui Tokusho (1327–1387) in 1380. It was at one time ranked as one of the **Jissatsu temples** ("Ten Distinguished Temples"), ranking below the Five Mountains in the **Gozan system**. It serves today as the main headquarters for the Kôgaku branch of the **Rinzai sect**.

Kôgaku-ji Ha

The **Kôgaku-ji** branch of Rinzai, one of the fourteen contemporary branches of the Japanese **Rinzai sect**. The main monastery for the branch is Kôgaku-ji, located in Yamanashi Prefecture. Bassui Tokusho (1327–1387) is regarded as the founder. The branch has sixty-two temples throughout Japan and claims approximately 30,100 adherents.

Kôgaku Sôen

The formal religious name of the prominent Rinzai master **Shaku Sôen** (1859–1919). See **Shaku Sôen**.

Kô Haku

"Lady White," Japanese for **Hou Po**, a clever female robber who appears in

Zen literature as the partner of Kô Koku, Lord Black. See **Hou Po**.

Kôhô

Japanese rendering of **Fa-hai**. See **Fa-hai**.

Kohô Kakumyô

(1271–1361) Japanese Rinzai **monk** of the Kamakura period (1185–1333). Kohô was the disciple of Shinchi **Kakushin** (1207–1298) and the second generation **patriarch** of the Hottô line of Japanese Rinzai **Zen**. He founded Unju-ji in Izumo and Daiyû-ji in Izumi. See also **Rinzai sect**.

Koji

"Lay person" or "**householder**," a Japanese term for a Buddhist believer who has not left the home life to become a **monk** or **nun**. In the modern period (1868–present), the term is often used as the final part of the posthumous Buddhist name given to the deceased as a part of a Japanese Buddhist funeral. See also **lay believer**.

Kôjô

Reality itself; the ultimate state of **satori**. The opposite of kôge, or phenomenal reality. Kôjô refers to the realm of absolute **equality**, which transcends all distinctions. The term literally means above or beyond, or to move upward or to progress. In the **Zen** school, the term is sometimes used for the third and highest level of a three part system of **kôan** practice; in this system, kôjô follows **Richi** and **kikan**.

Kôjû-shû

An alternative Japanese transliteration of **Hung-chou school**, an important Chinese **lineage** of early **Zen**. Also transliterated as Kôshû-shû. See **Hung-chou school**.

Kôke Zonshô

Japanese transliteration for **Hsing-hua Ts'ung-chiang** (830–888), a **Dharma** **heir** of **Lin-chi I-hsüan** (d. 867). See **Hsing-hua Ts'ung-chiang**.

Kô Koku

"Lord Black," Japanese for **Hou Hei**, a clever male robber who appears in **Zen** literature as the parter of Kô Haku (**Hou Po**), Lady White. See **Hou Hei**.

Kôkon Zazen

Evening session of **zazen**, one of the four periods of zazen (J. **shiji zazen**) observed daily in **Zen** monasteries. Although the exact hours differ by monastery, Kôkon zazen is held in the evening, sometime between seven and nine o'clock. See also **shiji zazen**.

Kokusan

The **black mountains**, a legendary region understood to be north of India. In Indian mythology, the black mountains are veiled in darkness and infested with evil demons. **Zen** masters sometimes use an allusion to this region as a metaphor for an unproductive mental state in which a person is hindered by delusions and discriminatory thinking.

Kokushi

"National Teacher," the Japanese rendering of the Chinese term *kuo-shih*. An honorific title conferred on prominent Buddhist masters by the emperor. The practice is said to have originated in India. The first **monk** to receive the honor in China was Fa-ch'ang in 550. In China, the masters designated as kokushi, usually served in some capacity as teachers of the ruling family at court.

In Japan, the term was first used during the Nara period (710–794) for a monastic officer responsible for overseeing the Buddhist monks and **nuns** in a given province. The practice of conferring the title as an imperial honor was transmitted later. **Emperor Hanazono** (1297–1348) first bestowed the posthumous title kokushi on **Zen** master **Enni Ben'en** (1202–1280) in 1312. After that time, the honor was often granted in Japan as a posthumous tribute for outstanding figures, although there are also examples of monks receiving the title during their lifetime.

In Zen texts, the title is sometimes used in reference to Nan-yang Hui-chung, the first Zen master to receive the honor in China. According to the tradition, Hui-chung was summoned to court by the emperor three times before he accepted the invitation. When he did finally go to court, he impressed the emperor so thoroughly that he received the title National Teacher.

Kokutai-ji

An important rural Rinzai monastery located in Takaoka, Toyama Prefecture. Its formal name is Machô-zan Kokutai-ji. It was founded by Jiun Myôi (1274–1345) in 1327. It serves today as the main headquarters for the Kokutai branch of the **Rinzai sect**.

Kokutai-ji Ha

The **Kokutai-ji** branch of Rinzai, one of the fourteen contemporary branches of the Japanese **Rinzai sect**. The main monastery for the branch is Kokutai-ji, located in Toyama Prefecture. Jiun Myôi (1274–1345) is regarded as the founder. The branch has thirty-five temples throughout Japan and claims approximately 2,200 adherents.

Komusô

"**Monk** of **emptiness**," The most commonly used name for members of the **Fuke sect** of Japanese **Zen Buddhism**. The exact derivation of the name is unknown. Komusô were half-monks and half-laymen, neither shaving their heads, nor wearing ordinary monk's robes. They lived a mendicant life, traveling through Japan begging for alms and playing the **shakuhachi**, a bamboo flute. During the Tokugawa period (1600–1867), the movement flourished,

attracting many rônin, or masterless **samurai**. At that time komusô wore a distinctive costume which included a bee-hive shaped bamboo hat. The hat completely hid the face and therefore effectively disguised the person's identity. For this reason, criminals sometimes posed as komusô, and the government eventually outlawed the group. See also **Fuke sect**.

Kongô Hannya Haramitsu Kyô

The Perfection of Wisdom Diamond Sutra (Sk. Vajra-cchedika-prajna-paramita-sutra), more commonly known as the Kongôkyô or Diamond Sutra. See **Diamond Sutra**.

Kongôjô

"Diamond vehicle," the Japanese translation for the Sanskrit term *Vajrayana*. See **esoteric Buddhism**.

Kongôkai Mandara

The Japanese name for the **Diamond-Realm Mandala**, one of two primary mandala used in **esoteric Buddhism**, especially within the **Shingon sect**. The Diamond Mandala represents the power of the diamond (**vajra**) of wisdom to overcome all ignorance. It consists of nine almost square rectangles arranged in three rows of three. The other primary mandala used in esoteric Buddhism is the Taizôkai Mandara (**Womb-Realm Mandala**). See **Diamond-Realm Mandala**.

Kongôkyô

Diamond Sutra, the popular abbreviated Japanese title for the Kongô Hannya haramitsu kyô (Sk. Vajra-cchedika-prajna-paramita-sutra). See **Diamond Sutra**.

Konkô

"Diamond," the Japanese translation for the Sanskrit word **vajra**. The diamond represents firmness and indestructibility in Buddhism. It is therefore used as a symbol for the **buddha** mind, which can cut through any obstruction.

Konkômyôkyô

(J. *Chingo Kokka No Sambukyô*) "Golden Light Sutra," the Japanese title for the Suvarna Prabhasottama Sutra, one of three scriptures used in Japanese **Buddhism** to protect the state. The Golden Light Sutra teaches that wherever a ruler honors the sutra and governs according to its teachings, the **four guardian kings** (J. Shitennô) will provide protection for the ruler, the nation, and its people. There are three major Chinese translations of the text (T. nos. 663–665). Japanese emperors beginning with Temmu (r. 672–686) had the sutra distributed at temples throughout the country, where it was recited and copied for the sake of the nation.

Konkô No Cho

Vajra pounder. Originally a weapon of war in ancient India, the vajra pounder was adopted as a religious implement in the **esoteric** traditions of **Buddhism**. The konkô no cho symbolizes the ability of the enlightened mind to cut through any **delusion**. In the **Zen** school, it is said that the konkô no cho represents the realization that "thusness" is not different from the **dharmas**.

Konshô

The evening bell which is sounded after sunset. It is customary in **Zen** monasteries to ring the evening bell 108 times to drive out all delusions. The number corresponds to the number of different kinds of **delusion** that are said to afflict human beings. As the person responsible sounds the bell, he or she simultaneously chants a sutra. On New Year's Eve, Zen monasteries sound the Konshô 108 times at midnight.

Koromo

A long monastic robe worn by Buddhist **monks** in China and Japan. In India, this style of robe was traditionally used as a sleeping garment. It is alternatively known as the jikitotsu. See also **kesa**.

Kôsen Sôon

(1816–1892) Japanese Rinzai **monk** of the late Tokugawa (1600–1867) and Meiji (1868–1912) periods who served as the **abbot** at **Engaku-ji** in Kamakura. His family name was Imakita, and he is often referred to as Imakita Kôsen. Kôsen is among the most important Rinzai masters of the modern period (1868–present). He studied Confucianism as a young man and only became a Buddhist monk at age twenty-five. He began as the disciple of Daisetsu Shôen (d. 1855) at **Shôkoku-ji** in Kyoto, with whom he practiced for seven years. Daisetsu then sent him to practice under Gisan Zenrai (d. 1877) in Okayama. It was from Gisan that Kôsen received his official recognition as a **Dharma heir**. Kôsen became abbot at Eikô-ji in Yamaguchi Prefecture in 1858, where he taught the daimyô, or military leader, of Iwakuni province and many other **samurai**. In 1862, he completed his most important work, the *Zenkai Ichiran* (*One Wave on the Sea of Zen*), a commentary on Confucian terms from a **Zen** perspective. After the Meiji Restoration, Kôsen gained further prominence. He was appointed as head of the Bureau of Religion and Education by the Meiji government. He also became abbot at Engaku-ji in 1875. As abbot, he developed Ryômô Kyôkai, an organization devoted to promoting the practice of Zen among the laity. His other writings include the *Kôroku* and the *Nempu*. His most important Dharma heir was **Shaku Sôen** (1859–1919). See also **Rinzai sect**.

Koshin Mida

"Amida within the self," the understanding that **Amida buddha** does not exist as an external reality outside one's own mind. Rather than rely upon the external power of Amida buddha as is the norm in **Pure Land** practice, other schools of **Mahayana Buddhism**, including **Zen**, shift the emphasis to one's own efforts of **meditation** on the true nature of the self.

Kôshô-ji

A Sôtô temple in Fukukusa, Japan, south of Kyoto. **Dôgen Kigen** (1200–1253) established a community there in 1233 a few years after he returned from China. The temple was officially consecrated in 1236. Dôgen constructed Kôshô-ji as the first Chinese-style **Zen** temple in Japan. It included a monks' hall (J. **Sôdô**), a **Dharma** hall (J. Hôdô), and a **Buddha** hall (J. **Butsudô**). See also **Sôtô sect**.

Koshushaku

"The **barbarian** with a red beard," a reference to **Bodhidharma**. The Chinese referred to all foreigners as barbarians and commonly believed that foreigners had red hair. Since Bodhidharma was an Indian **monk**, **Zen** texts often refer to him in this manner.

Kôshû-shû

An alternative Japanese transliteration of **Hung-chou school**, an important Chinese **lineage** of early **Zen**. Also transliterated Kôjû-shû. See **Hung-chou school**.

Kotsu

A small staff or baton used by a **Zen** master when instructing students or giving a sermon. The kotsu is usually about fifteen inches (35 cm) long, carved from wood or bamboo, and curved in the shape of a human spine. The master may use the kotsu to emphasize a point when speaking, to strike a student during a private interview (**sanzen**), or as a staff to rest upon when seated on the floor. The implement was originally used by government officials in China as a writing tablet, which was held at the chest during public audiences. The material (jade, ivory, or bamboo), indicated the official's rank. Also known as a nyoi.

Kotsu Jiki

To beg for food, one of the basic practices of the monastic life. According to the most ancient Buddhist tradition, **monks** and **nuns** sustain themselves by begging for food and not by any other form of labor. Begging is an ascetic practice, which reduces one's **attachment** to external possessions and concerns. In addition, monastic begging provides lay practitioners with the opportunity to build up **merit** through their generosity to monks and nuns. In the early tradition, monks and nuns begged daily for prepared food. While begging remains a standard practice in the **Zen** monasteries of East Asia, it is more common for monks to beg less frequently and to receive monetary donations or uncooked rice. See also **begging alms** and **lay believer**.

Kôyôboku No Zen

"Boxwood tree **Zen**." See **boxwood Zen**.

Kôzen Gokokuron

Discourse on the Propagation of Zen and the Protection of the Nation, a text in three parts (T. 80, no. 2543), composed by the Japanese Rinzai **monk Eisai** (1141–1215) in 1198. In the text, Eisai responds to criticisms of the newly introduced **Zen** teachings from members of established Japanese Buddhist sects. He maintains that promoting the practice of Zen will benefit the entire nation. This was the first work concerning Zen **Buddhism** written in Japan.

Krakucchanda Buddha

One of the **seven buddhas of the past** whose biographies appear at the beginning of the *Transmission of the Lamp* (Ch. ***Ching-te Chüan-teng Lu***; J. *Keitoku Dentôroku*) and other traditional accounts of the history of **Zen Buddhism** through the ages. Krakucchandra (J. Kuruson) is the fourth on the list and is identified as the first **buddha** of the present eon.

Kshatriya

(J. setteiri) The warrior class in India. According to the classical Hindu class system, the kshatriya were the second of four classes or castes, falling under the Brahmin or priestly class. Traditionally, kshatriyas had the responsibility to protect the people, either by governing in peacetime or fighting in wartime. Although Brahmanical texts clearly indicate that the priestly class was superior to the kshatriyas, kshatriyas did not always concede to priestly superiority. Buddhist texts, for example, often list the kshatriya as superior to the brahmins, rejecting the concept of priestly authority. **Siddharta Gautama**, the historical **Buddha**, was born into a warrior class family. According to the Buddhist texts, had the brahmins been the superior class, he would have been born a brahmin.

Basham, A. L. *The Wonder That Was India: A Survey of the History and Culture of the Indian Sub-Continent Before the Coming of the Muslims.* New York: Taplinger Publishing Co., 1968.

Kshitigarbha

The Sanskrit name for the "Earth Womb" **bodhisattva**. See **Jizô**.

Kû

"**Emptiness**," the Japanese translation of the Sanskrit term *shunyata*. See **emptiness**.

Ku

Suffering; one of the basic teachings of **Buddhism**. Ku is the standard Japanese translation of the Sanskrit term *duhkha*. See **suffering**.

Kuan-li-ssu

An important Chinese **Zen** monastery on **A-yu-wang-shan**. It was designated as one of the Five Mountains (Ch. wu-shan; J. **Gozan temples**), the most prestigious Zen monasteries in China.

Kuan-yin

(J. **Kannon**) "One who observes the sounds," the Chinese name for **Avalokiteshvara**, the **bodhisattva** of infinite **compassion** and mercy. Kuan-yin is among the most popular Buddhist deities in China and is universally revered in Chinese **Buddhism**, regardless of the sect or school. The name Kuan-yin is a rough translation of the original Sanskrit. It conveys the popular Buddhist understanding that Kuan-yin listens to the cries of **suffering** coming from **sentient beings** throughout the world. She will respond to rescue anyone in danger who cries out for help using her name. Kuan-yin can assume any corporeal shape and can enter any region, including **hell**, to save a believer.

Avalokiteshvara was consistently portrayed as masculine in Indian images and texts, but changes occurred in the Chinese iconography of the bodhisattva. Scholars cannot definitively explain the reasons for the transformation, but since at least the twelfth century, Kuan-yin has almost always been depicted as female in China. Early Chinese figures retained the masculine identity, but female versions began to appear as early as the fifth century. The most popular version takes the form of the white-robed Kuan-yin.

From an early period, Kuan-yin became the object of a popular cult dedicated to her; this remains true today. She is one of the most common subjects for miracle stories in popular Chinese literature, and **pilgrimage** to famous images of the bodhisattva is a common aspect of popular devotion. She is closely identified with several indigenous deities, including Miao-shan, a legendary Chinese princess who became a Buddhist nun, and who is now protective deity. Many scholars maintain that she has been completely transformed into a goddess in Chinese folk religion, although she is still revered in Chinese Buddhist temples. She is closely associated with childbirth in China, and women pray to her when they hope to conceive and when they are approaching childbirth.

Jesuit missionaries to China in the sixteenth century coined the name Goddess of Mercy for Kuan-yin. They noted the striking resemblance between female figures of the bodhisattva, especially the white-robed Kuan-yin, and Catholic images of the Virgin Mary. She is also known in Chinese as Kuan-shih-yin ("one who observes the sounds of the world") and Kuan-tzû-tsai ("the one who observes freely"). See also **Kannon**.

Kuan-yin Ching

Kuan-yin Sutra, the popular Chinese title for the "Kuan-shih-yin P'u-sa P'u-men P'in" ("The Universal Gateway of the **Bodhisattva** Perceiver of the World's Sounds"), which appears as the twenty-fifth chapter of the **Lotus Sutra**. The most common version of the sutra used in East Asia is the translation by **Kumarajiva**. The text has circulated independently and is sometimes regarded as a separate sutra. It is often recited at **Zen** rituals involving lay practitioners. See also **Avalokiteshvara Sutra**, **Kannonkyô**, and **lay believer**.

Kubutsuji

Nine Buddhist ritual actions performed as a part of the funeral of a prominent Buddhist **monk** or **nun**. They are 1) **nyûgan**, laying the corpse in the coffin; 2) **igan butsuji**, moving the coffin to the lecture hall; 3) **sagan butsuji**, closing the coffin lid; 4) **kashin**, hanging a portrait of the deceased in the lecture hall or at the front gate; 5) **taireishôsan**, a brief sermon on the **Dharma** in front of the coffin at the **taiya** service; 6) **kigan**, carrying the coffin to the cremation grounds; 7) **tencha butsuji**, offering hot tea, 8) **tentô butsuji**, offering hot sweetened water; and 9) **ako**, starting the cremation fire with a torch. Also pronounced kyûbutsuji.

Kuei-shan Ling-yu

(771–853; J. Isan Reiyû) Chinese **Zen** master of the T'ang dynasty (618–907) who, along with his disciple **Yang-shan Hui-chi** (807–883), founded the **Kuei-yang school** (J. Igyô-shû) of Zen. The Kuei-yang school is one of the so-called **five houses** (J. goke) of Chinese Zen. He was the **Dharma heir** of **Pai-chang Huai-hai** (720–814). Pai-chang appointed him **abbot** at a new monastery on Mount Kuei-shan, from which his popular name derives. Among his forty-one Dharma heirs, the most influential were the brothers Yang-shan and **Hsiang-yen Chih-hsien**.

Kuei-yang School

(J. Igyô-shû) A **lineage** of Chinese **Zen** active during the T'ang dynasty (618–907) and known as one of the so-called **five houses** of Zen. The lineage was founded by two Zen masters, **Kuei-shan Ling-yu** (771–853) and his **Dharma heir**, **Yang-shan Hui-chi** (807–883). The two developed a distinctive style of Zen practice, favoring silence and action over words. They also perfected the use of circular images as a Zen teaching device. The Kuei-yang school did not survive for long. It had already faded by the beginning of the Sung dynasty (960–1279), and its teachings were incorporated into the **Lin-chi school**.

Kufû

("work on" or "inquire into") **Zen** practice, especially seated **meditation** (J. **zazen**) or contemplation of a **kôan** during seated meditation. The expression may also be used to indicate intensive, single-minded meditation.

Kuge

The Japanese aristocracy, noble families associated with the imperial court. When **Buddhism** was first transmitted to Japan, it was limited to the kuge class. The kuge class became supporters of **Zen**, beginning in the Kamakura period

(1185–1333). They were especially interested in the highly refined culture of the **Gozan temples**, centers for the fine arts and literature during the medieval period (1185–1600).

Ku'in

The kitchen-office building, one of the seven core buildings (**shichidô garan**) within a traditional **Zen** monastery. In traditional layouts, the ku'in was located off to the right side of the Buddha hall (**butsudô**). The large kitchen-office complexes of medieval Zen monasteries housed not only the kitchen areas where the two daily meals were prepared for the whole monastic community, but also storage areas and administrative offices. The head administrator in the ku'in was the **tenzo**, or cook, one of the highest offices in the monastery hierarchy. The tenzo typically oversaw a large staff of assistants and **novices**. Other administrative officers (**tôhan**) likewise had their offices in the ku'in. Over the centuries, ku'in fell out of use in Japanese Zen monasteries; they were replaced by the smaller **kuri**.

Kujôe

"Nine-strip robe," one of three basic types of **kesa**, or monastic robes, worn by Buddhist **monks** and **nuns**. The nine-strip robe was originally called the samghati in Sanskrit. It is alternatively known in Japanese as the sôgyari or the daie, literally "great robe." The kujôe was originally designed to be worn as a formal outer garment, which monks and nuns donned whenever they had business outside the monastery grounds.

Kûkai

(774–835) Japanese Buddhist **monk** who founded the **Shingon sect** of Japanese **Buddhism**. Kûkai came from a noble class family and received a formal education in the Chinese classics. He later left school to pursue Buddhist practice. Kûkai traveled to China in 804, where he was initiated into the practices of **esoteric Buddhism**. He returned to Japan in 806 and eventually established the Shingon monastic headquarters on Mount Kôya.

Hakeda, Kûkai. *Major Works*. Trans. Yoshito S. Hakeda. New York: Columbia University Press, 1972.

Kumarajiva

(344–413; J. Kumarajû or Rajû) A Buddhist **monk** from Kucha, in Central Asia, who became the foremost translator of Buddhist texts from Sanskrit into Chinese. His father was Indian and his mother was the sister of the king of Kucha. He entered monastic life at a young age and studied both **Theravada** and **Mahayana** teachings. When the Chinese overran Kucha in 383, they took Kumarajiva captive. After being held for nearly twenty years, he was taken to Chang-an, the capital city of China, in 401. In China, Kumarajiva supervised a large team of linguists, including both Chinese and Central Asians, who produced new and revised translations of numerous texts, including the **Heart Sutra**, the **Diamond Sutra**, the **Lotus Sutra**, the **Vimalakirti Sutra**, and the basic treatises of the **Mâdhyamaka** school. His disciples became the founders of the **San-lun school**, based on the Mâdhyamaka teachings that Kumarajiva had transmitted. For this reason, Kumarajiva is regarded as one of the school's **patriarchs**.

Kumarajû

Japanese transliteration for **Kumarajiva**. Generally abbreviated to Rajû. See **Kumarajiva**.

Kung-an

"Public case," the original Chinese name for **kôan**, the teaching devices used in **Zen** practice. The term derives from the Chinese governmental tradition of publishing judicial cases that set precedent in law. See **kôan**.

Kunshin Goi

The **five ranks** of lord and vassal. An alternative expression of the five ranks developed by **Ts'ao-shan Pen-chi** (840–901). In this version of the formula, the lord represents ultimate reality and the vassal represents phenomenal existence. The five-part formula may be translated: 1) the lord sees the vassal; 2) the vassal faces the lord; 3) the lord alone; 4) the vassal alone; and 5) lord and vassal are one. See **five ranks**.

Kuri

A small monastery kitchen, traditionally used to prepare meals for the residents of the **abbot's** quarters and the guest quarters. The kuri was much smaller in size than the main kitchen-office, or **ku'in**, where meals for the majority of the monastic community were prepared. Over the centuries, Japanese **Zen** monasteries came to rely on the kuri rather than the ku'in, and the kuri became the administrative core for the monastery. Instead of gathering as a community to eat together in a central dining hall, most Japanese **monks** and **nuns** ate within their specific subtemples (**tatchû**) within the larger monastery complex. Meals were typically prepared at the small kuri which served the various subtemples.

Kuyô

Offerings made to express veneration, especially offerings made to the **three treasures**, the **Buddha**, the **Dharma**, and the **sangha**. The word *kuyô* is the Japanese translation of the Sanskrit term *puja*. Kuyô can include ritual offerings of food, flowers, **incense** and the like, presented to images of buddhas and **bodhisattvas**. It may also refer to the food, clothing, shelter, and other necessities that lay people provide for **monks** and **nuns**. See also **lay believer**.

Today, the most common usage of kuyô is for **memorial services** offered for the sake of deceased relatives. Other types of memorial services also exist, such as mizuko kuyô, or memorial services offered for the sake of miscarried or aborted fetuses. See also **four offerings**.

Ku Zôshi

"*The Phrase Book*," an anthology of 5,000 **Zen** phrases compiled in Japan by **Tôyô Eichô** (1438–1504), a **Dharma** descendant of **Kanzan Egen** (1277–1369) of the **Myôshin-ji** line of Rinzai Zen. Tôyô drew his material from **sutras**, **recorded sayings** of Chinese Zen masters, Taoist texts, Confucian texts, and Chinese poetry. He arranged the phrases according to length, including expressions of one to eight characters and parallel verses of five to eight characters. Tôyô's work circulated in manuscript form for several generations, but was never published. In the seventeenth century, someone using the pen name Ijûshi produced an expanded version of the *Ku Zôshi* under the title *Zenrin Kushû*, first published in 1688. See also *Zenrin Kushû*.

Kyô

The standard Japanese translation for *sutra*. The word is commonly appended to the title of a sutra, and may in some cases be pronounced gyô. See **sutras**.

Kyôgen Chikan

Japanese rendering of **Hsiang-yen Chih-hsien** (d. 898). See **Hsiang-yen Chih-hsien**.

Kyôsaku

The warning staff or admonition staff used during periods of seated **meditation** (**zazen**) to ward off drowsiness and distracted thoughts and to provide encouragement for meditators striving for **enlightenment**. Kyôsaku is the Japanese transliteration of the Chinese term preferred by the **Sôtô** school. In the Rinzai school, the same term is more often pronounced *keisaku*. The most obvious difference in the use of the Kyôsaku in the Sôtô school arises from differences in positioning during

Kyûdô, or "the Way of the Bow," is the modern Japanese term for archery.
Archery was introduced to Japan during the sixth century.

periods of meditation. Since meditators sit facing the wall in a Sôtô context, they may not always anticipate a blow from the Kyôsaku. In addition, the Kyôsaku is generally used only to strike the right shoulder in Sôtô, rather than both sides as is the case in Rinzai. See **keisaku**.

Kyôun-shû

Anthology of Crazy Cloud, a collection of **Zen** poetry composed in classical Chinese by **Ikkyû Sôjun** (1394–1481). The collection, two sections in length, was first published in 1642. Kyôun (Crazy Cloud) was Ikkyû's pen name.

Kyôzan Ejaku

Japanese rendering of **Yang-shan Hui-chi** (807–883). See **Yang-shan Hui-chi**.

Kyûdô

"The Way of the Bow," the modern Japanese term for archery. In earlier periods it was more commonly known as kyûjutsu, the art of the bow. Archery was introduced to Japan from the Asian mainland by the sixth century, long before **Zen** had developed in China. It first became associated with Zen practice during the medieval period (1185–1600), when several prominent archers studied and practiced Zen **meditation**. Eugen Herrigel wrote about the relationship between kyûdô and Zen in *Zen in the Art of Archery*.

Herrigel, Eugen. *Zen in the Art of Archery*. Trans. R.F.C. Hull. New York: Vintage Books, 1989.

L

Lan-ch'i Tao-lung

(1213–1278; J. Rankei Dôryû) A Yüan dynasty (1260–1368) **Zen** master from the Yang-ch'i **lineage** of Rinzai Zen, who traveled to Japan in 1246. Lan-ch'i was the first of several prominent Chinese **monks** who helped to establish exclusive Rinzai practice devoid of esoteric elements in Japan. In Kamakura, the regent **Hôjô Tokiyori** (1227–1263) invited Lan-ch'i to become the founding **abbot** of **Kenchô-ji**, the first strictly Rinzai monastery in Japan. Lan-ch'i modeled the monastery on Chinese examples; the grounds included such typical Zen structures as a communal **meditation hall** (**sôdô**). There were no buildings for esoteric practices and the rule observed allowed for no mixing of Rinzai with **esoteric Buddhism**. Lan-ch'i was later accused of being a Mongol spy and was twice exiled. See also **Rinzai sect** and **Yang-ch'i school**.

Lankavatara Sutra

(J. Ryôgakyô; Ch. Leng-ch'ieh Ching) Sutra When Entering Lanka, a **Mahayana** sutra set when the **Buddha** visited the island of Lanka and gave a sermon. Lanka is identified as being located to the south of India, and is generally thought to be a reference to Sri Lanka. The date and place of origin of the sutra are uncertain, although tradition holds that it was composed in India around the second century C.E. The Lankavatara Sutra provides an unsystematic review of several Mahayana teachings. It focuses primarily on the psychological workings of the mind, and it presents concepts such as the storehouse consciousness (**alaya consciousness**) and the **tathagata gharbha**. It explains that **enlightenment** is an internal transcendence of dualistic thought and that the **Dharma** may be transmitted without words, teachings later promoted by the **Zen** school. Indeed, the sutra is closely associated with Zen; in the early period of Zen's development in China, it was sometimes referred to as the Lankavatara school. According to Zen tradition, **Bodhidharma** handed down a copy of the Lankavatara Sutra to the Second Patriarch **Hui-k'o** (487–593) as a symbol of **Dharma transmission**. There are three Chinese translations (T. 16, nos. 670–672) of the sutra. **D. T. Suzuki** (1689–1966) translated the sutra into English, basing his work on the Sanskrit text.

Latter Age of the Dharma

(J. Mappô) According to a **Mahayana** Buddhist concept of history, the teachings and practice of **Buddhism** pass through three progressively deteriorating stages following Buddha's death. In each stage the **Dharma** is said to deteriorate until it ceases to exist. After the end of the third age, the world will await a new **buddha** to set the process back in motion. During the initial period, the Dharma survives intact, and the teachings, practice, and the attainment of **enlightenment** remain viable. During the second age, the teachings and practice remain, but enlightenment is no longer attainable. By the third and final age, the Dharma has deteriorated so thoroughly that even the practice of Buddhism becomes impossible. All that remains are the teachings, which cannot be truly followed or fully realized. This latter age of the Dharma is said to last for 10,000 years.

For many Buddhists, the latter age of the Dharma caused grave concern, in much the same way that the end of the millennium and predictions about the apocalypse concern some Christians. Calculations for the onset of the latter age of the Dharma differ in various parts of the Buddhist world. In East Asia, calculations are traditionally

The Laughing Buddha, or Maitreya, is a smiling monk with a protruding belly.
Small figures of the Laughing Buddha are commonly sold as charms.

based on 949 B.C.E. as the year of the Buddha's death. In addition, the first age may be calculated to last either 500 or 1,000 years. In China, Buddhists typically believed that the latter age commenced around the year 550 C.E. In Japan, where calculations were usually based on the longer interpretation, it was thought to begin around 1050 C.E. **Zen** Buddhists have not generally been as concerned about the concept of the latter age of the Dharma. This is because of the Zen understanding that enlightened masters of any age can teach the Dharma and that Zen practitioners continue to attain enlightenment. See also **three ages of the Dharma**.

Laughing Buddha

A popular name for **Maitreya**, especially when depicted as the Chinese **monk Pu-tai** (d. 916; J. Hotei). While early Buddhist images of the future **buddha** Maitreya depicted him as a graceful figure, sometime during the Sung dynasty (960–1279) an alternative portrayal became popular in China. The image of Pu-tai, regarded as an incarnation of Maitreya, is that of a smiling monk with a large belly protruding from his robes. He may be seated with his right leg raised or standing with his hands thrust over his head. Pu-tai was a historical figure, a Chinese **Zen** monk from the Sung dynasty, who became the subject of popular religious legend. After his death, Pu-tai was identified as an incarnation of Maitreya. Statues of Pu-tai are sometimes enshrined at Buddhist temples in East Asia as images of the future buddha Maitreya. Small figurines of Pu-tai are commonly sold as good luck charms.

Chên, Kenneth Kuan Shêng. *Buddhism in China: A Historical Survey.* Princeton, NJ: Princeton University Press, 1964.

Law of Causation

The Buddhist understanding of cause and effect, which is based on the understanding that all phenomena, whether physical or mental, have causes. Everything arises due to certain causes and conditions. When those causes and conditions cease to exist, the thing in question changes and passes out of existence. The Law of Causation is closely related to the concept of **codependent origination**, which is used to explain the origin and the possible cessation of **suffering**.

In addition, the Buddhist Law of Causation maintains that every intentional action necessarily produces an effect, whether in this lifetime or in a future life. In this regard, the Law of Causation is closely related to the concept of **karma**. Good actions necessarily produce positive fruits, and evil actions necessarily produce negative fruits.

Lay Believer

An ordinary member of a religious group who is neither ordained nor a member of a religious order of **monks** or **nuns**. Lay believers typically do not devote their entire lives to religious practice. In Buddhist contexts, lay believers are frequently called **householders**, indicating that their primary concern revolves around family life, unlike monks and nuns, who leave the home life when they enter the monastery. Lay Buddhists follow an abbreviated set of moral **precepts**, known as the **five precepts**, which enjoin the practitioner to abstain from killing, lying, sexual misconduct, stealing, and drinking alcohol. These are the first five precepts kept by all ordained Buddhists, although they are interpreted differently for lay people. For example, the third precept, which forbids monks and nuns from engaging in any sexual activity, is understood to preclude only improper sexual contact, including premarital and extramarital relations, for lay believers.

Layman P'ang

(740–803; J. Hô koji) P'ang Yun, a Chinese lay practitioner of **Zen Buddhism** and accomplished poet from the T'ang dynasty (618–907). Nothing is known of his youth. Married, with two children, P'ang practiced Zen throughout his life, receiving guidance from some of the leading masters of the day, including Shih-tou and **Ma-tsu Tao-i**. He attained **enlightenment** under Ma-tsu but refused to become a **monk**. In his later years, he gave away his home and took up an itinerant life. P'ang appears in case forty-two of the *Hekiganroku*. He is often compared to **Vimalakirti**, another prominent lay practitioner who attained enlightenment without ever taking the **tonsure**. P'ang left behind more than 300 poems, some of which still survive. There is an English translation of his **recorded sayings**, edited by Ruth Fuller Sasaki. See also **lay believer**.

Sasaki, Ruth Fuller, Yoshitaka Iriya, and Dana R. Fraser. *A Man of Zen: The Recorded Sayings of Layman P'ang*. New York: Weatherhill, 1971.

Lin-chi I-hsüan

(d. 867; Rinzai Gigen) Chinese **Zen** master of the T'ang dynasty (618–907), who is regarded as the founder of the Rinzai school of Zen **Buddhism**. Lin-chi had a distinctive teaching style, making use of shouts (J. **katsu**) and slaps to push his disciples toward an **enlightenment** experience. Little is known about Lin-chi's early life. He was born in Ts'ao prefecture sometime between 810 and 815 C.E. It is not known at what age he first entered monastic orders; he initially studied the **Vinaya** and various **Mahayana** teachings. Eventually, he traveled to Chiang-hsi to practice Zen at the monastery of **Huang-po Hsi-yün** (d. 850). The story of his enlightenment is quite famous within the tradition. After three years in Huang-po's community, Lin-chi had made little progress and had not once approached the master for direct instruction. The chief seat (J. **shuso**) at the monastery encouraged Lin-chi to ask the master about the cardinal principle of the **Dharma**. Three times Lin-chi asked Huang-po, and three times the master struck him with a blow. With Lin-chi on the verge of quitting the community in discouragement, Huang-po suggested that he visit Zen master Ta-yu. Lin-chi experienced enlightenment during his first interview with Ta-yu. He then returned to Huang-po, who recognized him as his **Dharma heir**. After ten more years of practice with Huang-po, Lin-chi went on a **pilgrimage** and eventually settled near the city of Chen-chou in a small temple called Lin-chi-yuan, from which he gained his popular name. He spent the last years of his life in a temple in Wei-fu. Lin-chi's **recorded sayings**, the *Lin-chi Lu* (*Sayings of Lin-Chi*), is among the most important texts within the Zen corpus. See also **Rinzai sect**.

Lin-chi Lu

The common abbreviation for *Lin-chi Ch'an-shih Yu-lu*, the *Recorded Sayings of Ch'an Master Lin-chi* (J. *Rinzai-roku*). See *Sayings of Lin-chi*.

Lin-chi School

(J. Rinzai-shû) One of two major schools of Chinese **Zen**, along with the **Ts'ao-tung school** (J. Sôtô). Lin-chi Zen is named for its founding **patriarch Lin-chi I-hsuan** (d. 867), one of the most famous Chinese Zen masters of the T'ang dynasty (618–907). The predominant Lin-chi style of practice uses **kôan** as the focus of attention during seated **meditation** (**zazen**). The Lin-chi style is also traditionally associated with the use of slapping and shouting (**katsu!**) as teaching devices.

The Lin-chi **lineage** first took shape during the T'ang dynasty and numbers among the **five houses** of Chinese Zen from that period. During the Sung dynasty (960–1279), the Lin-chi school divided into two major branches, the Yang-ch'i line (J. Yôgi-shû) and the Huang-lung line (J. Oryô-shû). Since the Sung dynasty, it has been the dominant form of Zen practice in China. The Lin-chi school was transmitted to Japan during the Kamakura period (1185–1333) and is known there as the **Rinzai sect**. See also **Huang-lung school** and **Yang-ch'i school**.

Lineage

Within the **Zen** school of **Buddhism**, it is very common to discuss the history of the school as a whole, or a segment of it in terms of lineage. Zen typically represents itself as a lineage of enlightened masters going back to **Bodhidharma** and the historical **Buddha**. Zen lineages are charted out in much the same way that family trees are drawn, presenting several generations of related Zen teachers and disciples. In a Zen context, however, lineage is not understood simply as a matter of historical relationships. It functions as a religiously charged concept and is understood to imply **Dharma transmission** from one generation to the next.

Lineage Chart

A listing from generation to generation of the **Zen** practitioners officially regarded as **Dharma heirs** within a segment of the Zen school. Lineage charts resemble family trees, mapping out the religious notion of **Dharma transmission**. They are a standard feature in the Zen school for presenting in graphic form the understanding that the Dharma is passed from master to disciple. Lineage charts typically begin with the historical **Buddha**, **Bodhidharma**, or another founding **patriarch**. The list then continues through the subsequent generations of patriarchs and masters.

Ling-yin-ssu

An important Chinese **Zen** monastery on **Pei-shan**. The monastery's full name was Ching-te Ling-yin-ssu. It was designated as one of the Five Mountains (Ch. wu-shan; J. **Gozan temples**), the most prestigious Zen monasteries in China.

Lion's Roar

An expression indicating intensity and power, since a lion's roar is said to possess the resonance of one hundred animals. **Buddhist scriptures** often apply the original Sanskrit expression "simha nada" (J. shishiku) to describe the unsurpassed quality of the **Buddha** preaching the **Dharma**.

Lotus Position

The body posture most commonly used for Buddhist **meditation**. In the full lotus position (J. **kekka fuza**), one sits cross-legged, placing the right foot on the left thigh and the left foot on the right thigh. In most schools of **Buddhism**, one places the hands palms up, the right hand resting on the left foot and the left hand on the right foot. In the case of **Zen** meditation, the right hand rests palm up on the left foot, and the left hand is placed above the right hand with the tips of the thumbs touching.

Lotus Sutra

(J. *Myôhô Rengekyô*) Popular name for the Saddharma-pundarika Sutra, the Scripture of the Lotus Flower of the Wondrous **Dharma**, one of the most important **Mahayana sutras**. The Lotus Sutra was originally composed in Sanskrit and was completed sometime around 200 C.E. It has been especially influential throughout East Asia, where it is widely accepted by all schools of **Buddhism**. In particular, the T'ien-t'ai, Tendai, and **Nichiren** schools are based on interpretations of the Lotus Sutra. There are several Chinese translations of the text, but by far the most popular was the one completed by **Kumarajiva** (T. 9, no. 262) in 406 C.E. There are several English translations from the Chinese text, including Leon Hurvitz's *Scripture of the Lotus Blossom of the Fine Dharma* and Burton Watson's *The Lotus Sutra*.

The Lotus Sutra presents a number of distinctive Mahayana teachings, in many cases providing the primary scriptural basis for Mahayana concepts.

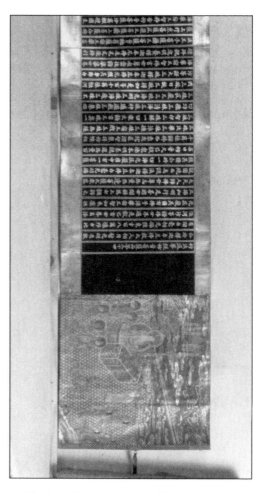

The Lotus Sutra was originally composed in Sanskrit around 200 C.E.

The sutra is set on **Vulture Peak** and is presented as the final sermon given by the **Buddha** before his death. For this reason, the sutra is said to represent the culmination of the Buddha's teachings, perfecting or superseding his earlier **sermons**, which are treated in the text as provisional. Through the use of colorful parables, including the stories of the **burning house** and the conjured city, the Buddha explains that he makes use of upaya, or **expedient means**, to prepare his followers for progressively advanced teachings. For this reason, followers of the **Theravada** (**Hinayana**) teachings who seek **nirvana** are actually on the same path as **bodhisattvas** of the Mahayana tradition who seek **buddhahood**. The sutra teaches that all **sentient beings** are capable of attaining

enlightenment and are on the path to buddhahood. Finally, the Buddha explains that he is not an ordinary human being who attained enlightenment, but a manifestation of an eternal Buddha. As a means of instructing others, the eternal Buddha assumes human form at various times in history, and then appears to pass into nirvana. See also **Tendai sect** and **T'ien-t'ai school**.

Tanabe, George J., Jr., and Willa Jane Tanabe. *The Lotus Sutra in Japanese Culture*. Honolulu, HI: University of Hawaii Press, 1989.

Lump of Red Flesh

A graphic expression used by the T'ang **Zen** master **Lin-chi I-hsüan** (d. 867) in reference to the human body or the human mind. Lin-chi I-hsüan contrasted the "lump of red flesh" (J. shaku-niku danjô) with the innate **Buddha Nature** within the self. A famous passage from the *Sayings of Lin-chi* says: "The master ascended the hall and said, 'Here in this lump of red flesh there is a True Man with no rank. Constantly he goes in and out the gates of your face. If there are any of you who don't know this for a fact, then look! Look!'"

Watson, Burton. *The Zen Teachings of Master Lin-chi: A Translation of the* Lin-chi lu. Boston, MA: Shambhala, 1993.

Mâdhyamaka

The Middle Doctrine school of early **Mahayana Buddhism** (J. Chûgan-ha), based on the writings of **Nagarjuna** (ca. 150–250 C.E.). The primary teachings of the school include the two truths and **emptiness** (shunyata). Mâdyamaka thought first developed in India but became extremely influential throughout East Asian Buddhism. In China and Japan, it became known respectively as the **San-lun school** and the **Sanron school**.

Mâdhyamika

A follower of the **Mâdhyamaka** school of **Mahayana Buddhism**. See **Mâdhyamaka**.

Mahakashyapa

(J. Makakashô or Kashô) One of the ten distinguished disciples of the **Buddha**, reknowned for his strict ascetic practice. Tradition has it that Mahakashyapa obtained enlightenment and became an **arhat** after only eight days as the Buddha's disciple. Because of his strict adherence to the ascetic life, Mahakashyapa became the head of the Buddhist community after the Buddha's death. He convened the First Buddhist Council at Rajagrha, at which the community composed the **Vinaya** and Sutra Pitaka, the first two sections of the **Tripitaka**.

Mahakashyapa came from a wealthy brahmin family, but from his youth was uninterested in worldly pleasures. He left the home life soon after his parents died and requested that the Buddha accept him as a follower. His request granted, Mahakashyapa folded his outer garment and offered it to the Buddha as a cushion. When the Buddha admired its softness, Mahakashyapa begged that the Buddha accept his robe, which was made from the same quality fabric. The Buddha agreed, offering his own tattered robe to Mahakashyapa in return. Mahakashyapa continued to wear the master's robe throughout his life, despite criticism from other disciples that his appearance was a discredit to the **sangha**, the community of Buddhist believers. **Zen** tradition regards this robe as the first **robe of transmission**.

Mahakashyapa is revered in the Zen school as the first of the twenty-eight Indian **patriarchs** of Zen. The first transmission of the Zen **Dharma** from Shakyamuni (**Siddharta Gautama**) to Mahakashyapa is a common theme in Zen literature. Once when the Buddha was lecturing to his disciples on **Vulture Peak**, he silently held up a flower. His disciples made no reply, unable to understand the Buddha's action. Only Mahakashyapa answered, responding to the Buddha with a smile. Seeing his smile, the Buddha said, "I have the True **Dharma Eye**, the wondrous mind of **nirvana**. I entrust it to Mahakashyapa." This story is the subject of several **kôan**, including case six of the *Mumonkan* and case 253 of the *Sanbyakusoku*.

Mahaprajna Paramita

(J. daihannya haramitta) "Great perfection of wisdom," an expression for the attainment of real or intuitive wisdom. **Dôgen Kigen** (1200–1253) used the term as the title for one essay in the *Shôbôgenzô*.

Mahavairochana Buddha

(J. Dainichi Butsu) The central of the five cosmic buddhas closely associated with the esoteric traditions of **Buddhism**. Originally, the epithet Vairochana, or "One who shines forth," was applied to Shakyamuni **Buddha** (**Siddharta Gautama**), but eventually, Vairochana came to be understood as an independent celestial buddha. Unlike other celestial buddhas, Mahavairochana is not thought to have existed first as a **bodhisattva**, but to exist eternally as a buddha. Mahavairochana Buddha is regarded as the embodiment of reality in the universe. Since his body, speech, and mind pervade the universe, many esoteric Buddhist practices focus on the three mysteries of body, speech, and mind as a means to identify with Vairochana.

Iconographically, Mahavairochana occupies the central position in the **Womb-Realm Mandala** and the **Diamond-Realm Mandala**, both of which are used extensively in the **Shingon sect**. He is sometimes depicted attended by the bodhisattvas Manjusri (J. **Monju**) and Samantabhadra (J. **Fugen**).

Mahayana Buddhism

(J. Daijô) "The Great Vehicle," one of the two (or three) major divisions within **Buddhism**, which incorporates a large number of distinctive schools of thought and styles of practice. Mahayana Buddhists adopted the name to contrast themselves with earlier forms of Buddhism, which they dubbed **Hinayana**, or "Lesser Vehicle." Mahayana is sometimes called Northern Buddhism because it predominates throughout East Asia, which lies to the north of Theravadan cultures. The various schools of Mahayana include the **Yogachara school**, the **Hua-yen school**, the **Pure Land schools**, the **Zen**, the **T'ien-t'ai school**, and many others. In addition, some scholars include the Vajrayana schools of Buddhism, including Tibetan Buddhism, under the general rubric of Mahayana.

Mahayana teachings are presented in a series of new scriptures that serve as a supplement to the early scriptures compiled in the original **Tripitaka**. Mahayana scriptures incorporate the Wisdom Literature, including the **Heart Sutra**, the **Diamond Sutra**, the **Lotus Sutra**, the **Avatamsaka Sutra**, the **Pure Land Sutras**, etc. Later Chinese and Japanese writings, including many texts from the extensive Zen corpus of literature, are also incorporated into the Chinese, Korean, and Japanese versions of the Tripitaka.

Mahayana Buddhism represents several new developments that diverged from the early Buddhist teaching and practice. These innovations first emerged in India from the first century B.C.E. through the third century C.E. and can be summarized under three basic areas. First, Mahayana teachings developed and expanded the concept of the **Buddha** to include the concept of an Eternal Buddha, who takes on specific form as the numerous historical and celestial buddhas. Second, the Mahayana teachings contrasted their understanding of the ideal practitioner of Buddhism, the **bodhisattva**, who demonstrates **compassion** to all **sentient beings**, with the earlier ideal of the **arhat**, who seeks only his or her own **enlightenment**. Finally, Mahayana thought built upon and extended the early teaching of No-Self (Sk. **Anatman**), which stressed the transient nature of the individual human self, thus developing the concept of **emptiness** (Sk. shunyata) which is said to characterize all phenomena (Sk. **Dharmas**). See also **esoteric Buddhism** and **three bodies of the Buddha**.

Main Temple

A Buddhist temple or monastery that serves as the institutional headquarters for a network of **branch temples**. The pattern of affiliation between main and branch temples (J. honji **matsuji**) emerged in Japan during the medieval period (1185–1600) and was later systematized in the early modern (1600–1867) and modern periods (1868–present). During the Tokugawa period (1600–1867), the government required that all Buddhist temples be affiliated in a sectarian hierarchy. The government limited the number of sectarian headquarters to a specified group of main monasteries and communicated with

Maitreya, the "future Buddha," is accepted throughout the Buddhist world as a symbol of hope.

the main temples, which were then responsible for conveying government regulations to the branch temples under their control. Main temples thus functioned as a part of the government's regulatory system designed to control many aspects of Japanese society, including **Buddhism**. The practice of temple networks continues today in Japan, although the separation of church and state in the post-World War II period has freed Buddhist main temples from any official governmental control. Most Buddhist temples in Japan are still affiliated as branch temples within an institutional sectarian structure under the administrative leadership of a main temple that serves as the sect's headquarters.

Maitreya

(J. Miroku) The Future **Buddha**, whom Shakyamuni Buddha (**Siddharta**

Gautama) is said to have designated as his successor. Other than Shakyamuni buddha himself, Maitreya is the only major cultic figure accepted throughout the Buddhist world, enjoying devotional popularity in both the **Mahayana** and the **Theravada** traditions. Buddhists believe that Maitreya currently resides as a highly advanced **bodhisattva** in **Tushita Heaven**, where he continues to perfect his bodhisattva practice in preparation for his final birth here in this world. As the future Buddha, Maitreya often serves as a symbol of hope for a better age, when human beings will find it easier to practice **Buddhism** more fully and attain **enlightenment**.

The most common form of Buddhist devotion to Maitreya focuses on building **merit** sufficient to warrant **rebirth** during Maitreya's future golden age. It is believed that those individuals fortunate enough to hear Maitreya preach the **Dharma** at that time will be able to attain enlightenment. In most Buddhist conceptualizations of time, it is understood that Maitreya will be born far in the distant future, millions of years from now. Before the dawn of the new age, the world must first pass through the tribulations of the end of the present age as the teachings of Shakyamuni buddha progressively fade away.

Another form of popular devotional practice once popular in East Asia focused on the hope of attaining rebirth in **Tushita Heaven** in the immediate future. Individuals born there would not only benefit from an environment more conducive to Buddhist practice, they would also have an opportunity to accompany Maitreya when he returns to this world. A believer hoping for rebirth in Tushita Heaven would seek to build merit and call upon Maitreya's assistance. This form of practice is quite similar to some forms of **Pure Land** belief. In fact, devotion to **Amida buddha** and hope for rebirth in his **Western Pure Land** later eclipsed devotion to Maitreya in East Asia.

In a few rare cases, East Asian Buddhists reinterpreted the mainstream Maitreya myth, transforming him into a messianic savior who would soon appear, or had already appeared, to usher in the millennial age. In some cases, political leaders in China claimed to be Maitreya to legitimate the rule. In other cases, Maitreya served as a rallying symbol for revolutionary political movements. The latent political and religious power of this variation of the Maitreya myth has not completely disappeared. In at least two new Japanese religions that have emerged in this century, founders were identified an incarnations of Maitreya.

Sponberg, Alan, and Helen Hardacre, eds. *Maitreya, the Future Buddha.* New York: Cambridge University Press, 1988.

Maka Hannya Haramitsu

"Great Perfection of Wisdom," the Japanese transliteration for *Mahaprajna Paramita*. See *Mahaprajna Paramita*.

Makakashô

The Japanese pronunciation of **Mahakashyapa**, the foremost disciple of the **Buddha** and the first Indian **patriarch** of **Zen**. See **Mahakashyapa**.

Makuragyô

A brief Japanese Buddhist service performed by a Buddhist **monk** over the body of the deceased immediately after death. Since the service is traditionally performed at the deathbed, it is known as the pillow sutra. Despite the name, there is no text bearing the name "Pillow Sutra," nor do the various Buddhist denominations employ a single common text for the deathbed service. The Makuragyô service is unique to Japanese Buddhist custom. The service typically includes the burning of **incense**, reading of a short passage from a sutra, and a brief sermon by a Buddhist priest. Throughout the service, the face of the deceased is covered with a white cloth, used as a shroud.

The custom of performing the pillow sutra became common in all denominations of Japanese **Buddhism** during the Tokugawa period (1600–1867). At that time, the Japanese government required that in every case of death, a Buddhist monk examine the body before filing a report and issuing a death certificate. Only then was permission granted for burial or cremation. The requirement was part of the Tokugawa government's effort to limit the spread of illegal religious groups, including Christianity. Buddhist monks played a role in the government's program by helping to ascertain that every Japanese was a member of a Buddhist temple, and not a member of an illegal religion. In earlier periods, the Makurakyô was a part of the wake, held throughout the night following death.

213

Mampuku-ji

The main monastery for the **Obaku sect** of Japanese **Zen**, located in Uji, a small city south of Kyoto. The full formal name is Obaku-san Mampuku-ji. The monastery was founded in 1663 by **Yin-yüan Lung-ch'i** (1594–1673), the founder of the Obaku sect. The monastery is distinctive in Japan, because it is constructed in the Ming Chinese style. It was originally modeled after Yin-yüan's home monastery, Wan-fu-ssu, in Fukien province. In addition to using Chinese architectural styles, Yin-yüan commissioned Chinese artisans to complete much of the carving and art work which adorns the temple buildings (**shichidô garan**).

Manbô

Japanese pronunciation of the Chinese characters meaning "**ten thousand Dharmas** (things)." This is a common East Asian Buddhist expression for everything in existence, the entire phenomenal world. The phrase is alternatively translated as the "myriad things." See **ten thousand Dharmas**.

Mandala

A sacred visual image often constructed of circles and rectangles, designed to symbolically depict the cosmos, the realm of a deity, or **buddha**. Originally developed in India, mandala (J. mandara) are generally used as aids in **meditation**. In the Buddhist world, they are most commonly associated with **esoteric Buddhism**, including Tibetan Buddhism and the East Asian schools of Shingon and Tendai Buddhism. Buddhist mandala generally incorporate images of various buddhas and **bodhisattvas**, or Sanskrit letters that symbolically represent them. Mandala may be temporary constructions or permanent images painted on scrolls. In Tibetan practice, mandala are images made from colored sand for specific rituals. In other cases, physical objects such as statues or religious implements may be arranged to form three-dimensional mandala. Mandala are not regularly used in the **Zen** school. See also **Diamond-Realm Mandala**, **Womb-Realm Mandala**, **Shingon sect**, and **Tendai sect**.

Mani

A mythical wish-fulfilling jewel obtained from a dragon king (**naga**) living in the sea. The jewel is spherical in shape, with a short pointed top, and is said to be capable of warding off calamities. In the eighth chapter of the **Lotus Sutra**, the mani is used as a metaphor for **buddhahood**. When the **Buddha** predicted perfect **enlightenment** for the five hundred **arhats**, they told a parable of a man with a jewel sewn to his garments. Not realizing that he had in his possession a jewel which would fulfill all his needs and wants, the man struggled and suffered to eke out a living, just as human beings, not realizing that they have the seed of buddhahood within themselves, suffer needlessly. In **Zen** texts, the mani is used in a similar manner as a symbol of the **Buddha Nature** that every individual possesses.

Manju-ji

An important Rinzai monastery in Kyoto. Manju-ji was designated as a **Jissatsu temple** for a time and was later designated one of the **Gozan temples** in Japan. Today it is a sub-temple of **Tôfuku-ji**. See also **Rinzai sect**.

Manjusri

The cosmic **bodhisattva** who represents the qualities of knowledge, wisdom, and **enlightenment** of the buddhas. Known as **Monju** in Japanese. See **Monju**.

Mantra

(J. shingôn) Sacred sounds, often with no literal meaning, which are believed to have intrinsic power. The Buddhist use of mantra derives from the Indian Hindu practice of using sacred sounds from the Vedas, the Hindu scriptures.

Zen monks and nuns are required to perform manual labor such as raking, cooking, or collecting firewood as a part of their monastic practice.

The **Buddhist scriptures** include mantras of various lengths, from one or two syllables to lengthy passages. In Buddhist contexts, mantras may be used as sacred formulas to ward off evil, to ensure good health, to bring rain in time of drought, and to acquire other practical benefits. They are also used as aids in **meditation**. The steady repetition of a mantra may help to focus the concentration and induce a meditative state. Mantra are used widely in the Buddhist world, and although they may be most closely associated with **esoteric Buddhism**, they are sometimes used within the **Zen** school. In the **Obaku sect** of Japanese Zen, for example, mantras are chanted during morning and evening services.

Manual Labor

Zen monks and **nuns** engage in manual labor (J. fushin or samu) as a regular part of their monastic practice. Activities such as raking the yard, collecting firewood, and cooking meals are interpreted by the Zen tradition as active forms of **meditation** that contribute to an individual's practice. The incorporation of manual labor into the Zen monastic lifestyle is said to date to the time of the fourth patriarch, **Tao-hsin** (580–651), when it was adopted as a necessity to insure the community's physical survival. Tao-hsin and his disciples, said to number over five hundred, lived a secluded life at Shuan-feng-shan, where they could not rely on the lay community to provide sufficient food supplies. They therefore undertook farming the land themselves, an activity traditionally forbidden to monks and nuns in the **Vinaya**. The requirement to participate in manual labor was later incorporated into the Zen **monastic codes**. **Pai-chang Huai-hai** (720–814), traditionally credited with creating the first monastic code specific to Zen, is said to have admonished his disciples, "A day without work, a day without food." Despite the traditional value placed on manual labor, not all members of the Zen monastic community engage in it on a daily basis. Certain monks and nuns are excused in order to concentrate more fully on meditation. Those who are otherwise occupied with administrative duties are also usually excused. See also **lay believer**.

Manzan Dôhaku

(1636–1715) Japanese Sôtô scholar-**monk** of the Tokugawa period (1600–1867) who initiated major reforms in the Sôtô school. Manzan was born in Bingo province, present-day Hiroshima Prefecture. He entered Buddhist orders at age six, and as a young man he traveled frequently with his master throughout the country. In 1651, they arrived in the capital city of Edo (now Tokyo). Manzan had numerous **enlightenment** experiences over the years. When he first met **Gesshû Shûko** (1616–1696), then **abbot** at **Daijô-ji**, in 1678, the master immediately acknowledged him as his **Dharma heir**. Two years later, Manzan succeeded Gesshû as abbot and served in that post for twelve years. Manzan carried out monastic reform in a number of ways, inspired by reading the works of the founder, **Dôgen Kigen** (1200–1253). Manzan studied the existing **monastic codes** available to him, including early Sôtô codes, such as Dôgen's *Eihei Shingi* and the *Keizan Shingi*, and the recently published *Obaku Shingi* of the **Obaku sect**. He prepared his own monastic code, the *Shôjurin Shingi*, for Daijô-ji. Based upon these texts, Manzan also argued

that **Dharma transmission** and **lineage** succession needed to be restored to comply with Dôgen's original understanding. His efforts to reinstitute "the seal of succession from one master" (J. **isshi inshô**) and "Dharma transmission from mind to mind" (J. **Menju shihô**) were successful.

Mappô

"The end of the Dharma," a term for the **latter age of the Dharma**, or the Age of the degenerate Dharma, the third and final period after the death of the historical **Buddha**. See **latter age of the Dharma**.

Mara

The Tempter, an evil deity in the Buddhist cosmology. The name *Mara* literally means "killer" or "death" in Sanskrit. Mara reigns in one of the six heavens in the realm of desire. In Buddhist legends, Mara is depicted as the personification of evil, a deity who prevents human beings from concentrating on religious practice by distracting them with various sensual pleasures and secular concerns. He can be seen as a special enemy of **Buddhism**.

Mara plays an important role in the stories of Shakyamuni's (**Siddahrta Gautama's**) life, especially the accounts of the **Buddha's enlightenment**. When the Buddha sat down to meditate under the **bodhi tree**, determined to meditate until he had achieved his goal, Mara set out to prevent him. He attempted to dissuade the Buddha from his course by tempting him with worldly benefits and attacking him with armies of demons. Understanding that Mara's promises and attacks are always illusory, the Buddha persevered and defeated Mara. In other Buddhist texts, Mara can be found causing trouble for the Buddha's disciples and other Buddhist practitioners.

Boyd, James W. *Satan and Mara: Christian and Buddhist Symbols of Evil*. Leiden, Netherlands: Brill, 1975.

Ling, Trevor Oswald. *Buddhism and the Mythology of Evil: A Study in Theravada Buddhism.* Rockport, MA: Oneworld, 1997.

Married Clergy

In most parts of the Buddhist world, Buddhist **monks** and **nuns** leave the ordinary life of a married **householder** to live celibate lives within the monastic community. In Japanese **Buddhism**, this is no longer the norm in the modern period (1868–present), and most Japanese Buddhist monks are actually married men with families. They are sometimes called priests in English, since the word *monk* implies celibacy in most contexts. The Jôdo Shinshû, or **True Pure Land sect**, was the first Japanese sect to allow its clergy to marry, beginning with the founder **Shinran** (1173–1262), who lived during the late twelfth and early thirteenth centuries. For many centuries, Jôdo Shinshû priests were the only married Buddhist clergy in Japan. During the Meiji period (1868–1912), the Japanese government lifted the legal sanctions against marriage for Buddhist monks. Although the **monastic code** was never actually changed, Buddhist monks began to marry, and it is now typical for Buddhist temples in Japan to be handed down within biological families, with sons inheriting the position of head monk from their fathers. The Japanese introduced the practice of married clergy to Korea during the years of occupation (1911–1945). The practice resulted in difficulties in the Korean Buddhist community after the end of the Second World War, when Korean Buddhists began to reassert the traditional monastic code of celibacy. See also **monastic celibacy**.

Masangin

"Three pounds of flax," a famous line attributed to the master Tung-shan Shou-chu (J. Tôzan Shusho; d. 900) from one of the most popular of the traditional **Zen kôan**. The kôan appears as case eighteen in the **Mumonkan**, case twelve in **Hekiganroku**, and case 172 in **Dôgen Kigen's** (1200–1253) **Sanbyakusoku**. It is commonly referred to as "Tôzan masangin," using the Japanese pronunciation. In the case, a **monk** asked Tung-shan, "What is the **Buddha**?" Tung-shan replied, "Three pounds of flax." Tung-shan's reply is similar to a "one word barrier" (**ichiji kan**), a device perfected by his teacher **Yun-men Wen-yen** (864–949) that is intended to push a disciple beyond rational discursive thought. Tung-shan himself said that words without any rational intention are living words, while words with rational intention are dead words.

Masen

"Polishing a tile," a reference to the famous classical **kôan** about the master Nan-yüeh Huai-jang (677–744) and his disciple **Ma-tsu Tao-i** (709–788). According to the story, Ma-tsu avidly practiced **zazen** in the hopes of attaining **enlightenment** and becoming a **buddha**. Nan-yüeh, aware that his disciple was becoming obsessed with **meditation** to such an extent that meditation itself constituted an obstacle to his progress, devised an ingenious method to overcome the problem. He sat outside his quarters polishing a coarse ceramic tile. Ma-tsu asked the master what he was trying to accomplish, and Nan-yüeh replied that he was making a mirror. When Ma-tsu exclaimed that he could not make a mirror by polishing a tile, Nan-yüeh retorted that neither could Ma-tsu make a buddha by practicing zazen.

Matsuji

A **branch temple** which has formal ties to a **main temple** or monastery (**honzan**). Most local Buddhist temples in Japan are branch temples that answer to a main monastery and that serve as the sect's headquarters. Historically, most relationships between branch temples and main temples go back to

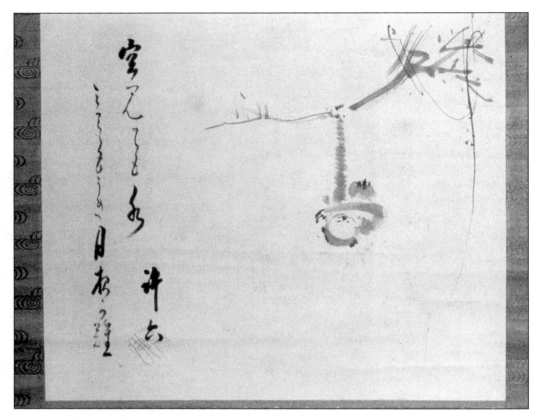

Matsuo Bashô is a famous Japanese writer best known for his poetry. The seventeenth-century calligraphy shown above is by Bashô, the painting by one of his students.

the founding of the branch temple. When a new temple was built, the patron usually invited a prominent **monk** to serve as the founding **abbot** (**kaisan**). The new temple would then be related to the temple or monastery from which the founding abbot came, and his disciples typically served subsequently as abbots. Relationships between branch temples and main temples were formalized officially during the Tokugawa period (1600–1867).

Matsuo Bashô

(1644–1694) One of the most famous Japanese writers of the Tokugawa period (1600–1867), who was deeply influenced by **Zen Buddhism**. Bashô is best known for his **Haiku** poetry, linked verse, and travelogues, which combine poetry and prose. Bashô's best known writings include *Hoku no hosomichi*, known in English as *The Narrow Road to the Deep North*, a

description of his final and longest journey undertaken to the northeastern provinces from 1689 to 1691.

Ma-tsu ssu-chia lu

Recorded sayings of the four houses of Ma-tsu. See **Ssu-chia Yu Lu**.

Ma-tsu Tao-i

(709–788; J. Baso Dôitsu) One of the most influential Chinese **Zen** masters of the T'ang dynasty (618–907). Ma-tsu was the **Dharma heir** of Nan-yüeh Huai-jang. He developed a dynamic teaching style, having learned from his master that sitting quietly alone was insufficient. According to accounts of his **enlightenment**, Ma-tsu was at one time overly absorbed by seated **meditation** and would do nothing else. When Nan-yüeh asked his student what he hoped to accomplish through all his meditating, Ma-tsu replied that he wanted to become a **buddha**. The master then took up a rough ceramic tile and began to rub it, and when Ma-tsu asked him what he was doing, the master replied that he was polishing the tile to make a mirror. Ma-tsu asked, "How can you hope to make a mirror from a tile?" The master replied, "How can you hope to make a buddha out of meditating?" Ma-tsu is famous for employing loud shouts and other shocking actions, such as striking students. These Zen teaching devices later characterized the Rinzai school, which descended from Ma-tsu's **lineage**. His Dharma heirs represent most of the dominant lineages of the period; they include **Pai-chang Huai-hai** (720–814), Nan-ch'üan P'u-yüan, and Ta-mei Fa-ch'ang. Ma-tsu is sometimes referred to as the "**Patriarch** of the House of Ma." See also **Rinzai sect**.

Maudgalyâyana

(J. Mokuren) One of the ten distinguished disciples of the **Buddha**, renowned as foremost in psychic powers. Maudgalyâyana came from a brahmin family and left the home life to become a follower of Sanjaya, one of the six non-Buddhist teachers mentioned in the **Buddhist scriptures**. Maudgalyâyana and **Shariputra**, another outstanding disciple of the Buddha, were close friends from boyhood and joined Sanjaya's community together. When they made their decision to leave Sanjaya and become disciples of Shakyamuni (**Siddahrta Gautama**), they led numerous other disciples to follow suit, creating tension. Maudgalyâyana suffered persecution because of his decision and was eventually killed by members of a rival religious group shortly before the Buddha's death.

Maudgalyâyana is best known in East Asian **Buddhism** for a story found in the **Ullambana** Sutra. According to the tradition, when Maudgalyayana's mother died, he used his psychic powers to learn her fate in the next **rebirth**. Maudgalyâyana searched through all the realms of existence and finally discovered that she had been reborn in **hell** as a **hungry ghost**. By means of his supernatural powers, Maudgalyâyana traveled down into hell and tried to offer his mother food and water to ease her **suffering**. She eagerly accepted his offering, but when she tried to eat it, it turned to fire in her mouth. Maudgalyâyana asked the Buddha how he could help his mother, and the Buddha instructed him to feed the entire assembly of **monks** at the end of the **rainy season retreat**. At that time, the community would have accumulated a large reserve of **merit** from their intensive practice and could transfer the merit to all hungry ghosts, thus easing the suffering of Maudgalyâyana's mother.

Medicine Buddha

The **buddha** of healing, called **Yakushi butsu** in Japanese and Bhaishajya-guru in Sanskrit. See **Yakushi butsu**.

Meditation

A general English term for a wide variety of introspective contemplative techniques used throughout the religious world. Meditation is one of the most basic elements of Buddhist practice, especially for **monks** and **nuns**. Within the Buddhist world, the different schools teach a wide variety of meditation styles, some of which include breathing practices, special body postures, visualization techniques, and different stages or levels of altered states of consciousness. The common goal of most forms of Buddhist meditation is the immediate realization of **enlightenment**.

The style of meditation practiced by members of the **Zen** school is commonly known as **zazen**, which simply means seated meditation. Zazen is usually performed while seated in the **lotus** or **half-lotus position**. It does not involve a complex series of levels or stages of attainment, nor do practitioners of zazen employ visual or mental images to focus the mind. In most cases, practitioners learn to observe their breathing, without seeking to

A meditation hall is specifically designed for seated meditation
and is equipped with special platforms and matting.

control the pattern. In some cases, especially in the Rinzai school of Zen, teaching devices known as **kôan** are used as the focus of Zen meditation. See also **lotus position** and **Rinzai sect**.

Meditation Hall

A hall specifically designed for the communal practice of seated **meditation** at a **Zen** monastery or temple. Meditation halls are equipped with raised meditation platforms typically covered with **tatami**, or rush matting. The term *meditation hall* may refer to the monks' hall (**sôdô**), since it served as the traditional location for seated meditation within Chinese and medieval Japanese Zen monasteries. Alternatively, it may refer to a separate hall used exclusively for meditation. The latter is much smaller than the traditional monks' hall, since residents do not use it for eating meals

or sleeping. Separate zendô of this type were introduced in Japan by the Chinese founders of the **Obaku sect** in the early Tokugawa period (1600–1867) and have since become common throughout all the sects of Japanese Zen.

Memorial Service

Buddhist ritual services (**kuyô**) that are held for deceased members of the community, both lay and monastic, to mark specific anniversaries of the date of death. The custom of holding memorial services for several years after death was first developed in China under Confucian influence. Initially, Chinese **Zen** monasteries developed a system of memorial services to commemorate the passing of **monks** and **nuns** from within the monastery community. When Zen spread to Japan, lay sponsors requested funeral and memorial services for their deceased family members. To accommodate this, Zen monks adapted the services originally designed for ordinary monks and nuns. Since the Tokugawa period (1600–1867), it has been customary that all Japanese receive funeral and memorial services from a Buddhist temple. The pattern of services currently used by the majority of Japanese Buddhist sects is related to the original Zen monastic rituals.

The actual pattern of memorial services differs slightly between the various school of **Buddhism** in Japan. In the initial period of mourning (J. **chûin**) immediately following the death, services were traditionally held every seven days for the first forty-nine days and then again on the hundredth day. Today, families rarely hold all seven seventh-day services; the first and last are the most common. Subsequent anniversary services gradually become less frequent, with the first anniversary service being the most important. In the Zen sect, it is typical for memorial services to be held on the first, third, seventh, thirteenth, seventeenth, twenty-third, twenty-seventh, and thirty-third years. In some cases, memorial services continue until the fiftieth anniversary. The cycle of services concludes with the thirty-third or fiftieth service, except in the case of extremely prominent members of the monastic community, such as the founder of a sect or **lineage**. See also **lay believer**.

Memorial Tablet
(J. **ihai**) A wooden tablet on which is written the name of a deceased individual. Memorial tablets have been used as part of East Asian funeral rituals since at least the second or third century in China. They were originally Confucian in origin, but were adopted by Chinese **Buddhism**. The custom of making memorial tablets was transmitted to Japan by the **Zen** school and became widespread during the Tokugawa period (1600–1867). According to modern Japanese Buddhist custom, items such as the posthumous Buddhist name, date of death, secular name, and age are inscribed on the memorial tablet. See **ihai**.

Menju Kuketsu
Face to face oral transmission of the **Dharma**. See **menju shihô**.

Menju Shihô
"**Face-to-face transmission**" of the **Dharma** from a **Zen** master to a disciple. The term refers to direct, one-on-one contact between the teacher and student, leading to formal recognition of the student as a **Dharma heir** through the conferral of **inka**. Used synonymously with **ishin denshin**.

Menpeki
To do **zazen** (seated **meditation**) facing a wall. The term literally means "facing a wall." The practice is said to derive from **Bodhidharma**, the traditional founder of **Zen** in China. According to Zen legend, Bodhidharma built himself a hermitage on Mount Sung outside the city of Lo-yang and spent nine years in meditation facing the steep face of the cliff. The hermitage was known as Menpeki-an, or "Wall-gazing hermitage." At Sôtô temples and monasteries, **monks** and **nuns** still meditate facing the wall, with their backs to the central aisle. The practice is also known as **hekikan** (Ch. pi-kuan). See **hekikan**.

Menzan Zuihô
(1683–1769) Japanese Sôtô scholar **monk** of the Tokugawa period (1600–1867) who carried out a major reformation of the **Sôtô sect**, which was inspired by his elder **Manzan Dôhaku** (1636–1715). Menzan was born in Higo province, in the Kumamoto area. He studied briefly under Manzan, but then became the disciple of Sonnô Sôeki (1649–1705). After Sôeki's death in 1705, Menzan undertook a thousand-day period of strict solitude at Rôba-an in Sagami.

221

He later became **abbot** at several leading Sôtô monasteries. He wrote several commentaries on **Dôgen Kigen's** (1200–1253) writings, the most important being the *Shôbôgenzô Shôtenroku*, an eleven-volume encyclopedic companion to the ***Shôbôgenzô***.

Merit

An expression commonly used in Buddhist texts in a manner roughly synonymous with "good **karma**." Buddhist practitioners, especially lay people, seek to build merit through good actions, since it is believed to confer benefits in one's present and future lives. The benefits of merit include long life, health, wealth, and a better **rebirth** in one's next lifetime. Activities such as keeping the **precepts**, giving donations to the monastic community, reading and copying **Buddhist scriptures**, sponsoring Buddhist rituals, and other similar actions are said to build one's merit. In addition, **Mahayana** teachings explain that merit may be shared from one individual to another. It is believed, for example, that the highly advanced buddhas and **bodhisattva** can assist ordinary **sentient beings** by transferring merit to them. See also **lay believer**.

Metsujinjô

The **meditation** of extinction, an advanced level of meditation in which all mental activity is extinguished. Practitioners in the **Theravada** tradition sought this meditative state as one of the ultimate states of mental tranquility. It is said that once attained, a practitioner can remain in meditation for up to seven days. Only those who have reached **enlightenment** and thus attained the stage of an **arhat** are capable of attaining the meditation of extinction. Also called metsujin **samadhi**.

Middle Path

An early name for Buddhism said to date back to the historical **Buddha** himself. In his first sermon, the Buddha admonished his followers to avoid the two extremes of sensual pleasure and severe asceticism. From his own life experience, the Buddha realized that neither of the extremes lead to **enlightenment**. He recommended instead a path that took a middle course between the two.

Mikkyô

"Secret teaching," Japanese name for **esoteric Buddhism**, especially the **Shingon** and **Tendai sects**. It is so named because practitioners are required to undergo initiation before they qualify for instruction. See **esoteric Buddhism**.

Mind and Body Drop-Off
See **shinjin datsuraku**.

Mind Ground

(J. shinji) A **Zen** expression for one's mental state. The mind is compared to a field or the ground because it is regarded as the source of all thoughts and experiences, including perceptions of all external phenomena. In some cases, the term refers to the mind of **enlightenment**.

Mind-to-Mind Transmission

An expression used to describe the authentic transmission of the **Dharma** in the **Zen** school from master to disciple, generation after generation. See **ishin denshin**.

Miroku

The Japanese name for the cosmic **bodhisattva Maitreya**, recognized throughout the Buddhist world as the future **Buddha**. Miroku resides for now in Tosotsuten (Sk. **Tushita heaven**), awaiting the appropriate time for birth in this world. See **Maitreya**.

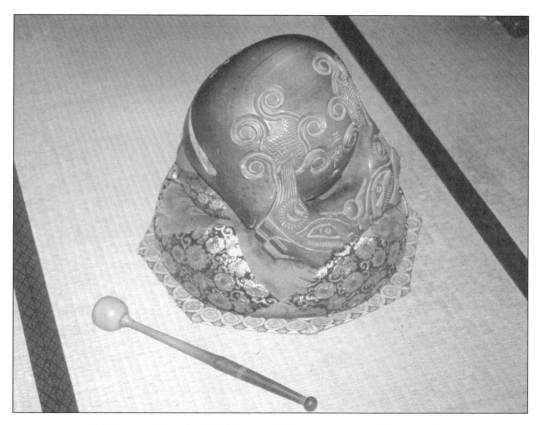

Mokugyo, or "wooden fish," is a musical instrument carved from a single block of wood. It is used to accompany Zen chanting.

Moji Zen

"Word and letter **Zen**" or "literary Zen," a derogatory expression for any Zen style which is overly concerned with words and literary pursuits rather than seeking a direct understanding of the **Dharma**. It is used synonymously with kattô Zen.

Mokugyo

A "wooden fish," a musical instrument used to accompany **chanting** in **Zen** monasteries. The shape of the instrument is globular, in the stylized shape of a fish with a bloated belly and a dragon's head. The exterior is engraved with markings to suggest the fish and dragon motif. The mokugyo is carved from a single piece of wood, with the center hollowed out. It is played by striking it with a padded stick. The mokugyo generally sits on a wooden stand, resting on a cushion.

According to one traditional account, the drum is made in the shape of a fish because fish never close their eyes to sleep, night or day. The image is intended to encourage Zen practitioners to forget about sleep and strive diligently in **meditation**. The mokugyo is a Ming-style instrument, introduced to Japan in the mid-seventeenth century by Chinese Obaku **monks** who founded the **Obaku sect** of Zen. Before that time, the word *mokugyo* was used for the wooden fish gong, known today as the **hô**, used to call **monks** to meals.

Mokuren

Japanese for **Maudgalyâyana**, one of the ten outstanding disciples of the **Buddha**, reknowned for his psychic powers. See **Maudgalyâyana**.

Mokushô Zen

"Silent illumination Zen," the practice of Zen characteristic of the Sôtô school of Zen **Buddhism**. Mokushô Zen involves practicing seated **meditation** without the use of a meditative device such as a **kôan** as a focal point. The term, pronounced *mo-chao ch'an* in Chinese, was originally coined by **Ta-hui Tsung-kao** (1089–1163) as a derogatory expression for the Zen style of his friend and rival **Hung-chih Cheng-chüeh** (1091–1157), which Ta-hui regarded as unorthodox. The opposite style of practice is known as **kanna Zen**, or "Kôan-gazing Zen." Although the term *mokushô Zen* is not always used in a negative sense, it is more common for people within the Sôtô tradition to refer to their style of meditation as **shikan taza**, or "just sitting."

Monastic Celibacy

Buddhist **monks** and **nuns** traditionally leave the ordinary secular life of **householders** (i.e., those who marry and have children) to lead celibate lives within the monastic community. Monastic celibacy dates to the historical **Buddha** and his immediate disciples, who left their families and possessions behind when they took the **tonsure**. It was common in the Indian culture of that time for religious seekers and holy people to forego sexual relations as a part of their religious practice. The **Vinaya**, or traditional Buddhist **monastic code**, required celibacy for all monks and nuns. Breaking the precept against sexual relations was one of only four violations that entailed expulsion from the community. Monastic celibacy represented one of the major stumbling blocks to **Buddhism's** initial acceptance in China and other areas in East Asia, since it was diametrically opposed to the dominant Confucian ethics, which demanded that every individual marry and rear children to fulfill the obligation of **filial piety** toward parents and family. Buddhist monastic celibacy was at first viewed as unfilial and destructive to the society, but Chinese Buddhists eventually came to interpret monastic celibacy as the highest form of filial piety. Today, monastic celibacy remains the norm throughout most of the Buddhist world. Japanese Buddhism represents the primary exception to this pattern: In Japan, although Buddhist nuns continue to lead celibate lives, most Buddhist monks are married men with families. See also **married clergy**.

Monastic Code

A collection of ethical **precepts** designed to govern the lives of **monks** or **nuns** living in religious communities. Within the Buddhist tradition, the earliest monastic code is the **Vinaya**, which constitutes one portion of the **Tripitaka**, the scriptures of **Theravada Buddhism**. According to Buddhist accounts, the regulations preserved in the Vinaya were actually established by the historical **Buddha** to regulate the activities of the **sangha**, the community of Buddhist believers, during his lifetime. The Buddha created regulations to meet various problems that arose within the community. The regulations typically convey the circumstances under which the individual rules were created and their specific purpose. The tradition maintains that the entire Vinaya was recited by the disciple **Upali** at the first Buddhist council held shortly after the Buddha's death. Later, tradition added to the Vinaya code as the need arose, and several versions of the Vinaya developed.

The **Zen** school developed its own genre of monastic codes, known in Chinese as ching-kuei and in Japanese as **shingi**, or "pure regulations." One of the distinctive features of the Zen codes is the requirement that all monks or nuns engage in **manual labor** as a regular part of their **monastic training**. Zen tradition maintains that the Chinese Zen master **Pai-chang Huai-hai** (720–814) composed the earliest Zen monastic code, the *Pai-chang Ch'ing-kuei* (J. *Hyakujô Shingi*), in the eighth or ninth century. Chinese codes were transmitted to Japan, where Japanese Zen masters designed their own versions to suit the Japanese context. **Dôgen Kigen** (1200–1253), the founder of Sôtô Zen, wrote one of the most famous Japanese examples, the *Eihei Shingi*.

Monju is the bodhisattva who represents knowledge, wisdom, and enlightenment.
This monk pays respect to an image of Monju in the meditation hall.

Monastic Training

The practice and discipline followed by a monastic community of **monks** or **nuns**. Buddhist monastic training is traditionally said to be divided into three parts: wisdom (J. egaku, Sk. **prajna**), morality (J. kaigaku, Sk. **sila**), and concentration (J. jôgaku, Sk. **samadhi**). See also **threefold training**.

Mondô

"Question and answer," a term for the discussion about the **Dharma** between a **Zen** master and disciple. In the classical Zen literature there are numerous exchanges between masters and disciples. In some cases, a student posed a question to the master, either to clarify an issue of personal concern or as a challenge. The master typically responded in a manner designed to push the student toward an immediate understanding of the Dharma. In other cases, the master would challenge an individual student or his entire assembly with a question. If a disciple answered the master's question with insight, the master could recognize the student's level of **enlightenment** in some way. It was very common for answers to take non-verbal forms such as shouts, slaps, or other gestures. Exchanges of this type became a common characteristic of Zen in T'ang dynasty China (618–907). Many of the classical examples of mondô were recorded and later served as the basis for **kôan**. Although Zen masters and disciples still engage in mondô, in many cases the practice has become stylized and scripted, lacking the spontaneity of the original exchanges.

Monju

The cosmic **bodhisattva** Manjusri, understood to represent the qualities of knowledge, wisdom, and **enlightenment** of the buddhas. Monju is often figured as an attendant of the **Buddha** (either Shakyamuni or Vairochana), standing on the left side of the triad. He is contrasted with the other attendant, the bodhisattva **Fugen**, who represents **meditation** and practice. Iconographically, Monju rides a lion, and carries in his hands a sutra and the sword of wisdom, which cuts through the hindrances to enlightenment.

Monju is a favorite figure in **Zen** art and literature, because of his close association with meditation. In many Zen monasteries, an image of Monju is enshrined as the main image in the **meditation hall** (zendô) or monks' hall (**sôdô**). A story about Monju's encounter with a Chinese Zen **monk** appears in the *Hekiganroku*, case thirty-five.

Monk

A male member of a religious monastic order. Given the many similarities between Christian and Buddhist monastic practice, the term *monk* has been adopted for Buddhist clerics. Like Christian monks, Buddhist monks typically live a celibate life within a monastic community devoted to religious practice, especially **meditation**. They share a similar tradition of taking **vows** and abiding by a **monastic code** that governs religious life in the monastery. Buddhist monks traditionally enter orders by taking on the **ten precepts** of a **novice**. A novice may later accept full **ordination** by undertaking the full set of 250 **precepts**.

Monks' Hall

One of the seven primary buildings (**shichidô garan**) which form the core of a **Zen** temple or monastery. Traditionally, the monks' hall served as the central living quarters for the majority of the monastic community and also as the dining hall and **meditation hall**. See **sôdô**.

Monna

Questions about the **Dharma**, usually addressed by a disciple to a **Zen** master. The term literally means "to ask a question." The term refers specifically to a question that a student asks during **mondô** (the question and answer session between master and student). In some cases, it applies to classical examples of questions drawn from Zen literature.

Moral Code

A set of **precepts** or ethical norms that govern the life and practice of religious individuals. See **precepts**.

Mount Gridhrakuta

"Vulture Peak," or "Mount of the Numinous Eagle" (J. Ryôjusen), a mountain outside the city of Rajagrha, India, where Shakyamuni **Buddha** (**Siddharta Gautama**) sometimes lived and taught. The mountain was probably so called because its profile resembles that of an eagle or vulture's head, or because flocks of vultures congregate there. In addition to the historical occasions when the Buddha gave **sermons** on Mount Gridhrakuta, the mountain is named as the legendary site for a number of later **Mahayana sutras**. The most famous sermon said to have been given at Vulture Peak was the **Lotus Sutra**. In Buddhist texts and art, Mount Gridhrakuta came to be envisioned as a transcendent mountain where wondrous events occurred, rather than the geographical site in India.

Within the **Zen** tradition, Mount Gridhrakuta is regarded as the site of the first authentic Zen transmission of the **Dharma** from Shakyamuni to **Mahakashyapa**. According to traditional accounts, once when the Buddha had a large audience of disciples gathered around him, he held up a flower without comment. No one in the audience said a word, except Mahakashyapa who smiled in response. The Buddha, understanding from the smile that Mahakashyapa had attained **enlightenment**, said, "I have the True Eye of the Dharma, the wondrous mind of **nirvana**, the true form of formlessness and the mysterious Gate of the Dharma. Without reliance on words or letter, in a special transmission outside the teachings, I entrust this to Mahakashyapa." Zen masters have often used this exchange as a **kôan**; it is included in the **Mumonkan** (case six) and the **Sanbyakusoku** (case 253). The Zen tradition regards the exchange as the first transmission of the Dharma from mind to mind without recourse to words.

Tanabe, George J., Jr. and Willa Jane Tanabe. *The Lotus Sutra in Japanese Culture*. Honolulu, HI: University of Hawaii Press, 1989.

Mount Sumeru

(J. Shumisen) According to Indian cosmology, Mount Sumeru, or Meru, is the highest mountain in the world and stands at the center of the universe. It is surrounded in each of the four cardinal directions by mountains, oceans, and continents. The continent to the south of Meru, the region where human beings dwell, is India, separated from Sumeru by the Himalayas. Mt. Sumeru is the axis of **heaven** and earth, understood as the dwelling place of the gods. **Indra** dwells in a palace at its summit, and the **four guardian kings** (shitennô) live on its slopes, each protecting his respective direction and associated continent. **Buddhism** adopted the earlier ancient Indian cosmology in its basic outlines, but made some alterations to suit its teachings.

Moxa

(J. yomogi or mogusa) A combustible substance obtained from the leaves of the mugwort plant. The English term is derived from the Japanese. People throughout East Asia have used moxa for centuries as a traditional medicine. Fibers from the mugwort are gathered together and formed into tiny cones, like **incense**. An individual lights a cone and holds it against the skin for a few minutes, causing mild burns. The burning sensation is said to be bearable, and the warmth that follows is pleasant. Moxa is applied to specific points on the body depending on the purpose of the treatment.

Zen monks traditionally use moxa treatments to ease minor ailments and discomfort, especially pain in the legs caused by long sessions of seated **meditation** (zazen). In this case, the practice of using moxa is not a form of asceticism, but a medicinal practice. There are some examples, however, of monks who used moxa treatments as a form of ascetic practice. In the latter cases, the burning is used to purify the mind of improper thoughts, especially sexual desires. Burning the forehead with moxa was also a traditional part of the **ordination** ceremony in China. This tradition survives in modified form in parts of Buddhist East Asia.

Mu

"No," "not," "nothing, "without." The Japanese translation of the Chinese word *wu*, a word of negation, which is used to negate other terms in much the same manner as the English prefixes a-, ab- or un-. When used in contrast to the word *u*, which means "existence" or "being," mu means "non-existence" or "non-being" as opposed to existence or being. In **Zen** texts, the expression *mu* often refers to the **Mu kôan**, or to the key phrase (**watô**) from the kôan.

Mu-an Hsing-t'ao

(1611–1684; J. Mokuan Shôtai) Chinese Obaku **monk** of the late Ming dynasty (1368–1644) who emigrated to Japan and assisted his master **Yin-yüan Lung-ch'i** (1594–1673) in founding the **Obaku sect** of **Zen** in Japan. Mu-an was born in Fukien province and took the **tonsure** at age nineteen at Wan-fu-ssu monastery, where Yin-yüan was **abbot**. He became Yin-yüan's **Dharma heir** in 1650. Mu-an initially remained in China when Yin-yüan left for Japan in 1654, but he then sailed for Japan the next year at Yin-yüan's request. In 1664, Mu-an succeeded his master and became the second abbot at **Mampuku-ji**. During his seventeen years as abbot, he oversaw the

227

A mudra is a hand gesture or other body posture used to indicate a state of enlightenment. This mudra is known as nebina gasshô in Japanese. It represents a firm and sincere heart.

construction of most of the monastery buildings. He also founded Zuishô-ji, the Obaku headquarters in the capital city of Edo (now Tokyo). Mu-an recognized over forty Dharma heirs, including Tetsugyû Dôki, **Tetsugen Dôkô** (1630–1682), and Chôon Dôkai. Mu-an is well known for his **calligraphy**; along with Yin-yüan and **Chi-fei**, he is known as one of the "three brushes of Obaku."

Mudra

Symbolic body postures, especially hand gestures, used in religious iconography and as a part of religious practice within various traditions, including several schools of **Buddhism** (J. ingei or inzô). The Sanskrit term literally means sign or seal. In Buddhist art, mudra are used to indicate the state of **enlightenment** or special attributes of a **buddha** or **bodhisattva**. The ritual use of mudra is associated most closely with **esoteric** and tantric forms of Buddhist practice. In these cases, the practitioner performs mudra while reciting related mantras as an aid to attain specific states of consciousness. Ritual use of mudra is not a regular feature of **Zen** practice.

Muen Botoke

The spirit of a dead person (**hotoke**) caught between the worlds of the living and the dead, unable to attain release. The term literally translates as "a **buddha** (or dead spirit) without **attachments**." To be without attachments in this context means to have no living family to offer the proper Buddhist **memorial services**. In Japanese folk belief, it is thought that such spirits wander in this world, unable to attain release on their own. See **wandering spirits**.

Muga

"No-Self," the Japanese translation for the Sanskrit term *Anatman*. See **Anatman**.

Mugaku Sogen

Japanese pronunciation for **Wu-hsüeh Tsu-yüan** (1226–1286), a Chinese Rinzai master who helped to establish the Rinzai school in Japan. See **Wu-hsüeh Tsu-yüan**.

Muhon Kakushin

See **Kakushin**.

Mujaku Dôchû

(1653–1744) A Japanese Rinzai **monk** of the Tokugawa period (1600–1867). Mujaku was born in Tajima, in modern day Hyôgo Prefecture. He became a monk at the age of seven and became the disciple of the Rinzai monk Jikuin Somon (1610–1677) at Ryôge-in, a subtemple of **Myôshin-ji**. He inherited the temple from Jikuin after his death. Mujaku also practiced under several other **Zen** masters and served three times as **abbot** of the main monastery Myôshin-ji. Mujaku was a leading Rinzai scholar monk of his day, and he pioneered philological studies of the Chinese Zen corpus, producing several commentaries and lexicons. Many of his scholarly works remain in use today. See also **Rinzai sect**.

Mujô

Impermanence, which characterizes all things that exist. Impermanence is one of the **three marks** of existence, along with **suffering** (dukkha) and No-Self (Sk. **Anatman**). According to the Buddhist understanding of reality, all things are impermanent and undergo constant change. Things arise, change, and eventually pass away. Nothing remains constant or unchanging for even a moment. Mujô is the Japanese translation for the Sanskrit concept anitya or the pali anicca.

Mujû Dôgyô

(1226–1313) Japanese Rinzai **monk** of the Kamakura period (1185–1333), also known as Mujû Ichien. Mujû became a monk at age nineteen and studied a wide variety of **Mahayana** teachings. Although he became a **Zen** monk and practiced as a disciple of Rinzai monk **Enni Ben'en** (1202–1280), he retained his interest in the mixture of Zen teachings and **esoteric Buddhism**. He is remembered primarily as the author of the *Shasekishû*, a collection of Buddhist stories and anecdotes. See also **Rinzai sect**.

Mujun Shiban

Japanese pronunciation for **Wu-chun Shih-fan** (1177–1249), a leading Chinese Rinzai **Zen monk** of the late Sung dynasty (960–1279). See **Wu-chun Shih-fan**.

Muken Jigoku

The Japanese translation for **Avici hell**, the hell of incessant suffering, the worst of the **eight hot hells** (hachinetsu jigoku). See **Avici hell**.

Mu Kôan

One of the most famous traditional **Zen kôan**, and the one Rinzai masters most often give to beginners as a focus for **meditation**. The so-called "Mu kôan" appears as the first case in the *Mumonkan*. A student once asked Zen Master **Chao-chou Ts'ung-shen** (778–897; J. Jôshû) if a dog has the **Buddha Nature**. Chao-chou answered, "**mu**." The word *mu* (Ch. wu) is a negation that can be translated as "no," "not," "nothing," "without." It is also used to express **emptiness**, the Buddhist characterization for ultimate reality. Since the time of **Hakuin Ekaku** (1685–1768), Japanese Rinzai has classified the Mu kôan as a **hosshin kôan**, that is, a kôan appropriate for beginners seeking **kenshô**, the initial **enlightenment** experience. The Mu kôan is also known as Jôshû's Dog, or Chao-chou's Dog. See also **Rinzai sect**.

Mumon Ekai

Japanese pronunciation for **Wu-men Hui-k'ai** (1183–1260), Chinese Rinzai master who authored the *Mumonkan*. See **Wu-men Hui-k'ai**.

Mumon Gensen

(1323–1390) A Japanese Rinzai **monk** of the Ashikaga period (1392–1568) who founded the **Hôkô-ji** line of Japanese Rinzai. Mumon was born in Kyoto, the son of **Emperor Go-daigo** (1287–1339). He entered Buddhist orders at age seven. At eighteen, he entered the **Zen** monastery **Kennin-ji** and practiced under Meisô Sôkan, Kaô Sônen, and Sesson Yûbai. In 1343, he traveled to Yüan-dynasty China where he visited many famous monasteries and practiced under various Zen masters. He received his formal **inka** in China. Mumon returned home to Japan in 1350 to escape chaos and warfare in China. He founded the monastery Hôkô-ji, in present day Shizuoka prefecture, in 1384. See also **Rinzai sect**.

Mumonkan

The Japanese title for the *Wu-mên kuan* (T. 48, no. 2005, pp. 292–299), a classic Chinese **Zen** text compiled by the Rinzai master **Wu-men Hui-k'ai** (1183–1260; J. Mumon Ekai) and edited by his disciple Tsung-shao (J. Shûshô). The work was completed in 1228 and first published in 1229. The full title in Japanese is *Zenshû Mumonkan, "The Gateless Gate of the Zen Lineage."* The text is comprised of forty-eight **kôan** from various sources, most of them extremely famous encounters in Zen history. To each kôan, Wu-mên provided a title and appended his own prose commentary and a verse.

Wu-mên explains in his preface to the *Mumonkan* that he collected the kôan cases to aid his own disciples in their practice. He wrote that he used "the cases of the ancient masters as brickbats to batter the gate and lead [his disciples] on according to their respective capacities" (Sekida, p. 26). The text has long been the most popular collection of kôan, used widely in the Zen world as a resource for training students. Many students of Zen begin their kôan practice with the first case of the *Mumonkan*, "Jôshû's 'Mu.'"

The Japanese Rinzai **monk** Shinchi **Kakushin** (1207–1298) first brought the collection to Japan in 1254. Kakushin traveled to China and practiced directly under Master Wu-mên's guidance. When Kakushin was leaving China to return home to Japan, the master gave him a copy of the *Mumonkan* as a departing gift. Kakushin's copy was a handwritten manuscript, copied by Wu-mên himself. All versions of the *Mumonkan* in use today in Japan are based on a wood block edition produced at Tosotsu-zan Kôon-ji in 1405. The *Mumonkan* has become popular in the West as well. There are several complete English translations, including Katsuki Sekida's *Two Zen Classics* (Weatherhill, 1977), Robert Aitken's *The Gateless Barrier* (North Point Press, 1990), and Zenkei Shibayama's *Zen Comments on the Mumonkan* (Harper & Row, 1974), among others. See also **Rinzai sect**.

Munen

No-thought, the Japanese translation of the Chinese term *wu-nien*, a basic **Zen** concept introduced in the **Platform Sutra**. See **no-thought**.

Muni

Sage or saint, in Sanskrit. Muni was originally an honorific title used for any outstanding religious teachers. In Buddhist texts, it refers specifically to the historical **Buddha**. The most commonly used name for the historical Buddha, Shakyamuni, is a compound word meaning "the Sage of the Shakya people," as **Siddharta Gautama** was born to a family from the **Shakya clan**.

Muni

(2) **Non-duality**, transcendence from the distinctions of ordinary perception. The Japanese term literally means "not two," since from the perspective of ultimate

Musical instruments, such as this sounding gong (mokugyo), are used in Zen monasteries to signal such things as the time of day and the beginning of ceremonies or rituals.

reality there are no distinctions such as good and bad, male and female, and so on.

Muryôju

"Infinite Life," another Japanese name for **Amida buddha**. See **Amida buddha**.

Muryôkô

"Infinite Light," another Japanese name for **Amida buddha**. See **Amida buddha**.

Mushin

No-mind, the Japanese translation of the Chinese term *wu-hsin*. Within the **Zen** school, the term is used synonymously with *munen*, "**No-thought**." See **No-thought**.

Musical Instruments

A variety of musical instruments are used in **Zen** temples and monasteries to announce times of day, provide cues to begin and end daily activities, and punctuate ritual ceremonies. In traditional monastic settings, verbal announcements are rendered unnecessary by the regular system of sounding instruments. The most common instruments include the following categories:

1) Bells. The largest of the monastery bells is the daishô, or **ogane**, which is generally made from cast bronze and hangs in a separate structure, the **shôrô**. Smaller versions of the same style of bell include the **denshô**, which hangs outside the Buddha hall, and the **kanshô**, which sits outside the master's quarters.

2) Drums. Taiko drums, called **hokku** and **saku** in a Zen context, are found in the Buddha hall. These large instruments rest horizontally on wooden platforms and may be played at both ends using wooden sticks. Another drum-like instrument found in monasteries is the wooden **mokugyo**, carved in the shape of a fish.

3) Gongs. One style of Buddhist gong is shaped like a bowl, typically made from cast bronze. Gongs rest on pillows, supported by a wooden stand, and are sounded by striking the rim with a padded stick. In Zen monasteries, the

larger version is called **keisu** and the smaller **shôkei**. There are also large wooden gongs, known as **hô**, which are carved in the shape of a fish with a pearl in its mouth.

4) Sounding Boards. There are basically two styles of sounding boards, the metal **umpan** and the wooden **han**. These boards are found throughout monastery grounds, hanging outside nearly every structure.

5) Small Hand Instruments. A variety of hand-held instruments that resemble tiny bells or gongs include the suzu, the rei, and the **inkin**. There are also wooden clappers called **hyôshigi**.

Musô Kai

"**Formless precepts**," the common Japanese abbreviation for the term *musô shinji kai*. See **musô shinji kai**.

Musô Shinji Kai

"**Formless precepts** of the mind-ground," the Japanese rendering of the original Chinese term derived from the **Platform Sutra** of the Sixth Patriarch. The concept of "formless precepts" is a distinctly **Zen** understanding of the Buddhist precepts, which sees them not as an external moral code, but rather as the naturally pure behavior which arises from the enlightened mind.

Musô Soseki

(1275–1351) Japanese Rinzai **monk** of the late Kamakura (1185–1333) and early Ashikaga (1392–1568) periods who was the most influential Gozan **Zen** master of his age. He is also known as Musô **Kokushi**, or National Teacher Musô, an honorific title that **Emperor Go-daigo** (r. 1318–1339) bestowed on him in 1335. Musô was born in Ise to a branch of the Minamoto family with imperial roots. He became a Buddhist monk at age eight and studied Shingon **Buddhism** for ten years before turning to Zen when his first teacher died. Musô traveled extensively on Zen **pilgrimage's** and studied with many of

the leading Japanese and Chinese Zen masters throughout Japan. He eventually became the **Dharma heir** of Kôhô Kennichi (1241–1316). Musô spent his early years in seclusion, practicing intently. He later gained the patronage of emperors and **shôgun** and was invited to serve as **abbot** at several important monasteries including **Nanzen-ji**, **Jôchi-ji**, and **Engaku-ji**. In 1339, Musô founded the Zen monastery **Tenryû-ji** as a memorial to the recently deceased Emperor Go-daigo, with the patronage of the shôgun Ashikaga Takauji (1305–1358). After his death, Musô received a total of six other honorific titles from successive emperors, including Fusai Kokushi, Genyû Kokushi, Buttô Kokushi, and Daien Kokushi. He is remembered for his contributions in the fields of Zen literature, especially poetry, and landscape gardening. An English translation of Musô's poetry and **sermons** was published by W. S. Merwin and Sôiku Shigematsu. See also **Gozan literature**, **Rinzai sect**, and **Shingon sect**.

Merwin, W. S., and Sôiku Shigematsu. *Sun at Midnight*. San Francisco, CA: North Point Press, 1989.

Musô Zange

"**Formless repentance**," the Japanese rendering of the original Chinese term derived from the **Platform Sutra** of the Sixth Patriarch. The concept of "formless repentance" is a distinctly **Zen** understanding of repentance based on the awareness that outward actions, whether good or evil, are ultimately empty. See **formless repentance**.

Myôan Eisai

(1141–1215) The Japanese **Zen** master traditionally credited with founding the **Rinzai sect** in Japan. He is most commonly known as **Eisai**, which may also be pronounced Yôsai. See **Eisai**.

Myôhô renge kyô

"The Scripture of the Lotus Flower of the Wondrous **Dharma**," the full Japanese title for the Saddharma pundarika, popularly known as the **Lotus Sutra**. See **Lotus Sutra**.

Myôô

"Shining lord," a class of fierce guardian deities who protect **Buddhism**, the **three treasures**, people, and the nation from evil. The word is a Japanese translation of the Sanskrit *Vidyaraja*. The myôô were adopted by Buddhism from Hindu mythology. They are understood in the Buddhist tradition to be manifestations of Dainichi, the **Buddha** Vairochana, capable of teaching the most stubborn unbelievers through the use of **mantra** (shingon). They are depicted as dramatically fierce figures, armed with weapons and having contorted faces, blazing eyes and hair of flames. A group of five myôô, known as godai myôô (the five great myôô), are especially revered in Japan as protective deities of the four directions and the center of the universe. They include Fûdô, Gôzanze, Gundari, Daiitoku, and Kongôyasha.

Although more closely associated with schools of **esoteric Buddhism** than **Zen**, the myôô are often represented at Zen temples as guardians. The most popular myôô in the Zen tradition, and in Japanese Buddhism in general, is **Fudô Myôô**. The Tokugawa period (1600–1867) Zen master **Suzuki Shôsan** (1579–1655), for example, recommended Fudô as an inspiration for Zen practitioners.

Myôshin-ji

A major Rinzai monastery, located in Kyoto. Its formal name is Shôbô-zan Myôshin-ji. The monastery was founded by retired **Emperor Hanazono** (r. 1308–1318) in 1337. The retired emperor took the **tonsure** in 1335, and converted one of his residences into a **Zen** temple. He invited **Kanzan Egen** (1277–1369) to serve as the founding **abbot**. The original structure of the temple was quite bare, and Egen lived a frugal existence there. He maintained a strict and rigorous style of Zen practice that continued to characterize the monastery throughout its history. The monastery never became associated with the **Gozan system** of ranking temples, nor with the literary and artistic concerns that characterized the **Gozan temples**. The temple was completely destroyed during the Onin War and rebuilt under the patronage of Emperor Go-Tsuchimikado in the late fifteenth century. It reached its greatest period of influence during the Tokugawa period (1600–1867), and today remains one of the most active monastic communities for training Zen **monks**. The monastery serves today as the main headquarters for the Myôshin-ji branch of the **Rinzai sect**. It sponsors the affiliated Hanazono College (J. Hanazono Daigaku), a major center for Zen studies in Japan.

Myôshin-ji Ha

The **Myôshin-ji** branch of Rinzai, the largest of the fourteen contemporary branches of the Japanese **Rinzai sect** in terms of both **branch temples** and adherents. The main monastery for the branch is Myôshin-ji, located in Kyôto. **Kanzan Egen** (1277–1369) is regarded as the founder. The branch has 3,431 temples throughout Japan and claims approximately 1,628,000 adherents.

Myôzen

See **Ryônen Myôzen**.

Naga

(J. ryû) Lesser gods and demigods from the Buddhist pantheon. Veneration of nagas dates back to pre-Hindu India. Nagas are serpent-like beings, sometimes said to resemble dragons. They reside in the sea, under the earth, or in the air, and control rainfall as well as the fertility of the land. The Buddhist tradition regards them as guardians of the **Dharma**, the teachings of the **Buddha**. According to some Mahayana legends, the Buddha entrusted his later Mahayana **sermons** to them, to be revealed to human beings only when they are prepared to hear the advanced teachings of **Mahayana Buddhism**.

Nagarjuna

(J. Ryûju) Indian **monk** who lived during the second or third century C.E. Nagarjuna was one of the outstanding philosophers of the early **Mahayana** tradition and was the founder of Madyamika school of early Mahayana. His most famous writing was the *Verses on the Middle Way* (***Mâdhyamaka Karikas***), which rejects wrong views. An English translation of the entire text was published by Garfield. His basic teaching is that all things are characterized by **emptiness**, including the concept of emptiness itself; he takes a middle view that rejects both an absolute conception of reality and an absolute negation of reality. Several schools of East Asian **Buddhism** regard him as a founding **patriarch**, including the **Pure Land schools**, the **esoteric** and tantric schools and the **Zen** school. The Zen tradition regards him as the fourteenth of the twenty-eight Indian patriarchs of Zen.

Garfield, Jay L., trans. *The Fundamental Wisdom of the Middle Way: Nagarjuna's* Mulamadhyamakakarika. New York: Oxford University Press, 1995.

Kalupahana, Nagarjuna. *The Philosophy of the Middle Way*. Albany, NY: State University of New York Press, 1986.

Streng, Frederick J. *Emptiness: A Study in Religious Meaning*. Nashville, TN: Abingdon Press, 1967.

Naikan

"Introspection," a form of inner contemplation in which attention is focused on the lower abdomen (**tanden**). The purpose of the practice is to build up and maintain the ki, or vital breath, within that power center of the body. This form of introspection can be carried out throughout the day during various activities. The **Zen** Master **Hakuin Ekaku** (1685–1768) advocated this form of introspection for therapeutic purposes.

Nampô Jômyô

(1235–1309) Japanese Rinzai **monk** of the Kamakura period (1185–1333) who traveled to China to study **Zen**. Nampô was born in what is now Shizuoka Prefecture to a branch of the Fujiwara family. He entered a Buddhist order at age fifteen at a local temple and traveled to **Kenchô-ji** in Kamakura to practice under the Chinese master **Lan-ch'i Tao-lung** (1213–1278) at age eighteen. In 1259, he sailed for China, where he became the disciple of **Hsü-t'ang Chih-yü** (1185–1269) at Hsüeh-tou-shan. Like Lan-ch'i, Chih-yü was from the Yang-ch'i **lineage** of Rinzai. Nampô accompanied Chih-yü to Ching-t'zu-ssu and **Ching-shan**, and in 1265 became his **Dharma heir**. He returned to Japan two years later.

In Japan, Nampô served as **abbot** first at Kôtoku-ji in Fukuoka, and then Sôfuku-ji, where he remained for thirty years. The emperor called him to Kyoto in 1304 to become abbot at **Manju-ji**. Later the Kamakura **bakufu** summoned him to Kamakura, where he served as abbot at Kenchô-ji. His leading Dharma heir was **Shûhô Myôchô** (1282–1337). He is more popularly known as Daiô Kokushi. His writings are recorded in the *Enzû Daiô Kokushi Goroku (The Recorded Sayings of the National Teacher Enzû Daiô)*. See also **Rinzai sect** and **Yang-ch'i school**.

Namu

The Japanese pronunciation of the Chinese characters used to transliterate the Sanskrit word *namas*. Namu expresses reverence, and is most commonly used in East Asian **Buddhism** with reference to the buddhas and the **three treasures** (**Buddha**, **Dharma**, and **sangha**). It may be used in formulaic expressions of faith when invoking the name of one or more buddhas, or when taking refuge (**kie**) in the three treasures. It may be variously translated into English as "Homage to. . .," "All praise to. . .," or "I take refuge in. . ."

Namu Amida Butsu

"All praise to **Amida buddha**." The Japanese pronunciation for the formula that followers of **Pure Land Buddhism** use most commonly to express their faith in and reliance on Amida buddha. The practice of calling on Amida's name using this formula is known as the **nembutsu**. According to Pure Land Buddhist belief, those who recite the nembutsu in faith will be reborn in Amida's **Western Pure Land**.

Namu Myôhô Rengekyô

"All praise to the Sutra of the Lotus Blossom of the Wondrous Dharma." Followers of **Nichiren Buddhism** recite this formula daily as an expression of their faith and reliance in the **Lotus Sutra**. The practice of reciting the formula is known as Shôdai or Daimoku. According to Nichiren belief, those who recite the Daimoku will become **buddhas** in the future.

Nan'in Engyô

Japanese transliteration of **Nan-yüan Hui-yung** (d. 930), a Chinese Rinzai master. See **Nan-yüan Hui-yung**.

Nan-shan

Mount Nan, literally Mount South, a mountain in modern day Hang-chou province, China, traditionally an important religious site for **Zen**. The mountain was the site for the Zen monastery **Ching-tzu-ssu**. Nan-shan became known as one of the Five Mountains (Ch. wu-shan; J. **Gozan temples**), the most prestigious Zen monasteries in China.

Nantô Kôan

"Difficult to pass through," the fourth of five categories of **kôan** distinguished by the Rinzai school of **Zen**. The kôan so designated are regarded as among the most difficult to understand. Since the time of the eighteenth century Japanese reformer **Hakuin Ekaku** (1685–1768), the Japanese school of Zen has used five categories of kôan to organize the ongoing process of kôan practice. After the practitioner has attained an initial **enlightenment** experience (**kenshô**), the student is guided through successive stages of kôan practice, each designed to deepen his or her understanding of Zen. Among the final stages are the Nantô kôan. See also **Rinzai sect**.

Miura, Isshû, and Ruth Fuller Sasaki. *The Zen Kôan*. New York: Harcourt, Brace & World, 1967.
Shimano, Eido T. "Zen Kôans." In *Zen: Tradition and Transition*. Ed. Kenneth Kraft. New York: Grove Press, 1988.

Nan-yüan Hui-yung

(J. Nan'in Engyô; d. 930) Chinese Rinzai **monk** of the late T'ang (618–907) and Five Dynasties period (907–960). Nan-yüan is also known as Pao-ying Ho-shang, or Master Pao-ying. He was the **Dharma heir** of **Hsing-hua Ts'un-chiang** (830–888), an important disciple of **Lin-chi I-hsüan** (d. 867). Although little is known of Nan-yüan, he played a crucial role in preserving the Rinzai **lineage**, and he was the first to make use of the **kôan** as a teaching device with his students. His only Dharma heir, **Feng-hsueh Yen-chao** (896–973), carried on the lineage. See also **Rinzai sect**.

Nanzen-ji, Kyoto, Japan.

Nanzen-ji

A major Rinzai monastery located in Kyoto. Its formal name is Zuiryû-zan Nanzen-ji. The monastery was founded by the retired emperor Kameyama (r. 1259–1274), who converted one of his residences into a **Zen** temple in 1293 and invited Mukan Fumon (1212–1291) to serve as the founding **abbot**. According to traditional accounts, soon after the retired emperor built a villa in the Higashiyama area of the capital, it became haunted. He requested that a Shingon **monk** from Tôdai-ji exorcise the grounds, but after conducting ritual **chanting** for ninety days, the monk was unsuccessful in exorcising the demons. The emperor next sought the help of Mukan Fumon, who is said to have solved the problem by taking up residence in the villa and practicing **meditation** for an extended period of time. To express his gratitude, the retired emperor converted the estate into a Zen monastery that then became the most powerful Zen monastery in the country and remained so for many generations. It was long ranked as the highest monastery in the **Gozan** (Five Mountain) **system**. The monastery grounds were completely destroyed during the Onin War (1466–1477) and were not restored until the early Tokugawa period (1600–1867). The monastery serves today as the main headquarters for the Nanzen-ji branch of the **Rinzai sect**. See also **Shingon sect**.

Nanzen-ji Ha

The **Nanzen-ji** branch of Rinzai, one of the fourteen contemporary branches of the Japanese **Rinzai sect**. The main monastery for the branch is Nanzen-ji, located in Kyoto. Mukan Fumon (1212–1291) is regarded as the founder. The branch has 427 temples throughout Japan and claims approximately 91,200 adherents. It now ranks second to **Myôshin-ji** in terms of temples and adherents.

Nehan

The Japanese transliteration of **nirvana**. See **nirvana**.

Nehandô

"**Nirvana hall**," the infirmary or sick room at a **Zen** monastery. See **nirvana hall**.

Nehan-e

Nirvana Festival, the day East Asian Buddhists commemorate the death, or perfect **nirvana** (Sk. **parinirvana**), of the historical Shakyamuni Buddha (**Siddharta Gautama**). Nehan-e is one of the **Sanbukki**, or three festivals commemorating major events in the Buddha's life. See **Nirvana Festival**.

Nehankyô

Commonly used Japanese abbreviation for the Daihatsu Nehangyô, the **Nirvana Sutra**. See **Nirvana Sutra**.

Nembutsu

"To think about the Buddha," a Buddhist practice that may either involve **meditation** on the **Buddha** or, more commonly, the invocation of the Buddha's name. Nembutsu is the Japanese pronunciation of the Chinese word *nien-fo*. In most cases, the buddha Amida serves as the focus of nembutsu devotion. The practice of **chanting** the nembutsu is especially associated with the **Pure Land schools** of East Asian **Buddhism**. All forms of the practice derive from the Pure Land scriptures, three **Mahayana sutras** devoted to the buddha Amida and his **Western Pure Land**.

Meditation on the Buddha or the Buddha's Pure Land is known more fully as kannen nembutsu. There are actually several styles of meditation on the Buddha, which may include visualization of the physical form of Amida and on the nature of the Pure Land. These meditative techniques are practiced primarily by **monks** and **nuns** as a part of their monastic practice. The goals of meditation on the Buddha are multiple. The immediate goal may be a vision of the Buddha or an **enlightenment** experience. The practitioner may also hope to be reborn in Amida's Pure Land (**ôjô**) in the next life.

The practice of verbally invoking the Buddha's name is known more fully as **shômyô** nembutsu. This practice generally involves the repetition of a formula of praise using the Buddha's name. The most common formula is, "**Namu Amida Butsu**," which may be translated "All praise to **Amida buddha**" or "I take refuge in Amida buddha." Since the invocation of the Buddha's name is an extremely simple practice to learn, its use is widespread among lay Buddhists as well as monastics. The ultimate goal of chanting the nembutsu depends on the faith of the believer. In many cases, people chant the name in order to gain **rebirth** in Amida's Pure Land. In the case of Jôdo Shinshû (Pure Land sect), believers chant the nembutsu in order to express gratitude to Amida for the promise of rebirth.

During the practice of chanting the nembutsu within the **Zen** school, it is most often the former style of meditation on the Buddha which is stressed. Zen masters will refer to the Buddha within the self (**koshin mida**) and the **Pure Land of the Mind Only** (yuishin no jôdo). In some cases, Zen masters encourage disciples to make use of the nembutsu as a **kôan**. The combined practice of Zen meditation and nembutsu was introduced to the Zen school by disciples of the Fifth Patriarch **Hung-jen**. It became common in Chinese Zen beginning in the tenth century and characterized all of Chinese Zen by the early Ming dynasty (1368–1644). It is still characteristic of the **Obaku sect** of Japanese Zen, introduced from China in the seventeenth century. See also **dual practice**, **lay believer**, and **Nembutsu kôan**.

Nembutsu Kôan

A **kôan** based upon the practice of **nembutsu**, or **chanting** the name of the **Buddha**. The Nembutsu kôan generally takes the form of a question, such as "Who chants the nembutsu?" Although the Nembutsu kôan is common in some parts of the **Zen** world, it is not derived from any traditional kôan collection or other classical Zen literature, but seems to have developed as a result of the **dual practice** of Zen and **Pure Land Buddhism** in Chinese monasteries during the Ming dynasty (1368–1644).

Nembutsu Kyôgen

A popular form of Japanese drama devoted to Buddhist themes, such as miracle stories or moral tales of karmic retribution. The plays are performed as pantomimes, with the actors dressed in colorful costumes and masks. Nembutsu kyôgen dates back several hundred years and is still performed today at Buddhist monasteries, such as Mibu-dera in Kyoto. The popular dramas are often comical in nature, but designed to convey Buddhist morals and teachings while entertaining the audience.

Nempu

"Chronology of years," **biography** of an important **Zen monk** or **nun**, composed to cover the life year by year. It is traditional for a leading disciple to record the biography of the master shortly after his or her death. Nempu represents a distinctive genre of Zen literature.

Nen

A Japanese word, which, when used as a noun, means "a thought," "a moment," or "a moment of thought." When used as a verb, it may mean "to think," "to contemplate," or "to remember." In some cases, such as in the expression **nembutsu**, it may alternatively mean to chant or recite.

Nenge Mishô

"Lifting a flower and smiling faintly," a reference to the **Zen** tradition's account of the first transmission of the **Dharma** from Shâkyamuni **Buddha** to **Mahakashyapa**, the first Indian **patriarch** of Zen. When Shâkyamuni

lectured on the Dharma to a group of disciples on **Vulture Peak**, he is said to have raised a flower and winked his eye without speaking a word. Only Mahakashyapa understood the Buddha's action, and he silently smiled his reply. Seeing Mahakashyapa smile, the Buddha recognized that he grasped the Dharma. According to Zen teachings, this event marks the beginning of the Zen school. The story is one of the most famous classical kôan, appearing as the sixth case in the *Mumonkan*.

Nenge Shunmoku

"Lifting a flower and winking an eye," a reference to the Zen tradition's account of the first transmission of the **Dharma** from Shakyamuni **Buddha** (**Siddharta Gautama**) to **Mahakashyapa**, the first Indian **patriarch** of Zen. The more common expression is **Nenge mishô**. See **Nenge mishô**.

Nenki

The anniversary of death. In Japanese Buddhist custom, **memorial services** (**hôji**) are held for deceased members of the monastic community on certain anniversaries of the death date. Although there is much variation in memorial practice throughout the denominations of Japanese **Buddhism**, the anniversaries most commonly observed are the first, third, seventh, thirteenth, seventeenth, twenty-third, twenty-seventh, and thirty-third. It is likewise customary for lay people to have similar memorial services held for deceased family members either at home or at the temple. **Zen** monasteries commemorate certain anniversaries of death on an annual basis, especially those of the sect's founder, the founder of the monastery, and other important personages. See also **lay believer**.

Nettetsugan

A red-hot iron ball; one of the punishments of **hell** dwellers described in Buddhist texts is being forced to swallow a ball of hot iron. According to **Lin-chi I-hsüan** (d. 867), any person who deceives others in this life will swallow hot iron in hell.

Nichimen Butsu, Gatsumen Butsu

"**Sunface buddha, Moonface buddha,**" the dying words of the Chinese **Zen** master **Ma-tsu Tao-i** (709–788), which appear as a **kôan** in case three of the *Hekiganroku*. Sunface buddha and Moonface buddha are two of the three thousand buddhas named in the Sutra of the Buddhas' Names (J. Butsumyôkyô; T. 14, nos. 440–442). According to the **sutra**, the lifespan of the Moonface buddha is twenty-four hours, while that of the Sunface buddha is 1,800 years. See **Sunface buddha, Moonface buddha**.

Nichiren

(1222–1282) Japanese Buddhist **monk** of the Kamakura period (1185–1333) who founded the Nichiren school of Japanese **Buddhism**. Nichiren was originally a Tendai monk and practiced and studied for some years on Mount Hiei. He became convinced that the **Lotus Sutra** was the ultimate teaching of Buddhism, and the only authentic teaching during the age of Mappô. He promoted the practice of **chanting** the title of the sutra using the formula "**Namu myôhô rengekyô**." Nichiren was twice exiled by Japanese authorities for his outspoken rejection of other schools of Buddhism. See also **Tendai sect**.

Nichiren Sect

A sect of Japanese **Buddhism** founded by the **monk Nichiren** (1222–1282) during the Kamakura period (1185–1333). The teachings and practices of the sect are based on Nichiren's understanding of the **Lotus Sutra**, which serves as the sect's principal scripture. Nichiren was originally a Tendai monk, and he studied the Lotus Sutra at the Tendai headquarters on Mount Hiei. **Chanting** the title of the sutra (using the formula "**Namu myôhô rengekyô**") is among the primary practices of Nichiren faithful. See also **Tendai sect**.

Nien-fo

"To think about the **Buddha**" Nien-fo refers to two types of Buddhist practices related to **Amidha buddha**. The first type involves some form of **meditation** on the Buddha or his **Pure Land**. The second, more common type of nien-fo practice includes the invocation of the Buddha's name. Practitioners generally chant the formula, "Na-mo A-mi-t'o fo," which may be translated "All praise to Amida buddha" or "I take refuge in Amida buddha." See **nembutsu**.

Nijô

Japanese for the **two vehicles**, namely those of **shravakas** and **pratyeka buddhas**. See **two vehicles**.

Nijûgoten

The twenty-five divisions of the night, from sunset to daybreak, which were traditionally announced in **Zen** monasteries using a wooden gong (J. **han**).

Ninyû

"**Two entrances**," the Japanese term for the two basic ways to attain an understanding of ultimate reality. Tradition maintains that **Bodhidharma**, the founder of **Zen**, first described the two entrances. The first entrance is **rinyû**, "the entrance through reason." This refers to studying the teachings of **Buddhism** as set out in the scriptures. The second entrance is **gyônyû**, "the entrance through practice." Zen Buddhism represents a form of gyônyû.

Ninyû Shigyôron

"Discourse on Two Entries and Four Practices," a **Zen** text traditionally attributed to **Bodhidharma**. See *Shôshitsu Rokumon*.

Niô are fierce guardian kings found on either side of a Zen temple gate.

Niô

"The two guardian kings." Two fierce figures of Kongô kings (vajra or Diamond kings) often found guarding either side of a temple gate. The two are identified by name as Misshaku (on the left) and Naraen (on the right). They are depicted as prepared for battle, ready to repulse demons and other forces of evil from entering temple grounds. The figure on the left has his mouth open, symbolically speaking the sacred sound "a"; the figure on the right has his mouth closed, pronouncing the syllable "Um." The two sounds together form the powerful mantra "AUM," a combination of the first and last letters in Sanskrit.

Niô Zen

"Guardian King **Zen**." A form of Zen practice recommended by the Tokugawa period (1600–1867) Zen master **Suzuki Shôsan** (1579–1655). Shôsan did not believe that beginners were capable of practicing what he called Nyôrai Zen, the **meditation** of the **Buddha**. He suggested that beginners visualize the form of the **Niô** in their minds and concentrate on the intense energy displayed by them. In some cases, he suggested that the meditator physically imitate the posture and facial expression of the Niô in order to generate the same levels of energy. The purpose of the exercise was to generate energy and direct it against the evil influences that hinder the meditation of a beginner.

King, Winston L. *Death Was His Kôan: The Samurai-Zen of Suzuki Shosan.* Berkeley, CA: Asian Humanities Press, 1986.

Tyler, Royall, trans. *Selected Writings of Suzuki Shosan.* Ithaca, NY: China-Japan Program, Cornell University, 1977.

Nirmanakaya

(J. ôjin) "Transformation body," one of three aspects or bodies of the **Buddha** according to the **Mahayana** understanding of the concept of Buddha. Nirmanakaya are manifestations of the eternal Buddha in this world, the so-called historical buddhas. These historical buddhas appear in human form to teach the **Dharma** to ordinary **sentient beings**. **Siddharta Gautama** is one example of nirmanakaya; the Mahayana tradition teaches that there have been innumerable others. See also **three bodies of the Buddha**.

Nirvana

(J. nehan) "Blowing out" or "extinction," the ultimate goal of Buddhist practice. The concept is associated with an enlightened state in which one has extinguished all passions and attained the highest wisdom. Having attained nirvana, one is no longer subject to the workings of **karma** or the process of **rebirth**. All **suffering**, **delusion**, and **attachment** are blown out in the state of nirvana. The final or perfect nirvana

Niô are typically depicted as prepared for battle, ready to fight evil demons.

(Sk. **parinirvana**) may be said to occur at the death of the enlightened individual. Although tradition has long maintained that nirvana cannot be adequately described with words, it is often discussed in positive terms as a blissful state of altered consciousness.

Nirvana Festival

In East Asian **Buddhism**, the celebration commemorating the death of the historical Shayamuni **Buddha** (**Siddharta Gautama**). As a part of the festival, followers display images depicting the Buddha entering his final or perfect **nirvana** (Sk. **parinirvana**) and chant the **Nirvana Sutra**. Traditionally, the festival was observed on the fifteenth day of the second month of the lunar calendar, but in Japan it is now observed on February 15, according to the solar calendar.

Unlike their East Asian counterparts who celebrate the major events in the Buddha's life on separate holidays, South and Southeast Asian Buddhists commemorate the Buddha's birth, **enlightenment**, and death on a single day, usually in May. See also **Buddha Day**.

Nirvana Hall

The infirmary or sick room at a **Zen** monastery. The name refers to the attainment of perfect **nirvana** (Sk. **parinirvana**), or the final passing into extinction that occurs when an enlightened person dies. **Monks** and **nuns** are cared for in the infirmary when they are too ill to continue with the normal temple life. Other names for the sick room include "hall for the prolongation of life" (**enjudô**) and anrakudô, the "hall of peace and pleasure."

Nirvana Sutra

(J. Nehankyô) The **Parinirvana** Sutra, a **Mahayana sutra** that presents itself as the final sermon given by the **Buddha** before his death. There are no Sanskrit versions extant, only Chinese translations (T. 12, nos. 374 and 375), the more important completed by Dharmakshema, a Buddhist monk of the fourth century C.E. The sutra gives an account of the Buddha's passage into parinirvana. Its basic teaching is that all **sentient beings** possess **Buddha Nature** and are capable of attaining **enlightenment**.

Nitai

"**Twofold Truth**," a **Mahayana** teaching that there are two levels or perspectives on reality. The two are daiichigitai, or absolute truth, and sezokutai, or conventional truth. See **Twofold Truth**.

Nitten Sôjo

Daily cleaning of a **Zen** monastery or temple. Every morning after breakfast, the resident **monks** or **nuns** participate in cleaning the temple buildings (**shichidô garan**) and grounds. Also called nitten samu.

Niu-t'ou School

(J. Gozu-shû) The **Oxhead school**, an important **lineage** of early Chinese **Zen** founded by **Fa-jung** (594–657), a **Dharma heir** of the Fourth Patriarch **Tao-hsin** (580–651). See **Oxhead school**.

Niwa Zume

Waiting period endured by new **Zen** trainees (**unsui**) before they are admitted to a Zen monastery for formal training. The term means to be left waiting at the entry gate (**genkan**), which is where the newcomer remains until the request for entry is accepted. Zen **postulants** formally request permission to enter a monastery for practice, but the initial request is always refused as a matter of form. The postulant then waits for a period of one to several days as a sign of his or her determination to practice Zen. Throughout the waiting period, the postulant sits at the edge of the raised platform in the entryway, with head bowed down over his or her baggage and hands held together in supplication. The practice is intended to test the resolve of trainees.

The Niwa Zume is a stylized version of traditional practices. Early Zen literature is filled with stories of masters testing the sincerity and determination of would-be disciples. Perhaps the most famous is the story of the Second Patriarch **Hui-k'o** (487–593), who stood patiently in the snow for several days awaiting recognition from **Bodhidharma**, the first patriarch. Finally, Hui-k'o cut off his arm with a sharp knife and presented it to Bodhidharma as a symbol of his deep commitment to the practice of Zen.

Suzuki, Daisetz Teitaro. *The Training of the Zen Buddhist Monk.* New York: Globe Press Books, 1991.

Nô Drama

A highly stylized form of Japanese drama and dance indirectly associated with **Zen Buddhism**. Nô, sometimes transliterated as Noh, was developed during the Ashikaga period (1392–1568) by Kan'ami (1333–1384) and his son Zeami (1363–1443) out of more popular forms of dance. The drama is performed by masked actors accompanied by musicians and a chorus. Although not all dramas portray Buddhist themes, the aesthetics of Nô and some of its themes are said to have been permeated by Zen influence.

No-Mind

A Buddhist concept used somewhat differently in various schools of thought. Within the **Zen** school, the term *no-mind* (mushin) refers to a state of detachment from the ordinary flow of discursive thought, which characterizes

Nô, a highly theatrical form of drama and dance, is performed by masked actors along with musicians and a chorus.

the state of **enlightenment**. The expression is used synonymously with **no-thought**. See **no-thought**.

Non-duality

The enlightened perspective of ultimate reality that transcends the distinctions of ordinary perception. The unenlightened individual experiences the world as a series of distinct phenomena, each perceived as different and judged as pleasant or unpleasant. From the perspective of ultimate reality, all phenomena are understood to be characterized by **emptiness** and are therefore without distinction. Reality is thus experienced as non-dual (J. **muni**); distinctions such as subject and object, **samsara** and **nirvana**, good and bad, male and female, and so on, are understood to be relative and not absolute.

Northern School

An important **lineage** of early Chinese **Zen** descending from **Shen-hsiu** (606?–706), a **Dharma heir** of the Fifth

Patriarch **Hung-jen** (601–674). The Northern school flourished for several generations before fading. It is not known if the lineage died out on its own or as a result of opposition from the **Southern school** of Zen. The division between the so-called Northern school of Shen-hsiu and the Southern school of **Hui-neng** (638–713) is regarded as one of the earliest splits within the Zen tradition. The names derive from the relative geographical location of the two lineages. Shen-hsiu and his lineage were active in the area north of the Yellow River and in the cities of Lo-yang and Ch'ang-an, while Hui-neng and his group were active in the south. According to traditional accounts of early Zen, the Northern school was an unorthodox form of Zen. It diverged from the orthodox Southern school in two ways. First, it taught a form of **gradual enlightenment**, which contravened the authentic Zen teaching of **sudden enlightenment**. Second, it followed an alternative lineage that did not recognize Hui-neng as the only valid

Sixth **Patriarch**. More recent research by Zen scholars, based on texts found at Tun-huang, has shown that this characterization is not historically accurate and was largely the creation of **Ho-tse Shen-hui** (670–762), a descendent of Hui-neng.

McRae, John R. *The Northern School and the Formation of Early Ch'an Buddhism*. Honolulu, HI: University of Hawaii Press, 1986.

No-Self

(J. Muga) The teaching of **Anatman**, one of the most basic and distinctive teachings of **Buddhism**. The concept of No-Self categorically denies that human beings possess a self-existent soul or self (Sk. **atman**) that is eternal, abiding, and unchanging. **Attachment** to the concept of such a false self is the fundamental cause of human **suffering**. Realization that no such self exists is understood as the basis for the attainment of **nirvana**, or release. See **Anatman**.

No-Thought

(J. munen) Detachment from the ordinary flow of discursive thought, which characterizes the state of **enlightenment**. No-thought is one of the most basic concepts of **Zen** introduced in the **Platform Sutra**. It is roughly equivalent of no-mind. No-thought does not imply the absolute absence of thought, a mental state that can be attained using some meditative techniques. Rather, no-thought describes a heightened state of awareness, in which one can respond without hindrance to any circumstance. No-thought describes the perspective of the enlightened mind, in which one realizes the nature of reality (i.e., one grasps the concept of **emptiness**). This allows one to think and respond to stimuli without clinging to thoughts or becoming attached to phenomena. The Platform Sutra says, "No-thought is not to think even when involved in thought . . . If you give rise to thoughts from your self-nature, then although you see, hear,

perceive, and know, you are not stained by the manifold environments, and are always free" (Yampolsky, pp. 138–139).

Yampolsky, Philip B. *The Platform Sutra of the Sixth Patriarch*. New York: Columbia University Press, 1967.

Novice

(J. **shami** and **shamini**) A person who has undergone an initial **ordination** as a **monk** or **nun**, but has not yet taken his or her final **vows**. In **Buddhism**, novices traditionally take refuge (**kie**) in the **three treasures** and accept the **ten precepts** as a part of their ordination. In accepting the ten precepts, the novice promises to refrain from killing, stealing, sexual misconduct, lying, drinking alcohol, eating after noon, enjoying secular entertainment, adorning the body, sleeping on a high (comfortable) bed, and handling gold and silver. Novices were accepted into the community under the guidance of a preceptor and a tutor, who respectively instructed the newcomer in the regulations of **monastic code** and the Buddhist teachings. The Buddhist monastic community did not traditionally accept children younger than eight, and in some cases fifteen, as a novices. A young novice had to reach the age of twenty before being allowed to proceed with full ordination.

Nun

A female member of a religious monastic order. Given the many similarities between Christian and Buddhist monastic practice, the term *nun* has been adopted for Buddhist clerics. Like their Christian counterparts, Buddhist nuns typically live a celibate life within a monastic community devoted to religious practice, especially **meditation**. They share a similar tradition of taking **vows** and abiding by a **monastic code** that governs religious life in the monastery. Unlike Christian nuns, however, Buddhist nuns are ordained and are therefore competent to conduct the same religious rituals as Buddhist **monks**. Buddhist nuns traditionally enter orders by taking on the **ten precepts** of a **novice**. A novice may later accept full **ordination** by undertaking the full set of 500 **precepts** for women.

Nyoi

A small curved staff or baton used by a **Zen** master when instructing students or giving a sermon. The term literally means "as one wishes." Nyoi are usually carved from wood or bamboo, and about fifteen inches long (35 cm). The master may use the nyoi to emphasize a point when speaking, to strike a student during a private interview (**sanzen**), or as a staff to rest upon when seated on the floor. Also known as a **kotsu**. See **kotsu**.

Nyorai

"Thus Come One," the Japanese translation of **Tathagata**. One of the **ten epithets for the Buddha**. The honorific title is commonly added to the name of a buddha, taking the place of the title Butsu, meaning buddha in Japanese. For example, **Amida buddha** may be alternatively referred to as Amida Nyorai. See **Tathagata**.

Nyoraizô

"Womb of the thus come one" or "Matrix of the **Buddha**," the Japanese translation of the Sanskrit term **Tathagata Garbha**. See **Tathagata Garbha**.

Nyûgan

Laying a corpse in the coffin, one of the nine ritual acts (**kubutsuji**) performed when a prominent Buddhist **monk** or **nun** dies. The deceased is placed in a round coffin in an upright seated position, as if he or she were meditating.

Nyûin

The installation of a new **abbot** at a **Zen** temple or monastery. The term literally means "to enter the temple." It is alternatively pronounced juen. In some cases, it may refer to the entry of a new **novice** to a Zen monastery. See **shinsanshiki**.

Nyusshitsu

Private instruction with the **Zen** master in the **abbot's** quarters. Sometimes pronounced Nisshitsu. The term literally means "entering the (master's) room." An alternative expression for shôeki.

Obaku-ban

The Obaku edition of the **Chinese Tripitaka**, composed by the Obaku **monk Tetsugen Dôkô** (1630–1682) in the late seventeenth century. Known as the Tetsugen edition, the Obaku-ban was Japan's first complete wood block version of the Chinese **Buddhist scriptures**. It was used as a standard edition in Japan until the modern *Taishô Daizôkyô* edition replaced it. Tetsugen traveled Japan raising funds for his Tripitaka project by preaching and collecting small donations from ordinary citizens. Meanwhile, craftsmen carved more than 60,000 blocks to complete the set of 6,956 bound volumes. The entire project took twelve years, from 1668 to 1680. Every volume of the set records the individuals, village associations, and Buddhist organizations who contributed to the effort.

According to popular legend, Tetsugen raised funds for the Obaku-ban project three times before the work was completed. First, a flood devastated the city of Osaka, and Tetsugen decided to spend the collected funds on disaster relief. The second time, he had almost raised the necessary amount when a famine struck the Kyoto-Osaka area. Tetsugen once again used his funds to feed the destitute. The third time, he collected donations and was able to complete his intended project. Tetsugen is known for both his work on the Tripitaka project and his participation in large-scale relief work.

Obaku Kiun

(d. 850) Japanese transliteration of **Huang-po Hsi-yün** (d. 850), one of the most important Chinese **Zen** masters of the T'ang dynasty (618–907). See **Huang-po Hsi-yün**.

Obaku Sect

The smallest of the three sects of **Zen Buddhism** in Japan. Obaku was founded by **Yin-yüan Lung-ch'i** (1594–1673) and a group of his disciples who emigrated from China, beginning in 1654. Obaku did not exist as an independent sect of Zen in China. Yin-yüan and his disciples descended from the Yang-ch'i **lineage** of the **Rinzai sect** of Zen. Its inclusion of **Pure Land** belief and practice, typical of all Zen lineages in China by the time of the Ming dynasty (1368–1644), is cited as one reason that Obaku became an independent sect distinct from Rinzai in Japan.

The main monastery for the Obaku sect is Obaku-san Mampuku-ji in the city of Uji, located to the south of Kyoto. Yin-yüan founded the monastery in 1661 with the permission and patronage of Tokugawa Ietsuna, the fourth Tokugawa shogun. The monastery in Japan bears the same name as Yin-yüan's home monastery in the Fukien province of southeastern China. The sect has approximately 462 temples and claims some 353,500 adherents. See also **Yang-ch'i school**.

Obaku Shingi

"The **Monastic Code** for the **Obaku Sect**," a text consisting of one section commonly attributed to **Yin-yüan Lung-ch'i** (1594–1673). The text, compiled by Kao-ch'üan Hsing-tun, was first published in 1673, the year of Yin-yüan's death. It governs the life and practice at the sect's main monastery, **Mampuku-ji**, as well as at other Obaku temples.

Obon

The Japanese version of the Festival of the Dead, celebrated during summer throughout Buddhist East Asia. The festival is based upon the **ullambana** ceremony, which traditionally closes the summer **rainy season retreat** on the fifteenth day of the seventh lunar month. The ceremony includes a feast offered up to the monastic community for those living beings **suffering** in **hell** as **hungry ghosts**. Since hungry ghosts cannot receive assistance directly, **offerings** of food are made to the **sangha**, and the **merit** is said to be transferred to the hungry ghosts to alleviate their suffering. As a part of Obon, Buddhist temples and many families in Japan continue to set up special altars and make offerings for the sake of hungry ghosts and other spirits who have no family to care for them. The festival has expanded to include many local folk traditions as well. In Japan, the focus of Obon now has more to do with honoring the spirits of the ancestors than with feeding hungry ghosts. The festival is usually observed from August 13 through August 15 and is the most important Buddhist festival of the year.

Traditionally, the Japanese travel back to their native villages for the Obon season, welcoming the spirits of their ancestors back to the world of the living. According to folk tradition, the spirits of the ancestors are said to travel back to the land of the living at Obon to visit their living descendants. To welcome the spirits and guide their passage, the celebrants light lanterns on the first evening of the festival. In preparation for the visit, families will carefully clean their Buddhist altar (J. **Butsudan**) and set out fresh flowers and **incense**. They may also set up a spirit altar, especially if they have suffered a loss since the last Obon festival. They participate in the customs of dancing, or Bon odori, intended to entertain both the living and the dead. At the end of the festival, people light farewell fires and say their goodbyes to the spirits, usually inviting them to return next year. Lantern boats, bearing the names of recently deceased individuals, may be lighted as a special send-off for the spirits who died within the last year. They are released on a river or dropped directly into the ocean and allowed to float out to sea.

Ogane, the largest temple bell on the grounds of a Buddhist monastery, is usually made of cast bronze and is intricately detailed.

Smith, Robert. *Ancestor Worship in Contemporary Japan*. Stanford, CA: Stanford University Press, 1974.

Offerings

Buddhist practitioners make ritual offerings as a regular part of their religious practice. **Monks**, **nuns**, and lay people alike may place offerings of **incense**, flowers, food, and other items before images of the **buddha** and **bodhisattvas** to express reverence and devotion. It is also traditional for lay people to make offerings to the monastic community and to individual monks and nuns as a means to build good **merit** and progress along the religious path of **Buddhism**. See also **four offerings** and **lay believer**.

Ogane

The largest temple bell on Buddhist monastery grounds. Ogane is the more popular transliteration of the characters that are formally pronounced "daishô." The ogane, which is usually made of cast bronze, hangs in a detached structure or bell tower (J. **shôrô**) specially designed for its display and ringing. Each one has a distinctive voice. They are prized as works of art for the deep, resonant sound they produce and the intricate designs in the casting. The large bell can be heard from afar when it is rung to signal events to the temple community. On the eve of the new year, most Buddhist temples ring the ogane 108 times to mark the passing of the old year. Each toll represents one of the 108 passions (or **afflictions**) that afflict human beings, and they are symbolically cast off in preparation for the new year.

Ogino Dokuon

(1819–1895) Japanese **monk** of the **Rinzai sect** of the late Tokugawa (1600–1867) and Meiji (1868–1912) periods who resisted government oppression of **Buddhism**. Born in Bizen province (Okayama Prefecture), Dokuon became the disciple of Daisetsu Shôen at **Shôkoku-ji**. He eventually became Daisetsu's **Dharma heir** and succeeded him as **abbot** in 1879. In 1872, as the official head of the combined **Zen** schools, Dokuon protested the Meiji government's policies toward Buddhism.

Oji Goi

The **five ranks** of princes. One of several formulaic expressions of the five ranks, originally developed by **Tung-shan Liang-chieh** (807–869) and **Ts'ao-shan Pen-chi** (840–901). In this version of the formula, titles of differing ranks of heirs to the throne are used allegorically to express the five ranks. The five-part formula may be translated as: 1) the crown prince, 2) an illegitimate son born to the ruler's concubine, 3) a vassal, 4) a military general, and 5) the king's younger brother. See **five ranks**.

Ojin

"Transformation body," the Japanese translation of the Sanskrit term *nirmanakaya*. Within the Mahayana Buddhist doctrine of the **three bodies of the Buddha** (J. sanshin), the nirmanakaya are the historical buddhas, manifestations of the eternal Buddha (J. hosshin; Sk. **Dharmakaya**) in this world. See **nirmanakaya**.

Ojô

The Japanese term for the ongoing cycle of birth and death that continues through numerous lifetimes. In the context of **Pure Land** Buddhist teachings, the term refers specifically to rebirth in Amida's **Western Pure Land**. See also **rebirth**.

Ojôyôshû

The Essentials of Salvation, a Japanese **Pure Land** text in three or six sections, composed by **Genshin** (942–1017) in 985. The *Ojôyôshû*, the first Pure Land text written in Japan, provided a theological basis for the later development of Japanese **Pure Land sects**.

Old-Woman Zen

Used in reference to the teaching style of some **Zen** masters who take great care in the training of students. The expression may be a form of praise, indicating that the master skillfully deals with disciples, or it may be derogatory, suggesting that the master is overly gentle with disciples or overly fastidious in his concern for detail. Zen texts abound with related expressions, such as grandmotherly concern (J. rôba shinsetsu and rôba tekkon), employed in much the same manner. See also **Rôba Zen**.

One-Finger Zen

(J. Tenryû isshitô or Isshitô Zen) A reference to the teaching style of the T'ang dynasty **Zen** master T'ien-lung (J. Tenryû) and his disciple **Chü-chih** (J. Gutei). According to tradition, when Chü-chi asked T'ien-lung to explain the essence of **Buddhism**, the master simply raised one finger. At that moment, Chü-chih was enlightened. From that time on, Chü-chih used this teaching device himself whenever disciples asked him questions about the **Dharma**. "One-finger Zen" is the topic of a famous case that appears in the *Mumonkan* and other **kôan collections**.

One Hand Kôan

(J. Sekishu kôan) The most famous **kôan**, attributed to the Rinzai master **Hakuin Ekaku** (1685–1768). The basic form of the kôan is, "What is the sound of one hand clapping?" Hakuin developed this kôan to be used by beginners as their first kôan. He believed that the One Hand kôan and the **Mu kôan** were the most effective meditative devices for attaining the initial experience of **enlightenment** (J. **kenshô**). See also **Rinzai sect**.

One Mind

(J. **Isshin**) The mind of **enlightenment** that perceives ultimate reality and transcends the dualism of ordinary thought and perception. The concept of "One mind" is presented in the *Awakening of Faith*, a Mahayana treatise attributed to **Ashvaghosha**. See also **Mahayana Buddhism**.

One Vehicle

(J. ichijô) The single path of **Buddhism**, encompassing all forms of Buddhism. The image of the one vehicle is presented in the **Lotus Sutra**, contrasted with earlier notions of the **three vehicles**. The Lotus Sutra teaches that all forms of Buddhism are paths to **enlightenment**, and together comprise the one great vehicle, or Mahayana.

One-Word Barrier

A **Zen** teaching device, which entailed a master using only one word in the original Chinese. See **ichiji kan**.

Orategama

A Japanese **Zen** text in three or four divisions, comprised of various letters (**kana hôgo**) composed by **Hakuin Ekaku** (1685–1768). The first edition, published in 1749, included three letters: one to Lord Nabeshima, one to a sick Zen monk, and one to a **Nichiren nun**. A later edition from 1751 appended additional letters in the *Orategama Zokushû*.

Ordination

A religious ritual symbolizing formal entry into a monastic community or religious profession. In **Buddhism**, ordination rituals marking the entry into monastic life as a **monk** or **nun** generally involve shaving the head to signify departure from ordinary lay life, reception of monastic robes, and the formal acceptance of the **precepts** that govern monastic life. In many schools of Buddhism, there are two levels of ordination: the initial ordination as a **novice** and full ordination as a monk or nun. Novices typically accept a smaller set of eight or ten monastic precepts, while fully ordained Buddhist monastics undertake the 250 precepts for monks or 500 precepts for nuns as set out in the **vinaya**. In Japan, many schools of Buddhism use a much shorter set of precepts known as the **bodhisattva precepts** at ordinations. See also **lay believer**.

Ordination Platform

In East Asia, Buddhist **ordinations** take place on specially constructed three-step platforms. See **kaidan**.

Original Enlightenment

(J. hongaku) The Mahayana teaching that all **sentient beings** innately possess the **Buddha Nature** and are capable of attaining **enlightenment**. Some schools of **Buddhism** teach that the seed of original enlightenment is gradually nurtured until one attains enlightenment, but in the **Zen** school, original enlightenment means that since we are already buddhas, it is only necessary to realize that within the self. This is the teaching of **sudden enlightenment**.

Original Face

(J. honrai no menmoku) A **Zen** expression for the original state of **enlightenment**, which Zen teaches that we all possess. The phrase *Original Face* is also commonly used in Zen texts to express the attainment of enlightenment (J. **satori**). For example, Zen Master **Tetsugen Dôkô** (1630–1682) wrote in his **Kana hôgo**, "Therefore, when the [proper] time comes and the causes [are ripe], you will suddenly overcome the darkness of ignorance [that has surrounded you] for innumerable **kalpas**. For the first time you will wake up from the long night of dreaming. You will clap your hands and laugh out loud. You will reveal your Original Face and illuminate the landscape of the original state."

Original Mind

(J. **Honshin**) A **Zen** expression used for one's true nature or **Buddha Nature**, which everyone possesses. The term is contrasted with the deluded mind of ordinary beings. Zen teaches that although everyone possesses the Original Mind of **enlightenment**, for most of us it is clouded by delusions. Through **meditation**, it is possible to realize the Original Mind or attain enlightenment.

Oryô Enan

(1002–1069) The Japanese name for **Huang-lung Hui-nan**, a Chinese **Rinzai sect** master of the Sung dynasty (960–1279). The name may also be alternatively transliterated Oryû Enan in Japanese. See **Huang-lung Hui-nan**.

Oryô School

The Japanese name for the **Huang-lung school**, a **lineage** of Chinese Rinzai. The characters are also transliterated Oryû in Japanese. In China, the Huang-lung school, active during the Sung dynasty (960–1279), was founded by the Chinese **Zen** master **Huang-lung Hui-nan** (1002–1069; J. Oryô Enan). In the late twelfth century, a Japanese Zen **monk** named **Eisai** traveled to China and became the **Dharma heir** of Hsü-an Huai-chang, an eighth generation master in the Huang-lung lineage. He then returned to Japan and transmitted the

lineage to his disciples there. In Japan, the Oryô school is regarded as one of the twenty-four lines of Japanese Zen. However, the school did not survive for long after Eisai's generation in either China or Japan. See also **Rinzai sect**.

Oshiku

Two days each month observed as days of rest at **Zen** monasteries, when the resident **monks** and **nuns** do not follow the regular schedule of **meditation** and ritual services. In the morning of oshiku days, monks and nuns help one another shave their heads and clean the monastery buildings and grounds. In the afternoon, they are free to attend to personal business. Oshiku are usually observed on the fourteenth and last day of each month.

Oshô

A title of respect used for senior **Zen monks** in Japan. Used in previous ages for any high-ranking monk, today the term *oshô* applies more specifically to **abbots**. In the Sôtô school, oshô indicates a monk who has already inherited the **Dharma** (J. shihô) from his master. Other schools of Japanese **Buddhism** use the same title for senior monks but may pronounce the characters differently. Tendai pronounces the word *Kashô*, whereas **Ritsu**, Shingon, and Jôdo Shinshû (**True Pure Land sect**) say *Wajô*.

Historically, the oshô was the Precept Master responsible for guiding a **novice's** practice, especially regarding the **monastic code**. Oshô is the Japanese translation of the term *Upadhyaya*, as the Precept Master was called in Sanskrit texts. In the ancient tradition, **novices** needed three teachers when they accepted the **precepts** at **ordination**. Of the three, the oshô was the person most directly responsible for the development of the new monk or **nun**. To serve as Precept Masters, monks or nuns were required to have practiced for ten full years beyond their full ordination. See also **Shingon sect**, **Sôtô sect**, and **Tendai sect**.

Other Power

(J. Tariki) Reliance upon the **merit** of a **buddha** or **bodhisattva** to attain spiritual progress on the path to **enlightenment**. Other Power is closely associated with the teachings of **Pure Land Buddhism**, encouraging faith in **Amida buddha** as the basic or solitary means for spiritual advancement. Other Power is contrasted with **Self Power** (J. Jiriki), the reliance on one's own merit and effort to attain enlightenment, which is characteristic of the **Zen** school.

Otôkan School

The Japanese Rinzai **lineage** centered at the monastery **Daitoku-ji** and **Myôshin-ji** in Kyoto. The name Otôkan derives from the honorific titles of its first three **patriarchs**: The *ô* from Daiô Kokushi (**Nampô Jômyô**; 1235–1309), the *tô* from Daitô Kokushi (**Shûhô Myôchô**), and the *kan* from Kanzan Kokushi (**Kanzan Egen**). Nampô founded the lineage during the Kamakura period (1185–1333), and under the Second and Third Patriarchs it became the dominant Rinzai lineage in Japan. The Tokugawa period (1600–1867) reformer **Hakuin Ekaku** (1685–1768) descended from this lineage. See also **Rinzai sect**.

Outflows

An alternate English translation for the Sanskrit term *ashrava*. See **defilements**.

Ox Cart

An image used for **Mahayana Buddhism** as the one path to **enlightenment**, drawn from the parable of the **burning house** recounted in the **Lotus Sutra**.

Oxhead School

(J. Gozu-shû) The Chinese Niu-t'ou school of **Zen**, an important **lineage** of early Chinese Zen founded by **Fa-jung** (594–657), a **Dharma heir** of the Fourth Patriarch **Tao-hsin** (580–651). The name derives from Ox-head Mountain (C. Niu-t'ou-shan) in Chiang-su where the headquarters of the school was located. The lineage thrived throughout the early centuries of the T'ang dynasty (618–907), continuing for eight or nine generations before it faded in the late ninth century. The Oxhead Zen teachings are said to have been transmitted to Japan by **Saichô** (767–822), the founder of the Japanese **Tendai sect**.

Oxherding Pictures

A series of ten drawings of an ox and an oxherder (J. **jûgyûzu**), which describe the process of **Zen** practice and **enlightenment**. The oxherder represents the Zen practitioner seeking enlightenment, while the ox represents the true self. The original pictures are attributed to the twelfth century Chinese Zen **monk** K'uo-an Shih-yuan (J. **Kakuan Shion**; d. 1234). The ten pictures are interpreted as graphic representations of ten stages of Zen practice: 1) seeking the ox, 2) finding its footprints, 3) seeing the ox, 4) catching the ox, 5) herding the ox, 6) riding the ox home, 7) forgetting the ox, but not the self, 8) forgetting both the ox and the self, 9) returning to the true self, and 10) entering the marketplace to bestow blessings on others.

P

Pagoda

(J. tô or tôba) A Buddhist religious structure found throughout East Asia characteristically possessing several stories with distinct rooftops forming a towerlike structure. The pagoda originally derived from the Indian **stupa**. Like stupas, pagodas are traditionally used to enshrine **relics** of the historical **Buddha** or other prominent holy men and women.

Pai-chang Ch'ing-kuei

(J. Hyakujô Shingi) The *Monastic Code of Pai-chang Huai-hai*, a **Zen** text traditionally regarded as the earliest Zen monastic code. The text, attributed to the T'ang master **Pai-chang Huai-hai** (720–814), exists in name only. There is no historical evidence that Pai-chang ever authored a **monastic code**, although references to a text by that title date back to the Sung dynasty (960–1279). In some cases, the term refers to the *Ch'ih-hsiu Pai-chang Ch'ing-kuei*, a Yuan dynasty synthesis of major Zen monastic codes of the Sung dynasty.

Pai-chang Huai-hai

(720–814; J. Hyakujô Ekai; alternatively transliterated Po-chang) Chinese **Zen monk** of the T'ang dynasty (618–907) and one of the most prominent masters of the day. Pai-chang is the disciple and **Dharma heir** of **Ma-tsu Tao-i** (709–788). His disciples include **Huang-po Hsi-yün** (d. 850). He is traditionally known as the author of the first Zen **monastic code**, the *Pai-chang Ch'ing-kuei*, although scholars no longer believe that he

authored such a text. Tradition maintains that Pai-chang systematized the monastic practice of Zen **Buddhism** in a manner distinctive from other forms of Chinese Buddhism of his day. He also established the requirement for daily **manual labor**, coining the rule, "A day without labor, a day without food."

Pali Canon

An alternative name for the Theravada **Buddhist scriptures**, better known as the **Tripitaka**. The earliest version was composed in the Pali language, hence the name. See **Tripitaka**.

P'ang Yun

(J. hô koji) Chinese lay practitioner of **Zen**, better known as **Layman P'ang** (740–803). See **Layman P'ang**.

Pao-lin Chuan

(J. Hôrinden) A Chinese **Zen** text in ten sections, recounting the **lineage** of Zen masters from the T'ang dynasty (618–907). The **monk** Hui-chu Chu-ling compiled the work in 801. It represents the traditional standard version of the Zen lineage.

Papiyas

(J. Hajun) An evil deity who reigns in the highest of the six heavens in the realm of desire. Papiyas is an enemy of **Buddhism**, determined to prevent the **Buddha** and his followers from practicing Buddhism and attaining **enlightenment**.

Parajika

(J. haraizai) Offenses entailing defeat; actions of a Buddhist **monk** or **nun** that are punishable by expulsion from the **sangha**. Parajika is the most serious category of offenses set out in the **vinaya**, the **monastic code** developed within the Theravada tradition. The vinaya identifies four parajika offenses for monks and eight for nuns. Monks are prohibited

East pagoda at Yakushi-ji (Medicine Buddha Temple), which was founded in Nara in 718 C.E.

from: 1) engaging in sexual intercourse, 2) stealing another person's belongings, 3) killing a human being, and 4) lying about one's spiritual accomplishments. Nuns, in addition, are prohibited from: 5) touching a man's body, 6) engaging in a forbidden activity with a man when filled with desire, 7) concealing the faults of another person at the assembly, and 8) breaking the rules of the assembly. See also **Theravada Buddhism**.

Wijayaratna, Mohan. *Buddhist Monastic Life: According to the Texts of the Theravada Tradition*. Trans. Claude Grangier and Steven Collins. New York: Cambridge University Press, 1990.

Parinirvana
(J. hatsu nehan) Final or perfect **nirvana**, the ultimate release attained when an enlightened person dies. The term *parinirvana* most often refers to the death of the historical **Buddha**, although it can be used more generally. When people attain **enlightenment** in this life, they are said to have reached the state of nirvana with residue. This means that although free from the workings of **karma**, they continue to live out the remainder of the present life. Such individuals are no longer subject to the ongoing cycle of birth and death, and at death attain complete release. Parivirnana is sometimes called nirvana without residue.

Parishioner System
A social system devised by the military government during the Tokugawa period (1600–1867) to control the Japanese populace. See **danka seido**.

Patriarch
(J. so, **soshi**, or **sobutsu**) An important leader recognized within a religious tradition as a founding figure. Although the Buddhist tradition rarely relies upon blood **lineage** for its leadership, the tradition makes wide use of familial terms, including the concept of patriarchs. Many Buddhist schools and sects acknowledge several historical teachers as their patriarchs. **Zen Buddhism** places an especially strong emphasis on the lineage of early patriarchs who created the Zen school and transmitted its **Dharma**. The Zen school acknowledges a lineage of patriarchs extending back from **Hui-neng** (638–713), the Sixth Chinese Patriarch, to the historical **Buddha** and beyond. According to Zen teaching, Shakyamuni (**Siddharta Gautama**) transmitted the Dharma to **Mahakashyapa**, the first Indian patriarch. The Dharma was then transmitted through twenty-eight Indian patriarchs. **Bodhidharma**, who traveled to China and passed on the Dharma there, is counted as the twenty-eighth Indian patriarch and the First Patriarch in China. Six Chinese patriarchs are acknowledged by all surviving Zen lineages. Later Zen teachers may also be known as patriarchs, for example, **Dôgen Kigen** (1200–1253) of the Japanese **Sôtô sect**.

Patriarch's Hall
A hall within a **Zen** monastic complex dedicated to the early Zen **patriarchs** and founders. See **soshidô**.

Pei-shan
(J. Hokusan) Mount Pei, literally Mount North, a mountain in modern day Hangchou province, China. The mountain was the site for the Zen monastery **Ling-yin-ssu** and became known as one of the Five Mountains (C. Wu-shan; J. **Gozan temples**), traditional religious sites and locations of the most prestigious Zen monasteries in China.

Pei-yung Ch'ing-kuei
Abbreviated title for the Ch'an-lin Pei-yung **monastic code**, a Chinese **Zen** monastic code in ten sections. Also known as the *Zenrin Biyô Shingi*, *Biyô Shingi*, or the *Shidai Shingi*, it was written by Tse-shan I-hsien and published in 1311.

Perfection of Wisdom Sutra

(J. **Daihannya Haramitsukyô**) An entire class of Mahayana literature comprised of approximately forty texts originally composed in Sanskrit. The **Heart Sutra** and the **Diamond Sutra** are two important texts in the Perfection of Wisdom literature that emerged in India between the second and sixth centuries C.E. Tibetan and Chinese translations also exist. The Perfection of Wisdom literature discusses the Mahayana concept that **emptiness** characterizes all of existence. In some cases, the title *Perfection of Wisdom Sutra* may refer specifically to the Perfection of Wisdom in Eight Thousand Lines, which is among the earliest examples of the Wisdom literature. See also **Mahayana Buddhism**.

Pien-wen

Tales of marvelous events, a genre of Chinese literature used to popularize stories from the life of the **Buddha** and from various **sutras**.

Pilgrimage

Traveling for religious purposes has been a part of the Buddhist tradition since the ancient period in India, and pilgrimage is still an important form of Buddhist ritual practice. As do pilgrimages in other religious traditions, Buddhist pilgrimages serve a number of purposes: they offer entertainment, the historical sites visited are educational, and the pilgrims may use the opportunity to reaffirm their commitment to Buddhism. For those less capable of undertaking the inward pilgrimage of **meditation**, the physical pilgrimage may represent a meaningful step on the **Buddhist path**.

In ancient Buddhism, pilgrimage was especially characteristic of lay Buddhist practice. Lay Buddhists traveled to two primary types of pilgrimage site—**stupas** constructed to house **relics** of the **Buddha**, and locations associated with crucial events in the Buddha's life. According to scriptural accounts, the Buddha himself made arrangements to

have his cremated remains distributed for the sake of lay devotion. Relics, including not only portions of the ash and bits of bone, but also personal effects such as the Buddha's robes and **begging bowl**, were eventually distributed throughout the Buddhist world. Pilgrimage routes also honored central locations from the Buddha's life, especially the wooded grove in Lumbini where he was born, the **bodhi tree** under which he attained **enlightenment**, the deer park outside **Benares** where he gave his first sermon, and the grove of **shala trees** in Kushinagara where he passed away.

Chinese and Japanese **monks** undertook long and often hazardous pilgrimages in search of the **Dharma**. Chinese monks like **Hsüan-tsang** (ca. 600–664) made the arduous trek across the deserts of Central Asia to visit India, where they could study Buddhism with Indian masters and acquire the written scriptures to carry home. A few generations later, the Japanese looked to China as the source of the Dharma in much the same way. Japanese monks risked the dangers of ocean crossings to visit China, where they could study Buddhism and acquire the texts and implements needed to transmit the tradition back to Japan.

Other forms of Buddhist pilgrimage also took root within East Asia, building upon the previously existing indigenous traditions. For example, the five peaks of Mount Wu-t'ai, originally a Taoist pilgrimage site, became closely associated with the cosmic **bodhisattva** Manjusri (J. **Monju**). Similarly, the Kumano and Kôya mountains in Japan, once associated with the powerful practices of indigenous asceticism, became holy sites for Japanese Buddhism, where holy men known as **Yamabushi** developed a syncretic asceticism based on the combination of Buddhist practice and indigenous beliefs.

The Japanese later developed junrei, a distinctive form of Buddhist pilgrimage that involves visiting a series of religious sites, usually a number of temples dedicated to a single buddha or bodhisattva. The most famous junrei circuits are the eighty-eight temples dedicated to Kôbô Daishi (J. **Kûkai**) on the island of Shikoku and the thirty-three **Kannon** temples in Saikoku. Even today, junrei pilgrims don the traditional garb of the religious traveler—white shirt, straw hat, and **walking staff**, which sets them apart from the ordinary world. Today, however, few Japanese pilgrims travel on foot. Most take buses that guide them along the set pilgrimage route. Junrei remains extremely popular; thousands of Japanese every year undertake a pilgrimage for religious and enjoyment purposes. Many say that their basic purpose is to acquire some practical benefit (J. **genze riyaku**) from the experience, the majority specifically hoping to resolve health concerns.

Zen pilgrimage, known as **angya** in Japanese, is a traditional part of the Zen monastic life. See also **lay believer**.

Pillow Sutra

A deathbed Buddhist service performed as a customary part of Japanese funeral rituals. See **Makuragyô**.

Pindola

(J. Binzuru) The first of the sixteen **arhats** venerated in East Asian **Buddhism**. Pindola, depicted with white hair and long eyebrows, developed supernatural powers—according to the tradition—and exhibited them rashly to impress ordinary people. The **Buddha** rebuked him for this and, for his inappropriate behavior, ordered him to postpone his own entrance into **nirvana** to assist **sentient beings**. In China, beginning in the early T'ang period (618–907), images of Pindola, called Pin-t'ou-lu in Chinese, were enshrined in temple dining halls as the holy **monk** of the hall (J. **shôsô**). Monks made an offering of food to him before every meal. In Japan, Pindola, known as Binzuru, is venerated for his healing powers. It is said that a person can be healed by touching the image.

Small images of Pindola are often found outside the main image hall. According to popular Japanese lore, Pindola sits outside the hall because he was expelled from the company of the other arhats for an act of indiscretion. It is said that he once admired a beautiful woman and commented on her appearance to others, an act of sexual misconduct for a monk. To request his assistance with health problems, Japanese supplicants touch the images of Binzuru and adorn him with knitted caps and bibs.

Pi-yen Lu

The *Blue Cliff Record*, one of the most popular collections of classical **Zen kôan**, compiled by the Chinese Rinzai master **Yüan-wu K'o-ch'in** (1063–1135; J. Engo Kokugon) in 1125. The text is more commonly known by its Japanese title, *Hekiganroku*. See *Hekiganroku*.

Platform Sutra

The Platform Sutra of the Sixth **Patriarch**, an important early **Zen** text, purporting to be the teachings of **Hui-neng** (638–713), the Sixth Chinese Patriarch of Zen. The Platform Sutra is the only Buddhist text called a sutra yet not considered to be the words of the **Buddha**. However, according to Zen understanding, an enlightened Zen master is no different from a buddha, and therefore the sermon may be regarded as a sutra. The Platform Sutra is divided into two sections, an autobiographical account of the Sixth Patriarch's early life and **enlightenment** and **sermons** presented by the patriarch to his disciples. The autobiographical section includes the famous account of the poetry contest that convinced the Fifth Patriarch to designate Hui-neng as his **Dharma heir** and the Sixth Patriarch.

The earliest extant version of the sutra (T. 48, no. 2007) is a ninth-century text discovered among the **Tun-huang manuscripts** in 1906. Its full title is The Southern School Sudden Teaching Supreme Mahayana Great Perfection of

Wisdom: The Platform Sutra Preached by the Sixth Patriarch Hui-neng Ta-shih at Ta-fan Temple in Shao-chou (J. Nanshû Tongyô Saijô Daijô Makahannya Haramitsu Kyô: Rokuso Enô Daishi Shôshû Daibon-ji Ni Oite sehô Suru No Dankyô). Philip Yampolsky translated this version into English under the title, *The Platform Sutra of the Sixth Patriarch* (New York: Columbia University Press, 1967).

The version of the sutra traditionally used within the Zen school is a Yuan dynasty text (T. 48, no. 2008) compiled by Tsung-pao in 1291. It is known as the Liu-tsu Ta-shih Fa-pao T'an-ching (J. Rokuso Daishi Hôbô Dankyô), or The Treasure of the Dharma Platform Sutra of the Sixth Patriarch. This version contains additional materials, including six epilogues by later masters. It is approximately twice the length of the earlier Tun-huang manuscripts.

Po-chang Huai-hai

Alternative transliteration of **Pai-chang Huai-hai** (720–814). See **Pai-chang Huai-hai**.

Posthumous Name

According to Japanese Buddhist practice, lay Buddhists receive a Buddhist name as a part of the funeral and **memorial services** following death. The Japanese terms *kaimyô* and *hômyô*, commonly translated as "posthumous name," actually denote the Buddhist names **monks** and **nuns** receive at **ordination**.

Postulant

A person who requests **ordination** from a monastic community. In some cases, a person requesting ordination must live the monastic life for a designated period of time and abide by a specified **monastic code** of conduct before being accepted by the community. In this case, the postulancy serves as a probationary period during which the community observes the newcomer to evaluate his or her suitability for monastic life. In other cases, postulants are underage individuals living in a monastery and preparing for ordination when they reach the minimum age.

In **Buddhism**, male candidates are not required to undergo a probationary period before ordination unless they are underage. If a young man is at least twenty years of age, he may receive full ordination immediately after being ordained as a **novice**. Although many young **monks** do spend some time practicing as a novice before undertaking full ordination, this is technically optional. In contrast, female novices are required to pass a two-year postulancy, regardless of age, before being permitted to move on to full ordination. The female novice is required to abide by the first six **precepts** of the novice during postulancy, a confusing requirement, since she will have already undertaken the full **ten precepts** to become a novice.

Wijayaratna, Mohan. *Buddhist Monastic Life: According to the Texts of the Theravada Tradition*. Trans. Claude Grangier and Steven Collins. New York: Cambridge University Press, 1990.

Prajapati

(J. Hajahadai, Makahajahadai) The aunt and foster mother of **Siddharta Gautama**, also known as Mahaprajapati. Siddharta's mother Maya died shortly after his birth, and his father **Suddhodana** married Prajapati to raise the child. Later, Prajapati became a lay disciple of the **Buddha** and requested permission to become a **nun**. According to traditional accounts, the Buddha initially rejected her request and only conceded to her pleas after **Ananda** interceded on her behalf. See also **lay believer**.

Prajna

(J. chie or hannya) Wisdom, the Buddhist concept of the absolute or perfect wisdom, which allows one to understand reality and perceive things as they really are. In **Theravada Buddhism**, prajna is the third part of the Buddhist training leading to **nirvana** and is built upon the training in morality (Sk. **sila**) and **meditation**. In **Mahayana Buddhism**, prajna refers specifically to the intuitive understanding of **emptiness** (Sk. shunyata). It is last of the **six perfections** (Sk. paramitas), which define the path of the **bodhisattva** toward **enlightenment**. See also **Perfection of Wisdom Sutra**.

Prajna Samadhi

The **samadhi** of perfect wisdom; the state of consciousness in which one realizes the reality of **emptiness** through wisdom. The realization of emptiness is regarded within the Buddhist tradition as the moment of **enlightenment**. Upon realizing that all things are ultimately devoid of any eternal, abiding, and unchanging quality, one can be said to understand things as they are rather than through a deluded mindset. See also **Perfection of Wisdom Sutra**.

Pratyeka Buddha

(J. engaku) A self-enlightened being; one that attains **enlightenment** solely through personal effort, without the benefit of hearing the teachings of a **buddha**. Pratyeka buddhas are solitary practitioners who have learned the **Dharma** on their own by contemplating the twelve-link chain of causation. They completely lack the ability to teach others. In the tradition of **Mahayana Buddhism**, pratyeka buddhas and **shravakas** are the **two vehicles** associated with **Hinayana Buddhism**, and they are regarded as inferior to the **bodhisattva**. See also **three vehicles**.

Precepts

(J. kai) The generic term for the ethical norms that govern the life and practice of religious individuals, especially Buddhists. Within **Buddhism**, distinct sets of precepts apply to different members of the Buddhist community. Lay Buddhists typically follow a set of **five precepts**: 1) not to kill living beings; 2) not to steal another's belongings; 3) to abstain from sexual misconduct; 4) not to lie; and 5) not to take intoxicants. These lay precepts, the first five of the **ten precepts** undertaken by ordained **novices**, are understood somewhat differently for lay people than for **monks** and **nuns**, although they are worded in the same way. In particular, the third precept against sexual misconduct is interpreted to preclude premarital and extramarital sexual contact for lay people, while it precludes all sexual conduct for monks and nuns. The ten precepts of the Buddhist novice continue with: 6) not to eat after noon; 7) not to adorn the body with perfume, flowers or jewelry; 8) not to participate in public entertainment such as dancing, plays, or singing; 9) not to use a luxurious bed; and 10) not to handle money. Although all of these precepts are worded in the negative form, they are understood to include positive action as well. For example, the first precept advocates actively protecting and caring for living beings.

Most fully ordained Buddhist monks and nuns also follow the **vinaya**, which comprise a much longer set of monastic precepts. The full list includes approximately 250 precepts for monks and 500 for nuns. These detailed rules, designed to govern all aspects of the shared life within the monastery, are not all regarded as being of equal importance. Violation of the most serious precepts might involve expulsion from the community, while a lesser offense might require temporary suspension, penance, or simple confession.

In **Mahayana Buddhism**, the **bodhisattva precepts** (J. bosatsukai) were developed, deriving from the **Brahma Net Sutra** (J. Bonmôkyô). The **ten heavy precepts** and **forty-eight light precepts** are intended to serve as the guiding principles of practice for a bodhisattva. All Mahayana Buddhists, monastic and lay, are enjoined to follow the ten heavy precepts, which include prohibitions against: 1) killing, 2) stealing, 3) sexual misconduct, 4) lying, 5) using intoxicants, 6) finding fault in others, 7) boasting about oneself, 8) envy, 9) anger and ill will, and 10) slandering the **three treasures**. The so-called light precepts involve a longer list of less serious offenses. In some schools of Japanese **Zen**, monks and nuns are ordained using the bodhisattva precepts rather than the precepts of the vinaya. See also **lay believer**.

Preta

(J. **gaki**) A **hungry ghost**. The Sanskrit word literally means a dead person, but the term is used specifically in the Buddhist tradition for one of the six possible realms of existence into which a person may be reborn after death. Preta suffer perpetual hunger that they cannot alleviate. See **gaki** and **hungry ghost**.

Prince Shôtoku

(574–622) Japanese regent who promoted **Buddhism** in Japan. See **Shôtoku Taishi**.

P'u-chi

(651–739; J. Fujaku) Chinese Buddhist **monk** known both as a **Zen** master and as a master of the **Hua-yen school**. P'u-chi was the **Dharma heir** and most important disciple of **Shen-hsiu** (606?–706), leader of the **Northern school**. Texts of his time often refer to him as the Seventh **Patriarch**, a title that seems to have been used for him during his lifetime. P'u-chi taught a large number of disciples, and the Northern school flourished under his direction.

P'u-hua

(J. Fuke) An eccentric Chinese **Zen monk** of the T'ang dynasty (618–907) about whom little is known. P'u-hua was the **Dharma heir** of P'an-shan Pao-chi. After P'an-shan died, P'u-hua traveled

around China. For a time he joined **Lin-chi I-hsuan's** assembly and became the famous master's friend, offering him assistance. Stories about him appear in the *Sayings of Lin-chi* (J. *Rinzai-roku*). P'u-hua is traditionally regarded as the founder of the **Fuke sect** of Zen.

Pure Land

(J. jôdo) Mahayana Buddhist concept of a celestial world or paradise created by a **buddha**. Buddhas are said to be capable of purifying a place and removing all hindrances for Buddhist practice by means of their limitless **merit**. The **Buddha Lands** they create are envisioned as ideal places for ordinary **sentient beings** to hear the Buddhist teachings and to practice and attain **enlightenment**. **Rebirth** in a Pure Land may be the immediate religious goal of a Buddhist believer, since attaining enlightenment there is far less difficult than on earth. Rebirth in a Pure Land is dependent not on the individual's merit or good **karma**, but on that of the Buddha or an associated **bodhisattva**. Having faith in the appropriate buddha, **chanting** his name, or **meditating** on him and his world may lead to rebirth in his land. In most contexts, the term *Pure Land* applies specifically to the **Western Pure Land** of **Amida buddha**, the most popular of the celestial buddhas.

In the **Zen** school, the concept of the Pure Land reflects an internal state of mind rather than a literal external place. That is, when one sees through the eyes of enlightenment, the ordinary world is transformed into a Pure Land.

Pure Land of the Mind Only

(J. yuishin no jôdo) A Mahayana teaching that the **Pure Land** does not literally exist as an actual world outside the self. According to this teaching, the ordinary concept of the Pure Land is reinterpreted as reflecting an internal state of mind. According to this understanding, the ordinary world, when seen through the eyes of **enlightenment**, is transformed into a Pure Land. The concept of the Pure Land of the Mind Only is shared by several schools of **Mahayana Buddhism**, including **Zen**.

Pure Land School

A form of **Mahayana Buddhism** that promotes faith in **Amida buddha** and teaches that individuals can attain salvation by being reborn in Amida's **Western Pure Land**. The scriptural basis for Pure Land teachings are the three **Pure Land Sutras**: the Larger Pure Land Sutra (J. Daimuryôjukyô), the Smaller Pure Land Sutra (J. Amidakyô), and the **Meditation** Sutra (J. Kammuryôjukyô). Although many Pure Land texts and concepts originated in India, the school did not develop there. Pure Land devotion took on distinct form as a school in East Asia, giving rise to several sects in China, Korea, and Japan. The primary practice of Pure Land devotion is **chanting** the name of Amida buddha, known in Japanese as the **nembutsu**.

Zen Buddhism and Pure Land became the two dominant schools of Buddhism in China. The first sects of Pure Land devotees took shape there in the fifth century C.E. Several prominent Chinese Buddhist **monks** are regarded as **patriarchs** of the Pure Land school, including Hui-yuan (344–416), T'an-luan (476–542), Tao-cho (562–645), and Shan-tao (613–681). Pure Land devotion was transmitted to Japan in the Heian period (794–1185). During the Kamakura period (1185–1333), it gave rise to several distinctive sects, including the Jôdo-shû founded by **Hônen** (1133–1212), the Jôdo Shinshû founded by **Shinran** (1173–1262), and the **Ji sect** founded by **Ippen** (1239–1289). The several **Pure Land sects** of Japanese Buddhism together represent the largest school of Buddhism in Japan.

Pure Land Sect

A sect of Japanese **Buddhism** founded by the **monk Hônen** (1133–1212) during the Kamakura period (1185–1333), known in Japanese as Jôdoshû. The teachings and practices of the sect are based on Hônen's understanding of the **Pure Land Sutras**, the sect's principal scriptures. Hônen was originally a **Tendai sect** monk, until he left Mount Hiei to establish a form of exclusive Pure Land practice. Pure Land Buddhism encourages placing one's faith in **Amida buddha** and achieving salvation through **rebirth** in his **Western Pure Land**. The primary practice of the sect is **chanting** the name of Amida, using the simple formula "**Namu Amida Butsu**."

Pure Land Sutras

(Sk. Sukhavati-vyuha Sutra; J. Daimuryôjukyô) Three Mahayana **sutras** that form the scriptural basis for the **Pure Land** teachings. The three scriptures include the Larger Pure Land Sutra; the Smaller Pure Land Sutra, or Amitabha Sutra (J. Amidakyô); and the **Meditation** Sutra (Sk. Amitayurdhyana Sutra; J. Kammuryôjukyô).

Purna

(J. Furuna) One of the ten outstanding disciples of Shakyamuni **buddha** (**Siddharta Gautama**), renowned for his eloquence and ability in debate. Purna was a Brahmin and a teacher of repute before he met Shakyamuni. His first encounter with the Buddha took place when he became determined to challenge Shakyamuni to debate, confident that he would defeat him. The Buddha quietly convinced Purna of the futility of debate, and Purna joined the **sangha** and became the Buddha's disciple.

Ishigami, Zenno. *Disciples of the Buddha*. Trans. Richard L. Gage and Paul McCarthy. Tokyo: Kosei Publishing Co., 1989.

Purple Robe

(J. shie) An honorific monastic robe bestowed on high-ranking **monks**, usually awarded by a reigning emperor. The color purple was not traditionally used for Buddhist monastic robes, but in China, the imperial court established a hierarchy of honorific robes classified by color for individuals who had performed meritorious service. Purple robes were ranked the highest. **Dôgen Kigen** (1200–1253) and Myôan **Eisai**, the founders of the Japanese **Sôtô sect** and **Rinzai sect** respectively, were the first to receive imperial purple robes in Japan. Unlike honorific titles, which are commonly granted posthumously, the purple robe is given to living masters.

Pu-tai

(d. 916; J. Hotei) An eccentric Chinese **Zen monk** who lived during the T'ang dynasty (618–907). Pu-tai lived the life of a homeless wandering monk in what is now Chekiang province. His actual family name is unknown, but he called himself Ch'i-tz'u. The name Pu-tai literally means "cloth sack" and was given to him by the people of the day, who took to calling him Master Cloth Sack because he always carried a large sack over his shoulder. It is said that he carried all of his worldly possessions in the sack and often stuffed in bits of leftover food he had received when begging.

He is always depicted as a humble person with a large, naked stomach protruding from his robes and carrying his staff and sack. In many cases, he is surrounded by children. Figures of Pu-tai, called the **Laughing Buddha**, are sometimes used in China and Japan as images of the future buddha **Maitreya** (J. Miroku). Obaku-san **Mampuku-ji**, the main monastery for Obaku Zen, has a statue of Pu-tai as Maitreya enshrined as the main image (J. **honzon**) in the Tennô-den. See also **Obaku sect**.

P'u-t'i-ta-mo

The Chinese rendering of **Bodhidharma**, commonly shortened to Ta-mo. See **Bodhidharma**.

R

Ragora

Japanese transliteration for **Rahula**, the son of the **Buddha**. See **Rahula**.

Rahula

(J. Ragora) **Siddharta Gautama's** son with his wife **Yashodhara**, born shortly before Siddharta determined to leave the home life and seek **enlightenment** as an ascetic. The name Rahula means "fetter" and suggests that Siddharta was already inclined toward religious life. Rahula, said to have joined the **sangha** at age nine and to have been fully ordained at age twenty, later became one of Shakyamuni's (Siddharta Gautama) leading disciples. He is numbered among the ten outstanding disciples of the **Buddha**. Rahula is reknowned for his dedication to training new **monks** and **novices**.

Ishigami, Zenno. *Disciples of the Buddha*. Trans. Richard L. Gage and Paul McCarthy. Tokyo: Kosei Publishing Co., 1989.

Rainy Season Retreat

(J. ango) A three-month period during the summer months when Buddhist **monks** and **nuns** retire to a temple or monastery for an intensive practice session. Traditionally the summer retreat was observed from the middle of the fourth lunar month through the middle of the seventh lunar month, roughly corresponding to the monsoon season on the Indian subcontinent. The custom dates back to the time of the historical **Buddha**, before the establishment of permanent monastic dwellings, when the Buddha and his disciples traveled throughout the year, taking only temporary shelter in the areas they visited. They only settled down for an extended period of time when the annual rainy season made travel inconvenient. Eventually, the Buddhist **monastic code** (Sk. **vinaya**) forbade travel during the rainy season, specifying that it be observed for a period of ninety days.

Zen monastic communities observe the rainy season retreat as one of two annual retreats. The other retreat falls during the severe winter months. Many monasteries now follow a Western calendar and keep the summer retreat from April 16 through July 15. During this retreat, monks and nuns observe a very strict version of the Zen monastic rules (J. **shingi**) and concentrate their efforts on making progress in **meditation**. Up to fourteen hours of the day are dedicated to seated meditation, and travel outside the temple is strictly limited for the duration of the retreat.

Rakusu

A small five-strip **kesa** that is commonly worn on a strap around the necks of **Zen monks** and **nuns** in China and Japan. This modification of the traditional kesa is worn over clothing to symbolically represent the patched robe of the **Buddha**. The design is not traditional to Indian **Buddhism**; it was created in China to allow more freedom of movement for Buddhist monks when they went begging or engaged in **manual labor**. Today, lay practitioners of Zen sometimes receive this garment when they take the **precepts**. See also **lay believer**.

Rankei Dôryû

The Japanese name for **Lan-ch'i Tao-lung** (1213–1278), a Chinese Rinzai master who helped to establish the **Rinzai sect** in Kamakura, Japan. See **Lan-ch'i Tao-lung**.

Rakusu, a small five-strip kesa commonly worn on a strap around the neck by Zen monks and nuns, represents the patched robe of the Buddha.

Rantô

An oval-shaped **stupa**, or memorial stone, used to honor deceased **Zen monks** and **nuns**. The oval stone, shaped like a bird's egg, rests upon a six- or eight-sided stone base. The term *rantô* literally means "egg stupa." They are also known as mûhôtô, or "seamless **pagoda**." In classical Zen literature, when the T'ang Zen master Nan-yang Hui-chung (d. 776), better known as Chung Kuo-shih, was near death, the emperor Tai-tsung (r. 762–779) asked how the master would like to be honored. The old monk responded that the emperor should build for him a seamless stupa.

Rebirth

Belief in a cycle of birth and death that continues through numerous lifetimes. The concept is shared by many religious traditions, including **Buddhism**. The term is sometimes used to translate the Sanskrit word ***samsara*** (J. rinne). In Buddhist contexts, it is a more accurate translation than **reincarnation**, since it does not necessarily imply the existence of an eternal soul.

Recorded Sayings

One of the most important and distinctive genres of **Zen** literature that developed first in China, where they are known as yu-lu, and continued in Japan, where they are called goroku. Recorded sayings preserve **sermons**, encounters with disciples, anecdotes, and other teachings of prominent Zen **monks** and **nuns** that disciples have collected and published after the masters' deaths.

Rei

A hand bell used in **Zen** monasteries during some sutra **chanting** services. Also pronounced rin. See **shôkei**.

Reincarnation

Belief that an eternal soul or essence is reborn in successive bodies. The concept of reincarnation is shared by many religious traditions. In the Indian traditions of Hinduism and Jainism, which accept the notion of a soul or eternal self, reincarnation is sometimes used to express the concept of **samsara**, the ongoing cycle of birth and death. Although the term is sometimes used similarly in a Buddhist context, it is not completely accurate, since **Buddhism** does not accept the concept of a soul.

Reitaku

Large and small handbells used by the **abbot** or another **monk** in leading various rituals. They are used, for example, while reading **sutras** during mealtime. Reitaku are played by shaking them. Small handbells are called rin or rei. See also **shôkei**.

Relative Truth

Conventional reality; the view of existence from which things may be said to exist in a relative sense and to be distinguished one from another. Relative Truth is generally contrasted with **Ultimate Truth**, the view of existence from which things are perceived to be empty. In **Mâdhyamaka** philosophy, for example, reality is spoken of at two levels, relative and ultimate. At the level of Relative Truth, or mundane reality, one may discuss things as having transitory existence. They arise due to causes and eventually pass away, leaving behind various effects. They cannot be said to have independent existence or to be permanent and unchanging. See also **emptiness**.

Relics

(J. sharira) Objects such as pieces of bone, hair, monastic robes, bowls, and other implements associated with religious figures and therefore regarded as in some sense sacred or powerful. Relics are a common feature in religious traditions throughout the world. In the Buddhist tradition, relics from the historical **Buddha** and other important Buddhist figures have been treated as objects of Buddhist veneration, especially among **lay believers**. The practice dates to the death of the Buddha, when pieces of bone collected from the Buddha's funeral pyre were distributed throughout the existing Buddhist community. Buddhist relics are commonly enshrined in special structures known as **stupas**, or **pagodas** as they are called in East Asia.

Renga

Linked verse, a genre of Japanese poetry indirectly associated with **Zen**. Renga are composed of alternating stanzas with 5-7-5 and 7-7 syllable lines, respectively. The first stanza of 5-7-7 syllables is known as the **hokku**. It developed into an independent genre known more commonly as **haiku**.

Restricted Area

Monastery grounds that are bounded and thereby restricted to practitioners only, especially ordained members of the Buddhist community. The concept derives from the practice in **Theravada Buddhism** of designating an **ordination** ground by setting up stone markers, known as sima stones. Sima stones may also be found at monastery entrances to designate monastery grounds in which the **monastic code** is observed as distinct from the secular world. In Japan, the term *kekkaiji* applied especially to Buddhist monastery complexes, such as those on Mount Hiei and Mount Kôya, where women were not allowed to enter.

Richi

Ultimate Truth; wisdom that perceives ultimate reality. The term is a combination of characters which literally mean "reality" and "wisdom." In the **Zen** school, the term is sometimes used for the first level of a three part system of **kôan** practice in which Richi precedes **kikan** and **kôjô**.

Rin

A small hand bell used in **Zen** monasteries during some sutra **chanting** services. Also pronounced rei. See **shôkei**.

Rin'i Monjin

Bowing with one's hands held in **gasshô** to greet the people on one's right and left in the **meditation hall** before beginning a session of seated meditation. The bow is performed facing one's own meditation cushion, not toward the other meditators; they bow in greeting in return.

Rinka

An expression for Japanese **Zen** monasteries and temples not affiliated with the **Gozan system**. The term literally means "below the grove" and was coined to contrast affiliated and unaffiliated temples. Monasteries within the Gozan system were commonly designated **sôrin**, literally, "grove" or "thicket." They were gradually associated more with literary and artistic pursuits than with Zen practice. Rinka monasteries, on the other hand, included almost all **Sôtô sect** temples and many **Rinzai sect** monasteries that remained independent. Rinka monasteries remained dedicated to the religious pursuit of **meditation** and **enlightenment**.

Rinne

Samsara, the ongoing cycle of birth, death, and **rebirth**. The term *rinne* is the Japanese translation of the original Sanskrit term, often translated as transmigration or rebirth in English. See **samsara**.

Rinsen Kakun

The Rinsen-ji House Code, a **Zen monastic code** devised by **Musô Sôseki** (1275–1351) for Rinsen-ji temple in 1339. The Rinsen kakun is among the first Zen monastic codes (J. **shingi**) written in Japan. It is an important resource for understanding Rinzai practice within the **Gozan system** during the Ashikaga period (1392–1568). A complete English translation appears in Martin Collcutt's *Five Mountains*. See also **Rinzai sect**.

Rinyû

"The entrance through reason," Japanese term for one of the Two Entries (J. **Ninyû**) to Buddhist **enlightenment**. The entrance through reason refers to studying the teachings of **Buddhism** as set out in the scriptures. It is the opposite of **gyônyû**, or the entrance through practice. See also **two entrances**.

Rinzai Gigen

(d. 867) The Japanese pronunciation for **Lin-chi I-hsuan**, the T'ang dynasty (618–907) Chinese **monk** who founded the Rinzai school of **Zen**. See **Lin-chi I-hsuan**.

Rinzai-roku

Japanese abbreviated title for the *Lin-chi Ch'an-shih Yu-lu*, the **recorded sayings** of Ch'an master Lin-chi. See *Sayings of Lin-chi*.

Rinzai Sect

One of three major sects of Japanese **Zen**, along with the **Sôtô sect** and the **Obaku sect**. Rinzai Zen is named for its founding **patriarch Lin-chi I-hsuan** (d. 867), one of the most famous Chinese Zen masters of the T'ang dynasty (618–907). Lin-chi is pronounced Rinzai in Japanese. The predominant Rinzai style of practice makes use of **kôan** as the focus of attention during seated **meditation** (J. **zazen**). The Rinzai style is also traditionally associated with the use of slapping and shouting (J. **katsu!**) as teaching devices to encourage the experience of **enlightenment**.

The **Lin-chi school** was established as a distinct **lineage** and sect in China and numbers among the **five houses** of

Chinese Zen of the T'ang dynasty. Since the Sung dynasty (960–1279), it has been the dominant form of Zen practice in China. During the Sung dynasty, the Lin-chi school divided into two major branches, the Yang-ch'i line (J. Yôgi-shû) and the Huang-lung line (J. Oryô-shû). Lin-chi Zen was transmitted to Japan during the Kamakura period (1185–1333). Traditionally, the sect regards the **monk Eisai** (1141–1215) as the founder in Japan, although the history is far more complex.

Today the Rinzai sect in Japan comprises fourteen lineages (J. ha), which are registered as independent institutions. These include: **Buttsû-ji Ha, Daitoku-ji Ha, Eigen-ji Ha, Engaku-ji Ha, Hôkô-ji Ha, Kenchô-ji Ha, Kennin-ji Ha, Kôgaku-ji Ha, Kokutai-ji Ha, Myôshin-ji Ha, Nanzen-ji Ha, Shôkoku-ji Ha, Tenryû-ji Ha**, and **Tôfuku-ji Ha**. See also **Huang-lung school** and **Yang-ch'i school**.

Rinzai-shû

Japanese for **Rinzai sect** of **Zen Buddhism**. Alternatively, it may refer to the Chinese **Lin-chi school** of Zen Buddhism. See **Rinzai sect** and **Lin-chi school**.

Ritsu

Vinaya, the **monastic code** of **Buddhism** which governs the lives of Buddhist **monks** and **nuns**. The Japanese word *ritsu* literally means laws, and the term is also used for secular legal codes. As a genre of Buddhist literature, ritsu texts form one portion of the **Sanzô**, or **Tripitaka**. The Sanskrit term *vinaya* refers specifically to the Theravada monastic codes, but the Japanese term *ritsu* is used in a general way to refer to more specialized Mahayana monastic codes, especially the **bodhisattva precepts** and **Zen** monastic codes (J. **shingi**), which in some cases supplemented and in others supplanted the traditional Theravada vinaya codes. See also **Theravada Buddhism**.

Ro

Defilements, outflows, or binding influences; the Japanese translation for the Sanskrit *ashrava*. Any mental activity that hinders one's attainment of **enlightenment** is a defilement. Sensual desires and **attachment** to false views are the most basic defilements to be extinguished through Buddhist practice. Ro is closely related to the concept bonnô (literally, "**afflictions** and delusions").

Rôba Zen

Old-Woman Zen or Grandmother Zen, an expression used for **Zen** teaching styles demonstrating the master's concern for his disciples. Just as a grandmother showers her grandchildren with affection, the master expresses **compassion** for his students. The compassion may be such that the master refrains from the harsher teaching methods often associated with Zen, yet a sharp blow may just as well be said to embody grandmotherly concern. Zen texts employ a number of expressions for grandmotherly concern, such as Rôba Shinsetsu and Rôba Tekkon. While Rôba Zen generally reflects a positive evaluation of a master, in some cases the term is used in a derogatory manner to criticize a master who is overly gentle.

Robe of Transmission

A **Dharma robe** passed from a **Zen** master to a disciple as a symbol of **Dharma transmission**. **Bodhidharma** bestowed the original robe of transmission on his heir, **Hui-k'o** (487–593), designating him as the Second Chinese **Patriarch** of Zen.

Rock Garden

Dry landscape gardens constructed of stone, sand, and moss, which are a form of **Zen** art. Known in Japanese as *kare sansui* (dry mountains and water), rock gardens are a common feature in Zen monasteries. The most famous examples include the gardens at **Ryôan-ji** and Kokedera, both in Kyoto. See **Kare sansui**.

Rôhatsu

The eighth day of the twelfth lunar month. Rôhatsu is the day East Asian Buddhists celebrate as **Bodhi Day**, the day on which the historical **Buddha** attained **enlightenment**. In Japan and other parts of the Buddhist world, Rôhatsu, also commonly pronounced rôhachi, is now celebrated on December 8.

Rôhatsu Sesshin

An intensive period of seated **meditation** (**sesshin**), traditionally from the first day of the twelfth lunar month to the eighth day. **Rôhatsu** literally means the eighth day of the twelfth lunar month. The Rôhatsu sesshin commemorates the **enlightenment** of Shakyamuni (**Siddharta Gautama**), the historical **Buddha**, which East Asian Buddhists believe occurred on Rôhatsu. During the sesshin, **monks** and **nuns** strive to imitate the determination shown by the Buddha when he sat down with the intention of meditating until he reached his goal of enlightenment. On the final night of the sesshin, participants sit up through the night without lying down to sleep (J. tetsuya). They do this in imitation of the Buddha, who sat in meditation through the night and attained enlightenment with the dawn. In some monasteries, monks refrain from lying down to sleep throughout all seven nights of the sesshin.

Buswell, Robert E., Jr. *The Zen Monastic Experience: Buddhist Practice in Contemporary Korea.* Princeton, NJ: Princeton University Press, 1992.

Rokkon

The **six sense organs**: eyes, ears, nose, tongue, body, and mind. These are paired with the six objects of perception (J. rokkyô), form (color and shape), sound, odor, taste, texture, and mental objects. The term *rokkon* literally translates as the six bases. The pairings of the six sense organs and their objects constitute the first six consciousnesses in the **Yogachara school** psychological system of the **eight consciousnesses**. See **six sense organs**.

Roku Chiji

(J. **tôhan**) The six stewards; the six senior **monks** at a **Zen** monastery who assist the **abbot** in managing the administrative aspects of the community, particularly economic matters. Together, they are known as the Eastern rank since their duties keep them largely in the eastern part of the temple grounds. The stewards include the offices of bursar (J. **tsûbun**), prior (J. **tsûsu**), supervisor (J. **kansu**), assistant supervisor (J. **fûsu**), cook (J. **tenzo**), labor steward (J. **shissui**), and supervisor of trainees (J. **ino**). Their counterparts in the Western rank (J. **seihan**) are known as the six prefects (J. roku chôsu). See **tôhan**.

Roku Chôsu

(J. **seihan**) The group of six senior **monks** who assist the **abbot** in the spiritual aspects of the monastic community. These prefects help train the community in **meditation**, monastic discipline, ritual procedures, and the study of religious texts. The prefects include the offices of chief seat (J. **shuso**), scribe (J. **shoki**), sutra prefect (J. **zôsu**), guest prefect (J. **shika**), bathkeeper (J. **chiyoku**), and prefect of the **Buddha** hall (J. **chiden**). They are also referred to as the Western rank because they work in the western area of the monastery. Their counterparts in the Eastern rank (J. **tohan**) are called the six stewards (J. roku chiji). See **seihan**.

Rokudo

Six Paramitas or the **six perfections**; an alternative Japanese term for ropparamitsu. See **six perfections**.

Rokudô

The **six paths**; the six realms of existence into which **sentient beings** are born. They include the realms of **hell** dwellers

(J. **jigoku**), **hungry ghosts** (J. **gaki**), animals (J. chikushô), human beings (J. ningen), evil demi-gods (J. **ashura**), and **heaven** dwellers (J. tenjô). See **six paths**.

Rokujin
The **six dusts** or **defilements**. A synonym for the six objects of perception (rokkyô). See **six dusts**.

Roku Jizô
Six **Jizô**, a grouping of six images of the **bodhisattva** Jizô. These figures represent Jizô's special willingness to enter any realm of samsaric existence to assist a sentient being. The six Jizô are: 1) Danda, who holds a human skull and saves those in **hell**; 2) Hôju, who holds a **mani** jewel and saves **hungry ghosts**; 3) Hôin, who saves animals; 4) Jiji, who saves **ashura**; 5) Jogaishô, who saves human beings; and 6) Nikkô, who saves **heaven** dwellers. See also **samsara**.

Rokumon
Six gates, also known as rokkonmon, a Japanese Buddhist expression for the six sense organs. See **six sense organs**.

Rokumotsu
The six items that **monks** are traditionally allowed as personal property. These include the outer robe with a lining, the unlined inner robe worn in toga fashion, the undergarment, a filtering bag used to filter out insects from drinking water, the **begging bowl**, and the **zagu**, a ritual sitting cloth.

Rokuso Dankyô
Japanese title for the **Platform Sutra** of the Sixth **Patriarch**. See **Platform Sutra**.

Ron
Japanese term for a commentary on a Buddhist sutra or a Buddhist philosophical treatise. *Ron* and *Ronzô* are standard translations for the Sanskrit term ***Abhidharma***.

Ronen
Year of the Donkey in Japanese. Something that will never occur, since there is no Year Of The Donkey in the traditional calendar used in East Asia. See **Year of the Donkey**.

Ropparamitsu
Six paramitas or perfections; six practices that describe the **bodhisattva's** path toward **enlightenment**. In Japanese they are: 1) fuse haramitsu (charity or giving); 2) **jikai** (observing the **precepts**); 3) ninniku (perseverance); 4) shôjin (energy); 5) zenjô (**meditation**); and 6) chie (wisdom; Sk. **prajna**). See **six perfections**.

Roshi
A respectful form of address for a **Zen** master, usually translated as "old master." However, the translation "venerable master" better suggests the original connotations of respect. In Zen, the meaning of the term differs according to time period and sect. It usually applies to any Zen master certified to guide others in meditative practice. In Western Zen contexts, male and female masters may be roshi.

In its broadest sense, Japanese may use the title *roshi* to refer to any senior or older **monk**. In the **Sôtô sect** today, it is often used in this manner, especially by younger monks as a polite form of address for the senior monks holding official positions at a monastery. In the contemporary **Rinzai sect**, only the **abbot** of a major monastery is addressed as roshi. The most limited application of the title *roshi* can be found within the Rinzai sect; here it may designate only the most exceptional Zen masters who have attained deep levels of **enlightenment** and are thus deemed qualified to guide the practice of others. Achieving this status normally requires thirty or more years of practice.

Kraft, Kenneth, ed. *Zen, Tradition and Transition*. New York: Grove Press, 1988.

Ryôan-ji is a Zen temple famous for its dry landscape garden
containing fifteen stones, raked sand, and moss.

Ryôan-ji

An important Rinzai **Zen** temple, located in northwestern Kyoto and famous for its lovely Zen garden. The temple was built under the patronage of the daimyô, or military leader, Hosokawa Katsumoto (1430–1473) in 1450. Hosokawa invited Giten Genshô (1396–1465) to serve as its founding **abbot**. For many generations it was a significant **branch temple** of nearby **Myôshin-ji**, but the temple suffered serious fire damage in the late eighteenth century and never recovered its former prominence. The Abbot's Garden, attributed to Sôami (d. 1525), is commonly regarded as the finest example of a Zen dry landscape garden (J. **kare sansui**). Its deceptively simple construction includes only fifteen oddly shaped stones and raked white sand; it is devoid of vegetation except moss. It is sometimes pronounced Ryûan-ji. See also **Rinzai sect**.

Ryôgakyô

Japanese title for the **Lankavatara Sutra**, "Sutra When Entering Lanka." See **Lankavatara Sutra**.

Ryôgen

The head **monk** of the reading room (**shuryô**) at a **Zen** monastery. The ryôgen is responsible for supervising monks' conduct in the reading room, where they read, study, and have tea after meals. Also called ryôshuso.

Ryôgon-gyô

Abbreviated Japanese title for the **Shuramgama Sutra** (T. 19, no. 945). The full Japanese title is Daibutchô Nyorai Mitsuin Shushô Ryôgi Shobosatsu Mangyô Shuryôgon-Gyô. See **Shuramgama Sutra**.

Ryôgon-ju

The **Shuramgama dharani**, a spell derived from the seventh division of the **Shuramgama Sutra**, which was used to exorcise evil spirits and ward off calamities. Its full title in Japanese is Daibutchô mangyô shuryôgon darani. It is alternatively abbreviated as the Daibutchô-ju. The Shuramgama dharani is one of the most commonly used dharani in the **Zen** school. It often appears as a part of Zen rituals, including **memorial services** and funerals. See **Shuramgama dharani**.

Ryôkan

(1758–1831) Japanese Sôtô **monk** of the Tokugawa period (1600–1867), best known for his **Zen** poetry, and popularly known as Daigu (sometimes spelled Taigu), or Great Fool. Born in Izumozaki, in Echigo province (now Niigata), the oldest son of a village headman, he began to study Zen at about sixteen and took the **tonsure** at a local Zen temple at age seventeen. In 1779, he moved to a larger Sôtô monastery in Bitchû and became the disciple of Kokusen. After Kokusen died, Ryôkan left the monastery, lived as a pilgrim monk for twenty years, and then returned to his native Echigo, where he lived in a hermitage on Mount Kugami. Translations of his poetry can be found in *Great Fool*, by Ryuichi Abe and Peter Haskel (University of Hawaii Press, 1996) and *One Robe, One Bowl*, by John Stevens (Weatherhill, 1988). See also **Sôtô sect**.

Ryôkan

(2) Second Barrier, the second of three sets of **kôan** used by some **Zen** monasteries in medieval Japan (1185–1600). The three sets were known as the first (J. **shokan**), second, and third barriers (J. **sankan**). The ryôkan were derived from the *Sayings of Lin-chi*.

Ryônen Myôzen

(1184–1225) Japanese Rinzai **monk**, a direct disciple of **Eisai**, best known as the teacher of **Dôgen Kigen** (1200–1253). Born in Ise, Myôzen was orphaned at age eight. He entered monastic life on Mount Hiei, where he studied Tendai Buddhist thought. After full **ordination** in 1199, he joined Eisai at **Kennin-ji**. There he practiced **Zen meditation** and eventually became Eisai's **Dharma heir**. Dôgen studied with him at Kennin-ji from 1217 to 1223, when the two traveled together to China. In China, Myôzen went to **Ching-te-ssu** on Mount T'ien-t'ung, where his master Eisai had likewise practiced. He became ill and died there in 1225. See also **Rinzai sect** and **Tendai sect**.

Ryôzen

Mount Gridhrakuta, or **Vulture Peak**. Ryôzen is the common Japanese abbreviation for Ryôjusen, which is more accurately translated "Mount of the Numinous Eagle." Ryôzen is important within the **Zen** tradition as the place where the **Buddha** transmitted the **Dharma** to **Mahakashyapa**. See **Mount Gridhrakuta**.

Ryûtaku Kaiso Jinki Dokumyô Zenji Nempu

"The Chronological **Biography** of **Zen** Master Jinki Dokumyô, Founder of Ryûtaku-ji," a biography of **Hakuin Ekaku** (1685–1768) in two parts, composed by **Tôrei Enji** (1721–1792), one of his leading disciples.

S

Saba

A few grains of rice set aside at daily meals in **Zen** monasteries for the sake of **hungry ghosts** (J. **gaki**). Before eating the meal, Zen **monks** and **nuns** perform a brief ritual called **shussan**, in which they remove a small amount of rice and recite a short verse. In other temples, the kitchen staff pours off the waste liquid used to rinse the eating bowls as an offering to the gaki. The tiny particles of food remaining in the water are said to be the perfect size for hungry ghosts' narrow throats.

Sabi

Loneliness, valued in traditional Japanese culture as an aesthetic quality. Art forms inspired by **Zen**, such as pottery, poetry, and drama, embody the styles of sabi and **wabi** (austere simplicity).

Sagan Butsuji

Closing the coffin lid. The sagan is one of nine ritual actions (J. **kubutsuji**) performed when an **abbot** or other prominent Buddhist **monk** or **nun** dies. See also **kubutsuji**.

Sai

The noontime meal at a **Zen** temple or monastery. Sai, the largest meal of the day, typically consists of rice, miso soup, pickles, and vegetables. Silence is observed at mealtimes; only chanting can be heard. At this meal, **monks** and **nuns** recite a five-part vow before they eat, remembering the labor that produced the food and the purpose for partaking of the meal.

The term was originally used for the Sanskrit **uposatha**, the twice-monthly observance days when monks and nuns reflected on their behavior and confessed any transgressions (violations) of the **monastic code**. In other contexts, it referred specifically to the monastic practice of abstaining from eating meals at inappropriate times.

Saichô

(767–822) Japanese Buddhist **monk**, founder of the **Tendai sect** of Japanese **Buddhism**. Saichô traveled to China in 804 and studied T'ien-t'ai teachings on Mount T'ien-t'ai. Returning to Japan, he established a major religious center on Mount Hiei where he transmitted T'ien-t'ai thought and other styles of Chinese Buddhist practice, such as **esoteric Buddhism**, various forms of **meditation**, and **Pure Land** teachings. He introduced the practice of ordaining monks using only the **bodhisattva precepts**. Saichô, commonly known by his posthumous title, Dengyô Daishi, was the first Japanese monk to receive the title "Daishi" (Great Teacher), an honor bestowed on him by the Emperor Seiwa. See also **T'ien-t'ai school**.

Saku

"Tea drum," the drum used in the Dharma hall (J. **hattô**) and the monks' hall (J. **sôdô**) at **Zen** monasteries to call the **monks** to tea. In the Dharma hall, the saku, which sits in the northwest corner, is sounded once at the beginning of the tea ceremony (J. **chanoyû**) and three times when tea is finished.

Samadhi

(J. sammai) Concentration; an intense state of mental concentration achieved through **meditation** in which the distinctions between subject and object are transcended. *Smadhi* is the Sanskrit term used in several religious traditions, including Hinduism, Jainism, and **Buddhism**. In Buddhism, samadhi refers to a state of "one-pointedness" achieved through the practice of meditation. Although samadhi is not the ultimate goal of Buddhist practice, it is regarded as the most conducive mental state for attaining **nirvana, or enlightenment**. The term *samadhi* is also used to describe Buddhist meditative training, one of the three traditional divisions of the **Eightfold Path** of Buddhism. In this case, it refers to the final three stages of the path: Right Effort, Right Mindfulness, and Right Concentration.

Samantabhadra

A cosmic **bodhisattva** representing the mercy, **meditation**, and practice of all the buddhas. Known as **Fugen** in Japanese. See **Fugen**.

Sambhogakaya

(J. hôjin) "Bliss Body" of the **Buddha**. According to Mahayana understanding, it is one of the three aspects, or bodies, of the Buddha. Sambhogakaya are manifestations of the eternal Buddha and they live and teach in other worlds. Various celestial buddhas, such as **Amida buddha**, who dwell in their own **Buddha Lands** and guide **sentient beings** born there are considered sambhogakaya. See also **Mahayana Buddhism** and **three bodies of the Buddha**.

Sambô

See **three treasures**.

Sambôe

See *Sanbôe*.

Sambô Kyôdan

See **Sanbô Kyôdan**.

Sammai

Concentration; an intense state of mental concentration achieved during **meditation**. Sammai, also written sanmai or zammai, is the Japanese transliteration of the Sanskrit term *samadhi*. See **samadhi**.

Samsara

The Sanskrit religious term for the belief in transmigration or **rebirth**, the ongoing cycle of birth, death, and rebirth. Samsara is a common teaching within several religious traditions originating in India, including Hinduism, **Buddhism**, and Jainism. The process of samsara depends upon the workings of **karma**, the actions one takes, and the moral consequences of those actions. Karma not only affects one's future in the present life, but also determines one's future rebirths. Since samsara was traditionally viewed as a relentless cycle of re-death, Indian religious traditions formulated means to escape from this cycle of **suffering**.

Samu

Manual labor, a regular part of the **Zen** monastic life. The word *samu* literally means "strenuous work" and typically involves working in the fields, sweeping the yard, or gathering firewood. See **manual labor**.

Samurai

Japanese warrior; the Japanese warrior class as a whole. The samurai class eventually replaced the nobility (J. **kuge**) as the ruling class in Japan. They gained military and political control of Japan during the Kamakura period (1185–1333) and maintained power until the modern period. According to the Confucian political and philosophical system, which prevailed during the Tokugawa period (1600–1867), the samurai class is designated as the highest of four social classes. The class system was abolished after the Meiji Restoration in the late nineteenth century.

Samurai leaders of the Kamakura period became generous patrons of **Zen** masters and built monasteries and temples throughout the country. Samurai governments continued to patronize Zen monasteries throughout the Kamakura (1185–1333), Ashikaga (1392–1568), and Tokugawa (1600–1867)

The Japanese warrior or samurai replaced the nobility as the ruling class of Japan. They remained in power until the modern period, when the class system was abolished.

periods. Yet few samurai seriously undertook the practice of **meditation** under the guidance of a Zen master. Many, however, called upon Zen **monks** as ritual specialists, especially for funeral services. Many samurai families were affiliated with a Zen sect and sponsored a Zen temple as their family temple (J. ujidera).

San'akudô

(J. akudô) The three **evil paths**, including **hell**, the realm of **hungry ghosts**, and the realm of animals. See **evil paths**.

Sanbô

Japanese for the **three treasures**: the **Buddha**, the **Dharma**, and the **sangha**. In Japanese they are Butsu, Hô, and Sô. See **three treasures**.

Sanbôe

"Illustrations of the **Three Treasures**," a collection of Buddhist stories in three parts, composed by Minamoto Tamenori (d. 1011) in 984. Tamenori designed the text to serve as an introduction to **Buddhism** for the imperial princess Enyûinnyôgo Takakonaishinnô after she took the **tonsure** as a **nun**. The text is divided into three sections, one for each of the three treasures. "The **Buddha**" relates **Jataka tales**, stories of the previous lives of the historical Buddha Shakyamuni (**Siddharta Gautama**). "The **Dharma**" includes stories of famous Japanese Buddhist figures. "The **Sangha**" relates the Buddhist calendar of rituals and festivals as they were observed in Japan at that time. Edward Kamens published a complete annotated translation of the text entitled *The Three Jewels*.

Kamens, Edward. *The Three Jewels: A Study and Translation of Minamoto Tamenori's* Sanbôe. Ann Arbor, MI: Center for Japanese Studies, University of Michigan, 1988.

Sanbô Kyôdan

Fellowship of the **three treasures**, a modern **Zen** movement for lay practitioners, established in Japan by Harada Sogaku (1871–1961) and his **Dharma heir** Yasutani Hakuun (1885–1973) in 1954. Sanbô Kyôdan, now an independent organization, was at one time affiliated with the **Sôtô sect**. The Zen style of the movement combines features from the **Rinzai sect** into its Sôtô style of practice. Despite its relatively small size in Japan, Sanbô Kyôdan has deeply influenced Zen in the West, especially in America. Zen teachers active in the West who have studied with the Sanbô Kyôdan include Robert Aitken, Philip Kapleau, Bernard Glassman, Maureen Stuart, and Richard Baker. See also **lay believer**.

Sanbukki

Three memorial days commemorating the historical **Buddha Siddharta Gautama's** birth, **enlightenment**, and death. In Japanese, the birth of the Buddha is formally called Kôtan-e but is more popularly known as **Hana Matsuri**, or Flower Festival. It was traditionally observed on the eighth day of the fourth lunar month, but in Japan it is now celebrated on April 8. The festival celebrating the Buddha's enlightenment under the **bodhi tree** is known as Jôdô-e, or **Rôhatsu**. It was traditionally observed on the eighth day of the twelfth lunar month but is now on December 8 in Japan. The **Nirvana Festival**, or Nehan-e, commemorating the Buddha's entry into the final **nirvana** at his death, was traditionally observed on the fifteenth day of the second lunar month and is now celebrated on February 15 in Japan. In South Asia and South East Asia, Buddhists celebrate the three events on a single day, usually in May.

Sanbutsuji

Three Buddhist ritual actions performed as a part of funerals and **memorial services**. They are 1) **tencha butsuji**, offering hot tea; 2) **tentô butsuji**, offering hot sweetened water; and 3) **ako**, the symbolic starting of the cremation fire with a torch.

Sanbyakusoku

"Three Hundred Cases," a collection of three hundred **kôan**, compiled by the Sôtô master **Dôgen Kigen** (1200–1253). The text is more widely known as the *Sanbyakusoku Shôbôgenzô*. It is composed in Chinese and may have originally been entitled simply *Shôbôgenzô*. In the *Sanbyakusoku*, Dôgen brings together traditional kôan materials that he collected in China while practicing under the Chinese master **Ju-ching** (1163–1228). It is possible that Dôgen composed the more famous *Shôbôgenzô* in Japanese as a commentary on the Chinese text.

Lost for several centuries, the *Sanbyakusoku* was discovered during the Tokugawa period (1600–1867) by Ein Shigetsu (d. 1764). Shigetsu's disciple, Honkô Katsudô, published the work, with a brief commentary on each case by his master. The text, published under the name *Nempyô Sanbyakusoku Funô Go*, caused some controversy in Japan. Sôtô scholars had long maintained that Dôgen completely rejected the use of kôan, so they initially denounced the *Sanbyakusoku* text as a forgery. Thus, the text does not usually appear in modern editions of the collected works of Dôgen. Scholars now accept the theory that Dôgen compiled the Chinese text, and they study it as a part of Dôgen's works.

In order to reduce confusion and distinguish between the Chinese *Sanbyakusoku Shôbôgenzô* and the Japanese language text, the former is sometimes called the *Shinji Shôbôgenzô*, the "*Shôbôgenzô* in Proper Characters," while the latter is known as the *Keji Shôbôgenzô*, the "*Shôbôgenzô* in Temporary Characters." See also **Sôtô sect**.

Sandai Sôron

Third Generation Schism, a sectarian dispute within the early **Sôtô sect** in Japan over who legitimately served as the third **abbot** at **Eihei-ji**, the main monastery. The various traditional accounts posit a serious conflict between Tettsu Gikai (1219–1309) and Gien (d. ca. 1313), two prominent disciples of **Dôgen Kigen** (1200–1253). Dôgen, founder and first abbot at Eihei-ji, appointed his disciple Ejô to serve as the second abbot. Ejô seems to have appointed Gikai to succeed him. Gikai assumed the post but faced serious difficulties during his tenure as abbot, and was eventually forced out of Eihei-ji. Gien then assumed leadership at the monastery. Gikai's departure is said to have created a schism within the nascent sect, which left Eihei-ji in decline for many years. In traditional versions of the schism, Gikai is often portrayed as a progressive who tried to popularize Sôtô by introducing new styles of ritual, while Gien is presented as a conservative who sought to maintain the traditional Sôtô practice.

Bodiford, William M. *Sôtô Zen in Medieval Japan*. Honolulu, HI: University of Hawaii Press, 1993.

Sandoku

Japanese for the **three poisons**: greed, anger, and ignorance. See **three poisons**.

San'e

"Three robes," the three types of **kesa** (Sk. kashaya) worn by **monks** and **nuns**. These include the five-strip robe (J. **gojôe**), originally an inner garment, the seven-strip robe (J. **shichijôe**), originally an outer garment worn inside monastery grounds, and the nine-strip robe (J. **kujôe**), originally an outer formal garment worn outside the monastery. See **kesa**.

San'e Ippatsu

"**Three robes, one bowl**," the most basic possessions of a Buddhist **monk** or **nun**. The term refers to the three types of **kesa** and the **begging bowl**, the only possessions monks and nuns were traditionally allowed to own. An alternate transliteration is sanne ippatsu. See **three robes, one bowl**.

Sangai

Three realms or three worlds of ordinary, unenlightened existence. In Japanese these are: 1) yokkai, the realm of desire; 2) shikikai, the realm of form; and 3) mushikika, the realm of no form. See **three realms**.

Sangai Yui Isshin

The **three realms** (of desire, form, and formlessness) are mind only. **Mahayana Buddhism** teaches that all phenomena experienced in ordinary life are actually the products of the mind. See **Consciousness Only**.

Sangaku

The Three Learnings. A Japanese expression for the **threefold training** of wisdom (J. egaku, Sk. **prajna**), morality (J. kaigaku, Sk. **sila**), and concentration (J. jôgaku, Sk. **samadhi**) in **Buddhism**. These three areas of learning are said to encompass the whole of Buddhist teaching and practice. **Zen** masters accept this basic Buddhist formula, identifying Zen **meditation** as the fundamental form of training in concentration. See **threefold training**.

Sange

Repentance for one's evil thoughts and actions. The Japanese translation of the Sanskrit term *kshama*.

Sangedatsumon

Three gates to emancipation, a reference to three kinds of **meditation**, or **gedatsu**. In Japanese these are: 1) kû gedatsu, release through meditation on **emptiness**; 2) musô gedatsu, release through meditation on no-attributes; and 3) mugan gedatsu, release through meditation on no desire. See **Three gates to emancipation**.

Sangemon

Repentance verse, a verse taken from the **Avatamsaka Sutra** and used to repent for evil deeds. The verse reads:

"All the karmic hindrances I have accumulated originated from passion, hatred, and ignorance. They are the product of my own physical, verbal, and mental misconduct. I confess them all."

Sangha

(J. sôgya or shu) The community of Buddhist believers, which includes the **four assemblies** of **monks** (J. **bhikkhu**), **nuns** (J. **bhikkhuni**), laymen (J. **upâsaka**), and lay women (J. **upâsikâ**). The community dates back to the lifetime of the **Siddharta Gautama**, the historical **Buddha**, who accepted lay and monastic followers during his forty-five years of traveling and teaching. The sangha is regarded as one of the **three treasures**, along with the Buddha and the **Dharma**, the Buddha's teachings. The sangha strives to live by the Buddha's teachings and to perpetuate them.

Many of Siddharta Gautama's followers venerated the Buddha and his teachings, but chose to continue to live as **lay believers** in the secular world. They practiced a modified form of the disciple in the monastic community. Other disciples abandoned their ordinary life to wholly dedicate themselves to the practice of **Buddhism** as monks and nuns.

In the early period of Buddhism's development, monks and nuns lived an itinerant life patterned on that of the historical Buddha, traveling much of the year from village to village, teaching others and seeking to fully realize for themselves the Buddhist goal of **nirvana**. They settled down only during the three-month rainy season (approximately July to October), because it made travel impractical. As a sign that they had completely abandoned ordinary **attachments** to material possessions, monks and nuns owned nothing other than their robes, **begging bowl**, and a few other minor items they could carry with them. Their other material needs were supplied by lay Buddhists.

In the early stage, the monastic community had no permanent dwellings, only temporary shelters. Over time, the monastic community developed patterns of returning to the same areas, building relationships with the local lay Buddhist community. Lay believers gradually built more permanent structures that the monks and nuns could use for the **rainy season retreat**. These structures were precursors to the major monasteries that lay devotees eventually built when the monastic community modified the practice of perpetual travel to allow for permanent residence.

The two parts of the sangha, lay and monastic, traditionally remain in close contact and support each other in a reciprocal relationship. Lay believers provide for the material necessities of monks and nuns by donating food, clothing, and shelter. Monks and nuns reciprocate by providing for the spiritual needs of the lay people, teaching them the Buddhist Dharma and allowing the lay people to build their **merit** through donations.

Sanji

Three Ages, a Japanese term for the **Three Ages of the Dharma**, three periods of progressive deterioration of the Buddhist teachings, practice, and attainment of **enlightenment**, which follow the death of the historical **Buddha**. The first age is **Shôhô**, the Age of the True Dharma; the second is **Zôhô**, the Age of the Semblance Dharma; and the third is Mappô, the **Latter Age of the Dharma**. See **Three Ages of the Dharma**.

Sanjô

The **three vehicles**, in Japanese. They are the vehicles of shômon (Sk. **shravaka**), engaku (Sk. **pratyeka buddha**), and bosatsu (Sk. **bodhisattva**). See **three vehicles**.

Sanjujôkai

The three pure **precepts**, representing the ideals of **Mahayana Buddhism** that **bodhisattvas** strive to realize. The precepts are: 1) do no evil, 2) do good, and 3) benefit all **sentient beings**. In the Sôtô **Zen** sect, **monks** and **nuns** take the three pure precepts as part of their **ordination**. The sanjujôkai constitute three of the sixteen **bodhisattva precepts** of Sôtô Zen (J. **jûrokujôkai**). See also **Sôtô sect**.

Sankan

Third barrier, the last of three sets of **kôan** used by some **Zen** monasteries in medieval Japan (1185–1600). The first and second barriers were known as **shokan** and **ryôkan**, respectively. The sankan, derived from the *Mumonkan*, were preceded by kôan sets from the *Hekiganroku* (*Blue Cliff Record*) and the *Sayings of Lin-chi*.

Sankikai

To take refuge (J. **kie**) in the **three treasures**: the **Buddha**, the **Dharma**, and the **sangha**. Literally, the term *sankikai* means the **precepts** of the three refuges, which are precepts in the context of **Zen ordination** rituals in the **Sôtô sect**. Sôtô **monks** and **nuns** take the three refuges as the first three precepts of the sixteen (J. **jûrokujôkai**) received at ordination. The formula "I take refuge in the Buddha; I take refuge in the Dharma; I take refuge in the sangha" is repeated three times.

Sanku

"The **three phrases**," a formulaic expression developed as a teaching device by **Lin-chi I-hsuan**, the founder of the Rinzai school of **Zen**. The term *sanku* is a Japanese rendering of the Chinese word *san-chu*. See **three phrases**.

Sanku

(2) **Three sufferings**. The three kinds of human **suffering** arise from sickness or hunger (J. kuku), separation from pleasure (J. eku), and the **impermanence** of things (J. gyôku). See **Three sufferings**.

Sankyô Itchi

"The **three teachings** are one," a traditional religious concept first developed in China, maintaining that **Buddhism**, Confucianism, and Taoism are essentially compatible and unified. The concept was widely accepted by Chinese **Zen** masters beginning in the Sung dynasty (960–1279) and spread throughout East Asia. In Japan, the same expression sometimes is interpreted to include Buddhism, Confucianism, and Shintô, the indigenous religion of the Japanese people.

Sankyû Nembutsu

The use of the **nembutsu**, that is, **chanting** the name of the **Buddha**, as a **kôan**. The so-called **Nembutsu kôan** generally takes the form of a question such as, "Who chants the nembutsu?"

San-lun School

"Three Treatises" school of Chinese **Buddhism**, the Chinese **Mâdhyamika** school that arose during the Southern and Northern dynasties. The school's name derives from the three Madhyamika texts on which its teachings are based: the Mâdhyamaka Karika (Treatise on the Middle; C. Chung-lun), Dvadashadvara-**shastra** (Treatise in One Hundred Verses; C. Po-lun) of **Nagarjuna**, and the Shata-shastra (Treatise of Twelve Categories; C. Shih-erh-men) of Aryadeva. **Kumarajiva** transmitted these texts to China, translating them into Chinese. Among Kumarajiva's Chinese disciples was **Seng-chao** (374–414), who wrote treatises on San-lun thought. The teachings were later systematized by the Korean master Chi-tsang (549–623). They were transmitted to Japan in the seventh century, where the school became known as the **Sanron school**.

Sanmai

See **sammai**.

Sanmi

Three levels, term used for a traditional three-part schema of **kôan** in the Sôtô school. The three levels are known as **Richi** (**Ultimate Truth**), **kikan** (devices), and **kôjô** (reality itself). See also **Sôtô sect**.

Bodiford, William M. *Sôtô Zen in Medieval Japan.* Honolulu, HI: University of Hawaii Press, 1993.

Sanmon

The large gate that serves as the main entryway into a **Zen** monastery, one of seven buildings forming the basic core of a Zen monastery (J. **shichidô garan**). The word *sanmon* is written with characters meaning either "mountain gate"—a reference to the fact that every Zen monastery regardless of location includes a mountain name as part of its full, formal name—or "triple gate." The typical architectural form is a two-story building with a tile roof, divided into three sections, hence the name triple gate. Massive doors hang in the center section, and images of the Two Guardian Kings (J. **Niô**) are usually displayed on the outer sections of the gate.

At **Rinzai sect** and **Obaku sect** monasteries in Japan, the gate stands independently, without any connections to other buildings or passageways. In medieval monasteries, the gate was incorporated into the outer wall of the monastery, making it the primary entrance for visitors and **monks** alike. Either way, the gate is regarded as the formal entrance to the monastery grounds.

The sanmon is the site for a number of formal Zen rituals, such as the installation ceremony for a new **abbots** and the formal greeting offered to visiting dignitaries.

Sanne-in Yuikai

The final instructions for Sanne-in, a set of admonitions composed by **Musô Sôseki** (1275–1351) in 1339 for his

The sanmon is a large gate at the entrance of a Zen monastery.

descendants at Sanne-in, a subtemple (J. **tatchû**) of Rinsen-ji. Also written san'e-in ikai.

Sanpai

Three lacquered wood tablets arranged in front of the main image (J. **honzon**) in the **Buddha** hall (J. **Butsuden**) at a **Zen** temple. Inscribed characters wish good fortune on the imperial family and other powerful patrons of the temple. The practice of using Sanpai originated in China during the Sung dynasty (960–1279). It was transmitted to Japan in the fourteenth century along with other Zen practices.

The inscriptions on the Sanpai differ from one period of Zen history to another. Sung dynasty tablets bore the inscriptions "Long Live the Emperor" on the center tablet and "Prosperity and Good Fortune to Patrons" and "Hail to the Lord of Fire" on the side tablets. Later, during the Yüan dynasty (1260–1368), the tablets read "Long Live the Emperor" in the center, "Gracious Years to the Empress" on the left, and "A Thousand Autumns for the Crown Prince" on the right. The Sung dynasty inscriptions were the norm in Japanese Zen temples, but during the Tokugawa period (1600–1867), the dedication to the fire deity was sometimes supplanted by a tablet with the inscription "Long Life and Prosperity for the **Shôgun**."

Collcutt, Martin. *Five Mountains: The Rinzai Zen Monastic Institution in Medieval Japan*. Cambridge, MA: Harvard University Press, 1981.

Sanpai

(2) Three bows or prostrations performed to indicate one's respectfulness in all actions, using the **gotai tôchi**, a full prostration on the floor. Repeating the bow three times is said to symbolize the three kinds of action (J. sango), those of body, speech, and mind. **Monks** and **nuns** typically perform sanpai before and after reciting the **sutras** at morning and afternoon services and on other occasions.

Sanron School

"Three Treatises" school, one of the Six Schools of Japanese **Buddhism** during the Nara period (710–794). This school of thought derived from the **San-lun school** of Chinese Buddhism, a system based on **Mâdhyamaka** philosophical writings. This name derives from the three Madhyamika texts on which its teachings are based: the Mâdhyamaka Karika (Treatise on the Middle; J. Chûron), Dvadashadvara-shastra (Treatise in One Hundred Verses; J. Hyakuron) of **Nagarjuna**, and the Shara-shastra (Treatise of Twelve Categories; J. Jûnimonron) of Aryadeva. **Kumarajiva** transmitted these texts to China, translating them into Chinese. The Korean **monk** Ekan (d. 1251), a disciple of Chi-tsang, transmitted the teachings to Japan in 625.

Sansammai

Three samadhi, three levels of samadhi, or realization. In Japanese these are: 1) kûzanmai, samadhi of **emptiness**; 2) musô zanmai, samadhi of no attributes; and 3) mugan zanmai, samadhi of no desire. See **three samadhi**.

Sanshin

Three bodies of the Buddha, a **Mahayana Buddhism** concept of the Buddha. In Japanese the three are hosshin (**Dharmakaya**), hôjin (**sambhogakaya**), and ojin (Sk. **nirmanakaya**). See **three bodies of the Buddha**.

Sanshu Sambô

Three ways of understanding the **three treasures**, as taught by **Mahayana Buddhism**. They are genzen sambô, jûji sambô, and ittai sambô, or the three treasures as manifest, as enduring, and as one. See **three treasures**.

Santai

The **Threefold Truth**, the Japanese name for the Tien-t'ai teaching. See **Threefold Truth**.

Sanzen

Going to see the **Zen** master for instruction. In the Rinzai school, the term is often used synonymously with the word *dokusan*, for the private interviews students have with the Zen master. Literally, sanzen means "practicing **meditation**." It may include **zazen** mediation, or to contemplate a **kôan** under the instruction of a Zen master. See also **Rinzai sect**.

Sanzô

The Japanese title for the **Tripitaka**, the three part scriptures of **Theravada Buddhism**. The term literally means "three storehouses," the rough equivalent of the "Three Baskets," indicated by the Sanskrit name. The three parts of the Sanzô include: 1) kyô (Sk. **sutras**), the **sermons** of the **Buddha**; 2) **ritsu** (Sk. **vinaya**), the monastic rules of discipline; and 3) **ron** (Sk. **shastras**), commentaries on the Buddha's teachings.

Sanzô

(2) Mountain **monk**; a humble term used by **Zen** monks referring to themselves. Sometimes pronounced *sansô*, the term

is used in much the same self-deprecating spirit as expressions like "this foolish monk" (sessô) or "this rustic monk" (yasô). Since all Zen monasteries have mountain names, all Zen monks can be called mountain monks, regardless of their monastery's location.

Historically, the term designated a monk living and practicing in the mountains. At one time, the **Tendai sect** monks from Mount Hiei were called "sanzô" to distinguish them from the temple monks living a more comfortable life in the capital city of Nara.

Sarei

(J. **chanoyû**) A tea ceremony held routinely at **Zen** monasteries. Sarei is held daily in the monks' hall (J. **sôdô**) or zendô (**meditation hall**) after the **monks** or **nuns** return from breakfast. At the morning tea service, attendance is checked to see that all monks or nuns are present. Daily tasks are assigned at the end of the sarei.

Sasaki Shigetsu

(1882–1945) Japanese Rinzai **monk** of the modern period who was influential in spreading **Zen** in the United States. Shigetsu is better known by his teaching name Sôkei-an Roshi, although his formal religious name is actually Sôshin Taikô. Shigetsu practiced as a lay person with **Shaku Sôkatash** and became his **Dharma heir**. He took the **tonsure** only after he had already received **inka**, or Dharma transmission. He traveled to the United States and in 1931 established The First Zen Institute of America in New York City. See also **Rinzai sect**.

Satori

Enlightenment, the immediate experience of reality. Satori, regarded as the goal of **Zen** Buddhist practice, is typically described as a state of understanding that transcends differentiation and duality. The term *satori* is the most common Japanese expression used for enlightenment within Zen texts. It is

often used as a synonym for **kenshô**. The character is alternatively pronounced "go" in Japanese. The Chinese pronunciation is "wu."

Sayings of Lin-chi

A text in one division (T. 47, no. 1985, pp. 495–506), which preserves the teachings of the T'ang dynasty **Zen** master **Lin-chi I-hsuan** (d. 866), the founder of the **Rinzai sect** school of Zen **Buddhism**. The *Sayings of Lin-chi* (J. *Rinzai-roku*) is among the most important classical Zen texts. It is comprised of three sections, the **recorded sayings** and **sermons**, interactions with disciples, and **pilgrimage** accounts. Some versions of the text include a biographical sketch appended at the end. The full Chinese title is *Chen-chou Lin-chi Hui-chao Ch'an-shih Yu-lu*, the "Recorded Sayings of Zen Master Lin-chi Hui-chao of Chen-chao." It is most often abbreviated as *Lin-chi Ch'an-shih Yu-lu* or simply *Lin-chi Lu*. The original text was compiled by Lin-chi's disciple San-sheng Hui-jan. A later edition, with a preface by Ma Fang, was completed by Yuan-chueh Tsng-yen in 1120. Complete English translations of the text include Ruth Fuller Sasaki's *The Record of Lin-chi* (Institute for Zen Studies, 1975) and Burton Watson's *The Zen Teachings of Master Lin-chi* (Shambhala, 1993).

Second Barrier

The second of three sets of **kôan** used by some **Zen** monasteries in medieval Japan (1185–1600). See **ryôkan**.

Second Patriarch

Usually refers to **Hui-k'o** (487–593) Ta-shih (487–593), the second Chinese **Patriarch** of **Zen**, who, tradition says, directly inherited the **Dharma** from **Bodhidharma**. In rare cases, the title applies to **Mahakashyapa**, the second Indian patriarch, who received the Dharma from Shakyamuni (**Siddharta Gautama**), the historical **Buddha**. See **Hui-k'o** and **Mahakashyapa**.

Segaki

A Buddhist ritual offered for the sake of **hungry ghosts** (J. **gaki**). Segaki is the common Japanese abbreviation for segaki-e, which literally means "ritual for **offering** alms to hungry ghosts." The ritual is held at Buddhist temples and monasteries throughout East Asia, particularly during the Festival of the Dead (J. **Obon**). Special altars are constructed, and **monks** and **nuns** chant **sutras** and offer rice and water to the beings **suffering** in **hell**. Segaki is regarded as an important ritual for those deceased souls who have no living relative to offer services for them. See **ullambana**.

Seian

The western retreat. An alternative expression for **seidô**. See **seidô**.

Seidô

Literally, the western hall, sometimes called seian, or western retreat. Seidô is a title of respect for former **abbots** residing at a temple other than the one at which they served as abbot. They are distinguished from **tôdô**, or the eastern hall, which are the retired abbots remaining at the temple where they served. Traditionally, these names derive from the halls where these high ranking **monks** lived. Today, the term *seidô* is used in the **Sôtô sect** as a title of respect for any high-ranking monk residing in a temple where he is not the abbot.

Seihan

The "Western rank," a group of monastic officers who assist the **abbot** with matters related to **meditation** and spiritual training of the community. Within every **Zen** monastery, administrative aspects of temple management are handled separately from spiritual aspects of monastic life. The distinct duties are entrusted to two sets of officers, referred to as the Western ranks and Eastern ranks (J. **tôhan**). Both ranks fall under the direction of the abbot, who is responsible for the operation of the community as a whole.

The Western rank of officers have this name because their primary duties are in monastic halls that are traditionally on the western side of the grounds. Officers of the Western rank, referred to collectively as the prefects (J. chôshu), include the chief seat (J. **shuso**), the scribe (J. **shoki**), the sutra prefect (J. **zôsu**), the guest prefect (J. **shika**), the bathkeeper (J. **chiyoku**), and the prefect of the **Buddha** hall (J. **chiden**).

Seiza

"Quiet sitting," an expression used for sitting calmly in **meditation**. It is alternatively pronounced **jôza**. Seiza may occasionally refer to **Zen** meditation, or more often, to the meditative practices of Sung or Neo-Confucianism. The term also refers to the traditional Japanese posture of sitting with buttocks resting on heels.

Seizan

West Mountain, the Japanese name for **Hsi-shan**, the monastery of the Fourth **Zen Patriarch Tao-hsin** (580–651). See **Hsi-shan**.

Sekiri Daruma

One Sandal **Bodhidharma**, Japanese reference to the story of Bodhidharma returning to India after his death while carrying a single straw sandal. See also **Straw Sandal Bodhidharma**.

Sekishu Kôan

The **Kôan** of One Hand, the most famous kôan created by **Hakuin Ekaku** (1685–1768). The basic form of the kôan is the question, "What is the sound of one hand clapping?" See **One Hand kôan**.

Sekkai

The explanation of the **precepts** given as a part of the **ordination** ceremony. On this occasion, the precept master explains the sect's configuration of monastic precepts. In most cases, these will include the three refuges and either the **ten precepts** from the Theravada tradition or the **bodhisattva precepts** of the Mahayana. In earlier usage, the term *sekkai* referred to the practice of reading or reciting the entire **monastic code** aloud twice each month at the **uposatha** assemblies. See also **Mahayana Buddhism** and **Theravada Buddhism**.

Sekkan

A flagpole located at the monastery gate from which a temple flag or **Dharma** banner (J. **setsuban**) is hung. The flag indicates that the resident **abbot** or head **monk** will be holding a sermon open to the public. The twenty-second case of the *Mumonkan* is entitled "Kashyapa's Flagpole." "**Ananda** once asked Kashyapa, 'Other than the golden robe, did the **World-Honored One** transmit anything else to you?' Kashyapa called to him, 'Ananda!' Ananda responded. Kashyapa said, 'Knock down the flag pole at the temple gate!'" This episode is used as a teaching device called a **kôan**, a cryptic passage from Zen literature that students use in meditation.

Sekkô Sôshin

(1408–1486) Japanese Rinzai **monk** of the Ashikaga period (1392–1568) who reinvigorated the **Zen** style at **Myôshin-ji** and restored its buildings and grounds after the devastation of the Onin War. He served as **abbot** at Myôshin-ji, **Daitoku-ji**, and other major Rinzai monasteries. He received the posthumous title Butsunichi Shinshô **Zenji** (Zen Master True Light of the Buddha's Sun). His four primary disciples were **Gokei Sôton** (1416–1500), **Keisen Sôryû** (1425–1500), **Tokuhô Zenketsu** (1419–1506), and **Tôyô Eichô** (1438–1504). See also **Rinzai sect**.

Self Power

(J. Jiriki) The endeavor to attain **enlightenment** through one's own efforts and **merit**, especially through the practices of **Buddhism**, including **meditation**. Self power is contrasted with **Other Power** (J. Tariki), the reliance on the merit of another being, such as a **buddha** or **bodhisattva**, for spiritual growth and advancement toward enlightenment. **Zen** Buddhism is among the schools of Buddhism that expect individuals to rely on their own efforts in order to attain enlightenment. Zen encourages believers to turn inward in meditation to seek realization of their true nature, rather than outward toward external objects of devotion. Other schools of Buddhism, most notably the **Pure Land schools**, encourage faith in a buddha as the basic means for spiritual advancement, recommending complete reliance on the power of the Buddha rather than on one's own religious practice.

Sembutsujô

(J. zendô) The **meditation hall** at a **Zen** monastery. Sembutsujô literally means "the place where buddhas are selected." Since most Zen practitioners attain **enlightenment** while practicing seated meditation, this term has come to be another name for the zendô.

Semmon Dôjô

The training hall at a **Zen** monastery; a Zen training monastery. The term usually refers to a place designated for the practice of **zazen** or other training in the practice of **Buddhism**. In the **Rinzai sect**, the term is most commonly used for its large training monasteries, including **Daitoku-ji** in Kyoto, **Kenchô-ji** and **Engaku-ji** in Kamakura, and **Myôshin-ji**, **Nanzen-ji**, and **Tenryû-ji**. In the **Sôtô sect**, the term may be used for the monks' hall (J. **sôdô**) at one of the main monasteries, **Eihei-ji** and **Sôji-ji**, where **monks** in training practice zazen.

Most local Zen temples in Japan are too small to include a training hall, and Zen **meditation** is not a regular part of the daily routine. These temples serve the surrounding community, providing services at festival times, as well as funeral and **memorial services** for member families. The larger monasteries, where monks receive their training, have daily Zen meditation and training. In some cases, interested lay people may have the option to join. See also **lay believer**.

Sendai

Shortened form of issendai. The Japanese rendering of the Sanskrit **icchantika**, a sentient being without the capacity to attain **enlightenment**. See **icchantika**.

Seng-chao

(374–414) Chinese Buddhist **monk** of the early Chinese **Mâdhyamaka** or **San-lun school**, one of the most important Buddhist thinkers of his day. His **biography** says that he came from a poor family and studied Taoist texts before turning to **Buddhism**. Seng-chao was the leading Chinese disciple of **Kumarajiva**, and together they translated **Buddhist scriptures** into Chinese. Seng-chao wrote the four-essay collection *Chao-lun*. His various works were highly influential among the **Zen** masters of the T'ang (618–907) and Sung (960–1279) dynasties.

Senge

A polite term commonly used to indicate the death of a **monk** or **nun**, especially a prominent individual. The term literally means "to move away." It can refer to the movement of a **bodhisattva** from one place (or lifetime) to another to save **sentient beings** trapped in the six realms of existence. This makes it a fitting euphemism for the passing of a Buddhist monk or nun.

Seng-ts'an

(d. 606; J. Sôsan) The Third Chinese **Patriarch** of **Zen**, according to tradition. Although nothing is known for certain about Seng-tsan, traditional Zen accounts maintain that **Hui-k'o** (487–593) designated him as his **Dharma heir** by presenting him with a copy of the **Lankavatara Sutra**, and that he, in turn, designated **Tao-hsin** (580–651) as his heir. See also **Hsin-hsin-ming**.

Senju

"Exclusive practice," a Japanese expression describing forms of **Buddhism** that stress a single form of practice to the exclusion or near exclusion of all others, especially the practice of **chanting** the **nembutsu**. Senju nembutsu is the exclusive practice promoted within some schools of **Pure Land** Buddhism. It rejects the efficacy of any other practice, such as reading **sutras** or **meditation**. **Zen** itself has been described as a form of exclusive practice stressing meditation over all other forms of practice.

Senju Darani

A Buddhist spell or **dharani** extolling the **merits** of the Senju Kannon, the Thousand-armed **Kannon**. The dharani, which includes eighty-two phrases and derives from the Senjukyô, is widely used in the esoteric schools of **Buddhism** and in the **Zen** sects. Senju darani is one common abbreviation for the Senju sengen kanzeon bosatsu emman muge daihishin darani. Also known as the Daihi darani or Daihi ju. See also **esoteric Buddhism**.

Sen No Rikyû

(1521–1591) Sôeki Rikyû, a Japanese **Zen monk** of the late Ashikaga period (1392–1568), best known as the foremost tea master of his time. Rikyû served as advisor and tea master to both Oda Nobunaga and Toyotomi Hideyoshi. Two schools of the tea ceremony (J. **chanoyû**), the Ura-senke and Omote-senke, continue to practice Rikyû's style.

Sentient Beings

Living beings. Although the term usually refers to human beings, **Buddhism** also recognizes sentient beings residing in **six paths** (J. rokudô), or levels of existence. The six realms encompass human beings, animals, heavenly beings, **hell** dwellers, **hungry ghosts**, and **ashura**, loosely translated as evil demi-gods. All sentient beings, even those dwelling comfortably in **heaven**, are caught in the cycle of reincarnation (Sk. **samsara**) and thus suffer and need to attain release through the practice of Buddhism. Since progress toward release can only be made by human beings, the focus of Buddhism remains on the human world.

Senzaki Nyogen

(1876–1958) Japanese **monk** of the **Rinzai sect** influential in spreading **Zen** to the West. Nyogen, the **Dharma heir** of **Shaku Sôen** (1859–1919), traveled to the United States and taught Zen to American disciples in both San Francisco and Los Angeles.

Seppô Gison

(822–908) Japanese transliteration of **Hsüeh-feng I-ts'un** (822–908), Chinese **Zen monk** of the late T'ang period (618–907). See **Hsüeh-feng I-ts'un**.

Sermons

There are several styles of sermons characteristic of **Zen** monastic practice in Japan, from formal, ritualized presentations to informal instruction. At **daisan**, or Great Assemblies, the **abbot** of a Zen monastery addresses the entire monastic community in the main hall, giving a formal **Dharma** lecture and allowing for subsequent questions and discussion. This formal sermon, known in Japanese as a **teishô**, usually includes the master's commentary on a particular **kôan** or a short passage from another classic Zen text. Abbots traditionally give less formal talks in their quarters to small groups of disciples; these are known as **shôsan**, or "Small Assemblies."

In addition to sermons presented orally to an audience, there are also Zen sermons preserved in written form. The general Japanese term for written sermons is **hôgo**, or "Dharma words." Hôgo likewise include a range of formal and colloquial styles. In general, formal hôgo are short texts in classical Chinese, while colloquial instructions, known as kanahôgo, are written in Japanese.

Seson

World-Honored One, the Japanese translation for the Sanskrit word *Bhagavat*, most commonly used in reference to Shakyamuni (**Siddharta Gautama**). See **World-Honored One**.

Sesshin

("encountering the mind," "collecting one's thoughts") Period of intensive meditative practice, traditionally seven days and nights, held periodically at **Zen** monasteries. During the sesshin, participants devote the entire day to **meditation**, nearly ceasing all their regular activities, such as **manual labor** and study. It is common for a monastic community to reduce the hours of sleep allowed each night during the sesshin. In some cases, the participants forego sleep altogether throughout the sesshin. Participants typically have the opportunity to visit with the Zen master for **dokusan** at least daily during sesshin. The master also traditionally gives **sermons**, or **teishô**, during the sesshin. In many monasteries, sesshin are held twice each year, in winter and in summer.

Setchô Jûken

(980–1052) Japanese transliteration of **Hsüeh-tou Ch'ung-hsien** (980–1052), Chinese **Zen monk** of the

Yun-men school from the early Sung dynasty (960–1279). See **Hsüeh-tou Ch'ung-hsien**.

Setsuban

A temple flag hung by the monastery gate to announce an upcoming lecture or service to the public. The temple flag will fly during retreat periods when a resident **abbot** offers regularly scheduled talks (J. **teishô**) or when there are special events, such as a visiting lecturer. In the **Sôtô sect**, the banner is used to announce the opening of the summer or winter retreats. The practice of using a banner to announce the location of a sermon is said to date back to Indian **Buddhism**. The temple flag is also known as Hôdô, or **Dharma** banner, and the flagpole is called a **sekkan**.

The twenty-ninth case of the *Mumonkan* involves a discussion of a setsuban flapping in the wind. Two **monks** were arguing about it; one said that it was the flag that moved, while the other maintained that it was the wind moving. Overhearing their discussion, the Sixth **Patriarch** stepped in and settled the matter, saying, "It is not the wind that moves, nor is it the flag that moves. It is your mind that moves."

Setsuwa

Short didactic stories or legends. These form a genre of Japanese literature that is closely associated with **Buddhism**. Setsuwa are usually placed in collections, such as the *Konjaku Monogatari*. Scholars believe that Buddhist **monks** and **nuns** used setsuwa in their popular preaching to teach lay people basic Buddhist concepts and virtues. See also **lay believer**.

Seven Buddhas of the Past

(J. kako shichibutsu) The seven buddhas from previous ages enumerated at the beginning of the *Transmission of the Lamp* (C. **Ching-te Ch'üan-teng Lu**; J. *Keitoku Dentôroku*) and other traditional accounts of the history of **Zen Buddhism**.

The group of seven buddhas includes **Vipashyin buddha**, **Shikhin buddha**, **Vishvabhu buddha**, **Krakucchanda buddha**, **Kanakamuni buddha**, **Kashyapa buddha**, and Shakyamuni buddha (**Siddharta Gautama**). The first three are said to have lived during the previous eon and the latter four in the present eon. Shakyamuni, an honorific name for Siddharta Gautama, who was presented as the most recent in a line of innumerable historical buddhas, serves as the pivotal figure who transmits the **Dharma** directly to **Mahakashyapa**, the first Indian **patriarch** of Zen. The account of the Seven Buddhas of the Past thus serves as a pre-history to the story of Zen proper.

With the exception of Shakyamuni buddha, the *Transmission of the Lamp* does not include stories recounting the lives of the buddhas of the past. The sections related to the first six buddhas follow a stylized format, including only a few standard biographical details, such as the place of birth, family name, and leading disciples. The text also provides a poem attributed to each buddha. Zen scholars regard the Shakyamuni buddha as the only historical figure in the list.

The opening passage of the *Transmission of the Lamp* indicates that the author selected seven individuals from the one thousand buddhas who appeared in recent eons. By portraying Shakyamuni buddha as the most recent in a line of historical buddhas, the text seeks to validate Zen not merely as a venerable tradition and an authentic school of Buddhism, but as the authentic form of Buddhism.

Sohaku, Ogata, trans. *The Transmission of the Lamp: Early Masters.* Wolfeboro, NH: Longwood Academic, 1989.

Seven Lucky Gods

Shichifukujin, seven deities revered in Japan as gods who bring good fortune. The deities are also understood as embodiments of various virtues. They are usually depicted sailing in a treasure ship (J. takarabune). Originally worshipped individually, they were eventually grouped together and became an object

Depiction of the Seven Lucky Gods, who bring good fortune.

of popular devotion starting in the fifteenth century. Now popularly identified as patron deities for a variety of occupations and trades, they include Daikoku and Ebisu, gods of business; **Bishamon**, the patron of doctors and travelers; Benten (or **Benzaiten**), the patron of the arts; Fukurokuju and Jurojin, the gods of learning; and Hotei, the patron of fortune tellers and liquor merchants.

Benzaiten, Bishamon, and Daikoku are from Indian mythology, while Hotei, Fukurokuju, and Jurojin are from Chinese mythology. Hotei was a historical person, the **Zen monk Pu-tai** (d. 916). Ebisu is an indigenous Japanese deity (J. **kami**). The Seven Gods of Fortune are associated with the New Year, when they are said to sail down from **heaven** to distribute good fortune for the coming year.

Seven Schools

(C. ch'i-tsung, J. shichishû) The seven **lineages** of Chinese **Zen** active during the Sung dynasty (960–1279). The seven schools include the earlier T'ang dynasty Zen lineages known as the **five houses**, along with two new Rinzai lineages founded during the Sung dynasty. The original five houses include the **Yun-men school** (J. Ummon-shû), the **Kuei-yang school** (J. Igyô-shû), the **Ts'ao-tung school** (J. Sôtô-shû), the **Lin-chi school** (J. Rinzai-shû), and the **Fa-yen school** (J. Hôgen-shû). The two additional branches of the Lin-chi school were the **Yang-ch'i school** (J. Yôgi-shû) and the **Huang-lung school** (J. Oryô-shû). These lineages are commonly referred to as the **five houses and seven schools**. See individual entries for more information. See also **Rinzai sect**.

Sexuality

Traditional **Zen** views of human sexuality fall comfortably within the broader realm of Buddhist morality. That is to say, human sexual behavior, especially sexual desire, is not regarded as inherently evil or good, but it is seen as one of the most powerful hindrances to religious practice and the attainment of **enlightenment**. Thus, for example, the **vinaya** texts specifically forbid all forms of sexual behavior for **monks** and **nuns**. The vinaya codes called for the automatic expulsion from the monastic community of any monk or nun who engaged in sexual intercourse. Although the Zen **monastic codes** are not an exact replication of the older vinaya codes, celibacy has been the expected norm in traditional Zen monasteries. Traditionally, appropriate sexual behavior for Buddhist lay practitioners includes sexual intercourse only within the confines of marriage.

Throughout the history of the Zen tradition, some masters have rejected some aspects of the Zen monastic code, including the traditional understanding of sexuality, eating meat, and drinking alcohol. Taking the view that all distinctions such as good and evil, moral and immoral are dualities that are transcended in enlightenment, certain Zen teachers have regarded sexual relations as permissible. This approach has been severely criticized by other Zen teachers as a misunderstanding of "Zen freedom" that leads to degenerate behavior.

Zen monasticism in Japan has undergone a significant change since the late nineteenth century. Within the various sects of Zen **Buddhism** in Japan today, most priests marry and raise families, although nuns continue to practice celibacy. In this regard, modern Japanese Zen differs from other modern forms of Zen in East Asia. In the West, where most Zen practitioners and teachers are lay people, marriage among the leadership is common. Indeed, the understanding of appropriate sexual behavior in Western Zen circles is changing so that it is not uncommon for Zen teachers in the West to accept committed sexual relations between unmarried couples, including homosexual relationships.

Shaba

This world; the world in which Shakyamuni **buddha** (**Siddharta Gautama**) teaches the **Dharma**. Shaba is a Japanese transliteration of the Sanskrit word *sahâ*, meaning "endurance," since in the ordinary world

The shakuhachi is a thin bamboo flute; its music is used to enhance the path to enlightenment.

all **sentient beings** must endure **suffering** and **samsara**, the ongoing cycle of death and rebirth.

Shaka

Japanese pronunciation of Shakya, the clan from northern India into which the historical **Buddha Siddharta Gautama** was born. In many contexts, the term *Shaka* is used as an abbreviated reference for the Buddha himself. See **Shakya Clan**.

Shakamuni

Japanese pronunciation of Shakyamuni, an honorific title for **Siddharta Gautama**, the historical **Buddha**. See **Siddharta Gautama**.

Shaka Nyorai

"Shakya **Tathagata**" or "Thus Come One Shakya," referring to the **Buddha** Shakyamuni (**Siddharta Gautama**). Shaka Nyorai is a commonly used Japanese name for **Siddharta Gautama**, the historical Buddha. The Buddha was born to the **Shakya clan** in India, which is pronounced "Shaka" in Japanese. See **Siddharta Gautama**.

Shakuen Eichô

(d. 1247) A Japanese Rinzai **monk** of the Kamakura period (1185–1333), one of the leading disciples of **Eisai**. Eichô was originally a Tendai monk and studied **esoteric Buddhism**. He became Eisai's disciple in Kamakura and practiced **meditation** under his guidance. Eisai recognized him as a **Dharma heir** in the **Zen** tradition, but Eichô remained committed to the esoteric tradition. He continued to practice a mixed form of Buddhism, combining Zen meditation with many elements of esoteric ritual and thought, placing heavier emphasis on esoteric practice. His primary contribution to the **Rinzai sect** of Zen was through his disciples. He founded Chôraku-ji, a Tendai temple in the Kantô region, where **Jinshi Eison** (1195–1272), Muhon **Kakushin** (1207–1298), and **Enni Ben'en** (1202–1280) became his students and were first introduced to Zen. See also **Tendai sect**.

Shakuhachi

A long bamboo flute with five finger holes associated with the **Fuke sect** of **Zen Buddhism**. According to Fuke teachings and practice, playing the shakuhachi and hearing its music are conducive to attaining **enlightenment**.

Shakuniku Danjô

"A **lump of red flesh**," the graphic expression used by the **Zen** master **Lin-chi I-Hsuan** for the human body or the human mind. Lin-chi distinguishes the lump of red flesh from the **Buddha Nature** innate within the self. See **lump of red flesh**.

Shaku Sôen

(1859–1919) Japanese Rinzai **monk**, also known by his religious name Kôgaku Sôen, one of the most important **Zen** masters of the modern period. He was the disciple and **Dharma heir** of **Kôsen Sôon** (1816–1892) who sent him to Keiô Gijuku (later to become Keiô University) so that the young monk would receive an education appropriate for the new era of modern Japan. After Sôen completed his practice under Kôsen, he traveled to Ceylon to study **Theravada Buddhism**. He also visited Siam (now Thailand) and China. Shaku inherited the position of **abbot** at **Engaku-ji** when his master died in 1892. The next year, he attended the World Conference of Religions in Chicago. He was the first monk from the **Rinzai sect** to visit the West, and he visited two more times. Three of Sôen's disciples also were influential in introducing Rinzai to the West: **Shaku Sôkatsu** (1870–1954), **D.T. Suzuki** (1870–1966), and **Senzaki Nyogen** (1876–1958).

Shaku Sôkatsu

(1870–1954) Japanese Rinzai **monk** of the modern period, also known by his religious name Tetsuô Sôkatsu. Sôkatsu was the adopted son and primary **Dharma heir** of **Shaku Sôen** (1859–1919). Sôkatsu originally practiced **Zen** as a lay person under the guidance of **Kôsen Sôon** (1816–1892). After Kôsen died, he took the **tonsure** and became the disciple of Sôen. When he had received **inka**, or the Dharma transmission, Sôkatsu made a **pilgrimage** throughout Japan, Burma, and Siam (now Thailand). Sôkatsu never lost his interest in promoting Zen practice among lay people. He revived the Ryômô Kyôkai, a lay organization of Zen practitioners, and dedicated his career to guiding its members. In 1907, he traveled to California with a group of disciples to establish a Zen center there, but decided that the time was not yet ripe for transmitting the Dharma to America. He returned to Japan in 1910. One of his Dharma heirs, **Sasaki Shigetsu** (1882–1945), later completed the mission to the United States. See also **lay believer** and **Rinzai sect**.

Shakya Clan

Family from which **Siddharta Gautama** descended. The Shakya clan were warrior class (**kshatriya**) and the ruling family of a small republic in the northeastern region of the Indian subcontinent, now Nepal. At the time of the **Buddha**, they remained self-governing, with **Kapilavastu** as their capital.

Shakyamuni

"The Sage of the **Shakya Clan**," an honorific title for the historical **Buddha, Siddharta Gautama**, who founded **Buddhism**. The Buddha was born to the Shakya clan, a people from northern India (now Nepal). Buddhists commonly refer to Siddharta as the Shakyamuni buddha. See **Siddharta Gautama**.

Shala Trees

(*Vatica robusta*) According to the Buddhist tradition, the historical **Buddha** lay down to die in the town of Kushinagara between two shala trees, commonly referred to as twin shala trees; that is, trees with two trunks. The Buddha's death is known as **parinirvana**, or perfect **nirvana**. The trees were blooming out of season, and the Buddha requested that his disciple **Ananda** prepare a couch between two of them. In some accounts, the blossoms fell and the trees withered when he died. The grove of shala trees is called the crane grove (J. kakurin) because in other accounts, the tradition says that the trees blossomed with pure white flowers after the Buddha died, as if a flock of cranes had landed.

Shami

The Japanese term for a male **novice** who has received the initial **ordination**, based on the **ten precepts** of the novice. A shami has received the **tonsure**, meaning that he shaves his head and wears monastic robes. He will continue to train at a monastery until prepared to accept full ordination. In the past, most novices were teenagers who were too young to qualify for full ordination, normally allowed at age twenty. In medieval Japan (1185–1600), the term *shami* was also used for lay Buddhists and self-ordained **monks** who practiced outside the confines of monastic **Buddhism**. See also **lay believer**.

Shamikai

The novice precepts based on the **monastic code** (Sk. **vinaya**) of **Theravada Buddhism**. See **ten precepts**.

Shamini

The Japanese term for a female **novice** who has received the **ten precepts** of the novice at an initial **ordination** ceremony. She shaves her head and wears novice's robes until prepared to accept the full ordination.

Shamon

Japanese for shramana, an ascetic **monk** or **nun**. In Japanese, the word most often simply denotes a Buddhist monk or nun. See **shramana**.

Shao-lin-ssu

(J. Shôrin-ji) The Chinese Buddhist monastery on Mount Sung, near the former capital city of Lo-yang, where the Indian **monk Bodhidharma** is traditionally said to have remained for nine years seated in **meditation** facing a wall at Shao-lin-ssu.

Shari

Relics, especially of the historical **Buddha** or another important Buddhist figure. Shari is the Japanese transliteration of the Sanskrit term *sharira*. See **relics**.

Sharihotsu

Japanese for **Sharirputra**, one of the ten distinguished disciples of the **Buddha**, known for his deep wisdom. See **Sharirputra**.

Sharirputra

(J. Sharihotsu) One of the ten outstanding disciples of the **Buddha** and reknowned as foremost in wisdom. Sharirputra was born to the brahmin class and, along with his boyhood friend **Maudgalyâyana**, left the home life to become a follower of the skeptic Sanjaya. Sharirputra met a disciple of the Buddha and determined from a short exchange that the Buddha's teaching was the wisdom he had been seeking. The two friends then decided to become disciples of the Buddha and joined the **sangha**. They brought with them scores of Sanjaya's other disciples as well. Because of his brilliance, Sharirputra soon distinguished himself as one of the Buddha's leading disciples. Many years later, when the Buddha was nearing death, Sharirputra asked the Buddha for permission to die. He died shortly before the Buddha's passing.

Ishigami, Zenno. *Disciples of the Buddha*. Trans. Richard L. Gage and Paul McCarthy. Tokyo: Kosei Publishing Co., 1989.

Sharira

Relics, especially of the historical **Buddha** or another important Buddhist figure. *Sharira* is the Sanskrit term. See **relics**.

Shasekishû

Collection of Sand and Stone, a text in ten sections compiled by the Japanese

Rinzai **monk Mujû Dôgyô** (1226–1313) and completed in 1283. The text contains a series of popular Buddhist stories or **setsuwa**, many of them humorous in tone. Robert E. Morrell has published an English translation under the title *Sand and Pebbles* (SUNY Press, 1985). See also **Rinzai sect**.

Shashu

Hand position used in **Zen** monasteries when entering and leaving the **meditation hall**. The left hand forms a fist around the thumb, and the right hand covers the left. The hands are held, fist toward the chest, in front of the body with forearms straight.

Shastra

(J. **ron**) A genre of religious instructional literature common to all the religious traditions of Indian origin, including **Buddhism**. In a Buddhist context, a shastra is a commentary on a Buddhist sutra or a Buddhist philosophical treatise. Shastras compose a major portion of the **Buddhist scriptures**.

Shaven-Headed Layman

A **Zen monk** who focuses on literary or artistic pursuits as the primary concern of his practice. Although the monk may pursue Buddhist literature and art, the approach to the material is usually secular. The Rinzai master **Musô Sôseki** (1275–1351) used the expression "shaven-headed laymen" in contrast to the three grades of disciples that he had encountered: those of high, medium, and low ability. He asserted that shaven-headed laymen were not worthy of being classified as disciples at all; even disciples with low capacities for Zen practice were superior to those with a secular mind set. See also **Rinzai sect**.

Shen-hsiu

(606?–706; J. Jinshû) Chinese **Zen monk** of the early T'ang dynasty (618–907), commonly regarded as the founder of

the **Northern school** of early Zen. Contemporary scholars conclude that Shen-hsiu was a leading disciple of **Hung-jen** (601–674), the Fifth Patriarch, and one of the most important Zen masters of his day. Born in Hunan province to an aristocratic family, he renounced the home life at an early age. At age twenty, he took the full **precepts** at T'ien-kung ssu in Lo-yang. In 651, he traveled to Huang-mei and practiced with Hung-jen for several years. Scholars believe that after Hung-jen's death in 674, Shen-hsiu became the leader of the **East Mountain school**. Shen-hsiu spent the majority of his teaching career at Tu-men ssu in Ching-chou, where he led a large community of monks. In 701, he traveled back to Lo-yang and spent the last years before his death working there and in Chang-an. The community that he founded in Ching-chou remained active for several generations. It would later become known (and disparaged) as the Northern school, so designated by **Ho-tse Shen-hui** (670–762).

However, these historical accounts of Shen-hsiu's role in early Zen differ significantly from traditional accounts. The traditional account is based on a section of the **Platform Sutra**, which explains how **Hui-neng** (638–713), rather than Shen-hsiu, became the rightful Sixth Patriarch. In the biographical section of the sutra, Shen-hsiu is portrayed as the highest ranking disciple in Hung-jen's assembly, but one who does not fully grasp the **Dharma**. On one occasion, the Fifth Patriarch asked his disciples to present him with verses demonstrating their understanding of the Dharma so that he could designate an heir as the Sixth Patriarch. Shen-hsiu wrote a verse that the master deemed insufficient. When another member of the assembly, Hui-neng, responded to Shen-hsiu's verse with one of his own, Hung-jen secretly named him the Sixth Patriarch. This account became the orthodox version of early Zen history, and Shen-hsiu fell into obscurity.

Cremation is one of the shichibutsuji, or seven ritual actions, performed at the funeral of a prominent Buddhist monk or nun.

McRae, John R. *The Northern School and the Formation of Early Ch'an Buddhism*. Honolulu, HI: University of Hawaii Press, 1986.

Shen-hui

(670–762; J. Jinne) Chinese **Zen monk** of the T'ang dynasty (618–907). His full name is **Ho-tse Shen-hui** (670–762). See **Ho-tse Shen-hui**.

Shichi

"The **four wisdoms**," the Japanese translation of the Sanskrit term *catvari jnanani*. Within the context of early Buddhist texts, shichi refers to the realization of the **four noble truths**. This can be obtained by the **arhat**, the ideal practitioner of **Theravada Buddhism**. Within the Mahayana tradition, **bodhisattvas** strive to attain shichi, which characterize a **Buddha**. The four wisdoms are: 1) Daienkyôchi, Great Perfect Mirror Wisdom; 2) Byôdôshôchi, Universal Nature Wisdom; 3) Myôkansatchi, Marvelous Observing Wisdom; and 4) Jioshosatchi, Perfecting of Action Wisdom. See **four wisdoms**.

Shichibutsuji

Seven Buddhist ritual actions performed as a part of the funeral of a prominent Buddhist **monk** or **nun**. They are: 1) **nyûgan**, laying the corpse in the coffin; 2) **igan butsuji**, moving the coffin to the lecture hall; 3) **sagan butsuji**, closing the coffin lid; 4) **kigan**, carrying the coffin to the cremation grounds; 5) **tencha butsuji**, offering hot tea; 6) **tentô butsuji**, offering hot sweetened water; and 7) **ako**, starting the cremation fire with a torch. See also **kubutsuji**.

Shichidô Garan

The seven monastic halls that form the basic core of all **Zen** temples and monasteries. These seven include: the **Dharma** hall (J. **hattô**), which serves as the main assembly hall for **sermons**; the **Buddha** hall (J. **butsden**), in which the primary Buddha image is enshrined; the monks' hall (J. **sôdô**), where the **monks** or **nuns** sleep, eat and meditate; the kitchen-office (J. **ku'in**), where meals are prepared and the senior monastery staff have offices; the latrines (J. **tôsu**); the mountain gate (J. **sanmon**), which serves as the formal entrance to the monastic compound; and the bath-house (J. **yokushitsu**). According to **Mujaku Dôchû** (1653–1744), a Tokugawa scholar monk, the traditional layout of the seven halls can be represented graphically in the shape of a human body. The buildings are conceived in anthropomorphic fashion, with the Dharma hall as the head, the Buddha hall as the heart, and so forth, as shown in the diagram. This layout was probably a Ming Chinese style of Zen monasteries, introduced into Japan by the **Obaku sect**.

The term *shichidô garan* may also refer generically to any Buddhist monastery from any Buddhist school. The Zen list differs somewhat from the basic buildings found in other monasteries. A typical list from another Buddhist school would include a golden hall (J. kondô), a lecture hall (J. kyôdô), a **stupa** (J. tô), a dining hall, a bell tower (J. **shôrô**), a storehouse for sacred texts (J. kyôzô), a separate **meditation hall** (J. zendô), a **founder's hall** (J. kaisandô), and the monks' hall (J. **sôdô**).

Shichifukujin

The **seven lucky gods** revered in Japan. See **seven lucky gods**.

Shichijôe

"Seven-strip robe," one of three basic types of **kesa**, or monastic robes, worn by Buddhist **monks** and **nuns**. The seven-strip robe was originally called the uttarasangha in Sanskrit. It is alternatively known in Japanese as the uttarasô. The shichijôe is designed to be worn as an outer garment and was originally the basic robe that monks and nuns wore inside the monastic community.

Shichishû

(C. ch'i-tsung) "**Seven school**," a Japanese expression used to describe the seven lineages of **Zen** active during the Sung dynasty (960–1279) in China. In other contexts, the expression may refer to seven sects and schools of Japanese **Buddhism**, including the **Ritsu** sect, the **Hossô school**, the **Sanron school**, the **Kegon school**, the **Tendai sect**, the **Shingon sect**, and the **Zen** sect. See **seven schools**.

Shidai

The **four great elements**: earth, water, fire, and wind. See **four great elements**.

Shidô

Hall within a Buddhist temple or monastery in which mortuary tablets (J. **ihai**) for deceased lay members are enshrined. **Sutras** are chanted daily within the shidô (a practice known as *shidô fugin* in Japanese), and other **offerings** are made periodically to commemorate anniversaries of specific individuals' deaths. See also **lay believer**.

Shidô Bu'nan

(1603–1676) Japanese Rinzai **monk** and Zen master of the early Tokugawa period (1600–1867). Bu'nan was born to a commoner family in Sekigahara, in Mino province, where his father ran an inn. Although he became familiar with **Zen** practice as a young man, he did not become a monk until 1654, when he was already fifty-one years old. His teacher was **Gudô Tôshoku** (1579–1661). His only **Dharma heir** was **Dôkyô Etan** (1642–1721), the teacher of **Hakuin Ekaku** (1685–1768). See also **Rinzai sect**.

Shichidô garan, Nanzen-ji.

Shie

Purple robe, Japanese term for an honorific monastic robe bestowed on high ranking **monks**. See **purple robe**.

Shigu seigan

The **four great vows** of a **bodhisattva**. Various versions of the vows are used in different schools of **Buddhism**. The version used by the **Zen** school is based upon a passage from the Tun-huang edition of the **Platform Sutra**. In Japanese it reads: 1) Shujô muhen seigan do (**Sentient beings** are innumerable, I vow to save them all); 2) Bonnô muhen seigan do (The **afflictions** are innumerable, I vow to extinguish them all); 3) Hômon muhen seigan gaku (The **Dharma** is immeasurable, I vow to master it all); and 4) **Mujô butsudô** seigan jô (The Buddhist Way is unsurpassed, I vow to attain it). Zen **monks** and **nuns** recite these vows daily as a part of morning and evening services.

Shihokkai

Four realms of reality, an alternate expression for shishu hokkai. See **four realms of reality**.

Shiji No Kuyô

Japanese for "**four offerings**," which one may appropriately offer to a **buddha**, **monk**, or **nun**. See **four offerings**.

Shiji Zazen

"**Four periods of meditation**," which are traditionally observed daily in a **Zen** monastery. (Alternately rendered Shiji no **zazen**.) Although they are not mentioned in the *Zen'en Shingi*, both **Eisai** and **Dôgen Kigen** (1200–1253) mention that the four periods of Zazen were observed in the Chinese Zen monasteries of the Sung dynasty (960–1279) that they visited. The custom was then transmitted and preserved in Japanese Zen monasteries. The times and duration of the periods differ somewhat from

295

monastery to monastery. The traditional names for the four periods are: 1) **Goya zazen**, held early in the morning before daybreak; 2) **Sôshin zazen**, held later in the morning, after breakfast; 3) **Hoji zazen**, held in the afternoon; and 4) **Kôkon zazen**, held in the late evening.

Shijûhachikyôkai

The **forty-eight light precepts**. The secondary set of **bodhisattva precepts**, as presented in the Bonmôkyô (Sk. **Brahma Net Sutra**). The forty-eight light and **ten heavy precepts** (J. Jûjûkinkai) together comprise the complete set of bodhisattva precepts. For a full listing of the Shijûhachikyôkai, see John Stevens, *The Marathon Monks of Mount Hiei* (Shambhala, 1988. pp. 24–25.)

Shijûzai

"**Four grave offenses**" in Japanese. See **four grave offenses**.

Shika

The Guest Prefect at a **Zen** monastery, one of the six offices (J. chôsu) of the Western rank held by a senior **monk**. The guest prefect's responsibilities include the entertainment of official visitors and the care of itinerant monks (J. **unsui**). Because **pilgrimage** is a traditional part of the Zen monastic life, Zen monasteries maintain guest accommodations (J. kakusu) to house visiting monks. The shika sees to the visitor's material needs during his stay. In addition, since all new arrivals seeking entry to the monastery come under his supervision, the shika plays a very important role within the monastic community. During a newcomer's probation period (J. **tanga zume**), the shika observes and evaluates the candidate to determine his suitability for entering the monastery. Also called the tenkaku or tenbin.

Shikai

"**Dead ashes**," a metaphoric expression used to describe the mental state of a person who has extinguished all harmful passions and **attachments**. The word often applies to **Theravada Buddhism** masters who attain the meditative level of extinction (J. **metsujinjô**). See **dead ashes**.

Shikan

"Tranquility and contemplation," the Japanese translation for chih-kuan, the form of Buddhist **meditation** devised by the **T'ien-t'ai school** master **Chih-i** (538–597). The term derives from the Sanskrit words *samatha* (tranquillity) and *vipashyana* (contemplation). Shikan was transmitted to Japan by **Saichô** (767–822) and is the characteristic **Tendai sect** style of meditation.

Shikan Taza

Style of seated **Zen meditation** without the use of a **kôan**, the style characteristic of the **Sôtô sect** of Zen. The expression literally means "earnest meditation," or "seated meditation only." **Dôgen Kigen** (1200–1253), the founder of Japanese Sôtô, advocated shikan taza as the ideal form of Buddhist practice. He identified shikan taza with **enlightenment** itself.

Shikatsu

"**Four shouts**," the Japanese rendering of the Chinese expression ssu-ho. The four kinds of shouts is a formulaic expression developed by **Lin-chi I-hsuan**, founder of Rinzai **Buddhism**, which explains how he used loud shouting (**katsu!**) as a teaching device for his disciples. See **four shouts**.

Shike Goroku

Japanese title for the *Ssu-chia Yu Lu*, the *Recorded Sayings of the Four Houses*. See *Ssu-chia Yu Lu*.

Shiketsu

An implement made from soft bamboo or wood that was traditionally used in place of toilet paper. It translates literally as "outhouse stick." The term appears in several **Zen** texts, including Case 21 of the *Wu-men Kuan* (J. *Mumonkan*). In that passage, a **monk** asks master **Yun-men Wen-yen** (864–949), "What is **Buddha**?" Yun-men replies, "A dried outhouse stick." Yun-men's answer is shocking not only because the implement was generally regarded as defiled, but also because of the vulgarity of the expression itself. Like a loud shout or a sharp slap on the face, the Yun-men's shocking reply cuts off the discursive and discriminatory thought suggested by the student's question.

Shikhin Buddha

One of the **seven buddhas of the past** whose biographies appear at the beginning of the *Transmission of the Lamp* (C. **Ching-te Chüan-teng Lu**; J. *Keitoku Dentôroku*) and other traditional accounts of the history of **Zen Buddhism** through the ages. Shikhin (J. Shiki) is second on the list and is identified as the 999th **Buddha** of the previous eon.

Shikunichi

Days of the month containing the numerals 4 or 9; that is, the 4th, 9th, 14th, 19th, 24th and 29th of each month. At **Zen** monasteries, these days are observed as free days on which **monks** and **nuns** help one another to shave their heads, wash their clothing, take a bath, and attend to other chores. See also **oshiku**.

Shila

Sanskrit pronunciation of the more commonly used Pali word *sila*. See **sila**.

Shinbun Ritsu

(C. **Ssu-fen Lu**) *The Vinaya in Four Categories of Dharmagupta*, the version of the **vinaya** that became the standard in East Asian **Buddhism**. The text was translated into Chinese and transmitted to Japan in the eighth century. The Japanese **Ritsu** school was based on the study and careful observance of this version of the Theravada **monastic code**. See *Ssu-fen Lu*.

Shinchi

"**Mind ground**," a **Zen** expression for one's mental state. The mind is compared to a field or the ground because it is regarded as the source of all thoughts and experiences, including perceptions of all external phenomena. In some cases, the term refers to the mind of **enlightenment**. Alternatively pronounced "Shinji." See **mind ground**.

Shinchi Kakushin

See **Kakushin**.

Shingi

Zen monastic codes, which set out the proper conduct for life and practice within the Zen monastic community. Shingi may be literally translated as "pure regulations." It is the Japanese pronunciation of the Chinese term *ching-kuei*. Shingi represent a distinctive genre of Zen literature. Zen tradition maintains that the T'ang master **Pai-chang Huai-hai** (720–814) composed the earliest shingi, the *Pai-chang Ch'ing-kuei* (J. *Hyakujô Shingi*), in the eighth or ninth century. Scholars no longer believe that this text ever existed. Recent scholarship suggests that the earliest Zen monastic codes actually date to the Sung dynasty (960–1279). Chinese codes were transmitted to Japan beginning in the twelfth century. Many Japanese shingi were likewise composed, including the *Eihei Shingi* written by **Dôgen Kigen** (1200–1253). In some cases, shingi are written to govern conduct within a particular monastery. In other cases, they are designed for more general use within a sect or school of Zen.

Shingon Sect

Japanese school of **esoteric Buddhism** founded by **Kûkai** (774–835) during the Heian period (794–1185). Esoteric Buddhism first developed in India and was transmitted to China in the eighth century. Although this school did not give rise to a separate school of Buddhism in China, Kûkai was initiated into its teachings and practice when he studied in China. When he returned to Japan, he established an independent sect and systematized the teachings. The primary texts for the school are the Mahvairochana Sutra (J. Dainichikyô) and the Vajrashekhara (J. Kongôchôkyô). Shingon literally means "true word," and is the Japanese translation for **mantra**. Shingon ritual makes use of mantra, **mudra** and **mandala**.

Shingyô

Heart Sutra, the common, abbreviated Japanese title for the **Prajna** Paramita Hrdaya Sutra. The most popular Chinese translation (T. 8, no. 251) is that completed by **Hsüan-tsang** (ca. 600–664) in 648. The Japanese version of the text is composed of only 268 characters. The full title in Japanese is Maka Hannya Haramitta Shingyô. See **Heart Sutra**.

Shin'in

"Seal of the mind," a **Zen** expression for transmission of the **Dharma** between master and disciple. Shin'in is a common abbreviation for busshin'in (**inka**), "seal of the Buddha's mind."

Shinji Ike

Heart-shaped pond; a pond created to resemble the Chinese character for "heart." Shinji ike are sometimes found in monastery gardens, such as the gardens at **Tenryû-ji** and Saihô-ji, both located in western Kyoto.

Shinjin Datsuraku

"Dropping off body and mind," an expression used in Sôtô **Zen** for the experience of **enlightenment**, which **Dôgen Kigen** (1200–1253) identified with the practice of seated **meditation**. The expression derives from traditional accounts of Dôgen's enlightenment experience during an intensive summer retreat at a Chinese Zen monastery where he resided for a time. Dôgen and his fellow **monks** were sitting in meditation when the man beside him fell asleep. Dôgen suddenly attained enlightenment when he heard his master **Ju-ching** (1163–1228) shout at his sleepy neighbor, "When you study under a master, you must drop off the body and mind. What is the use of single-minded, intense sleeping?"

Scholars now believe that the original expression employed by Ju-ching may have actually been "Dropping off **dust** from the mind." Although they are not homonyms in the original Chinese, in Japanese, the two expressions are pronounced identically. It is theorized that Dôgen either cleverly reinterpreted the verse or fortuitously misheard it. See also **Sôtô sect**.

Kodera, Takashi James. *Dôgen's Formative Years in China: An Historical Study and Annotated Translation of the* Hokyo-ki. Boulder, CO: Prajña Press, 1980.

Shinjinmei

Japanese title of the "**Hsin-hsin-ming**," a verse attributed to **Seng-ts'an** (d. 606), the Third Chinese **Patriarch**. See **Hsin-hsin-ming**.

Shinnin

True person, the Japanese pronunciation of the Chinese word *chen-jen*. The concept derives from the Taoist tradition, and the Taoist philosopher Chuang-tzu who used the term as an expression for a Taoist expert who perfectly understands the **Tao**. The expression was later adopted by Chinese Buddhists to translate the Sanskrit word "**arhat**," the ideal Buddhist practitioner who has realized **nirvana**. See **true person of no rank**.

Shinnyo

"**True Thusness**," the Japanese translation for the Sanskrit term *tathata*. See **True Thusness**.

Shinran

(1173–1262) Japanese Buddhist **monk** who founded the **True Pure Land sect** (J. Jôdo Shinshû). Shinran was born to a branch of the Fujiwara family and was the son of Hino Arinori. He began his Buddhist training at age nine as a Tendai monk and spent twenty years on Mount Hiei, where he first became acquainted with Pure Land teachings. He left Mount Hiei in 1201 when he was twenty-nine to become a disciple of the Pure Land teacher **Hônen** (1133–1212). A few years later, he married Eshin-ni. In 1207, when Honen offended the emperor, Honen and his disciples, including Shinran, were exiled from Kyoto. Shinran was sent to Echigo province, where he remained until he was pardoned in 1211. He continued to teach in rural areas for many years, spreading the Pure Land faith in the Kantô region. He returned to Kyoto in 1235 and lived there until his death in 1262. See also **Tendai sect**.

Shinsanshiki

Ordination ceremony for a new **abbot** at a **Zen** monastery. An announcement of the ceremony is posted outside the main monastery gate. The newly appointed abbot first rests in a room prepared for his use (J. angesho) and then is greeted formally there by the senior temple officers and lay sponsors, with whom he exchanges bows and shares tea. The supervisor of the **meditation hall** (J. **ino**) rings a bell to summon the entire monastic assembly, at which time the new abbot, monastery officers, and assembled **monks** form a procession and enter the monastery gate. Inside the gate, the abbot gives a brief **Dharma** sermon (J. **hôgo**) and offers **incense**. The group proceeds to the monks' hall (J. **sôdô**), where the abbot once again speaks a few words and lights incense. He then formally hangs up his staff, symbolic of taking up residence in the monastery, and moves on to the **Buddha** hall, where he again gives a brief sermon and offers incense. Here he lays out a ritual cloth (J. **zagu**) and prostrates himself three times (J. sanbai). He stops at the shrine for the local guardian deity (J. dojijin) and says some words of the Dharma. He then proceeds to the **founder's hall** where he gives his final sermon, offers incense, and bows three times. Finally, he enters the abbot's quarters, where he formally accepts the room and receives the monastery's seal. See also **lay believer**.

Shinshin

The "**True Mind**," a **Zen** expression for one's true or original nature, which is said to be **Buddha Nature**. The realization of Shinshin is synonymous with **enlightenment**.

Shinshû

The common abbreviation for Jôdo Shinshû, the **True Pure Land sect** of Japanese **Buddhism**. The sect is generally referred to as Shinshû in Japan, as well as in Western countries to which it has been transmitted. See **True Pure Land sect**.

Shion

The **four obligations** or the four debts of gratitude. See **four obligations**.

The shippei was traditionally used to discipline meditating monks,
but today is considered mostly symbolic.

Shippei

Bamboo staff used as a ritual implement by **Zen** masters. The shippei is
made from a split piece of bamboo,
which is bound with wisteria vine and
then lacquered. It is bent like a bow
and measures approximately sixty to
one hundred centimeters in length.
Chinese Zen masters would use the
shippei to strike students as a teaching
device. It is now used primarily as a
symbol of the Zen master's authority.

Shiroku Benreitai

See **shiroku no bunshô**.

Shiroku No Bunshô

A Chinese style of composition dating to
the Southern and Northern dynasties
(5th–6th c.) with alternating lines of four
and six characters. It is known formally
in Japanese as Shiroku benreitai. The
style was used by **Zen** masters in both
China and Japan.

Shiryôken

The **four discernments** (C. ssu-liao-
chien), a teaching device used by the
Chinese master **Lin-chi I-hsuan**, founder
of the **Rinzai sect** of **Buddhism**. The four
viewpoints are: 1) datsunin fudakkyô, the
negation of subject and the affirmation of
object; 2) dakkyô fudatsunin, the negation of object and the affirmation of subject; 3) ninkyô ryôgudatsu, the negation
of both subject and object; and 4) ninkyô
gufudatsu, the affirmation of both subject
and object. See **four discernments**.

Shishiku

"Lion's roar," the Japanese translation
of the Sanskrit expression *simha nada*.
See **lion's roar**.

Shishô

The four manners of birth: from
a womb, from an egg, from moisture,
and from metamorphosis. See **four
kinds of birth**.

Shisho

Succession certificate, a document presented to a **Zen** disciple by his or her master to certify transmission of the **Dharma**. Documents of succession typically include a listing of the **lineage** of the newly certified teacher, providing the names of founding **patriarchs** and more recent descendants, down to the master and new **Dharma heir**. In some cases, shiso may trace the lineage back to **Bodhidharma** or Shakyamuni **buddha** (**Siddharta Gautama**). In practical terms, the shiso certifies that the recipient is qualified to train students and to serve as **abbot** or head **monk** at a Zen temple or monastery. Shiso is also the title of one essay in **Dôgen Kigen's** (1200–1253) *Shôbôgenzô*.

Shishu Hokkai

"**Four realms of reality**," the Japanese name for the **Hua-yen school** concept that describes reality using four levels of existence or **Dharma** realms. In Japanese, the four realms are: 1) jihokkai, the realm of phenomena; 2) rihokkai, the realm of reality; 3) rijimuge hokkai, the realm of interpenetration of phenomena and reality; and 4) jijimuge hokkai, the realm of interpenetration of phenomena and phenomena. The school is also known as Shihokkai. See **four realms of reality**.

Shisô

Four aspects of phenomenal existence. Buddhist thought includes several such listings of aspects of existence. Shisô may refer to birth (J. shô), old age (J. rô), sickness (J. byô), and death (J. shi)—the basic kinds of **suffering** endured by all living beings. It may refer to four phases of change that characterize everything that exists: coming into existence or birth (J. shô), continuing (J. jû), changing (J. i), and passing out of existence or death (J. metsu). Shisô may also refer to four erroneous views of the self mentioned in the **Diamond Sutra**: existence of a real self (J. **gasô**), an individual self (J. ninsô), a sentient soul (J. jushasô), and an eternal soul (J. shujôsô).

Shissui

The labor steward at a **Zen** monastery, one of the six administrative offices of the monastic community. The shissui position is held by a senior **monk** responsible for organizing **manual labor** crews and assigning specific tasks. He oversees all construction, maintenance, and repair of temple buildings (J. **shichidô garan**); all large-scale cleaning operations; and all field work related to planting and harvesting crops. In most cases, the shissui manages labor done by lay workers, attendants, and **novices**. When a project is more labor intensive, such as planting or harvesting crops, the shissui may call upon the entire monastic community to participate in the project. The post generally rotates on a yearly basis. See also **lay believer** and **temple positions**.

Shitennô

Japanese for the **four guardian kings**. See **four guardian kings**.

Shiza

Dead sitting, a derogatory expression used to describe incorrect or ineffective forms of seated **meditation**. See **dead sitting**.

Shôbôgenzô

The Treasury of the Eye of the True **Dharma**, a **Zen** expression for the essential truth of **Buddhism**. According to traditional Zen accounts of the first transmission of the Dharma from Shakyamuni **buddha** (**Siddharta Gautama**) to his disciple **Mahakashyapa**, such as found in the sixth case of the *Mumonkan*, the Buddha declared that he possessed the Shôbôgenzô and that he entrusted it to Mahakashyapa. *Shôbôgenzô* is also the title that **Dôgen Kigen** (1200–1253), founder of the **Sôtô sect** of Zen in Japan, chose for his magnum opus (greatest written work).

Shôbôgenzô

(2) Treasury of the True **Dharma Eye**, the master work of **Dôgen Kigen** (1200–1253), the founder of the **Sôtô sect** in Japan. The text is comprised of ninety-five separate essays (ninety-two in some editions), composed over a period of twenty-two years, from 1231 to 1253. Dôgen wrote the essays in Japanese, a departure from the norm at the time, which was using classical Chinese for writings on **Buddhism**. Dôgen intended the work to eventually include 100 essays, but he died before completing the project. In addition to the Japanese language text, Dôgen compiled a second text in Chinese, also called the *Shôbôgenzô*. The latter text's full title is *Shôbôgenzô Sambyakusoku*, and it is a set of three hundred **kôan** that Dôgen collected while he was in China.

There are several partial translations of the *Shôbôgenzô* in English, including *How to Raise an Ox* (Center Publications, 1978) and *Sounds of Valley Streams* (State University of New York, 1989), both by Francis Cook; *Zen Master Dôgen*, by Yûhô Yôkoi (Weatherhill, 1976); and *Moon in a Dewdrop* by Kazuaki Tanahashi (North Point Press, 1985). A complete translation in several volumes has been published under the title *Master Dôgen's* Shôbôgenzô by Gudo Waju Nishijima and Chodo Cross (Windbell Publications, 1994).

A second text, written by the Chinese Rinzai master **Ta-hui Tsung-kao** (1089–1163), also bears the *Shôbôgenzô* name in Japanese. Its Chinese title is ***Cheng-fa Yen-tsang***.

Shôbôgenzô Benchû

A commentary on **Dôgen Kigen's** *Shôbôgenzô* in twenty-two parts, written by the Tokugawa **monk Tenkei Denson** (1647–1735). The Benchû was the first line-by-line commentary on the *Shôbôgenzô*. Tenkei rejected some of the original chapters and made substantial changes to several others. He criticized Dôgen's ungrammatical reading of Chinese passages in many places and disagreed with Dôgen on many substantive issues. He rejected, for example, Dôgen's tendency to criticize great **Zen** masters of the past. Tenkei worked on the study for a period of about four years, from 1726 to 1729, but it was not published until 1881.

Shôbôgenzô Zuimonki

A collection of **Dôgen Kigen's Dharma** talks and instructions given to his disciples. The material was recorded and edited by Dôgen's leading disciple, Koun Ejô (1198–1280). Dôgen gave the talks between 1235 and 1237 while he was still at **Kôshô-ji** in the Kyoto area. The *Zuimonki*, as it is often abbreviated, is extremely popular in the **Sôtô sect** because of its easy literary style. It represents the earliest Japanese example of the **Zen** genre known as "**recorded sayings**" (J. goroku), first developed in China. Ejô recorded Dôgen's talks in Japanese, but he did not translate them into formal Chinese, as was the norm in Japan. Instead, he left the text in colloquial Japanese. The text was first printed in 1651, and the scholar **monk Menzan Zuihô** (1683–1769) published an improved edition in 1769. Matsunaga Reihô published an English translation under the title *A Primer of Sôtô Zen*.

Matsunaga, Reihô, trans. *A Primer of Sôtô Zen: A Translation of Dôgen's* Shôbôgenzô Zuimonki. London: Routledge and K. Paul, 1972.

Shodô

"The Way of Writing," a Japanese term for the art of **calligraphy**. It is also known as Shojutsu. See **calligraphy**.

Shôdô

"Holy path," or the **steep path**, an expression used for those forms of **Buddhism**, especially **Zen**, which encourage personal striving toward **enlightenment** through the practices of **meditation** and observance of **precepts**. See **steep path**.

The Japanese shôgun or military general acts as the head of state.

Shôeki

Private instruction with the **Zen** master in the **abbot's** quarters. The term literally means "asking for instruction." It is another expression for nisshitsu or **nyusshitsu**. See **nyusshitsu**.

Shôgen Sûgaku

The Japanese pronunciation for **Sung-yüan Chung-yueh** (1132–1202), a Chinese Rinzai master. See **Sung-yüan Chung-yueh**.

Shogo Kôten

The sounding of a wooden gong (J. **han**) to announce the twenty-five divisions of the night, from sunset to daybreak. This was traditionally done throughout the night in **Zen** monasteries.

Shôgun

A military general or commander; most often used as a shortened form of Seii-Tai-Shôgun, a title conferred by the Japanese imperial court on a military leader who serves as the acting head of state. Seii-Tai-Shôgun literally means the "General who quells **barbarians**," reflecting its origins. In the eighth century, the title was bestowed by the reigning emperor upon military leaders who fought for the imperial court against the indigenous Ainu people. Later, the title was borne by military dictators who only theoretically wielded power delegated to them by the emperor, since during the Kamakura (1185–1333), Ashikaga (1392–1568), and Tokugawa (1600–1867) periods, Japanese emperors were largely figureheads. The shôguns ruled through authority based on their own military power. They possessed the title for life and passed it on to hereditary successors, creating dynastic governments called **bakufu**, or shogunates. Many shôgun maintained strong relations with **Zen Buddhism** as lay sponsors and, in a few rare cases, as lay practitioners. See also **lay believer**.

Shôhô

The True **Dharma**, in Japanese; the first of the **Three Ages of the Dharma** that follow the death of the historical **Buddha**. During the Age of True Dharma, the Buddha's teachings remain intact, as perfect as they were during his lifetime. Throughout the age, Buddhists continue to practice and follow the **Buddhist path**, and some individuals attain **enlightenment**. According to some versions of the theory of the Three Ages, including those most popularly accepted in China, the first age lasts for 500 years. Other interpretations, including the most prevalent in Japanese **Buddhism**, set the time span at 1,000 years.

Shôichi Ha

A Japanese Rinzai **lineage** founded by **Enni Ben'en** (1202–1280), which was closely associated with the **Tôfuku-ji** monastery in Kyoto. The lineage was one of the dominant lineages within the **Gozan system** of Rinzai **Zen**. The name of the lineage derives from Shôichi **Kokushi** (National Teacher Sagely Unity), the posthumous title bestowed on Ben'en by the **Emperor Hanazono** (1297–1348). See also **Rinzai sect**.

Shôjô

"Lesser Path" or "Small Path," the Japanese translation for Hinayana. See **Hinayana Buddhism**.

Shôju Dôkyô Etan Anju Anroku

"The Biography of Hermitage Master Shôju Dôkyô Etan," composed by **Tôrei Enji**. The short text is a biography of Dôkyô Etan, known more popularly as

Shôju Rôjin. Dôkyô was a **Dharma heir** of **Shidô Bu'nan** (1603–1676) and is regarded as the most important **Zen** teacher for **Hakuin Ekaku** (1685–1768). See also **Dôkyô Etan**.

Shôjurin Shingi

A study of Sôtô and other **Zen monastic codes** prepared by **Manzan Dôhaku**, the Tokugawa period (1600–1867) reformer, between 1680 and 1691. Manzen based his work on traditional **Sôtô sect** codes, including the *Eihei Shingi* attributed to **Dôgen Kigen** (1200–1253), and the *Keizan Shingi*, attributed to **Keizan Jôkin** (1268–1325). He also made use of codes from the Tokugawa period, such as the *Undo Jôki*, composed by his master Gesshû, and the *Obaku Shingi* of the **Obaku sect**.

Shôju Rôjin

"The Old Man of Shôju Hermitage," a nickname for **Dôkyô Etan** (1642–1721). See **Dôkyô Etan**.

Shojutsu

"The art of writing," a Japanese term for the art of **calligraphy**. It is also known as shodô. See **calligraphy**.

Shokan

First barrier, the first of three sets of **kôan** used by some **Zen** monasteries in medieval Japan (1185–1600), which were known as the first, second (J. **ryôkan**), and third barriers (J. **sankan**). The first shokan were derived from the *Hekiganroku* (*Blue Cliff Record*), the second from the *Sayings of Lin-chi*, and the third from *Mumonkan*.

Shôkei

A percussion instrument used in **Zen** temples to accompany **chanting** during Buddhist services. The shôkei is a much smaller version of the **keisu**, without a separate wooden stand. Like the keisu, the shôkei is cast in bronze and shaped like a **begging bowl**. It rests on a small cushion and is played by striking the rim with a wooden stick. Unlike the larger keisu, which is played throughout sutra chanting, the shôkei is used to signal specific transitions during the service. For example, it signals the end of sutra chanting and marks the transition to circumambulating inside the **Buddha** hall during a service. Also called rin or rei. See also **reitaku**.

Shôken

(J. **dokusan**) A **Zen** practitioner's first interview with the Zen master, at which time he or she is officially accepted as a disciple. The shôken occurs after the student has passed an initial probationary period in the temple, known as the **tanga zume**. At the shôken, the disciple formally meets with the master, requests guidance, and, traditionally, makes a small monetary donation, or "**incense money**," to establish the master-disciple relationship. If the master finds the student's request sincere, the individual will be formally accepted as a disciple.

Shoki

A clerical officer or scribe, one of the six prefects (J. chôshu) of a **Zen** monastery. The prefects, known collectively as the Western rank (J. **seihan**), aid the **abbot** in managing the spiritual direction of the monastic community. The scribe's duties include the preparation of all official monastic documents and correspondence. For this reason, the scribe needs familiarity with Zen documentary styles and a good hand at **calligraphy**. Traditionally, the shoki handled both internal and external correspondence, but today the post is generally divided between two individuals. The shoki handles formal documents and external matters, while one of the **jisha** serving the abbot handles informal and internal matters.

Shôkoku-ji

A major **Rinzai sect** temple located in Kyoto. Its formal name is Mannen-zan

Shôkoku-ji. Ashikaga Yoshimitsu (1358–1408), the third Ashikaga **shôgun**, built the temple in 1382 as a symbol of his power. **Musô Sôseki** (1275–1351) was posthumously named the founding **abbot**. Although originally conceived as a branch of **Tenryû-ji**, it later became independent and was ranked as one of the Five Mountains, or **Gozan temples** of Kyoto. It was completely destroyed during the Onin War (1466–1477) and later restored. It now serves as the headquarters for the Shôkoku-ji branch of Rinzai **Zen**.

Shôkoku-ji Ha

The **Shôkoku-ji** branch of Rinzai, one of the fourteen contemporary branches of the Japanese **Rinzai sect**. The main monastery for the branch is the Shôkoku-ji temple, located in Kyoto. **Musô Sôseki** (1275–1351) is regarded as the branch founder. The branch has 119 temples throughout Japan and claims approximately 53,750 adherents.

Shômon

"Voices hearers," the Japanese translation for the Sanskrit term *shravaka*. Shômon refers to the immediate disciples of the historical **Buddha** who had the opportunity to hear the Buddha preach firsthand. The **Mahayana Buddhism** tradition also uses the term for those individuals who study the Buddha's teachings and contemplate them in an attempt to attain **enlightenment** for themselves, in contrast to bosatsu (Sk. **bodhisattvas**), who strive to aid others as well as themselves. See **shravaka**.

Shômyô

To chant verses from the **sutras**. The term originally referred to one of five traditional forms of linguistic study in India, *sabda-vidya* in Sanskrit. In East Asian **Buddhism**, it came to refer to a melodic style of ritual **chanting** set to music. Shômyô is usually performed by **monks** in front of an image of the

Buddha. The chanting style is also known in Japanese as **bonbai**. Shômyô was first introduced to Japan in the ninth century by the **monk Ennin** (793–864), who learned the practice in China. It became popular in the esoteric schools of Japanese Buddhism, the **Shingon sect**, and the **Tendai sect**. Shômyô styles also exist in Japanese **Zen**.

Matsunaga, Daigan, and Alicia Matsunaga. *Foundation of Japanese Buddhism*. 2 vols. Los Angeles, CA: Buddhist Books International, 1976.

Shonan

The first seventh day service, a **memorial service** held seven days after death, according to Japanese Buddhist custom. The shonan is the first of seven memorial services, which are held at seven-day intervals throughout the primary period of mourning (J. **chûin**) following a death. For lay Buddhists, the shonan is traditionally the occasion on which the deceased receives a posthumous Buddhist name (J. **kaimyô**) from the family temple. It includes an **ordination** ceremony, in which the presiding **monk** symbolically confers the **precepts** on the deceased. See also **lay believer**.

Shôrin-ji

Shao-lin-ssu, the Chinese Buddhist monastery on Mount Sung. See **Shao-lin-ssu**.

Shôrô

The bell tower that houses the **ogane**, the largest temple bell. Shôrô are open structures of support beams covered by a tile roof. The ogane hangs under the roof, with a swinging beam (J. **shumoku**) hanging horizontally beside the bell. The bell is sounded by pulling back the beam with the attached guide ropes and allowing it to strike the outside of the bell. The shôrô becomes the focus of the monastic community and the neighboring lay members on New

Year's Eve when, just before midnight, a service is held beside the shôrô and the ogane is struck 108 times, one for each of the 108 human failings. Each sounding of the bell symbolically expels the previous year's failures in preparation for the new year. See also **lay believer**.

Shôsan

"Small assembly," informal instruction given by the **Zen** master to a small number of disciples in the **abbot's** quarters. The shôsan are distinguished from the **daisan**, the large formal assemblies which include all resident **monks** or **nuns**.

Shôshitsu Rokumon

A collection of six **Zen** essays, all of which are traditionally attributed to **Bodhidharma** (T. 48, no. 2009). The word *Shôshitsu* (C. Shao-shih) refers to the hermitage on Mount Sung where Bodhidharma practiced **meditation**, and it is often used as another name for Bodhidharma. The title therefore can be translated as "The Six Gates of Bodhidharma." Scholars believe that the six texts are later compositions, probably written during the T'ang dynasty (618–907). They were originally written as independent texts and later collected under a single title. Exactly when the collection was put together is unknown, but the oldest extant copy is a Japanese edition published in 1647.

The first essay is written in verse and called the Hsin-ching Sung (J. Shingyô Ju), or "Verses on the **Heart Sutra**." The other five are prose texts, entitled P'o-hsiang Lun (J. Hasô Ron), "On Breaking Through Form"; Erh-chung-ju (J. Nishu'nyû), "Two Ways of Entrance"; An-hsin fa-mên (J. Anjin Hômon), "The Gate of Peaceful Mind"; Wu-hsing lun (J. Goshô Ron), "On Awakened Nature"; and *Hsüeh-mo lun* (J. Ketsumyaku Ron), "On the Blood **Lineage**." Three of the six essays are translated into English in Red Pine's *Zen Teaching of Bodhidharma*.

The shôrô is the tower that houses the ogane, or temple bell, and is the site of a special New Year's Eve bell-ringing ceremony.

Shôsô

An image of a **buddha** or **bodhisattva** enshrined in the middle of the **meditation hall**, the monks' hall (J. **sôdô**), and other buildings in a **Zen** monastery. The term literally means "holy monk" in Japanese. The practice of enshrining holy monks seems to have originated in China. By the early T'ang period (618–907), images of the **arhat Pindola** were commonly enshrined in the dining hall at Buddhist temples. Today, the figure most often enshrined in the meditation hall is the bodhisattva Manjusri (J. **Monju**). Other images, such as **Mahakashyapa**, Pindola, and **Subhuti** are sometimes also used. In the **shuryô**, or reading room, **Kannon** usually serves as the shôsô.

Shôsô Jisha

The formal name for the attendant **monk** (J. **jisha**) assigned to care for the **shôsô** ("holy monk"), the image of a **buddha** or **bodhisattva** enshrined in the monks' hall (J. **sôdô**) or **meditation hall**.

Shôtoku Taishi

(574–622) Prince Shôtoku, a Japanese imperial regent of the Asuka period who is regarded as the founder of **Buddhism** in Japan. Shôtoku was the second son of Emperor Yômei. He served as regent from the age of nineteen, during the reign of his aunt, Empress Suiko. Shôtoku is said to have written and promulgated the Seventeen Article Constitution (Jûshichijô Kempô), a statement about good government that mentions Buddhist principles as one basis for political and social life, although the actual authorship of the Constitution remains in doubt among scholars. He is also known as a Buddhist scholar in his own right and as a patron of the Buddhist clergy. Tradition credits Shôtoku with writing three commentaries on Buddhist **sutras** (the **Lotus Sutra**, the **Shrimala Sutra**, and the **Vimalakirti Sutra**), the first Buddhist texts composed in Japan. He is also known for sponsoring the construction of seven major Buddhist temples, including Shitennô-ji in Osaka and Hôryû-ji near Nara. After his death, Shôtoku was regarded as an incarnation of the **bodhisattva Kannon**, and he is often portrayed accordingly in iconography.

Shouting

Zen masters, especially in the Rinzai school, characteristically make use of powerful, sudden shouts as an expression for a state of perception beyond analytical thought. The shout was first used as a teaching device by the Chinese T'ang dynasty master **Ma-tsu Tao-i** (709–788) but is most closely associated with **Lin-chi I-hsuan**, founder of the Rinzai school. Zen masters may use a loud shout to push a disciple beyond the web of discursive and analytical thought. In other cases, a disciple may respond to the master with a shout to indicate comprehension that goes beyond words. See **katsu!**

Shôyôroku

The Japanese title for the *T'sung-jung Lu*, a collection of one hundred classical Zen **kôan** with prose commentary and verses. It was first published in 1224 (T. 48, no. 2004) under the long title *Wang-sung Lao-jên P'ing-ch'ang T'ien-t'ung Chüeh Ho-shang Sung-ku Ts'ung-jung-an Lu*. The text consists of a series of **sermons** on classical kôan and related verses given by the Chinese **Sôtô sect** master Wang-sung Hang-hsiu (1166–1246; J. Banshô Gyôshû). Wang-sung based his commentaries on the *Sung-ku Po-tsê* (J. *Juko Hyakusoku*), an earlier collection of one hundred kôan compiled by **Hung-chih Cheng-chüeh** (1091–1157; J. Wanshi Shôgaku), a Chinese Sôtô master from the same **lineage**. The abbreviated title means "The record of the [hermitage of] serenity," referring to the hermitage where Wang-sung gave his lectures.

The *Shôyôroku* represents Wang-sung's second lecture series on the *Sung-ku Po-tsê*. He gave the first series early in his teaching career, but the manuscript of those sermons was lost during the confusion of the Mongol invasion. Later in his life, his disciples requested that he give his commentary a second time. They recorded his sermons and published the text. For each kôan case, the *Shôyôroku* includes five parts: Wang-sung's introduction, the original kôan, Wang-sung's prose commentary on the case, Hung-chih's verse, and Wang-sung's commentary on the verse.

Although Sôtô Zen may not focus on kôan practice as intently as Rinzai, the *Shôyôroku* holds an important place within the Sôtô tradition. It is often said that it enjoys a high status in the Sôtô school, comparable to that of the **Hekiganroku** in the Rinzai school. Indeed, Wang-sung, who gave his lectures a hundred years after the publication of the *Hekiganroku*, styled his own work on its general format. In terms of the cases included, the *Shôyôroku* shows significant overlap with both the *Hekiganroku* and the **Mumonkan**. These three are the classic collections of Zen kôan. Thomas Cleary published a full translation of the text in English under the title *The Book of Serenity*. See also **Rinzai sect**.

Cleary, Thomas. *The Book of Serenity*. Boston, MA: Shambhala, 1998.

Shozan

"Various mountains," the designation for the lowest rank of temples within the **Gozan system** of Chinese and Japanese **Zen** monasteries. In the original Chinese system, the lowest tier was a group of approximately thirty-five provincial temples known as chia-ch'a, or "major temples." In Japan, the number of shozan temples rose to more than 250 temples throughout the country. Unlike temples in the higher tiers, the shozan were not formally ranked, nor did they receive government funding. They were primarily smaller regional temples, housing no more than forty to fifty **monks**.

Shôzômatsu

The Japanese term for the **Three Ages of the Dharma**, three periods of progressive deterioration in the Buddhist teachings, practice, and attainment of **enlightenment**, which follow the death of the **Buddha**. The first age is **Shôhô**, the Age of the True Dharma; the second is **Zôhô**, the Age of the Semblance Dharma; and the third is Mappô (written with characters read separately as "matsu" and "hô"), the **Latter Age of the Dharma**. See **Three Ages of the Dharma**.

Shramana

An ascetic **monk** or **nun** who strives for **enlightenment**. Shramana (J. shamon) have left the home life and taken on the life of a wandering holy person. They avoid evil and do good, not in the hope of a better **rebirth**, but as a part of their practice to attain release from **samsara**, the ongoing cycle of birth and death. Ascetics practice equanimity; that is, controlling their emotions and reducing their **attachments** to material and spiritual aspects of life. They practice **ahimsa**, or non-injury to other **sentient beings**. The Sanskrit term has been used by both Buddhists and Jains for their monks and nuns.

Shravaka

(J. shômon) Those who hear the teaching of the **Buddha** and attain **enlightenment** by contemplating the **Dharma**. The Sanskrit word literally means "one who hears." It originally applied to the immediate disciples of the historical Buddha who heard him teach directly, and it may still be used in that limited fashion. It may also apply to any individual striving to follow the path forged by the historical Buddha. Shravakas aim at becoming **arhats**, that is, individuals who become enlightened by their own strenuous efforts. To reach that end, shravakas contemplate on the **four noble truths** and practice the **Eightfold Path**. In Mahayana teaching, shravakas are one of the **two vehicles** of the Hinayana tradition, which are contrasted with the **one vehicle** of the Mahayana tradition. Since shravakas are said to strive only for themselves, they are regarded as inferior to **bodhisattvas**. See also **three vehicles**.

Shrimala Sutra

Short name for the Shrimaladevi Shimhanada **Sutra**, the sutra of the **lion's roar** of Queen Shrimala, a Mahayana sutra comprised of one section (T. 12, no. 353). The sutra presents itself as the teachings of Queen Shrimala, a lay Buddhist. The text teaches about the **Tathagata Garbha** theory, concerning the potential inherent in each sentient being to attain **buddhahood**. See also **lay believer**.

Shu

Assembly, the entire community living in a Buddhist monastery; sometimes used as an alternative Japanese translation for **sangha**. See **sangha**.

Shû

Japanese term which may be translated as school, sect, denomination, or **lineage**, depending on the context. Shû is typically appended to the name of a religious institution, such as Rinzai-shû (**Rinzai sect**) or Sôtô-shû. See **lineage**.

Shugendô

A form of Japanese religious ascetic practice that draws upon Buddhist and Shintô teachings. Practitioners, known as **Yamabushi**, undertake austerities in the mountains in order to accumulate mystical powers. The legendary mountain ascetic En-no-Gyôja, also known as En-no-Ozunu, is regarded as the founder. Shugendô first emerged as an organized tradition during the Heian period (794–1185). Throughout its history, the movement has been closely associated with the **Tendai sect** and **Shingon sect** of **esoteric Buddhism**.

Shûhô Myôchô

(1282–1337) A Japanese Rinzai **monk** of the Kamakura period (1185–1333), better known by his honorific title Daitô Kokushi. Myôchô is regarded as one of the founders of the **Otôkan school** which became one of the most important in the development of Japanese Rinzai **Zen**. He was born in Harima province (modern day Hyôgo Prefecture) near Osaka. At age ten, he entered Buddhist orders at a Tendai temple. In 1301, he traveled to Kamakura where he became a disciple of Kôhô Kennichi (1241–1316) at **Manju-ji**. He later became the disciple of **Nampô Jômyô** (1235–1309), whom he had followed to Kamakura. He received **inka**, or the transfer of Dharma, from Nampô at the early age of twenty-five. After Nampô's death, Myôchô returned to Kyoto where he established a small hermitage and gathered disciples. With imperial patronage, the hermitage was eventually expanded to a full monastery and named **Daitoku-ji**. His most important **Dharma heirs** were **Kanzan Egen** and **Tettô Gikô** (1295–1369). Myôchô received several imperial honors, including the honorific title Kôzen Daitô Kokushi (National Teacher Great Lamp That Propogates Zen) from **Emperor Hanazono** (1297–1348), bestowed during the master's lifetime, and the title Daijun Kyôshin **Kokushi** from **Emperor Go-Daigo** (1287–1339), conferred posthumously. The monastery, Daitoku-ji, and Myôchô's lineage through Kanzan Egen produced one of the most influential Rinzai lines in Japan. See also **Rinzai sect** and **Tendai sect**.

Shujô

Walking staff used by **Zen monks** and **nuns** when traveling on **pilgrimages**. See **walking staff**.

Shukke

To leave the home life; a Japanese expression for the process of becoming a member of the Buddhist monastic community. When a lay person (J. **koji**) is ordained as a **monk** or **nun**, the individual leaves behind the ordinary life and responsibilities of the **householder** and accepts the **precepts** of monastic life. See also **ordination**.

Shuku

Rice gruel, one of the main dietary staples at traditional **Zen** temples and monasteries. According to Buddhist **monastic codes**, **monks** and **nuns** are technically allowed only one full meal each day, generally eaten at the noon hour. In East Asian monasteries, rice gruel has long been used as a supplement to maintain bodily strength and alleviate unnecessary discomfort. Shuku is served to resident monks or nuns in the morning and again in the evening. Rice gruel preserves the simple lifestyle appropriate to the monastic life and represents a frugal use of temple resources. It is also said to have many medicinal benefits. Since shuku is served for breakfast, the term sometimes is used synonymously with breakfast. Shuku is the more formal term; it is more commonly called kayu or okayu. The ten benefits one receives from eating shuku are called **shukuyûjûri**.

Shukuha Fugin

Sutra **chanting** which is performed after the morning meal.

Shukushin

Prayer services held regularly on the first and fifteenth day of each month at **Zen** monasteries for the health and well-being of the secular authorities. On these occasions, the **abbot** ascends the high seat in the main hall and addresses the assembly, giving a sermon on the **Dharma**. He also burns **incense** and prays for the health of the emperor and prosperity for the nation.

Shukuyûjûri

The ten benefits associated with eating **shuku**, or rice gruel. According to a traditional **Zen** verse, rice gruel improves

Shuku, or rice gruel, is a dietary staple of Buddhist monks and nuns.

one's complexion, builds stamina, promotes longevity, provides comfort, purifies one's speech, is easily digested, does not cause gas, alleviates hunger, alleviates thirst, and is simple to prepare.

Shumidan

The raised platform in the **buddha** hall or **Dharma** hall on which the image of the Buddha is enshrined. The term literally means "platform of **Mount Sumeru**" and symbolizes the center of the cosmos.

Shumisen

Mount Sumeru, in Japanese. Often abbreviated as Shumi or Misen. See **Mount Sumeru**.

Shûmitsu

Japanese rendering of **Tsung-mi** (780–840), a Chinese Buddhist **monk**. See **Tsung-mi**.

Shumoku

A large wooden beam used to sound the large monastery bell, the **ogane**. The beam hangs, suspended horizontally with ropes, beside the bell. To sound the bell, the shumoku is drawn back, often with guide ropes, and brought forward to strike the side of the bell. The term may also be used for smaller wooden mallets used to strike smaller temple bells and gongs.

Shûmon Kattôshû

A **Zen kôan** collection in two sections, compiled in Japan during the Tokugawa period (1600–1867). The compiler and date of first publication are unknown. The text includes 272 kôan, primarily from classical Chinese Zen sources. A few are of Japanese origin. The work remains a basic resource within the Japanese **Rinzai sect** today.

Shûmon Mujintô Ron

"On the Eternal Lamp of **Zen**," a text in two sections (T. 81, 581a–605b) composed by **Tôrei Enji** under the pen name Fufu-an. The preface is dated 1751 by the author, but the text was first published in 1800. Tôrei wrote the text while he was living in Kyoto, where he undertook an intense period of solitary **meditation** after his initial **enlightenment** experience. As a result of his severe discipline he became ill, contracting tuberculosis. Told that his condition was terminal and that he would not live long, Tôrei wrote in the preface that he regretted being unable to lead others to enlightenment. He therefore decided to record the basic teachings of Zen **Buddhism** as they were taught to him by **Hakuin Ekaku** (1685–1768). The text is divided into ten sections that describe the progressive system of Zen practice designed by Hakuin. The text became highly influential in the **Rinzai sect**, which continues to use it as an introduction to Hakuin Zen.

Shûmon Rentô Eyô
Japanese title for "The T'ien-sheng Record of the Widely Extending Lamp," (C. *Tsung-men Lien-teng Hui-yao*). See *Tsung-men Lien-teng Hui-yao*.

Shun'ô Reizan
(d. 1399) Japanese Rinzai **monk** of the late Kamakura period (1185–1333). He was the **Dharma heir** of **Bassui Tokushô** (1327–1387). He worked in the Kantô area and founded Kôon-ji in Hachioji, near present day Tokyo. He is best known for publishing the authoritative Japanese edition of the *Wu-men Kuan* (J. *Mumonkan*) in 1405. See also **Rinzai sect**.

Shunyata
"**Emptiness**," the fundamental Mahayana Buddhist concept regarding ultimate reality and one of the definitive concepts within Mahayana thought. The Sanskrit term is also rendered "Void" or "Nothingness." Shunyata asserts that all phenomena, including **sentient beings**, inanimate objects, and ideas, are empty of self-nature. This teaching denies as false the ordinary perception that things in the phenomenal world possess an independent existence that is unchanging and eternal. The teaching is based on the realization of Dependent Coorigination; that all phenomena are relative and dependent on causation. To say that all things are empty means that they are interdependent, arise out of causal factors, and are continually susceptible to change. See **emptiness**.

Shuramgama Dharani
A **dharani**, or spell, derived from the seventh section of the **Shuramgama Sutra**. One of the most commonly used dharani in the **Zen** school, it often appears as a part of rituals, including **memorial services** and funerals. The dharani may be used to exorcise evil spirits and ward off calamities and is therefore sometimes used to pray for rain, for recovery from serious illness, and the like. It is known in Japanese as the Ryôgon-ju or the Daibutchô-ju, alternate abbreviations for Daibutchô mangyô shuryôgon darani.

Shuramgama Sutra
Heroic Valour Sutra, a title shared by two distinct Mahayana **sutras**. The earlier text, more properly known as the Shuramgama **Samadhi** Sutra (T. 15, no. 642), is a work in two sections that describes a form of **meditation** known as shuramgama samadhi. This text was translated into Chinese by **Kumarajiva**. The later sutra, a text of ten sections (T. 19, no. 945), is an apocryphal scripture originally composed in Chinese. It is a discourse on the workings of the mind and includes some description of esoteric practices. The latter Shuramgama Sutra was widely influential in the **Zen** school.

Shuryô
The Reading Room in a **Zen** monastery where **monks** study and have tea after meals. The word *shuryô* literally means

"monks' quarters," but the hall is not used for sleeping or meditating. It typically has an image of **Kannon** enshrined in the center as the **shôsô**, and desks are arranged around the perimeter of the hall on raised **tatami** platforms for reading and study. **Dôgen Kigen** (1200–1253) composed a brief set of regulations for conduct in the shuryô, called the *Kisshôzan Eiheiji Shuryô Shingi.*

Shohei, Ichimura. *Zen Master Eihei Dôgen's Monastic Regulations* Washington, DC: North American Institute of Zen and Buddhist Studies, 1993.

Shuryôgon-gyô

Japanese title for the **Shuramgama Sutra** (T. 19, no. 945), often abbreviated to Ryôgon-gyô. The full Japanese title is Daibutchô Nyorai Mitsuin Shushô Ryôgi Shobosatsu Mangyô Shuryôgon-Gyô. See **Shuramgama Sutra**.

Shuso

"Chief Seat," the highest ranking officer in a **Zen** temple after the **abbot**. The shuso is one of six monastic officers, or prefects (J. chôshu), known collectively as the Western rank (J. **seihan**). Together, the prefects assist the abbot in managing the spiritual direction of the monastic community. However, the shuso directs all activities within the monks' hall (J. **sôdô**) and **meditation hall**. He is entrusted with guiding the meditation practice of the other resident **monks**. Thus, to be qualified for appointment as shuso, a monk must have many years of experience in the practice of Zen meditation, usually more than ten years.

The word *shuso* literally means "head seat" or "chief seat," a reference to the shuso's place beside the abbot on the meditation platform. There are several other terms used for the same office, including daiichiza, jôza, shushu, rissô, zagen, and zentô.

Shussan

A daily ritual performed at mealtime in **Zen** temples for the sake of **hungry ghosts** (J. **gaki**). Before eating, each **monk** or **nun** sets aside a few grains of rice or a small amount of another food item (J. **saba**) as an offering to the hungry ghosts who suffer perpetual hunger. The offering is accompanied by a brief verse. According to Ichimura Shohei in his translation of **Dôgen Kigen's monastic code**, monks at **Eihei-ji** today chant the verse, "Oh, host of hungry ghosts, Now I make an offering of food for you. This food is offered widely in all ten regions, For all those of ghost spirits." (Shohei, p. 120).

Shohei, Ichimura. *Zen Master Eihei Dôgen's Monastic Regulations* Washington, DC: North American Institute of Zen and Buddhist Studies, 1993.

Shutara

A Japanese transliteration of sutra. See **sutra**.

Shûtô Fukkô

Restoration of the **lineage** system, a reform movement within the Japanese **Sôtô sect** during the Tokugawa period (1600–1867) to restore **Dôgen Kigen's** original system of **Dharma** succession. In the centuries before the Tokugawa period, it became common practice for Sôtô **monks** to accept Dharma seals (J. **inkas**) from several masters, often switching lineages when they changed temple residence. The seventeenth century Sôtô reformer **Manzan Dôhaku** objected to the practice and argued strenuously for a return to **isshi inshô**. Manzan and **Baiyû jikushin** (1633–1707) petitioned the Japanese government to mandate the restoration of isshi inshô. In 1703, their petition was accepted and Dharma succession in Sôtô temples was regularized.

Shuya

Nightly fire watch, traditionally performed after sunset and again at bedtime each night at **Zen** monasteries. The person responsible for acting as watchman walks around the temple grounds, beating wooden clappers and **chanting** a special **dharani** to ward off fire and other calamities.

Siddharta Gautama

Indian religious teacher who became known as the **Buddha**, regarded as the founder of **Buddhism**. Siddharta Gautama was born around 586 B.C.E. in a small kingdom in the northwestern region of the Indian subcontinent, in what is now Nepal. Little has been established about his life with historical certainty, but traditional biographies abound. The most important traditional account of the Buddha's life is the *Buddhacharita*, a text written several centuries after his death. What follows is a summary of traditional accounts of his life.

Tradition maintains that Siddharta was born the son and heir of **Suddhodana**, the king of **Kapilavastu** of the **Shakya clan**. His mother, Maya, conceived the child when she saw a white elephant enter her body during a dream. When the time for her delivery approached, she traveled home to her own people. She gave birth to Siddharta in a grove called Lumbini; the child emerged miraculously from her side without causing his mother any pain. The child immediately took seven steps and declared that this was to be his final birth. Within a few days, Maya passed away, and Siddharta was raised by his maternal aunt **Prajapati**.

Ashita, a seer and interpreter of signs, visited the newborn and informed Suddhodana that his son was destined to renounce the world and become a great religious teacher. The father was determined to protect the child from any awareness of **suffering** and by doing so steer him away from a religious quest. Siddharta grew up within the protective confines of the court. When he came of age, he married a woman named **Yashodhara**, who bore him a son named **Rahula**. At about this time, Siddharta decided to leave the court and travel out into the city to experience something of the world. His father, concerned that Siddharta would be distressed by evidence of poverty and disease among the populace, cleared the streets of the old, the poor, and the infirm. Siddharta ventured out with his charioteer four times, and on each occasion encountered a part of life his father had hoped to conceal. On the first venture, Siddharta saw an old person and learned that all human beings age. On the second outing, he met a person riddled with disease and learned that all people suffer illness. Next, he encountered a corpse being carried to the cremation grounds and realized that all who are born will eventually die. Finally, he encountered a wandering mendicant who had forsaken ordinary life to seek release from suffering. The young prince determined to do the same.

At the age of twenty-nine, Siddharta left his home and family to become a homeless wanderer, seeking a solution to the problems of human suffering. He practiced different forms of **meditation** under various teachers, mastering each technique thoroughly but finding that it was not the solution he sought. Deciding that meditation itself is not the goal, Siddharta began to practice asceticism. He joined a group of five ascetics and practiced increasingly severe austerities for several years. Emaciated nearly to the point of physical collapse, Siddharta concluded that asceticism alone is insufficient, and, at age thirty-five, he began to follow a path of his own devising.

First, Siddharta accepted food offered to him by a woman who took him to be the incarnation of a deity. The other mendicants rejected him as a failure in religious practice. Eventually, when he had recovered his strength, Siddharta sat down under a tree to meditate, determined to continue

This scroll depicts the death of Buddha (Siddharta Gautama).
It is located in the Kannon building of the Bukkokuji Zen temple in Japan.

until he reached his goal. First he withstood the temptations and attacks of **Mara**, the god of desire and death, who sensed that Siddharta would soon escape the power of death. Siddharta remained firm and meditated throughout the watches of the night, attaining increasingly higher states of awareness. During the first watch, he became aware of the cycles of his former births. In the second watch, he gained an understanding of the life and death of all **sentient beings** in the universe. During the third watch, he realized the concepts now known as the basic teachings of Buddhism. Finally, as the morning star rose at the end of the fourth watch, Siddharta attained **nirvana**, the state of complete **enlightenment**.

The Buddha, as he now could be called, remained in mediation for seven days. He reflected on the truths he had realized and decided that they would be too difficult for others to grasp. **Indra** and Brahma, two popular Indian deities, visited him and begged him to reconsider. The Buddha then decided to teach others and began a lengthy career as a wandering religious teacher. His first disciples were the five mendicants, who attained enlightenment during his first sermon. He went on to teach several members of his family, including his father, his aunt and foster mother **Prajapati**, who became the first **nun**, and his son Rahula, who became a **monk**.

The Buddha taught for the rest of his life, spending forty-five years wandering throughout the Ganges River region. He gathered hundreds of disciples who formed the basis of the Buddhist order. When he was about eighty years old, the Buddha died. Some accounts say that his death was caused by tainted pork offered to him by a lay disciple. Before his death, he designated no successor to lead the order. Instead, he asked his disciples to continue to live according to his teachings and to "be each his own light." The Buddha instructed his disciples to cremate his corpse and distribute the ashes as **relics** throughout the Buddhist community. See also **lay believer**.

Sila

Morality, ethics, and conduct conducive for progressing toward **enlightenment**. In some cases the term may refer to religious **precepts**, such as those undertaken by Buddhist lay people, **monks**, and **nuns**. In Buddhist contexts, sila (morality, ethics, and conduct) is one part of the **threefold training**; **prajna** (wisdom) and **samadhi** (concentration) are the other two parts. Sila is the first and most basic of the three types of training. In terms of the **Eightfold Path**, sila is associated with right speech, right action, and right livelihood. For lay people, sila implies undertaking the **five precepts** of the laity; for Buddhist monks and nuns, it implies keeping the **ten precepts** of **novices** (and the entire **monastic code** for the fully ordained). In the Mahayana tradition, sila is closely associated with the **six perfections** of the **Bodhisattva** Path. See also **lay believer**.

Silent Illumination Zen

Style of seated **meditation** characteristic of the Sôtô school of **Zen**, which refrains from **kôan** as the focus of meditation. See **mokushô Zen**.

Silver Mountain, Iron Wall

(J. ginzan teppeki) **Zen** expression for **enlightenment**. The mind of enlightenment is compared to a mountain or wall that cannot be climbed by ordinary means, since it cannot be attained through ordinary, discriminating thought. For example, case 57 of the **Hekiganroku** says, "When you have not penetrated it, it stands before you like a silver mountain or an iron wall. When you have penetrated it, you yourself are the silver mountain and iron wall."

Silver Pavilion, Kyoto, Japan.

Silver Pavilion

Ginkaku-ji, the popular name for the Rinzai **Zen** temple Jishô-ji, located in eastern Kyoto in the Higashiyama area. The temple was originally designed and constructed by the eighth Ashikaga **shô-gun** Yoshimasa (1436–1490) as a retirement villa in 1482. It was designed to be a match for the **Golden Pavilion** in northwestern Kyoto, and Yoshimasa's original plans called for the pavilion to be covered in silver leaf, hence the popular name. Yoshimasa never actually completed this portion of the plan because he was unable to raise the necessary funds. The villa was constructed immediately following the devastating Onin War (1466–1477), and the economy had not yet recovered to support such an ambitious project. The villa was converted to a Zen temple after Yoshimasa's death in 1490, and **Musô Sôseki**

(1275–1351) was posthumously named the founding **abbot**. The Golden Pavilion and the Silver Pavilion are regarded as the finest examples of Gozan architecture from the Ashikaga period (1392–1568). See also **Rinzai sect**.

Sin

An action or mental state that alienates a person from God; a theological concept common to several religious traditions in the West, including Judaism, Christianity, and Islam. **Buddhism** does not have any concept directly analogous to Western notions of sin. In particular, Buddhism does not accept the premise that a personal and omnipotent deity determines proper conduct or metes out reward and punishment. Instead, Buddhism teaches the concept of **karma**, which functions as an impersonal law, like the laws of nature.

According to the Buddhist understanding of karma, good actions necessarily produce good effects and evil actions necessarily produce bad effects.

Six Dusts

A common synonym for the six objects of perception (J. rokkyô), which include form (color and shape), sound, odor, taste, texture, and mental objects. They are referred to as the six dusts (J. rokujin) or **defilements** because **attachment** to them defiles the originally pure mind. In the **Platform Sutra**, the Sixth Patriarch says, "The **Dharma** of **no-thought** means: even though you see all things, you do not attach to them . . . Even though you are in the midst of the six dusts, you do not stand apart from them, yet are not stained by them. . ." (Yampolsy, p. 153)

Yampolsky, Philip B. *The Platform Sutra of the Sixth Patriarch*. New York: Columbia University Press, 1967.

Six Gates

(J. rokumon) The **six sense organs**: the eyes, ears, nose, tongue, body, and mind. See **six sense organs**.

Six Paths

(J. rokudô) The six realms of existence into which **sentient beings** caught in the ongoing cycle of **samsara** may be reborn. The realms are arranged hierarchically from best to worst: **heaven** dwellers, **ashuras**, human beings, animals, **hungry ghosts**, and **hell** dwellers. The realms are depicted as existing on different levels of the cosmos. Hell is understood to be an extensive region beneath the earth where sentient beings undergo a variety of punishments. Hell has many regions, descending from cold hells to progressively hotter hells. Hungry ghosts suffer from perpetual and insatiable hunger. They are said to live either on the outskirts of hell or as invisible beings on the periphery of the human world. The earth is the location for the animal and human realms, while ashuras, deities, and other heaven dwellers live in the atmosphere above the earth or in the heavens above that.

Rebirth into one of the six realms is determined by the **karma** accumulated during the previous lifetime, that is, by an impersonal law of cause and effect. The three higher destinies reward good behavior and are regarded as good outcomes. The three lower destinies involve varying degrees of **suffering** as punishment for wicked behavior. These are the so-called **evil paths**. Despite the recognition that some destinies are better than others, all six are equally part of the ongoing cycle of samsara, characterized by suffering. This means that no existence is permanent, and **impermanence** itself is seen as a form of suffering. For example, individuals born into heaven, despite the pleasures of their current existence, are subject to death once their good karma has been exhausted. They will then inevitably fall into a lower rebirth.

Of the upper **three realms**, the human is the most important because only human beings can make spiritual progress toward **enlightenment**, which entails escape from the cycles of samsara. Being born as a human being is regarded, therefore, as a rare and precious opportunity. The realm of the ashuras has ambiguous status in the tradition. Ashuras are demi-gods who fight continually with other deities. Although they rank higher on the scale than humans, the tradition sometimes interprets their violent nature as a form of punishment.

The **Zen** tradition often interprets the six realms in a metaphoric sense and sees the various realms as creations of the human mind in the present existence. Individuals who are pugnacious and eager to fight transform themselves into ashuras. People who greedily grasp at possessions and refuse to practice the virtue of generosity are already hungry ghosts, and those who kill others have already fallen into hell.

Six Perfections

(J. ropparamitsu) The six paramitas, which can be understood as virtues or practices undertaken by **bodhisattvas** as they progress toward **enlightenment**. Bodhisattvas undertake the practice of the six perfections in order to build **merit**, which they then transfer to other **sentient beings**. The six paramitas include: 1) charity or giving (Sk. dana), which includes the sharing of material goods, **Dharma** instruction with others, and the willingness to give up one's life for the sake of another; 2) observing the **precepts** (Sk. **sila**), which includes controlling one's body, speech, and mind; 3) patience or perseverance (Sk. kshanti), which means endurance of pain and hardship and forgiveness of injury without anger or agitation; 4) vigor (Sk. virya), which refers to boundless energy and willingness to overcome one's faults and cultivate virtues; 5) **meditation** (Sk. dhyana), in which the bodhisattva enters various meditative states but does not accept **rebirth** in a **heaven** or **Pure Land**; and 6) wisdom (Sk. **prajna**), the stage at which the bodhisattva fully realizes Buddhist teachings of reality, including **emptiness**, **codependent origination**, and No-Self (Sk. **Anatman**).

Six Sense Organs

(J. rokkon) The eyes, ears, nose, tongue, body, and mind; also called the six gates (J. rokumon). The senses are compared to gates, since it is through the senses that we perceive the stimuli of form, sound, smell, taste, texture, and thought. According to the Buddhist understanding of perception, the senses include not only the five senses normally recognized in Western thought, but the mind as well. Just as the eyes perceive shape and color and the ears sound, the mind perceives mental images and thoughts.

Sixth Patriarch

The title usually refers to **Hui-neng** (638–713), the Sixth Chinese **Patriarch** of **Zen**. Tradition says Jui-neng directly inherited the **Dharma** from the Fifth Patriarch **Hung-jen** (601–674). In some classical texts deriving from the **Northern school**, the title may refer to **Shen-hsiu** (606?–706), another **Dharma heir** of Hung-jen. See **Hui-neng**.

Skandha

(J. un) Literally, a heap. **Buddhism** uses the term in reference to the component parts that comprise all existent things, including the human self. See the **five skandhas**.

Skillful Means

See **expedient means**.

Small Vehicle

(J. Shôjô) Literal English translation of **Hinayana**, a derogatory name for ancient and **Theravada Buddhism**. The term was coined by proponents of **Mahayana Buddhism**, to contrast it with their own "great vehicle." See **Hinayana Buddhism**.

So

"**Patriarch**," a founder of a school, sect, or **lineage** of **Buddhism**. See **patriarch**.

Sôan

A grass hut or hermitage used for solitary **Zen** life and practice. Sôan are sometimes located in rural or mountainous areas, where individual **monks** and **nuns** practice far from the distractions of urban life and a large monastic community. In other cases, sôan are built on monastery grounds, sometimes in the middle of a city.

Sôan

(2) Departing from the monastery; seeing off a **Zen monk** or **nun** who is leaving on **pilgrimage**.

Sobutsu

The **patriarchs** and the **Buddha** who transmit the **Dharma**. When translated as Patriarch-Buddha, it refers specifically to Shakyamuni buddha (**Siddharta Gautama**). **Zen** masters sometimes use the term *sobutsu* to emphasize the Zen teaching that all human beings are originally enlightened beings and that an enlightened person is no different from a buddha or patriarch. For example, the Chinese Zen Master **Lin-chi I-Hsuan** explained in one of his **sermons**, "Bring to rest the thoughts of the ceaselessly seeking mind, and you'll not differ from the Patriarch-Buddha. Do you want to know the Patriarch-Buddha? He is none other than you who stand before me listening to my discourse." (Sasaki, p. 7) See also **busso**.

Sasaki, Ruth Fuller. *The Record of Lin-chi*. Kyoto, Japan: The Institute for Zen Studies, 1975.

Sôdô

The monks' hall, one of the seven primary buildings (J. **shichidô garan**) that form the core of a **Zen** temple or monastery. Traditionally, the sôdô was the central spiritual center of a Zen monastery, where the monastic community ate, slept, and practiced seated **meditation** together. In traditional layouts, it is located to the left of the **Buddha** hall. Inside the monks' hall, meditation platforms line the walls and are grouped in the central areas. In China, the platforms are covered with rush matting in summer and rugs in winter. In Japan, they are covered with **tatami** matting. Resident **monks** or **nuns** are traditionally assigned a small mat on one of the meditation platforms in the hall. There they sit in meditation, take their daily meals, and sleep. At the center of the inner hall is a raised altar with an image of the halls' patron, the "holy monk" (J. **shôsô**), usually the **bodhisattva** Manjusri (J. **Monju**). Facing the "holy monk" at the entrance is the **abbot's** chair. The outer part of monks' hall includes space for walking meditation (J. **kinhin**) and platforms for administrative officers, attendants, and other staff to take meals and meditate.

The sôdô was one of the most characteristic halls of Zen monasteries in China and became characteristic of early Japanese Zen monasteries as well. Traditional use of the monks' hall fell out of common practice in Japan during the Ashikaga period (1392–1568), when it became common for monks and nuns to reside and practice in separate subtemples. Despite efforts to revive communal living and practice in the sôdô by restoration movements within Rinzai and Sôtô Zen during the Tokugawa period (1600–1867), few monks' halls operate in the traditional manner today. Most monasteries have adopted the Obaku custom of maintaining a separate **meditation hall** (J. zendô). See also **Obaku sect**, **Rinzai sect**, and **Sôtô sect**.

Sôgya

Sangha, the community of Buddhist practitioners. See **sangha**.

Sôgyari

The nine-strip outer garment worn by Buddhist **monks** and **nuns**. Sôgyari is the Japanese transliteration of the Sanskrit term *samghati*. See **Kujôe**.

Sôhei

Warrior **monks**, the Japanese term used for armed Buddhist monks who served as soldiers within a monastic army. Sôhei were a common feature for many centuries in Japanese **Buddhism**, despite the fact that bearing arms and going into battle are strictly forbidden by the Buddhist **monastic code**. Throughout the medieval period (1185–1600), powerful Buddhist monasteries in Japan raised and maintained armies from among the ranks of resident monks. These armies protected the monastery's interests against rival Buddhist institutions, the imperial court, military government (J. **bakufu**) forces, and other competitors. The practice began in the early Heian period (794–1185) and continued until the early modern period (1600–1867). In the late sixteenth century, the last warrior monks were defeated and disarmed by Oda Nobunaga and Toyotomi Hideyoshi. Monasteries subsequently had no opportunity to rearm because the Tokugawa military government established and enforced strict monastic codes prohibiting monastic armies.

Sôhei were drawn from the lower ranks of the monastic community, including low-ranking monks and unordained servants residing on temple grounds, but not including the scholar monks. Sôhei generally came from the lower social classes. They not only served as soldiers in times of need, but also were responsible for carrying out much of the regular **manual labor** necessary to keep a large monastic community in operation.

Sôji-ji

A major Sôtô **Zen** monastery in Yokohama and one of two main monasteries for the **Sôto sect** in Japan. The original Sôji-ji was located in what is now Ishikawa Prefecture. It was founded by the Hossô **monk** Gyôgi (668–749) and was called Shogaku-ji. In 1321, the Sôtô master **Keizan Jôkin** inherited Shogaku-ji, then a **Ritsu** sect temple. Keizan converted it into a Sôtô monastery and renamed it Sôji-ji. The **Emperor Go-Daigo** (1287–1339) raised Sôji-ji's rank to a main monastery (J. **honzan**), making it equal to **Eihei-ji**. The monastery grew in prominence under the direction of its second **abbot**, Gasan Jôseki, attracting a great many resident monks and building a large network of **branch temples** throughout rural Japan. The original monastery was completely destroyed by fire in 1898, and Sôji-ji was then established at its present location in Yokohama. See also **Hossô school**.

Sôjô

The Japanese pronunciation for **Seng-chao** (374–414), an early Chinese Buddhist scholar-**monk**. See **Seng-chao**.

Sôkei

The Japanese pronunciation for Ts'ao-hsi, an alternative name for **Hui-neng** (638–713), the Sixth Patriarch. See **Hui-neng**.

Sôkei-an

(1882–1945) The teaching name of **Sasaki Shigetsu**, the Japanese Rinzai master who was influential in introducing **Zen** to the West. He founded The First Zen Institute of America in New York City in 1931. See also **Sasaki Shigetsu**.

Sokkô Roku Kaien Fusetsu

A text comprised of one section that records a series of **sermons** (J. **teishô**) given in 1740 by **Hakuin Ekaku** (1685–1768) on *The Recorded Sayings of Master Hsu-t'ang Lu* (J. *Kidô Roku*). The sermons were recorded and revised by two of Hakuin's disciples. The text was first published in 1743. *Sokkô Roku* was the title Hakuin used for *The Recorded Sayings of Master Hsu-t'ang Lu*. The *Fusetsu* is one of Hakuin's most important works and serves as a basic introduction to his understanding of **Zen** teaching and practice. In the sermons, Hakuin promotes the traditional use of **kôan** (J. **kanna Zen**) as a means to attain **enlightenment** and sharply criticizes silent illumination Zen (J. **mokushô Zen**). Norman Waddell published an English translation of the text under the title *The Essential Teachings of Zen Master Hakuin* (Shambhala, 1994).

Sôkô Shinsai

Tsao-kung, the Chinese god of the hearth who protects the kitchen fire. This Chinese folk deity came to be enshrined in the kitchens of Chinese **Zen** temples, and the practice was later transmitted to Japanese Zen temples. **Dôgen Kigen** (1200–1253) specifically required that a ritual of **chanting** verses from the **sutras** be offered on a daily basis to Sôkô Shinsai by the kitchen staff before the noon meal.

The worship of Sôkô Shinsai is an ancient practice in China, dating back to the second century B.C.E. Sôkô Shinsai, sometimes called the kitchen god, is a popular and important deity for ordinary Chinese, since he is associated with personal longevity and with the kitchen fire, a potent symbol of family unity. He sits above the hearth throughout the year observing the words and deeds of family members. Once each year he visits **heaven** to report on the family's actions, thus determining the longevity of individual family members. On the twenty-third day of the twelfth lunar month, the family sends Sôkô Shinsai off to heaven by burning the paper image of him that hangs above the stove throughout the year. Traditionally, they smear his mouth with something sweet so that he will make a pleasant report about their behavior. On New Year's Eve, they paste up a new image to mark the beginning of the New Year.

Shohei, Ichimura. *Zen Master Eihei Dôgen's Monastic Regulations.* Washington, DC: North American Institute of Zen and Buddhist Studies, 1993.

Thompson, Laurence G. *Chinese Religion, An Introduction.* Fifth Edition. Belmont, CA: Wadsworth Publishing Co., 1996.

Sokuhi Nyoichi
The Japanese name for **Chi-fei Ju-i** (1616–1671), an Obaku **monk** who emigrated from Ming China to Japan. See **Chi-fei Ju-i**. See also **Obaku sect**.

Sômon
The outer gate of a **Zen** monastery. The sômon is much smaller than the **sanmon**, the main monastery gate. In earlier periods, monasteries had three gates, with the sômon being the outermost of the three.

Sôrin
A **Zen** monastery or temple. The word literally means "thicket" or "grove." It derives from an Indian expression, *pindavana*, which was used for an assembly of religious mendicants. In Japan, sôrin was used as a common designation for all of the Japanese Zen monasteries that comprised the **Gozan system**. Zen temples that were not part of the Gozan system were designated **rinka**, literally meaning "below the grove."

Sôsan
(d. 606) The Japanese pronunciation for **Seng-ts'an**, the Third Chinese **Patriarch** of **Zen**. See **Seng-ts'an**.

Sôsan
(2) A general form of **sanzen** in which disciples gather as a group to receive instruction from the **Zen** master.

Sôsan
Morning instruction, a sermon given in the morning after breakfast. The sôsan takes place in the **Dharma** hall and is addressed to the entire assembly.

Soshi
"**Patriarch**," a founder of a Buddhist school, sect, or **lineage**. Sometimes used in **Zen** texts as a reference for **Bodhidharma**, traditionally regarded as the founder of Zen **Buddhism**.

Soshidô
Patriarch's hall, a monastery building in which images and/or mortuary tablets of the founder of the sect or the monastery are enshrined. In some cases, images of earlier patriarchs, such as **Bodhidharma** or **Lin-chi I-Hsuan**, may also be enshrined in the soshidô.

Sôshin Zazen
Morning session of meditation, one of the four periods of **zazen** (J. **shiji zazen**) observed daily in **Zen** monasteries.

Although the exact hours differ by monastery, sôshin zazen is held after breakfast, sometime between nine and eleven o'clock in the morning.

Sôtô Sect

One of three major sects of Japanese **Zen**. The **Rinzai sect** and **Obaku sect** are the other two. Sôtô Zen developed from the Chinese **Ts'ao-tung school** (J. Sôtô) of Zen. Its name derives from two of its founding **patriarchs, Tung-shan Liang-chieh** (807–869; J. Tôzan) and **Ts'ao-shan Pen-chi** (840–901; J. Sôzan), who were active during the T'ang dynasty (618–907). The predominant style of Sôtô focuses on single-minded devotion to seated **meditation** (J. **zazen**) without the use of **kôan** or other devices.

The Ts'ao-tung **lineage** was established as a distinct lineage and sect in China and numbered among the **five houses** of Chinese Zen of the T'ang dynasty. During the Sung dynasty (960–1279), Ts'ao-tung was one of two major forms of Zen practice in China. Unlike the Lin-chi lineage which championed kôan practice, Ts'ao-tung masters preferred a style of meditation known in Japanese as *shikan taza*, "earnest meditation," or "seated meditation only." The Ts'ao-tung style of Zen was transmitted to Japan during the Kamakura period (1185–1333) by the Japanese **monk Dôgen Kigen** (1200–1253), who established **Eihei-ji** as the main monastery for the new sect. After his death, the sect developed further under the guidance of **Keizan Jôkin**, sometimes known as the Second Patriarch. Keizan and other Sôtô monks successfully established Sôtô as a popular form of **Buddhism**, especially among the warrior class. Today, Sôtô remains among the largest sects in Japan, with almost 15,000 temples and over six million members. See also **Lin-chi school**.

Sôtô-shû

Japanese for **Sôtô sect** of **Zen Buddhism**. It also may refer to the Chinese **Ts'ao-tung school** of Zen Buddhism. See **Sôtô sect** and **Ts'ao-tung school**.

Southern School

An early school of Chinese **Zen**, generally regarded by the tradition as the orthodox **lineage** of **Hui-neng** (638–713), the Sixth Patriarch, from which all surviving lineages of Zen claim descent. **Ho-tse Shen-hui** (670–762), a disciple of Hui-neng, adopted the name Southern school to distinguish his master's lineage from the so-called **Northern school** of **Shen-hsiu** (606?–706). The names of the two schools derive from the relative geographical location of the two lineages. Shen-hsiu and his lineage were active in the area north of the Yellow River and the cities of Lo-yang and Ch'ang-an, while Hui-neng and his group were active in the south. According to Shen-hui and the later tradition, the Southern school preserved the Sixth Patriarch's teaching of **sudden enlightenment**, as opposed to the Northern school's preference for **gradual enlightenment**. Recent scholarship has questioned the historical accuracy of this story of the doctrinal schism between the two schools.

Sôzan Honjaku

The Japanese pronunciation for **Ts'ao-shan Pen-chi** (840–901), a Chinese **Zen monk** and co-founder of the Chinese Sôtô school. See **Ts'ao-shan Pen-chi**.

Ssu-chia Yu Lu

Recorded Sayings of the Four Houses, a text in six sections containing the recorded sayings of four famous Chinese **Zen** masters of the T'ang (618–907) dynasty: **Ma-tsu Tao-i** (709–788), **Pai-chang Huai-hai** (720–814), **Huang-po Hsi-yün** (d. 850), and **Lin-chi I-hsuan** (d. 866). The compiler and date of the original publication are unknown, but a subsequent edition was published by

Chieh Ning in 1607. The text is also known as the *Ma-tsu Ssu-chia Lu*.

Ssu-fen Lu

(J. *Shinbun Ritsu*) *The Vinaya in Four Categories of Dharmagupta*, one of several versions of the **monastic code** of **Theravada Buddhism** translated into Chinese, and the version that became the standard in East Asian **Buddhism**. The text explains the general regulations for **monks** and **nuns** in the first section; the regulations for receiving the **precepts** and for preaching in the second section; the regulations for retreats, repentance, clothing, and medication in the third section; and the regulations related to housing and miscellaneous items in the fourth section. The text was transmitted to China in the fifth century C.E, and translated into Chinese by Buddhayashas. The Chinese Buddhist monk Tao-hsuan (596–667) founded the Lu school, or **Vinaya** school, based on the study and careful observance of this text.

Steep Path

(J. *shôdô*) Also known as the holy path, an expression used for those forms of **Buddhism**, especially **Zen**, which encourage personal striving toward **enlightenment** through the practices of **meditation** and observance of **precepts**. The steep path contrasts with the **easy path** of faith, characteristic of **Pure Land** Buddhism, in which the individual relies upon the **merit** of a **buddha** or **bodhisattva**. **Nagarjuna** is said to have originated the distinction between the easy and steep paths in a chapter on easy practice in the *Shih-chu-p'i-p'o-sha-lun* (J. *Jûjûbibasharon*).

Storehouse Consciousness

The **alaya consciousness**, part of the Yogachara (J. Hossô) system of human psychology. In this schema, the storehouse consciousness (J. arayashiki) is the fundamental level of human consciousness that stores previous experiences and constitutes the lense through which all other experiences are evaluated. The storehouse is the eighth (J. hasshiki) and deepest level of consciousness. The **Zen** school has generally accepted and adopted the Yogachara view of human psychology as the theoretical basis for its own thought. See **alaya consciousness**.

Straw Sandal Bodhidharma

Refers to the story of **Bodhidharma** returning to India after his death with one straw sandal. According to the legend preserved in the *Ching-te Ch'iian-teng Lu* (J. *Dentôroku*), some three years after Bodhidharma had died and been buried in China, a Chinese official named **Sung Yun** was returning to China from a mission to India and encountered the master somewhere in Central Asia. The master carried a single straw sandal in his hand. When the emissary asked where he was going, the master replied that he was returning to India. The official reported this encounter to the emperor on his return to the capitol. The emperor ordered Bodhidharma's grave opened for inspection. They found the coffin completely empty, save for a single straw sandal. Because of this story, Bodhidharma often appears in **Zen** art carrying a single sandal (J. **sekiri daruma**).

Stupa

Buddhist structure used to enshrine **relics** of the historical **Buddha** or another important religious figure, or to mark a religiously significant location. In early **Buddhism** and still today in Theravada communities, stupas symbolically represent the historical Buddha and serve as the principal objects of worship for lay Buddhists. While Theravadan believers understand that the Buddha passed into **nirvana** and that he is not present to be worshipped in the sense that a deity is, stupa worship nevertheless serves as a reminder of the founder and his teachings. The structures are not designed for worshippers to enter. Believers circumambulate the stupa in

The stupa is a Buddhist shrine used to preserve relics of the historical
Buddha, or to mark a religiously significant site.

the clockwise direction; they may also prostrate themselves before it or make **offerings** of flowers.

Traditional stupas are derived in form from the burial mounds constructed for Indian royalty. They are dome-shaped structures resting on a square or circular base. From the top of the dome, a metal pole rises, supporting umbrella-shaped discs, which symbolize the Buddha's spiritual royalty. They may also represent the **bodhi tree**, under which the Buddha attained **enlightenment**. Some stupas include covered or enclosed walkways around the exterior designed for circumambulation. In China, the traditional form of the stupa underwent significant change. The East Asian form of the stupa, known as a **pagoda** (J. tô or tôba), is a multistoried tower with distinct rooftops for each level. The most common style of pagoda has three or five stories. See also **lay believer**.

Subhuti

(J. Shubodai) One of the ten outstanding disciples of the **Buddha**, renowned for his understanding of No-Self (Sk. **Anatman**) and **emptiness** (Sk. shunyata). Before becoming a disciple of the Buddha, Subhuti is said to have been plagued by a constant state of anger, causing him to perpetually lash out at others. Under the Buddha's guidance, Subhuti practiced **meditation** on loving kindness and attained **enlightenment**, making him an **arhat**. Because of his deep understanding of the teaching of Anatman, Mahayana **sutras** often depicted Subhuti expounding the teaching of shunyata.

Ishigami, Zenno. *Disciples of the Buddha*. Trans. Richard L. Gage and Paul McCarthy. Tokyo: Kosei Publishing Co., 1989.

Subtemple

A Buddhist temple that is built within a larger monastery complex and does not have legal status independent of the monastery. Large Japanese **Zen** monasteries often have a number of smaller subtemples, known in Japanese as **tatchû**. In most cases, subtemples were originally constructed by leading Zen masters as personal residences after their retirement. See **tatchû**.

Succession Certificate

The document that a qualified **Zen** master presents to a disciple to certify the individual as a designated **Dharma heir**. The succession certificate indicates that the recipient is qualified to train students and to serve as **abbot** or head **monk** at a Zen temple or monastery. Documents of succession generally take the form of **lineage charts**, presenting the Dharma ancestors of the newly certified teacher. See **shisho**.

Sudden Enlightenment

Zen understanding that **enlightenment** is attained immediately and not gradually through stages. The teaching of sudden enlightenment (J. tongo or tongaku) appears in the **Platform Sutra** of the Sixth Patriarch and is associated with the **Southern school** of Chinese Zen. It came to be regarded as the orthodox position. The teaching of **gradual enlightenment** is traditionally associated with the **Northern school**, although scholars have shown that this is not historically accurate.

Suddhodana

(J. Jôbonnô) The personal name of Suddhodana Gautama, the father of **Siddharta Gautama**, the historical Buddha. Suddhodana was the ruler of **Kapilavastu**, a small republic in northern India, during the sixth century B.C.E. This country, the land of the **Shakya clan**, was at the time a semi-autonomous part of the larger kingdom of Koshala. The region is now part of Nepal. Suddhodana and his wife, Maya, had a son named Siddharta, who later became known as Shakyamuni Buddha. Since Maya died shortly after giving birth, Suddhodana married her sister **Prajapati** to raise the young prince. According to traditional accounts of the Buddha's life, Suddhodana objected to his son pursuing a religious life and tried to preclude that possibility by limiting his son's exposure to the harsher realities of human life. Later in life, he became a devoted lay disciple of the Buddha. See also **lay believer**.

Suffering

According to the Buddhist understanding of reality, suffering characterizes all aspects of ordinary existence. The primary goal of Buddhist practice is **nirvana**, or **enlightenment**—the elimination of all suffering. Suffering (Sk. dukhha; J. ku) is one of the **three marks** of existence, along with **impermanence** (Sk. anitya) and No-Self (Sk. **Anatman**).

The Buddhist understanding of suffering is closely associated with the **four noble truths**. The first of the noble truths, called the teaching of suffering (Sk. duhkha), states that all life is suffering. Birth, death, old age, illness, separation from what one loves or desires, and contact with what one despises are all forms of suffering. Even aspects of life that may be seen as pleasurable involve the eventual suffering of loss or separation due to the transitory nature of existence. The second and third noble truths indicate that desire is the cause of suffering and that cutting off desire leads to the elimination of suffering. The fourth noble truth teaches that the way to eliminate desire and end suffering is to follow the **Eightfold Path** of **Buddhism**.

Sugyôroku

Japanese title for the *Tsung-ching Lu*, by **Yung-ming Yen-shou** (904–975). See *Tsung-ching Lu*.

Suibokuga

Black ink painting, or ink drawing; a style of monochromatic painting commonly used by **Zen monks** and **nuns** to express their understanding of the **Dharma**. The paintings may be landscapes or may depict famous Zen **patriarchs** and stories from the past.

Sumie

Black ink painting, or ink drawing. See **suibokuga**.

Sunface Buddha, Moonface Buddha

(J. Nichimen Butsu Gatsumen Butsu) Two **buddhas** named in chapter seventeen of the Sutra of the Buddhas' Names (J. Butsumyôkyô; T. 14, nos. 440–442), a listing of three thousand buddhas of the past, present, and future. According to the sutra, the life span of the Sunface buddha is 1,800 years, while the Moonface buddha survives only one day and one night. Just before he died, the Chinese **Zen** master **Ma-tsu Tao-i** (709–788) is said to have spoken the words "Sunface buddha, Moonface buddha." This account takes the form of a **kôan** in case 3 of the *Hekiganroku*.

Sung-shan

(J. Sû-zan) Mount Sung, a mountain in Honan province, China, near the old capital city of Lo-yang, which was the site of many Buddhist monasteries. According to **Zen** legend, the founder **Bodhidharma** sat in **meditation** for nine years at **Shao-lin-ssu**, a Buddhist monastery on Mount Sung.

Sung-yüan Chung-yueh

(1132–1202; J. Shôgen Sôgaku) Chinese Rinzai **monk** of the Sung dynasty (960–1279). Sung-yüan became the **Dharma heir** of Mi-an. Although Sung-yüan died without naming a successor, one of his disciples was designated as his heir after his death. His **lineage** thus extended to that of **Nampô Jômyô** (1235–1309) and **Shûhô Myôchô**

(1282–1337), an important lineage in Japanese Rinzai. Sung-yuan appears in case 20 of the *Wu-men Kuan* (J. *Mumonkan*). See also **Rinzai sect**.

Sung Yun

Chinese government official of the sixth century who plays a small role in the traditional **biography** of **Bodhidharma**. According to legend, Sung Yun encountered Bodhidharma in Central Asia as he was returning home to China from India. He noticed that Bodhidharma was carrying a single sandal in his hand. On reporting on his mission, Sung Yun realized that he had seen Bodhidharma on the very day of his death. When Bodhidharma's tomb was opened, all that was found inside was a single sandal. See also **Straw Sandal Bodhidharma**.

Susoku-kan

Breath-counting contemplation, an introductory form of **meditation** in which one calms the mind by counting one's breaths. Susoku-kan is generally regarded as a **Theravada Buddhism** practice, derived from anapana sati. Although it is explicitly rejected by some **Zen** teachers, many Zen students first learn to meditate by counting their inhalations and exhalations. There are different styles, but the most common is to count one on the inhalation, two on the exhalation, three on the inhalation, and so on up to ten. One then begins the process again with one inhalation.

Sutras

Sermons or discourses of a **buddha**, especially sermons attributed to Shakyamuni (**Siddharta Gautama**), the historical Buddha. The sutras are a genre of Buddhist literature and one of the three basic divisions in the Theravada **Buddhist scriptures** (Sk. **Tripitaka**). According to the Buddhist tradition, the sermons of the historical Buddha were preserved as the sutras by **Ananda**, who was able to recite them from memory after the Buddha's death. The early sutras were first recorded in Pali and Sanskrit and later translated into Tibetan and Chinese. The Mahayana sutras were composed later by other Buddhist masters, but like the Theravadan sutras, are generally attributed to the historical Buddha. In a few cases, Mahayana sutras present themselves as the discourse of another buddha. The **Zen** text known as the **Platform Sutra** of the Sixth Patriarch is the only text referred to as a sutra but not attributed to a buddha.

Suzuki, Daisetsu Teitaro

(1869–1966) Daisetsu Teitaro Suzuki, a Japanese **Zen** scholar and teacher of the modern period who was instrumental in introducing Zen to the West. Suzuki was born in Kanazawa to a **samurai** family. His father was a physician who died when Suzuki was only six, leaving the family in poverty. While attending college, he studied Zen as a lay person under the Rinzai master Imakita Kosen and his **Dharma heir** Soyen Shaku at **Engaku-ji** in Kamakura. Because of Suzuki's ability to speak and write in English, Soyen sent him to the United States in 1897, where he lived and worked for a number of years. He later returned to Japan, and there married Beatrice Erskine Lane in 1911. Together they founded *The Eastern Buddhist*, an English-language journal. After World War II, Suzuki returned to the United States and taught at several American universities, including the University of Hawaii, Claremont College, and Columbia University. He again returned to Japan and continued to write until his death at age 96. His many books in English include *Essays in Zen Buddhism* (in three volumes), *An Introduction to Zen Buddhism*, *The Training of the Zen Buddhist Monk*, and *The Zen Kôan as a Means of Attaining Enlightenment*. Suzuki also contributed many scholarly translations of Buddhist texts, especially those important for Zen Buddhism. See also **lay believer** and **Rinzai sect**.

Suzuki Shôsan

(1579–1655) Japanese **Zen monk** from the early Tokugawa period (1600–1867), loosely associated with Sôtô Zen. Shôsan was born in Mikawa (Aichi prefecture), to a **samurai** family. As a young man he fought for Tokugawa Ieyasu at the crucial battles at Sekigahara (1600) and Osaka Castle (1614–1615). He took the **tonsure** and became a monk late in life, at age forty. He continued to serve the Tokugawa **bakufu** in his new capacity as a Buddhist monk. In particular, he participated in establishing methods for controlling Christianity, which was banned at that time.

Shôsan was not a part of the Sôtô Zen institutional structure, nor any other established Buddhist sect. He never established his **lineage** or created an independent school to carry on his teachings after his death. He acted as a freelance agent, promoting his own brand of Buddhist practice among the warrior and commoner classes. He strongly advocated Buddhist practice within the confines of ordinary life, stressing the religious character of one's inherited profession. The style of Zen **meditation** that he recommended is sometimes known as **Niô Zen**. He also promoted **chanting nembutsu** as an appropriate religious practice for commoners. His writings include *Roankyô* (Donkey-Saddle Bridge), *Ha-kirishitan* (Christianity Crushed), *Môanjô* (A Trustworthy Staff for the Blind), *Banmin Tokuyô* (Meritorious Way of Life for All), and *Nembutsu Zôshi* (Nembutsu Notes). See also **Sôtô sect**.

King, Winston L. *Death Was His Kôan: The Samurai-Zen of Suzuki Shosan*. Berkeley, CA: Asian Humanities Press, 1986.

Ooms, Herman. *Tokugawa Ideology: Early Constructs, 1570–1680*. Ann Arbor, MI: Center for Japanese Studies, University of Michigan, 1998.

Tyler, Royall, trans. *Selected Writings of Suzuki Shosan*. Ithaca, NY: China-Japan Program, Cornell University, 1977.

Suzuki Shunryû

(1904–1971) Japanese Sôtô master of the modern period who taught **Zen** in the United States. Although Shunryû's father was a Zen priest, he did not become his father's heir. Instead, he left home and became the disciple of Gyakuju So-on. Shunryû first came to the United States in 1959 to serve as the priest for a Japanese immigrant community at the Sôtô Zen Mission temple in San Francisco. He began to attract American disciples and later founded the San Francisco Zen Center in 1962. His American **Dharma heirs** include Richard Baker. A collection of Shunryû's Dharma talks is published under the title *Zen Mind, Beginner's Mind*. See also **Sôtô sect**.

Suzuki, Shunryû. *Zen Mind, Beginner's Mind*. New York: Walker/Weatherhill, 1970.

T

Ta-hsiu Cheng-nien

(1215–1289; J. Daikyû Shônen) Chinese Rinzai master of the late Sung dynasty (960–1279) who helped to transmit Rinzai **Zen** to Japan. In China, Ta-hsiu became the **Dharma heir** of Shih-chi Hsin-yueh. In 1269, he came to Japan at the invitation of **Hôjô Tokiyori** (1227–1263). He served as **abbot** at several Kamakura Zen temples, including **Jufuku-ji**, **Kenchô-ji**, and **Engaku-ji**, and was the founding abbot at **Jôchi-ji**. He received the posthumous title Butsugen **Zenji** (Zen Master Buddha's Source). See also **Rinzai sect**.

Ta-hui Tsung-kao

(1089–1163; J. Daie Sôkô) Prominent Chinese Rinzai master of the Sung dynasty (960–1279) who was a leading Rinzai teacher of his day. He is said to have taught more than 2,000 disciples. Ta-hui became the **Dharma heir** of **Yüan-wu K'o-ch'in** (1063–1135), a strong proponent of **kôan** practice and author of the kôan collection the *Hekiganroku*. Despite his own dedication to the use of kôan and his master's connection with the text, Ta-hui was responsible for destroying the original version of the *Hekiganroku*. Ta-hui collected all the printed copies of the text that he could find and burned them, and also destroyed the original woodblocks. Some scholars believe that Ta-hui did this because his disciples became too reliant on the written word.

Ta-hui is best known in the **Zen** tradition for his emphasis on the use of kôan rather than what he called "silent illumination Zen" (J. **mokushô Zen**). He and his friend **Hung-chih Cheng-chüeh** (1091–1157), a leading Sôtô master of the day, entered into a famous controversy about the proper approach to Zen **meditation**. While Ta-hui favored the contemplation of kôan during seated meditation as the best approach for achieving **enlightenment**, Hung-chih preferred meditation without the use of kôan. Ta-hui's style of meditation, which has become known as "kôan gazing Zen" (J. **kanna Zen**), still characterizes practice within the Rinzai school. Ta-hui received the posthumous title Pu-chueh **Ch'an-shih** (Zen Master Deep Insight). See also **Rinzai sect** and **Sôtô sect**.

Cleary, Christopher, trans. *Swampland Flowers: The Letters and Lectures of Zen Master Ta Hui*. New York: Grove Press, 1977.

Taikô Gyôyû

(1163–1241) Japanese Rinzai **monk** of the early Kamakura period (1185–1333) and a leading disciple of **Eisai**. Gyôyû was born and raised in the Kamakura area. He became a Buddhist monk at an early age in the Shingon tradition of **esoteric Buddhism**, and he served for a time as an attendant at the Tsuruoka Hachiman Shintô shrine in Kamakura. Gyôyû was already advanced in age when he became Eisai's disciple at **Jufuku-ji**; however, he succeeded Eisai as **abbot** at Jufuku-ji when the master died. He did not forsake the Shingon teachings and practice, but advocated a mixed form of **Zen** and esoteric Buddhism. See also **Rinzai sect** and **Shingon sect**.

T'ai-p'o-shan

(J. Taihaku-zan) Mount T'ai-p'o, a mountain in China's modern day Che-chiang province, which was traditionally an important religious site for **Zen**. Mount T'ai-p'o was the site for the Zen monastery **Ching-te-ssu**, home to such famous Zen masters as **Hung-chih Cheng-chüeh** (1091–1157) and **Ju-ching** (1163–1228). The Japanese Zen masters **Eisai**, **Dôgen Kigen** (1200–1253), and

Ryônen Myôzen (1184–1225) visited the mountain and practiced at Ching-te-ssu. T'ai-p'o-shan became known as one of the Five Mountains (C. wu-shan; J. Gozan temples), the most prestigious Zen monasteries in China.

Taireishôsan

A brief sermon on the **Dharma** given as a part of the funeral services for a prominent Buddhist **monk** or **nun**. It is traditional for **sermons** to mark virtually every stage of the funeral process for prominent members of the monastic community. The taireishôsan is the sermon given in the lecture hall in front of the coffin on the **taiya**, the night before the funeral. It is one of nine ritual actions (**kubutsuji**) comprising the funeral services for prominent individuals.

Taishaku

Short form for Taishakuten; Japanese for **Indra**, an ancient Indian god of war. Indra reigns in a palace above **Mount Sumeru**, from which he serves as a guardian for Buddhist teachings and believers. See **Indra**.

Taishakuten

Japanese for **Indra**, an ancient Indian god of war. Often shortened to Taishaku. See **Indra**.

Taishô Daizôkyô

Modern Japanese edition of the Mahayana **Buddhist scriptures**, an extended version of the **Chinese Tripitaka**. The full name of the edition is the Taishô Shinshû Daizôkyô, the Newly Revised Tripitaka of the Taishô Era. The project was first started in 1924 during the Taishô period and was completed in 1932. The Taishô Daizôkyô includes 100 volumes which incorporate several types of text: 1) translations from the early Theravada tradition which formed the original Sanskrit Tripitaka; 2) translations of Mahayana **sutras** originally composed in Sanskrit; 3) apocryphal texts composed in Chinese but represented as translations; 4) texts composed by and attributed to Chinese authors; 5) texts composed by Japanese authors; 6) indices; and 7) iconography and illustrations.

Taiya

The evening before a Buddhist funeral or **memorial service**. The term *taiya* also refers to the rituals performed on that night. When a prominent Buddhist **monk** or **nun** dies, for example, a brief sermon known as the **taireishôsan** is addressed to the monastic community. Thus the taireishôsan is one example of a taiya.

Taiza Monjin

Bowing with one's hands held in **gasshô** to greet the people on the opposite side of the **meditation hall** before beginning a session of seated meditation. The bow is performed with one's back to one's own meditation position after one has already greeted the meditators to one's right and left (J. **rin'i monjin**). The meditators on the other side, in turn, bow together in greeting.

Taizôkai Mandara

The Japanese title for the **Womb-Realm Mandala**, one of the two primary mandala used in **esoteric Buddhism**, especially the **Shingon sect**. The Womb Mandala consists of a series of twelve concentric rectangles. The central portion of the mandala depicts an open lotus blossom with eight petals. The **buddha** Dainichi (Sk. Mahavairochana) sits in the center of the lotus, surrounded by four buddhas and **bodhisattvas**. Other Buddhist deities inhabit the other rectangular halls. The second primary mandala is the Kongôkai Mandara (**Diamond-Realm Mandala**). See **Womb-Realm Mandala**.

Taking Refuge

Called **kie** in Japanese. In Indian culture, to take refuge in a person or concept indicates that one has made a deep personal commitment. In a religious context, refuge does not imply a place to hide but rather a source of strength. See **Kie**.

Takuan Sôhô

(1573–1645) Japanese Rinzai master of the early Tokugawa period. (1600–1867) Takuan was born into a **samurai** family in Hyôgo province. Although his family were **Pure Land** Buddhists and he began his education at a Pure Land temple, Takuan soon moved to a **Zen** temple to continue his education. He eventually followed his Zen teacher to Kyoto, where he practiced under Shun'oku Sôen at **Daitoku-ji**. He received **inka**, the Dharma transfer, from Ittô Shôteki. Takuan was appointed **abbot** at several monasteries, including Daitoku-ji. In 1628, he was exiled to Yamagata by the Tokugawa military government for his role in the so-called purple robe affair (when the military government stripped away imperial honors that they had not authorized). He was pardoned in 1632 and returned to Kyoto. The third Tokugawa **shôgun** Iemitsu named him founding abbot for Tôkai-ji in Shinagawa, near Edo. Takuan is perhaps best known for his writings on the relationship between swordsmanship (J. **kyûdô** or kyûjutsu) and Zen. See also **Rinzai sect**.

Takuhatsu

To seek alms; a basic part of the practice of monastic **Buddhism**. The term literally means to take up the **begging bowl**. The practice originated in ancient India, where various religious groups, including that of the historical **Buddha**, subsisted on the food they received as donations from lay people. Takuhatsu may refer to **monks** and **nuns** begging for prepared food on a daily basis, as was the norm in the early tradition. It may also refer to begging for alms in other forms, as is more commonly done in East Asia. **Zen** monks typically beg in small groups, walking through the streets, announcing their presence with

the word *Hô*, or **Dharma**. They may also chant **sutras** for the sake of their benefactors. **Lay believers** offer them donations, usually money or uncooked rice. In the autumn, monks and nuns go out into the countryside to beg for daikon, which are Japanese radishes, during the harvest season. Takuhatsu is also known as Jihatsu or Kotsujiki. See also **begging alms**.

Takujû Kosen

(1760–1833) Japanese Rinzai **monk** of the Tokugawa period (1600–1867) who is regarded as the founder of the **Takujû school** of Japanese **Zen**. Takujû was the **Dharma heir** of **Gasan Jitô** (1727–1348), a leading disciple of the reformer **Hakuin Ekaku** (1685–1768). He and his Dharma brother **Inzan Ien** (1751–1814) are credited with completing the process of systematizing **kôan** practice within the **Rinzai sect**. Takujû was born in Tsushima, near the city of Nagoya. He became a Buddhist monk at Sôken-ji in Nagoya at age fifteen and began a **pilgrimage** looking for a suitable master at age nineteen. He visited Gasan at Tôki-an and decided to join his assembly. Takujû requested permission to live separately and to be relieved of all of his monastic duties in order to concentrate exclusively on **meditation**. His request granted, he attained **kenshô** in a matter of ninety days. He then resumed his normal duties and practiced under Gasan for fourteen years. Gasan acknowledged him as a Dharma heir. Takujû then returned to his home temple Sôken-ji where he lived quietly for twenty years. He was appointed **abbot** at **Myôshin-ji** in 1813 and received a **purple robe**. This spread his reputation and he gathered a community of disciples at Sôken-ji. He also attracted many **lay believers**. He is especially known for the quality of his lectures on the Zen corpus. He received the **posthumous name** Daidô Enkan **Zenji** (Zen Master Round Mirror of the Great Way).

Takuhatsu is the process of monks and nuns seeking alms, such as money or rice.

Takujû School

One of two major forms of Japanese Rinzai **Zen** founded by **Takujû Kosen** (1760–1833), a second generation descendent of **Hakuin Ekaku** (1685–1768). All active lineages of Rinzai Zen in Japan today descend from either the Takujû or the **Inzan schools**. The teaching methods and Zen style of the two schools are nearly identical. Together they encompass what is often known as "Hakuin Zen." See also **Rinzai sect**.

Tan

The assigned place on the raised platform in the monks' hall (J. **sôdô**) or the **meditation hall** (J. zendô) where a resident **monk** or **nun** sits in meditation, takes daily meals, and sleeps. The term also refers to the platform as a whole. Tan generally line the interior walls of the hall and may also be placed in the central area. The platform is usually two to three feet high and covered with rush or **tatami** mats. The depth of the tan depends upon its use. In the monks' hall, the tan measures approximately three and one-half by seven feet, deep enough to accommodate a person stretched out to sleep. In the meditation hall, the tan are typically more shallow. The term also refers to the individual nameplates designating the occupant of each position on the raised platform.

Tanbutsu

"Paying homage to the **Buddha**," usually by a verse of praise. **Zen monks** and **nuns** pay homage to the Buddha at certain meals, by reciting a verse of ten Buddha names. There are also special rituals known as tanbutsu-e, in which the names of 3,000 Buddhas recorded in the Sutra of the Buddhas' Names (J. Butsumyôkyô; T. 14, nos. 440–442) are chanted. The tanbutsu-e is observed at some Zen monasteries.

Tanden

The lower abdomen, specifically the region between the navel and the pelvis. The word *tanden* literally means "Field of Cinnabar." Various systems of Asian **meditation** identify the tanden as the central core of the individual, one of the body's natural energy centers. In Taoism and **Zen Buddhism**, the tanden is said to be the location of one's vital breath, or ki. One method of Zen concentration focuses the attention on the tanden, especially its movement while breathing. It is known more popularly as the **hara**.

Tanden

(2) Simple or direct transmission; the transmission of the **Dharma** from a **Zen** master to a disciple.

Tanga

Literally meaning to pass the night, the term denotes the practice of traveling **monks** taking lodging for a single night at a time at various monasteries along their route. **Zen** monasteries maintain a guest hall, administrated by the guest prefect (J. **shika**), for the sake of offering such lodging. Newly admitted trainees also spend a period of time in the guest hall. See also **tanga zume**.

Tanga Zume

A probationary period lasting a few days, when a new **Zen postulant** is first accepted by a monastery for training. During the tanga zume, the trainee is not yet admitted into the monastery proper to practice with the rest of the assembly. For a few days, the postulant resides alone in a guest hall specifically designed and maintained for temporary lodging. The term *tanga* literally means "to pass the night" and is the word used for the practice of traveling **monks** stopping at a temple for a night's lodging in the guest room. Before being admitted to the monastery for the tanga zume, the trainee undergoes another initial waiting period, known as the **niwa zume**. During that period of time, the trainee is left waiting in the entryway.

During the three to seven days of the tanga zume probation, the postulant remains alone, passing the days in quiet **meditation**, isolated from other monks. The probation period is a further test of the postulant's determination to practice Zen. It provides the administrator of the temple an opportunity to observe the candidate and evaluate his or her suitability to monastic life. At the end of the probation period, the postulant is given formal permission to enter the monastery and instructed in the rules of the monastic community.

Suzuki, Daisetz Teitaro. *The Training of the Zen Buddhist Monk.* New York: Globe Press Books, 1991

Tan-i

The place within the monks' hall (J. **sôdô**) or the **meditation hall** (J. zendô) assigned to a particular **monk** or **nun**. Each tan-i is marked with a sign bearing the occupant's name. Positions within the hall are assigned based upon seniority determined by the date of entry into monastic orders.

Tanjôge

The birthday verse of **Siddharta Gautama**, who would later become the **Buddha**. According to the Buddhist tradition, immediately after his birth in the Lumbini Garden, the newborn Siddharta is said to have taken seven steps in each of the four cardinal directions, pointed his right hand to **heaven** and his left to the earth, and declared his intention to attain **enlightenment**. There are several different versions of the verse. The most popular version of the birthday verse in East Asia is the following: "In the heavens above and on the earth below, I alone am worthy of respect. The triple world is filled with **suffering**; I will ease that suffering."

Tanka

"Short verse," a genre of Japanese poetry; one of two standard forms of **waka**. Tanka are composed of five lines of verse, having 5-7-5-7-7 syllables, respectively.

Tanpyô

The nameplate hanging above the raised platform in the monks' hall (J. **sôdô**) or the **meditation hall** (J. zendô) indicating the individual **monk** or **nun** assigned to occupy that spot. Also called the tanban or simply **tan**.

Tao

"Way" or "path," a Chinese term used extensively in East Asian religious and philosophical traditions. On the simplest level, the term *Tao* (J. dô) designates different religious and philosophical traditions. **Buddhism**, for example, may be referred to as the Way of the **Buddha**. Used alone, the word *Way* often suggests the most appropriate style of human life or the most effective course of human action. In Buddhist contexts, Tao has two basic meanings. It may be used to describe the practice of Buddhism, that is, the way to attain **enlightenment**. Alternatively, in rare examples, it is used as a term for enlightenment itself.

Tao-che Ch'ao-yüan

(d. 1660; J. Dôsha Chôgen) Chinese Rinzai master of the Ming dynasty (1368–1644) who was among the earliest Chinese **monks** to travel to Japan during the early Tokugawa period (1600–1867). Tao-che served as head monk for a Chinese **Zen** monastery in Nagasaki, and he also attracted many Japanese students interested in practicing with a Chinese master. His most prominent Japanese disciple was **Bankei Yôtaku** (1622–1693). Tao-che came from the same **lineage** as **Yin-yüan Lung-ch'i** (1594–1673), the founder of Obaku Zen, and is commonly regarded as a forerunner of the Obaku Zen movement. He returned to China shortly before his death. See also **Obaku sect** and **Rinzai sect**.

Tao-hsin

(580–651; J. Dôshin) The Fourth Chinese **Patriarch** of **Zen**, according to traditional accounts. Tao-hsin was a Chinese Zen master of the Sui dynasty and founder of the **East Mountain school** of early Zen. According to traditional biographies, he was born in Ho-nei in Hunan province. He practiced under **Seng-ts'an** (d. 606) on Mount Huan-kung for eight or nine years and became his **Dharma heir**. He eventually settled on Mount Shuang-feng in Huang-mei, where the Fifth Patriarch **Hung-jen** (601–674) numbered among his disciples.

McRae, John R. *The Northern School and the Formation of Early Ch'an Buddhism.* Honolulu, HI: University of Hawaii Press, 1986.

Tariki

Other Power, the Japanese term for seeking **enlightenment** through reliance on the **merit** of a **buddha** or **bodhisattva**. See **Other Power**.

Ta Sheng Ch'i-hsin-lun

The Awakening of Faith in Mahayana (J. Daijô Kishinron), a treatise in **Mahayana Buddhism** traditionally attributed to **Ashvaghosha**. The text survives only in Chinese, and scholars now believe it was originally composed in Chinese rather than Sanskrit. Two Chinese versions exist, said to be translations completed by Paramartha (T. 32, no. 1666) around 550 C.E. and by Shiksananada (T. 32, no. 1667) around 700 C.E. See *Awakening of Faith*.

Tassu

The **Zen monk** charged with conducting **memorial services** for a Zen **patriarch** or founder. Services are generally held in the presence of a portrait of the master,

Floors covered with tatami mats in a building near Mount Haguro, Japan.

another sort of image, or the memorial tablet (J. **ihai**). They may also be conducted at the grave site or a **stupa** especially dedicated to the master. In later usage, the term *tassu* sometimes refers to the head monk at a subtemple within the complex of a large monastery.

Tatami

Floor matting made from straw or rush, used as the traditional flooring in Japanese structures, including family homes and monastery buildings. Each tatami mat is approximately three and one-half feet by seven feet. Rooms are often measured in terms of tatami mats.

In **Zen** monasteries, the raised platforms (J. **tan**) in the monks' hall (J. **sôdô**) and the **meditation hall** are covered with tatami. Each resident **monk** or **nun** is assigned one full tatami mat in the monks' hall for living space; this allows each person sufficient space to stretch out to sleep. The tatami mats in the meditation hall are generally more shallow, since practitioners do not need to lie down in the meditation hall.

Tatchû

A small subtemple within a larger **Zen** monastery complex. Subtemples are a unique feature of Japanese Zen monasteries, not based upon any Chinese model. During the Kamakura (1185–1333) and Ashikaga (1392–1568) periods, it became common for senior Zen **monks** to build tatchû within the precincts of the monastery in which they had served as **abbot**. After retiring from office, they used the tatchû as personal residences. Often the masters' disciples also took up residence at the tatchû and continued to practice under the master's immediate supervision. In some cases, the tatchû functioned as monasteries in their own right with numerous monks in residence, drawing the focus away from the original main monastery. After the master's death, **Dharma heirs** inherited the subtemple as a part of the master's personal possessions. In this way, subtemples typically remain within the **lineage** of the founding master. Before the modern period, tatchû were not treated as independent temples. For this reason, they did not generally have formal mountain names typical of Zen temples. Since the Meiji period (1868–1912), many of them have acquired legal status as independent **branch temples**.

The term *tatchû* may also refer to the grave site of the founder of a monastery or another leading master. After a senior **monk** died, it was traditional for his or her disciples to construct a memorial **pagoda** or another small structure within the precincts of the monastery. This tatchû was then used as the site for **memorial services** offered for the sake of the deceased master.

Tathagata

(J. nyorai) Thus Come One, in Sanskrit. One of the ten epithets used for the **Buddha**. The Sanskrit word can also be understood to mean "Thus Gone One," but it is rarely rendered that way in the English translation. The tathagata is an individual who has attained perfect **enlightenment** and gone to or come from a realization of truth. Having followed the path of the buddhas, the tathagata understands Thusness, or things as they really are. **Siddharta**

Gautama, the historical Buddha, apparently referred to himself after his enlightenment using this title.

Tathagata Garbha

(J. Nyoraizô) "The womb of the thus come one," or the "matrix of **buddhahood**," a Mahayana Buddhist concept. The term has two basic meanings in the tradition. First, it may refer to the potential inherent in each sentient being to attain buddhahood, the seed of **enlightenment** which may be perfected. Used in this sense, it is identical with the concept of **Buddha Nature**. Second, the term may refer to the matrix or environment in which enlightenment develops. In this latter sense, it is closely associated with the concept of the **alaya** (or storehouse) **consciousness**.

Tea Ceremony

A Japanese art form closely associated with **Zen Buddhism**. See **chanoyû**.

Teihatsu

Tonsure, shaving the head. Buddhist **monks** and **nuns** initially shave off their hair at **ordination** as an indication of their break from ordinary secular life and their dedication to monastic practice. See **tonsure**.

Teishô

Expounding the principles of the **Dharma**. The term is most commonly used for the formal **Zen sermons** given by the Zen master for his or her disciples during periods of intensive Zen practice (J. **sesshin**). Teishô typically take place in the Dharma hall (J. **hattô**) with the entire assembly present. The master speaks from the high seat (J. **hôza**) set up on the central dais (raised platform). The sermon itself takes the form of a commentary on a classical Zen text, such as the *Sayings of Lin-chi* or the *Wu-men Kuan* (J. *Mumonkan*). Teishô are not, however, lectures in the academic sense; they are immediate presentations of the master's understanding of the Dharma. Alternate terms include teiyô and teikô.

Temple Buildings

There are seven monastic halls which form the basic core of any **Zen** monastery. The seven include the **Dharma** hall (J. **hattô**), the **Buddha** hall (J. **Butsuden**), the monks' hall (J. **sôdô**), the kitchen-office (J. **ku'in**), the latrines (J. **tôsu**), the mountain or triple gate (J. **sanmon**) and the bathhouse (J. **yokushitsu**). These seven halls are known collectively as **shichidô garan** in Japanese. See **shichidô garan**.

Temple Positions

The highest ranking **monk** or **nun** at a large training monastery is the **abbot** (J. **jûji** or chôrô), who is responsible for the management of the monastery as a whole. This means that the abbot serves as both the senior administrator who oversees the monastery staff and the **Zen** master who directs the **monastic training** of the resident monks or nuns. In order to fulfill these responsibilities, the abbot of a major monastery relies upon a large staff of senior officers who assist with either the administrative aspects of management or the spiritual aspects of monastic training. These two types of responsibility are entrusted to two distinct sets of officers, referred to as the Eastern rank (J. **tôhan**) and Western rank (J. **seihan**).

The Eastern rank is the group of monastic officers who assist the abbot with matters related to the secular administration of the community. Officers of the Eastern rank, referred to collectively as the stewards (J. chiji), include the bursar (J. **tsûbun**), who is the chief financial officer; his three assistants, the prior (J. **tsûsu**), the supervisor (J. **kansu**), and the assistant supervisor (J. **fûsu**); the cook (J. **tenzo**), who oversees the kitchen staff; the labor steward (J. **shissui**), who oversees construction projects, repair, maintenance, and farm work; and the supervisor of trainees (J. **ino**), who manages activities in the monks' hall (**sôdô**).

The "Western rank" is the group of monastic officers who assist the abbot with matters related to **meditation** and training of the community. Officers of the Western rank, referred to collectively as the prefects (J. chôshu), include: the chief seat (J. **shuso**), who is second only to the abbot and directly responsible for guiding the other resident monks in their meditation practice; the scribe (J. **shoki**), who handles official correspondence and prepares formal documents; the sutra prefect (J. **zôsu** or **chizô**), who serves as the librarian and cares for the monastery's book collection; the guest prefect (J. **shika**), who receives guests and admits **novices** seeking entry into the community; the bathkeeper (J. **chiyoku**); and the prefect of the **Buddha** hall (J. **chiden**), who cleans the hall and prepares it for ritual use.

Temple Regulations

Regulations from two sources, the monastic community and external authorities, which govern life and practice within a **Zen** Buddhist temple or monastery. First, there are the internal regulations created by the community itself. There are Zen **monastic codes**, a special genre of Zen literature known as **shingi** in Japanese. There also may be internal regulations written by the founder of a monastery or sect to govern his or her own community. In addition to internal regulations, Zen communities often must answer to external authorities. In many parts of the Buddhist world, secular governments create official regulations to control Buddhist monastic communities. During the Tokugawa period (1600–1867) in Japan, for example, the Tokugawa military government (J. **bakufu**) enacted a special series of regulations related to Buddhist temples and monasteries. These regulations, known as **jiin hattô**, were designed to control Buddhist growth and the activities of **monks** and **nuns**.

Tenbôrin

"**Turning the Wheel of the Dharma**," in Japanese, an image used for the **Buddha** teaching the Dharma. See also **Wheel of the Dharma**.

Tencha Butsuji

A Buddhist ritual in which hot tea is offered in veneration to the **Buddha**, the **patriarchs**, or a deceased individual. Tencha is performed as one of the nine ritual actions (J. **kubutsuji**) making up the funeral services for an **abbot** or another prominent member of the monastic community. It is also one of the three ritual actions which characterize Buddhist funerals for ordinary **monks** and **lay believers**. See also **sanbutsuji**.

Tendai Sect

Sect of Japanese **Buddhism** founded by **Saichô** (767–822) in the early ninth century. Its headquarters is the **Enryaku-ji** monastery on Mount Hiei, just east of Kyoto. Tendai teachings draw heavily upon those of the **T'ien-t'ai school** of Chinese Buddhism, from which it drew its name. As in T'ien-t'ai, the primary textual base of Tendai Buddhism is the **Lotus Sutra**. The Chinese T'ien-t'ai and Japanese Tendai systems are not identical, however, because Tendai teachings incorporate elements from other forms of Buddhism, including **esoteric Buddhism** rituals, **Pure Land meditation**, and the **bodhisattva precepts**. Tendai was among the most active schools of Japanese Buddhism throughout the classical and medieval periods. All of the founders of the so-called Kamakura period (1185–1333) schools of Buddhism, including Rinzai and Sôtô **Zen**, emerged from the Tendai school. See also **Rinzai sect** and **Sôtô sect**.

Ten Directions

The term literally refers to the four cardinal directions (east, west, north, and south), the four intermediate directions (northeast, northwest, southeast, and southwest), and up and down. The expression *ten directions* appears frequently in Buddhist texts as a general reference for the entire world or the entire cosmos.

Tendoku

"Revolving reading," a method of speed reading the **sutras** by turning the pages. In tendoku, one does not read or recite the entire sutra word for word. Rather, one recites a few lines from the beginning, middle, and end of the text, and then fans the pages to complete the process. Using this method, it is possible for a small group of **monks** to "read" the entire **Chinese Tripitaka** in a single short ceremony. Japanese **Zen** temples today continue to hold tendoku ceremonies at specified times of year. In many temples, for example, monks recite the 600 sections of the Great **Perfection of Wisdom Sutra** (J. Daihannya Kyô) at New Year's assemblies, using the tendoku method. At **Mampuku-ji**, the main monastery of Obaku Zen, the monks read the entire Chinese Tripitaka in a dramatic New Year's Eve service. In addition, tendoku services may be offered at irregular times as an extraordinary means to build **merit** for special purposes, such as when someone is seriously ill. Tendoku is regarded as the opposite of Shindoku, or "true reading." See also **Obaku sect**.

Ten Epithets for the Buddha

Ten honorific phrases (J. **jûgô**) used to express the qualities of the **Buddha** Shakyamuni (**Siddharta Gautama**): 1) **Tathagata**, or Thus Come One; 2) **Arhat**, or a Holy One Worthy of Veneration; 3) Fully **enlightened one**; 4) Possessor of Wisdom and Practice; 5) Well Gone One; 6) Knower of the World; 7) Unsurpassed; 8) Guide for Human Beings; 9) Teacher of Gods and Human Beings; and 10) the Buddha, the **World-Honored One**.

Ten Evil Acts

The ten most serious offenses of body, speech, and mind (J. jûaku). They are: 1) killing a living being, 2) stealing, 3) sexual misconduct, 4) lying, 5) slander, 6) using language that causes dissension among others, 7) idle talk, 8) greed, 9) giving way to anger, and 10) holding wrong views. The first three are the evil acts of the body, four through seven are the evil acts of speech, and eight through ten are the evil acts of the mind. They are the opposite of the **ten good acts** (jûzen).

Ten Good Acts

The ten good actions related to body, speech, and mind (J. jûzen). Most often they are presented in negative terms as refraining from the **ten evil acts** (J. jûaku): 1) not killing, 2) not stealing, 3) not engaging in sexual misconduct, 4) not lying, 5) not slandering, 6) not using language that causes dissension among others, 7) not engaging in idle talk, 8) not acting out of greed, 9) not giving way to anger, and 10) not holding wrong views. They can also be interpreted in positive terms. The three good actions of the body are saving **sentient beings**, giving generously, and abiding by sexual norms. The four good actions of speech are truthfulness (this counts as two, since it is the positive interpretation of not lying and not slandering), gentle speech, and using language to reconcile disputes. The three good actions of the mind are having generosity, having loving kindness, and holding right views.

Ten Great Disciples of the Buddha

The most prominent of **Siddharta Gautama's** immediate disciples (J. Jûdai Deshi), each traditionally honored for special aptitude in one aspect of Buddhist practice: **Ananda**, foremost in hearing the **Dharma**; **Anuruddha**, foremost in divine insight; **Katyayana**, foremost in analyzing the teachings; **Mahakashyapa**, foremost in ascetic practice; **Maudgalyâyana**, foremost in psychic powers; **Purna**, foremost in debate; **Rahula**, foremost in training young **novices**; **Shariputra**, foremost in wisdom; **Subhuti**, foremost in understanding the teaching of **emptiness**; and **Upali**, foremost in keeping the **precepts**.

Of these ten, the **Zen** school holds Mahakashyapa and Ananda in special regard as the first two Indian **patriarchs** of Zen. According to traditional accounts, Shakyamuni transmitted the Dharma to Mahakashyapa mind to mind, without reliance on verbal teaching, on **Vulture Peak**. The Buddha held up a flower to his assembled disciples and Mahakashyapa alone responded with a smile. Mahakashyapa then transmitted the Dharma to Ananda. See individual entries for further information.

Ishigami, Zenno. *Disciples of the Buddha*. Trans. Richard L. Gage and Paul McCarthy. Tokyo: Kosei Publishing Co., 1989.

Tengu

A fantastical creature from Japanese folklore, described as appearing half human and half bird. The tengu has a long nose or beak, wings, glittering eyes, and a human body with arms and legs. Many stories about tengu appear in popular literature from the medieval period through the modern period. The tengu is closely associated with the mountains and may be regarded as the special guardian of forests and large trees. Perhaps for this reason, when tengu assumes a human form it disguises itself as **Yamabushi**, a Japanese mountain ascetic who wears distinctive robes.

The tengu is generally understood to be an enemy of **Buddhism**. It is often depicted setting fire to Buddhist temples or kidnapping Buddhist **monks**. While holding monks captive, tengu corrupt them by offering them sumptuous food which is actually dung. Tengu also kidnap children, carrying them away from ordinary human existence.

The tengu, a half-human, half-bird creature of Japanese folklore,
is thought to be the special guardian of forests.

Even when the children escape and return home, they are damaged by the experience and never fully recover.

Blacker, Carmen. *The Catalpa Bow.* Boston, MA: Unwin, 1989.

Ten Heavy Precepts

(J. jûjûkai or jûjûkinkai) The primary **precepts** of the **Bodhisattva** Path, derived from the Bonmôkyô (Sk. **Brahma Net Sutra**). The ten heavy precepts include prohibitions against 1) killing, 2) stealing, 3) sexual misconduct, 4) lying, 5) using intoxicants, 6) finding fault in others, 7) boasting about oneself, 8) envy, 9) anger and ill will, and 10) slandering the **three treasures**. The ten heavy precepts differ from the **ten precepts** in that they were not originally used for ordination of monks and nuns, but were to be observed by all Buddhists including lay people. A secondary set of **forty-eight light precepts** fill out the full **bodhisattva precepts** which guide those practicing **Mahayana Buddhism**. See also **lay believer**.

Tenjô Tenge Yuiga Dokuson

"In the heavens above and on the earth below, I alone am worthy of respect." According to the Buddhist tradition, **Siddharta Gautama**, who would later become the **Buddha**, spoke these words immediately after his birth in the Lumbini Garden. The entire verse is known in Japanese as the **Tanjôge**, or the birthday verse.

Tenkei Denson

(1648–1735) Japanese Sôtô **monk** of the Tokugawa period (1600–1867) who was one of the leading early modern scholars of **Dôgen Kigen's** writings. Tenkei was born in Kii, present-day Wakayama Prefecture, and became a Buddhist monk at age eight. He became the **Dharma heir** of Gohô Kaion and served as **abbot** at **Sôji-ji** and other important Sôtô monasteries. He opposed Manzan's reform efforts to restore the practice of **isshi inshô**, receiving **inka**, or Dharma transfer, from only one master. Tenkei defended the **in'in ekishi** system of changing Dharma **lineage** according to the temple at which one serves as abbot. His literary works include the *Shôbôgenzô Benchû*, the first early modern commentary on Dôgen's master work. See also **Sôtô sect**.

Ten Precepts

The most important **precepts** in the **vinaya**, the Buddhist **monastic code** formulated by the **Theravada Buddhism** tradition. Male and female **novices** accept the ten precepts (J. jikkai) at their initial **ordination**. The ten precepts are: 1) not to kill living beings, 2) not to steal, 3) to abstain from sexual misconduct; 4) not to lie, 5) not to take intoxicants, 6) not to eat after noon, 7) not to adorn the body with perfume, flowers, or jewelry, 8) not to participate in public entertainment including dancing, plays, or singing, 9) not to use a luxurious bed, and 10) not to handle money. These precepts form the basis for all monastic practice, providing the foundation upon which **monks** and **nuns** add training in **meditation** and wisdom.

The ten precepts of the novice are sometimes compared with the Ten Commandments found in Judaism and Christianity. The basic rationales for the two codes, however, differ significantly. While the Western traditions understand their moral code to be the ethical norms determined by God and revealed in scripture, the Buddhist monastic code is not based on any form of divine revelation. The ten precepts represent behavior in keeping with the Buddhist **Dharma** and describe a lifestyle which is conducive to the attainment of **enlightenment**. Alcohol, perfume, and secular entertainments are not precluded because they are in any sense wrong or evil in and of themselves. Rather, they are regarded as distractions that may interfere with meditative concentration. Likewise, the **Buddha** recommended that monks and nuns not eat after the noon hour in order to maximize their powers of concentration.

Not all **Zen** monks and nuns are ordained with the ten precepts based on the Theravada vinaya, since Chinese ordination practices underwent some alteration in the context of Japanese **Buddhism**. Sôtô monks and nuns in Japan, for example, receive the **bodhisattva precepts** based on Mahayana texts in place of the ten precepts. The Chinese and Korean Zen traditions and the Obaku school in Japan continue to use the ten precepts for novices. See also **Obaku sect** and **Sôtô sect**.

Ten Realms

The ten levels of living beings recognized by the Mahayana tradition. The ten realms (J. jikkai) include 1) **hell** dwellers, 2) **hungry ghosts**, 3) animals, 4) human beings, 5) **ashura**, 6) **heaven** dwellers, 7) **shravakas**, 8) **pratyeka buddhas**, 9) **bodhisattvas**, and 10) **buddhas**. The lower six realms, from hell dwellers through heaven dwellers, constitute the realms of ordinary **sentient beings**, while the upper four are the realms of **enlightenment**. Ordinary sentient beings do not understand the world as it really is and are thus caught in the cycle of **samsara**. Based on their behavior, they are reborn within the six lower realms. Shravakas and pratyeka buddhas have made progress by realizing the concept of **emptiness**. They have not perfected their Buddhist practice, since they do not embody **compassion** for other sentient beings. Bodhisattvas not only understand emptiness; they practice compassion. Buddhas have attained perfect enlightenment and understand the world as it actually is. See also **six paths**.

Swanson, Paul L. *Foundations of T'ien-T'ai Philosophy: The Flowering of the Two Truths Theory in Chinese Buddhism*. Berkeley, CA: Asian Humanities Press, 1989.

Tenrinnô

"The Wheel-Turning King," Japanese for **Cakravartin**, the ideal monarch in Indian mythology. See **Cakravartin**.

Tenryû-ji

A major **Rinzai sect** monastery located in western Kyoto. Its formal name is Ryôkin-zan Tenryû-ji. It was founded by **Musô Sôseki** (1275–1351) in 1339, as a memorial to the recently deceased **Emperor Go-Daigo** (r. 1318–1339). It was constructed on the site of an imperial villa donated by retired emperor Kôgon (r. 1332–1333). Musô received the support and patronage of the Ashikaga **bakufu**, including the **shôgun** Takauji (1305–1358). The project was funded, in part, by the proceeds of a trading mission to China undertaken by the bakufu in 1342 specifically to raise funds for the temple. Tenryû-ji was ranked among the **Gozan temples** (Five Mountain temples) of Kyoto. It contains some of the loveliest landscape gardens in Kyoto, one said to have been designed by Musô himself. The temple serves today as the headquarters for the Tenryû-ji branch of Rinzai **Zen**.

Tenryû-ji Ha

The **Tenryû-ji** branch of Rinzai, one of the fourteen contemporary branches of the Japanese **Rinzai sect**. The main monastery for the branch is Tenryû-ji, located in the Saga area of Kyoto. **Musô Sôseki** (1275–1351) is regarded as the branch founder. The branch has 103 temples throughout Japan and claims approximately 82,600 adherents.

Tenshô Kôtôroku

Japanese title for the ***T'ien-sheng Kuang-teng Lu***, "The T'ien-sheng Record of the Widely Extending Lamp." See ***T'ien-sheng Kuang-teng Lu***.

Ten Stages of a Bodhisattva

Ten stages in the development of **buddha**-wisdom which are used to describe the bodhisattva's progress along the path toward complete **enlightenment** (J. **jûji** or jucchi). The stages are set out in one chapter of the **Avatamsaka Sutra**. They are: 1) the stage of joy in benefitting oneself and others (Sk. pramudita bhumi); 2) the stage of freedom from all defilement (Sk. vimala bhumi); 3) the stage of emitting the light of wisdom (Sk. prabhakari bhumi); 4) the stage of radiance with wisdom (Sk. arcishmati bhumi); 5) the stage of being difficult to conquer (Sk. sudurjaya bhumi); 6) the stage at which reality is manifested before one's eyes (Sk. abhimukhi bhumi); 7) the stage of going far (Sk. duramgama bhumi); 8) the stage of immovability (Sk. acala bhumi); 9) the stage of attaining of expedient wisdom (Sk. sadhumati bhumi); and 10) the stage of the cloud of the **Dharma** (Sk. dharmamegha bhumi).

Ten Thousand Dharmas

An expression for all things in existence, the entire phenomenal world. In this case, the Sanskrit word ***Dharma*** does not refer to the teachings of **Buddhism** but has a meaning similar to the English word "things." The earlier Buddhist tradition used the word *Dharma* to refer to a limited number of building blocks of phenomenal existence, which we experience as a multitude of mental and physical entities. In East Asia, the term came to refer to the things of the phenomenal world itself, including physical and mental objects. In Chinese thought, the number 10,000 is used to express completion, all-inclusiveness. Hence, the phrase "ten thousand things" (J. manbô) is better understood to mean "all things."

Tentô Butsuji

A Buddhist ritual in which hot, sweetened water is offered in veneration to the **Buddha**, the **patriarchs**, or a deceased individual. Tentô is performed as one of the nine ritual actions (J. **kubutsuji**) comprising the funeral services for an **abbot** or another prominent member of the monastic community. It is also one of the three ritual actions which characterize Buddhist funerals for ordinary **monks** and **lay believers**. See also **sanbutsuji**.

Tenzo

Chief cook, or kitchen head, at a **Zen** monastery, one of the six administrative offices of the monastic community whose role is to oversee the practical administration of the monastery. The tenzo oversees the monastery kitchen and is responsible for all aspects of food preparation and procurement. He or she generally has a large staff of assistants to aid in meal preparation and service. The role of chief cook is crucial to the smooth operation of the monastery and is therefore a position reserved for a senior member of the community. **Dôgen Kigen** (1200–1253) wrote the "**Tenzo Kyôkun**," a famous essay on the responsibilities of the tenzo which is included in the *Eihei Shingi*. See also **temple positions**.

Tenzo Kyôkun

"Instructions for the Cook," a text in one section by **Dôgen Kigen** (1200–1253). Dôgen composed this essay in 1237, when he was residing at Kôshôji near the city of Kyoto. It contains Dôgen's reflections on the responsibilities of the head kitchen **monk**, or **tenzo**, one of the most important officials within a **Zen** monastery, and stories from Dôgen's travels to China. The "Tenzo Kyôkun" was published as the first section of the *Eihei Shingi*. There are two recent English translations, in *Dôgen's Pure Standards for the Zen Community*, by Taigen Daniel Leighton and Shohaku Okamura (State University of New York Press, 1996), and in *Zen Master Eihei Dôgen's Monastic Regulations*, by Ichimura Shohei (North American Institute of Zen and Buddhist Studies, 1993).

Tera

The Japanese term for temple, which commonly refers to Buddhist temples and monasteries. When used as a part of a temple's name, the same word may be pronounced "dera." An alternate transliteration of the same character, "ji," generally appears as a part of any Buddhist temple's name. Tera may refer to a small local temple with only one building or a large monastery complex with several subtemples consisting of numerous structures.

Te-shan Hsuan-chien

(782–865) Chinese **Zen** master of the T'ang dynasty (618–907). Te-shan was the **Dharma heir** of Lung-t'an Ch'ung-hsin. His **lineage** encompasses both the **Yun-men school** and the **Fa-yen school** of Zen, through his disciple **Hsüeh-feng I-ts'un** (822–908). Te-shan is best known for striking students with a stick as a means to provoke an **enlightenment** experience. He appears in many traditional **kôan** cases in the large **kôan collections**.

Tetsugen Dôkô

(1630–1682) Japanese Obaku **monk** of the Tokugawa period (1600–1867), best known for producing the **Obaku-ban**, the first complete woodblock edition of the **Chinese Tripitaka** produced in Japan. Tetsugen was born in Kumamoto province on Kyûshû to a Shinshû (**True Pure Land sect**) family. He entered Buddhist orders at age twelve and trained as a Shinshû monk. He later converted to **Zen** at age twenty-six, when he met **Yin-yüan Lung-ch'i** (1594–1673), the founder of Obaku Zen. He eventually became the **Dharma heir** of **Mu-an Hsing-t'ao** (1611–1684), the second Obaku **patriarch**. Tetsugen died of a fever he contracted while feeding the hungry during a famine in Osaka. See also **Obaku sect**.

Tetsugen-ban

An alternative name for the **Obaku-ban**, the Obaku edition of the **Chinese Tripitaka** produced through the efforts of the Obaku **monk Tetsugen Dôkô** (1630–1682). See **Obaku-ban**.

Tettô Gikô

(1295–1369) Japanese Rinzai **monk** of the late Kamakura (1185–1333) and early Ashikaga (1392–1568) periods. Tettô was born in Izumo and became a Buddhist monk at age six. He began his practice of **Zen** at **Kennin-ji**, where he took the **precepts** at age nineteen. Dissatisfied with the Gozan style of Zen, he became a disciple of **Shûhô Myôchô** (Daitô Kokushi) at **Daitoku-ji**. Tettô was one of the master's leading **Dharma heirs**, and he assumed the position as second **abbot** at Daitoku-ji when Daitô passed away in 1338. His leading disciples included Gongai Sôchû. He received the posthumous titles Daiso Shôbô **Zenji** (Zen Master Great Patriarch of the True Eye) and Tennô Daigen Kokushi (National Teacher Great Manifestation of Heavenly Response). See also **Rinzai sect**.

Theravada Buddhism

"The Way of the Elders," the name used to designate the school of **Buddhism**, which flourishes today in South Asia and South East Asia, as well as a general term for the teachings of early Buddhism. The Theravada school, one of several early Buddhist sects, was originally founded in Sri Lanka in the third century B.C.E. At that time it was one among several early sects of Buddhism. Scholars now apply the term more broadly, since it was the only sect in the region which survived into the modern period. Theravada Buddhism is sometimes called **Hinayana**, a pejorative term meaning Lesser Vehicle (J. Shôjô). The school is contrasted with the **Mahayana Buddhism** tradition, or Great Vehicle, which developed later and spread throughout East Asia.

Third Barrier

The last of three sets of **kôan** used by some **Zen** monasteries in medieval Japan (1185–1600). See **sankan**.

Third Generation Schism

A sectarian dispute within the early **Sôtô sect** in Japan over who legiti-, mately served as the third **abbot** at **Eihei-ji**, the sect's main monastery. See **Sandai Sôron**.

Third Patriarch

The title usually refers to **Seng-ts'an** (d. 606), the Third Chinese **Patriarch** of **Zen** who, tradition says, directly inherited the **Dharma** from the Second Patriarch **Hui-k'o** (487–593). See **Seng-ts'an**.

Thirty-two Marks of a Buddha

Developed from a pre-Buddhist concept of the physical marks that distinguish a **cakravartin**, or universal monarch, from ordinary human beings. The thirty-two marks (J. sanjûnisô) were associated with the **Buddha**, and Buddhist art often portrays him possessing some of these marks. Some slight variation exists in different texts. A typical list would include: 1) a cone-shaped protrusion on top of the head, 2) curly hair, 3) a smooth forehead, 4) a white tuft of hair between the eyebrows, 5) blue eyes with lashes like a bull, 6) forty teeth, 7) perfectly even teeth, 8) pure white teeth, 9) four white canine teeth, 10) saliva that makes all food taste good, 11) a proud jaw like a lion, 12) a long, slender tongue, 13) a beautiful voice, 14) full, strong shoulders, 15) well-formed hands, feet, shoulders, and head, 16) full armpits, 17) golden skin, 18) long arms which reach his knees, 19) an upper body like a lion's, 20) armspan equal to his height, 21) body hair that curls to the right, 22) body hair that stands up, 23) penis concealed in a sheath, 24) full, rounded thighs, 25) well-arched feet, 26) soft hands and feet, 27) webbed fingers and toes, 28) soles marked with the thousand-spoked **Wheel of the Dharma**, 29) slender fingers, 30) flat soles that rest firmly on the ground, 31) long legs, and 32) slender legs like a deer.

Three Ages of the Dharma

(J. Sanji) The Buddhist concept, developed in India, that the **Dharma** taught by the historical **Buddha** would begin to degenerate over time after his death. The concept coincides with other Indian conceptions of cyclical decline over periods of time leading to the emergence of a new age. According to the concept, the Dharma passes through three ages, the Age of the True Dharma, the Semblance Dharma, and the Degenerate Dharma. After the Dharma of the Buddha has completely degenerated and disappeared altogether from the world, a new buddha will emerge to teach the Dharma. The degenerative process then begins anew.

While the concept of the Three Ages (J. Sanjji or Shôzômatsu) took initial shape in India, it was only fully developed and systematized in East Asia. The **T'ien-t'ai school** master Hui-ssu (515–577) was among the first to clearly define the ages and determine the time spans involved. Other Buddhist thinkers altered the time spans somewhat, but the basic system that became widely accepted throughout the East Asian Buddhist world can be outlined as follows:

1) During the Age of True Dharma, the Buddha's teachings remain intact as they were during his lifetime. Buddhists can practice and follow the **Buddhist path**, and some highly advanced individuals attain **enlightenment**. By Hui-ssu's reckoning, this age lasts for 500 years. Other interpretations popular in Japanese **Buddhism** set the time span at 1,000 years.

2) During the Age of Semblance Dharma, the teachings have begun to deteriorate. What remains has the appearance of the true Dharma but is no longer perfect. In this intermediate stage, people continue to practice Buddhism as they did in the earlier age, but the full realization of the teachings and the attainment of enlightenment are no longer possible. This period lasts for 1,000 years.

3) Finally, during the Age of Degenerate Dharma, the Dharma has deteriorated so thoroughly that even the practice of Buddhism becomes impossible. All that remains are the teachings, which can neither be truly followed nor fully realized. This **Latter Age of the Dharma** (J. Mappô), as it is commonly called, lasts for 10,000 years.

Since East Asian Buddhists traditionally accept the year 949 B.C.E. as the date of the Buddha's death, they believed that the Age of the Degenerate Dharma (Latter Age of the Dharma) began in 550 or 1050 C.E., depending on their interpretation of the time span of the first age. (The date 949 B.C.E. is historically inaccurate. The Buddha actually died circa 560 B.C.E. However, the earlier date served an important purpose for East Asian Buddhism, since it placed the Buddha several centuries before Confucius, rendering Buddhism the more venerable tradition!) The belief in the Three Ages was so widespread in China and Japan that almost all schools of East Asian Buddhism responded to it in some way.

The **Zen** school most commonly rejects the notion that practice and enlightenment are inaccessible in the present age. Zen teaching maintains that the Dharma, transmitted from mind to mind throughout the generations starting with Shakyamuni Buddha (**Siddharta Gautama**), remains the True Dharma.

Matsunaga, Daigan, and Alicia Matsunaga. *Foundation of Japanese Buddhism.* 2 vols. Los Angeles, CA: Buddhist Books International, 1976.

Three Baskets

Literal translation of the Sanskrit "**Tripitaka**," the **Buddhist scriptures**. See **Tripitaka**.

Three Bodies of the Buddha

The **Dharma** body (Sk. **Dharmakaya**), the bliss body (Sk. **sambhogakaya**), and the transformation body (Sk. **nirmanakaya**) of the **Buddha**. The concept of the three bodies (Sk. trikaya; J. sanshin) is a Mahayana understanding of the Buddha, formulated to clarify the various and often confusing teachings related to the different types of buddhas that developed within the tradition. Ancient **Buddhism** and the Theravada tradition recognize Shakyamuni (**Siddharta Gautama**), the historical Buddha, as the one and only Buddha, who, with his death, passed out of existence. Over time the Mahayana tradition not only developed alternative understandings of Shakyamuni himself, it came to recognize numerous other historical and cosmic buddhas. In addition, the Mahayana tradition regarded all of these historical and cosmic buddhas as manifestations of an eternal Buddha.

First, the Dharma or truth body is understood to be the eternal Buddha that represents the source of all the manifestations of the Buddha in various times and places. The Dharma body is closely identified with the Mahayana concept of **emptiness** (Sk. shunyata). Second, the bliss body of the Buddha is associated with the various celestial buddhas like **Amida buddha** who dwell in their own **Buddha Lands** and guide **sentient beings** born there. Third, the transformation body signifies the manifestations of the Buddha in this world, the historical buddhas, of whom Siddharta Gautama is but one example. These historical buddhas appear in order to teach the Dharma to ordinary sentient beings.

Three Essentials of Zen

(J. sangen san'yô) According to the **Zen** teachers, the sincere practice of Zen requires three essential elements, Great Trust (J. **Daishinkon**), Great Doubt (J. **Daigi**), and Great Resolve (J. **Daifunshi**). The Three Essentials were first discussed by the Yüan dynasty (1260–1368) Rinzai master Kao-feng Yüan-miao (1238–1295) in a text entitled *Zen Essentials* (*Kao-feng Ho-shang Ch'an-yao*; J. *Kôhô Ôshô Zen'yô*). The Japanese Rinzai master **Hakuin Ekaku** (1685–1768) drew upon Kao-feng's writings and likewise stressed the Three Essentials for his own disciples. First, the Zen practitioner must place great trust in the Buddhist teachings, the path of Zen, and his or her own individual teacher. Second, through the practice of seated **meditation** and the use of **kôan**, the practitioner must produce and break through the Great Doubt to attain **enlightenment**. Third, the practitioner must preserve a deep determination to persevere in Zen practice. See also **Rinzai sect**.

Threefold Training

Wisdom (Sk. **prajna**), morality (Sk. **sila**), and concentration (Sk. **samadhi**). These three areas of learning and practice encompass the whole of the traditional **Buddhist path**. Wisdom begins with intellectual training in the teachings of **Buddhism**. Morality is ethical training, which involves keeping the Buddhist **precepts** and coming to understand the premises on which the code is based. Concentration includes a variety of forms of meditative training. In practical terms, Buddhists, both lay and monastic, begin with morality as the basis of practice. Intellectual and meditative training are most often understood to be the proper concern of **monks** and **nuns**.

Buddhists traditionally use the threefold training (J. sangaku) as an abbreviated formula which encompasses all the elements of the **Eightfold Path**. In this context, wisdom is said to be composed of right views and intention; morality, of right speech, action, and livelihood; and concentration, of right effort, mindfulness and concentration. In Mahayana contexts, one more often finds references to the threefold training than to the Eightfold Path.

Threefold Truth

A Chinese Buddhist elaboration on the earlier Mahayana concept of **Twofold Truth**. **Chih-i** (538–597), the founder of the **T'ien-t'ai school** of **Buddhism**, developed the concept to avoid problems arising from viewing the Twofold Truth originally set out by **Mâdhyamaka** as though it were an absolute dichotomy. In addition to the levels of **Ultimate Truth** and **Relative Truth**, the Threefold Truth (J. santai) adds the perspective of the middle path. From this perspective, the ultimate reality of **emptiness** and the relative reality of ordinary existence are seen as one.

Three Gates to Emancipation

Three kinds of **meditation** which lead to release (J. sangedatsumon). These are: 1) meditation on **emptiness**, especially as it regards the self; 2) meditation on no-attributes, the concept that all phenomena lack ultimate reality; and 3) meditation on no desire, because since phenomena lack ultimate reality, there is nothing to desire.

Three Marks

Buddhist teaching that all of existence is characterized by **suffering** (Sk. duhkha), **impermanence** (Sk. anitya), and No-Self (Sk. **Anatman**).

Three Phrases

A formulaic expression developed by **Lin-chi I-hsuan**, the founder of the Rinzai school of **Zen**, as a teaching device. It is based on a passage from the *Sayings of Lin-chi*:

"A **monk** asked, 'What is the First Phrase?' The master said, 'When the seal of the Three Essentials is revealed, the vermilion dots are seen to be merged, and yet, without resort to discussion, host and guest are distinct.'

'What is the Second Phrase?' The master said, 'How could Miao-chie permit Wu-cho to question him? How can skill in the use of expedients go against the power to cut through the myriad streams?'

'What is the Third Phrase?' The master said, 'Look at the puppets playing on the stage! All their jumps and jerks depend upon the person behind.'"

These phrases became known in Chinese as san-chu and in Japanese as sanku. The later Rinzai tradition used the formula as a **kôan**. The tradition does not have a unified understanding of the meaning of the phrases. See also **Rinzai sect**.

Three Poisons

(J. sandoku) Greed, anger, and ignorance. These are the three fundamental obstructions to **enlightenment**, sometimes called **afflictions** (J. bonnô), which can also be identified as the basic causes of **suffering**.

Three Pounds of Flax

A famous answer given by the **Zen** master Tung-shan Shou-chu (J. Tôzan Shusho; d. 900) which became a popular **kôan** in the classical tradition. See **Masangin**.

Three Realms

The world of unenlightened beings is divided into three realms (J. sangai), according to the Buddhist tradition. The lowest level is the realm of desire, which includes **hell** dwellers, **hungry ghosts**, animals, human beings, **ashura**, and some **heaven** dwellers. In these levels of existence, **sentient beings** experience sexual desire, hunger, thirst, and other forms of sensual desire. The realm of form includes some of the higher heavens, in which the inhabitants experience no sensual desires. The realm of formlessness

Buddhist monks and nuns wear the traditional three robes and carry
one begging bowl as they travel about seeking alms.

includes the very highest heavens, in which beings have no physical form and exist in meditative states.

Three Robes

Buddhist **monks** and **nuns** traditionally wear the three types of monastic robes (J. san'e), or **kesa** (Sk. kashaya). These three include an undergarment (Sk. antarvasa; J. **gojôe**), an ordinary outer garment (Sk. uttarasangha; J. **shichijôe**), and a formal outer garment (Sk. samghati; J. **kujôe**). The first robe served as underwear during daytime hours and was worn alone while sleeping and working on temple grounds. The second robe was worn during the day inside the temple grounds. The third robe was worn over the others whenever a monk or nun ventured outside monastery grounds. See **kesa**.

Three Robes, One Bowl

(J. san'e ippatsu) The most basic possessions of a Buddhist **monk** or **nun**, which are regarded as symbolic of the monastic life. Traditionally, monks and nuns were allowed to own only three **kesa** and one **begging bowl** as their personal property.

Three Samadhi

Three levels of **samadhi** or realization (J. sansammai). These are: 1) samadhi of **emptiness**, in which one realizes that there is no abiding and unchanging self; 2) samadhi of no attributes, in which one realizes that all phenomena lack ultimate reality; and 3) samadhi of no desire, in which one realizes that since phenomena lack ultimate reality, there is nothing to desire.

Three Sufferings

The three kinds of human **suffering** (J. sankû) that arise from sickness or hunger, separation from pleasure, and the **impermanence** of things.

Three Teachings

(J. sankyô) An expression used throughout East Asia for the three major religious traditions of the region, namely, **Buddhism**, Confucianism, and Taoism. In some cases, Japanese used the term *three teachings* in reference to Buddhism, Confucianism, and Shintô, substituting the Japanese indigenous religion for Taoism. There were many thinkers, including some Buddhist masters, who taught the principle that the three teachings are one. See also **Sankyô itchi**.

Three Teachings as One

A traditional religious concept popular throughout East Asia which maintains that **Buddhism**, Confucianism, and Taoism (or sometimes Shintô) are essentially compatible. See **Sankyô itchi**.

Three Treasures

(J. sambô) The **Buddha**, the **Dharma**, and the **sangha**; that is, the Buddha; his teachings, especially as they are preserved in the **Buddhist scriptures**; and the community of believers, especially the community of **monks** and **nuns**. These three things function as the core objects of faith for Buddhists and serve as resources for Buddhist belief and practice. All Buddhists, regardless of school or denomination, revere the three treasures. Buddhists express their faith in them through a ritual formula known as "taking refuge" (J. **kie**), a universal practice throughout the Buddhist world. Taking refuge in the three treasures is the ritual action through which one embarks upon the **Buddhist path**, and it is therefore used as a part of initiation rituals, including **ordinations**. In addition, Buddhists regularly repeat the formula as a means of reaffirming their commitment to the tradition. Despite the unifying structure provided by the three treasures throughout the Buddhist world, differences in various schools' interpretations naturally arise. (For instance, Theravada Buddhism recognizes only the historical Buddha, Siddharta Gautama, Mahayana Buddhism recognizes many different Buddhas.)

Mahayana Buddhism teaches that there are three ways of understanding the three treasures (J. sanshu sambô): as manifest (J. genzen sambô), as enduring (J. jûji sambô), and as one (J. ittai sambô). The manifest three treasures refers to the treasures as they existed during the lifetime of the historical Buddha: Shakyamuni buddha (**Siddharta Gautama**) himself, his teachings expressed in words and **sermons**, and the community of his immediate disciples. The enduring three treasures refers to the ongoing forms of the treasures as they have continued to exist since the Buddha's death: images of the Buddha preserved in art, the written scriptures which convey his teachings, and the existing Buddhist monastic community. The conception of the three treasures as one affirms that from the perspective of ultimate reality, the three treasures transcend distinctions.

The **Zen** school maintains faith in the three treasures, including the recognition of the manifest, enduring, and unified perspectives. Zen texts tend to stress, however, the need to recognize that the Treasures are not realities external to the believer, but rather are inherent within the self. In the **Platform Sutra**, the Sixth Patriarch admonishes, "Good friends, I urge you to take refuge in the three treasures in your own natures. The Buddha is **enlightenment**, the Dharma is truth, and the sangha is purity." (Yampolsky, p. 145).

Yampolsky, Philip B. *The Platform Sutra of the Sixth Patriarch*. New York: Columbia University Press, 1967.

Three Vehicles

The Mahayana tradition originally recognized three paths or vehicles (J. sanjô) leading to **enlightenment**: those of **shravakas, bodhisattvas**, and **pratyeka buddhas**. Shravaka buddhas rely upon the teachings of the **Buddha** and strive to become **arhats**. That is, they aspire to attain enlightenment for themselves. Their practice is based upon the contemplation of the **four noble truths** and the **Eightfold Path** as taught by the historical Buddha. Bodhisattvas follow the Bodhisattva Path, striving to perfect their practice of the **six perfections**. Their goal is to become buddhas and to lead all other **sentient beings** to the same goal. Unlike the bodhisattvas, who embody **compassion** for others, shravakas are said to focus selfishly on their own attainment of enlightenment. Pratyeka buddhas are self-enlightened beings who achieved an understanding of the **Law of Causation** on their own, without the benefits of learning the **Dharma** from another buddha. However, pratyeka buddhas cannot share what they have learned with others. They are completely isolated practitioners. The Mahayana tradition deems the vehicles of pratyeka buddhas and shravakas to be inferior to that of the bodhisattva.

The so-called **two vehicles** are associated with the Hinayana tradition. Mahayana uses the pejorative expression meaning "Lesser Vehicle" for ancient **Buddhism** and **Theravada Buddhism**. The vehicle of the bodhisattva is identified as the Great Vehicle, or Mahayana. The **Lotus Sutra** took the teachings of the three vehicles one step further and denied that three distinct vehicles actually exist. By means of the parable of the **burning house** found in chapter three of the Lotus Sutra, the Buddha explains that all three vehicles can be reduced to the single Great Vehicle, the **one vehicle** of Mahayana. In effect, the Lotus Sutra identifies pratyeka buddhas and shravakas as bodhisattvas who misunderstand the ultimate nature of the **Buddhist path**.

T'ien-sheng Kuang-teng Lu

"The T'ien-sheng Record of the Widely Extending Lamp," (J. *Tenshô Kôtôroku*) a chronicle of early **Zen** history, presented in the biographies, **sermons**, and anecdotes of prominent Zen masters. The biographies begin with Shakyamuni **Buddha (Siddharta Gautama)** and continue down through the Chinese **patriarchs** and to the masters of the early eleventh century. The text was written by the nobleman Li Tsun-hsu (d. 1038), a lay practitioner of Rinzai Zen, in 1036. Li placed special emphasis on the Rinzai **lineage** and included the *Sayings of Lin-chi* (Ch. *Lin-chi Lu*; J. *Rinzai-roku*) in its entirety. It is the second of the five Zen chronicles known collectively as the *Five Records of the Lamp* (J. *Gotôroku*). See also **lay believer** and **Rinzai sect**.

T'ien-t'ai School

Chinese school of **Buddhism**, systematized by **Chih-i** (538–597) in the sixth century. The school draws its name from Mt. T'ien-t'ai in Chekiang, the headquarters of the school where Chih-i lived and taught. T'ien-t'ai thought draws heavily upon **Nagarjuna's** writings. The school's primary teaching of the **Threefold Truth** is a Chinese elaboration of Nagarjuna's teaching of **Twofold Truth**. Chih-i created a synthesis of all the various Buddhist teachings and **sutras** by dividing the life of the historical **Buddha** into five time periods. In this system, the **Lotus Sutra** represents the final and supreme teaching of the Buddha. T'ien-t'ai thought was transmitted to Japan in the ninth century by **Saichô** (767–822) where it became the primary basis for the **Tendai sect**.

T'ien-t'ung Ju-ching
(1163–1228) Chinese Sôtô master better known as **Ju-ching**. See **Ju-ching**.

T'ien-t'ung-shan
Mount T'ien-t'ung, also an alternate name for Mount T'ai-p'o, in modern-day Che-chiang province, China. See **T'ai-p'o-shan**.

Ti-Tsang
Chinese name for the **bodhisattva** Kshitigarbha, popularly known by his Japanese name **Jizô**. See **Jizô**.

Tô
Pagoda, or **stupa**, a Buddhist structure designed to house **relics**. The Japanese term tô is the standard translation for the Sanskrit word stupa. Also known in Japanese as tôba or sotoba. See **stupa**.

Tôan
Literally, the eastern retreat. The term is used as a variant term for **tôdô**.

Tôdô
Literally, the eastern hall; alternately, tôan, the eastern retreat. It is a title of respect given to a retired **abbot** of a **Zen** temple. Retired abbots residing in the temple where they previously served as abbot are called tôdô, because they traditionally live in the eastern hall. In contrast, retired abbots who served at a different temple are called **seidô**, or western hall. In the modern period, the term is used by both the **Rinzai sect** and the **Obaku sect** to designate one of ten possible ranks a **monk** may hold.

Tôfuku-ji
A major **Rinzai sect** monastery, located in the Higashiyama area of Kyoto. Its formal name is E'nichi-zan Tôfuku-ji. It was named for the magnificent Nara temples Tôdai-ji and Kôfuku-ji, which it was intended to rival in grandeur. It was founded by **Enni Ben'en** (1202–1280) in 1239 with the patronage of the regent Kujô Michiie (1193–1252). The monastery remained closely associated with the Fujiwara family for many years. Although it was built to be primarily a **Zen** monastery, the original grounds included structures for Shingon and Tendai esoteric rituals. It was ranked among the **Gozan temples** (Five Mountain temples) of Kyoto. The monastery suffered damage on several occasions throughout its history. Various political leaders have funded restoration projects, and many of the present structures were built or restored in 1938. The monastery serves today as the headquarters for the Tôfuku-ji branch of Rinzai Zen and is an active monastery in terms of meditative practice. See also **Shingon sect** and **Tendai sect**.

Tôfuku-ji Ha
The **Tôfuku-ji** branch of Rinzai, one of the fourteen contemporary branches of the Japanese **Rinzai sect**. The main monastery for the branch is Tôfuku-ji, located in the Higashiyama area of Kyoto. **Enni Ben'en** (1202–1280) is regarded as the branch founder. The branch has 372 temples throughout Japan.

Tôhan
The Eastern rank, a group of monastic officers who assist the **abbot** with matters related to the secular administration of the community. Within every **Zen** monastery, responsibilities for the administrative aspects of temple management are handled separately from the spiritual aspects of

monastic life, such as **meditation** and training. The distinct duties are entrusted to two sets of officers, referred to as the Eastern and Western (J. **seihan**) ranks. Both ranks fall under the direction of the abbot, who is responsible for the smooth operation of the community as a whole.

The Eastern rank of officers are so called because their primary duties keep them in the monastic halls traditionally situated on the eastern side of the grounds. Officers of the Eastern rank, referred to collectively as the stewards (J. chiji), include the bursar (J. **tsûbun**), the prior (J. **tsûsu**), the supervisor (J. **kansu**), the assistant supervisor (J. **fûsu**), the cook (J. **tenzo**), the labor steward (J. **shissui**), and the supervisor of trainees (J. **ino**). See the respective entries for the specific duties of each office. See also **temple positions**.

Tokuhô Zenketsu

(1419–1506) Japanese Rinzai **monk** of the Ashikaga period (1392–1568). Tokuhô was born in Mino, in present day Gifu Prefecture. He was a seventh generation descendent of **Kanzan Egen's Myôshin-ji** line. **Sekkô Sôshin** (1408–1486) trained Tokuhô to be his **Dharma heir** and Tokuhô became one of his four principal disciples. He served as **abbot** at **Daitoku-ji**, Myôshin-ji, and other major Rinzai monasteries. After his death, he received the title Daijaku Jôshô **Zenji** (Zen Master Ever Illuminating Nirvana). See also **Rinzai sect**.

Tokusan Senkan

The Japanese pronunciation for **Te-shan Hsuan-chien** (782–865), a Chinese **Zen monk**. See **Te-shan Hsuan-chien**.

Tômyô E'nichi

Japanese pronunciation for **Tung-ming Hui-jih** (1272–1340), a Chinese Sôtô **Zen monk**. Alternatively pronounced Tômei. See **Tung-ming Hui-jih**.

Ton

A measure indicating a certain number of blows with a cane. In secular Chinese society, striking with a cane was commonly used to punish criminals. One ton was generally equivalent to forty or sixty blows with the cane. In the **Zen** school, Zen masters sometimes struck disciples with the cane as a teaching device to shock them out of ordinary patterns of discursive thought. This practice was not intended as a punishment for misbehavior, but as a means to trigger an **enlightenment** experience. In the Zen context, one ton is thought to indicate ten or twenty blows with the cane.

Tongaku

"Sudden teaching," an alternate expression for tongo, **sudden enlightenment**. See **sudden enlightenment**.

Tongo

"Sudden enlightenment," the Japanese term for the **Zen** teaching that **enlightenment** is achieved immediately rather than gradually or in stages over an extended period of time. The term is contrasted with zengo, or **gradual enlightenment**. See **sudden enlightenment**.

Tonsure

Shaving the head when becoming a **monk** or **nun**. One speaks of a person taking the tonsure when they join a monastic order. The word derives from the Roman Catholic monastic practice of shaving the top of the head and leaving a thin outer band of hair. The practice of shaving the head when entering monastic orders exists in numerous religious traditions throughout the world and is generally regarded as a symbol of leaving behind the ordinary secular life. In the Christian West, monks traditionally shaved a portion of their heads when they first entered orders and continued to do so as a regular part of monastic life.

When one becomes a Buddhist monk or nun, he or she is given tonsure, the ritual shaving of the head.

Throughout the Buddhist world, both monks and nuns completely shave their heads at **ordination** and continue to do so at regular intervals. Men also shave all facial hair. At many Japanese Zen monasteries, shaving days are observed at five-day intervals, falling on days with a four or a nine (J. **shiku-nichi**). Shaving days are generally also cleaning days; monks and nuns do their laundry and clean the temple grounds after assisting one another with shaving. The Buddhist tonsure not only distinguishes the monastic community from ordinary **householders**, it effectively reduces the worldly distinctions between the genders. In some Buddhist areas and in some time periods, the tonsure is more a symbolic gesture, and only a portion of the hair is cut, especially for women.

Tôrei Enji

(1721–1792) Japanese Rinzai **monk** of the Tokugawa period (1600–1867) who was a direct **Dharma heir** of **Hakuin Ekaku** (1685–1768). Enji was born in Kanzaki, modern-day Shiga Prefecture, to the Nakamura family. His maternal family was an important Shintô **lineage**, and Enji maintained connections to Shintô practice and thought throughout his life. He entered Buddhist orders at age nine. He was later ordained by a Rinzai monk and soon made his way to Shôin-ji to practice under Hakuin. After an initial **enlightenment** experience, he spent many years in solitary practice in Kyoto, beginning in 1746. He received Hakuin's **inka**, or Dharma transfer, and a **Dharma robe** in 1748. Hakuin purchased and restored two temples for his favorite disciple. In 1755, Hakuin restored Ryûtaku-ji in the neighboring village of Mishima in Izu. Tôrei, as he was now called, resided at Ryûtaku-ji for twenty years. Hakuin later bought Shidô-an in Edo, which Tôrei used when he lectured in Edo. Tôrei became a writer and lecturer of high repute. His literary works include the *Shûmon Mujintô Ron*, the *Goke Sanshô Yôro Mon*, the *Kaisan Shidô Bu'nan Anju Zenji Anroku*, the *Shôju Dôkyô Etan Anju Anroku*, and the *Ryûtaku Kaiso Jinki Dokumyô Zenji Nempu*. He received the posthumous title Butsugo Jinshô Zenji (Zen Master Guardian of the Buddha Illuminator of the Gods). See also **Rinzai sect**.

Tortoise Hair

A **Zen** expression used to undermine or ridicule belief in something that does not exist. In particular, Zen teachers apply the term *tortoise hair* (J. kimô) to the belief that one has an abiding, eternal self, or that the phenomena of everyday life have ultimate reality when they do not. Tortoise hair is often paired as an expression with rabbits' horns.

Tosotsuten

Japanese for **Tushita heaven**, the current abode of the future **Buddha**, Miroku (Sk. **Maitreya**). See **Tushita Heaven**.

Tôsu

The latrine, one of the seven buildings (J. **shichidô garan**) that form the core of a **Zen** monastery. The term literally means "the eastern office", a reference to its traditional location. The Zen **monastic codes** provide extensive instructions on proper etiquette in the latrine. Before using the latrine, for example, **monks** were enjoined to contemplate on the **compassion** of Ususama **Myôô**, a deity willing to purify even the foulest place. Images of Ususama Myôô are often enshrined in the tôsu as the presiding deity. **Incense** was burned in the hall not only to freshen the air, but as a part of proper ritual behavior. Traditional latrines are no longer used in Japanese monasteries.

Tôyô Eichô

(1438–1504) Japanese Rinzai **monk** of the Ashikaga period (1392–1568). Tôyô was born in Mino, in present-day Gifu Prefecture. He was a seventh generation descendent of **Kanzan Egen's Myôshin-ji** line. He became the **Dharma heir** of **Sekkô Sôshin** (1408–1486) and was one of his four principal disciples. He served as **abbot** at **Daitoku-ji**, Myôshin-ji, and other major Rinzai monasteries. The Rinzai reformer **Hakuin Ekaku** (1685–1768) was a later descendant in Tôyô's **lineage**. His literary works include the *Ku Zôshi*. See also **Rinzai sect**.

Tôzan

East Mountain, the Japanese name for **Tung-shan**, the monastery of the Fifth **Zen Patriarch Hung-jen** (601–674). See **Tung-shan**.

Tôzan Ryôkai

The Japanese pronunciation for **Tung-shan Liang-chieh** (807–869), a Chinese **Zen monk**, co-founder of the Chinese Sôtô school. See **Tung-shan Liang-chieh**.

Transformation Body

One of **three bodies of the Buddha** according to the Mahayana understanding of the concept of the Buddha. Called *nirmanakaya* in Sanskrit. See **nirmanakaya**.

Transmission of the Lamp

(J. *Keitoku Dentôroku*) The ***Ching-te Ch'üan-teng Lu***, a collection of **Zen** biographies of Indian and Chinese Zen masters compiled by Tao-yuan and edited by Yang I (968–1024) in 1004, during the Ching-te era of the Sung dynasty (960–1279). The text provides a traditional version of the authentic Zen **lineage** from the **Seven Buddhas of the Past** through the Chinese masters of the Sung dynasty.

The title *Transmission of the Lamp* is sometimes used to refer to the entire genre of Zen literature which provides biographies of eminent masters arranged to convey the history of **Dharma transmission**. These texts serve a variety of purposes. They honor the masters of the past, and thereby legitimate the Zen school as a whole or a specific lineage. They also give information about the teaching styles of all the important masters of a given period and provide teaching material Zen masters can use with their own students. Most of the kôan used throughout the Zen tradition derive from this literature. See ***Ching-te Ch'üan-teng Lu***.

Tripitaka

The **Buddhist scriptures**, especially those of early **Buddhism** and **Theravada Buddhism**. The Tripitaka proper, a collection of thirty-one Theravadan texts, represents the oldest collection of Buddhist scriptures, portions of which date back to the second century B.C.E. For several centuries, the scriptures were preserved orally, and there are therefore different versions. The texts were eventually recorded in Pali and later translated into Sanskrit, Tibetan, and Chinese. The term *Tripitaka* (J. **sanzô**) is sometimes used more loosely for the later **Mahayana** collections of the scriptures which contain many additional Mahayana **sutras** and commentaries.

Tripitaka literally means "Three Baskets," and the scriptures of the original are divided into three distinct sections or baskets, each representing a different type of teaching. The first basket is the **vinaya**, which sets out the **monastic code** governing the lives of Buddhist **monks** and **nuns**. According to tradition, **Upali**, a leading disciple of the **Buddha**, recited the entire vinaya at the first Buddhist council held shortly after the Buddha's death. The second basket, known as the sutras or discourses, preserves the **sermons** given by the historical Buddha. Tradition maintains that **Ananda**, another important disciple, likewise recited the sutras at the first council. Finally, the **Abhidharma** basket includes commentaries on the Buddha's teachings written by later Buddhist scholars. Because the Triptaka was originally preserved in Pali, the Theravada collection is commonly known as the Pali Canon. Later Mahayana collections are sometimes known as Tibetan or **Chinese Tripitaka**. The Japanese refer to the Chinese Tripitaka as the **Daizôkyô** or **issaikyô**.

True Mind

A **Zen** expression for one's true or original nature, which is said to be **Buddha Nature**. The realization of True Mind is synonymous with **enlightenment**.

True Person of No Rank

An expression coined by the T'ang **Zen** master **Lin-chi I-hsuan** for an enlightened individual. According to one famous passage in the ***Sayings of Lin-chi***, the master said, "Here in this lump of red flesh there is a true person with no rank. Constantly he goes in and out the gates of your face. If there are any of you who don't know this for a fact, then look! Look!" (Watson, p. 13) Lin-chi used the term *true person* in contrast to "the **lump of red flesh**," the ordinary human person. Like other Zen teachers, Lin-chi stressed that every individual possesses an innate **Buddha Nature** and that one needs only to recognize it to be enlightened. The enlightened being and the ordinary person differ only in the real-

Woodblock plate bearing part of the Tripitaka, or Buddhist scriptures, from the Obaku-ban at Hôzô-in.

ization of innate **enlightenment**, so the true person is already present in the ordinary person.

The concept of the true person (Ch. chen-jen; J. shinnin) derives from concepts and terminology from both classical **Buddhism** and Taoism. Taoists first used the term *true person* to describe an ideal Taoism adept who had attained a high level of wisdom. Chinese Buddhists originally adopted the Taoist concept as a translation for the Sanskrit *arhat*, a Buddhist practitioner who has attained **nirvana**. Lin-chi describes the true person as "without rank," suggesting complete freedom from external limitations based on social classification and other form of categorization.

Watson, Burton. *The Zen Teachings of Master Lin-chi: A Translation of the* Lin-chi Lu. Boston, MA: Shambhala, 1993.

True Pure Land Sect

A sect of Japanese **Buddhism** founded by the **monk Shinran** (1173–1262) during the Kamakura period (1185–1333), known in Japanese as Jôdo Shinshû. The teachings and practices of the sect are based on Shinran's understanding of the **Pure Land Sutras**, which serve as the principal scriptures. Shinran was originally a Tendai monk until he left Mount Hiei to become the disciple of **Hônen**, a proponent of exclusive Pure Land practice. True Pure Land Buddhism encourages placing one's faith in the **Amida buddha** and achieving salvation through **rebirth** in his **Western Pure Land**. The primary practice of the sect is **chanting** the name of Amida, using the simple formula "**Namu Amida Butsu**." See also **Tendai sect**.

True Thusness

Things as they are; absolute reality. One of the standard English translations for the Sanskrit term *Tathata* (J. Shinnyo). It is alternately translated as "suchness." True Thusness is a **Mahayana Buddhism** concept which came to be a key notion for **Zen Buddhism**. True Thusness is beyond the distinctions of ordinary discursive thought and is perceived immediately by the enlightened mind. It is closely associated with the concept of *shunyata*, or **emptiness**; True Thusness expresses the same reality as the positive concept of emptiness.

Ts'ao-hsi

A mountain in China which is sometimes used as an alternative name for **Hui-neng** (638–713), the Sixth **Patriarch**, who resided there. See **Hui-neng**.

Tsao-kung

Sôkô Shinsai, the Chinese God of the hearth who protects the kitchen fire. See **Sôkô Shinsai**.

Ts'ao-shan Pen-chi

(840–901; J. Sôzan Honjaku) Chinese **Zen** master, who, along with his **Dharma** master **Tung-shan Liang-chieh** (807–869), is known as a co-founder of the **Ts'ao-tung school** (J. Sôtô) of Chinese Zen. Tung-shan entrusted Ts'ao-shan with the doctrine of the **five ranks**, a teaching then exclusive to their **lineage**, as a sign of his **Dharma transmission**. Ts'ao-shan is said to have systematized the teaching.

Ts'ao-tung School

One of two major schools of Chinese **Zen**, along with the **Lin-chi school**. Ts'ao-tung Zen is named for two of its founding **patriarchs**, **Tung-shan Liang-chieh** (807–869) and his disciple **Ts'ao-shan Pen-chi** (840–901), who rank among the leading Chinese Zen masters of the T'ang dynasty (618–907). The predominant style of Ts'ao-tung practice focuses on single-minded devotion to seated **meditation** (**zazen**) without the use of **kôan** or other devices. The Ts'ao-tung **lineage** is traditionally numbered among the **five houses** of Chinese Zen from the T'ang dynasty. It was transmitted to Japan during the Kamakura period (1185–1333) by the Japanese **monk Dôgen Kigen** (1200–1253). It is known there as the **Sôtô sect**.

Tsûbun

The bursar at a **Zen** monastery. This office was added by the Japanese to the original Chinese list of six administrative offices within the monastic community whose role is to oversee the practical administration of the monastery. (These positions together are called the chiji or **tôhan**.) The bursar was the chief financial officer responsible for the overall economic welfare of the community. In that capacity, the bursar supervised the activities of the other three financial officers within the administration, the **tsûsu**, the **kansu**, and the **fûsu**. In some cases, the bursar served as the chief officer in the Eastern Rank and oversaw all six of the chiji. In medieval Japan (1185–1600), the bursar often acted as a moneylender to raise additional funds for the upkeep of the temple. See also **temple positions**.

Tsung

Chinese term which may be translated as school, sect, denomination, or **lineage**, depending on the context. Pronounced "shû" in Japanese. See **lineage**.

Tsung-ching Lu

(J. Sûgyôroku) A Chinese Buddhist text by **Yung-ming Yen-shou** (904–975), in 100 sections and composed in 961. In the text, Yung-ming provides a syncretic overview of various **Mahayana Buddhism** schools of thought and argues that the teachings of **Zen** are identical with those of the "**Consciousness Only**" school, **San-lun school**, **Hua-yen school**, and **T'ien-t'ai school**.

Ts'ung-jung Lu

The Book of Serenity, a classic collection of one hundred **Zen kôan** with verses and prose commentaries, first published in 1224. Known more commonly by its Japanese title, the *Shôyôroku*. See *Shôyôroku*.

Tsung-men Lien-teng Hui-yao

(J. *Shûmon Rentô Eyô*) "A Collection of Essential Material of the Zen Sect's Successive Records of the Lamp," in thirty sections. It was compiled by Hui-weng Wu-ming in 1183. It includes material derived from the *Ching-te Ch'üan-teng Lu*, the *T'ien-sheng Kuang-teng Lu*, and the *Chien-chung Ching-kuo Hsu-teng Lu*, as well as additional materials drawn from **recorded sayings** of several **Zen** masters of the Sung dynasty (960–1279). It begins with the **Seven Buddhas of the Past** and continues down through the masters of the Southern Sung dynasty, the time period of the compiler. This text represents the fourth of the five Zen chronicles of Zen biographies known collectively as the *Five Records of the Lamp* (J. **Gotôroku**).

Tsung-mi

(780–840; J. Shûmitsu) Chinese Buddhist **monk** of the T'ang dynasty (618–907) who is regarded as a **Zen** master in the **lineage** of **Ho-tse Shen-hui** (670–762) and as the fifth and final **patriarch** of the **Hua-yen school** of **Buddhism**. In Zen contexts, he is more commonly known as Kuei-feng Tsung-mi because of his residence at Kuei-feng monastery. Tsung-mi's writings include the *Yuan-jen Lun* (J. *Gennin Ron*), often used as a primer of **Mahayana Buddhism** teachings, and *Ch'an-yuan Chu-ch'uan-chi Tu-hsu* (J. *Zengen Shozenshû Tojo*), which distinguishes five styles of **meditation** and three schools of early Zen: the Northern, Southern, and **Ho-tse schools**.

Tsûsu

Chief Supervisory Officer or Prior at a **Zen** monastery, one of the six administrative offices of the monastic community. Along with the supervisor (J. **kansu**) and the assistant supervisor (J. **fûsu**) who are under his direct supervision, the prior is one of three financial officers responsible for the economic management of temple resources. See also **temple positions**.

Tung-ming Hui-jih

(1272–1340; J. Tômyô Enichi) Chinese Sôtô **Zen monk** of the Yüan dynasty who emigrated to Japan in 1309. Although he was himself a Sôtô master, he served as **abbot** at several Rinzai monasteries in Kamakura, including **Kenchô-ji** and **Engaku-ji**. See also **Rinzai sect** and **Sôtô sect**.

Tung-shan

East Mountain (J. Tôzan), the popular **Zen** name for Mount Feng-mu in present-day Hupeh, where the Fifth **Patriarch Hung-jen** (601–674) established his monastery. The mountain is also known as Huang-mei-shan (J. Obai-zan) or Yellow Plum Mountain, and Wu-tsu-shan (J. Goso-zan), or Fifth Patriarch Mountain. The name East Mountain was coined to contrast Hung-jen's monastery from that of his predecessor **Tao-hsin** (580–651), whose monastery was known as **Hsi-shan** (J. Seizan), or West Mountain. See also **East Mountain school**.

Tung-shan Liang-chieh

(807–869; J. Tôzan Ryôkai) Chinese **Zen** master, who along with his **Dharma heir Ts'ao-shan Pen-chi** (840–901), is known as a co-founder of the **Ts'ao-tung school** (J. Sôtô) of Chinese Zen. Tung-shan was the Dharma heir of Yun-yen T'an-sheng. Known as a poet, he composed the *Wu-wei Sung*, the classic verse of five stanzas on the **five ranks**, one of the distinctive teachings of his **lineage** of Zen. Tung-shan's prominent disciples included Ts'ao-shan and Yun-chu Tao-ying.

Tun-huang Caves

Caves located in the Tun-huang (J. Tonkô) oasis in northwestern China, near the desert. The caves house a number of Buddhist temples, where numerous carved and painted images are preserved. The earliest wall murals date back to at least 344, and the process of painting continued through the end of the Sung dynasty (960–1279), leaving an important record of Chinese art through nearly 1,000 years. In cave number sixteen, an important collection of written manuscripts, mostly Buddhist texts, was discovered early in the twentieth century. See also **Tun-huang manuscripts**.

Tun-huang Manuscripts

A collection of Chinese texts recovered from one of the **Tun-huang caves** (J. Tonkô), in northwestern China. The manuscripts were first discovered by a farmer in 1900; Western scholars later removed several thousand of the texts for study. There were two major Western expeditions to the caves to collect manuscripts: one led by Sir Aurel Stein in 1907, the other led by Paul Pelliot in 1908. Portions of the collection can now be found at the British Museum, the Bibliotheque National in Paris, and the National Library in Peking. Among the manuscripts found at Tun-huang are a large number of important early **Zen** texts, including the oldest extant copy of the **Platform Sutra**.

Turning the Wheel of the Dharma

An image used for the **Buddha** teaching the **Dharma**. See also **Wheel of the Dharma**.

Turning Word

A word or expression that reveals the speaker's depth of understanding of the **Dharma**, or one that turns or shifts listener's point of view, thereby leading to a sudden experience of insight or **enlightenment**. Turning word is a translation of the Japanese expression tengo or **ittengo**.

Tushita Heaven

According to Buddhist cosmology, the fourth of six heavens in the Realm of Desire. Tushita heaven (J. Tosotsuten) is currently the abode of the **bodhisattva Maitreya**, the future **buddha**. For this reason, Tushita is sometimes referred to as Maitreya's **Pure Land**. All future buddhas must reside there for a time while they perfect their practice as bodhisattvas in preparation for their final birth into this world. Once born in this world, the future buddha will attain final **enlightenment**, become the Buddha, and preach the **Dharma**. Traditional biographies of Shakyamuni buddha (**Siddharta Gautama**) generally begin with accounts of his life in Tushita heaven before his final **rebirth** as Siddharta Gautama.

For believers devoted to Maitreya, Tushita heaven may serve as an object of contemplation just as Amida's Pure Land is contemplated by devotees of **Amida buddha**. Tushita heaven is regarded as easily accessible through meditative states, because of its close proximity to this world. Believers may also regard Tushita as an otherworldly paradise into which they hope to be reborn as a reward for meritorious life. Rebirth in Tushita heaven is said to provide the practitioner with an opportunity to attain the bodhisattva stage of non-reversal. See also **Maitreya**.

Twelve-Link Chain of Causation

An early Buddhist teaching designed to explain the causes for human suffering and the reasons for continued bondage in the cycle of birth, death, and rebirth. The Twelve-Link Chain of Causation includes a series of interrelated conditions. A standard rendering of the Twelve-Link Chain includes: 1) ignorance, 2) dispositions, 3) consciousness, 4) name and form, 5) six senses (the five senses plus the mind), 6) sensory stimulation, 7) feeling, 8) desire, 9) attachment to things and persons, 10) becoming, 11) birth, 12) aging, dying, and sorrow.

Ignorance refers specifically to the ordinary person's lack of awareness of the four noble truths of Buddhism, which explain reality as it is. This does not mean merely an ignorance of the teachings in an intellectual sense, but a failure to perceive the world through an awareness of them. Ignorance leads to dispositions; that is, the creation of karmic consequences for one's mental and physical actions. The karmic dispositions create tendencies of thought and behavior which characterize one's consciousness.

Karmic dispositions can lead to consciousness in this life and also as a legacy for future lives. Consciousness takes shape in a sentient being with both mental and physical attributes, known as Name and Form. This sentient being then makes use of the six senses to explore the world through sensory stimulation. This exploration leads to feelings or responses to sensory stimuli, including evaluations of which experiences are pleasant and which are unpleasant. These feelings then lead to desires, to possess the pleasant and avoid the unpleasant. Desire leads to specific attachments to things and people. Attachments create the fuel for the ongoing process of change that will lead not to the attainment of enlightenment, but to a subsequent birth after this life; ultimately this continuation of ignorance leads to aging, dying, and sorrow in the next life. The chain thus forms a circle.

It is likewise traditional to discuss the chain in reverse order, to discuss how one may bring suffering to an end by cutting off ignorance through the wisdom of the Buddhist teachings. The tradition recognizes two places at which one may cut the twelve-link chain of causation, by cutting off ignorance or by reducing desires. The **Eightfold Path** of Buddhism is designed to cut the chain at these two intersections and thus end the cycle of suffering, birth, and death.

Two Entrances

Two **Buddhist paths**, or ways, which allow one to attain an understanding of ultimate reality. The concept is spelled out in the "Discourse on Two Entries and Four Practices" (J. *Ninyû Shigyôron*), an essay attributed to **Bodhidharma**. The first entrance to the way of **Buddhism** is through reason, which includes studying the teachings as they are set out in the scriptures. The second entrance is through practice. Bodhidharma explicitly mentions four types of practice: endurance of hardships, adapting to circumstances, seeking nothing, and practicing in conformity with the **Dharma**.

Twofold Truth

Mahayana teaching that reality may be viewed from two perspectives (J. Nitai), either the absolute or the relative and conventional. From the perspective of absolute truth, all things that exist are characterized by **emptiness**. This means that nothing possesses an unchanging and eternal essence; all things arise from causes and are conditioned by circumstances. From this perspective all ordinary distinctions dissolve, and all things appear as equal and undifferentiated. From the perspective of relative or conventional truth, however, things do possess a transitory existence, and it is possible to distinguish them one from the other. The concept of Twofold Truth was developed by thinkers in the Madyamika school of **Buddhism** and expressed most clearly in the writings of **Nagarjuna**.

Two Vehicles

(J. nijô) **Shravakas** and **pratyeka buddhas**, as well as their Buddhist practices.
The **Mahayana Buddhism** tradition recognizes **three vehicles** leading to
enlightenment: those of shravakas,
pratyeka buddhas, and **bodhisattvas**.
The first two vehicles are often identified with the Hinayana tradition and are
generally regarded as inferior to the
Bodhisattva Path. Shravaka buddhas
rely upon the teachings of the **Buddha**
and strive to attain enlightenment for
themselves. Unlike bodhisattvas,
shravakas are said to focus selfishly on
themselves. Pratyeka buddhas are self-
enlightened beings who neither learn
from others nor teach others the
Dharma they realize for themselves.

U

Udraka Ramaputra

One of two Indian **meditation** masters with whom **Siddharta Gautama**, the historical **Buddha**, studied before he attained **enlightenment**. Udraka Ramaputra taught a form of yogic meditation leading to a state of concentration known as "the attainment of neither perception nor non-perception." According to traditional accounts, Siddharta mastered Ramaputra's technique and was declared competent to teach. He chose to leave Ramaputra's community because he found the teaching and the meditative states insufficient.

Ullambana

(J. Urabon-e or **Obon**) A Buddhist ceremony traditionally held immediately following the close of the summer retreat, which ends on the fifteenth day of the seventh lunar month. The ullambana service is offered to ease the **suffering** of **sentient beings** living in **hell** as **hungry ghosts**. According to the traditional accounts based on the Urabon **Sutra**, the ceremony was first established by the historical **Buddha**. **Maudgalyâyana** (J. Mokuren), one of the Buddha's leading disciples, was renowned for the supernatural abilities he developed through his meditative practices. When his mother died, Maudgalyayana used his abilities to search for her and learn her fate in the next **rebirth**. Maudgalyayana searched through all the realms of existence, and finally discovered that his mother had been reborn in hell as a hungry ghost. Again relying on his supernatural powers, Maudgalyayana traveled down into hell and tried to offer her food and water to lessen her plight. When she took his offering, it turned to fire in her mouth, and she could not eat it. Maudgalyayana then consulted with the Buddha to ask how he could effectively help his mother. The Buddha instructed him to feed the assembly of **monks** at the end of the **rainy season retreat**, when they had accumulated a large reserve of **merit** from their intensive practice. The merit earned from feeding the monastic community and all of the merit accumulated throughout the retreat would be transferred to the hungry ghosts, thus easing the suffering of Maudgalyayana's mother and all other hungry ghosts.

Ultimate Truth

The absolute view of reality (J. **Richi**); one of two (or sometimes three) levels of truth, or perspectives of reality recognized by Mahayana philosophical thought. From the perspective of ultimate truth, all things that exist are characterized by **emptiness**. This means that nothing possesses an unchanging and eternal essence; all things arise from causes and are conditioned by circumstances. From this perspective all ordinary distinctions dissolve, and all things appear as equal and undifferentiated. Ultimate Truth is generally contrasted with **Relative Truth**. See also **Mahayana Buddhism**.

Ummon Bun'en

(864–949) Japanese pronunciation of **Yun-men Wen-yen**, founder of the **Yun-men school** of early Chinese **Zen Buddhism**. See **Yun-men Wen-yen**.

Ummon School

The Japanese name for the **Yun-men school**, a **lineage** of Chinese **Zen** active during the T'ang dynasty (618–907). See **Yun-men school**.

An umpan, a sounding board made of bronze, at Zuiryu-ji in Osaka, Japan.

Umpan

A flat, bronze gong or sounding board in the stylized shape symbolic for clouds, used to call **monks** to meals and to signal other events. The word literally means "cloud plate." Cloud motifs are common on monastic implements because they symbolize freedom from **attachment**. Umpan hang outside the kitchen (**kuri**) and the dining hall. They may be sounded to signal meal times or the end of a **zazen** session. Wooden boards (**han**) hanging on various buildings throughout the temple grounds are sounded simultaneously to alert the members of the community beyond the range of the umpan.

Umpo Zenjô

(1572–1653) Japanese Rinzai master from the early Tokugawa period (1600–1867). Little is known about the teachings of this master, who came from the **Myôshin-ji lineage**. He is famous primarily for his prominent disciple, **Bankei Yôtaku** (1622–1693), one of the best-known figures of the period. See also **Rinzai sect**.

Waddell, Norman. *The Unborn: The Life and Teaching of Zen Master Bankei, 1622–1693*. New York: North Point Press, 2000.

Un

"Pile" or "heap," the Japanese translation of the Sanskrit term *skandha*. See **five skandhas**.

Unborn

(J. fushô) A Mahayana expression for absolute reality, often paired with the term *undying*. In contrast to **samsara**, in which **sentient beings** are subject to an ongoing cycle of birth, **suffering**, and death, **nirvana** is said to be unborn, or non-arising. The term *unborn* was originally used in the Theravada tradition as an epithet for **arhats**, who were no longer subject to the workings of birth and death because of their **enlightenment**. They were therefore said to be unborn and undying. This concept also appears in Mahayana philosophy. While all existing things appear to be created and pass away, Mahayana teachings insist that everything is ultimately characterized by **emptiness**, possessing no independent and eternal essence to be created or distorted. Thus, all things are considered unborn and undying. The Tokugawa **Zen** teacher, **Bankei Yotaku**, championed the teaching that all people innately possess the unborn **Buddha** mind, which makes them all buddhas without realizing it. Since his work is closely associated with the concept of the unborn, his style of Zen is often called "Unborn Zen" (J. fushô zen). See also **Mahayana Buddhism** and **Theravada Buddhism**.

Unsei Shukô

(1535–1615) Japanese transliteration of Yün-ch'i Chu-hung, a Chinese Buddhist **monk** from the Ming dynasty (1368–1644), who advocated the **dual practice** of **Zen meditation** and **chanting** the **nembutsu**. See **Chu-hung**.

Unsui

(J. kôun ryûsui) Clouds and water; an abbreviation for moving clouds and flowing water. The Japanese term refers specifically to **Zen postulants** who seek entry into a monastery and for **novices** undergoing training in Zen practice. They seek the Way (**Tao**) by traveling from master to master as freely as passing clouds and flowing water. It may also refer to pilgrim **monks** or **nuns**, since they are without permanent homes and travel without many physical possessions to weigh them down. The term can be applied more broadly for any practitioner of Zen, since followers of Zen attempt to move freely through life, without the constraints and limitations of **attachment**, like free-floating clouds or flowing water.

Upali

(J. Ubari) A barber from **Kapilavastu** who became a leading disciple of the **Buddha**. Upali is counted among the ten outstanding disciples of the Buddha due to his great dedication to the **monastic code**, the **vinaya**. At the first Buddhist council convened after the Buddha's death, Upali recited all the instructions formulated by the Buddha to regulate the life of the community and the circumstances under which these rules were created. This became the vinaya, one of the three sections of the **Tripitaka**.

Ishigami, Zenno. *Disciples of the Buddha*. Trans. Richard L. Gage and Paul McCarthy. Tokyo: Kosei Publishing Co., 1989.

Upâsaka

The Sanskrit term for Buddhist laymen, one of the **four assemblies** of the Buddhist **sangha**, or community. To become an upâsaka, a man first pledges his commitment by taking refuge (**kie**) in the **three treasures**: the **Buddha**, the **Dharma** and the sangha. He then promises to live his life by the **five precepts**. Lay practice dates back to the lifetime of the historical Buddha, who accepted lay people as his disciples. **Lay believers** remain involved in secular life and their practice of Buddhism is usually less extensive than **monks** and **nuns**. They keep the **precepts** and build **merit** by supporting the monastic community through donations. See also **Upâsikâ**.

Upâsikâ

A laywoman who practices **Buddhism**; the Sanskrit term for one of the **four assemblies** of the Buddhist **sangha**, or community. Like her male counterpart, the **upâsaka** (J. ubai), a woman becomes a lay Buddhist by establishing her connection with Buddhism in the ritual act of taking refuge (**kie**) in the **three treasures**: the **Buddha**, the **Dharma** and the sangha. In addition, she commits herself to keeping the **five precepts** of the layperson. See also **lay believer**.

Upaya

(J. hôben) The original Sanskrit term usually rendered in English as **expedient means**. Upaya refers to any teaching device employed by a **buddha** or another Buddhist teacher to convey aspects of the **Dharma** to individuals. The full Sanskrit term is upaya-kaushalya, which may be alternatively translated into English as skillful or expedient means. See **expedient means**.

Uposatha

(J. fusatsu) A meeting of the Buddhist **sangha**, or community, held twice a month for reflection and repentance. In India, a month was divided into two fifteen-day periods based on phases of the moon. Uposatha was observed on the last days of each period at the full moon and the new moon. In Theravada Buddhist monasteries, the rituals related to the uposatha include reading and explaining the **vinaya**, the portion of the **Tripitaka** containing the **monastic code**. In Mahayana monasteries in East Asia, the **bodhisattva precepts** or the Bonmôkyô (**Brahma Net Sutra**) were sometimes substituted. These rituals provide **monks** and **nuns** the opportunity to reflect on their actions over the two-week period and to confess any offenses committed during that time. **Lay believers** also have the opportunity to participate on uposatha days. The more devout may spend the day and night at the monastery and take on additional **precepts**, temporarily abiding by the monastic code for **novices**. This means that in addition to following the **five precepts** for a layperson, they abstain from all sexual relations, do not eat after the noon hour, and do not sleep on a comfortable bed.

The observance of uposatha days remains an important part of Theravada Buddhist practice for the monastic and lay communities, but it is only rarely observed by Mahayana lay Buddhists. The Fusatsushiki, as the uposatha ceremony is known in Japanese, is still a part of **Zen** monastic practice. See also **Mahayana Buddhism** and **Theravada Buddhism**.

Urabon-e

The full name of the Buddhist festival more popularly known as **Obon**, the Japanese observance of the **Festival of the Dead**. See **Obon**.

Uttarasô

The seven-strip outer garment worn by Buddhist **monks** and **nuns**. Uttarasô is the Japanese transliteration of the Sanskrit term *uttarasangha*. See **shichijôe**.

Vairocana Buddha

A common abbreviation for **Mahavairochana Buddha**, the great cosmic Buddha associated with **esoteric Buddhism**. See **Mahavairochana Buddha**.

Vajra

(J. kongô or **konkô**) "Diamond" in Sanskrit. The diamond represents firmness and indestructibility in Buddhism. It is therefore used as a symbol for the **Buddha** mind, which can cut through any obstruction. The term *vajra* may also be used as an abbreviated name for a vajra pounder, a religious implement used within the **esoteric Buddhist** tradition. During rituals, they are held as symbolic weapons that can cut through delusion. Originally, vajra pounders were weapons used in ancient India. There are several types of vajra pounders: they may have a single prong, three prongs, or five prongs. The single-pronged vajra represents the singularity of reality; the three-pronged vajra represents the Three Mysteries, which are practices related to body, speech, and mind; and the five-pronged vajra represents the Five Wisdom Buddhas, which are the five buddhas either at the center of the **Diamond-Realm Mandala** or the **Womb-Realm Mandala**.

Vajrayana Buddhism

(J. Kongôjô) Diamond Vehicle, a Sanskrit name for Tantric or **esoteric Buddhism**. Vajrayana is sometimes regarded as the third major school or vehicle of Buddhism, along with Theravada and Mahayana. Other scholars classify it as a form of **Mahayana Buddhism**. See **esoteric Buddhism**.

Vegetarian Feasts

The practice of offering vegetarian feasts to the monastic community at a Buddhist temple arose as a means for lay Buddhists to build **merit**. Many laypeople regularly offer alms to **monks** and **nuns** making their daily begging rounds. In East Asia, where monks and nuns do not usually beg, lay Buddhists sometimes sponsor feasts at the monastery or another location to build merit for special occasions. These may include the illness or death of a loved one, the approaching birth of a child, or the coronation of a new leader. See also **lay believer** and **vegetarianism**.

Vegetarianism

Throughout East Asia, it is traditional for practicing Buddhists, particularly the monastic community of **monks** and **nuns**, to maintain a strict vegetarian diet. The teaching of **ahimsa**, or non-injury of all **sentient beings**, is the philosophical basis for Buddhists to refrain from eating meat. Buddhists recognize that, like human beings, animals are sentient beings living and **suffering** in one of the **six paths** of existence (rokudô). The vegetarian diet is intended to reduce the suffering inflicted on animals and is thus an expression of Buddhist **compassion**.

The observance of vegetarianism at Buddhist temples and monasteries is based on the **precepts** against killing, but vegetarian practice has changed from ancient times. The early **monastic codes** (**vinaya**) still observed in **Theravada Buddhism** do not strictly forbid monks and nuns to consume meat. Rather, the codes instructed them to accept and eat any food which lay people donate to them on their daily begging rounds. To express a preference for any type of food, including vegetarian dishes, was strictly forbidden. So long as an animal was not killed expressly to feed the monk or nun, they committed no offense by accepting meat and eating it. In addition, the early codes forbid monks and nuns to prepare food in the monastery for

It is traditional for Buddhist monks and nuns to adhere to a strict vegetarian diet, based upon the principle of ahimsa, or noninjury of all sentient beings.

themselves. The **bodhisattva precepts** observed in the Mahayana tradition of East Asia, however, explicitly forbid eating animal flesh. As a rule, the monastic communities in East Asia do not depend directly on **lay believers** for food preparation. Monasteries maintain their own kitchens where they prepare their own vegetarian meals.

Zen monasteries throughout East Asia maintain the general Mahayana practice of strict vegetarianism, in some areas developing a unique **Zen cuisine**. While the food served in Zen monasteries on ordinary days is very simple vegetarian fare, the monastery food prepared for festival occasions may be quite elaborate. Many temples enjoy reputations for the quality of their food. It should be noted that in the modern period in Japan (1868–present), many Zen Buddhists, including ordained clergy, do not maintain a strict vegetarian diet outside of the monastic context. Indeed, since the Meiji period

(1868–1912) when the government made observance of the monastic code a matter of personal preference, strict observance of vegetarianism outside the monastery has become the exception rather than the rule. See also **Mahayana Buddhism** and **vegetarian feasts**.

Vessel of the Dharma

An expression used to describe an individual with a deep capacity to master the Buddhist **Dharma**. In the **Zen** school, it refers to a Zen practitioner who is capable of attaining **enlightenment** and is worthy to transmit the Dharma. See also **hôki**.

Vimalakirti

(J. Yuima or Bimarakitsu) A wealthy lay Buddhist from Vaishali, India, who was a contemporary of Shakyamuni (**Siddharta Gautama**), the historical

Buddha, and appears as the leading character in the Vimalakirti **Sutra**. In the sutra, Vimalakirti is depicted as the perfect lay **bodhisattva**, capable of cleverly and effectively using **expedient means** to teach the most profound Mahayana concepts. One teaching device that Vimalakirti employs is his own illness; bedridden, he draws visitors into his sickroom, where he instructs them in the **Dharma**. (The words used to describe Vimalakirti's sickroom, "ten-foot-square room" or **hôjô**, is the term employed by the **Zen** school for the **abbot's** quarters at a Zen monastery.) Hearing of the illness, the Buddha suggests that his most prominent disciples go to inquire about Vimalakirti's health. One by one, each disciple declines the mission, describing an earlier occasion in which he was bested by the layman and received a lesson in the Dharma, a role reversal for **monk** and lay practitioner. Finally, Manjusri (J. **Monju**) agrees to visit Vimalakirti and all of the disciples accompany him. The sutra reaches its climax in their exchange about the meaning of **emptiness**, in which Vimalakirti surpasses the others by answering with silence.

Vimalakirti is a popular figure throughout the schools of East Asian **Buddhism** precisely because he practiced Buddhism and attained **enlightenment** as a lay person. Vimalakirti sometimes appears in Zen texts, including case 84 of the *Hekiganroku*, which recounts his discussion with Manjushri. See also **lay believer** and **Mahayana Buddhism**.

Thurman, Robert A. F., trans. *The Holy Teaching of Vimalakirti: A Mahayana Scripture*. University Park, PA: Pennsylvania State University Press, 1976.

Vimalakirti Sutra

The Vimalakirti Nirdesha Sutra, "Sutra of the Teaching of Vimalakirti," a Mahayana sutra about a wealthy lay Buddhist named Vimalakirti who was a contemporary of Shakyamuni (**Siddharta Gautama**), the historical **Buddha**. In the sutra, Vimalakirti is depicted as the perfect **bodhisattva**, capable of cleverly and effectively using **expedient means** to teach the most profound Mahayana concepts. One such teaching device that Vimalakirti employs is his own illness; bedridden, he draws visitors into his sickroom, where he instructs them in the **Dharma**. Hearing of the illness, the Buddha suggests that his most prominent disciples go to inquire about Vimalakirti's health. One by one, the disciples all decline the mission. Each one describes an earlier occasion in which he was bested by the layman and received a lesson in the Dharma, a role reversal for **monk** and lay practitioner. Finally, Manjusri (J. **Monju**) agrees to visit Vimalakirti, and all of the disciples accompany him. The sutra reaches its climax in their exchange about the meaning of **emptiness**, in which Vimalakirti surpasses the others by answering with silence.

The Vimalakirti Sutra is widely popular in East Asia, where at least six translations were made into Chinese. It is a favorite sutra in the **Zen** school, where Vimalakirti's roaring silence became the subject of a traditional **kôan**. The most commonly used Chinese translation of the sutra is the Wei-mo-chieh So-shuo Ching (J. Yuimakitsu Shosetsukyô), completed by **Kumarajiva** (T. 14, no. 475) in three parts. A complete English translation was done by Robert Thurman under the title *The Holy Teaching of Vimalakirti: A Mahayana Scripture*. See also **lay believer** and **Mahayana Buddhism**.

Thurman, Robert A. F., trans. *The Holy Teaching of Vimalakirti: A Mahayana Scripture*. University Park, PA: Pennsylvania State University Press, 1976.

Vinaya

(J. **ritsu** or binaya) The Buddhist **monastic code**, which governs the lives of Buddhist **monks** and **nuns**. The vinaya texts constitute one portion or basket of the Theravada **Buddhist scriptures**, which are known as the **Tripitaka**. According to Buddhist accounts, the regulations preserved in the vinaya were actually established by the historical **Buddha** to regulate the activities of the Buddhist **sangha**, or community, during his lifetime. The Buddha created new regulations as various problems arose within the community. The texts typically convey the specific purpose of each rule and the circumstances under which it was created. The tradition maintains that the entire vinaya was recited by the disciple **Upali** at the first Buddhist council held shortly after the Buddha's death. The later tradition added to the vinaya code as the need arose, and several versions of the vinaya developed.

The version of the vinaya that became the standard in East Asia is the "Vinaya in Four Categories of Dharmagupta" (J. *Shinbun Ritsu* or *Ssu-fen Lu*). Dharmagupta is a school of **Theravada Buddhism**. The first section outlines the regulations for monks. The second explains the regulations for receiving the **precepts** and for preaching. The third describes the regulations for retreats, repentance, clothing, and medication. The fourth section explains the regulations related to housing and miscellaneous items. Vinaya schools arose in China and Japan based on this version of the code. These included the Lu school in China and the Ritsu school in Japan.

Traditionally, the vinaya was recited twice a month at the **uposatha** ceremony. These readings provided monks and nuns the opportunity to reflect upon their actions and confess to any major breaches of the code. The vinaya prescribes the appropriate punishment for various offenses, dividing them into four categories. First were the most serious offenses entailing defeat (Sk. **parajika**); these require immediate expulsion from the monastic community. Second were the offenses that required temporary suspension and public repentance. The third category requires repentance and forfeiting the object involved. The fourth requires simple repentance.

Vipashyin Buddha

(J. Bibashi) One of the **Seven Buddhas of the Past** whose biographies appear at the beginning of the *Transmission of the Lamp* (Ch. ***Ching-te Ch' uan-teng Lu***; J. *Keitoku Dentôroku*) and other traditional accounts of the history of **Zen Buddhism** through the ages. Vipashyin is the first **buddha** named and is identified as the 998th buddha of the previous eon.

Vishvabhu Buddha

(J. Bishabu) One of the **Seven Buddhas of the Past** whose biographies appear at the beginning of the *Transmission of the Lamp* (Ch. ***Ching-te Ch' uan-teng Lu***; J. *Keitoku Dentôroku*) and other traditional accounts of the history of **Zen Buddhism** through the ages. Vishvabhu is the third **buddha** named and is identified as the 1,000th buddha of the previous eon.

Vows

(J. gan) There are several types of vows undertaken by Buddhist practitioners. First there are various sets of **precepts** undertaken by **lay believers**, **novices**, and fully ordained **monks** and **nuns**, which are sometimes spoken of as vows. The precepts are common to both Theravada and Mahayana. In addition, followers of **Mahayana Buddhism**, both lay and ordained, recite the four **bodhisattva vows**. See also **Theravada Buddhism**.

Vulture Peak

(J. Ryôjusen) **Mount Gridhrakuta**, a mountain in Magadha, India, where the **Buddha** is traditionally said to have given many **sermons**, including the **Lotus Sutra**. Vulture Peak is important within the **Zen** tradition, because it is there that the Buddha transmitted the **Dharma** to his disciple, **Mahakashyapa**.

Wabi

Poverty, or austere simplicity, valued in the Japanese cultural tradition as an aesthetic quality. The various art forms inspired by **Zen**, such as pottery, poetry, and drama, are said to embody the styles of wabi and **sabi** (loneliness).

Waka

Japanese poetry, which is written in two standard forms: **tanka** and **chôka**. In Japan, waka is contrasted with **kanshi**, poetry composed in Chinese.

Walking Staff

(J. shujô) **Zen monks** and **nuns** traditionally carry a long walking staff when traveling on a **pilgrimage**. The walking staff is also carried by Zen masters as a symbol of authority at **ordinations** and is hung on the wall during formal lectures given in the Dharma hall (J. **hattô**). It is said that the walking staff derives from the classical Buddhist tradition. According to the Theravadan **monastic code** (**vinaya**), the **Buddha** allowed old and infirm monks and nuns to use a walking stick. See also **Theravada Buddhism**.

Wandering Spirits

A folk concept in Japan referring to spirits of the dead who wander in search of release from their endless **suffering**. The Japanese term *muen botoke* literally means "a **buddha** without **attachments**," but is more accurately understood as the spirit of a dead person (**hotoke**) caught between worlds, unable to attain release. The spirit may have been forgotten or may have died without surviving family to offer the appropriate **memorial services** (**hôji**). It is also said that individuals who die without resolving deep emotional problems, such as intense jealousy, rage, or resentment, may be trapped in a similar state. Such spirits are said to wander in the world of the living, seeking food and comfort, dependent on the living to ease their suffering. Services such as segaki (**ullambana**) are offered for their benefit.

Wanshi Shôgaku

(1091–1157) Japanese transliteration of **Hung-chih Cheng-chüeh** (1091–1157), Chinese Sôtô **Zen** master of the Sung period (960–1279). See **Hung-chih Cheng-chüeh**.

Wan-shou-ssu

An important Chinese **Zen** monastery on Chin-shan. The monastery's full name was Hsing-sheng Wan-shou-ssu. It was designated as one of the Five Mountains (Ch. wu-shan; J. **Gozan temples**), the most prestigious Zen monasteries in China.

Warrior Monks

Armed **monks**, known as **sôhei** in Japanese, who fought to protect the interests of Japanese Buddhist monasteries and temples throughout the medieval period (1185–1600). The practice of monasteries raising armies from among their own ranks began in the Heian period (794–1185) and continued until the last warrior monks were defeated and disarmed by the military leaders Oda Nobunaga (1534–1582) and Toyotomi Hideyoshi (1536–1598), who helped unify Japan in the late 16th century. See **sôhei**.

Wasan

Hymn or devotional verse, usually in praise of a **buddha**, a **bodhisattva**, a **patriarch**, or some other Buddhist figure. Together, wasan form a genre of Japanese Buddhist literature, common to all schools of Japanese **Buddhism**. In the **Zen** school, the best known wasan is the **Zazen wasan**, composed by **Hakuin Ekaku** (1685–1768) in praise of the practice of seated **meditation**.

Watô

The primary word or expression that summarizes a **kôan**. Watô literally means "head of thought." When a student contemplates a kôan as a part of meditative practice, one word or phrase from the original kôan may become the primary focus of attention. For example, when contemplating the "**Mu kôan**," the first case from the *Mumonkan*, the single sound "**mu**" becomes the watô for most practitioners. Sometimes the term is used more generally as an alternative expression for kôan.

Way

(J. Tô or Dô) The most commonly used English translation for the Chinese word **Tao**, which may also be rendered "path." See **Tao**.

Western Pure Land

The celestial world created by **Amida buddha**, where ordinary individuals may easily attain **enlightenment**. It is called Sukhavati in Sanskrit and Gokuraku in Japanese. According to the **Pure Land** scriptures, when Amida was still a **bodhisattva**, he made a series of **vows**. Among these was a vow to attain **buddhahood** only if he could create a pure land were even the weak could be reborn, hear the **Dharma**, and easily practice Buddhism. A lengthy description of the Western Pure Land is provided in the three **Pure Land Sutras**, especially the Larger Pure Land Sutra.

Western Rank

The monastic officers who guide the **meditation** practice and training at a **Zen** monastery. See **seihan**.

Wheel of the Dharma

One of the most common images used for the Buddhist **Dharma**, or teachings, is a wheel. Known as dharmachakra in Sanskrit, and hôrin in Japanese, the image goes back to the most ancient period in Buddhist history. By using a wheel to symbolize the **Buddha** and the Dharma, the Buddha's teachings are compared to the **Cakravartins'** great wheels. Just as the Cakravartin use their wheels to subdue the secular world, the Buddha uses the Dharma to crush all delusions and lead people to **enlightenment**.

There are three traditional levels of meaning in the image of the Wheel of the Dharma based upon its roundness, its power to crush, and its ability to turn. First, the Wheel of the Dharma's roundness symbolizes its perfection and completeness; the Dharma is unsurpassed and lacking in nothing. Second, the Dharma crushes the false views held by **sentient beings** in the same way that the Cakravartin's wheel crushes political resistance. Third, just as a wheel can turn and move freely, the Dharma can be transmitted anywhere it is taught.

The Wheel of the Dharma is most closely identified with the teachings presented in the first sermon in **Benares**, which explains the concepts of the **middle path**, the **four noble truths**, and the **Eightfold Path**. In Buddhist iconography, the wheel is commonly drawn with eight spokes, representing the Eightfold Path. In the early centuries, before the Buddhist tradition used human representations of the Buddha, the wheel was a popular image for veneration.

Wheel of Life

An image created by the Buddhist tradition to graphically systematize the teachings about existence in the world of **samsara**, the ongoing cycle of birth and death. It is called Bhavachakra in Sanskrit and Urin in Japanese, literally translated as "the wheel of existence."

The Wheel of the Dharma is one of the most common Buddhist images, symbolizing perfection and completeness.

At the center of the wheel, forming the hub, are three animals: a cock, a snake, and a pig, symbolizing greed, anger, and ignorance. These three **afflictions**, known collectively as the **three poisons**, are the forces that keep the cycles of samsara in motion. The spokes of the wheel depict the six realms of existence: the realms of **heaven**, **ashuras** (protective spirits), human beings, animals, **hungry ghosts**, and **hell**. Individuals are reborn into one of these realms depending on the karmic accumulation from their previous existence. The outer rim of the wheel represents the twelve causal links in the chain of **codependent origination** that are responsible for human **suffering**. **Mara**, the demon who represents **impermanence** and death, holds the whole wheel in his mouth and claws.

Whisk

A religious implement that **Zen** teachers carry as a symbol of their authority. They are known as **hossu** in Japanese. Zen whisks are usually made from horse hair attached to a short staff. Originally, Buddhist **monks** in India carried the whisk to clear the ground in front of them as they walked to avoid inadvertently killing any small insects in their path.

Womb-Realm Mandala

(J. Taizôkai Mandara) One of the two primary **mandala** used in **esoteric Buddhism**, especially the **Shingon sect**, to symbolically depict the realm of divinity. The Womb-Realm Mandala represents **Mahavairochana's enlightenment**, which pervades the entire cosmos and is inherent in all **sentient beings**. Through **compassion**, this seed of **Buddha Nature** that each sentient being possesses can lead one to enlightenment. The mandala depicts twelve rectangular halls; the central hall encompasses an eight-petalled lotus, with the eleven other halls forming concentric rectangles around it. At the center of the lotus sits the buddha Mahavairochana (J. Dainichi Butsu), the central buddha of esoteric Buddhism. Mahavairochana is surrounded by four other buddhas, one in each of the petals in the four cardinal directions, and by four **bodhisattvas** in the intermediate petals. Other Buddhist deities inhabit the various halls surrounding the central lotus blossom. Over 400 buddhas, bodhisattvas, and other Buddhist deities are depicted on the mandala. The mandala is based upon a description from the Mahavairochana Sutra (J. Dainichkyô), although some variant versions exist. The other major mandala is the **Diamond-Realm Mandala** (J. Kongôkai Mandara).

Ishida, Hisatoyo. *Esoteric Buddhist Painting.* Trans. E. Dale Saunders. New York: Harper & Row, 1987.

Yamasaki, Taiko. *Shingon: Japanese Esoteric Buddhism.* Trans. Richard and Cynthia Peterson. Ed.Yasuyoshi Morimoto and David Kidd. Boston, MA: Shambhala, 1988.

World-Honored One

(J. Seson) An honorific title used for any worthy religious teacher, especially Shakyamuni (**Siddharta Gautama**), the historical **Buddha**. World Honored One is an English translation of the Sanskrit word Bhagavat. The combined expression "the Buddha, the World-Honored One" forms one of the **ten epithets for the Buddha**. The Buddha is worthy of honor because he attained perfect **enlightenment** and thereby benefits all **sentient beings**. **Zen** literature often refers to the Buddha simply as the World-Honored One.

Wu

No, not; a Chinese word of negation. See **mu**.

Wu

(2) **Enlightenment**; **satori**. Wu is the Chinese pronunciation of the same character transliterated as "satori" in Japanese. See **satori**.

Wu-an P'u-ning

(1197-1276; J. Gottan Funei) Chinese Rinzai **Zen monk** of the Yüan dynasty (1275–1368) who helped to establish Rinzai Zen in Japan. Wu-an emigrated to Japan in 1260, perhaps to escape the unrest in China. He received the sponsorship of the regent **Hôjô Tokiyori** (1227–1263) and served as **abbot** at **Kenchô-ji**, a monastery in Kamakura. Wu-an eventually recognized Tokiyori as his **Dharma heir**. He returned to China after Tokiyori's death. See also **Rinzai sect**.

Wu-chia

(J. goke) "**Five houses**," a Chinese expression used to describe the five distinctive styles of **Zen** characteristic of the five different **lineages** which developed during the T'ang dynasty (618–907) in China. See **five houses**.

Wu-chun Shih-fan

(1177–1249; J. Bushun Shiban) Chinese Rinzai **monk** of the late Sung dynasty (960–1279), a leading master in the Yang-ch'i **lineage** (J. Yôgi) in the thirteenth century. Although Wu-chun never visited Japan, he had a strong impact on the development of Rinzai **Zen** in Japan through his Japanese disciple, **Enni Ben'en** (1202–1280), and Chinese disciples **Wu-hsüeh Tsu-yüan** (1226–1286) and **Wu-an P'u-ning** (1197–1276). See also **Rinzai sect** and **Yang-ch'i school**.

Wu-hsüeh Tsu-yüan

(1226–1286; J. Mugaku Sogen) Chinese Rinzai **monk** of the late Sung dynasty (960–1279), who helped establish the Rinzai school in Japan. Wu-hsueh was the **Dharma heir** of **Wu-chun Shih-fan** (1177–1276). He immigrated to Japan in 1279 at the invitation of the Japanese regent **Hôjô Tokimune** (1251–1284). Wu-hsueh served as the **abbot** of **Kenchô-ji** and was the founding abbot of **Engaku-ji**. See also **Rinzai sect**.

Wu-men Hui-k'ai

(1183–1260; J. Mumon Ekai) Chinese Rinzai **monk** of the Sung dynasty (960–1279), best known as the compiler of the *Wu-men Kuan* (J. *Mumonkan*). Wu-men was the **Dharma heir** of the Zen master Yueh-lin Shih-kuan of the Yang-ch'i **lineage** (J. Yôgi). He attained **enlightenment** fairly early in life, and began teaching at the age of thirty-six. He developed his collection of classical **kôan** as an aid in teaching his own disciples. He eventually became the founding **abbot** at Hu-kuo Jen-wang-ssu in Hangchow by imperial decree. His disciples include the Japanese monk Shinchi **Kakushin** (1207–1298). See also **Rinzai sect** and **Yang-ch'i school**.

Wu-men Kuan

The Gateless Gate, the most popular collection of classical **Zen kôan**, compiled by the Chinese Rinzai master **Wu-men Hui-k'ai** (1183–1260) in 1228. The text is more commonly known by its Japanese title, *Mumonkan*. See *Mumonkan*.

Wu-tsu Fa-yen

(d. 1104; J. Goso Hoen) Chinese Rinzai **monk** of the Sung dynasty (960–1279), an early master in the Yang-ch'i **lineage**. Fa-yen was a native of Szechwan and did not enter monastic orders until he was thirty-five. He initially studied "**Consciousness Only**" teachings, but later looked for a **Zen** teacher. He first became the disciple of Yuan-chien Fa-yuan, and then Shou-tuan **Ch'an-shih**, from whom he received **Dharma transmission**. He lived for many years as Wu-tsu-shan, the popular name for **Huang-mei-shan**, from which his name derives. See also **Rinzai sect** and **Yang-ch'i school**.

Wu-tsu Hung-jen

(J. Goso Gunin) "The Fifth **Patriarch Hung-jen**." See **Hung-jen**.

Yabukôji

A **kana hôgo** written by **Hakuin Ekaku** (1685–1768) for Ikeda Tsugumasa (1702–1776), the daimyô or lord of Okayama in 1753. Hakuin describes the practice of Zen and commends the use of the **One Hand kôan** (J. Sekishu kôan). The *Yabukôji* is alternatively known as the *Sekishu No Onjô*. A translation of the *Yabukôji* appears in Yampolsky's *The Zen Master Hakuin: Selected Writings* (Columbia University Press, 1971).

Yakuseki

In Zen temples, they use the term *yakuseki* as a euphemism for the evening meal or the last meal of the day. This is a meal that is eaten in the evening in violation of the monastic rule; the term literally means "medicine stone." The **vinaya** or Buddhist **monastic code** developed within the Theravada tradition explicitly forbids **monks** and **nuns** to eat after the noon hour. Medicinal stones originally referred to heated stones that monks and nuns held against their abdomens in the evening to ease the sensation of hunger and to provide warmth in cold weather. In the Mahayana temples of East Asia, although Buddhist monks and nuns continued to abide by the same monastic code, eating an evening meal has become common practice in most monasteries. It has been argued that the purpose of allowing an evening meal is medicinal in intention, that it is used as a preventive against illness rather than as a concession to personal comfort. The term first appears in Zen monastic codes (**shingi**) in the early

thirteenth century. See also **Mahayana Buddhism** and **Theravada Buddhism**.

Yakushi Butsu

(Sk. Bhaishajya-guru Vaidurya-prabha) The **Buddha** of Healing; known as Bhaishajya-guru in Sanskrit. His full Japanese name is Yakushi Rurikô, meaning the "Medicine Master of Emerald Light." Tradition says that Yakushi was a great medicine king who took twelve **vows** while still a **bodhisattva**; one of the vows was to cure all **sentient beings** from **suffering** from disease. Yakushi now reigns as the buddha of the Eastern **Pure Land** of Pure Emerald. He is venerated as the Medicine Buddha throughout East Asia, where he has enjoyed more popularity than in India. Worship of him as a means of curing illness and ensuring longevity are ancient practices in China and Japan, dating back to the earliest Buddhist period in Japan. Although Zen temples typically enshrine an image of Shakyamuni Buddha (**Siddharta Gautama**) as the main image (**honzon**), many smaller Zen temples in the countryside have images of Yakushi.

In Japan, Yakushi is sometimes identified with **Pindola**, the healing **arhat**, who is also known as Binzuru in Japanese. Pindola can often be found outside the main hall, since according to popular Japanese lore he was expelled from the company of the other arhats. It is said that he committed an act of sexual indiscretion when he admired a beautiful woman. People adorn smaller images of Yakushi or Binzuru with knitted caps and bibs to request his assistance with health problems.

In iconography, Yakushi is often depicted seated in **meditation** or standing, holding a medicine bowl in his left hand while his right hand is raised in the **mudra**, indicating that those approaching should have no fear. He may be included in a buddha triad, standing on the left with Shakyamuni in the middle and **Amida buddha** on

Yakushi Butsu is the great Buddhist medicine king who vowed to cure all beings of disease and illness.

the right. Alternatively, Yakushi may be depicted standing in the center of his assistants, Nikkô and Gakkô Bosatsu, the bodhisattvas of sunlight and moonlight.

Getty, Alice. *The Gods of Northern Buddhism: Their History and Iconography*. New York: Dover Publications, 1988.

Saunders, E. Dale. *Mudra: A Study of the Symbolic Gestures in Japanese Buddhist Sculpture*. Princeton, NJ: Princeton University Press, 1985.

Yama

(J. **Emma**) Lord of the realm of the dead in Hindu and Buddhist mythology. In Buddhist mythology, Yama assumes authority over humans after death and judges their actions, both good and evil. Based on his review of a person's deeds, Yama determines whether the individual deserves punishment or rewards, and assigns them to a **heaven** or **hell**, accordingly. Yama himself reigns over the various hells, where souls of the dead are punished until their evil **karma** is exhausted.

Yama originally appeared in ancient Indian mythology, where he was a benign deity who cared for the souls of the dead in heaven. Yama became the ruler of the dead as the first human being to die and discover the path to that realm. He came to be regarded as a deity, and the guardian of the south, the region of deceased souls. He was carried over into Hindu mythology as the king of hell, a much darker and more frightening figure. In Hindu iconography, Yama is depicted as a terrifying figure. His body is green and he wears red robes. He rides on the back of a buffalo and carries a club and noose to capture souls when they die. He not only judges souls after death, but has an army of assistants to inflict cruel punishments on those found guilty of wicked acts. Yama also has a female counterpart, called Yamî, who reigns over the female residents of hell. Beliefs about Yama underwent significant changes in East Asian **Buddhism**.

Yamabushi

Mountain ascetics in Japan who practice **shugendô**, a religious practice that blends beliefs and practices from different traditions. Yamabushi combine intense physical austerities and mystical practices that build spiritual power with the teachings and practice of Buddhism. Yamabushi traditionally provide services of healing and exorcism. They display their spiritual power at religious rituals by walking across beds of glowing embers or climbing ladders of sharpened sword blades. Most Yamabushi are affiliated with either the **Tendai** or the **Shingon sect** of Japanese Buddhism.

Yang-ch'i School

A **lineage** of Chinese Rinzai Zen that first became active during the Sung dynasty (960–1279); it is known as one of the so-called **seven schools** of Zen. The lineage was founded by the Zen master Yang-ch'i Fang-hui (992–1049; J. Yôgi Hôe), a seventh generation descendent of **Lin-chi I-hsuan**. By the end of the Sung dynasty, the Yang-ch'i school was the dominant lineage of Rinzai in China. It was within this school that **kôan** practice fully developed and flourished. Descendants of this lineage include **Wu-men Hui-k'ai** (1183–1260) the compiler of the *Wu-men Kuan* (J. **Mumonkan**); and **Ta-hui Tsung-kao** (1089–1163) author of the *Hekiganroku*. In the thirteenth and fourteenth centuries, several prominent Chinese masters and their Japanese disciples transmitted the lineage to Japan, where it became known as the **Yôgi school**. All active Rinzai lineages in Japan are branches of the Yang-ch'i lineage, with the exception of the Obaku school. See also **Obaku sect** and **Rinzai sect**.

At a firewalking ceremony, the Yamabushi walk across the hot, glowing coals first;
then laypeople are allowed to cross.

Yang-shan Hui-chi

(807–883; J. Kyôzan Ejaku) Chinese **Zen** master of the T'ang dynasty (618–907) who, along with his **Dharma** master **Kuei-shan Ling-yu** (771–853), founded the **Kuei-yang school** (J. Igyô-shû) of Chinese Zen. The Kuei-yang school is one of the so-called **five houses** (J. goke) of Chinese Zen. Yang-shan founded a temple on Mount Yang-shan, from which his popular name derives. Yan-shan perfected the use of the circle, long a symbol of perfection in Chinese thought, as a Zen teaching device.

Yasen Kanna

Zen treatise composed by **Hakuin Ekaku** (1685–1768) in 1757. The text is comprised of one section. The name is sometimes transliterated as *Yasen*

Kanwa. In the text, Hakuin addresses the problem of the "**Zen sickness**," which commonly afflicts those who meditate extensively. He describes in detail his own difficulties with meditation-related physical and mental illness. He recounts his visits to a Taoist master named Hakuyû, who taught him an effective cure, the introspective practice known as *naikan*. See also **meditation**.

Yashodhara

The wife of **Siddharta Gautama**, before he renounced his home life and became the **Buddha**. She was also the mother of **Rahula**. Later in life she became a disciple of the Buddha and joined the order of **nuns**.

Year of the Donkey

(J. Ronen) A Zen expression for something that will never happen. Each year in the twelve-year cycle of the traditional Chinese calendar is named for an animal of the zodiac. Since there is no Year of the Donkey, it designates an impossible event.

Yin-yüan Lung-ch'i

(1594–1673; J. Ingen Ryûki) Chinese monk in the **Rinzai sect**. Yin-yüan lived late in the Ming dynasty (1368–1644) and founded the **Obaku sect** of Zen in Japan. Yin-yüan was born in the Fukien province in southern China. He entered monastic life at age twenty-nine at Wan-fu-ssu monastery. He practiced first under the Chinese Rinzai master, Mi-yun Yüan-Wu (1566–1642), and later became the **Dharma heir** of Mi-yun's successor, Fei-yun T'ung-Jung (1593–1661). Yin-yüan became the abbot of Wan-fu-ssu in 1637. He accepted an invitation from the Chinese émigré community in Nagasaki and immigrated to Japan in 1654, at the age of sixty-two. Yin-yüan was the most prominent Chinese monk to travel to Japan in several generations, and he attracted many Japanese disciples. Yin-yüan eventually received the patronage of the Japanese military government and founded Obaku-san **Mampuku-ji**, the head monastery for the Obaku sect, in the city of Uji. Yin-yüan served as abbot for only a year before retiring in 1664 in favor of his disciple **Mu-an Hsing-t'ao** (1611–1684). Yin-yüan lived out his years of retirement at Mampuku-ji, composing portions of the *Obaku Shingi*, the **monastic code** for the Obaku sect, during that time. He was granted the posthumous title Daikô Fushô **Kokushi** (National Teacher Great Illumination Shining Widely) from retired emperor **Gomizunoo** (1596–1680).

Yogachara School

A school of **Mahayana Buddhism** first developed in India in the fourth or fifth century C.E., based on the writing of two scholar **monks**, Asanga and his brother, Vasubandhu. The school is often referred to as the "**Consciousness Only**" school, because it teaches that the phenomenal world that we experience is actually a product of our conscious minds. The primary teachings of the school include the storehouse consciousness (**alaya consciousness**) and the Three Natures of reality. The first of the Three Natures of reality is the mistaken view that the perceived world is made of permanent essences or souls. The second nature is the view that all things are changing or mutually dependent. The third nature is the view of absolute reality. In the seventh century, the Yogachara school was transmitted to China, where it became known as the **Fa-hsien school**, and to Japan where it is known as the **Hossô school**.

Yôgi School

The Japanese name for the Yang-ch'i **lineage** of the Chinese **Rinzai sect**. In China, the **Yang-ch'i school** first became active during the Sung dynasty (960–1279). It was founded by the Chinese Zen master Yang-ch'i Fang-hui (992–1049; J. Yôgi Hôe). By the end of the Sung dynasty, the Yang-ch'i school was the dominant lineage of Rinzai in China. In the thirteenth and fourteenth centuries, several prominent Chinese masters and their Japanese disciples transmitted the lineage to Japan, where it became known as the Yôgi school. All active Rinzai lineages in Japan are branches of the Yang-ch'i lineage, with the exception of the **Obaku sect**.

Yôjô Taimitsu

(1141–1215) "The Yôjô **lineage** of Tendai **esoteric Buddhism**," the name used by Myôan **Eisai** (1141–1215) for his own lineage of Zen, a combination of Rinzai Zen with esoteric practice. Eisai is traditionally regarded as the founder of Rinzai Zen in Japan. He began his career as a **monk** in the **Tendai sect** on Mount Hiei, and was fully trained in the esoteric practices and teachings of the Tendai school. Although Eisai hoped to promote an exclusive practice of Zen in Japan such as he had experienced in China, it was not practical in his day. He therefore continued to incorporate esoteric rituals and teachings in his Zen school. He named his lineage after the Yôjô valley on Mount Hiei. See also **Rinzai sect**.

Yôkô-ji

A Japanese Sôtô monastery in what is now Ishikawa Prefecture. Around the year 1313 C.E., the Sôtô master **Keizan Jôkin** (1268–1325) built a small **meditation** retreat on the grounds of Yôkô-ji, then a Shingon temple. Sometime later, perhaps in 1325, Keizan received funds to restore the temple and convert it into a Sôtô monastery. He renamed it Tôkoku-san Yôkô-ji. See also **Shingon sect** and **Sôtô sect**.

Yokushitsu

The name for the bathhouse in a **Zen** monastery. Yokushitsu is one of the seven buildings (**shichidô garan**) that make up the core of every Zen monastery. While it is a physical necessity to have a bathhouse, in the monastery it is intended to be a place of contemplation as well. Zen **monastic codes** carefully specify regulations for the proper behavior and demeanor while using the bath. An appropriate subject for **meditation** on bath day, for example, is "the touch of water," a reference to an episode in case 78 of the *Hekiganroku*. "Long ago, there were sixteen bodhisattvas. At bath time, they entered the water according to usual order. They were suddenly enlightened by the touch of the water. So, Zen worthies, do you understand this?"

According to the Zen monastic codes, one day every two weeks is set aside as bath day, a day when the ordinary monastic routine is not observed. The bath is heated, and the residents of the monastery enter the bath based on their order of seniority. While **monks** and **nuns** wash daily to maintain proper hygiene, in many monasteries hot water is only available in large quantities on bath day. Traditionally the fuel used to heat the bath is dead leaves and other refuse gathered while cleaning the temple grounds, although many monasteries now use more modern methods.

Yômyô Enju

(904–975 C.E.) Japanese rendering of **Yung-ming Yen-shou** (904–975). See **Yung-ming Yen-shou**.

Yôsai

(1141–1215) An alternative pronunciation for **Eisai**, the Japanese **Zen** master of the Kamakura period (1185–1333) traditionally credited with founding the **Rinzai sect** in Japan. Some scholars have argued that Yôsai was the original pronunciation that the master used himself. Both readings are possible, but Eisai is used more commonly in secondary materials. See **Eisai**.

Yūan-wu K'o-ch'in

(1063–1135; J. Engo Kokugon) A Chinese **Zen** master from the Sung dynasty (960–1279) who is best known as the compiler of the *Hekiganroku*. K'o-ch'in was a disciple of **Wu-tsu Fa-yen** (d. 1104), from the **Yang-ch'i school** (in Japan, the **Yôgi school**) of the **Rinzai sect**. He became one of the most popular Zen masters of his day, with disciples from lay and monastic circles. K'o-ch'in received several imperial titles and honors, and is also known by the honorific title Yūan-wu **Ch'an-shih** (J. Engo Zenji), bestowed upon him by the emperor Kao-tsung of the Southern Sung dynasty. His most important heir was the master **Ta-hui Tsung-kao** (1089–1163). K'o-ch'in based the *Hekiganroku* on an existing **kôan** collection edited by **Hsüeh-tou Ch'ung-hsien**, to which he added notes and commentary. See also **lay believer**.

Yuige

Death poems, a genre of **Zen** literature. It is customary for a Buddhist master to record a final verse before death. In most cases, the verse is intended as a final instruction for the master's disciples and may be an expression of the master's understanding of the **Dharma**.

Yuima

The common abbreviation for Yuimakitsu, the Japanese name for **Vimalakirti**, the lay **bodhisattva** who plays the leading role in the **Vimalakirti Sutra**. In Japan, he is also sometimes referred to as Yuima Koji, the Layman Vimalakirti. See **Vimalakirti**.

Yuimakyô

The popular abbreviated Japanese title for the **Vimalakirti Sutra**. The term generally refers specifically to **Kumarajiva's** Chinese translation of the sutra, the Yuimakitsu Shosetsukyô (Ch. Wei-mo-chieh So-shuo Ching; T. 14, no. 475). See **Vimalakirti Sutra**.

Yuishiki

"**Consciousness Only**," the Japanese term for the Mahayana Buddhist teaching that all phenomena that one experiences as external realities are manifestations of one's consciousness or mind. The doctrine was developed first within the **Yogachara school** in India. Yogachara teachings, especially the treatises attributed to the Indian scholar monks Asanga and Vasubandu, inspired the Chinese **Fa-hsien school**. This in turn served as the basis for the **Hossô school** of Nara Buddhism in Japan. See **Consciousness Only**.

Yuishin No Jôdo

Pure Land of the Mind Only, the Japanese rendering of a teaching shared by several schools of **Mahayana Buddhism**, including **Zen**. See **Pure Land of the Mind Only**.

Yu-lu

The Chinese term for **recorded sayings**, one of the most important and distinctive genres of **Zen** literature. See **recorded sayings**.

Yün-ch'i Chu-hung

(1535–1615; J. Unsei Shukô) One of the leading Chinese Buddhist monks of the Ming dynasty (1368–1644). See **Chu-hung**.

Yung-ming Yen-shou

(904–975; J. Yômyô Enju) A Chinese Sung dynasty **Zen** master famous for his syncretic approach to **Buddhism**. Yung-ming stressed the basic unity between the doctrines set out in the **sutras** and the understanding achieved through Zen **meditation** (J. kyôzen itchi). He advocated combining Zen practice with the **Pure Land** Buddhist practice of the **nembutsu** (Ch. nien-fo), recitation of the name of **Amida buddha**. He pioneered this form of **dual practice**, which later became a dominant force in Chinese Buddhism. Yung-ming is regarded as a **patriarch** in the **Pure Land school** as well as a Zen master from the **lineage** of **Fa-yen Wen-i** (J. Hôgen). Yung-ming's primary literary work is the *Tsung-ching Lu* (J. *Sugyôroku*).

Yun-men School

(J. Ummon-shû) A **lineage** of Chinese **Zen** active during the T'ang (618–907) and Sung (960–1279) dynasties and known as one of the so-called **five houses** of Zen. The lineage was founded by the Zen master **Yun-men Wen-yen** (864–949). It flourished during the early Sung dynasty, but was later absorbed into the dominant Lin-chi lineage. Yun-men developed a distinctive teaching style, which included sharp blows with the staff, shouts, and abrupt answers to disciples' questions, known as "one-word barriers" (ichiji kan). These pithy remarks and longer exchanges between

Yun-men and his disciples became the subject of numerous **kôan** used in the later Zen tradition. It was a Zen **monk** from the Yun-men school, **Hsüeh-tou Ch'ung-hsien**, who first collected and commented upon the one hundred cases that later became the *Hekiganroku*. Although the Yun-men school did not survive beyond the Sung dynasty, its literature ensured that it had an enduring influence on the later tradition. See also **Lin-chi school**.

Yun-men Wen-yen

(864–949; J. Ummon Bun'en) Chinese Zen **monk** of the T'ang dynasty (618–907), founder of the **Yun-men school** of early **Zen Buddhism**. Yun-men was born in Chia-hsing. He took his monastic **vows** at age twenty, and began his Buddhist carrier studying the **vinaya**. A few years later, he went out on **pilgrimage**, seeking a master. He practiced under two important Zen masters of the day. He first attained **enlightenment** under Ch'en Tsun-su (better known as Mu-chou), a direct disciple of **Huang-po Hsi-yün** (d. 850), and later became the **Dharma heir** of Hsueh-feng. Yun-men taught in southern China for thirty years. He first became **abbot** at Ling-shu-yuan in 919, under the patronage of Liu Yan. He later built a monastery on Mount Yun-men, from which his popular name derives. Yun-men became famous for his "one-word barriers" (**ichiji kan**), short, pithy replies to questions from his disciples. Many of these interchanges became the subjects for classical **kôan**. Selections from Yun-men's **recorded sayings** are translated by Urs App in *Master Yunmen: From the Record of the Chan Master "Gate of the Clouds"* (Kodansha International, 1994).

Z

Zabuton

A square cushion used during seated **meditation**. Also called **zaniku**. See **zaniku**.

Zafu

A small, round pillow used during seated **meditation (zazen)**. Following the Sôtô manner of zazen, the meditator sits directly on the zafu, which is resting on a larger cushion called a zabuton or **zaniku**. When seated in the proper position for zazen, the backbone falls just above the center of the zafu, so that half of the cushion is behind one's back. According to **Dôgen Kigen** (1200–1253), the founder of the **Sôtô sect**, the zafu is used in conjunction with the larger cushion to raise the backside above the level of the knees, which then rest on the larger mat. The practice is still followed within the Sôtô sect.

Zagu

A square ritual cloth used for sitting and for making formal prostrations. The zagu is one of the six personal possessions (**rokumotsu**) of a **monk** or **nun**. The size of the cloth was officially determined in the monastic codes, but larger monks are allowed to use a larger size for practical reasons.

Zaike

A lay Buddhist. This Japanese term literally means a **householder**, or someone who lives at home. Although the word can refer to anyone living a secular life, it most often denotes Buddhist **lay believers**. The term originated because

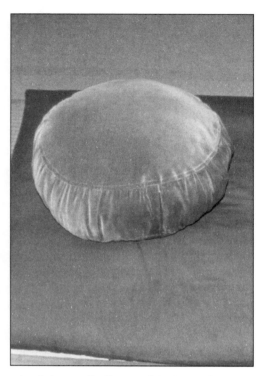

A zafu is a small pillow used during meditation; it rests upon a zabuton.

of the contrast in the location and manner of practice between the lay and monastic communities in **Buddhism**. Buddhist **monks** and **nuns** leave the home life (**shukke**) to join the monastic community, so it became the practice to refer to lay believers as householders.

Zammai

Concentration; an intense state of mental concentration achieved during **meditation**. Zammai, also written *zanmai* or *sammai*, is the Japanese transliteration of the Sanskrit term *samadhi*. See **samadhi**.

Zaniku

A square pillow or mat used during seated **meditation (zazen)**. The zaniku is just large enough to accommodate a person sitting in the **lotus position**. In the Sôtô manner of meditation, the zaniku rests on the **tatami**, with the **zafu**, a smaller, round cushion, placed upon it. It is also called zabuton. See also **Sôtô sect**.

Zazen

"Seated **meditation**," the style of Buddhist meditation characteristic of the **Zen** school. Zazen is traditionally performed while seated cross-legged in the full **lotus** or **half-lotus position**; in Korean monasteries, the quarter lotus position is more often adopted. In the quarter lotus position, one sits with one leg pulled up against the bottom of the opposite thigh, with the other leg bent with the knee pointing upward. In most cases, the practitioner sits on a thick cushion, wearing loose clothing. The hands are held in the cosmic **mudra**, palms up with the left over right and thumbs lightly touching. The body posture is straight, with ears parallel to shoulders, and nose in line with the navel. Teeth and lips are held shut, but the eyes remain slightly open, gazing downward. Breathing may be observed, but is not controlled; nor is an effort made to empty the mind or control the flow of thought. Thoughts are allowed to arise and pass away.

Zazengi

"Manual of Zen Meditation," the Japanese title for any one of several manuals describing the proper method of seated **meditation** (**zazen**). The title most commonly refers to the *Tso-ch'an I*, a Chinese **Zen** text that appears in the **Ch'an-yuan Ch'ing-kuei** (J. *Zennen Shingi*) composed by the Chinese Zen master, Chang-lu Tsung-tse. It is also used as an abbreviated title for **Dôgen Kigen's** (1200–1253) *Fukan Zazengi*, which forms one chapter in the **Shôbôgenzô**. Dôgen's essay is based on Tsung-tse's earlier work.

Zazen Wasan

"A Hymn to Zazen," a popular devotional verse written in Japanese by the eighteenth-century Rinzai reformer, **Hakuin Ekaku** (1685–1768). Rinzai **monks** and lay practitioners of **Zen** continue to chant the verse as a devotional practice today. The verse opens with the line, "**Sentient beings** are intrinsically **Buddha**. Just like ice and water—apart from water there is no ice; apart from sentient beings there is no Buddha." A full English translation of the verse can be found in Isshu Miura's and Ruth Fuller Sasaki's *Zen Dust* (Harcourt, Brace & World, 1966). See also **lay believer**, **Rinzai sect**, and **zazen**.

Zazen Yôjinki

"Notebook on Zen Practice," a commentary in one section on the practice of seated **meditation** (J. **zazen**) written by **Keizan Jôkin** (1268–1325), the second **patriarch** of the **Sôtô sect** in Japan. The text was first published in 1680 by the Sôtô scholar-monk Manzan. The Zazen yôjinki describes the practice of meditation following the style developed by the founder of the Sôtô sects, **Dôgen Kigen** (1200–1253). Keizan based his text on Dôgen's earlier **Zen** manual, the *Fukan Zazengi*. The Sôtô sect continues to use the Zazen yôjinki as a beginner's manual on how to meditate. Two English translations have been published: *The Sôtô Approach to Zen* by Matsunaga Reihô, and *Timeless Spring* by Thomas Cleary.

Cleary, Thomas. *Timeless Spring: A Sôtô Zen Anthology*. New York: Weatherhill, 1980.
Matsunaga, Reihô. *The Sôtô Approach to Zen*. London: Routledge & Kegan Paul, 1972.

Zen

"Meditation," the Japanese abbreviation for *zenna*, which is the Japanese pronunciation for the Chinese word *ch'anna*. Ch'anna and zenna are the standard transliterations for the Sanskrit term *dhyana*. In Japanese texts, the term *Zen* may be used broadly for any style of meditation, whether Buddhist or not. It often refers specifically, however, to **zazen**, the style of seated meditation practiced within the Zen school of **Buddhism**. In addition, the term *Zen* is used to designate the Zen school, or Zen teachings and Zen practice in general.

Zen cuisine consists of vegetarian food served at Zen Buddhist
monasteries to monks and nuns, as well as to the general public.

Zen tradition explains its history in terms of simple transmission of the **Dharma** from one master to another, which historians no longer accept as factually accurate. Tradition maintains that the Indian monk **Bodhidharma** was the first Zen **patriarch** to travel to China to spread Zen practice in East Asia. He is said to have transmitted the Zen teachings and style of practice to his Chinese disciple, **Hui-k'o** (487–593), known as the Second Patriarch. Hui-k'o then transmitted the Dharma to his disciple, the Third Patriarch **Seng-ts'an** (d. 606), and so on through **Hui-neng** (638–713), recognized as the Sixth Patriarch. Tradition says that Bodhidharma taught that all human beings innately possess the **Buddha Nature**. He is said to have taught a form of seated meditation designed to allow the individual to grasp the workings of the mind, to recognize one's own Buddha Nature, and thus attain **enlightenment**.

The actual history of Zen Buddhism's development in China presents a much more complex process. Zen first arose in China sometime during the T'ang dynasty (618–907), several centuries after Buddhism had entered the country. The Chinese had long expressed special interest in the Buddhist meditative texts that were imported from India and Central Asia and translated into Chinese. Chinese meditation masters began to develop styles of practice appropriate for the Chinese cultural context. In the sixth and seventh centuries, before one can accurately speak of Zen Buddhism as an independent school of Chinese Buddhism, small communities of Buddhist meditators took shape at monasteries and hermitages located in mountainous areas. From these early communities, the precursors of Zen emerged, including the **East Mountain school**. By the eighth century, Zen took the form of distinct **lineages** of Zen masters who identified themselves as the heirs of earlier **patriarchs**, including Bodhidharma and Hui-k'o. The latter portion of the T'ang dynasty, the ninth and tenth centuries, are regarded as the golden age of Zen in China. It was during this period that masters such as **Ma-tsu Tao-i** (709–788), **Pai-chang Huai-hai** (720–814), **Huang-po Hsi-yün** (d. 850), **Yun-men Wen-Yen** (864–949), **Tung-shan Liang-chieh** (807–869), and **Lin-chi I-hsuan** were active.

Zen took on a distinctive institutional form during the Sung dynasty (960–1279), when Zen **monastic codes** were compiled. It was during the same period that most of the classical textual sources, such as the **recorded sayings** of the masters, collections of **kôan**, and the compendia of biographies were compiled. The kôan emerged during this period as an important meditative device among some Zen masters, especially those in Lin-chi's Rinzai **lineage**. By the late Sung dynasty, only a few major Zen lineages survived, out of which came the two primary schools of Chinese Zen, the **Rinzai sect** and the **Sôtô sect**. Both schools were transmitted to Japan during the late twelfth through the thirteenth century.

The founder of Sôtô Zen in Japan was **Dôgen Kigen** (1200–1253), who traveled to China. In China, he practiced under a Chinese master and became his **Dharma heir**. The transmission of Rinzai Zen was much more complicated, involving the efforts of several Chinese monks who emigrated to Japan and Japanese monks who visited China. Nevertheless, the Japanese monk, Eisai, is traditionally recognized as the founder of Japanese Rinzai. A third school of Japanese Zen, the Obaku school, emerged centuries later, during the early Tokugawa period (1600–1867). Obaku was founded by the Chinese monk **Yin-yüan Lung-ch'i** (1594–1673) and a small group of his disciples, who immigrated to Japan in the mid-sixteenth century. In the twentieth century, Zen Buddhism has spread throughout the Western world, and is developing new monastic and lay styles of practice appropriate for Western culture. See also **lay believer** and **Obaku sect**.

Zenbyô

Japanese for "**Zen sickness**," an ailment that may arise as a result of practicing Zen meditation. See **Zen Sickness**.

Zenchishiki

A good friend in the **Dharma**. Literally the term means "good and knowledgeable." Often used in reference to the person who first introduced one to the practice of **Buddhism**, or someone who guided one along the **Buddhist path**.

In Zen literature, the term usually refers to an excellent teacher of the Buddhist way or, more specifically, one's Zen master. The term may also be used as a polite form of address; in the **Platform Sutra**, for example, the Sixth **Patriarch** addresses his audience using the expression.

Zen Cuisine

Zen monasteries are sometimes known for their vegetarian cuisine. In Japan, monasteries may serve food to the general public in an affiliated restaurant or in the monastery dining hall. While the ordinary diet for Zen **monks** and **nuns** is quite simple, fancier food is usually prepared for special occasions. See also **vegetarianism**.

Zendô

The **meditation hall** at a Zen monastery or temple. The term *zendô* refers to the monks' hall (J. **sôdô**), which served as the traditional location in Chinese and medieval Japanese Zen monasteries for seated meditation, meals and sleeping; zendô may also refer to a separate hall used exclusively for meditation. The latter are much smaller than the traditional monks' hall, since residents do not use them for eating meals or sleeping. They were introduced in Japan by the Chinese founders of the **Obaku sect** in the early Tokugawa period (1600–1867) and have since become common throughout all the sects of Japanese Zen. See **meditation hall**.

Zen'en Shingi

"The **Zen monastic code** of the Yuan dynasty," the Japanese title for the *Ch'an-yuan Ch'ing-kuei*. Also transliterated as *Zennen Shingi* and *Zen'on Shingi*. See *Ch'an-yuan Ch'ing-kuei*.

Zenga

Zen painting, a general term that encompasses several styles or genres, including ink painting (J. **suibokuga**), landscapes, and portraits of Zen masters (J. **chinsô**).

Zengen Shozenshû Tojo

Japanese title for the *Ch'an-yuan Chu-ch'uan-chi Tu-hsu*, a text by **Tsung-mi** (780–840). See *Ch'an-yuan Chu-ch'uan-chi Tu-hsu*.

Zengo

"Gradual enlightenment," the Japanese term for the belief that enlightenment may be achieved in stages over an extended period of time. See **gradual enlightenment**.

Zengyô

"Gradual teaching," teachings based on the concept of gradual enlightenment. See **gradual teaching**.

Zenji

"**Zen** master" or "**Meditation** master," a Japanese title of respect used to address accomplished Zen **monks** and **nuns**. The Chinese pronunciation of the same characters is Chan-shih. Originally the term distinguished masters who instructed others in meditation from **Dharma** masters, or **hosshi**. Historically, Zenji was also a formal honorific title bestowed on outstanding Zen monks by the imperial court in China and Japan.

Zenjô

Meditation; the state of mental concentration achieved while meditating or the practice associated with it. Zenjô represents the Japanese pronunciation of a Chinese word used to translate the Sanskrit term *dhyana*. The word *zenjô* can be used in a number of ways, since its component parts allow for different interpretations. The character *zen* can be used alone to mean dhyana, the practice of meditation. The character *jô* can be translated as **samadhi**, the state of mental concentration typically achieved through the practice of meditation. While the Sanskrit term *dhyana* does not apply exclusively to the **Zen** style of meditation, the word *zenjô* is sometimes used synonymously with **zazen**, the word for seated Zen meditation. See **meditation** and **zazen**.

Zenkai Ichiran

"One Wave on the Sea of **Zen**," a Zen treatise in one part, which is one of the most important works of Zen literature written in the modern period (1868–present). A monk in the **Rinzai sect**, **Kôsen Sôon** (1816–1892), also known as Imakita Kôsen, composed the text for the daimyô, or military leader, of the Iwakuni province in 1862. It argues for the basic compatibility between Confucianism and Zen. Large portions of the work provide commentary on Confucian terminology and sayings as seen from the Zen perspective.

Zenkan Sakushin

Japanese title for the *Ch'an-kuan Ts'e-chin* (To Encourage Zealous Study of the Zen Barriers). See *Ch'an-kuan Ts'e-chin*.

Zenkiku

A woven ball made of animal hair that was used to prevent **monks** from falling asleep during sessions of seated **meditation**. The ball would be tossed at monks who were nodding off to stop them from falling asleep. The practice is no longer observed in Zen monasteries.

Zenmon Kishiki

"**Zen monastic code**," the Japanese title for the "**Ch'an-men Kuei-shih**." See **Ch'an-men Kuei-shih**.

Zennasu

A practitioner or trainee of **meditation**, a Zen **monk** or **nun**. The term *zenna* is the Japanese translation of the Sanskrit word dhyana, or **meditation**.

Zennen Shingi

"The Zen **monastic code** of the Yüan dynasty," the Japanese title for the ***Ch'an-yuan Ch'ing-kuei***. Also transliterated as *Zen'en Shingi* and *Zen'on Shingi*. See ***Ch'an-yuan Ch'ing-kuei***.

Zen'on Shingi

"The Zen **monastic code** of the Yüan dynasty," the Japanese title for the ***Ch'an-yuan Ch'ing-kuei***. Also transliterated as *Zennen Shingi* and *Zen'en Shingi*. See ***Ch'an-yuan Ch'ing-kuei***.

Zenpan

A board used to provide support during **zazen** (seated **meditation**) so that the meditator can rest or even nap while seated in the **lotus position**. The board is long and narrow, measuring approximately 21 inches long (52 cm), 2.4 inches wide (6 cm), and less than half an inch thick (10 mm). The zenpan has a small, round hole cut toward the top. In some cases, a cord was passed through the hole and attached to wall behind, such that the person meditating could rest on a diagonal against the flat of the board. Today, it is rested flat across the knees or used as a chin rest to prop up the head.

Zenrin Biyô Shingi

Japanese title for the ***Pei-yung Ch'ing-kuei***, a Chinese **Zen monastic code** published in 1311. See ***Pei-yung Ch'ing-kuei***.

Zenrin Kushû

"A Collection of Phrases from the Zen Garden," a compilation of 6,000 quotations drawn from various **Buddhist scriptures**, Zen texts, and non-Buddhist sources. At least since the time of the eighteenth-century Rinzai reformer, **Hakuin Ekaku** (1685–1768), Rinzai masters and students have relied upon the *Zenrin Kushû* as a resource for **jakugo**, or capping verses, which are used as a regular part of **kôan** practice. Portions of the text have been translated into English in Sasaki and Miura's *The Zen Kôan* and Shigematsu's *A Zen Forest*.

The *Zenrin Kushû* is based upon an earlier anthology of 5,000 Zen phrases known as the ***Ku Zôshi***, compiled by **Tôyô Eichô** (1438–1504). Tôyô drew his material from **sutras**, **recorded sayings** of Chinese Zen masters, Taoist texts, Confucian texts, and Chinese poetry. He arranged the phrases according to length, beginning with single-character expressions, continuing with phrases of two characters through eight characters, and interspersing parallel verses of five through eight characters. Tôyô's work circulated in manuscript form for several generations until the seventeenth century. At that time, a person using the pen name Ijûshi produced an expanded version of the text that was first published in 1688 under the title *Zenrin Kushû*. See also **Rinzai sect**.

Miura, Isshû, and Ruth Fuller Sasaki. *The Zen Kôan*. New York: Harcourt Brace & World, 1967.

Shigematsu, Soiku, trans. *A Zen Forest: Sayings of the Masters*. New York: Weatherhill, 1992.

Zenshitsu

The hall or room at a Zen temple or monastery in which seated meditation (**zazen**) is practiced. The term sometimes refers to the **abbot's** quarters (**hôjô**) at a Zen monastery. By extension, it can also be used as an indirect reference to the abbot himself. In other contexts not related specifically to the Zen school of **Buddhism**, the word *zenshitsu* may refer to small meditation hermitages that individual **monks** and **nuns** built for themselves to provide a secluded location for meditative practices.

Zen Sickness

An illness of the body or mind that arises as a result of practicing **zazen**, especially when practicing without proper guidance from a qualified master. Although different physical and mental illnesses may occur, the most common ailment is a form of **delusion** and hallucination. Meditators routinely experience a variety of phenomena when meditating, which can easily be misunderstood. If the condition goes unchecked, it commonly leads to false understanding regarding one's practice and a false sense of **enlightenment**. The seventeenth-century Rinzai master, **Hakuin Ekaku** (1685–1768), discusses Zen sickness in his *Orategama* and *Yasen Kanna*. See also **Rinzai sect**.

Dumoulin, Heinrich. *Zen Buddhism: A History, Vol. 2: Japan*. Trans. James W. Heisig and Paul Knitter. New York: Macmillan Publishing Company, 1994.
Yampolsky, Philip B., trans. *The Zen Master Hakuin: Selected Writings*. New York: Columbia University Press, 1971.

Zensô

"Meditation monk," a Buddhist **monk** or **nun** who practices some form of meditation. In many cases, the term refers specifically to Zen monks or nuns.

Zensu

A Zen trainee or Zen **monk** or **nun**. A shortened form of **Zennasu**. See **Zennasu**.

Zôhô

The Semblance **Dharma**, in Japanese; the second of the **Three Ages of the Dharma** following the death of the historical **Buddha**. The Age of Semblance Dharma follows the Age of the True Dharma, when the Buddha's teachings remained perfect. During the second age, the teachings have begun to deteriorate somewhat, so that what remains has only the appearance of the true Dharma. In this intermediate stage, people continue to practice **Buddhism** as they did in the earlier age, but the full realization of the teachings and the attainment of enlightenment are no longer possible. The period lasts for 1,000 years.

Zôsu

Sutra prefect at a **Zen** monastery, one of the six senior officers from the Western rank (**seihan**) of the monastery. Also known as the chief librarian, or **chizô**. The sutra prefect is responsible for the proper care of the monastery's collection of books and scrolls, which includes the preservation of texts and the acquisition of new materials. The zôsu is usually a **monk** widely educated in Buddhist literature, especially the Zen corpus. In a contemporary Zen monastery, the position is often held by a highly trained Zen scholar-monk.

Abe, Ryuichi, and Peter Haskel, trans. *Great Fool: Zen Master Ryôkan: Poems, Letters, and Other Writings*. Honolulu, HI: University of Hawaii Press, 1996.

App, Urs., trans. *Master Yunmen: From the Record of the Chan Master "Gate of the Clouds."* New York: Kodansha International, 1994.

Aitken, Robert, trans. *The Gateless Barrier: The Wu-mên Kuan*. San Francisco, CA: North Point Press, 1990.

Barnes, Nancy J. "Women in Buddhism." In *Today's Woman in World Religions*. Ed. Arvind Sharma. Albany, NY: State University of New York Press, 1994.

Basham, A. L. *The Wonder That Was India: A Survey of the History and Culture of the Indian Sub-Continent Before the Coming of the Muslims*. New York: Taplinger Publishing Co., 1968.

Bielefeldt, Carl. *Dôgen's Manuals of Zen Meditation*. Berkeley, CA: University of California Press, 1988.

Blacker, Carmen. *The Catalpa Bow*. Boston, MA: Unwin, 1989.

Blofeld, John. *The Zen Teaching of Huang Po on the Transmission of Mind*. Boston, MA: Shambhala, 1994.

Bodiford, William M. "Dharma Transmission in Sôtô Zen." In *Monumenta Nipponica* Vol. 46, No. 4 (Winter, 1991).

——. *Sôtô Zen in Medieval Japan*. Honolulu, HI: University of Hawaii Press, 1993.

Boyd, James W. *Satan and Mara: Christian and Buddhist Symbols of Evil*. Leiden: Brill, 1975.

Broughton, Jeffrey. *Kuei-feng Tsung-mi: The Convergence of Ch'an and the Teachings*. New York: Columbia University Press, 1975.

Buswell, Robert E., Jr. *The Zen Monastic Experience: Buddhist Practice in Contemporary Korea*. Princeton, NJ: Princeton University Press, 1992.

Chên, Kenneth Kuan Shêng. *Buddhism in China: A Historical Survey*. Princeton, NJ: Princeton University Press, 1964.

Chung-Yuan, Chang. *Original Teachings of Ch'an Buddhism: Selected from the* Transmission of the Lamp. New York: Grove Press, 1982.

Cleary, Christopher, trans. *Swampland Flowers: The Letters and Lectures of Zen Master Ta Hui*. New York: Grove Press, 1977.

Cleary, Thomas. *The Book of Serenity*. Boston, MA: Shambhala, 1998.

——. *Timeless Spring: A Sôtô Zen Anthology*. New York: Weatherhill, 1980.

Collcutt, Martin. *Five Mountains: The Rinzai Zen Monastic Institution in Medieval Japan*. Cambridge, MA: Harvard University Press, 1981.

Conze, Edward. *Buddhist Scriptures: A Bibliography*. Ed. Lewis Lancaster. New York: Garland, 1982.

Cook, Francis Harold. *How to Raise an Ox: Zen Practice as Taught in Zen Master Dôgen's* Shobogenzo. Los Angeles, CA: Center Publications, 1978.

——. *Sounds of Valley Streams.* Albany, NY: State University of New York Press, 1989.

Covell, Jon Carter, and Shobin Yamada. *Unraveling Zen's Red Thread; Ikkyu's Controversial Way.* Elizabeth, NJ: Hollym International Corporation, 1980.

Cowell, E. B. et al., eds. *Buddhist Mahayana Texts.* New York: Dover Publications, 1969.

de Visser, Marinus Willem. *The Arhats in China and Japan.* Berlin: Oesterheld and Co., 1923.

——. "The Bodhisattva Ti-Tsang in China and Japan." *Ostasiatische Zeitschift* 2 (1913).

Dumoulin, Heinrich. *Zen Buddhism: A History.* 2 vols. Trans. James W. Heisig and Paul Knitter. New York: Macmillan Publishing Company, 1994.

Garfield, Jay L., trans. *The Fundamental Wisdom of the Middle Way: Nagarjuna's* Mulamadhyamakakarika. New York: Oxford University Press, 1995.

Getty, Alice. *The Gods of Northern Buddhism: Their History and Iconography.* New York: Dover Publications, 1988.

Groner, Paul. *Saichô: The Establishment of the Japanese Tendai School.* Honolulu, HI: University of Hawaii Press, 2000.

Hakeda, Kûkai. *Major Works.* Trans. Yoshito S. Hakeda. New York: Columbia University Press, 1972.

Hakeda, Yoshito S., trans. *The Awakening of Faith.* New York: Columbia University Press, 1967.

Harvey, Peter. *An Introduction to Buddhism: Teachings, History and Practices.* Cambridge: Cambridge University Press, 1990.

Herrigel, Eugen. *Zen in the Art of Archery.* Trans. R. F. C. Hull. New York: Vintage Books, 1989.

Haskell, Peter. *Bankei Zen: Translations from the Record of Bankei.* New York: Grove Press, 1984.

Hori, Ichiro. *Folk Religion in Japan: Continuity and Change.* Ed. Joseph M. Kitagawa and Alan L. Miller. Chicago, IL: University of Chicago Press, 1968.

——, et. al, eds. *Japanese Religions: A Survey by the Agency for Cultural Affairs.* Tokyo: Kodansha International, 1972.

Hsu, Sung-peng. *A Buddhist Leader in Ming China; The Life and Thought of Han-shan Te-ch'ing, 1546–1623.* University Park, PA: The Pennsylvania State University Press, 1979.

Hurvitz, Leon, trans. *Scripture of the Lotus Blossom of the Fine Dharma.* New York: Columbia University Press, 1982.

Ishida, Hisatoyo. *Esoteric Buddhist Painting*. Trans. E. Dale Saunders. New York: Harper & Row, 1987.

Ishigami, Zenno. *Disciples of the Buddha*. Trans. Richard L. Gage and Paul McCarthy. Tokyo: Kosei Publishing Co., 1989.

Kalupahana, Nagarjuna. *The Philosophy of the Middle Way*. Albany, NY: State University of New York Press, 1986.

Kamens, Edward, trans. *The Three Jewels: A Study and Translation of Minamato Tamenori's* Sanboê. Ann Arbor, MI: Center for Japanese Studies, University of Michigan, 1988.

Kapleau, Philip. "The Private Encounter with the Master." In *Zen, Tradition and Transition*. Ed. Kenneth Kraft. New York: Grove Press, 1988.

Kent, Richard K. "Depictions of the Guardians of the Law: Lohan Painting in China," In *Latter Days of the Law: Images of Chinese Buddhism, 850–1850*. Ed. Marsha Weidner. Honolulu, HI: University of Hawaii Press, 1994.

King, Winston L. *Death Was His Kôan: The Samurai-Zen of Suzuki Shosan*. Berkeley, CA: Asian Humanities Press, 1986.

——. *In the Hope of Nibbana: An Essay on Theravada Buddhist Ethics*. LaSalle, IL: Open Court, 1964.

Kodera, Takashi James. *Dôgen's Formative Years in China: An Historical Study and Annotated Translation of the* Hokyo-ki. Boulder, CO: Prajña Press, 1980.

Kraft, Kenneth, ed. *Zen, Tradition and Transition*. New York: Grove Press, 1988.

La Fleur, William R. *The Karma of Words: Buddhism and the Literary Arts in Medieval Japan*. Berkeley, CA: University of California Press, 1983.

——. *Liquid Life: Abortion and Buddhism in Japan*. Princeton, NJ: Princeton University Press, 1992.

Leighton, Taigen Daniel, and Shohaku Okamura. *Dôgen's Pure Standards for the Zen Community*. Albany, NY: State University of New York Press, 1996.

Liebenthal, Walter. *Chao Lun: The Treatises of Seng-chao*. Hong Kong: Hong Kong University Press, 1968.

Ling, Trevor Oswald. *Buddhism and the Mythology of Evil: A Study in Theravada Buddhism*. Rockport, MA: Oneworld, 1997.

Matsunaga, Daigan, and Alicia Matsunaga. *Foundation of Japanese Buddhism*. 2 vols. Los Angeles, CA: Buddhist Books International, 1976.

Matsunaga, Reihô, trans. *A Primer of Sôtô Zen: A Translation of Dôgen's* Shôbôgenzô Zuimonki. London: Routledge and K. Paul, 1972.

——. *The Sôtô Approach to Zen*. London: Routledge & Kegan Paul, 1972.

McRae, John R. *The Northern School and the Formation of Early Ch'an Buddhism*. Honolulu, HI: University of Hawaii Press, 1986.

Merwin, W. S., and Soiku Shigematsu. *Sun at Midnight*. San Francisco, CA: North Point Press, 1989.

Miura, Isshû, and Ruth Fuller Sasaki. *Zen Dust: The History of the Kôan and Kôan Study in Rinzai (Lin-chi) Zen*. New York: Harcourt, Brace & World, 1967.

——. *The Zen Kôan*. New York: Harcourt, Brace & World, 1967.

Morrell, Robert E. *Sand and Pebbles: The Tales of Muju Ichien, a Voice for Pluralism in Kamakura Buddhism*. Albany, NY: State University of New York Press, 1985.

Nearman, Rev. Hubert, O.B.C., *The Denkôroku or The Record of the Transmission of the Light by Keizan Zenji*. Mount Shasta, CA: Shasta Abbey, 1993.

Nishijima, Gudo Waju, and Chodo Cross. *Master Dôgen's* Shôbôgenzô. Woking, Surrey: Windbell Publications, 1994.

Ooms, Herman. *Tokugawa Ideology: Early Constructs, 1570–1680*. Ann Arbor, MI: Center for Japanese Studies, University of Michigan, 1998.

Paul, Diane Y. *Women in Buddhism: Images of the Feminine in Mahayana Tradition*. Berkeley, CA: University of California Press, 1985.

Pine, Red, trans. *The Zen Teaching of Bodhidharma*. San Francisco, CA: North Point Press, 1989.

Pye, Michael. *Skillful Means: A Concept in Mahayana Buddhism*. London: Duckworth, 1978.

Reader, Ian. "Zazenless Zen: The Position of Zazen in Institutional Zen Buddhism." *Japanese Religion*. Vol. 14, No. 3 (1986).

Reischauer, Edwin O., trans. *Diary: The Record of a Pilgrimage to China in Search of the Law*. New York: Ronald Press Co., 1955.

——. *Enniu's Travels in T'ang China*. New York: Ronald Press Company, 1955.

Reynolds, Frank E., and Charles Hallisey. "The Buddha," In *Buddhism and Asian History*. Eds. Joseph M. Kitagawa and Mark D. Cummings. New York: Macmillan, 1987.

Robinson, Richard H., and William L. Johnson. *The Buddhist Religion: A Historical Introduction*. Belmont, CA: Wadsworth Publishing Co., 1996.

Sasaki, Ruth Fuller. *The Record of Lin-chi*. Kyoto, Japan: The Institute for Zen Studies, 1975.

Sasaki, Ruth Fuller, Yoshitaka Iriya, and Dana R. Fraser. *A Man of Zen: The Recorded Sayings of Layman P'ang*. New York: Weatherhill, 1971.

Saunders, E. Dale. *Mudra: A Study of the Symbolic Gestures in Japanese Buddhist Sculpture.* Princeton, NJ: Princeton University Press, 1985.

Sekida, Katsuki, trans. *Two Zen Classics:* Mumonkan *and* Hekiganroku. Ed. A. V. Grimstone. New York: Weatherhill, 1977.

Shibayama, Zenkei. *Zen Comments on the* Mumonkan. Trans. Sumiko Kudo. New York: Harper & Row, 1974.

Shigematsu, Soiku, trans. *A Zen Forest: Sayings of the Masters.* New York: Weatherhill, 1992.

Shimano, Eido T. "Zen Kôans." In *Zen, Tradition and Transition.* Ed. Kenneth Kraft. New York: Grove Press, 1988.

Shohei, Ichimura. *Zen Master Eihei Dôgen's Monastic Regulations.* Washington, DC: North American Institute of Zen and Buddhist Studies, 1993.

Smith, Robert. *Ancestor Worship in Contemporary Japan.* Stanford, CA: Stanford University Press, 1974.

Sohaku, Ogata, trans. *The Transmission of the Lamp: Early Masters.* Wolfeboro, NH: Longwood Academic, 1989.

Sponberg, Alan, and Helen Hardacre, eds. *Maitreya, the Future Buddha.* New York: Cambridge University Press, 1988.

Stevens, John. *The Marathon Monks of Mount Hiei.* Boston, MA: Shambhala, 1988.

——. *One Robe, One Bowl.* New York: Weatherhill, 1988.

Streng, Frederick J. *Emptiness: A Study in Religious Meaning.* Nashville, TN: Abingdon Press, 1967.

Strong, John S. *The Experience of Buddhism: Sources and Interpretations.* Belmont, CA: Wadsworth Publishing Co., 1995.

——. *The Legend of King Ashoka; A Study and Translation of the* Asokavadana. Princeton, NJ: Princeton University Press, 1983.

Suzuki, Daisetz Teitaro. *Essays in Zen Buddhism (First Series).* London: Rider, 1970.

——. *Manual of Zen Buddhism.* New York: Grove Press, 1960.

——. *The Training of the Zen Buddhist Monk.* New York: Globe Press Books, 1991.

Suzuki, Shunryû. *Zen Mind, Beginner's Mind.* New York: Walker/Weatherhill, 1970.

Swanson, Paul L. *Foundations of T'ien-T'ai Philosophy: The Flowering of the Two Truths Theory in Chinese Buddhism.* Berkeley, CA: Asian Humanities Press, 1989.

Taishô Shinshu Daizôkyô. Ed. Takakusu Junrirô. Tokyo: Taishô Issaikyô Kankokai, 1924–1932. 85 vols.

Tanabe, George J., Jr., and Willa Jane Tanabe. *The Lotus Sutra in Japanese Culture.* Honolulu, HI: University of Hawaii Press, 1989.

Tanahashi, Kazuaki. *Moon in a Dewdrop.* San Francisco, CA: North Point Press, 1985.

Thompson, Laurence G. *Chinese Religion, An Introduction.* Fifth Edition. Belmont, CA: Wadsworth Publishing Co., 1996.

Thurman, Robert A. F., trans. *The Holy Teaching of Vimalakirti: A Mahayana Scripture.* University Park, PA: Pennsylvania State University Press, 1976.

Tyler, Royall, trans. *Selected Writings of Suzuki Shosan.* Ithaca, NY: China-Japan Program, Cornell University, 1977.

Tzu, Mou. "The Disposition of Error." In *Sources of Chinese Tradition.* Compiled by Wm. Theodore De Bary and Irene Bloom. New York: Columbia University Press, 1999.

Ueda, Yoshifumi, and Dennis Hirota. *Shinran: An Introduction to His Thought.* Tokyo: Hongwanji International Center, 1989.

Varley, Paul, and Kumakura Isao. *Tea in Japan: Essays on the History of Chanoyu.* Honolulu, HI: University of Hawaii Press, 1989.

Waddell, Norman. *The Essential Teachings of Zen Master Hakuin: A Translation of the* Sokko-roku Kaien-fusetsu. Boston, MA: Shambhala, 1994.

——. *The Unborn: The Life and Teaching of Zen Master Bankei, 1622–1693.* New York: North Point Press, 2000.

Waddell, Norman, and Masao Abe, trans. "Dôgen's *Bendôwa.*" *Eastern Buddhist.* Vol. 4, No. 1 (1971): 88–115.

Watson, Burton, trans. *The Lotus Sutra.* New York: Columbia University Press, 1993.

——. *The Zen Teachings of Master Lin-chi: A Translation of the* Lin-chi Lu. Boston, MA: Shambhala, 1993.

Wijayaratna, Mohan *Buddhist Monastic Life: According to the Texts of the Theravada Tradition.* Trans. Claude Grangier and Steven Collins. New York: Cambridge University Press, 1990.

Williams, Paul. *Mahâyâna Buddhism: The Doctrinal Foundations.* New York: Routledge, 1989.

Wu, Ch'eng-en. *Monkey.* Trans. Arthur Waley. New York: Grove Press, 1994.

Yamasaki, Taiko. *Shingon: Japanese Esoteric Buddhism.* Trans. Richard and Cynthia Peterson. Ed. Yasuyoshi Morimoto and David Kidd. Boston, MA: Shambhala, 1988.

Yampolsky, Philip B. *The Platform Sutra of the Sixth Patriarch.* New York: Columbia University Press, 1967.

——, trans. *The Zen Master Hakuin: Selected Writings.* New York: Columbia University Press, 1971.

Yôkoi, Yûhô, and Daizen Victoria. *Zen Master Dôgen: An Introduction with Selected Writings.* New York: Weatherhill, 1976.

A

abbot, **1–2**, 4, 33, 49–50, 52, 54, 58–60, 71, 73, 75, 80, 82, 84, 95, 107, 109, 111–112, 114, 117–118, 121–122, 126, 130, 132–133, 135, 140, 142, 150, 152–158, 162, 165–168, 171–172, 178, 180, 185, 187, 189, 196, 199, 201, 204, 216, 218, 222, 227, 229, 232–234, 236, 245, 248, 250, 264, 268–269, 272, 275, 278, 282–283, 285–286, 290, 299, 301, 303, 305–306, 310, 313, 317, 320–321, 326, 330, 332, 337–339, 341, 343, 345, 352–353, 355, 359, 369, 374–375, 383, 390

Abhidharma, **2**, 10, 38, 268, 356

Abihidharma literature, 2

Acts of the Buddha. See Buddhacharita

afflictions, **2–3**, 14, 26, 30, 33, 94, 96, 158, 248, 266, 295, 348, 373

Agama Sutras, **3**

Age of the Degenerate Dharma. *See* Latter Age of the Dharma

agyo, **3**, 172

ahimsa, **3–4**, 309, 367. *See also* lay believer

Aikuô. *See* Ashoka

Aitken, Robert, viii, 274

ajari, **4**, 159. *See also* Shingon sect, Sôtô sect, and Tendai sect

ako, **4**, 199, 275, 293. *See also* sanbutsuji

akudô. *See* evil paths

alaya consciousness, **4–5**, 10, 55, 77, 88, 125, 139, 204, 324, 337, 380. *See also* Fa-hsien school and Hossô school

alcohol and intoxicants, 12, 78, 93, 111, 125, 139, 153, 161, 168, 170, 206, 244, 258–259, 288, 341–342

ama no hakkikai, **5**

Amida buddha, **5–6**, 7, 30, 35, 37, 45, 53, 75–76, 108, 114, 124, 129, 136, 138, 165, 196, 213, 231, 235, 237, 239, 245, 251, 259–260, 272, 347, 357, 360, 372, 376. *See also* dual practice and koshin mida

Amida's vows, **5–6**. *See also* Amida buddha

Amitayus. *See* Amida buddha

Ananda, **7**, 22, 167, 257, 283, 290, 327, 340, 356. *See also* arhat

Anatman, **7–8**, 14, 55, 82, 109, 152, 211, 229, 244, 319, 325–326, 348

Ancestor Worship in Contemporary Japan (Smith), 40, 151, 247

andae. *See* gojôe

andô. *See* anjadô

ango, **8**. *See also* Sôtô sect

anger, 2–3, 33, 76–77, 148, 168, 180, 259, 319, 340,–341, 348, 373

angya, **8–9**, 129, 256

animals, 4, 13, 19, 66, 81, 86, 133, 139, 191, 208, 223, 226, 229, 234, 251, 314, 318, 340, 342, 345, 348, 367, 373, 378, 388

anja, **9**, 10, 119, 163, 181

anjadô, 8–9, **10**. *See also* lay believer

anroku, **10**

Anuruddha, **10**, 167, 340

anuttara samyak sambodhi, **10**

App, Urs, 150, 383

Arada Kalama, **10**

arayashiki. *See* Alaya consciousness

archery. *See* kyûdô

architectural styles, 40, 108, 111–112, 115–116, 252, 283, 294, 317, 324–325, 336

arhat, 7, **10–12**, 24, 27, 47, 55, 64, 91, 96, 100, 167, 171, 182, 210–211, 214, 222, 256, 293, 299, 307, 309, 325, 339, 351, 357, 365, 376

The Arhats in China and Japan (de Visser), 12

arrogance, 2–3, 33

art, ix, 149, 12 32, 43–44, 48, 50–51, 65, 82, 100, 102, 107, 115–116, 120–121, 126, 167, 170, 179, 226, 228, 248, 251, 271, 292, 327, 345, 360, 371, 388

ascetic practices, **12–13**, 19, 119

Ashikaga period (1392–1568; Japan), 17, 62, 111, 116, 140, 151, 184, 203, 232, 242, 265, 272, 283–284, 305, 317, 320, 337, 343, 345, 353, 355

Ashita, **13**, 182, 314

Ashoka, **13**, 16, 30, 43, 191. *See also* lay believer

ashura, **13–14**, 86, 98, 161, 268, 285, 318, 342, 348, 373

Ashvaghosha, **14**, 16, 35, 58, 249, 335

Asuka period (5th–6th c.; Japan), 307

atman, 7, **14**, 19, 37, 64, 93, 106, 244

attachment, viii, 2, 4, 7, 13, **14**, 19, 24, 33, 54, 63, 65, 75, 77, 91, 94, 109, 162, 182, 197, 228, 241, 244, 266, 276, 296, 309, 318, 364–365, 371

Avalokiteshvara, **14–15**, 45, 109, 175–176, 198

Avalokiteshvara Sutra, **15**, 176, 178, 199. *See also* lay believer

Avatamsaka Sutra, **15–16**, 55, 94, 102, 145, 153, 182, 211, 276, 343

Avici hell, **16**, 91, 110, 229

Awakening of Faith, **16**, 58, 249, 335. *See also* Shingon sect

The Awakening of Faith (Hakeda), 16

A-yu-wang-shan, **16**, 198

B

baitô, **17**

Baiyû Jikushin, **17**, 313

Baker, Richard, viii, 274

bakufu, 1, **17**, 140, 159, 234, 304, 320, 328, 338, 343. *See also* samurai

ball of doubt, **17**, 56, 109

banka, **17**

Bankei Yôtaku, 13, **17–18**, 155, 335, 364–365. *See also* Rinzai sect

dembôin. *See* inka

Dengyô Daishi. *See* Saichô

Denkôroku, **64**, 185. *See also* Sôtô sect

The Denkôroku or The Record of the Transmission of the Light by Keizan Zenji (Nearman), 64

Denshin Hôyô. See Ch'uan-hsin Fa-yao

denshô, **65**, 125, 231

Dentôroku. See Ching-te Ch'üan-teng Lu

"Depictions of the Guardians of the Law: Lohan Painting in China," *Latter Days of the Law: Images of Chinese Buddhism* (Kent), 12

deshi, **65**

Devadatta, **65**

devas, **65**. *See also* six paths

Devil's Cave. *See* Kikutsuri

de Visser, Marinus Willem, 12, 165

dharani, 45, 56, 63, **66**, 75, 284, 312, 314

Dharma, 1–4, 6–7, 12–14, 16, 19, 24, 27, 30, 32, 34, 36–37, 39, 43, 45, 50, 52, 59, 62, **66**, 67, 69, 71, 87–88, 90, 93, 95–97, 99–100, 104, 106–107, 112, 115, 119, 126–127, 130–132, 134–135, 138–139–140, 145–146, 149, 151, 153–156, 158, 161, 166, 168, 171, 174, 182, 189, 196–197, 199, 201, 204, 207–208, 210–211, 213, 221–223, 225–226, 233–235, 238, 241, 249–250, 254–255, 258, 270, 274, 276–277, 281, 283, 285–286, 288, 292, 294–295, 298–299, 301–302, 304, 309–311, 313, 318–319, 322, 327, 331–332, 334, 337–338, 340, 342–343, 345–347, 350–351, 358, 360–362, 365–366, 368–370, 372, 379, 382, 386–388, 390. *See also* lay believer

Dharma combat, **66–67**

dharmadhatu, **67**, 134

Dharma doll, 63, **67–68**

Dharma eye, 47, **68**, 71, 92, 210, 302. *See also* Sôtô sect and lay believer

Dharma gate, **68**, 135

Dharma hall. *See* hattô

Dharma heir, 17–18, 48, 50, 54, 60, 63, **68–69**, 72, 82, 84, 88–90, 107, 109, 111–112, 117, 121, 126, 139–143, 145–146, 152, 154–155, 166, 178, 182, 185, 194, 196, 199, 207, 216, 218, 221, 227, 232, 234–235, 242–243, 248, 251–252, 256, 259, 270, 274, 280, 284–285, 289–290, 294, 301, 304, 310, 312, 319, 326–330, 332, 335, 337, 341, 344–345, 353–355, 359, 374–375, 380, 383, 387. *See also* lay believer and Sôtô sect

Dharmakaya, **69**, 132, 138, 248, 280, 347

Dharma King, **69**, 138

Dharma robe, 59–60, **69**, 71, 133, 266, 355

Dharma Seal. *See* inka

Dharma Seat. *See* Hôza

Dharma transmission, 27, 51, 59, 64, 69, **71**, 80, 88, 106–107, 118, 139, 145, 147, 154, 156, 174, 182, 204, 207, 216, 266, 356, 358, 375. *See also* Sôtô sect

"Dharma Transmission in Sôtô Zen," *Monumenta Nipponica* (Bodiford), 107, 154

Dharma Wheel. *See* Wheel of the Dharma

dhyana. *See* meditation

Diamond-Realm Mandala, **71–72**, 195, 211, 214, 331, 367, 374

Diamond Sutra, 57, **72**, 146, 195, 200, 211, 255, 301

Diary: The Record of a Pilgrimage to China in Search of the Law (Reischauer), 84

Disciples of the Buddha (Ishigami), 7, 10, 182, 260, 262, 291, 325, 340, 365

"The Disposition of Error," *Sources of Chinese Tradition* (Tzu), 91

Dô. *See* Tao

dôban, **72**

Dôgen Kigen, vii, 4, 8, 26, 29, 37, 46–47, 58–59, 63–64, **72–73**, 76, 79, 85, 99, 102, 104, 108, 122, 129, 150, 166, 169, 173–174, 176, 181, 189, 197, 210, 216–217, 222, 224, 254, 261, 270, 275, 295–298, 301–302, 304, 313, 321, 323, 330, 341, 344, 358, 384–385, 387. *See also* Tendai sect

Dôgen's Formative Years in China: An Historical Study and Annotated Translation of the Hokyo-ki (Kodera), 298

Dôgen's Pure Standards for the Zen Community (Leighton and Okamura), 80, 344

dojidô, **73**

dôjô, **73**

dokkaku. *See* pratyeka buddha

dokusan, **73–74**, 176, 280, 285, 305. *See also* Obaku sect and Rinzai sect

Dôkyô Etan, **74**, 121, 172, 294, 304

dônai, **74**

donkatsukan, **74**. *See also* Rinzai sect

dora, **74**

Dôsha Chôgen. *See* Tao-che Ch'ao-yüan

Dôshin. *See* Tao-hsin

Dôshô, **74**, 139, 141. *See also* Yogachara school

dôshu. *See* ino

dôsu. *See* ino

doubt, 2–3, 33

dropping off body and mind. *See* shinjin datsuraku

dual practice, 6, 53, **75**, 88, 125, 237–238, 365. *See also* Rinzai sect

duhkha. *See* suffering

Dumoulin, Heinrich, 84, 390

dust, **75**, 104, 162, 298. *See also* five dusts and six dusts

E

Early Modern period (1600–1867; Japan), 103–104, 211, 320

Eastern rank. *See* tôhan

East Mountain school, **76**, 292, 335, 359, 386

easy path, **76**, 324

Edo (Tokyo), Japan, 74, 216, 228, 312

ehatsu. *See* three robes, one bowl

Eichô. *See* Shakuen Eichô

Eigen-ji, **76**, 158. *See also* Rinzai sect

Eigen-ji Ha, **76**, 266

eight cold hells, **77**, 120, 128, 159

eight consciousnesses, 55, **77**, 125, 267. *See also* "Consciousness Only" and Yogachara school

Eightfold Path, 10, 26, 36, 38, 41, **77–78**, 84, 98, 125, 272, 309, 316, 326, 347, 351, 361, 372

eight hot hells, 16, **78**, 120, 128, 159, 229

eight precepts, **78**, 120, 125. *See also* lay believer

eighty minor marks of a buddha, **78**

Eihei-ji, 73, **79**, 173, 185, 275, 283, 313, 321, 323

Eihei Shingi, 46, 73, **79–80**, 216, 224, 304, 344. *See also* Sôtô sect

Eisai, vii, 45, 63, 72, **80**, 84–85, 143, 166–167, 187–188, 197, 232, 261, 266, 270, 289, 295, 330, 380–381

Eka Daishi. *See* Hui-k'o

Emma, **80–81**, 378

Emmei Jikku Kannonkyô, **81**

Emmei Jikku Kannonkyô Reigenki, **81**

Emperor Go-Daigo, 61, **81**, 185, 230, 232, 310, 321, 343

Emperor Hanazono, 61, **81–82**, 124, 178, 194, 233, 304, 310

Empress Wu, **82**

emptiness, 7, 26, 35, 37, 54–55, 69, 72, **82**, 85–86, 92, 99, 105, 113, 124, 155, 162–163, 167, 191, 195, 198, 210–211, 229, 234, 243–244, 255, 258, 264, 276, 280, 312, 319, 325, 340, 342, 347–349, 358, 361, 363, 365, 369

Emptiness: A Study in Religious Meaning (Streng), 234

engaku. *See* pratyeka buddha

Engaku-ji, 60, **82–83**, 116, 134, 156, 196, 232, 283, 290, 328, 330, 359, 374. *See also* Rinzai sect

Engaku-ji Ha, **83**, 266

engi. *See* co-dependent-origination

engi (2), **83**

Engo Kokugon. *See* Yüan-wu K'o-ch'in

enju, **83**

enjudô, 75, **83**, 241

enlightened one, 34, 37, **83**, 119, 167, 339

enlightenment, viii, 2, 5, 10, 12, 14–15, 17–20, 25–27, 30–34, 36–39, 41–42, 44, 46, 50, 52, 55–57, 59, 63–66, 68–69, 71–75, 77, 82–83, **84**, 85–88, 94, 96–97, 102–103, 108–113, 117–119, 121, 124, 129, 132, 134, 137–138, 141–142, 146–147, 149–150, 152, 154–159, 161–163, 165, 167, 170, 172, 184, 188, 190, 192, 201, 204, 206, 209, 211–212, 214, 216–219, 222, 225–226, 228–229, 235, 237, 241–244, 249–252, 254–256, 258–259, 262, 265–268, 272, 274, 277, 281, 283–284, 288–289, 296–299, 302, 304–305, 309, 312, 316, 318–319, 321, 324–326, 330, 334–335, 337, 342–344, 346–348, 350–351, 353, 355–357, 360, 362–363, 365, 368–369, 372–375, 383, 386, 390

gradual enlightenment, **117**, 140, 243, 323, 326, 353, 388

sudden enlightenment, 117, 140, 146, 243, 249, 323, **326**, 353

Enni Ben'en, **84**, 195, 229, 289, 304, 352, 374. *See also* Rinzai sect, Tendai sect, and Yang-ch'i school

Ennin, **84**, 306. *See also* T'ien-t'ai school

Enniu's Travels in T'ang China (Reischauer), 84

Enô. *See* Hui-neng

Enryaku-ji, **84–85**, 129, 187, 339. *See also* Tendai sect

enshû, **85**. *See also* Tendai sect

ensô, **85**, 149

equality, 42, **86**, 194

esoteric Buddhism, 37, 66, 71, 81, **86**, 140, 162, 174, 187, 195–196, 200, 204, 214–215, 222, 228–229, 233–234, 271, 284, 289, 298, 309, 330–331, 339, 367, 373, 380

Esoteric Buddhist Painting (Ishida), 72, 374

Essays in Zen Buddhism (Suzuki, D. T.), 141, 328

The Essential Teachings of Zen Master Hakuin: A Translation of the Sokko-roku Kaien-fusetsu (Waddell), 121, 321

evil paths, 4, 14, **86**, 180, 274, 318. *See also* six paths

expedient means, 39, 68, **87**, 92, 109, 131, 208, 366, 369

The Experience of Buddhism: Sources and Interpretations (Strong), 29, 91, 148–149

F

face-to-face transmission, **88**, 221

Fa-ch'ih, **88**, 132

Fa-hai, **88**, 194

Fa-hsien school, 5, 55, **88**, 138, 380, 382

Fa-jung, **88**, 117, 140, 242, 251

farming, 4, 83, 215, 301

fasting, 12, 161, 244, 258, 288, 266

Fa-yen school, **89**, 92, 131, 142, 288, 344

Fa-yen Wen-i, **89**, 92, 131, 382. *See also* Hua-yen school

Feng-hsueh Yen-chao, **89**, 103, 235. *See also* Rinzai sect and T'ien-t'ai school

K

Photo Credits

About the Author

Helen J. Baroni, Ph.D., is an associate professor in the department of religion at the University of Hawaii at Manoa. She received a bachelor of arts from Grinnell College in 1981, a master's degree in divinity from the Princeton Theological Seminary in 1984, and both a master's degree (1990) and a doctorate degree (1993) in philosophy from Columbia University.

From 1990 to 1991, Dr. Baroni was a visiting research fellow at the International Research Institute for Zen Buddhism of Hanazozo College in Kyoto, Japan. She was awarded a Japan Foundation Dissertation Fellowship in 1990, a Weatherhead Fellowship in 1992, and a grant from the Harvard Pluralism Project in 1998. Dr. Baroni has published a number of journal articles on Japanese religions. She is also the author of *Obaku Zen: The Emergence of the Third Sect of Zen in Tokugawa, Japan*, published by the University of Hawaii Press (2000).